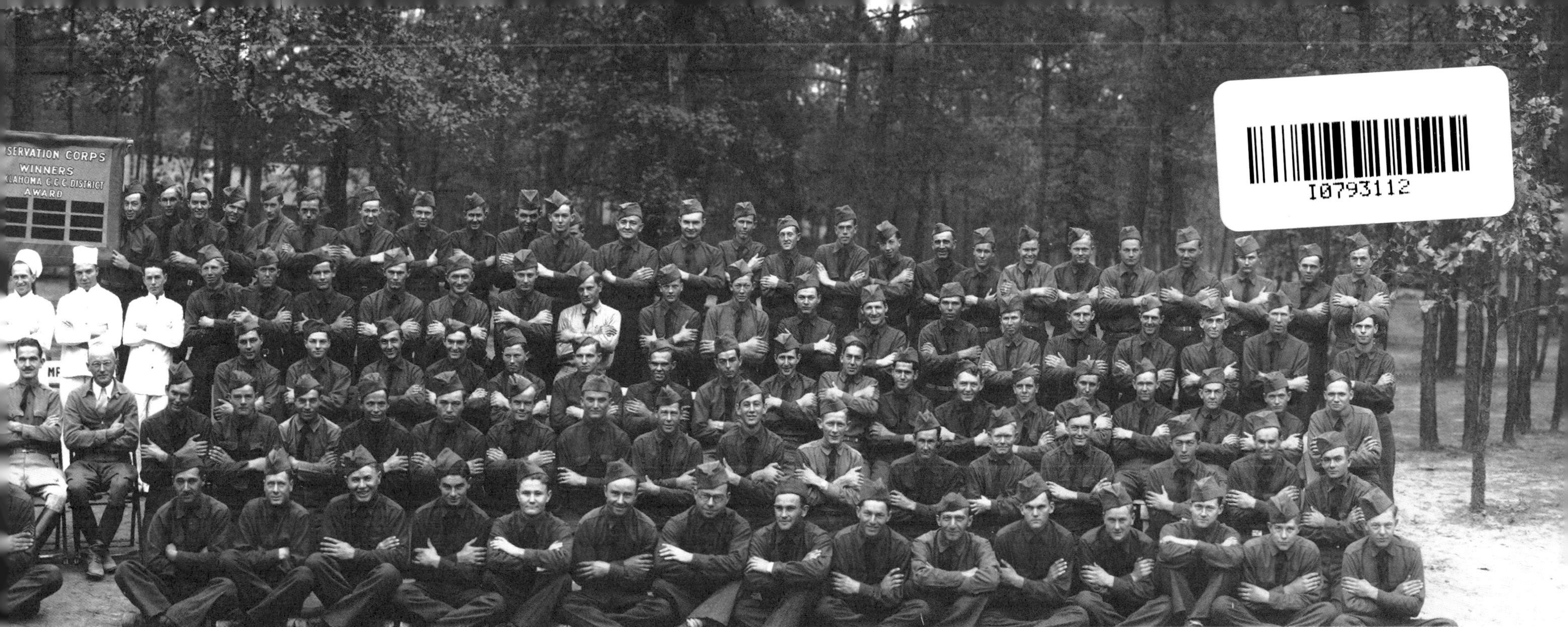
SERVATION CORPS
WINNERS
KLAHOMA C.C.C. DISTRICT
AWARD

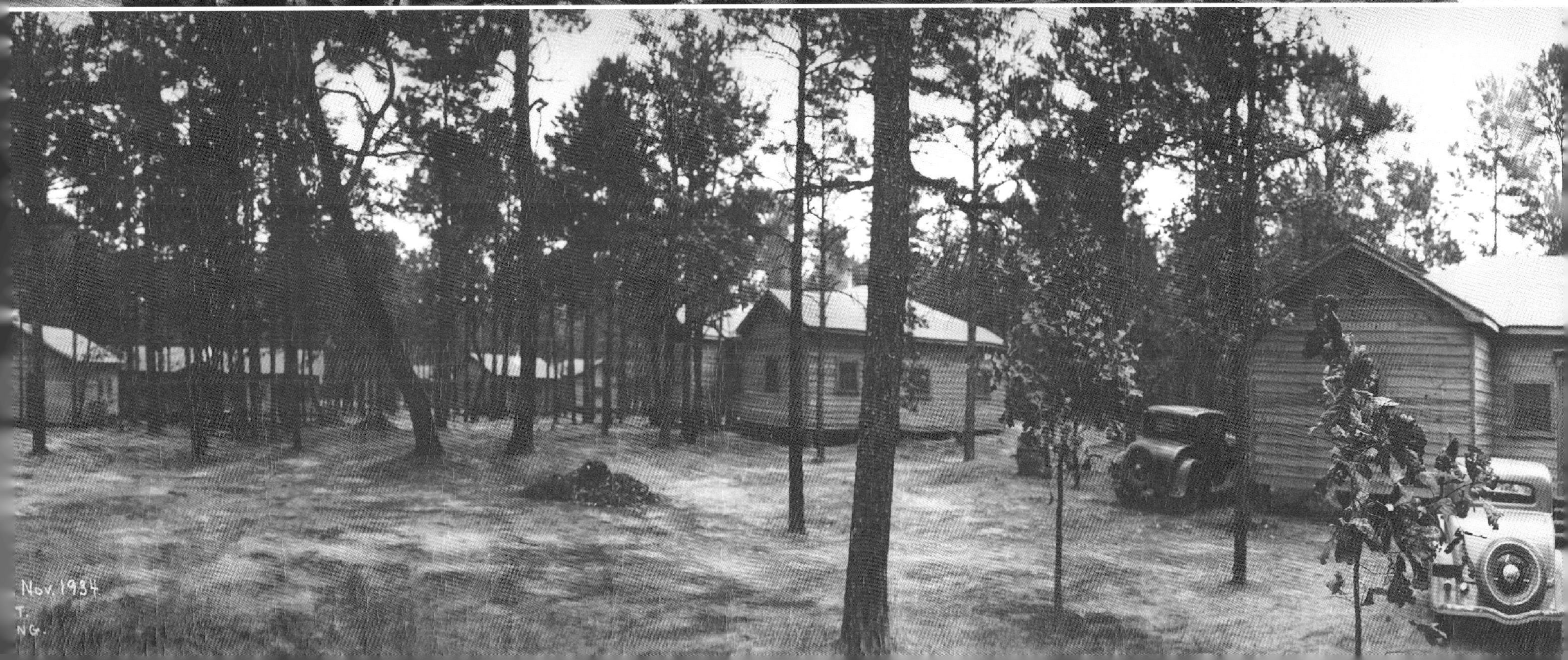
Nov. 1934

# PRESERVING LIVES

Other books by Hank O'Neal

*Eddie Condon's Scrapbook of Jazz*
*A Vision Shared*
*Allegra Kent's Water Beauty Book*
*Berenice Abbott—American Photographer*
*Life Is Painful, Nasty and Short*
*All the King's Men (photographs only for limited edition)*
*Charlie Parker—The Funky Blues Date*
*The Ghosts of Harlem*
*Gay Day—The Christopher Street Parade*
*Berenice Abbott Vol. 1*
*Berenice Abbott Vol. 2*
*XCIA'S Street Art Project*
*Berenice Abbott—Early New York*
*Berenice Abbott—The American Scene*
*Berenice Abbott—Greenwich Village*
*Berenice Abbott—Deep Woods*
*Berenice Abbott—Route One*
*Berenice Abbott—Paris Portraits*
*A Vision Shared—40th Anniversary Edition*
*Internationale Jazzfestival Bern*

# PRESERVING LIVES

## An American Family's Scrapbook

**Hank O'Neal**

TCU Press

Fort Worth, Texas

Library of Congress Cataloging-in-Publication Data

Names: O'Neal, Hank, author.
Title: Preserving lives : an American family's scrapbook / Hank O'Neal.
Description: Fort Worth, Texas : TCU Press, 2018.
Identifiers: LCCN 2017042022 (print) | LCCN 2017059168 (ebook) | ISBN 9780875656922 | ISBN 9780875656748 (alk. paper)
Subjects: LCSH: O'Neal, Harold (Harold Lee), 1910-1972. | Christian, Sarah Beatrice, 1914-1968. | Married people--United States--Biography.|
Scrapbooks--United States. | O'Neal, Hank--Family.
Classification: LCC CT275.O5527 (ebook) | LCC CT275.O5527 O54 2018 (print) |
DDC 306.872--dc23
LC record available at https://urldefense.proofpoint.com/v2/url?u=https-3A__lccn.loc.gov_2017042022&d=DwI-FAg&c=7Q-FWLBTAxn3T_E3HWrzGYJrC4RvUoWDrzTlitGRH_A&r=O2eiy819IcwTGuw-vrBGiVdmhQxMh2yxeggw9ql-TUDE&m=qCRhZP4RMjLzf5jMsey6XaUlnCIbz1nSUPyzRA3UTmA&s=XqHOv_6XnRzOYmixfAPw_I15_40rimSm5MpBHx-S04CQ&e=

TCU Press

TCU Box 298300
Fort Worth, Texas 76129
817.257.7822
www.prs.tcu.edu
To order books: 1.800.826.8911

Designed by Bill Brammer
www.fusion29.com

*For Sarah and Harold*

## Contents

# Introduction

*The dream doesn't die until the dreamer does and maybe not even then.*

This is the story of two people, each born more than a century ago, ordinary people now long dead, mostly forgotten, resting silently and anonymously together under a simple headstone in a modest cemetery in East Texas, just a few miles from where their life together began many years earlier. Two ordinary people, who lived ordinary lives, just like the sentiment in the Sondheim song, except for one thing. Their life together was almost perfect and nothing is ever perfect in a Sondheim show, except possibly the show itself. Maybe there are hundreds of thousands, maybe millions of people who have similar stories. I don't know about that. I only know about this one, and this is what happened, and as I look back on it everything seems so very simple—almost as if it was planned perfectly. In some ways, as the story has unfolded today, it almost appears as if it is still being planned or perhaps guided in some peculiar way.

Harold and Sarah were born into families of limited means and circumstance. Harold in Dallas, in 1910; Sarah in Tyler, in 1914. In 1910, Dallas was not *Big D A Double L A S* and full of skyscrapers and big oil businesses or even big hair, and in 1914 Tyler wasn't the Rose Capital of the World. That would all come later. No, it was much simpler than that.

Harold's father, Lewis Henry O'Neal, born 1878, was a carpenter, and his wife Abbie Nicholson, born 1884, was a housewife. Each was a child of dirt farmers who eked out a hard living in East Texas. At one point, looking to better his station in life, Lewis's father William traded his farm in Chandler for a saloon in Athens, but it didn't work out. He went back to the land and took most of his children with him, but Lewis left the land, struck out on his own, and took his carpenter skills to Dallas, where Harold and his two brothers were born. All the boys learned their father's trade while working with him but also other skills at Bryan Technical High School. Abbie didn't have a very good run of it; she died of renal asthma in 1922 at the age of thirty-eight. I've seen a picture of her when she was about thirty, and she looks twice that age. Lewis had a longer life; he died of cancer in 1957.

Little is known of Harold during the teens and early 1920s. There is one picture of him in a goat cart with his two brothers that is pasted in my baby book, and Sarah has written under the picture *Harold O'Neal, Sr., 5 months*. There's another of him at about age five or six with his brother Raymond and a dog, as well as a formal portrait, at maybe nine or ten,

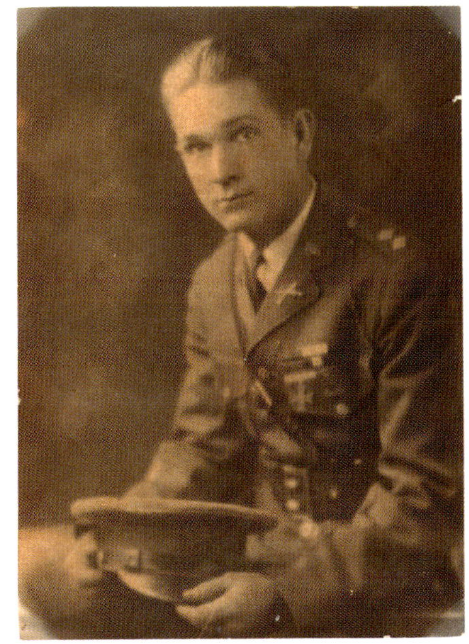

Harold, age 17 in ROTC uniform, Dallas, 1927

wearing a nice jacket, possibly provided by the photographer. Then there is nothing until 1927.

Harold loved carpentry; he worked with his hands until his hands could no longer hold a tool, but he didn't want it to be his profession. He must have taken ROTC training at Bryan Tech, and being ambitious with a bit of larceny in his heart, he lied about his age—claiming to have been born in 1909—and became a reserve lieutenant in the US Army in

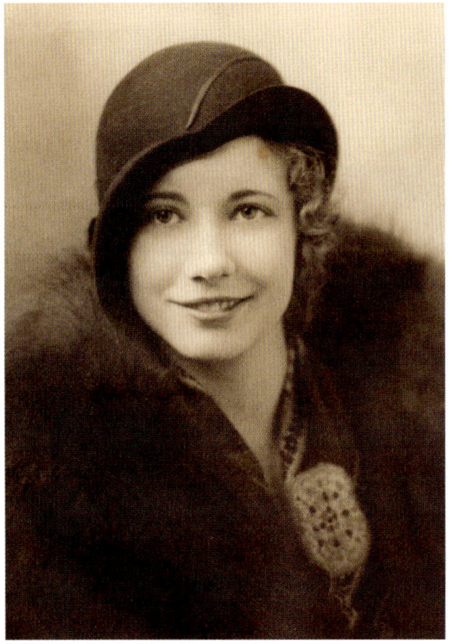

Sarah, age 16, Tyler 1930

1928. By 1929 he was teaching ROTC in Amarillo, Texas. He was only nineteen.

Tyler, Texas, was a small town of less than ten thousand in 1914. The O'Neal and Nicholson families had been in Texas for many years, as had Sarah's mother's family, but Sarah's father had migrated to Texas from Georgia. Curtis Austin Christian was born in Elbert County in 1884. His only claim to fame from his days in Georgia is that around 1900 he was the pitcher for a baseball team from just across the county line in Royston, Georgia. Normally this would be of little interest except that one of his teammates was the legendary Ty Cobb, claimed by some to be the greatest baseball player of all time. A picture of the team was reproduced in *Life* magazine in 1952.

Etta Beatrice Kelly was born near Garden Valley, Texas, in 1886, a town that no longer really exists except on maps and ancient records. There are unconfirmed family legends that the Kelly family was from the Atlanta area and had loose links to the fictional O'Hara family and Margaret Mitchell. Curtis and Beatrice met and were married in Tyler on April 19, 1911. Sarah Beatrice was the first child, and she was photographed and other aspects of her life documented regularly from the time she was three months old until the late 1950s, and all this documentation was saved.

Women usually live longer than men, but just as had been the case with Harold's mother, Beatrice Kelly Christian also died young, in 1947, after a long illness. Curtis hung on for another twenty years, dying in a nursing home in 1967. Sarah had brought him to upstate New York to be close to her, and when he was moved, the old family home in Tyler was rented for a few dollars a month.

Things had changed with the end of World War I; America was being transformed, and these changes would last for two decades. The first decade couldn't have been more different from the second. In the 1920s, the Jazz Age and the horrors of Prohibition swept America while mores and economies changed faster and faster. Things changed faster in big cities, more slowly in the backwaters, and Harold and Sarah were part of these changes, the much slower part, because they were in East Texas.

Toward the end of the second half of the Roaring Twenties, life for most was all about two things: the Great Depression and how to get out of it, as well as no jobs and how to find one. Harold and Sarah were also part of these circumstances, but because they were in the backwater of East Texas where things took longer and because of something called Daisy Bradford No. 3, their circumstances were hard but hardly dire. And these two ordinary but very fortunate people became part of the transformation of America and the beginning of what would later be known as the *American Dream*, especially among the chattering political class and sociologists looking for pegs upon which to hang various theoretical hats. These two young people didn't even know they were part of it or that it was happening; it was just the way things were, at least for them.

When Harold was beginning his career in the Army, Sarah was just a year from completing high school. She was bright and precocious, would graduate in 1930 at the age of sixteen, was the editor of her high school yearbook, an accomplished pianist, and in some ways it seems the belle of the ball.

In the fall of 1930, Harold was tending to his first ROTC students in Amarillo, but Sarah was younger and still leading the life of a happy middle-class teenager in Tyler, Texas. Her father's drug store was struggling but still in operation, and she was a dreamer—about the boy down the street and the much prettier but unavailable boys she saw on the movie screens and in magazines she read at the drugstore soda fountain. She began a scrapbook in which she pasted pictures of the movie stars she liked best. Ramon Novarro was her favorite. She was so innocent she had no idea the gorgeous Novarro didn't like pretty young girls like her, that he preferred pretty young boys.

As the Depression depressed much of America, it took a while for its impact to reach East Texas, and the truth is, the impact was less in East Texas than in most places in the country. Few of the farmers and storekeepers in East Texas were big players in the stock market, so when Black Thursday wiped out Wall Street on October 24, 1929, it didn't wipe out many locals, but it did hurt Sarah's father, who had given credit to far too many people who had sick babies and/or grandmothers who had the shorts and couldn't stop coughing. Sarah's comfortable middle-class life was cramped slightly, but she kept dreaming and saving pictures of movie stars.

Then, less than a year later, while Harold and Sarah were still leading separate lives, unknown to one another, a much more important date occurred in their lives and those of their friends and neighbors. Later, it became known as Black Friday, September 5, 1930, when it was determined there was oil in the Woodbine sands underneath a well known as Daisy Bradford No. 3, and then a month later an oil well exploded in the middle of nowhere, in a field four or five miles northwest of Henderson, and began gushing thousands of gallons of black gold every day. Then a few months later there was Black Sunday, December 28, 1930, when twenty miles to the north in Kilgore, the Lou Della Crim No. 1 came in, a well capable of producing ten thousand barrels of oil per day.

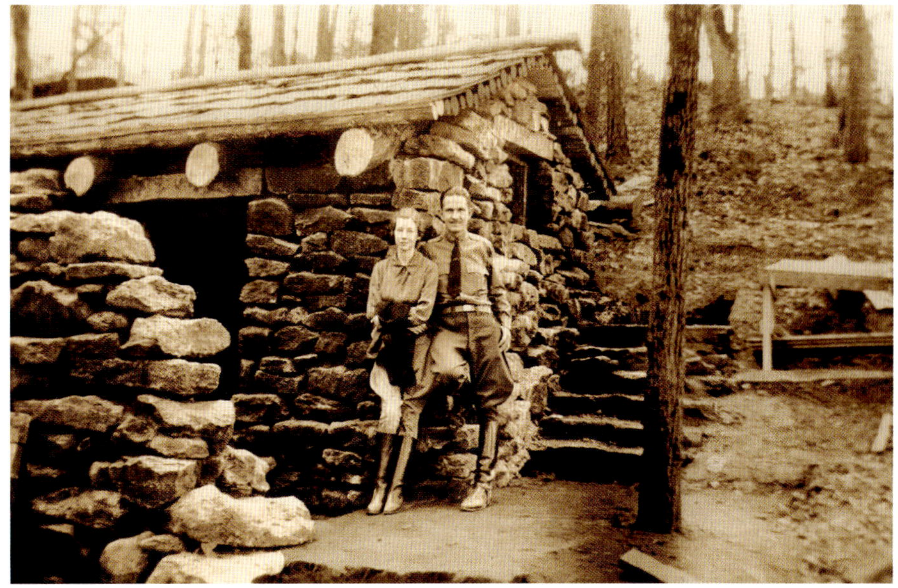

Harold and Sarah, Caddo Lake, 1934

The second well proved the East Texas oil patch was at least twenty miles long, the largest known oil field in the world, and nothing was ever the same. This discovery prevented the depths of the Depression from ever reaching into this pocket of East Texas, and Kilgore, the town in which Harold and Sarah eventually settled, saw its population grow from seven hundred or so when the Lou Della Crim came in to nearly ten thousand within a year. Some may think it unfair to call the area a backwater, but when those wells came in there were few paved roads, no sewers, hardly any services, and heavy rains had water backed up everywhere.

But the Great Depression did have an impact on Harold and Sarah, and it had nothing to do with the oil boom. Harold was still in the army, teaching in Amarillo, when he met Sarah on March 19, 1932. The job was decent, but it kept him far away from Sarah in Tyler and in

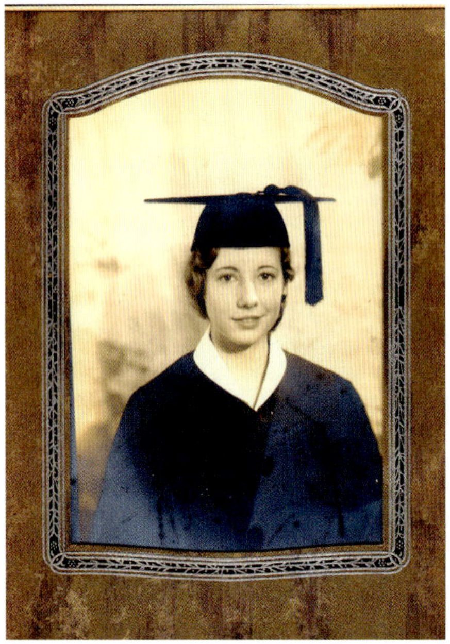

Sarah, May 26, 1932,
graduation from Tyler Junior College

Waco, where she was in school at Baylor University.

After they met and the sparks flew and the bells rang, it was clear to both of them that Harold had to find a military job in East Texas. But what kind of job could he find in a country that had thirteen million unemployed men looking for work? As it turned out, there was an answer right around the corner, and he didn't have to wait long. The timing couldn't have been more perfect.

In November 1932, a few months after Sarah and Harold met, an aristocratic man with a liberal streak named Franklin Delano Roosevelt was elected president. He was inaugurated on March 4, 1933, having every intention of putting as many of those thirteen million unemployed men back to work as quickly as possible. He had a plan, and it only took him thirty-three days to get started.

On April 5, 1933, President Franklin D. Roosevelt signed the legislation that created the most popular of his New Deal programs, the Civilian Conservation Corps. The CCC, as it came to be known, provided employment for young men, unmarried and unemployed, ages 18-25. It provided the young men with food, housing, educational instruction, medical attention, and clothing, as well as a salary of $30 a month, roughly a dollar a day, $25 of which was sent home to their parents.

In exchange, the young men did hard work: they planted billions of trees, built roads and bridges, fixed up state and national parks, and most importantly, built over eight hundred state parks throughout the country. Army officers were in charge of the young men who built these parks, and between the years 1933 and 1938 Harold was the officer in charge of building three of them. These assignments in East Texas allowed the two young lovers to be together on weekends and during holidays, all of which led to a secret marriage across the state line in Benton, Louisiana, in mid-1935, and an official one a few months later in Tyler.

His superiors always thought he was older, but Harold was only twenty-three when he first commanded units building parks near Denison (Loy Park, 1934), Karnack (Caddo Lake State Park, 1934-38), Daingerfield (Daingerfield State Park, 1935-38), and Bogata (1936). Officially, there was no segregation allowed in the CCC, but Harold's company at Bogata was entirely black. This experience would serve him well in coming years, particularly during World War II in the South Pacific and in his second career in education that followed his nearly two decades of military service.

During these years the overly romantic and very much in love Sarah kept an illustrated diary and scrapbooks of her adventures with Harold.

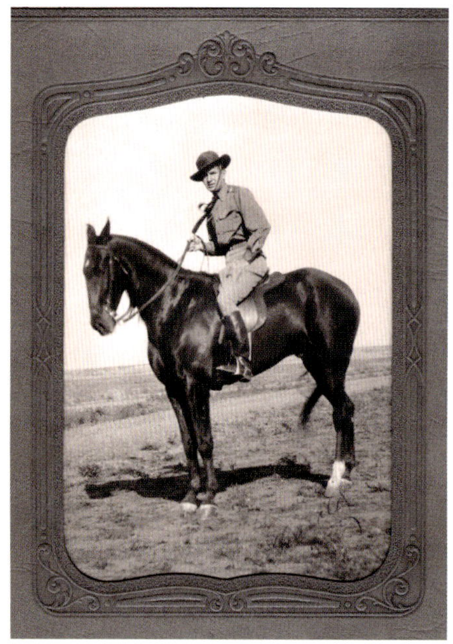

Harold, Amarillo, 1931

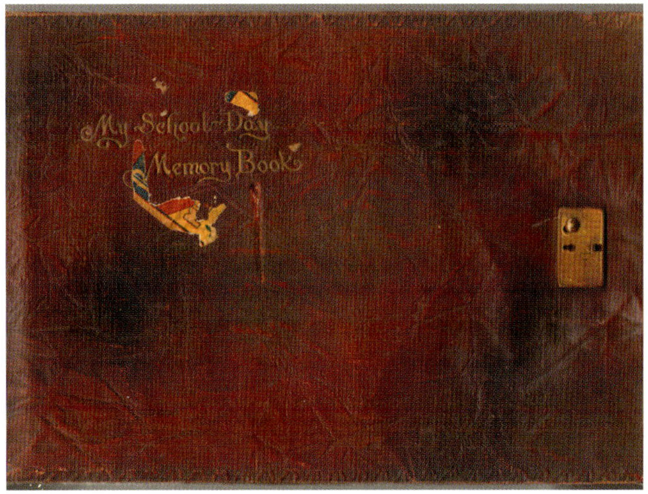


Sarah's 1930s Scrapbook

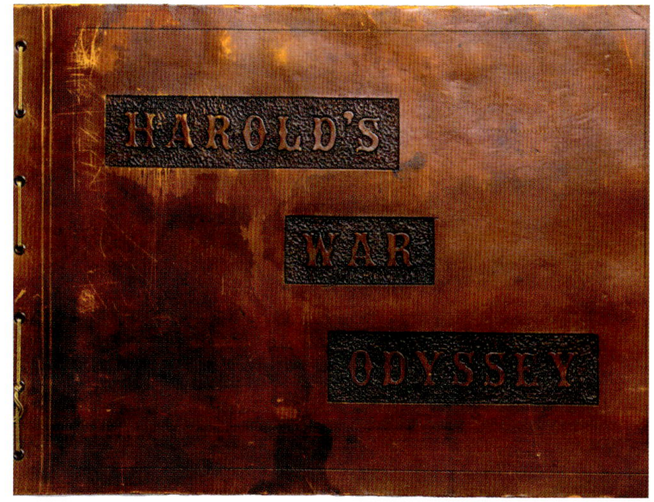


Harold's War Odyssey

If you look at her diary entries and the clippings and pictures she pasted in her scrapbooks, it's clear she was still a dreamer, a naïve, romantic young girl who dreamed of someday moving into a modest cottage stocked with pots and pans, and maybe a radio and an electric Victrola, and cups and saucers and plates that matched. She had no idea that she and Harold were in their own innocent way pursuing the American Dream, but they were. They didn't know that the rules were if you worked hard and were honest and forthright and fair and humane and did the right thing and studied hard and saved your money and went to church on Sundays, all things were possible. The reason they didn't know it is that this is what they were inclined to do anyway.

And of course, with an occasional bump in the road, that's what happened. With the coming of World War II and America's dominance after the Allied victories and the surge in industry, employment, and educational opportunities, there was rapid growth in the standard of living of the American middle class. The dream came true for millions of Americans, and Harold and Sarah were swept up with it.

They had been brought together by accident, were able to be married because of the first New Deal program, endured three years apart because of World War II, but survived and prospered after the war because of the benefits of the last New Deal program, the GI Bill of Rights. Harold was a career soldier, but after eighteen years that career ended in 1946-1947 because of illness and disease, either brought on or exacerbated by his service in the Pacific Theater during World War II.

At the time of the Japanese surrender Harold was officially Major O'Neal, the commander and Provost Marshall of the Fourteenth Corps of the First Cavalry Division. Sarah was still a housewife, in command of me and a tiny apartment in Fort Worth, Texas. Harold often said he was a "chief of police" in Japan, by which I presume he meant his military police company supervised part of a city. The city was Sendai, but he didn't keep the job very long; he was covered with what he called "jungle rot," was suffering from tropical sprue, and weighed about 116 pounds. When he was sent home in the fall of 1945, he first went to Fort Sam Houston, then back to the apartment Sarah maintained in Fort Worth, stayed for a few months, and then went to back and forth to Fort Sam Houston where it was hoped he might be cured or at least stabilized. While hospitalized, Harold taught himself how to work with leather and began fashioning a scrapbook that would illustrate his years in the Pacific Theater. He would call it Harold's War Odyssey.

Many months of treatment provided no relief; he was declared unfit for duty, was discharged due to permanent medical disability, and returned permanently to Fort Worth. But fortunately the possibility of pursuing the dream was still intact, as it was for so many other returning servicemen. The GI Bill plus his medical disability payments of $147 a month enabled him to enroll as a freshman at Texas Christian University in 1946. He worked overtime, and six years later had a BA and MA from TCU and a Doctorate in Education from Indiana University, and would never be unemployed until he retired in 1970. It worked that way, once upon a time.

Along the way, both Harold and Sarah became part of the dream realized by a generation that worked hard at and believed in their dreams and what they were doing, with a comfortable home of their own, new cars every so often, appliances to make life easier, and every expectation that it would be even better for their only child, which, of course, it was. And when in the mid-1950s it all came together with their own home, a new car, and an upstairs and downstairs telephone, it was just the natural progression of things.

When these two young people began their journey, the idea of the American Dream wasn't something they thought about or scholars wrote about or politicians wailed about. That would all come later when the official dream was codified, along with a lot of other things, and became a catch phrase, to be analyzed and studied while being attained by fewer and fewer people. But in those years the way Harold and Sarah lived their lives was just the way it was, the way it was supposed to happen, once upon a time. They were just trying to be with one another, to get by as comfortably as possible, but with modest expectations, to find their own way and build a future for themselves and their only child. Which is just what they managed to do.

This is their story in pictures, illustrations, and words, mostly pictures and illustrations.

# Harold

## November 22, 1910–March 19, 1932

**IN 1910, DALLAS, TEXAS WAS THE FIFTY-EIGHTH LARGEST CITY IN THE UNITED STATES** with slightly less than one hundred thousand citizens. It was the largest city in Texas, a status it would maintain into the 1920s, when it was displaced by Houston. It was a cosmopolitan center, soon to be home of a branch of the Federal Reserve Bank (1911), Southern Methodist University (1915), and already the home of the tallest building west of the Mississippi, as well as the most prominent inland cotton market in the country.

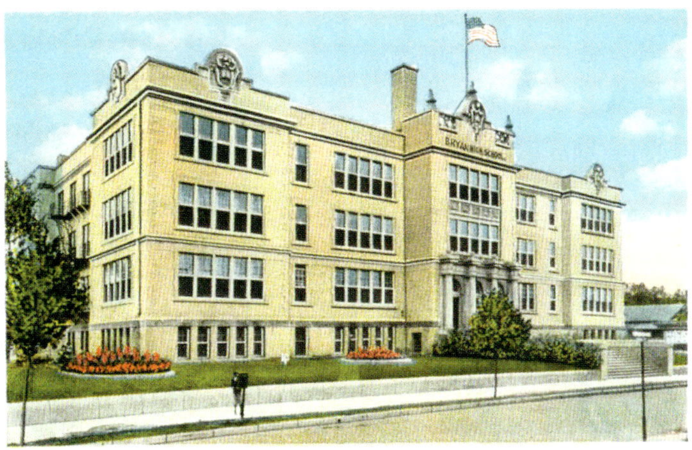

Bryan High School, Dallas, Texas

It was, however, still a mixture of the Deep South, the Wild West, and everything in between. There was at least one widely reported lynching that year, and probably a few others that went unnoticed. In the most notorious reported event, a black man, Allen Brooks, accused of molesting a white child, was attacked by a mob inside the Dallas courthouse and thrown out a second story window. It was reported that he landed on his head. Conveniently for the lynch mob, he already had a rope around his neck when he hit the ground, it having been placed around his neck while still in the courthouse, and even though he may have been killed by the fall, just to make sure they dragged Brooks a few blocks and strung him up from the Elks Arch, a prominent landmark.

On the positive side, a few months later, Booker T. Washington spoke before a biracial audience at Fair Park, so in this instance and in many others, civility prevailed. Harold O'Neal was born in this city of extremes on November 22. As it turned out, he was inclined to side with civility.

The city was in the midst of a building boom, a boom that would continue through and beyond the Depression; a good place for a skilled carpenter to make his home and raise a family, although the legendary Neiman-Marcus store would not be completed until 1913, and the famous, sometimes infamous, Woodlawn Sanitarium was also three years in the future and twenty-five years into the future of the family into which Harold would marry.

Harold's father, Lewis Henry O'Neal, born 1878, was a carpenter, and his wife Abbie Nicholson, born 1884, was a housewife. He was lucky to have been born at all because so many of the men and women in his family died young. His grandmother was consumed in a grass fire, his mother was stricken by catarrh in 1895, and two of his stepmother's sisters died of typhoid fever. Pneumonia claimed yet another family member, and a few others had cancer. They lived hard lives, and it was not a healthy family, a tradition that lasted through Harold's generation.

Lewis and Abbie were each children of subsistence farmers who eked out a difficult living in East Texas. Sometimes the eking was harder than others. The size of the family farms ranged all the way from 1,900 acres to fewer than one hundred, and sometimes they were forced to farm rentals, both in Texas and a few times in Oklahoma. At one point, in 1905, looking to raise his standard of living, Lewis's father William traded his farm near Chandler for a saloon in Athens, bought a home, and moved the family twenty-five miles to begin a new life. Two years later, in 1907, Athens voted itself dry, and the saloon went bankrupt. William lost his home, and he and his family went back to the land, where he struggled picking cotton or truck and dirt farming until the end of his long and very hard life in 1932. The lives of his children were only slightly better than his own.

Lewis had enough of the struggle and uncertainty of itinerant farming and was nearing thirty when everything collapsed in Athens. He decided not to return to the land and took his carpenter skills to Dallas, where Harold and his brother Raymond (1907) were born. The oldest boy, Cecil, was born in 1902, in Chandler. In 1917 the family migrated to Oklahoma City but returned to Dallas in 1921. All the boys learned their father's trade while working with him, and Harold and Raymond learned other skills at Bryan Technical High School, from which Raymond graduated in 1926 and Harold in 1929. The oldest brother, Cecil, finished high school in Oklahoma City and was the first of three brothers to travel outside Texas and Oklahoma, but he returned to Dallas and carpentry in the 1920s.

Harold's mother, Abbie, was worked hard and died of renal asthma in 1922 at the age of 38, or maybe it was 36. Her tiny eight-line death notice in a Dallas newspaper was clipped and saved in a family scrapbook.

It read: *O'Neil, - Mrs. Abbie O'Neil, 36, died Saturday in Vickery, Texas. She is survived by her husband, C. P. O'Neil and thre sons, Raymond, Cecil and Harold O'Neil. Funeral services were held at 2 o'clock Monday afternoon at the Weiland parlors.* The paper managed to misspell O'Neal four times, change her husband's name from Lewis Henry to C. P., and invent a new word, "thre," which might be a misspelling of either "three" or possibly "their." Plus there's the question about age, thirty-six or thirty-eight? Odds are that she was thirty-eight. I've seen a picture of her when she was in her early thirties, and she looks twice that age.

Lewis had a longer life; he remarried in 1926 (Marie Hicks), remained in the Vickery section of Dallas, and died of cancer in 1957.

Except for the death of Abbie in 1922, the Vickery period was one of some stability for the Lewis O'Neal family. Today, Vickery is known as a quaint section in northeast Dallas with older landmarked bungalows in various architectural styles. When Lewis arrived in 1921 there were few houses, but a good deal of surveyed land. He felt it was an ideal place for a carpenter to build a home and perhaps find work building homes for others.

At the time Vickery had a population of less than two hundred people, and a few stores and churches. There would soon be more families and they would need housing. Over the years the population fluctuated, but not too much, and when Vickery was annexed by the City of Dallas in 1945 it had a population of about one thousand.

Little is known of Harold during the teens and early 1920s. The family was not affluent by any means, but when they returned to Dallas and settled in Vickery, Lewis and his children's carpentry skills were put to use, and they earned a decent living. They built a modest but attractive bungalow in the newly developing Dallas subdivision.

It was of a scale and style similar to the home Sarah's father had built in Tyler. There was even a black Ford to go with the house; some time before her death in 1922, Abbie posed with the car. She looks like a tough lady, but she wasn't tough enough to beat the asthma that killed her.

There are few family pictures from this period except for items discovered in an old memory book compiled from photographs saved by Cecil O'Neal and assembled by someone else, possibly

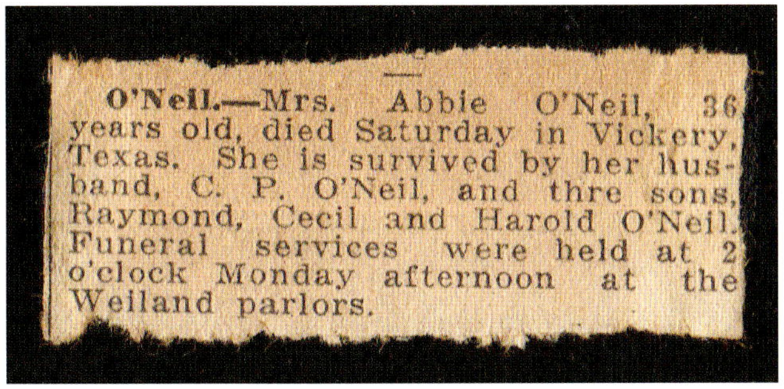

O'Neil.—Mrs. Abbie O'Neil, 36 years old, died Saturday in Vickery, Texas. She is survived by her husband, C. P. O'Neil, and thre sons, Raymond, Cecil and Harold O'Neil. Funeral services were held at 2 o'clock Monday afternoon at the Weiland parlors.

Abbie Nicholson O'Neal obituary, 1922

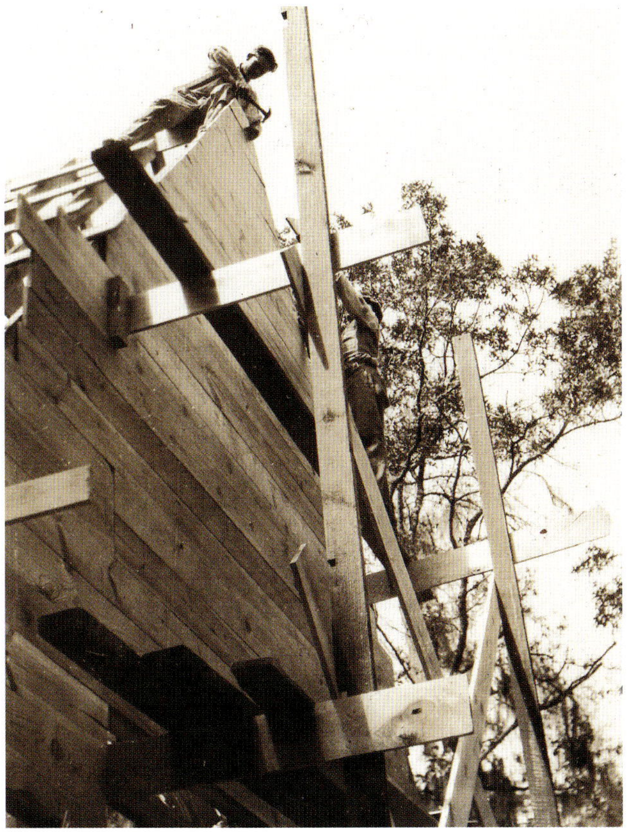

Building a home in Vickery (early 1920s)

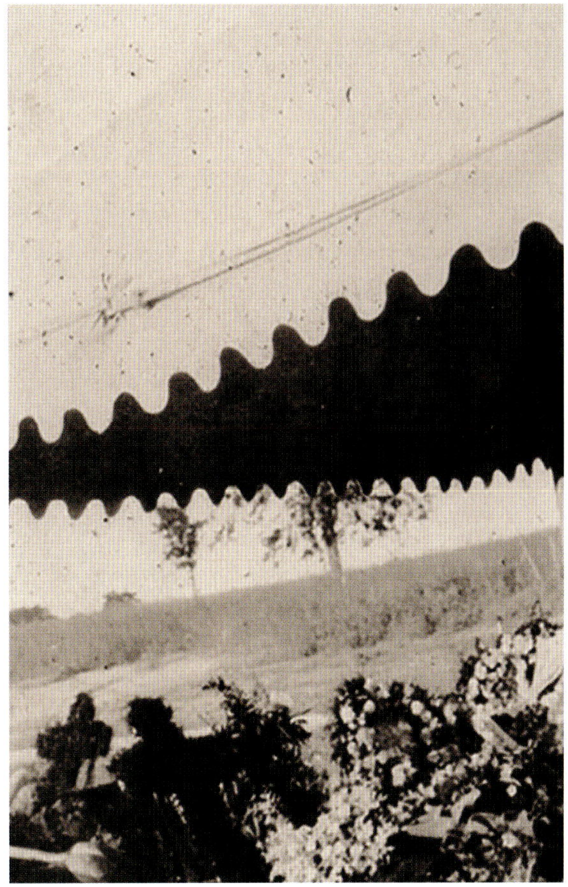

Abbie's grave, Vickery, Texas, 1922

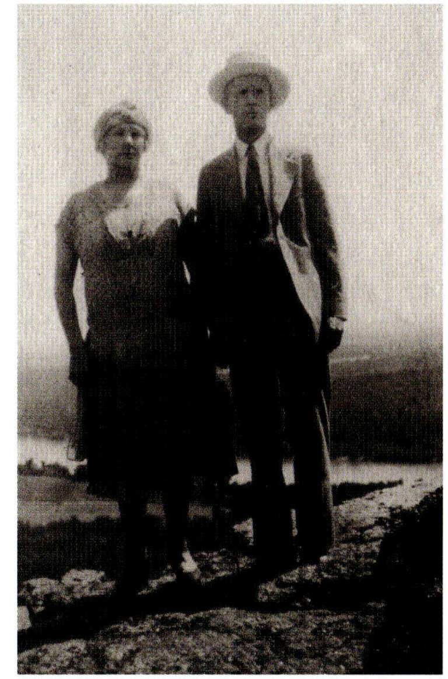

Lewis and Marie O'Neal (early 1930s)

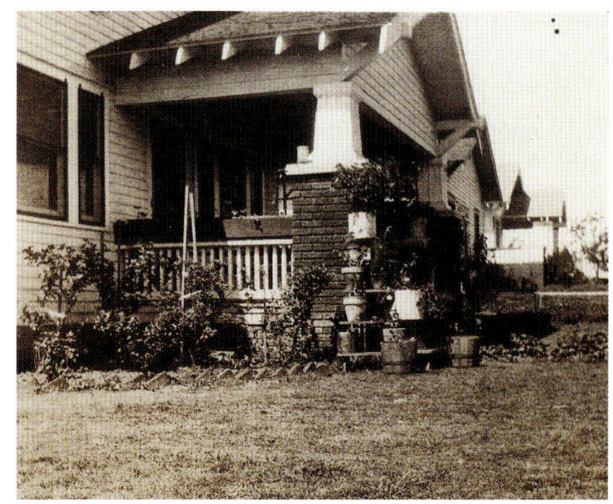

The O'Neal Home in Vickery

his wife, Maudelle Kidd, to whom he was married in 1928. There is one picture of Cecil and Raymond sitting on a forlorn donkey and another of Harold in a goat cart with his two brothers that is pasted in my baby book and Sarah has written under the picture *Harold O'Neal, Sr., 5 months*.

There's another of him at about age five or six with his brother Raymond and a dog. It is casual and out of focus. There are also three formal portraits, one of Harold, at maybe nine or ten, and another of Abbie and her three sons. All the brothers are wearing nice jackets, possibly provided by the Rembrandt Studio, a well-equipped studio on Main Street in Oklahoma City. The third portrait is also of Cecil, a few years earlier, dressed as a smart young man, looking ready to be cast in a gangster movie of the period.

Cecil O'Neal's scrapbook is filled with snapshots of activities in Vickery and other small towns as well as invitations, dance cards, playbills, tickets, his mother's funeral notice, building projects, concerts, masquerade balls, menus, graduation notices, and other sorts of ephemera. On many occasions Lewis and Abbie O'Neal were listed as chaperones at dances sponsored by clubs or fraternal organizations, dances with names like the "June Toddle" or "Turkey Dance." The bands that played had jazz age names like the Tex "A" Jazzers, the Original Footwarmers, the Night Riders, Frisco Jazz Orchestra, and best of all, the Rat's Hill Orchestra. And they played the hot songs of the day like "Sister Kate," "Hot Lips," "Aunt Hager's Blues," "Haunting Blues," and "Lonesome Mama," as well as the ever-popular "Got to Cool My Doggies Now," whatever that means. Songs almost lost in time, but how fascinating it is that the bands listed the songs they intended to play on dance cards and flyers.

In addition to the hot jazz bands there were times set aside for more serious kinds of music. Dallas has always been a magnet for great classical artists, for symphonies and opera performances and recitals. Even in 1923, when three long-forgotten vocalists, headlined by Mrs. Helen Fouts Cahoon, and four instrumentalists presented an evening of song at the Bush Temple that featured the music of Beethoven, Mozart, Grieg, Arenski, and the still very much alive and well Percy Grainger. This may have been the first time his music was performed in Dallas. It may also have been the first time Harold was exposed to this kind of music, music that stayed with him the rest of his life.

At the same time there was just enough of the Wild West and pseudo-gangster culture in and around Dallas to encourage some of Cecil and Harold's friends to pose as much-too-heavily armed but well-dressed gangsters. The would-be gangster's molls posed languidly on the bumper of their getaway car, and this was a decade before the exploits of the infamous Texas outlaw

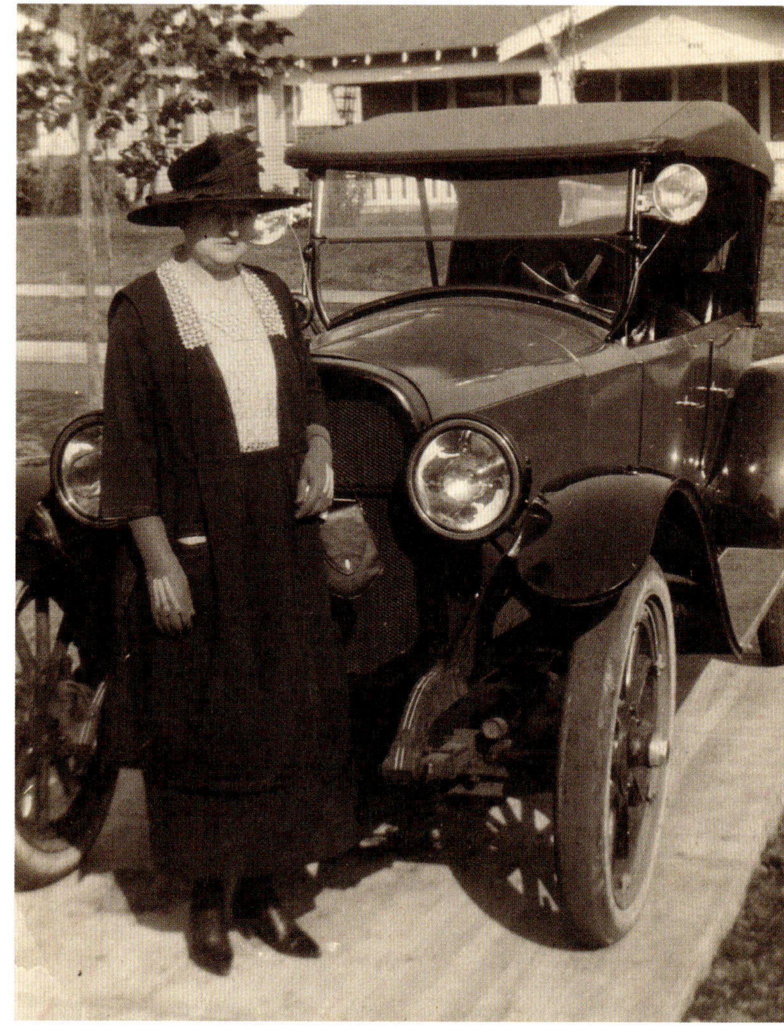

Abbie Nicholson O'Neal with the family Ford

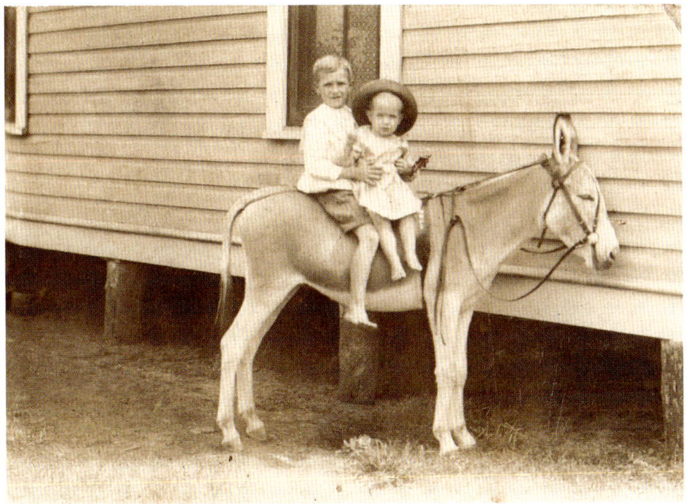

Raymond and Cecil on a donkey, Dallas, 1909

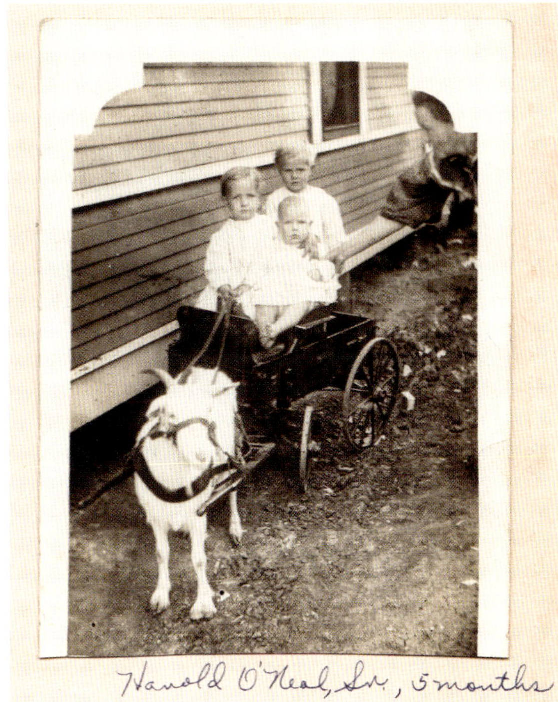


Harold, Raymond, and Cecil in a goat cart, Dallas, 1911

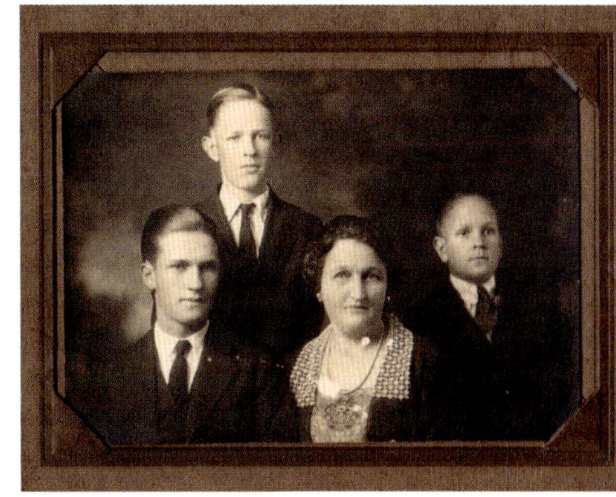

Cecil, Raymond, Abbie, and Harold O'Neal, Oklahoma City, circa 1917-18

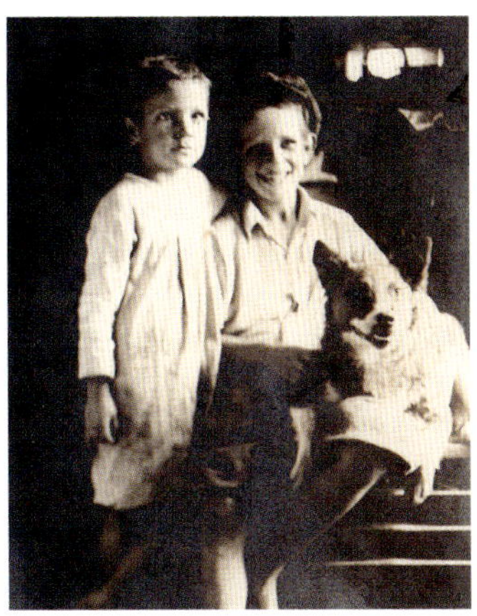

Harold, Raymond, and a dog, Dallas, circa 1914

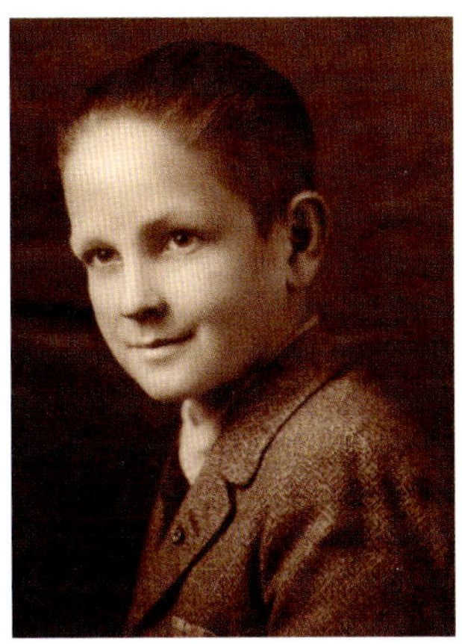

Harold, age 10, Oklahoma City, 1920

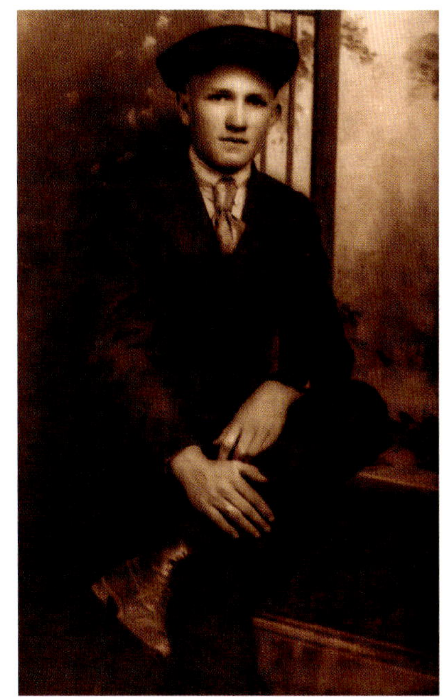

Cecil O'Neal, Dallas, mid-1910s

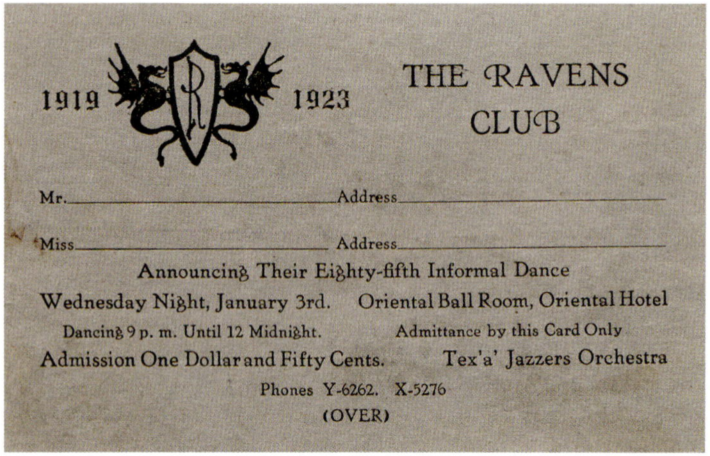

1919 R 1923

THE RAVENS CLUB

Mr.________________ Address________________

Miss________________ Address________________

Announcing Their Eighty-fifth Informal Dance

Wednesday Night, January 3rd. Oriental Ball Room, Oriental Hotel

Dancing 9 p. m. Until 12 Midnight. Admittance by this Card Only

Admission One Dollar and Fifty Cents. Tex'a' Jazzers Orchestra

Phones Y-6262. X-5276

(OVER)

Ravens Club informal dance ticket, January 3, 1923

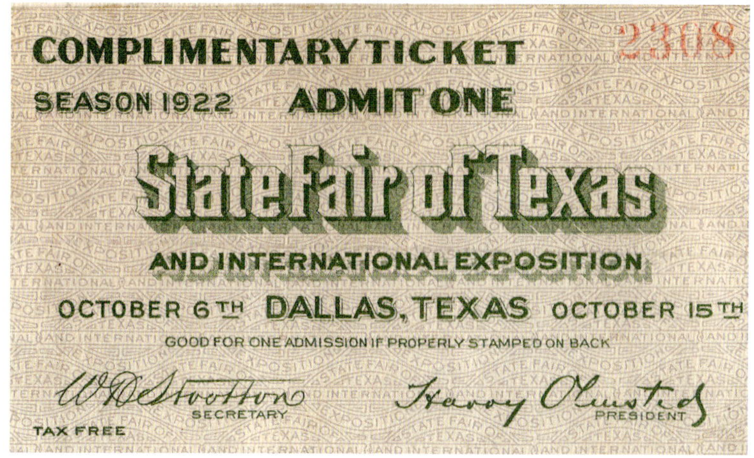

2368

COMPLIMENTARY TICKET

SEASON 1922 ADMIT ONE

State Fair of Texas

AND INTERNATIONAL EXPOSITION

OCTOBER 6TH DALLAS, TEXAS OCTOBER 15TH

GOOD FOR ONE ADMISSION IF PROPERLY STAMPED ON BACK

W. H. Stratton, SECRETARY  Harry Olmsted, PRESIDENT

TAX FREE

State Fair of Texas, Dallas, 1922

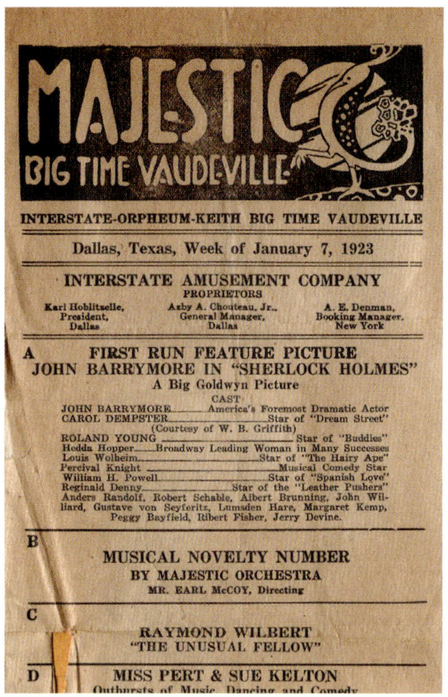

MAJESTIC

BIG TIME VAUDEVILLE

INTERSTATE-ORPHEUM-KEITH BIG TIME VAUDEVILLE

Dallas, Texas, Week of January 7, 1923

INTERSTATE AMUSEMENT COMPANY

PROPRIETORS

Karl Hoblitzelle, President, Dallas — Asby A. Chouteau, Jr., General Manager, Dallas — A. E. Denman, Booking Manager, New York

A — FIRST RUN FEATURE PICTURE

JOHN BARRYMORE IN "SHERLOCK HOLMES"

A Big Goldwyn Picture

CAST

JOHN BARRYMORE ........ America's Foremost Dramatic Actor
CAROL DEMPSTER ........ Star of "Dream Street"
(Courtesy of W. B. Griffith)
ROLAND YOUNG ........ Star of "Buddies"
Hedda Hopper ........ Broadway Leading Woman in Many Successes
Louis Wolheim ........ Star of "The Hairy Ape"
Percival Knight ........ Musical Comedy Star
William H. Powell ........ Star of "Spanish Love"
Reginald Denny ........ Star of the "Leather Pushers"
Anders Randolf, Robert Schable, Albert Brunning, John Willard, Gustave von Seyferitz, Lumsden Hare, Margaret Kemp, Peggy Bayfield, Ribert Fisher, Jerry Devine.

B — MUSICAL NOVELTY NUMBER

BY MAJESTIC ORCHESTRA

MR. EARL McCOY, Directing

C — RAYMOND WILBERT

"THE UNUSUAL FELLOW"

D — MISS PERT & SUE KELTON

Outbursts of Music, Dancing and Comedy

Majestic Theater Big Time Vaudeville, January 7, 1923

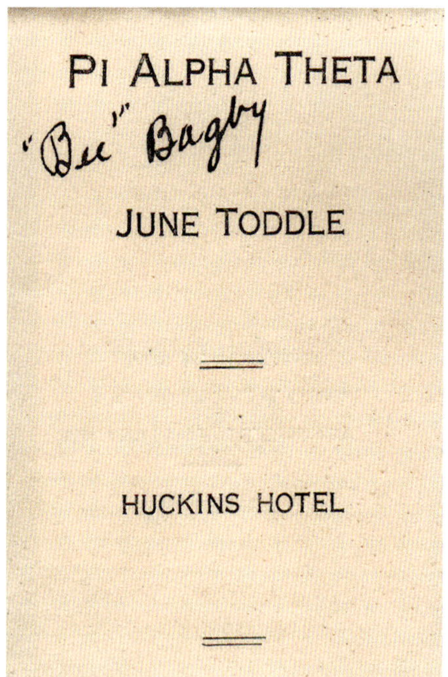

PI ALPHA THETA

"Bee" Bagby

JUNE TODDLE

HUCKINS HOTEL

Pi Alpha Theta June Toddle

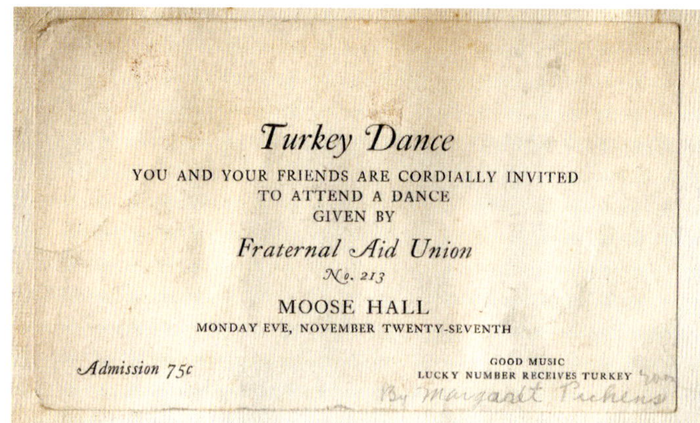

*Turkey Dance*

YOU AND YOUR FRIENDS ARE CORDIALLY INVITED TO ATTEND A DANCE GIVEN BY

*Fraternal Aid Union*

*No. 213*

MOOSE HALL

MONDAY EVE, NOVEMBER TWENTY-SEVENTH

*Admission 75c*

GOOD MUSIC

LUCKY NUMBER RECEIVES TURKEY

Turkey Dance

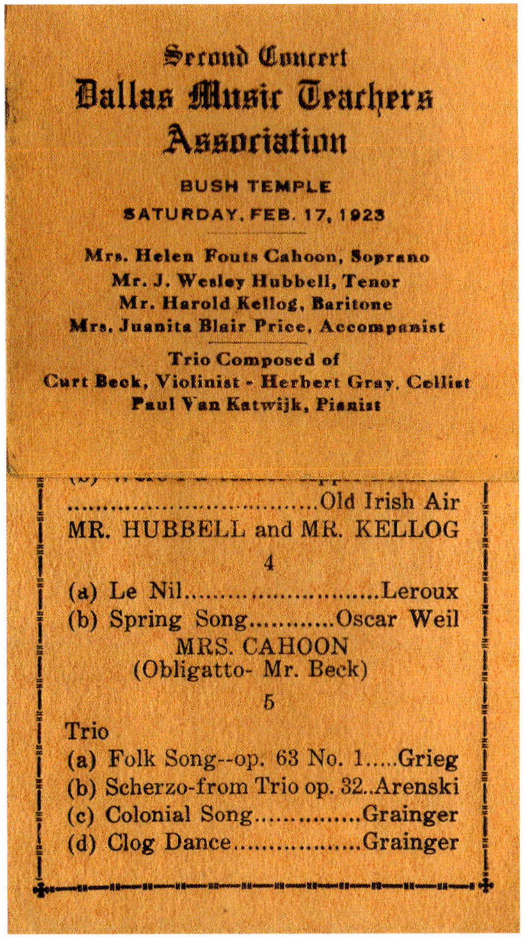

Second Concert
Dallas Music Teachers Association

BUSH TEMPLE

SATURDAY, FEB. 17, 1923

Mrs. Helen Fouts Cahoon, Soprano
Mr. J. Wesley Hubbell, Tenor
Mr. Harold Kellog, Baritone
Mrs. Juanita Blair Price, Accompanist

Trio Composed of
Curt Beck, Violinist - Herbert Gray, Cellist
Paul Van Katwijk, Pianist

..................................Old Irish Air
MR. HUBBELL and MR. KELLOG

4

(a) Le Nil............................Leroux
(b) Spring Song...........Oscar Weil
MRS. CAHOON
(Obligatto- Mr. Beck)

5

Trio
(a) Folk Song--op. 63 No. 1.....Grieg
(b) Scherzo-from Trio op. 32..Arenski
(c) Colonial Song...............Grainger
(d) Clog Dance..................Grainger

Concert, Dallas, February 17, 1923

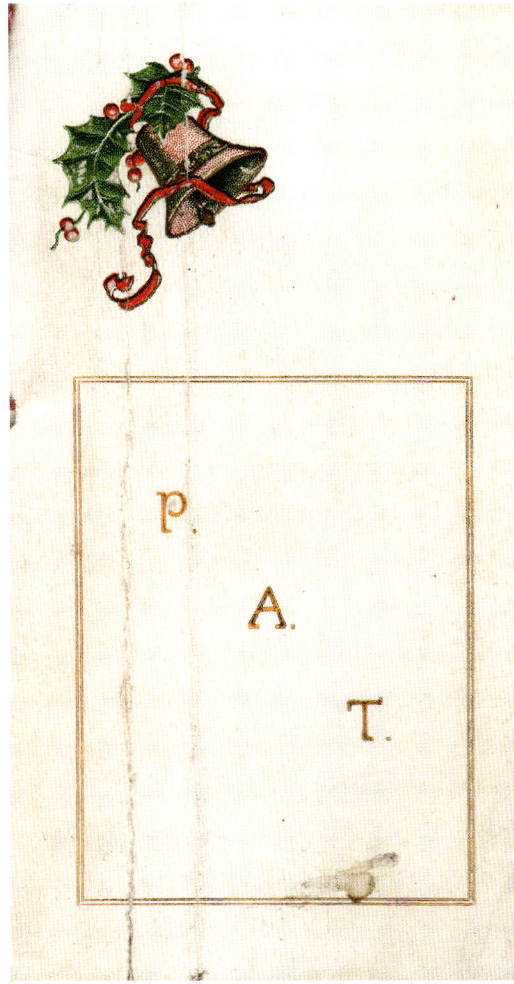


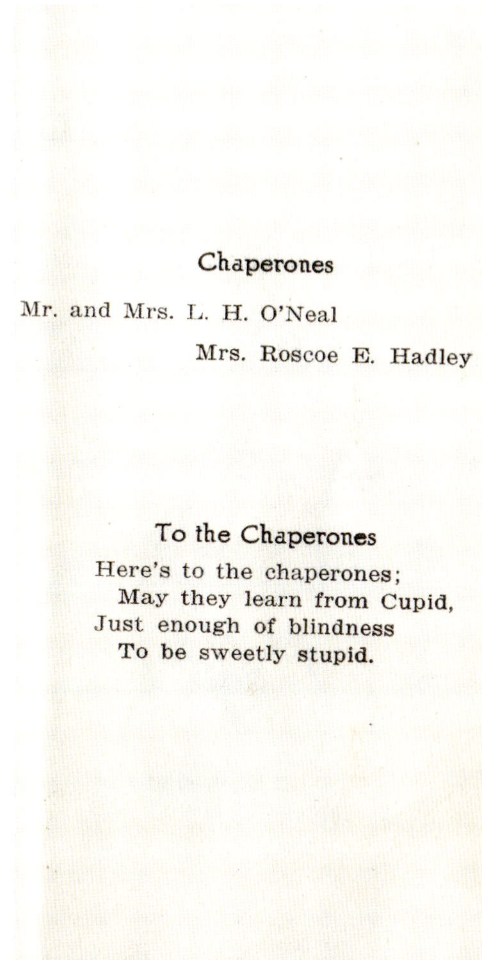

Chaperones

Mr. and Mrs. L. H. O'Neal
Mrs. Roscoe E. Hadley

To the Chaperones

Here's to the chaperones;
May they learn from Cupid,
Just enough of blindness
To be sweetly stupid.

Chaperones

## Sunday afternoon gangsters

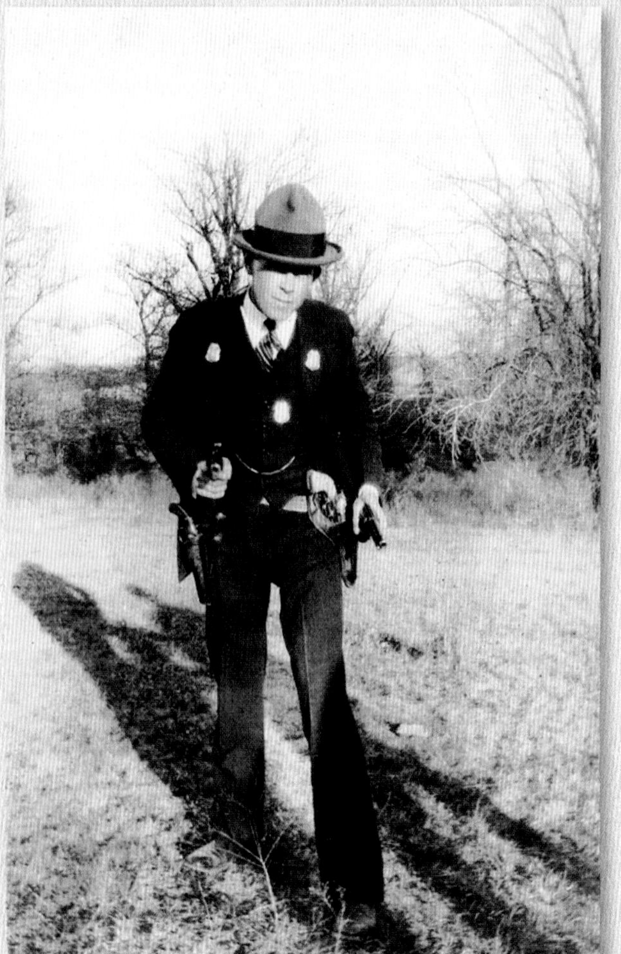

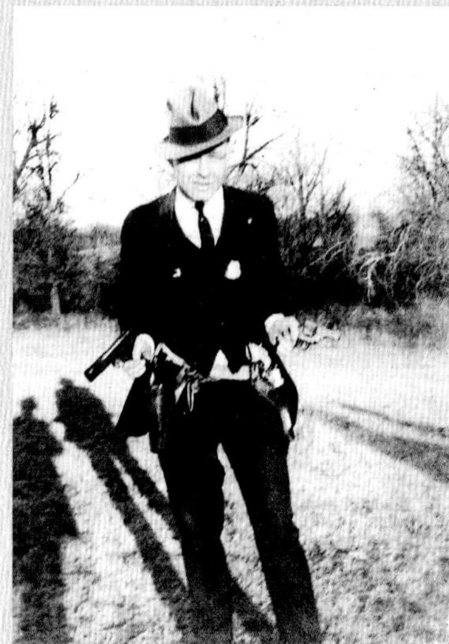

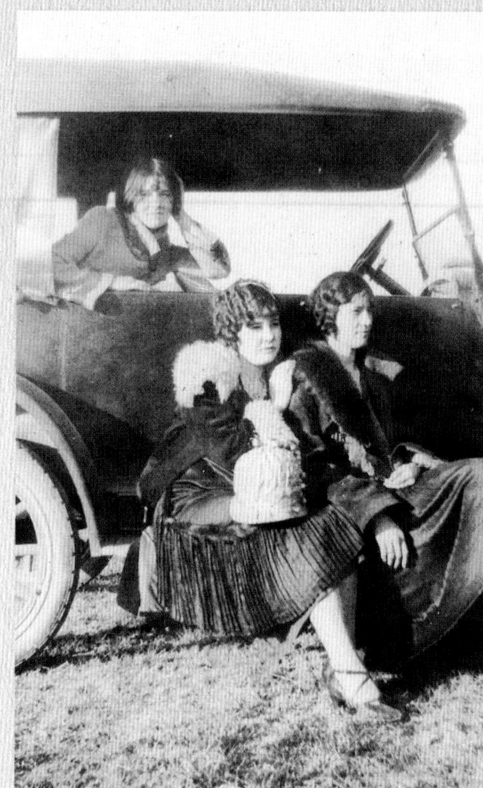

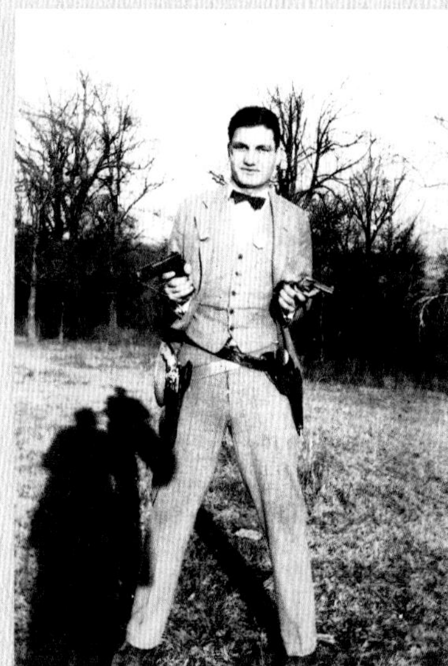

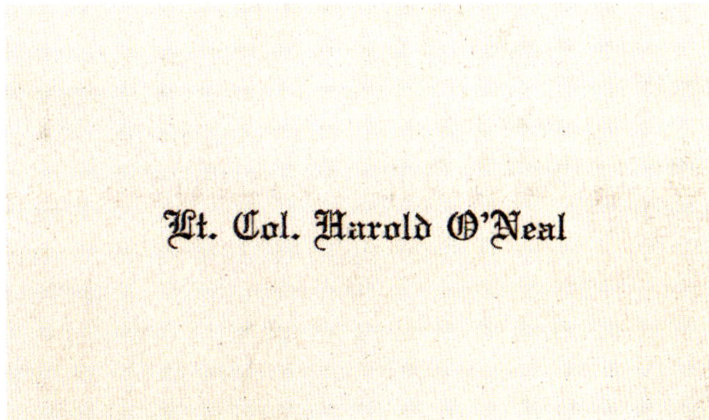


gang, Bonnie and Clyde. A fourteen-year-old Harold probably thought this was a terrific Sunday outing.

Harold loved carpentry; he worked with his hands and woodworking tools until age and strength issues prevented him from doing so, but he didn't want it to be his profession, and woodworking was never more than a serious hobby. In addition to regular studies, he undertook ROTC training at Bryan Tech, discovered he was skilled in matters military, and began saving paperwork to prove it. He enrolled in the Junior Division of the Reserve Officers' Training Corps on January 31, 1926, and an oversized document from the Reserve Officers' Training Corps of The Dallas High Schools proclaimed on January 30, 1928, that the Superintendent of Schools appointed Harold O'Neal a Cadet Second Lieutenant in the Infantry Section Reserve Officers' Training Corps of the Army of the United States, Junior Division. On September 17, 1928, he was promoted to First Lieutenant, and one year later, on September 16, 1929, a few short weeks before the stock market crash on October 29, he was promoted once again, but this time to Lieutenant Colonel. It is unclear how he managed to bypass Captain and Major, but he was so sure the promotion was real that he had calling cards printed that read: *Lt. Col. Harold O'Neal.* He was actively looking for a military assignment elsewhere, and a certificate dated January 1930 states, "Lt. Col. O'Neal was cadet commanding officer of First Battalion and discharged his duties in a very satisfactory manner."

Harold was ambitious and not only wanted a job but wanted that job to be as an army officer. He knew that he would be looked on differently as an officer and a gentleman, and having spent part of his high school years in ROTC training, recognized there might be job opportunities for him to become an instructor in other schools in Texas. He knew he looked dashing in his military uniform, and lied about his age, claiming to have been born in 1909. He became a reserve lieutenant in the US Army in late 1929. His military records reflected the 1909 birthdate for the next fifteen years.

The Great Depression caused massive unemployment and disruption of many lives, and there may have been some retraction in the US Army, but it did not affect Harold. Perhaps his superiors recognized a good junior officer in the making and decided to take a chance on him, but his reserve army position and teaching skills led him to his first non-carpentry-related job. Early in 1930, just a few months out of Bryan Tech, at the real age of nineteen, he was scheduled to begin teaching ROTC at the high school in Amarillo, Texas. From this point on his life is well documented in words and pictures.

In the summer of 1930 Harold undertook a month of training at Camp Dallas in Mineral Wells, Texas, the last time he would take part in such activity for many years. A few months later he was in the midst of the fall semester at Amarillo High School, as Lieut. O'Neal, in charge of the training of at least 150 cadets in the high school's ROTC program. His cadets were divided into four companies. He was also the sponsor of The Diamond & Disc Club, an organization that included a dozen cadet officers, and the NCO Club, which included thirty-eight noncommissioned cadet officers.

If the school yearbook is any indication, the ROTC department had a very successful year. In the spring of 1931 the graduating class of Amarillo High School published its annual yearbook, *La Airosa*. It is a handsome, well-produced 252-page book, filled with features common to yearbooks in those years. The most popular girl and boy, best athlete, class wit, favorite teacher, all the clubs, all the sports, big pictures of seniors and little pictures of sophomores, medium-sized pictures of the teachers, dozens of pages of candid pictures, many pages of "compliments of" ads in the back, and four pages for autographs.

There are also four pages of full-page formal portraits of four very pretty girls, under the heading "Favorites." The favorite senior was Sara Moreland; the junior, Helen Mode; the sophomore, Elizabeth Wilson; and the football queen was Ruth Virginia Perdue. There is nothing unusual about this except for one thing: Sara Moreland, a beautiful young girl who is pictured throughout the yearbook, seems unusually prominent. Who was Sara Moreland and what was her relationship with the young man pictured in the faculty section with the caption H. L. O'Neal, Commandant of Cadets?

Sara was the senior class favorite; she was also the sponsor of ROTC Company B. There is a full page cut-out picture of Harold surrounded by Sara and the three other sponsors. This meant Sara and the three others must have interacted regularly with the handsome twenty-year-old Commandant of Cadets. On the page facing the cut-out pictures is a snapshot of the four girls with Harold that is captioned "It looks as tho they adore army life."

The yearbook is Harold's copy, and when issued he was no more than a couple of years older than the girls in these pictures. Next to her picture Sara has written *I wish you lots and lots of luck, Sara*. Nothing unusual here either except she has also boldly signed the page marked "Autographs" *Sara Moreland TAG '31*. There are only two other signatures on the page, both girls, Jean Walker and Charlotte Allen. Again, a commonplace kind of thing, but there is something else.

Sara must have been a popular and

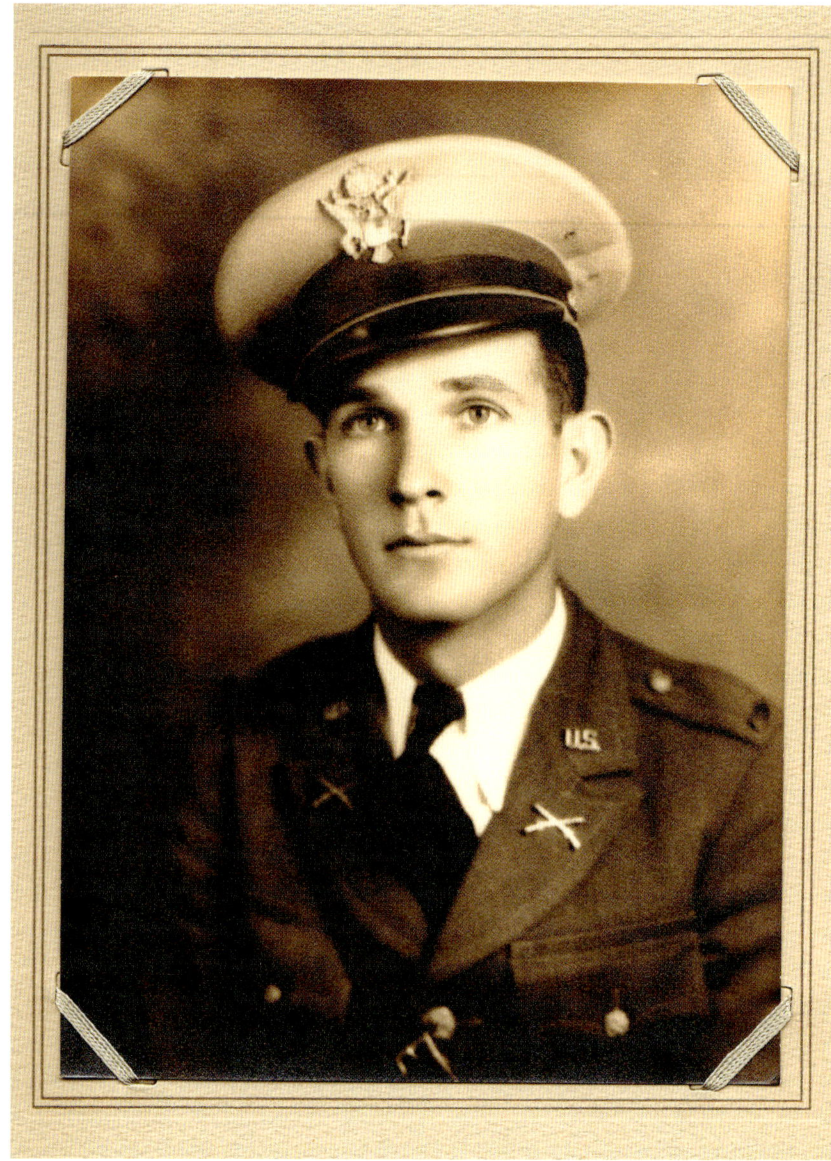

Dallas, 1929

SARA MORELAND

I wish you lots, & lots of luck, Sara

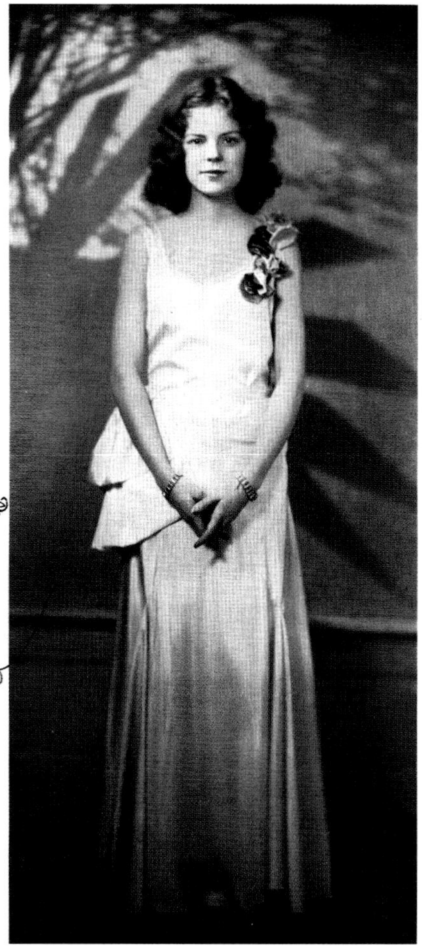

Sara Moreland, Amarillo, 1931

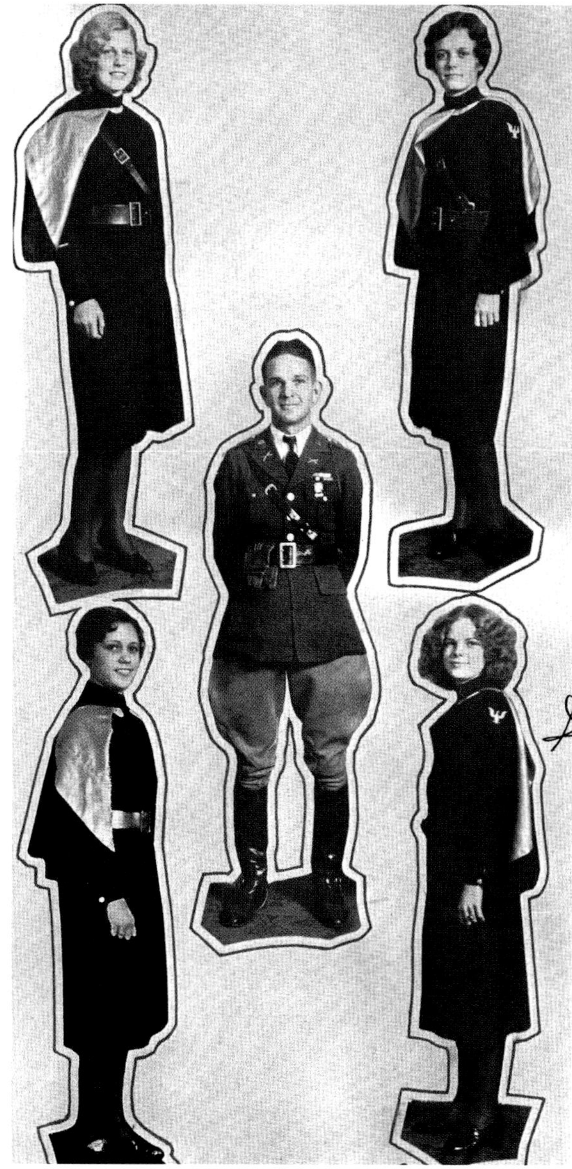

R. O. T. C. SPONSORS

HELEN MODE
Company D

HELEN ANDERSON
Company A

LT. L. H. O'NEAL
Supervisor

LOUISE DOCHE
Company C

SARA MORELAND
Company B

Sara

Harold with ROTC sponsors

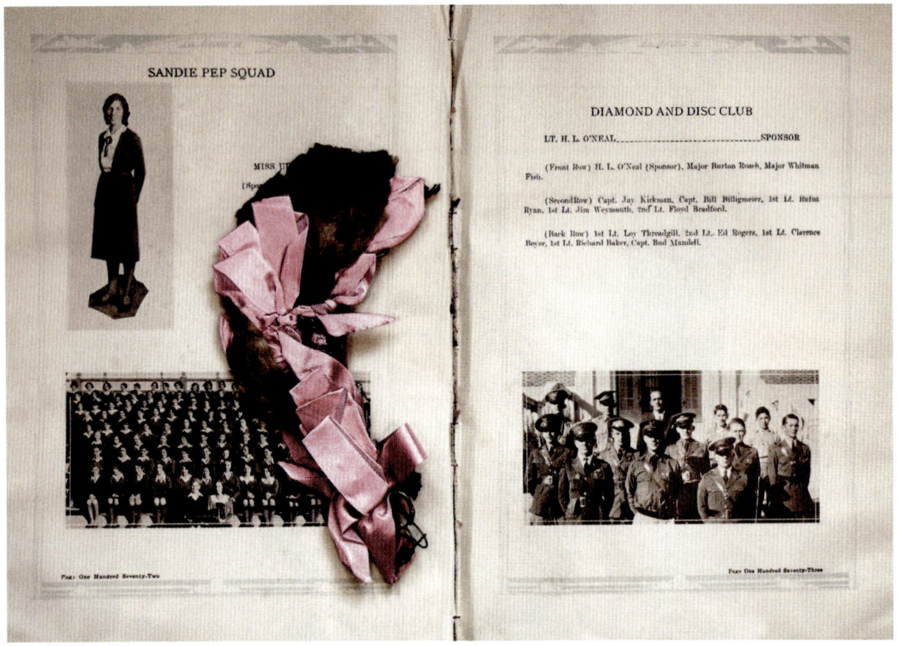


Eighty-six-year-old corsage

active girl. There are many other pictures of her scattered throughout the yearbook, particularly in the Features section. She has signed every picture *Sara*. On one two-page spread she has signed three pictures, including one standing next to "Lt. H.L. O'Neal Supervisor." But there is more. In the full-page portrait, Sara is wearing a white dress and a corsage above her left breast. Pressed between pages 172 and 173 is a now eighty-five-year-old corsage that looks remarkably similar to the one Sara is wearing in her portrait. She is the only one of the "Favorites" to be favored with a corsage. And for some unknown reason a corsage was saved in this old yearbook, possibly never opened until eighty-five years later. The bundle of faded flowers has even split the otherwise perfect binding between pages 172 and 173. She has also signed half a dozen other pictures through the book.

Sara turns up twice in the pages of the *Amarillo Globe-Times* in 1931 and 1933 and once again on February 15, 1938, as a "cotillionette" at the Cotillion Dance where she is described as *Sara Moreland in orchid chiffon, bodice made of shaded violet with bouffant skirt. And you can't imagine who her date was. It was Adair Barlow.* She was in her mid-twenties in 1938 and was still unmarried, which was unusual for a gorgeous "Favorite" at a time when people tended to get married younger than today.

No one will ever know what happened between Harold and Sara, but it is not too far-fetched to wonder if Sara was the girl that was left behind? In that last social notice from 1938 she was described as wearing a gown with the same colors as the ribbons still enveloping the preserved corsage. It seems likely that Harold and Sara were close, but it ended when the young Commandant of Cadets met another Sarah, one about the same age, in the spring of 1932—a girl he'd marry twice in 1935.

# Sarah

## January 7, 1914 – March 19, 1932

**TYLER, TEXAS, JANUARY 1914,** a bustling little East Texas agricultural town of less than ten thousand, trying to find its way in the world in midwinter. It had been founded sixty years earlier on one hundred acres that had been acquired by the founding fathers for $150, and was now a place where a lot of people thought anything was possible because the peach trees had come back after the blight that had occurred around the turn of the century. A couple of years earlier, 750,000 tons of peaches had been harvested, so many peaches there weren't enough train cars to transport them to eager customers, and piles of rotting peaches were strewn along the railroad tracks, dumped when the last cars were filled. And the farmers who'd switched from peaches to roses after the turn-of-the-century blight killed hundreds of thousands of trees were also beginning to turn a good profit, which would ultimately enable Tyler to become the Rose Capital of America by the 1920s. A century later it is not producing as many rose bushes as it once did at its peak in the 1950s, when twenty million rose bushes a year were shipped all over the world, but it still keeps the title on signs and its website just for old time's sake, and every year in October they have a marvelous rose festival to prove it. There are also a few peach orchards, but not nearly as many as one hundred years earlier.

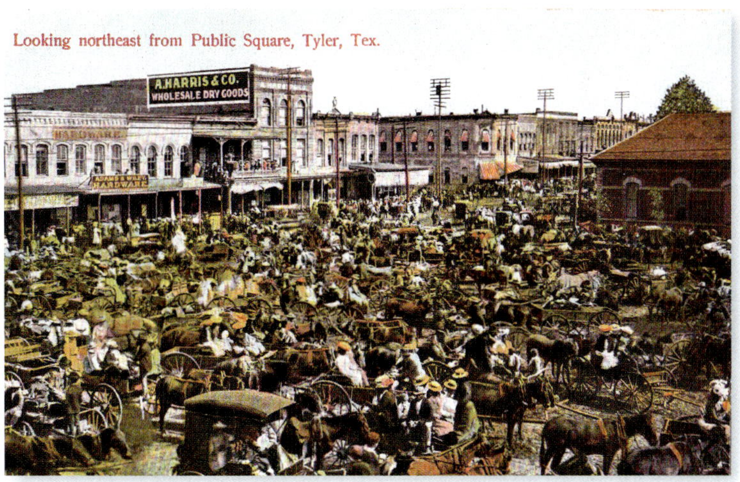


When Sarah was born in 1914, there were no serious highways connecting Tyler to the outside world as there were in Dallas; US 80 was a decade or more in the future, and the other roads to surrounding towns like Kilgore, Longview, Lindale, and Mineola were only modest at best. The major railroads also bypassed Tyler; the old Cotton Belt Route eventually served Tyler, but even in 2018 to catch a passenger train requires a trip to Mineola. Transportation would remain a problem for some time; it was not easy to get there, or leave once you had.

The O'Neal and Nicholson families had been in Texas for many years, as had Sarah's mother's, but Sarah's father had migrated to Texas from Georgia. Curtis Austin Christian was born in Elbert County in 1884. His only claim to fame from his days in Georgia is that around 1900 he was a good pitcher for a baseball team from just across the county line in Royston, Georgia. I can attest to his ability. He could still throw a ball hard enough to sting my gloved hand when he was in his sixties. One of his teammates on that kids' team in Georgia was the legendary Ty Cobb, who some feel to be the greatest baseball player of all time. A picture of the team was reproduced in *Life* magazine in 1952. Curtis is the one holding the ball in the front row. A diminutive Ty Cobb is to his right, next to the boy with the *R* on his sweater. All of this made a great difference to me. In 1954 and 1955 Ty Cobb was my pen pal; we exchanged half a dozen letters. That he knew Curtis made a difference.

Etta Beatrice Kelly was born near Garden Valley, Texas, in 1886, a town that once had a post office and a store, but in 2018 consisted of a stop sign, no public buildings, and few of any other kind. Old tax records from those years indicate that her father, J. W. Kelly, owned 240 acres in 1879 and paid $11.26 for the privilege of doing so. But he must have worked hard and done well because seven years later, the year Sarah's mother was born, he paid $22.41 on 400 acres.

There are family legends about the Kelly family being from the Atlanta area, with loose links to the fictional O'Hara family and Margaret Mitchell, but family legends are hard to prove beyond the dinner table and front porch gossip. It is an interesting story, and a photograph was once circulated of one of the Kelly girls from Georgia who was allegedly the model for Scarlett O'Hara. Family members visited ruins of the old Kelly plantation in the 1930s, and there was a meeting with Margaret Mitchell. Maybe there's a grain of truth in there somewhere.

The romance between Curtis and Beatrice was later described in some detail by Curtis's sister after his death, but the primary details are that they had known one another for many years and were married in Tyler on April 19, 1911. Sarah Beatrice was the second child and first daughter. She was doted on, and photographs of her as an infant and at every other stage of her life filled scrapbooks and photo albums, all of which were carefully saved along with documents from church and school and assorted treasured keepsakes in folders and boxes. They still survive.

Sarah's father died in 1967, and in April of that year, his younger sister, Roba, wrote a letter to Sarah describing their life in Georgia and Texas in the years leading up to the turn of the century.

*Curtis, Cyrus and Judson and I played together, went to school together and shared our happy childhood together. In the spring we hunted out the first wild flowers, climbed trees to find the first bird's eggs in their nests, but we didn't bother the eggs. We watched them so closely that the mother bird thought we belonged to the family. Where we lived out on the farm in Georgia we had all kinds of flowering shrubs, spring huckleberries and when we could persuade mother to go with us our whole morning would be spent in the woods.*

*In the fall we had haws getting ripe, fall huckleberries, hickory nuts and black walnuts. Curtis, being older, was always a step or two ahead of the rest of us. Mother always made us rake the leaves on Saturday morning before*

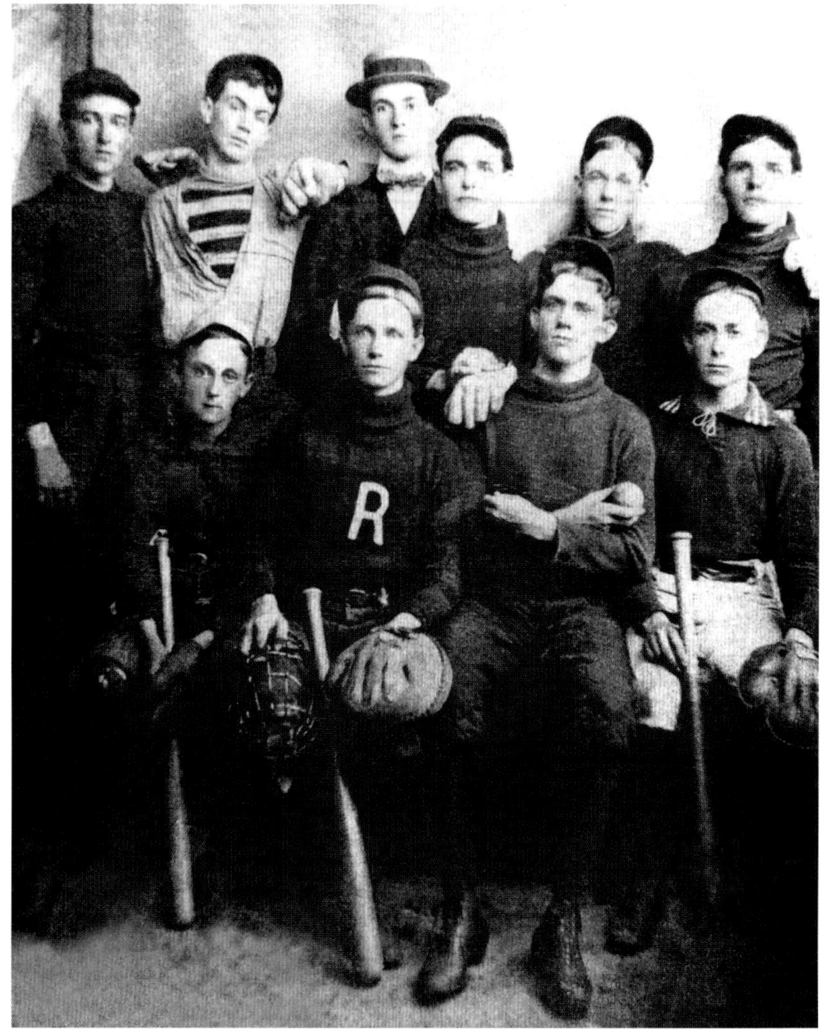

C. A. Christian (front row, holding ball), Ty Cobb (front row, far left, holding bat)

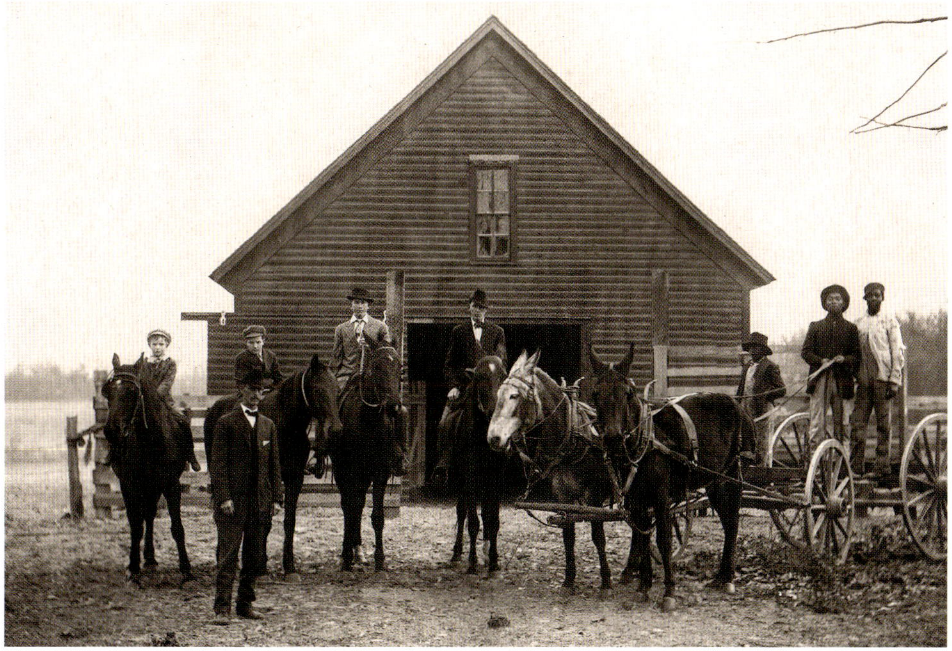

The Kelly clan at their farm, near Garden Valley

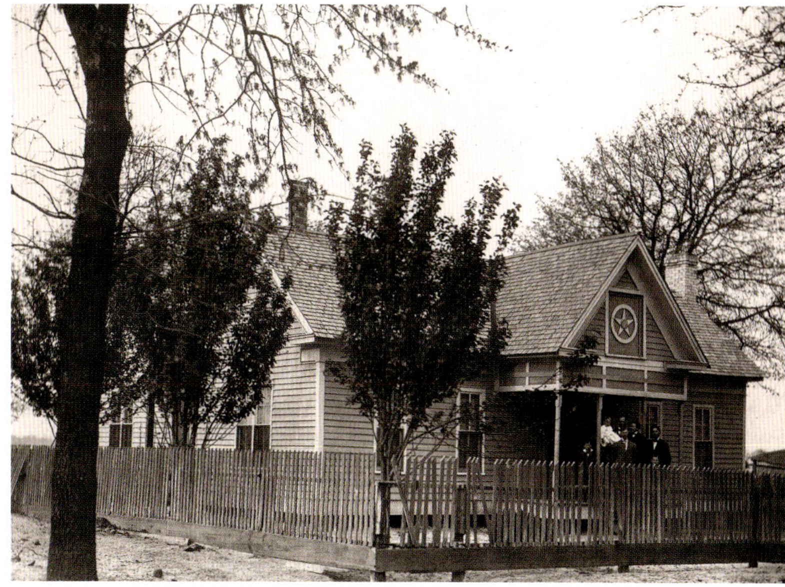

The Kelly home near Garden Valley

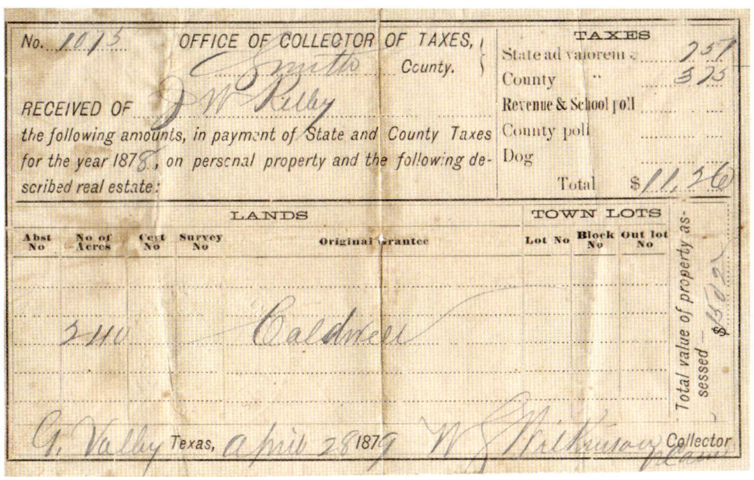

No. 1073 OFFICE OF COLLECTOR OF TAXES, Smith County.

RECEIVED OF J W Kelly

the following amounts, in payment of State and County Taxes for the year 1878, on personal property and the following described real estate:

| TAXES | |
|---|---|
| State ad valorem | 7 51 |
| County " | 3 75 |
| Revenue & School poll | |
| County poll | |
| Dog | |
| Total | $11 26 |

LANDS / TOWN LOTS

| Abst No | No of Acres | Cert No | Survey No | Original Grantee | Lot No | Block No | Out lot No |
|---|---|---|---|---|---|---|---|
| | 240 | | | Caldwell | | | |

Total value of property assessed — $502

G. Valley Texas, April 28 1879 W J Wilkinson Collector

1878 Tax Record

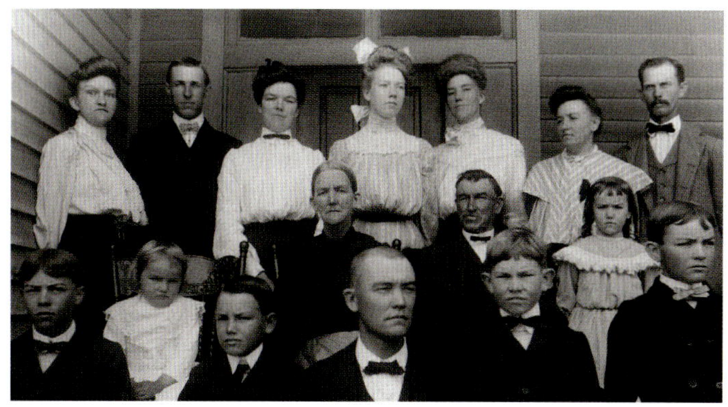

The Kelly family at the turn of the century, Beatrice Kelly, top center *she let us go nutting in the afternoons. When mother wasn't with us we roamed the pastures, dug steps in the "big gully" and never had a care in the world.*

*An end came to this idyllic situation when we moved to town to take advantage of better schools. We were still a close-knit family but didn't have the fun together we had on the farm. We made friends in town and we were privileged to attend church every Sunday. We grew older and learned to play the organ a little. We all learned to sing with daddy and mother joining in. With our schoolwork, our chores and our family entertainment we were content.*

*A great upheaval occurred in the family when daddy decided to move to Texas. He made the move when all the children were with him. Curtis was getting to be a big boy so he decided he had had enough schooling, that he would get a job and help the family. He worked as a carpenter and the money he received cheered him and made him think he had done the right thing. The next year he went to live at your Grandfather Kelly's and farmed his land. Your mother was quite too young then for him to notice much. But later on he remembered the nice shy little girl he hadn't noticed.*

*The next year Mr. Norman of Kaufman offered Curtis good pay to run his alfalfa farm. This was a grueling job and soured him on farm work. When he came home on a visit he always managed to see the girl at the Kelly place who was growing up. When the year was over and he came back home, he announced he was going back to school, that there must be an easier way to make a living than running an alfalfa farm.*

*He went back to high school, not being embarrassed to be in classes with younger boys and girls. He then went to Huntsville, where he received a teacher's certificate, but deciding he didn't want to teach he went to pharmacy school, and went to work as a druggist. All these years he had kept in touch with the blond girl at the Kelly place. He was working his way through school, and before he finished some of the others had jobs and could help a bit. Your Uncle Broadus got very upset because he sold his calf and sent the money to Curtis, and he bought his girl, your mother, an engagement ring. He fussed no end about that.*

*School over, a job secured, wedding bells were in order, and soon Curtis had a family of his own. His great sorrow in losing his firstborn seemed to cast a shadow over his life for a time, but his love for his others was beautiful to see. This is the picture I want you to keep in your mind at this time of final separation: Forget the last few trying years; roll back the frustrations and inconveniences; and dip into the pot of former days. Paint red and blue where frustrations have been. You had a life with your parent that was blessed with love and happiness. Paint over the last few years and see only the bright years behind.*

*Curtis never wrote me without mentioning what a treasure you were. Martha was further away and didn't get to administer to him as you did and he always spoke of you as "true blue." The family appreciates you too. You were his own family, but he was our family too, and we loved him and all his. I have tried not to cry, but when happy memories come, I don't seem able to hold back the tears.*

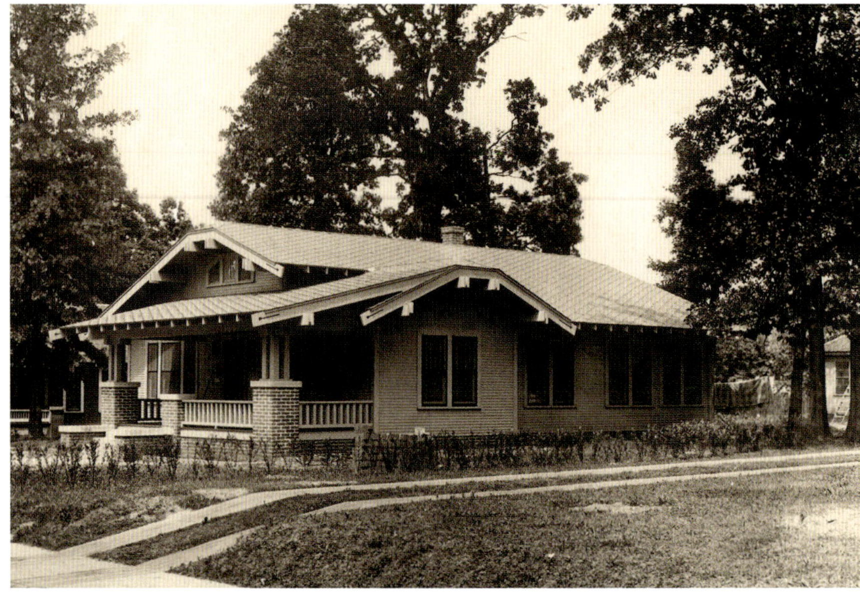

508 South Bonner Avenue

Sarah's mother and father settled in Tyler and began a family as well as a business. Sarah was born in 1914. A brother, known as little C. A., had been born a year earlier but was dead before his fourth birthday. Her sister, Martha, was born in 1916, and then her mother

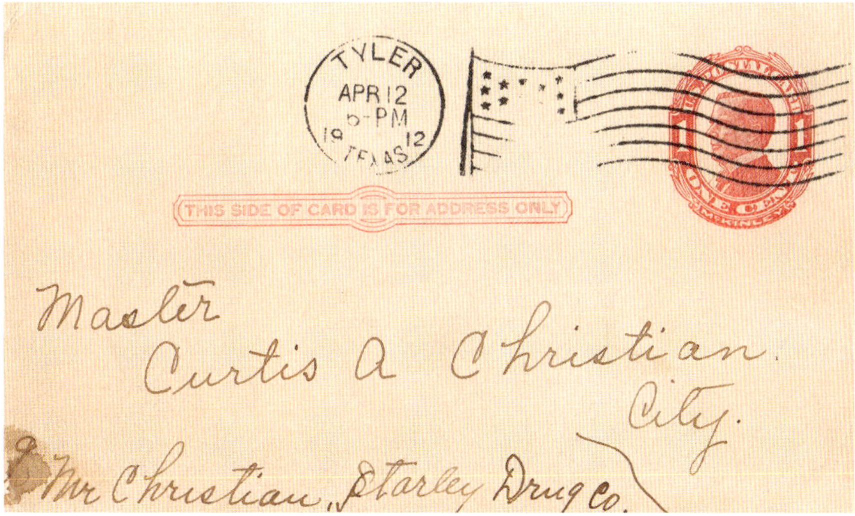


Master
Curtis A Christian.
City.
% Mr Christian, Starley Drug Co.

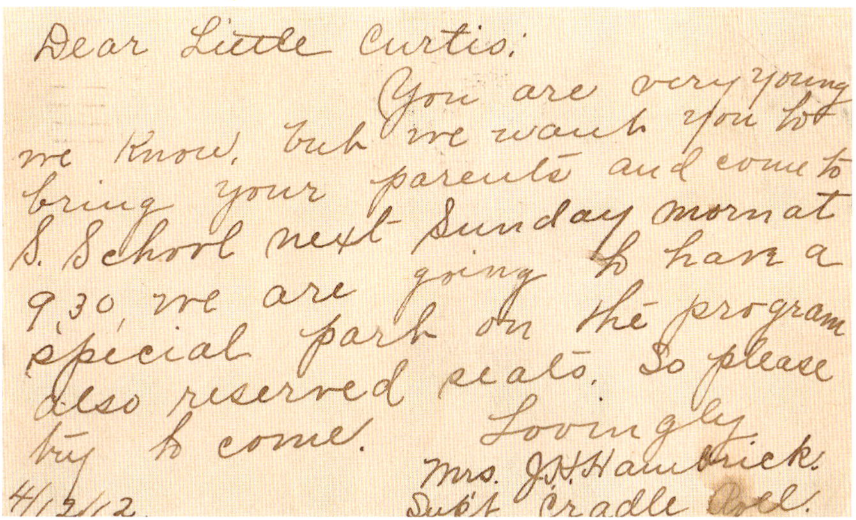

Dear Little Curtis:
You are very young we know, but we want you to bring your parents and come to S. School next Sunday morn at 9.30, we are going to have a special part on the program also reserved seats. So please try to come. Lovingly
Mrs. J.H. Hambrick.
Sup't Cradle Roll.
4/12/12

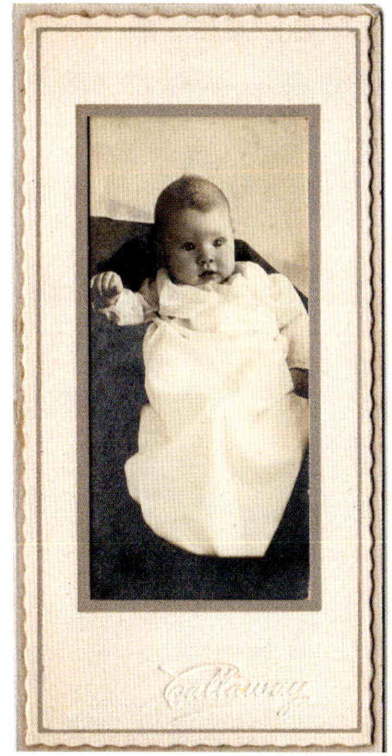

Martha Christian, 3 months and 20 days

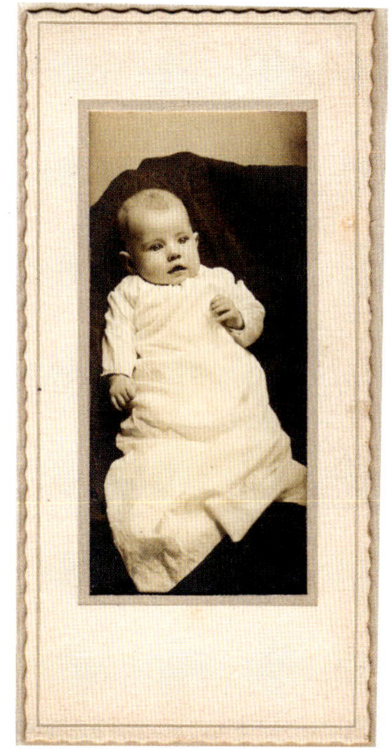

Sarah Christian, 3 months and 28 days

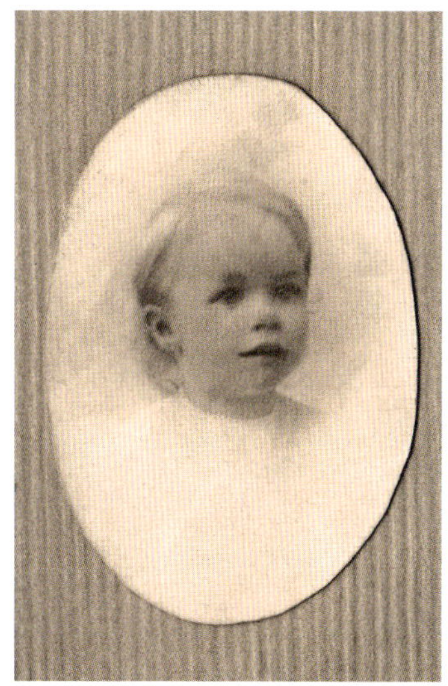

C. A. Christian, 18 months, August 1913

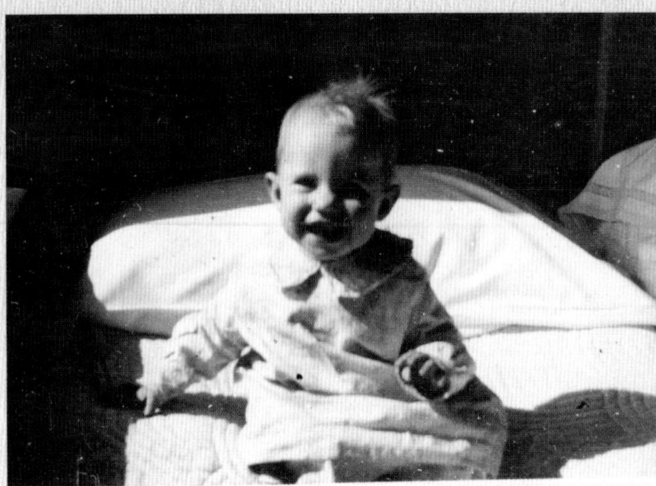

1914

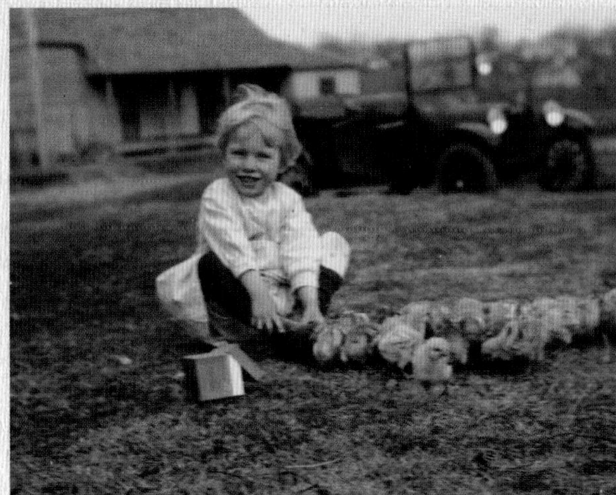

1917

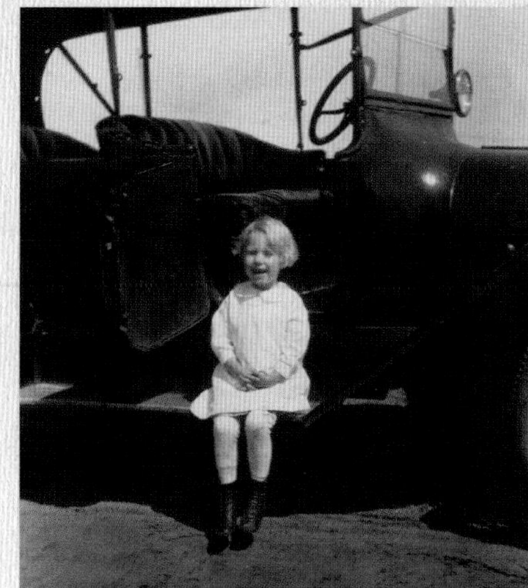

1918

## Sarah, 1914-1931

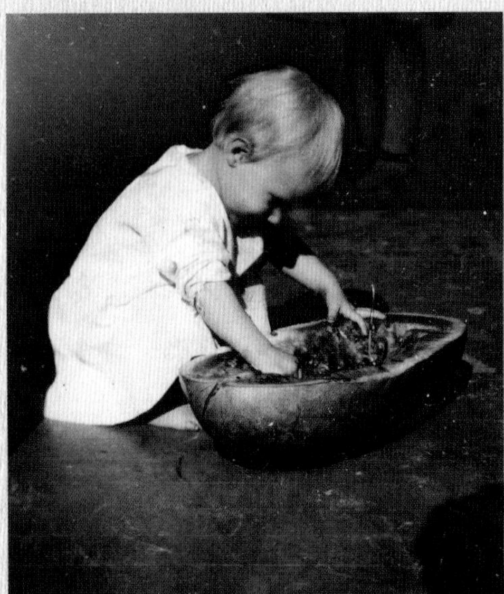

1915

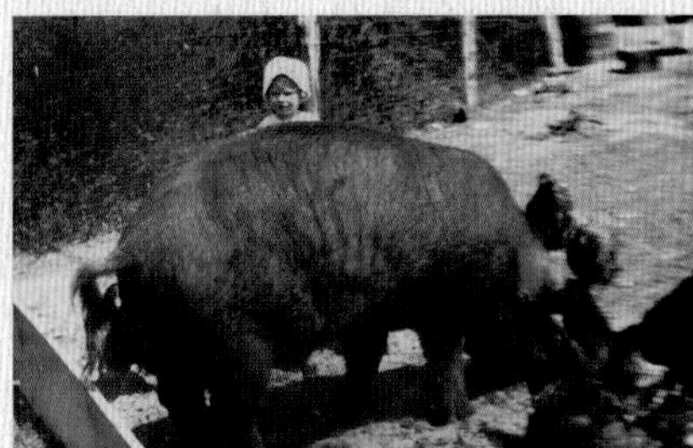

1916

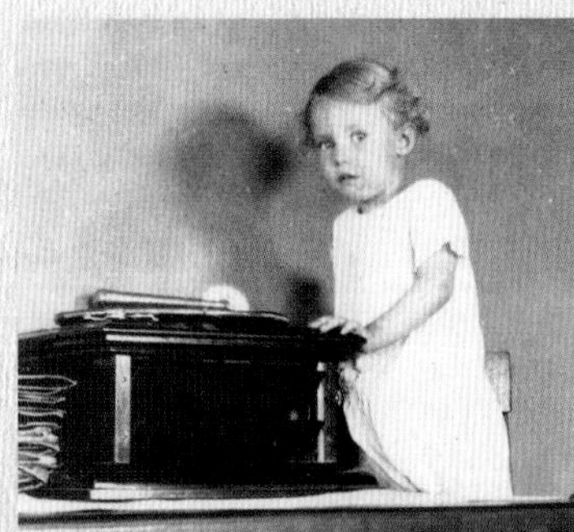

1916

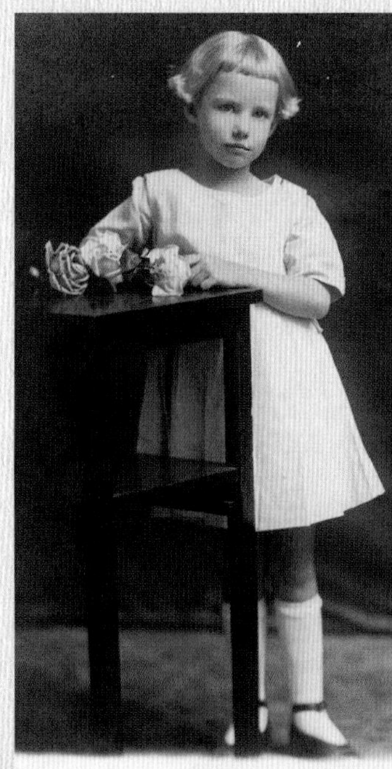

1919

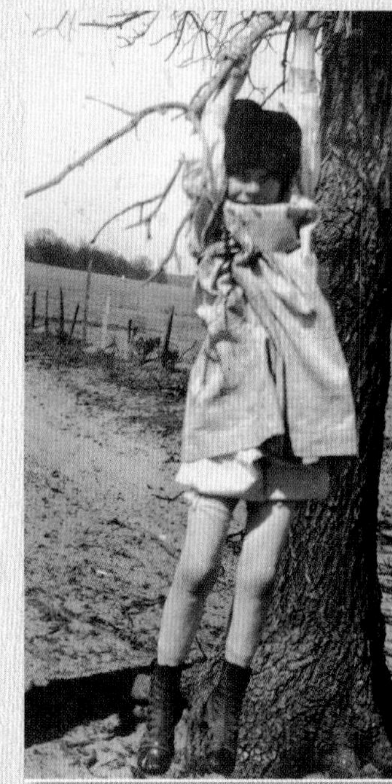

1920

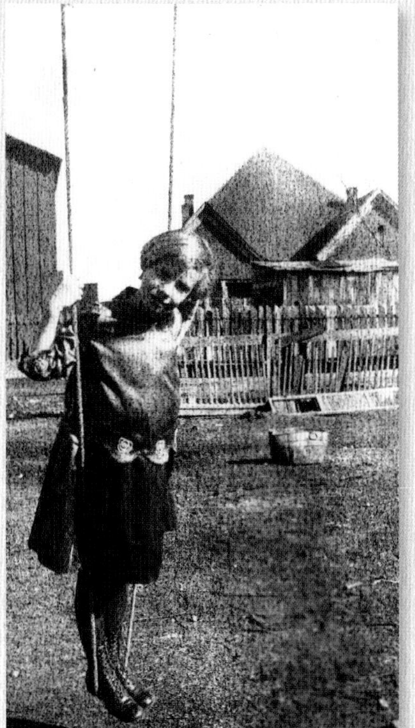
1921

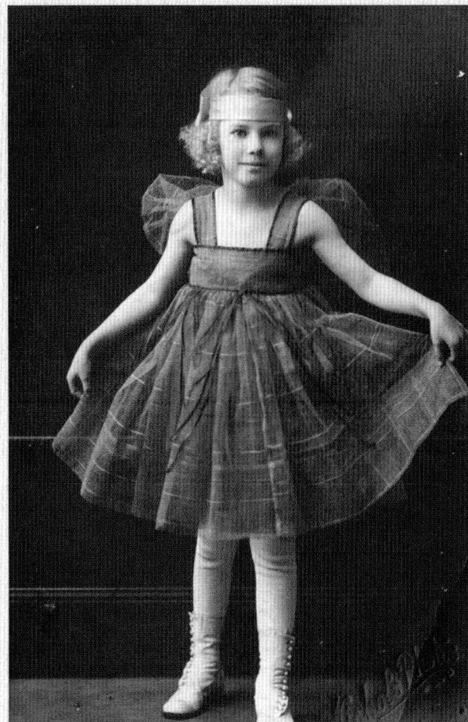
1922

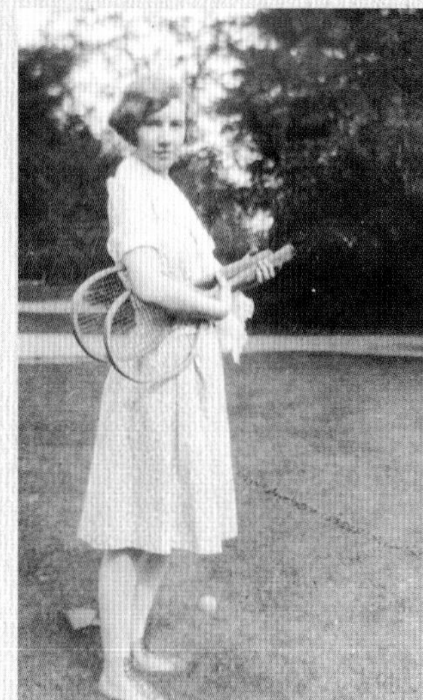
1927

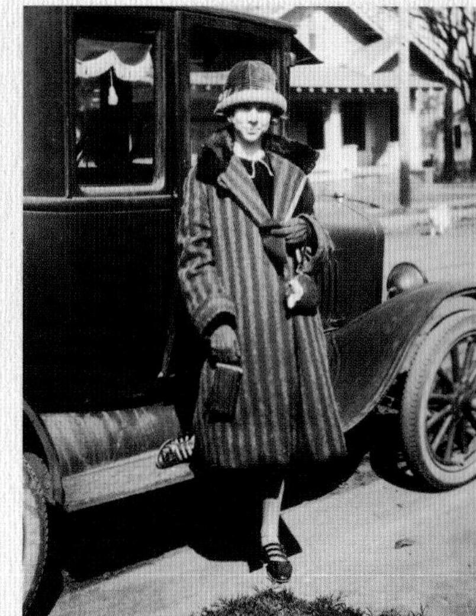
1925

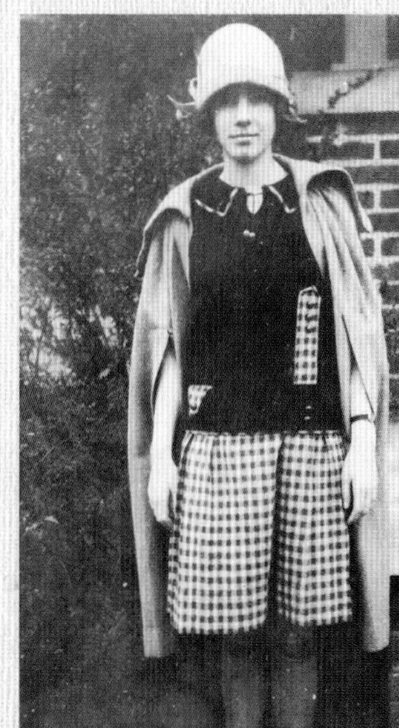
1926

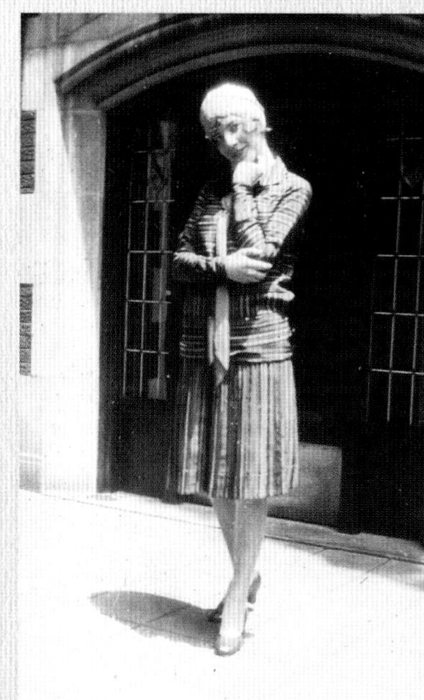
1930

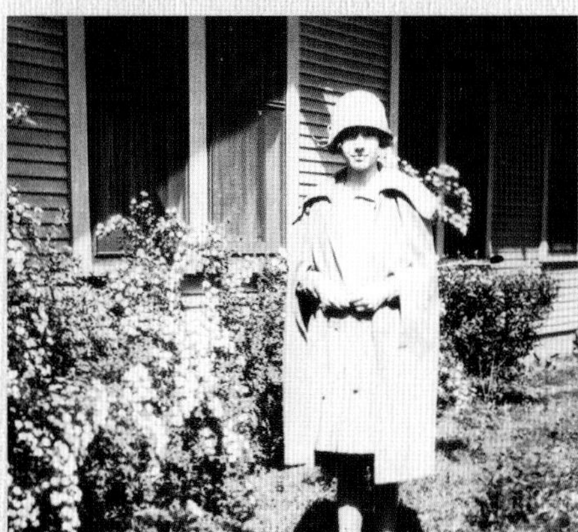
1926

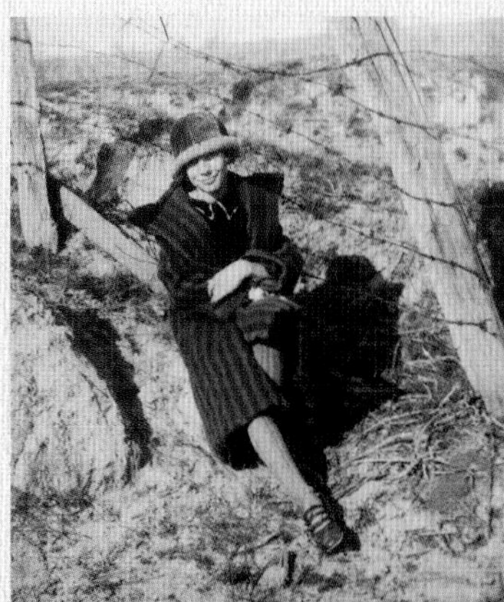
1924

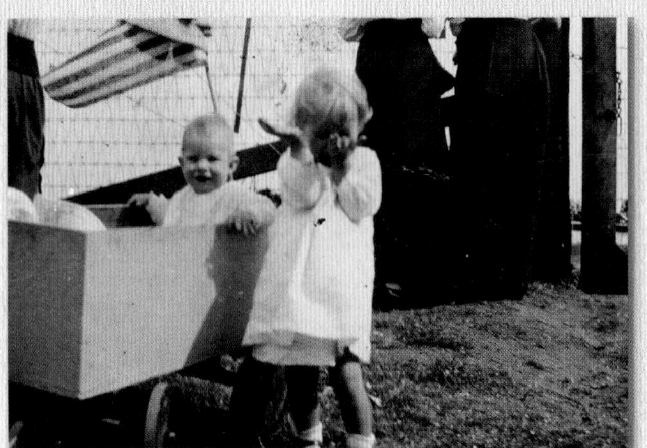

1914

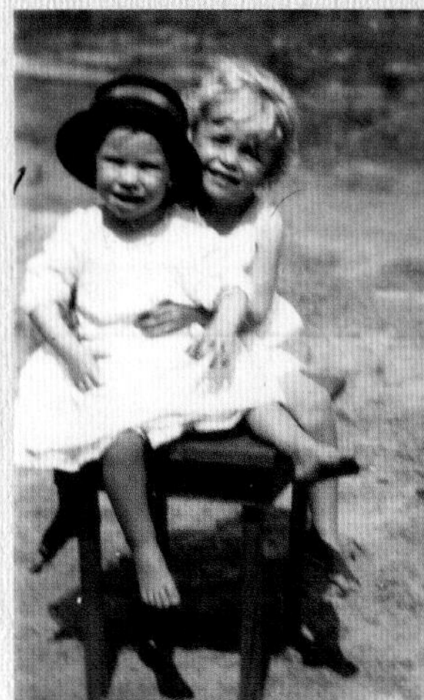

1915

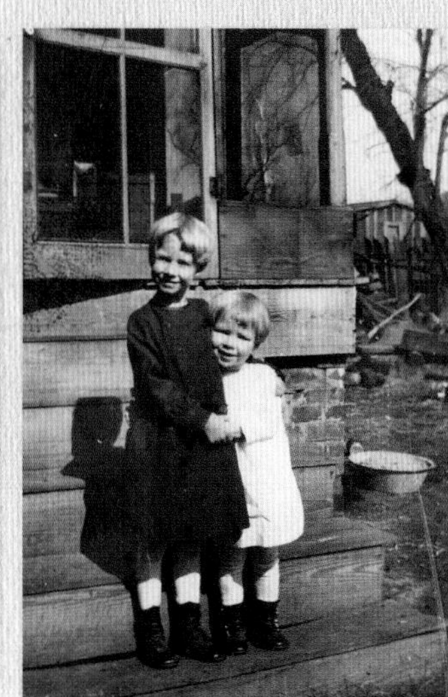

1919

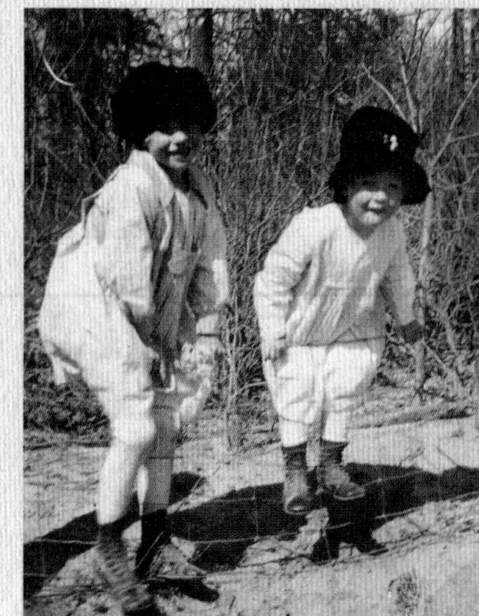

1920

## C. A., Sarah, and Martha, 1914-1930

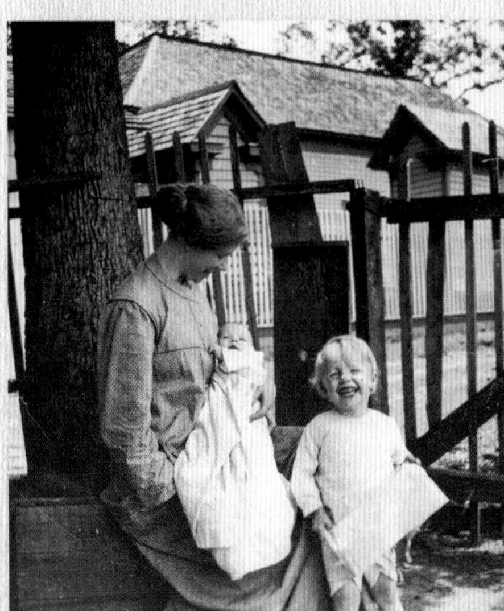

1916

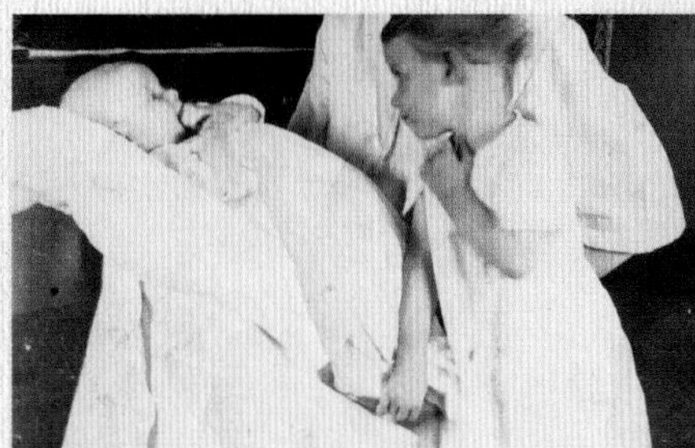

1916

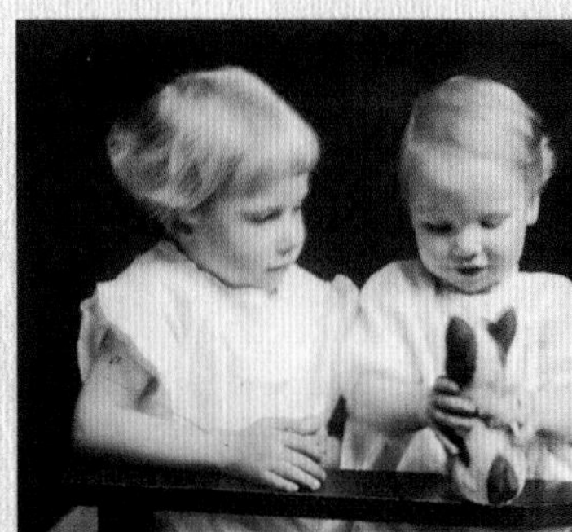

1917

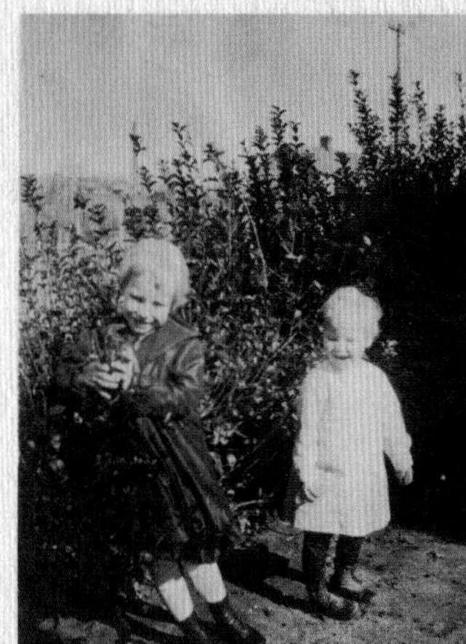

1918

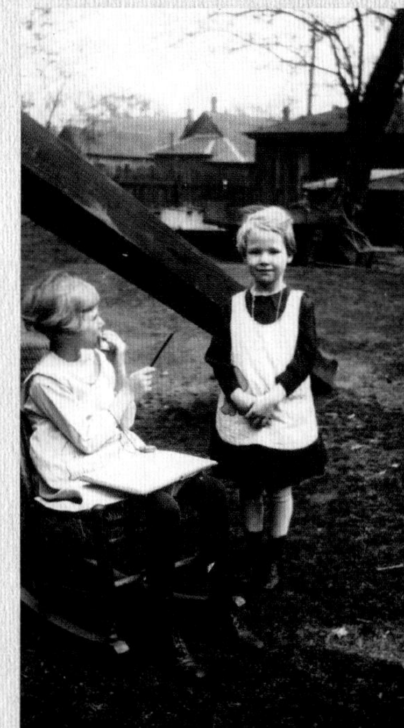

1921

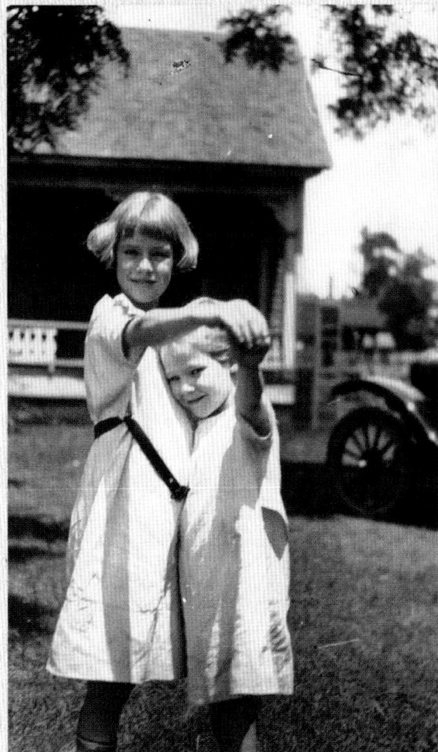
1922

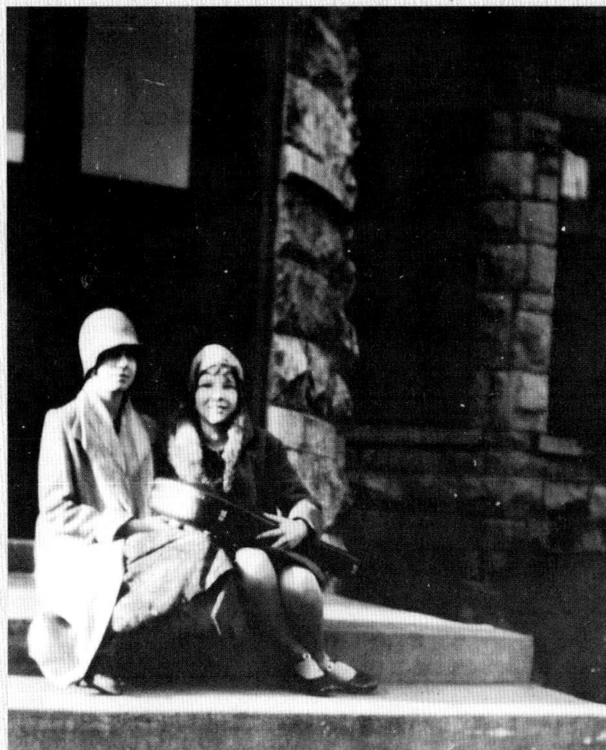
1928

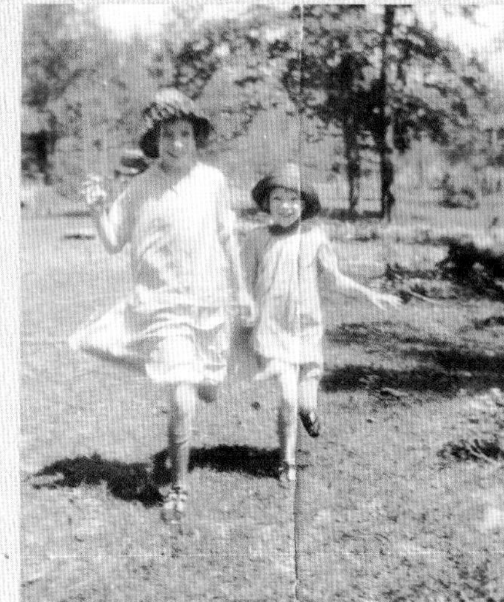
1923

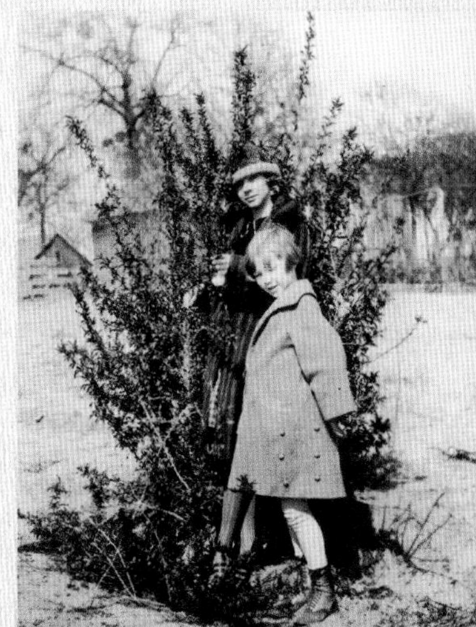
1924

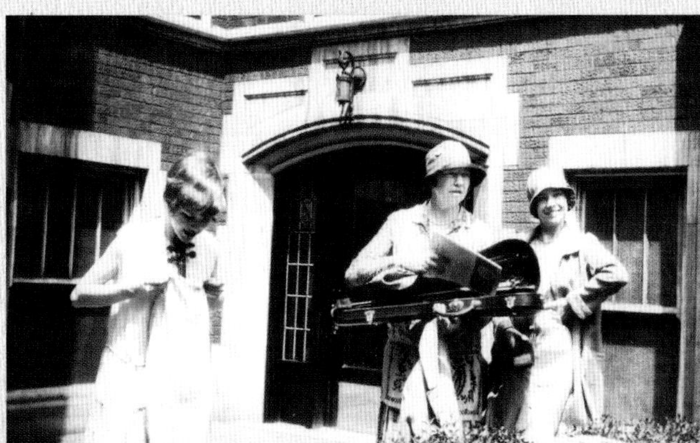
1930

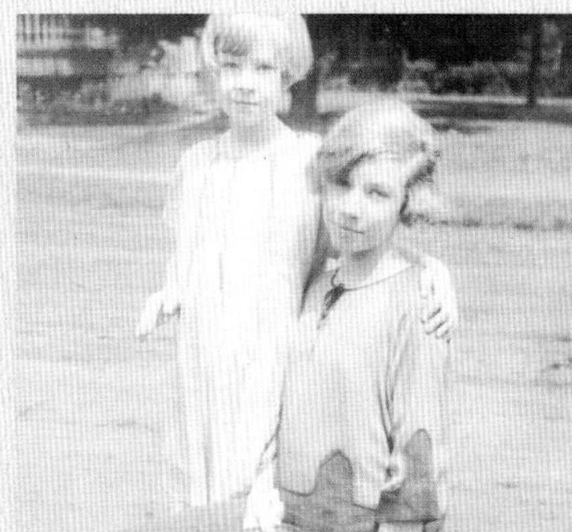
1925

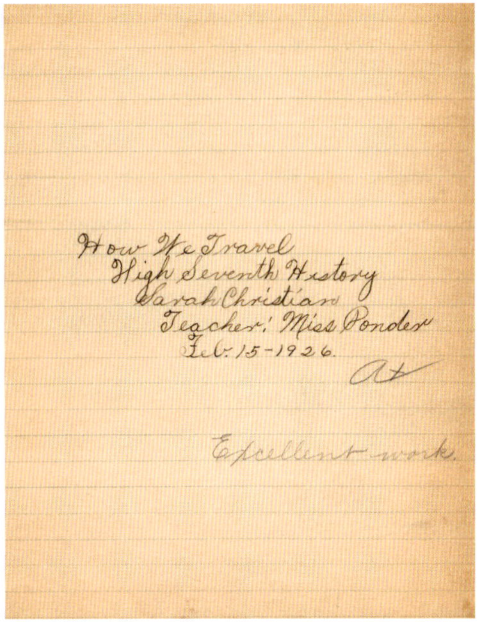
How We Travel
High Seventh History
Sarah Christian
Teacher: Miss Ponder
Feb. 15-1926.
A+
Excellent work.

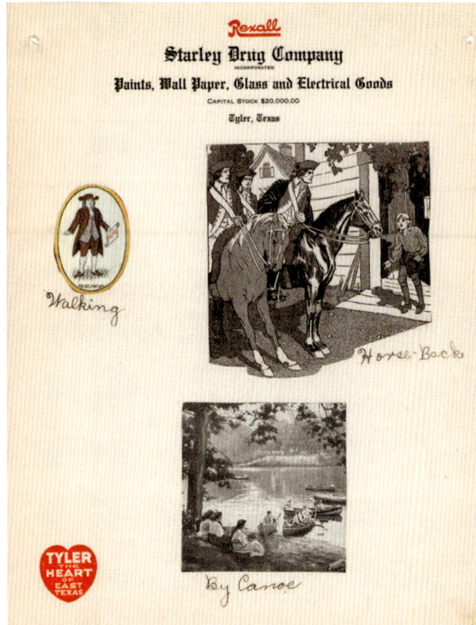
Rexall
Starley Drug Company
Incorporated
Paints, Wall Paper, Glass and Electrical Goods
Capital Stock $20,000.00
Tyler, Texas
Walking
Horse-Back
By Canoe
Tyler The Heart of East Texas

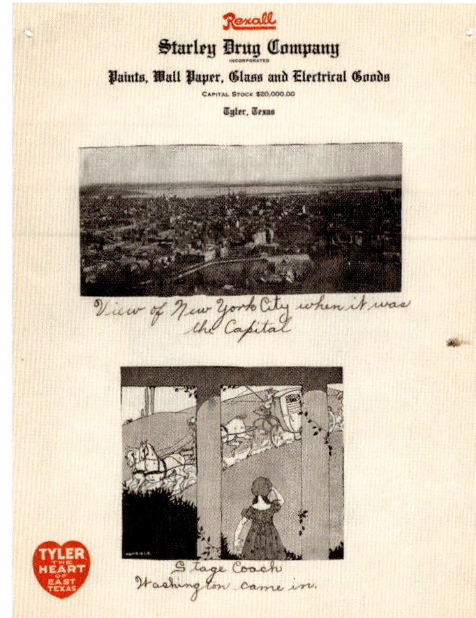
Rexall
Starley Drug Company
Incorporated
Paints, Wall Paper, Glass and Electrical Goods
Capital Stock $20,000.00
Tyler, Texas
View of New York City when it was the Capital
Stage Coach Washington came in.
Tyler The Heart of East Texas

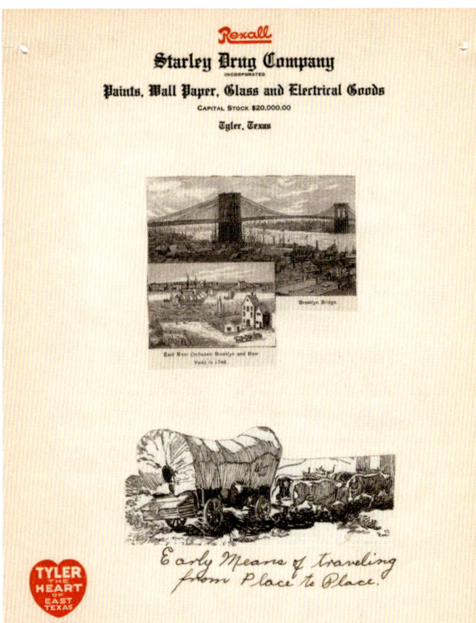
Rexall
Starley Drug Company
Incorporated
Paints, Wall Paper, Glass and Electrical Goods
Capital Stock $20,000.00
Tyler, Texas
Early Means of traveling from Place to Place.
Tyler The Heart of East Texas

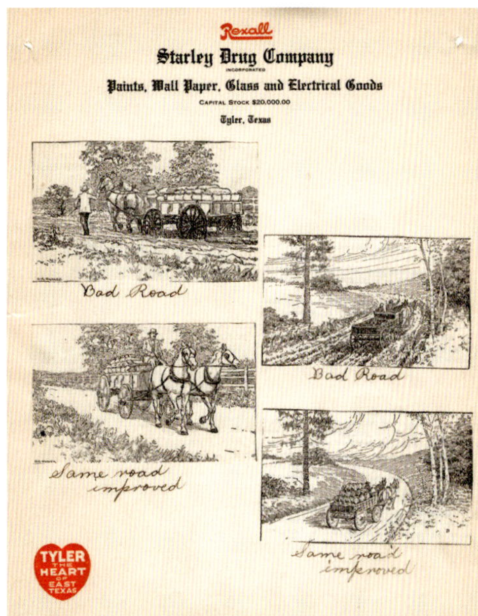
Rexall
Starley Drug Company
Incorporated
Paints, Wall Paper, Glass and Electrical Goods
Capital Stock $20,000.00
Tyler, Texas
Bad Road
Bad Road
Same road improved
Same road improved
Tyler The Heart of East Texas

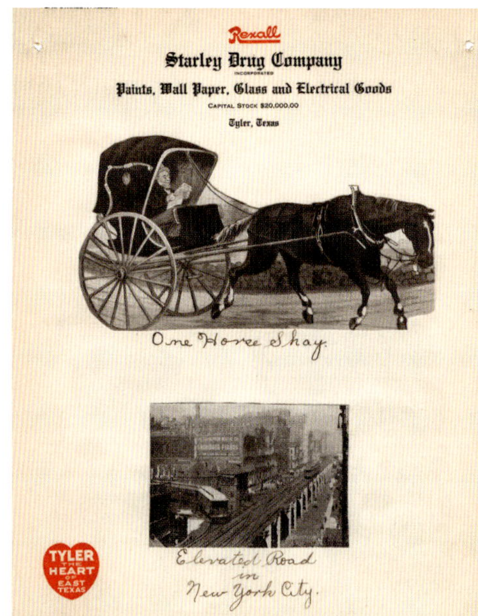
Rexall
Starley Drug Company
Incorporated
Paints, Wall Paper, Glass and Electrical Goods
Capital Stock $20,000.00
Tyler, Texas
One Horse Shay.
Elevated Road in New York City.
Tyler The Heart of East Texas

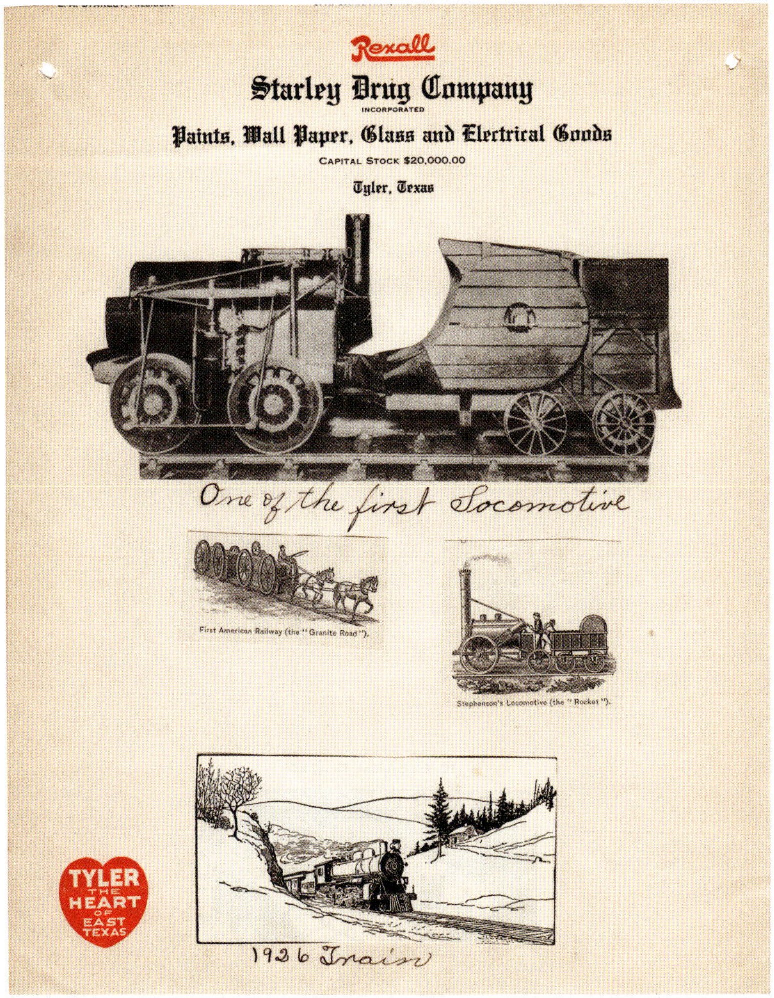
Rexall
Starley Drug Company
INCORPORATED
Paints, Wall Paper, Glass and Electrical Goods
Capital Stock $20,000.00
Tyler, Texas
One of the first Locomotive
First American Railway (the "Granite Road").
Stephenson's Locomotive (the "Rocket").
1926 Train
TYLER
THE
HEART
OF
EAST
TEXAS

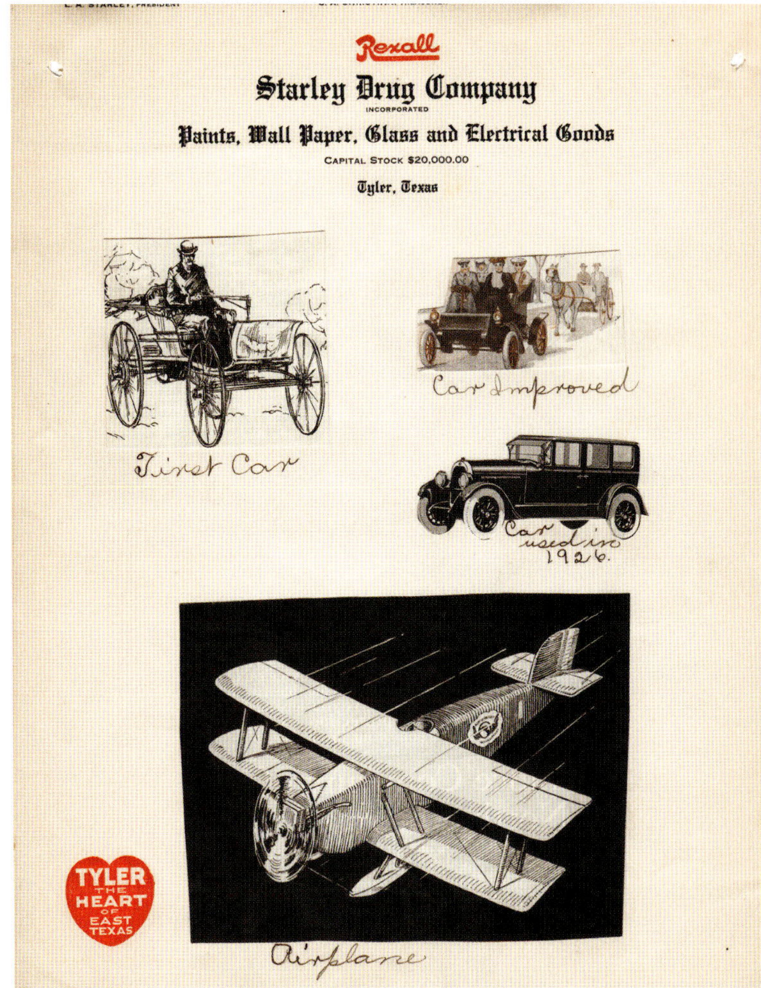
Rexall
Starley Drug Company
INCORPORATED
Paints, Wall Paper, Glass and Electrical Goods
Capital Stock $20,000.00
Tyler, Texas
First Car
Car Improved
Car used in 1926.
Airplane
TYLER
THE
HEART
OF
EAST
TEXAS

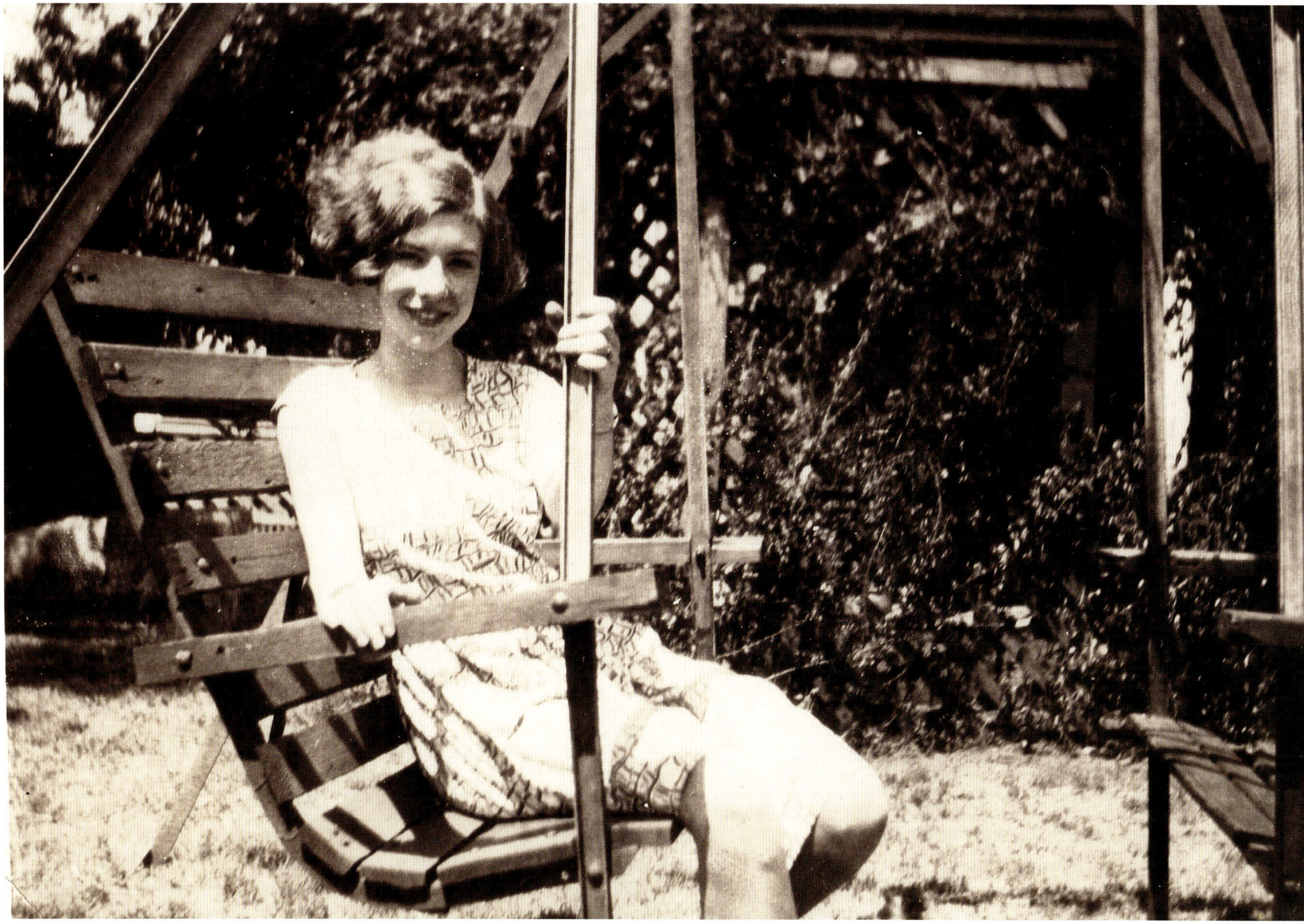

1930

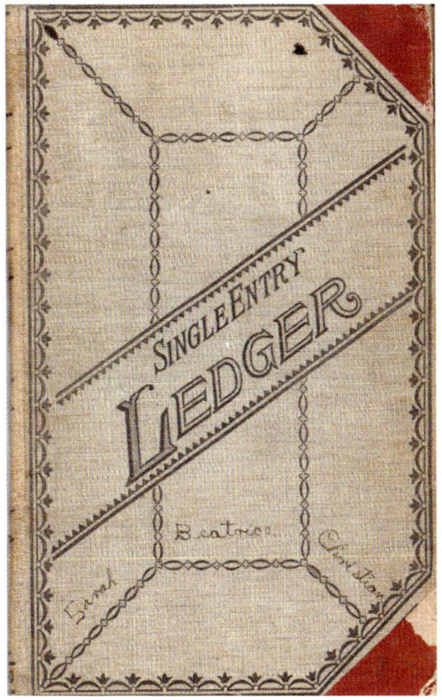


The First Scrapbook

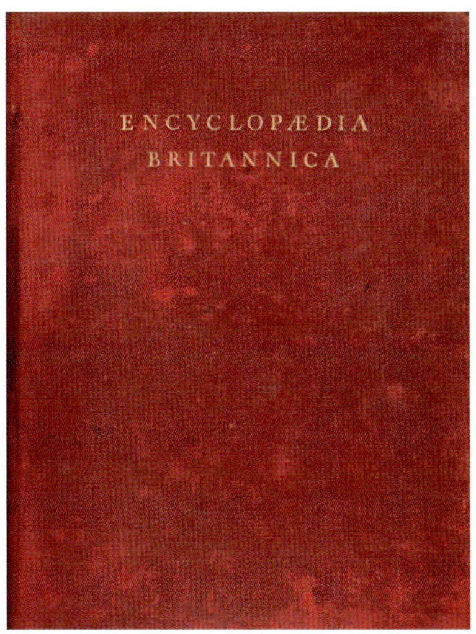


The Second Scrapbook

was done. Three children in three years is a strain. All the while, Curtis was planning and working toward building a successful business. He clearly achieved a measure of success by 1919 when, with Rebecca and L. K. Starley, he became a partner in the Starley Drug Store, issuing $20,000 in stock, and occupying a multistory building well situated on the courthouse square at Broadway and Ferguson.

Sarah grew up surrounded by pills and patent medicines, soda fountains, photo finishing, movie star magazines on the racks, the latest records, and all the notions that a three-story department store-like drug store offered in those days. There were even birds for sale on the third floor. She also grew up in a loving home; her father built a home for his family close enough to the drugstore that he could walk to work. It was a comfortable bungalow on a nice street where his girls lived and excelled in grade schools with names like Douglas and Gary, under teachers with unusual names like Lulu and Meusie and with ordinary ones like Mary. When Harold died and was buried in Tyler fifty years later, Mary Bourne, Sarah's favorite teacher from high school, was at the funeral. There are hundreds of snapshots of a happy family, mostly of Sarah and Martha, seemingly without a care in the world, just like snapshots of millions of other families.

Time passed and Sarah went on to Tyler High School, where she continued to excel until 1929, when she and her sister were whisked away to Chicago so Martha could study violin in a fancy school. They were quickly whisked back after the stock market crash in the fall of that year, because the money ran out.

But a few years before the trip to Chicago Sarah began the first of four scrapbooks. The first, in an old ledger book, filled with school-girl essays, romantic and emotional poems, and the literary efforts of a barely teenage girl; the source of the essays is unclear, perhaps copied from magazines, perhaps a few original, some written in longhand, others typed out on inexpensive paper and pasted in the ledger book.

The origin of the poems is easier to trace because Sarah seems to have been horrified by World War I and typed out and saved *The Fool* by Robert Service, on paper liberated from a rival drug store, and John McCrea's *In Flanders Fields* on Starley Drug Store stationery. These were two of the most popular and moving poems to have emerged from the war. It never occurred to her she would have to face a world war in her own life, when she would constantly worry about the safety of someone who would enter her life a few years in the future.

In 1929 *The Encyclopedia Britannica* produced its Fourteenth Edition. It was sold widely, even at a drugstore in Tyler, where Sarah came upon a copy of Volume One. Perhaps thinking she would find an article about an aardvark and everything else that began with the letter *A*, she instead discovered a blank book. It was the same size as the regular volumes of the encyclopedia but was filled with hundreds of blank pages. It was just a salesman's sample, but to her it was perfect for a scrapbook. This, her second scrapbook, was filled with postcards of Chicago, pictures clipped from movie star magazines, real pictures real movie stars sent her, sentimental lyrics from her favorite love songs, and even a story she'd clipped from the *Delineator*, "From Here To Heaven"—a love story by Dixie Willson about "a little girl with a fluff of pale gold hair" that sang the words "I want to travel the road from here to heaven with you—you—no one but you."

Two men seemed to fascinate her in those days: the movie star Ramon Novarro and Charles Lindbergh. She collected dozens of pages from movie star magazines that followed the exploits of the gorgeous but closeted Novarro and pasted them in her scrapbook. Sarah did the same with pictures and articles that followed the exploits of the famous aviator while he was still a national hero. She was fifteen and already a romantic, dreaming of the boys in the movie star magazines and those she saw at the picture show, handsome aviators flying overhead, and maybe even those closer to home and far more available in her classroom. To prove she was in her classroom regularly and excelled at every turn, she saved every report card she received between the years 1921 and

NUNNALLY'S CANDIES

# IRION DRUG COMPANY

ESTABLISHED 1904
107 WEST FERGUSON STREET
TYLER, TEXAS

EASTMAN KODAKS

THE FOOL

"But it isn't playing the game, he said
And he slammed his books away;
"The latin and Greek I've got in my head
Will do for a duller day."
"Rubbish!" I cried; The bugle call
Isn't for the lad from school;"
D'ye think H'ed listen? Oh, not at all;
So I call him a fool; A fool

Now there's his dog by his empty bed,
And his flute he use to play,
And his favorite cat- But
Dick- he's dead.
Somewhere in France they say;
Dick with his rapture of song and sun,
Dick of the yellow hair,
Dicky, whose life had but begun
Carrion cold out there.

Look at his prizes all in a row;
Surely a hint of fame,
Now he's finished with, nothing to show
Doesn't it seem a shame?
Look from the window, All you see
Was to be his one Day;

Forrest and furrow, lawn and lea,
And he goes and chucks it away,
Chucks it away to die in the dark
Somebody saw him fall,
Part of him mud, part of him blodd,
The rest of him not at all,
And yet I'll bet he was never afraid,
And he went as the best of'em go,
For his hand was clentched on his broken blade
And his face was turned to the foe.

And I called him a fool;
Oh, how blind was I!
And the cup of my grief's abrim,
Will the Glory of the States every die
So long as we've lads like him?
So long as we've fond and fearless fools,
Who, spurning fortune and fame,
Turn out with the fallying cry of their schools
Just bent on playing the game?

A Fool? Ah No, He was more than wise,
His was the proudest part,
He died with the Glory of Faith in his eyes,
And the Glory of Love in his heart,
And though there's never a grave to tell
Nor a cross to mark his fall;
Thank God, We know that he battled well,
In the last Great Game of All.

"The Fool" by Robert Service

L. A. STARLEY, PRESIDENT C. A. CHRISTIAN, TREASURER MRS. C. A. CHRISTIAN, SECRETARY

Rexall

# Starley Drug Company

INCORPORATED

Paints, Wall Paper, Glass and Electrical Goods

CAPITAL STOCK $20,000.00

Tyler, Texas

IN FLANDERS FIELD.
JOHN MC CRAE.

In Flanders fields the poppies grow
Between the crosses, row on row
That mark our places, and in the sky
The larks, still bravely singing, fly,
Scarce heard amid the guns below.

We are the dead; short days ago
We lived, felt dawn, saw sunset glow,
Loved and were loved, and now we lie
In Flanders Fields.

Take up our quarrel with the foe!;
To you from failing hands we throw
The torch; be yours to hold it high
If ye break faith with us who die
We shall not sleep, though poppies grow
In Flanders Field.

O God Speed Old Glory.

God speed Old Glory when she takes the road to France,
Through the thundering of the legions where the bugles play
advance God speak; The fight is mine, Carry you my conquering
lance; God Speed Old Glory On!

God speed Old Glory first and foremost in the fight,
Fling her far, O God of Battles, in the van for the right,
Lift our hearts up oto our freedom flag of Red and Blue and White,
God Fling Old Glory Far.

God Guard Old Glory clean through battle grime and sweet
Consecrate the men who serve her so that none may ee'ver forget,
How the honor of the colors lies within his keeping yet,
God guard Old Glory clean!

Go bring old Glory home in honor, might and pride,
Battle-black and bullet slashed and stripes streaming wide,
Gorgeous with the memories of men who greatly died-
God Bring Old Glory Home!

TYLER THE HEART OF EAST TEXAS

"In Flanders Fields" by John McCrae and "A Godspeed" by Mary Raymond Shipman Andrews

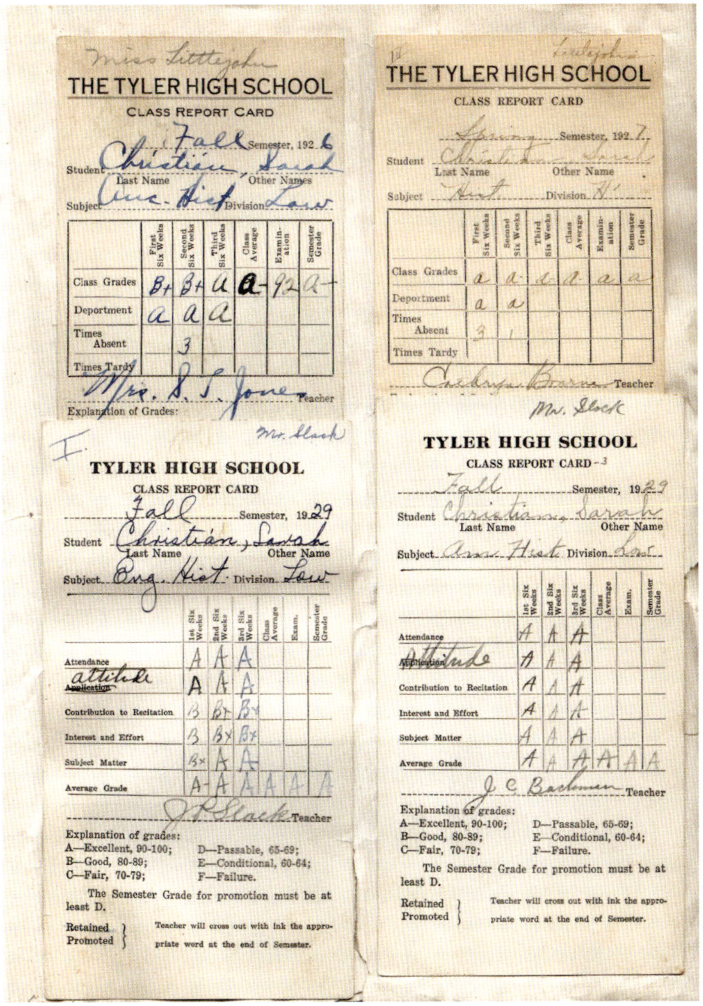

THE TYLER HIGH SCHOOL
CLASS REPORT CARD
Fall Semester, 1926
Student Christian Sarah
Last Name Other Names
Subject Anc. Hist Division Low

| | First Six Weeks | Second Six Weeks | Third Six Weeks | Class Average | Examination | Semester Grade |
|---|---|---|---|---|---|---|
| Class Grades | B+ | B+ | a | a- | 92 | a- |
| Deportment | a | a | a | | | |
| Times Absent | | 3 | | | | |
| Times Tardy | | | | | | |

Mrs. S. S. Jones Teacher
Explanation of Grades:

THE TYLER HIGH SCHOOL
CLASS REPORT CARD
Spring Semester, 1927
Student Christian Sarah
Last Name Other Name
Subject Hist Division H'

| | First Six Weeks | Second Six Weeks | Third Six Weeks | Class Average | Examination | Semester Grade |
|---|---|---|---|---|---|---|
| Class Grades | a | a | a | a | a | a |
| Deportment | a | a | | | | |
| Times Absent | 3 | 1 | | | | |
| Times Tardy | | | | | | |

Teacher

TYLER HIGH SCHOOL
CLASS REPORT CARD
Fall Semester, 1929
Student Christian, Sarah
Last Name Other Name
Subject Eng. Hist Division Low

| | 1st Six Weeks | 2nd Six Weeks | 3rd Six Weeks | Class Average | Exam. | Semester Grade |
|---|---|---|---|---|---|---|
| Attendance | A | A | A | | | |
| Attitude | A | A | A | | | |
| Contribution to Recitation | B | B+ | B+ | | | |
| Interest and Effort | B | B+ | B+ | | | |
| Subject Matter | B+ | A | A | | | |
| Average Grade | A- | A | A | A | A | A |

J. P. Slack Teacher
Explanation of grades:
A—Excellent, 90-100; D—Passable, 65-69;
B—Good, 80-89; E—Conditional, 60-64;
C—Fair, 70-79; F—Failure.
The Semester Grade for promotion must be at least D.
Retained / Promoted } Teacher will cross out with ink the appropriate word at the end of Semester.

TYLER HIGH SCHOOL
CLASS REPORT CARD
Fall Semester, 1929
Student Christian, Sarah
Last Name Other Name
Subject Am. Hist Division Low

| | 1st Six Weeks | 2nd Six Weeks | 3rd Six Weeks | Class Average | Exam. | Semester Grade |
|---|---|---|---|---|---|---|
| Attendance | A | A | A | | | |
| Attitude | A | A | A | | | |
| Contribution to Recitation | A | A | A | | | |
| Interest and Effort | A | A | A | | | |
| Subject Matter | A | A | A | | | |
| Average Grade | A | A | A | A | A | A |

J. C. Bachman Teacher
Explanation of grades:
A—Excellent, 90-100; D—Passable, 65-69;
B—Good, 80-89; E—Conditional, 60-64;
C—Fair, 70-79; F—Failure.
The Semester Grade for promotion must be at least D.
Retained / Promoted } Teacher will cross out with ink the appropriate word at the end of Semester.

Report Cards

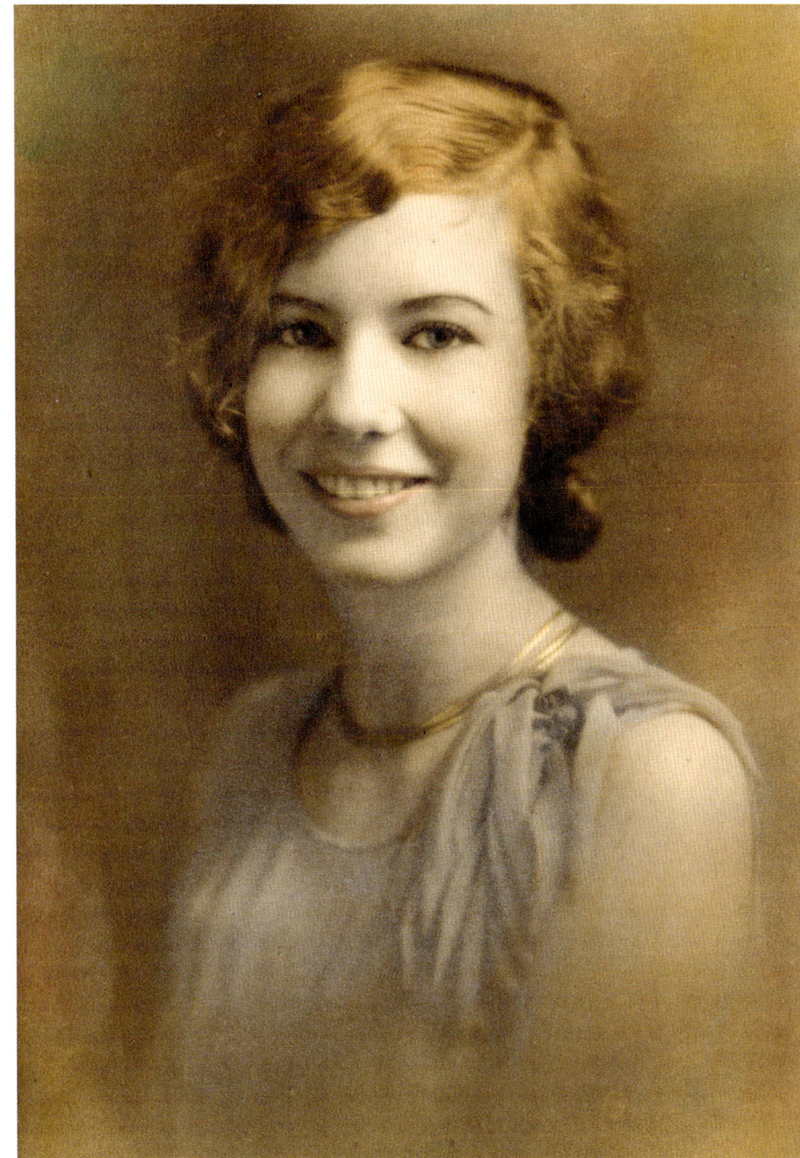

Sarah in Chicago, 1928

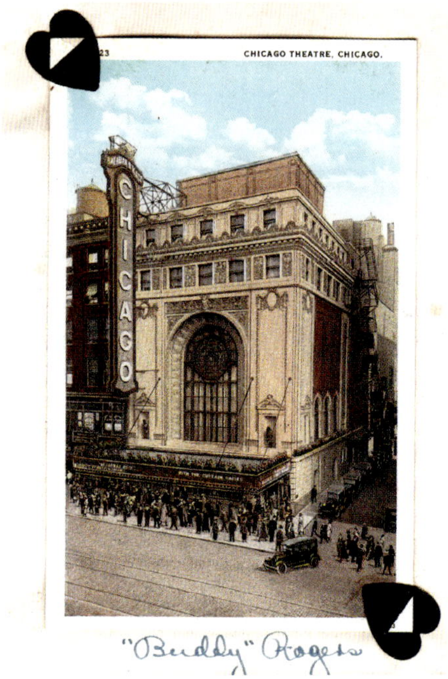


The Chicago Theater with Buddy Rogers

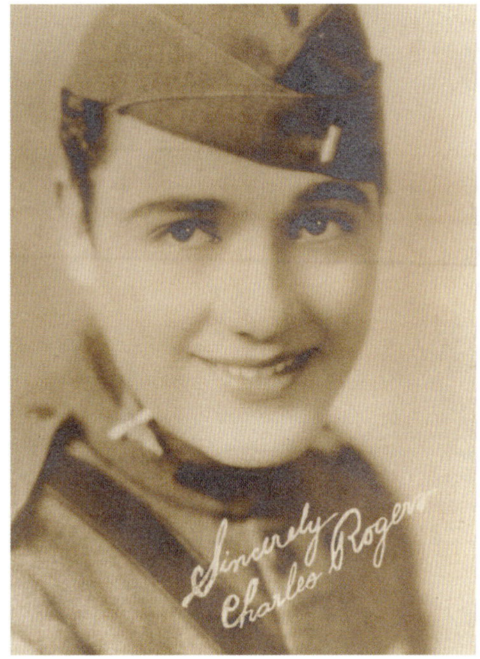


Buddy Rogers

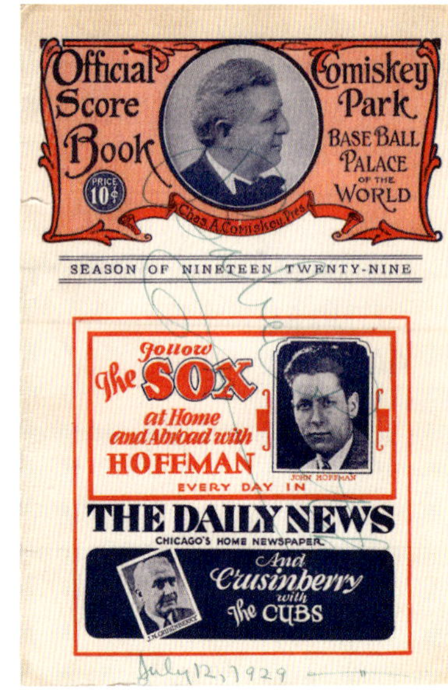


Yankees vs. White Sox

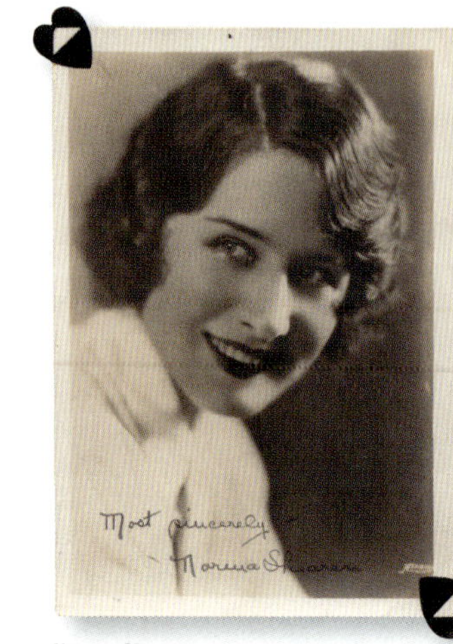


Norma Shearer

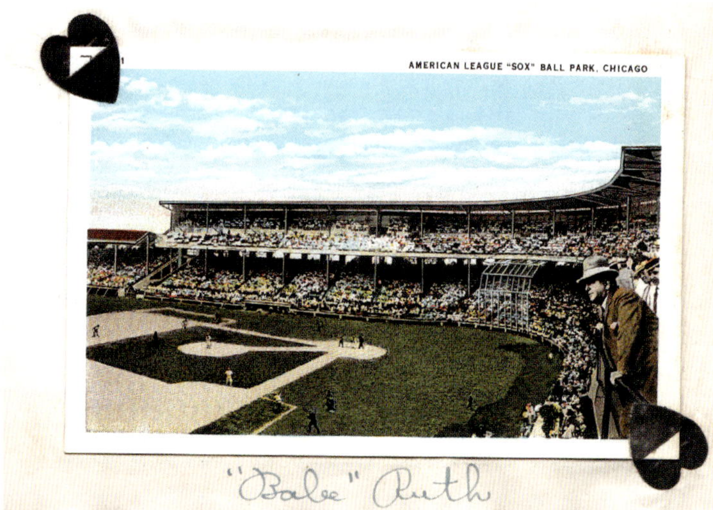


Babe Ruth

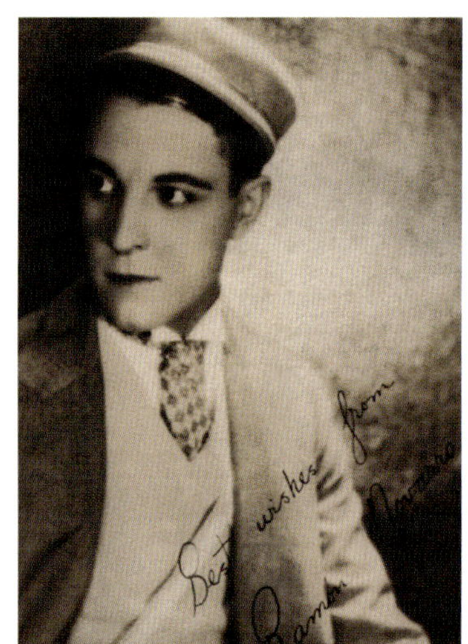


Ramon Novarro

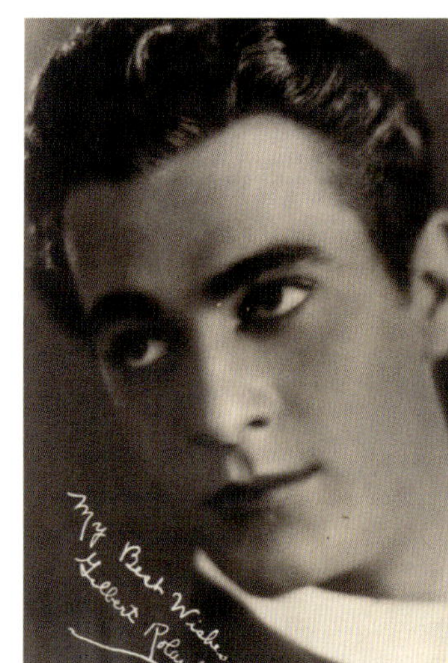


Gilbert Roland

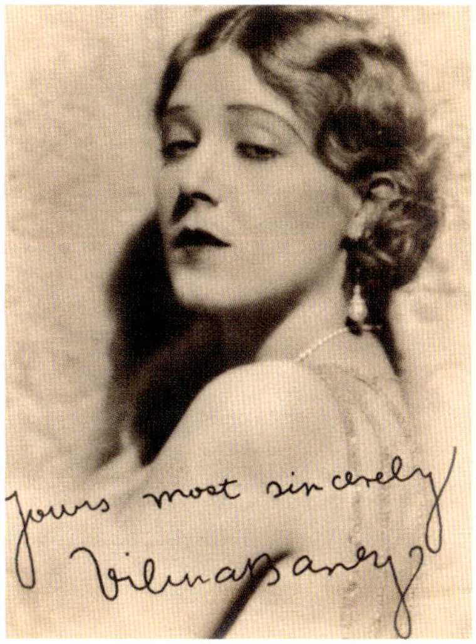


Vilma Bankey

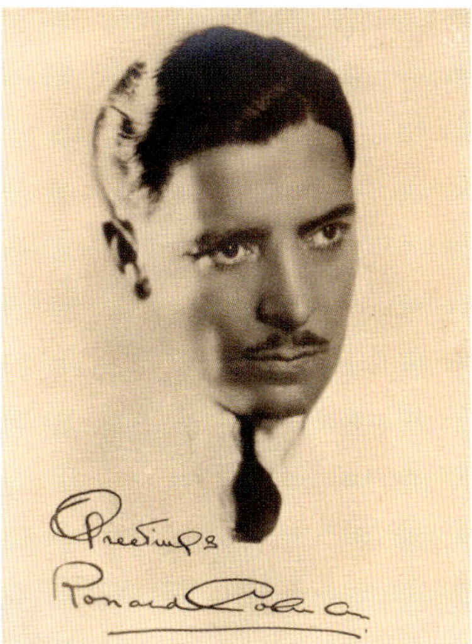


Ronald Coleman

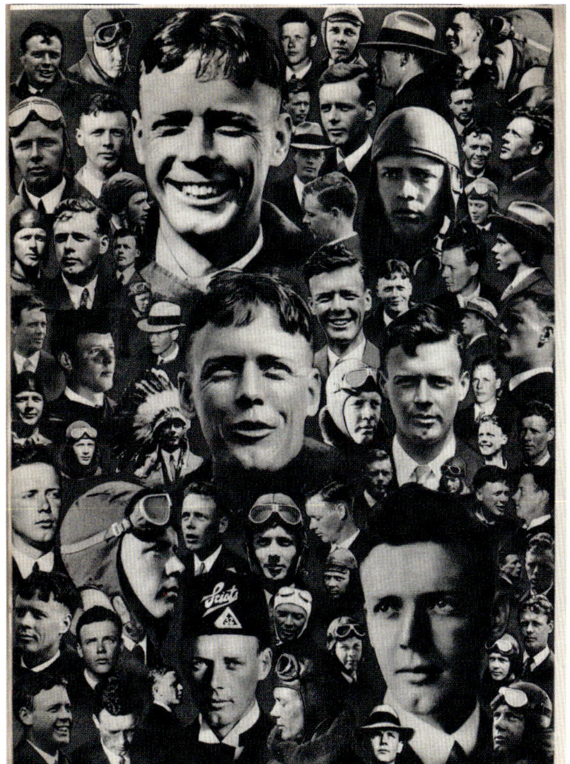

**All in Two Years** When Lindbergh hopped off for Paris on the morning of May 20, 1927, he was almost unknown as a flyer. Next evening he was a world hero. Since then he has made flying visits to every state in the Union, and blazed air trails over the wilds of Mexico and Central America. In all he has flown about 100,000 miles, and probably has received more honors than any other young man in history. Here he is in poses showing every mood.

Charles Lindbergh

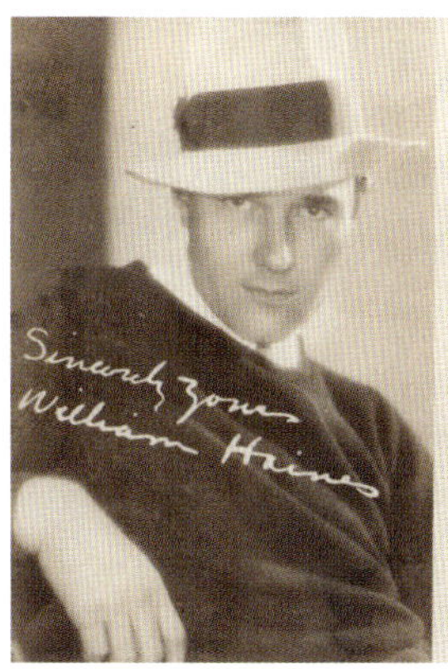


William Haines

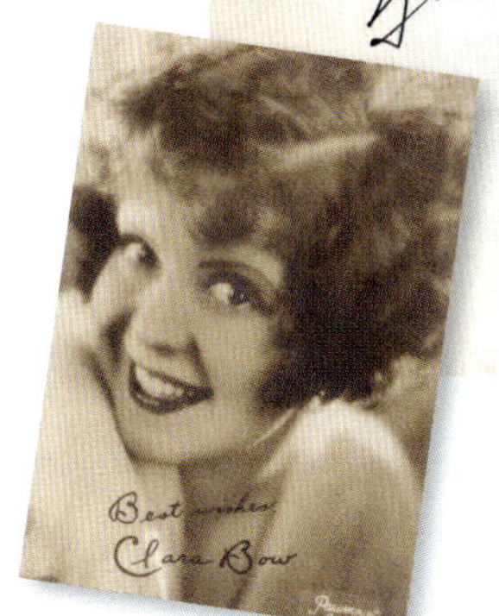


Clara Bow

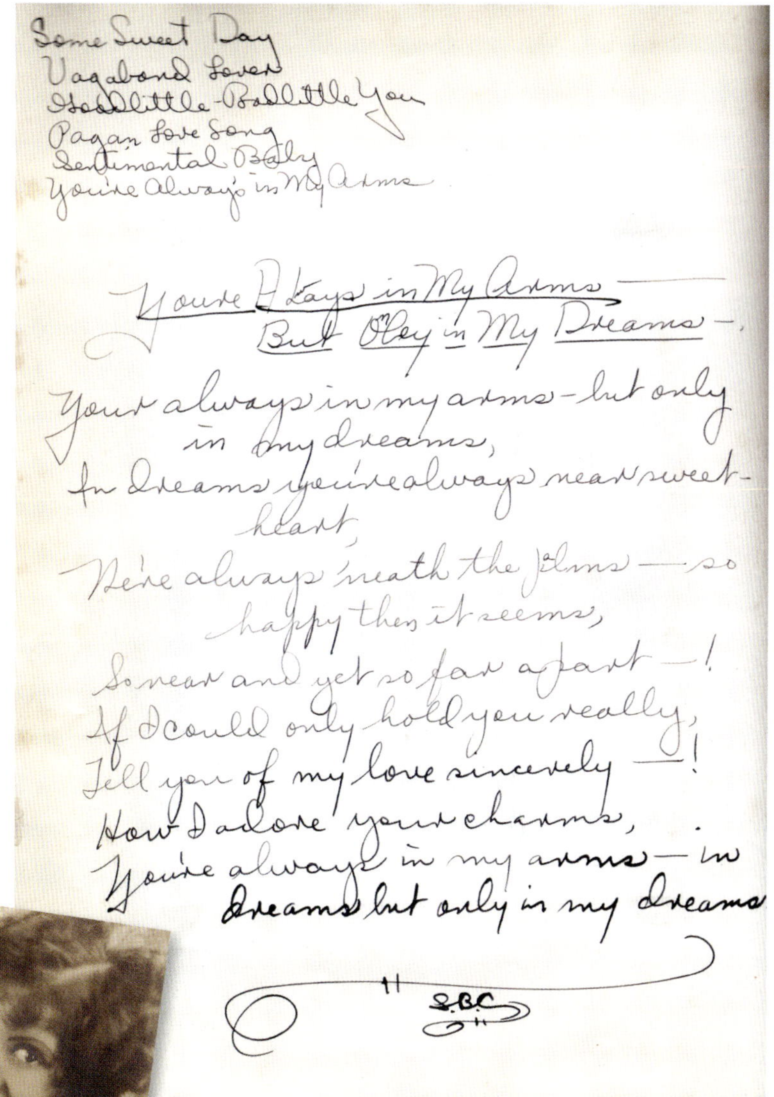

Some Sweet Day
Vagabond Lover
Goodlittle-Badlittle You
Pagan Love Song
Sentimental Baby
You're Always in My Arms

You're Always in My Arms —
But Only in My Dreams —

Your always in my arms — but only
in my dreams,
In dreams you're always near sweet-
heart,
We're always 'neath the palms — so
happy then it seems,
So near and yet so far apart —!
If I could only hold you really,
Tell you of my love sincerely —!
How I adore your charms,
You're always in my arms — in
dreams but only in my dreams

S.B.C.

Love and Dreams

**Yearbook**

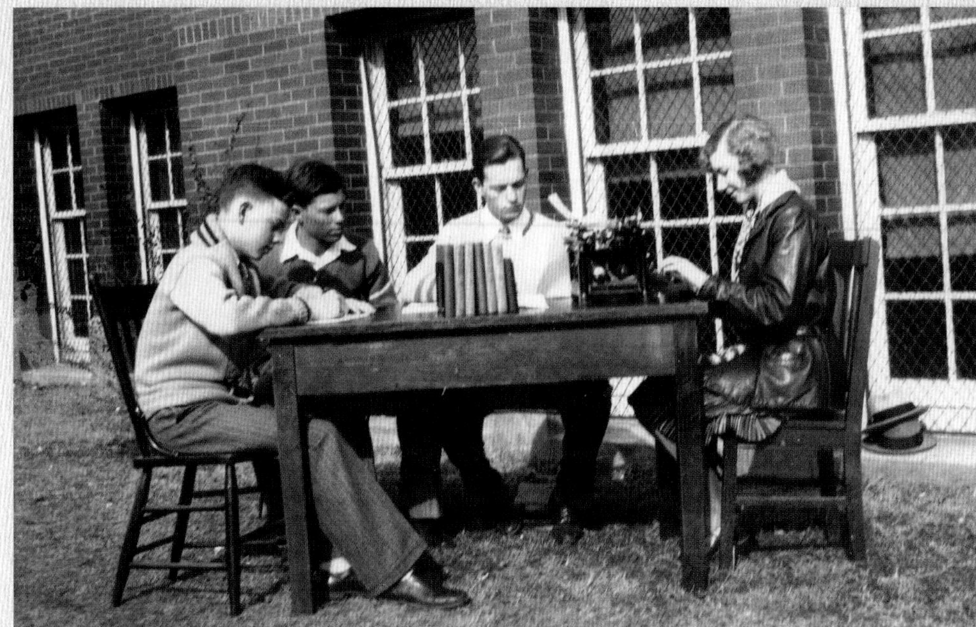

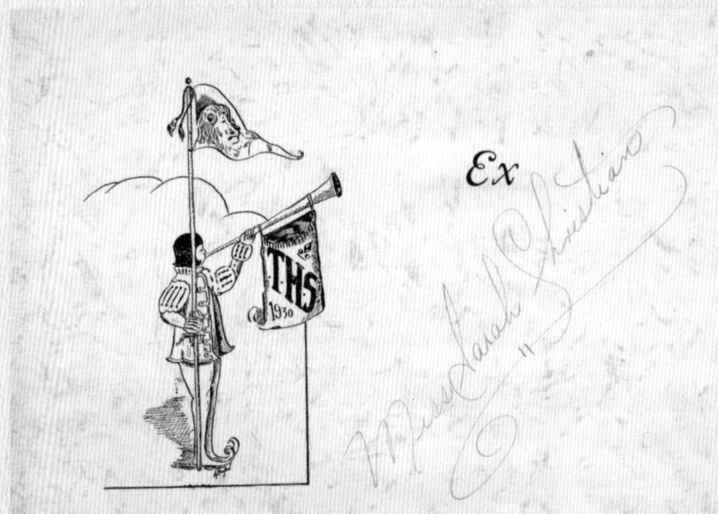

THE ALCALDE STAFF

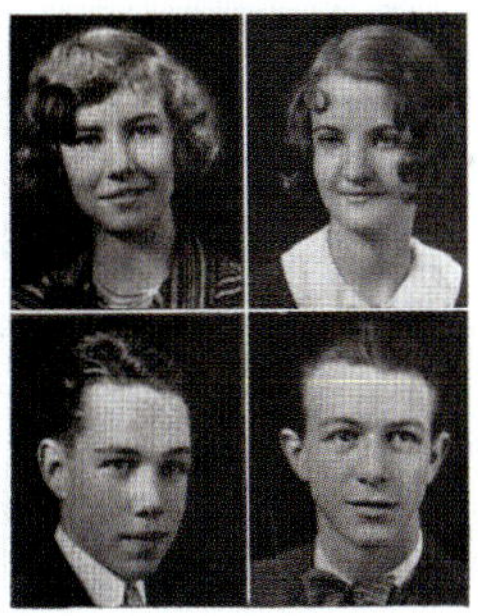

Sarah Christian . . . . . . . *Editor*
Louise Boren . . . . . . . *Co-Editor*
Olney Davis . . . . *Business Manager*
Mitchell Smith . *Advertising Manager*

Griffin, Jones, Murphy, Mardock, Quinn, Peters
Dean, Wooten, Darnell, Albertson, Starnes, Shuford
Zarr, Stovall, Smyre, Bedell, Neely, Glass

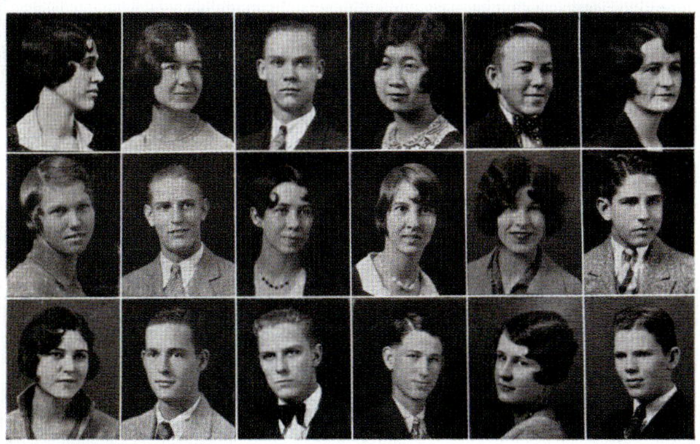



## Batting Average

| *Name—* | *Times at Bat* | *Hits* | *Put Outs* | *Errors* |
|---|---|---|---|---|
| Dorothy Mae Perdue | Eternally | Always | Anybody | Her beauty |
| Louise Clarkston . . | With Ruth | Often | Too many | Prowling |
| Ruth Hutchison . . | With Louise | After dark | When awake | Lindale |
| Sarah Christian . . | Friday night | Many | J. C. | Few |
| Eula Cardwell . . . | In "autos" | "Jellies" | Frequently | Fishing |
| Alinda Martin . . | Away from home | All possible | Good food | Her wise cracks |
| Ava Norton . . . . | Any time | Hard | We wonder? | A mirror |
| LaNelle Dean . . . | Plenty | Plenty | Plenty | Plenty |
| Louise Martindale . | Dances | Okla. City | 3 guesses | Public speaking |
| Virginia Buster . . . | When riding | Her brother | Nobody | "Teeny" |

### Sarah Christian

**J. C. C., Latin Club, Honor Roll Club, Alcalde Staff, Pep Squad.**

*"She's clever and she's smart,*
*She travels the road to everyone's heart."*

1929 and pasted them in this scrapbook.

Her turn in the big city of Chicago was short-lived and was to be her last experience away from East Texas for many years. Sarah returned to Tyler for her senior year, edited her high school yearbook, where her class picture is captioned *She's clever and she's smart, she travels the road to everyone's heart.* On page 124, ten of the most popular girls are listed in baseball terms. Sarah Christian: Times at Bat: Friday Night; Hits: Many; Put Outs: J. C.; Errors: Few. On the opposite page is a tiny ad that reads: *STARLEY DRUG COMPANY North Broadway Soda Fountain and Luncheonette Best Place In Tyler To Eat*.

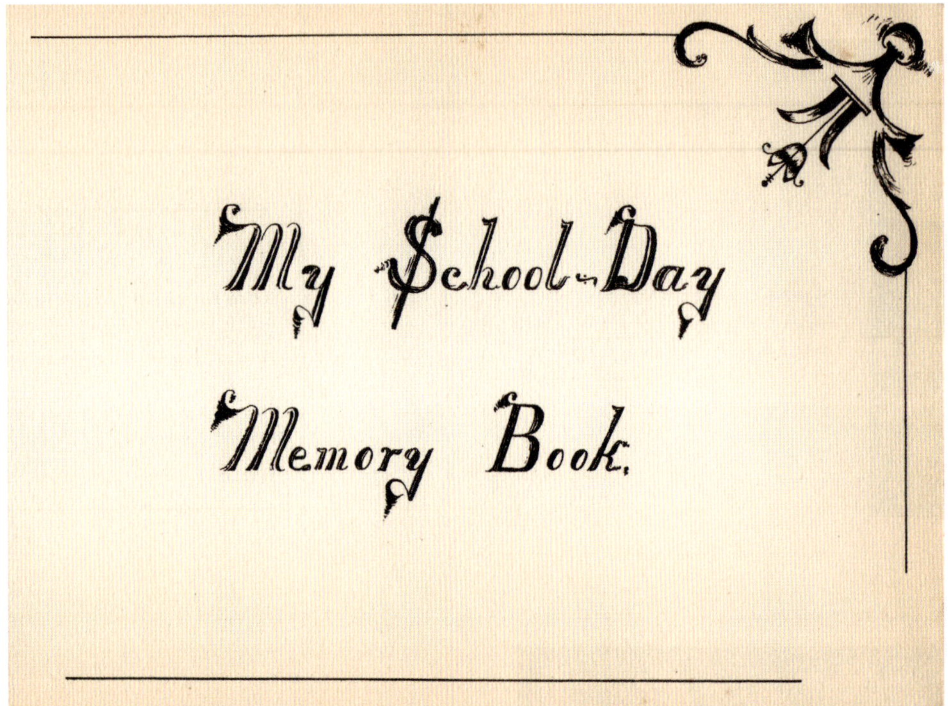


That year Sarah ended her childhood, enrolled at Tyler Junior College, closed her scrapbook filled with pictures of movie stars, and began another filled with real boys from East Texas, real romance in the back seat of a car, and dreams that could be realized. *My School Day Memory Book* begins with a seventeen-year-old girl and details fragments of two short-lived romantic encounters, then a few years of real courtship, a secret marriage, a real one a few months later and the run-up to World War II. Her memory book is a visual reminder of a time when there was a sense of innocence in some parts of the land, when life was not only simpler, but when something as seemingly meaningless as a candy wrapper or a torn movie ticket could have a poignant meaning all its own, when it was not only easier to fall in love but easier for that love to last.

It was also easier to dream of tomorrow and how tomorrow would be so much better than today, and there wasn't anyone in church, or at school, or on the radio, or in the movies, or on the street corner, or in the newspaper or magazines saying this wasn't so. In fact, in all those places people were telling the Harolds and Sarahs of the world that it was so. Even at the height of the Great Depression in 1932, there was hope in the hearts of many, and perhaps that's what made the dream of tomorrow come true for so many Americans from those years, and why it isn't coming true for as many today.

# The Oil Patch

## October 5, 1930

**THERE WERE ALWAYS A FEW PEOPLE, MOSTLY OUTSIDERS, WHO THOUGHT THERE WAS OIL IN EAST TEXAS.** Lots of oil, right under their feet, but they didn't have any money to do anything about it, so most of them didn't. There were a few locals who thought the same thing, but they didn't have any money either and sold leases for their land to the outsiders for fifty cents an acre or maybe as much as a dollar. Sometimes they got paid; sometimes it was just speculation and a promise to pay.

In 1930 the ravages of the Great Depression hadn't taken such a heavy toll on East Texas, but that was largely because there wasn't much of anything there to take. Life had always been hard; there was little industry other than logging in the largely agricultural land, and East Texas was in the midst of a three-year drought and recurring crop failures. It was poor country. Much of the land was considered worthless, so worthless banks wouldn't even foreclose on it. They had foreclosed on so much they didn't know what to do with it anymore. There was no one who could buy it, and even if they had the funds to do so, no one wanted to buy it because no one was eager to invest in the next crop failure.

Towns like Longview and Kilgore and Henderson had a few paved streets but not many; public services were few, and in many ways all these small towns were backwaters. Tiny settlements like Winona and the even smaller Starrville were even more primitive than Longview or Kilgore. How primitive? Harold and many of his relatives lived in or near Winona and Starrville or in the immediate countryside. One of his relatives, Sam Gary, who lived near Starrville, wanted to get electricity to his farm. This meant cutting down trees, trimming them so they could be used to string electric lines, digging holes, setting the trees masquerading as telephone poles in place, and then running his own wire to the closest location that had an electrical line.

This all changed on October 3, 1930, when the Daisy Bradford No. 3 came in near Henderson, in a field that an outsider, "Dad" Joiner, had leased from the widow Daisy Bradford. Joiner had speculated for years in East Texas and had

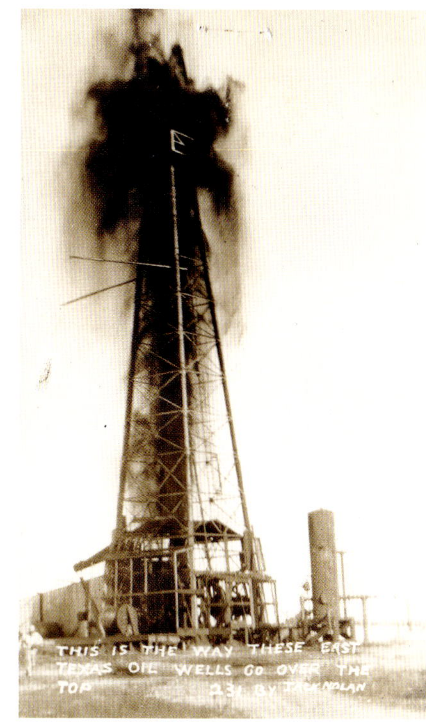


Early 1930's East Texas Oil Well

worked on this lease for over a year; his first two attempts with Daisy Bradford No. 1 and No. 2 had come up dry. But No. 3 was a success, in a field at least four miles from the nearest paved road, and when it happened oil leases skyrocketed. Leased acreage prices went even higher on December 28, 1930, when oil came in ten miles north on the farm of another widow, Lou Della Crim.

The Lou Della Crim No. 1 was many times larger than the widow's well to the south. Nobody knew how big the field was, but they figured it out within a few months. It wasn't very wide, mostly four or maybe five miles wide with a bulge west of Longview, and about fifty miles long, from south and west of Henderson to north of Longview.

Soon it became a stampede, a lawless, unorganized stampede. Little towns were overrun and overwhelmed, tent cities and shantytowns sprang up, some burned down only to be rebuilt a few miles away, roads were ruined, wells and streams polluted. In some places there was no good water for miles around, nor was there any semblance of law and order. People were robbed and murdered with impunity. Old churches were used to house criminals; people who were thought to have broken the loose laws of the land were chained together because there was nothing else to do with them. Wells were drilled in cemeteries, making dead people and their relatives wealthy overnight, if only for a minute; in some places the Texas Rangers had to be called in to restore order. A stretch of the newly built US Highway 80 was deemed the most dangerous stretch of road in America. Prostitutes wandered about freely wearing little more than nightgowns, and what law enforcement there was looked the other way because they'd been paid off—in cash and kind—to let the girls alone.

Every law imaginable was broken, and because things were moving so fast there often weren't even laws to break. A tipsy man trying to cross Commerce Street in Kilgore might fall over and be lost and drowned in a sea of mud until found by accident a month later. Or maybe he'd been shot and was just left to sink out of sight. Land and leases were stolen from ignorant, often illiterate landowners, particularly the uneducated blacks. Trucks full of hot oil vanished into waiting tank cars. Sometimes the oil was hotter than usual and an oil well exploded, often for no apparent reason. East Texas had become the Wild West, although it wasn't the west, it was the piney woods of East Texas. But because of the cushion provided by oil and all the work and industry related to it, many people in East Texas were able to ride out the Great Depression better than people in other parts of the country.

There were no more than three producing wells in the East Texas oil patch at the end of 1930, but within three months wells in East Texas were producing 160,000 barrels of oil a day. By

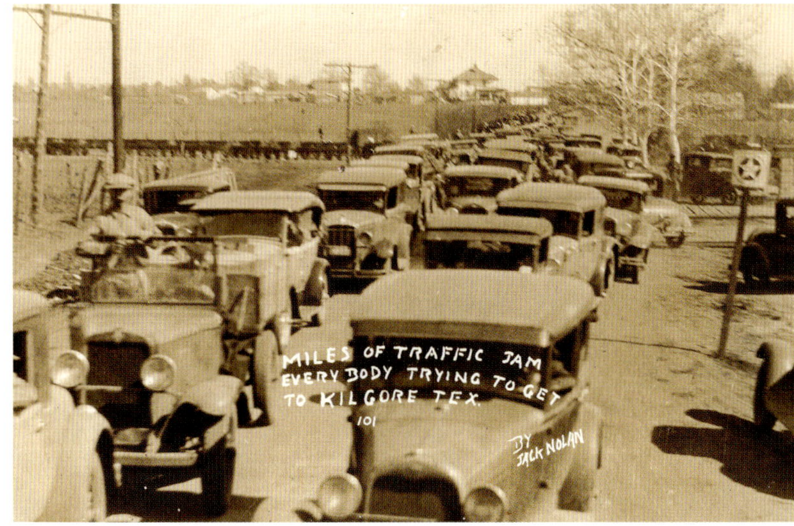


Traffic jam near Kilgore

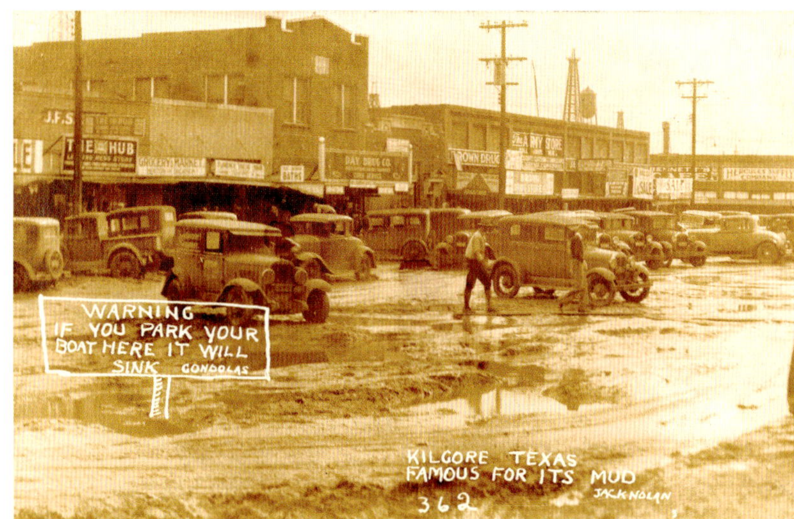


Muddy streets in Kilgore

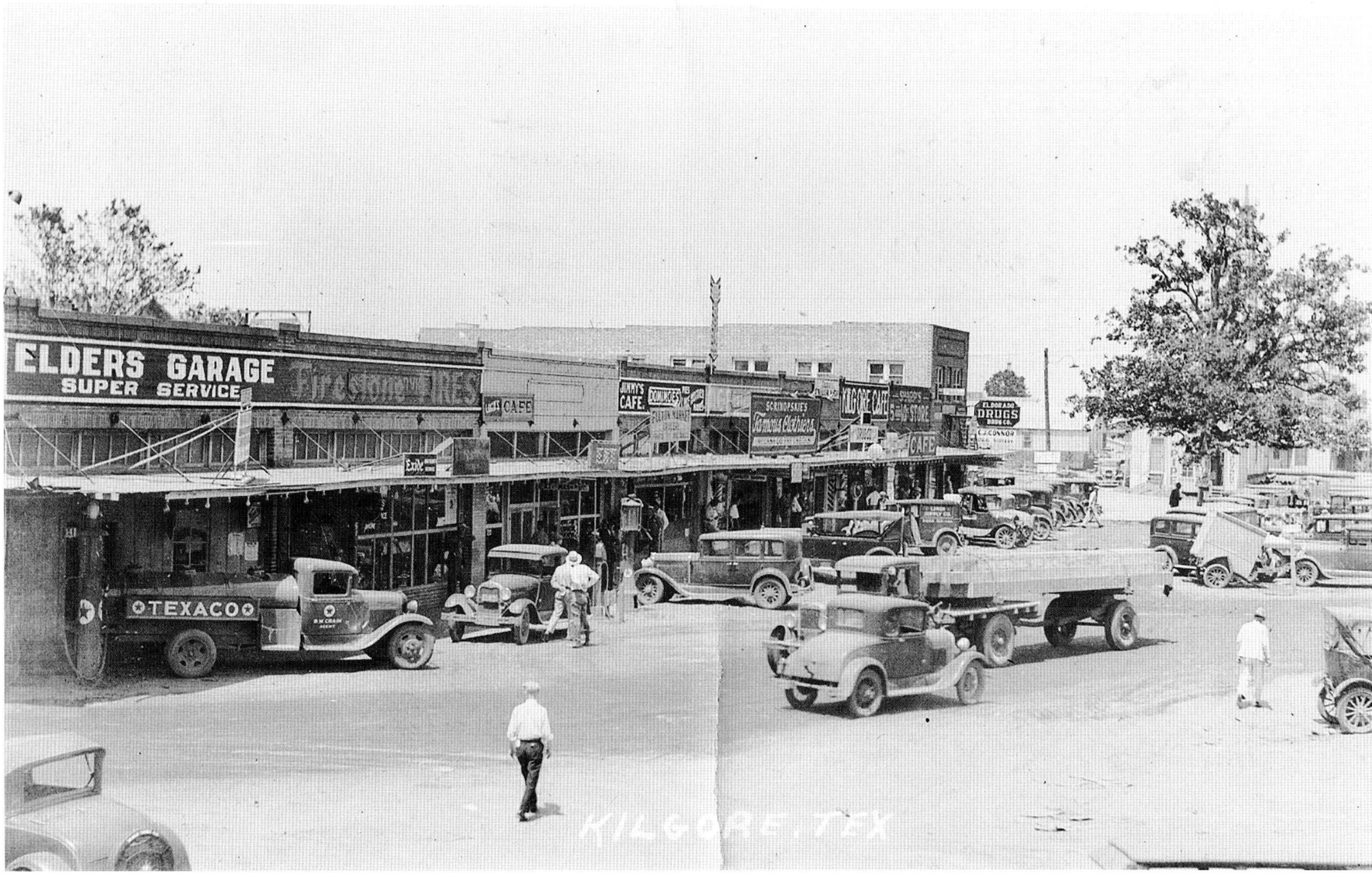
ELDERS GARAGE
SUPER SERVICE
TEXACO
CAFE
JIMMY'S CAFE
KILGORE CAFE
ELDORADO DRUGS
KILGORE. TEX

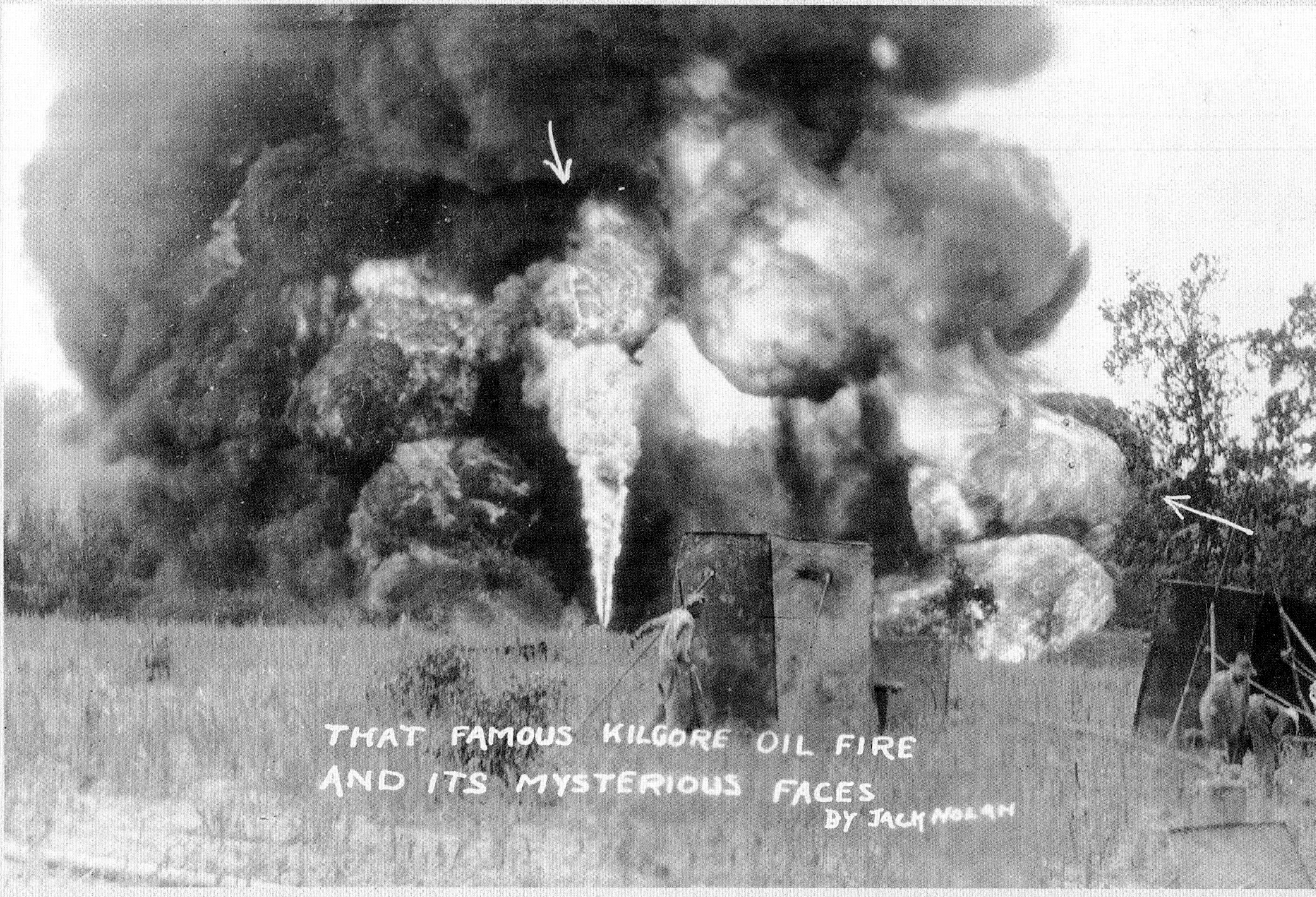


Fighting an oil well fire

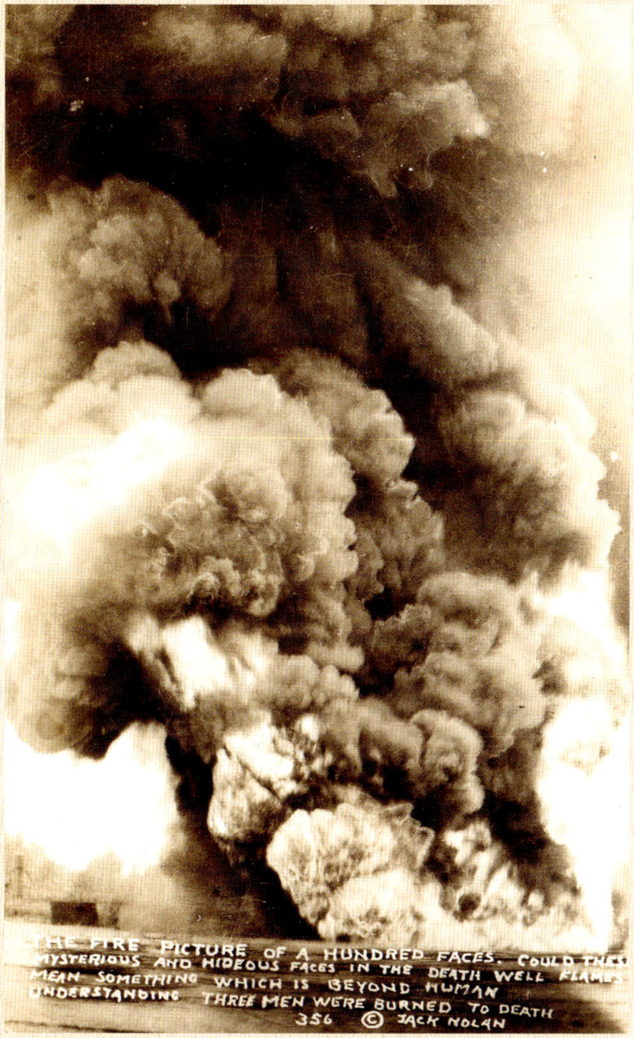


Deadly oil well explosion and fire

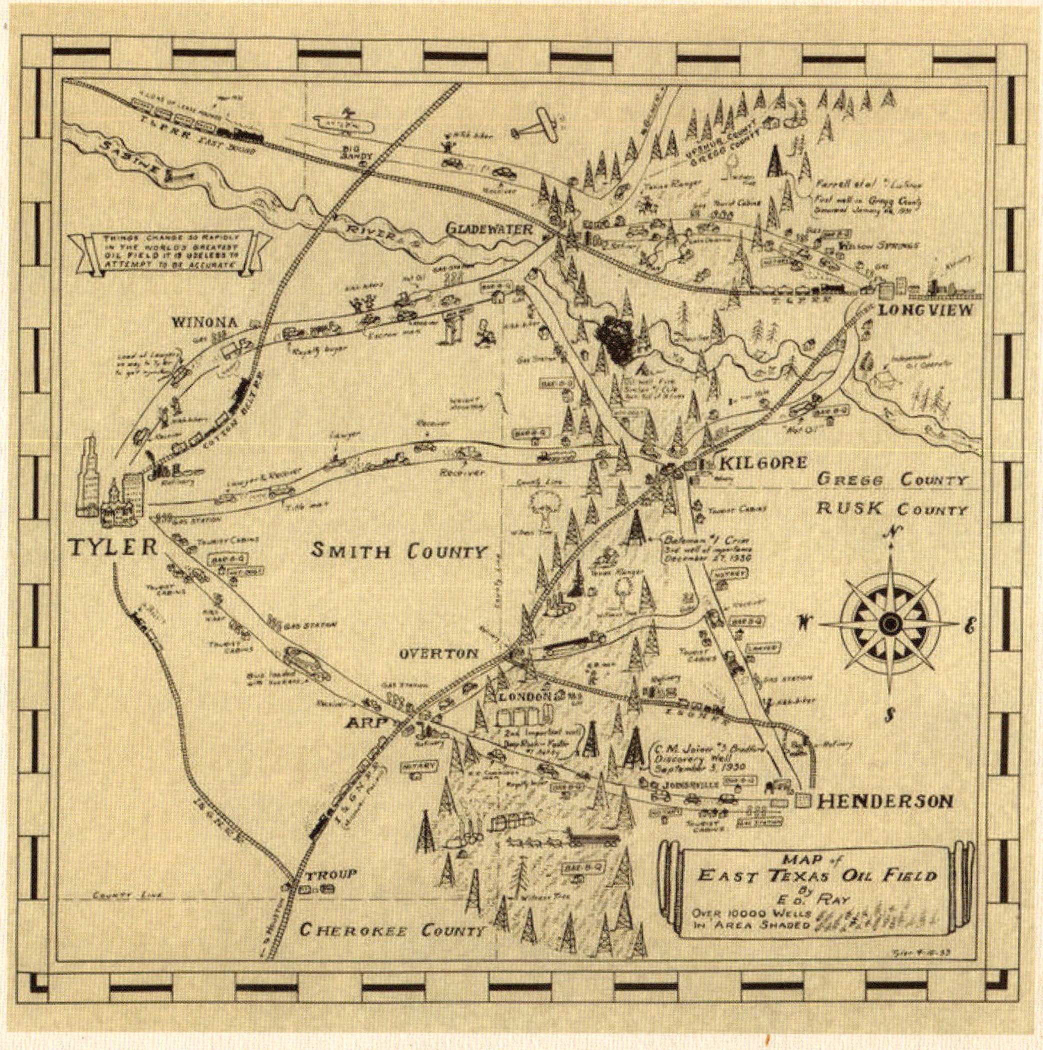


East Texas Oil Field

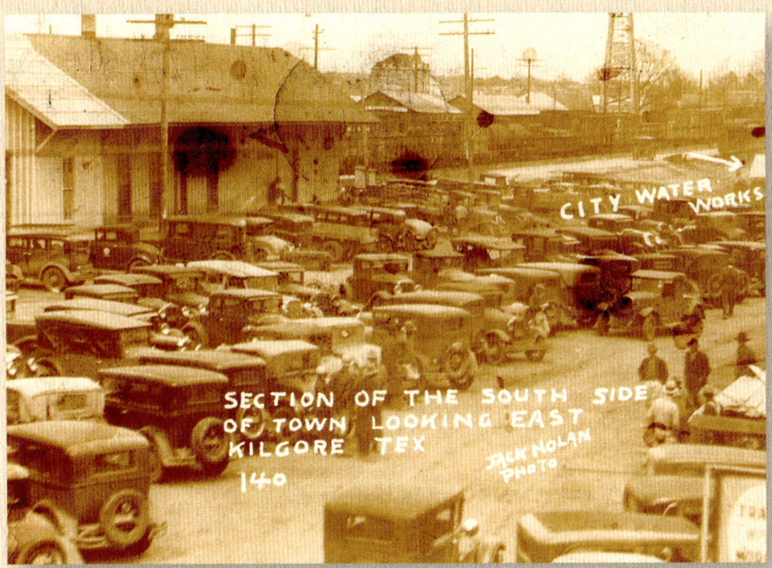
CITY WATER WORKS
SECTION OF THE SOUTH SIDE OF TOWN LOOKING EAST KILGORE TEX
140
JACK NOLAN PHOTO

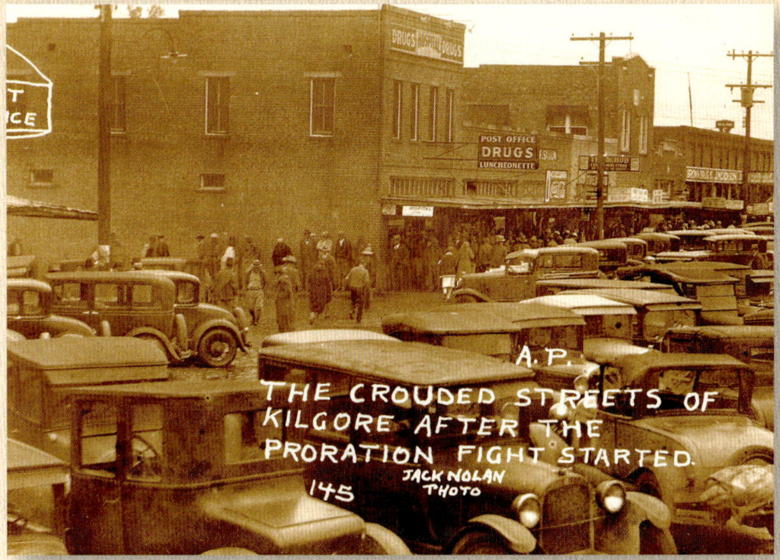
POST OFFICE
DRUGS
A.P.
THE CROUDED STREETS OF KILGORE AFTER THE PRORATION FIGHT STARTED.
145
JACK NOLAN PHOTO

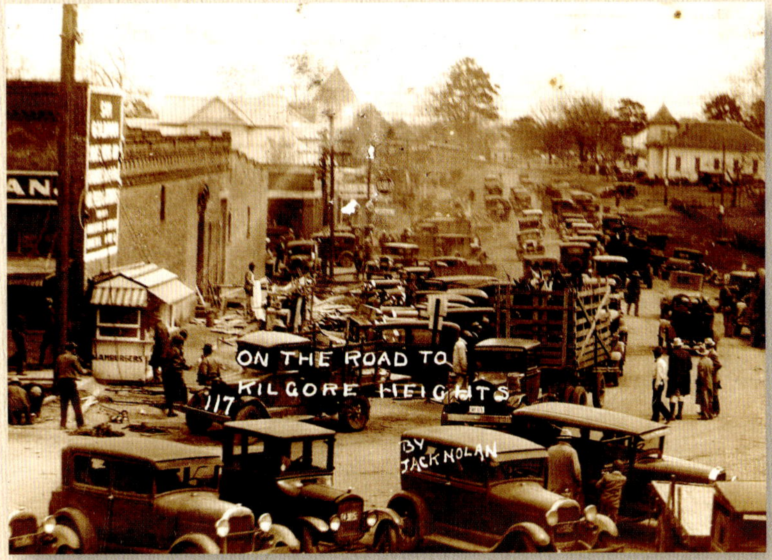
ON THE ROAD TO KILGORE HEIGHTS
117
BY JACK NOLAN

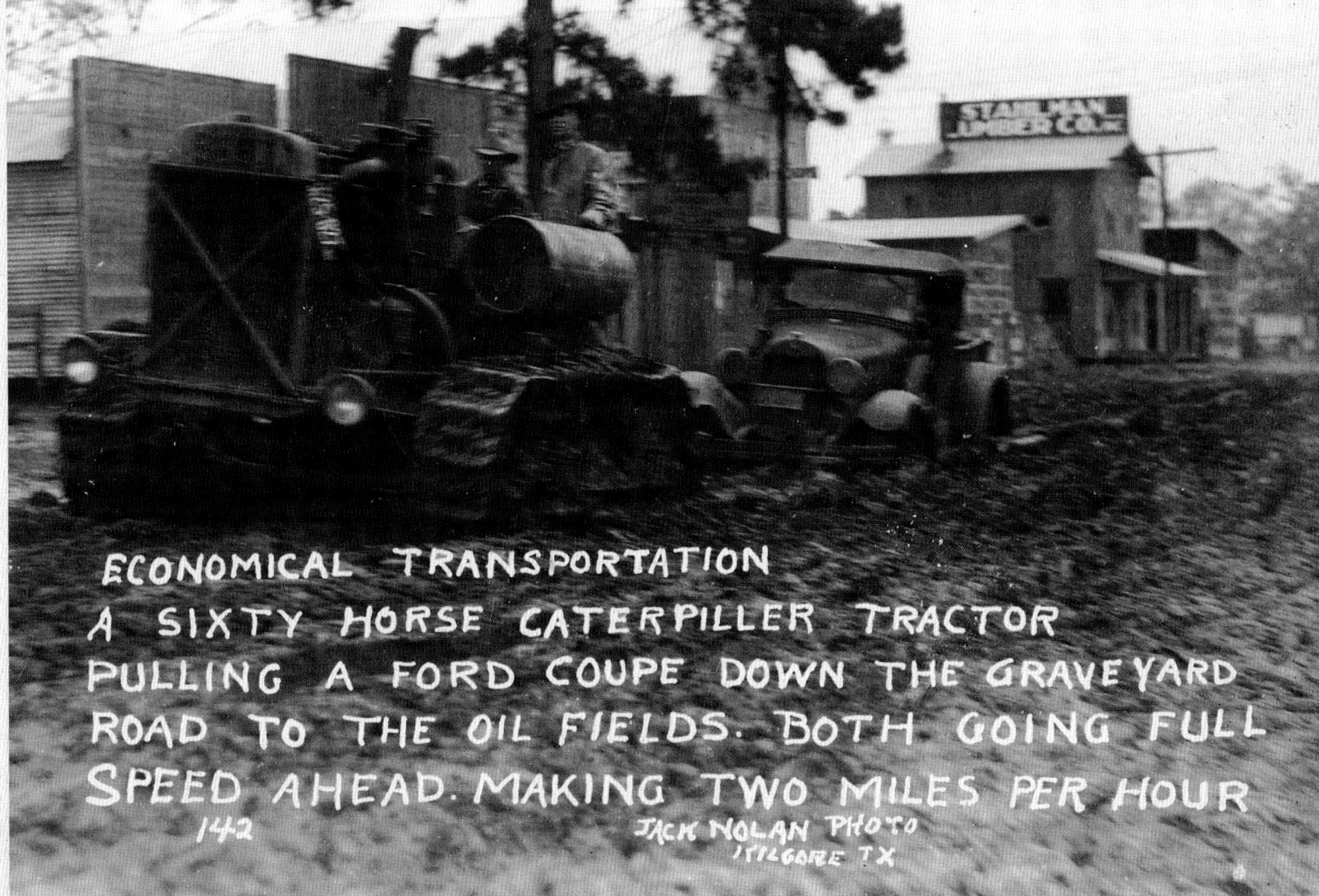
ECONOMICAL TRANSPORTATION
A SIXTY HORSE CATERPILLER TRACTOR
PULLING A FORD COUPE DOWN THE GRAVEYARD
ROAD TO THE OIL FIELDS. BOTH GOING FULL
SPEED AHEAD. MAKING TWO MILES PER HOUR
142
JACK NOLAN PHOTO
KILGORE TX

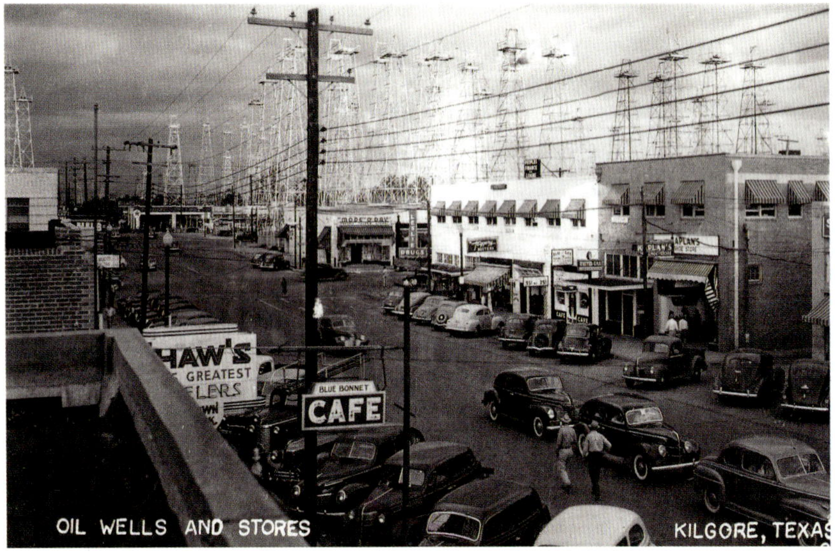


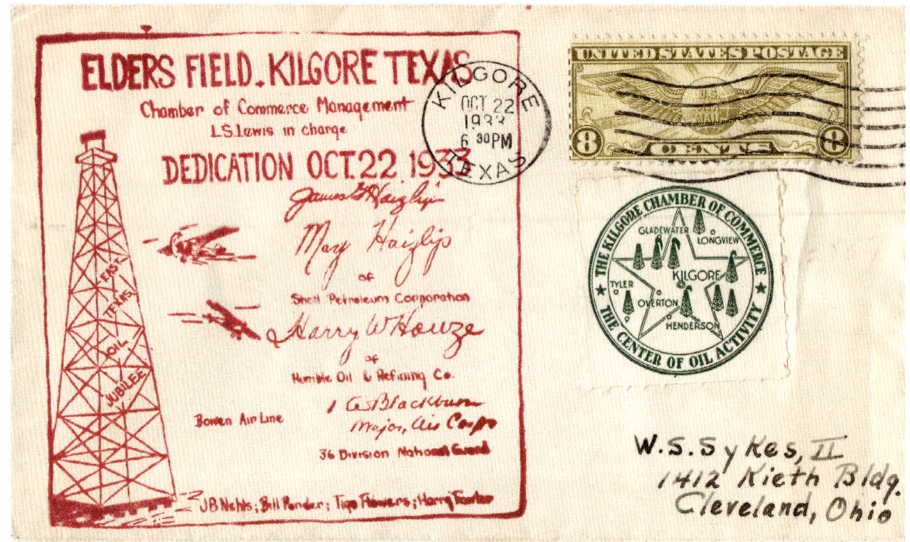


Downtown Kilgore circa 1940

the summer of the same year production was even greater, and prices had begun to plummet. Before the East Texas field came in the going price for oil throughout most of the United States was roughly $1.00 barrel. Within six months it was sometimes as little as a dime in East Texas. Even when prices fell and lawlessness continued unabated, no one stopped drilling, and by mid-1934 there were over thirteen thousand producing wells in the oil patch. All this activity defined East Texas and shaped the lives of its residents for years to come.

Kilgore was the epicenter of the oil business in Texas, and it is the town to which Harold and Sarah would come in 1938, and where their first and only child would be born in 1940. Except for one very distant relative on Harold's side, no one in either of the families prospered directly from the oil boom, but indirectly the oil patch was of great help.

Kilgore became an unusually wealthy town, and within a decade, during the 1930s, it established a fine school system, including a junior college, movie theaters, a library, exclusive residential neighborhoods, and solid infrastructure. The school system would eventually employ Harold; oil would power the ships, airplanes, and other vehicles used throughout World War II; and most of the ships on which Harold sailed, airplanes in which he was transported, and Jeeps in his military police company were fueled in part by petroleum products that originated in the East Texas oil patch. By the end of the war these fields were not producing at such incredible capacity, but during the war they were crucial.

# Harold and Sarah

## March 19, 1932

**HAROLD AND SARAH'S STORY TOGETHER BEGAN ON A SATURDAY AFTERNOON IN A TINY EAST TEXAS TOWN, WINONA, IN 1932.** How tiny? There were maybe as many as four hundred residents. The town had been founded in 1870, and then prospered a bit when the Tyler Tap Railroad built a station in the town.

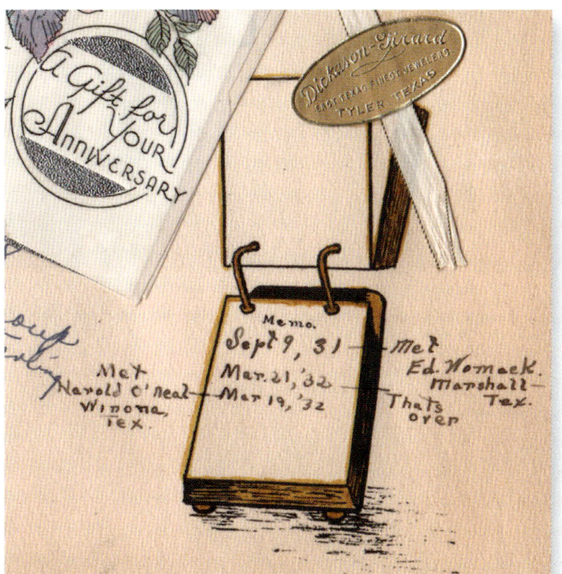


The first meeting

By the mid teens there were about six hundred residents, a bank, two hotels, a few grocery/general stores, a gasoline station, cotton gins, at least three churches, and a small newspaper. After the war, the population grew a bit, but with the advent of the Depression it plummeted. At least half the residents left town, which is where the population was when Harold met Sarah.

Winona is on the outer reaches of northern Smith County. In those years, the residents mostly derived their incomes from the sandy soil, usually the top foot or so. The outer reaches of the East Texas oil patch didn't extend to Winona. But after years and years of agricultural boom and bust, mostly with cotton farming, the rose boom that began in Tyler after the turn-of-the-century peach blight made its way to Winona. By 1940 over half the rose bushes sold in the United States came from Smith County, and farms in and around Winona played their part in supplying these plants. There was even a special building along the railroad tracks that was used for nothing but storing rose bushes for transport.

But for a young couple looking for amusement or entertainment, unless they wanted to look at a rose field or listen to a radio or a Victrola, they had to go somewhere else, usually a town or city with a picture show and or maybe a road house in a county or town that wasn't dry. Winona was close to other towns; Tyler was only a dozen miles away, Longview about thirty, Kilgore a little more than twenty, Mineola and Gilmer about twenty-five. But sometimes a moonlit night and a Victrola would do.

This is how it began, in the words of a just-turned eighteen-year-old girl and her twenty-two-year-old soon-to-be suitor. It was just before springtime, mid-March in Winona, Texas. Winona, a place where the bus stopped every so often and the train even less, but where there was a new paved road that went all the way to Tyler, which made the twelve-mile journey an easy one.

The town was in good repair; there were handsome houses along Dallas Street and Church Street, the churches were new and well maintained, Starnes's General Store had a good selection of almost anything anyone would expect in a general store, and gasoline at the station on the road to Tyler was cheap and plentiful. Most of the buildings standing then are standing today, but almost all are vacant. Many are in disrepair, and others have fallen down. But no one was thinking about that or much of anything else on a Saturday night in 1932 that offered the promise of endless possibilities for romance, a ride in an open car, dancing somewhere to a wind-up Victrola or even the radio.

Sarah had come on the new road from Tyler with her friend, Alpha Verne Wells, and Alpha's boyfriend and eventual husband, Lance Lowery. Lance and Alpha Verne were Sarah's friends from Tyler High School. Harold was visiting for the weekend, probably with his brother Cecil, who lived in Winona, or possibly with other relatives in nearby Starrville. Starrville was once a thriving little town, but the railroad passed it by a few decades earlier and it went slowly downhill. By 1932 it was much smaller than Winona.

In 2018 Starrville consists of a church, an always-empty meeting hall, and a handful or residents. Most of the former citizens of this hamlet reside in its picturesque rural cemetery, including Alpha Verne Wells and Lance Lowry. There is still space available, just for the asking. In rural cemeteries like these, if there is space you can often stake out a claim by simply leaving a piece of paper in a jelly jar. But no one who is eighteen or even twenty-two ever thinks about such things, especially on a moonlit night in an open car. It is unclear who furnished the car.

And so began a seemingly flawless sequence of events that led to thirty-six years together, never apart except for three years during World War II. Everything seemed to come together naturally, at just the right time, under the perfect circumstances. The dreams came true, not without some effort, but looking back at it from today it appears almost perfect.

On one level, it wasn't very complicated, a boy and a girl fall in love, possibly the first real love for each, a love for one another that was completely and forever, but what makes their story fascinating is how this innocent love affair that worked so perfectly for them was able to take place with so many complicated events and circumstances swirling around them. These were events that would unfold rapidly over the next dozen years, and then more slowly and methodically until the mid-1950s. Harold and Sarah were swirled along with them.

As Harold and Sarah began their lives together in 1932, they couldn't imagine these events that would utterly transform not only the immediate world in which they lived, but the entire world that everyone lived in. Simply look at what happened between the years 1932 and 1954, not just in their lives but the lives of everyone in the United States and rest of the world.

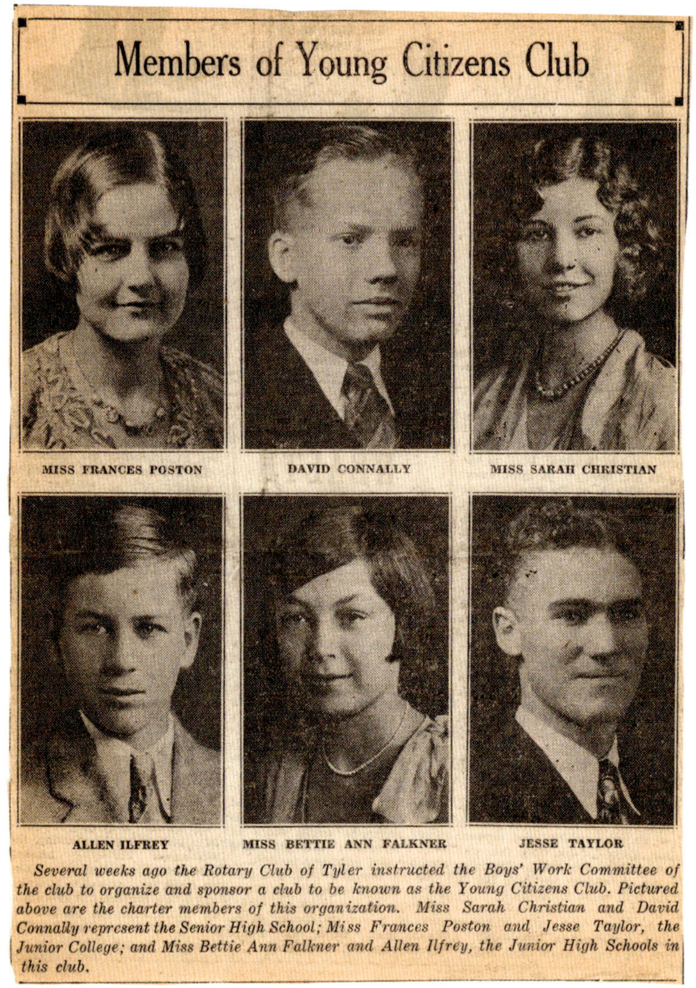
Members of Young Citizens Club

MISS FRANCES POSTON — DAVID CONNALLY — MISS SARAH CHRISTIAN

ALLEN ILFREY — MISS BETTIE ANN FALKNER — JESSE TAYLOR

*Several weeks ago the Rotary Club of Tyler instructed the Boys' Work Committee of the club to organize and sponsor a club to be known as the Young Citizens Club. Pictured above are the charter members of this organization. Miss Sarah Christian and David Connally reprcsent the Senior High School; Miss Frances Poston and Jesse Taylor, the Junior College; and Miss Bettie Ann Falkner and Allen Ilfrey, the Junior High Schools in this club.*

# Holidays.

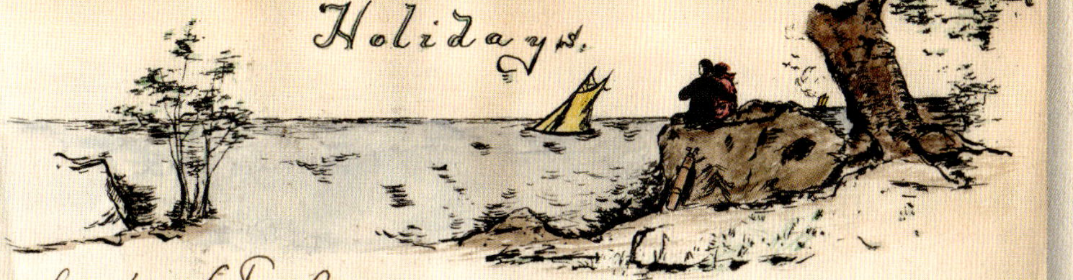

March 19, '32, Saturday — 5:00 aft - 12:00 Night
Met Harold O'Neal about 5:00. I had gone home with Alpha Verne Wells for the week-end. That night Lance, Alphy, Harold and I went riding — Beautiful moon, open car.

March 20, '32, Sunday 11 morn. - 9:00 Night
This afternoon we four went horse-back riding. Started about 2:00 o'clock. Went to a pretty pine grove. — Heavenly time. That night we danced — Harold and I. He took my address — Then I came home.

Friday, April 1, '32 — 4:30 aft - 11:30 Night
Alphy and I went down to Winona with Jimmy. Alphy's sister met us. We got Harold and took him to Starville. Again we danced. Ate supper. At 7:30 - we went to see a play which Lance was in. Then Lance and Harold brought us home.

Saturday, April 9, 32 — 7:30 aft - 1:30 Night
Lance came after Alphy and I. We went to Sandflat. Harold came. We sat in the car. Harold had his brother's car — Heavenly. We got all mixed up. Harold left about 1:30 that night — Fun - gee!

Sunday April 10, '32 2:30 aft - 9:30 Night.
Lance and Alphy came down. Went to show. Saw Richard Barthlemess in "Alias the Doctor." That

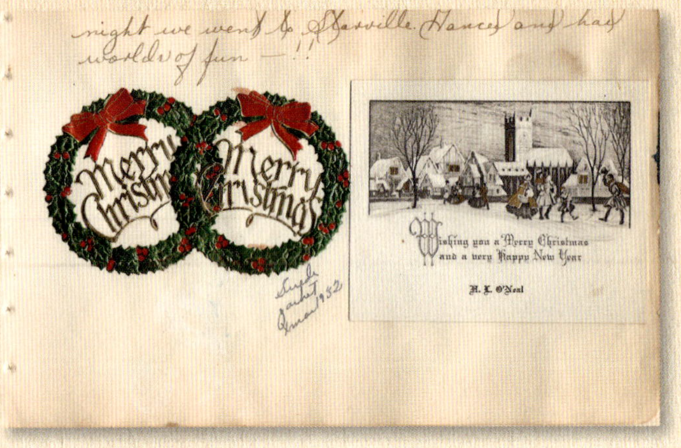


W. A. McINTOSH, SUPERINTENDENT OF SCHOOLS
GEO. M. WADDILL, BUSINESS MANAGER

R. B. NORMAN, PRINCIPAL SENIOR HIGH SCHOOL

HAROLD L. O'NEAL, 2ND LIEUT. INF. RES. COMMANDANT OF CADETS

WAR DEPARTMENT

R. O. T. C.

*The Senior High School*

~~*Amarillo, Texas*~~

Winona, Texas
March 23,1932

Dear Sarah:

Greetings little Mary Sunshine. This letter is to remind you of something that you had forgotten. During the unforgetable week-end while you were in our fair city you got in debt. For several compliments I passed upon you I was promised two five cent pieces and three pennies, making a total of thirteen cents. This is to remind you that you left here Sunday evening without paying me the thirteen cents. Now just to show you how free hearted and what a good sport I am I will make the following proposition. If you will oblige me by paying the above sum the next time I see you I will then in return do the following. Take the afore mentioned amountof sheekles and squander it in this manner. With the dime I will buy each of us a ice cream cone or a cold drink ( if the drink cost a dime I will drink it and then tell you how good it was). Then with the remaining three cents I will buy some pepermints (knowing you enjoy them) and we will divide them accordingly. How does this suit you? After taking a careful estimate of the situation I think that it is very reasonable. Let me know what sort of a reaction you are going to take so I will know whether to head for the river bottomsor come to Tyler.

Waiting your reply I remain,
As ever,

Harold

P.S. Lance and I will be in Tyler some evening this week. If you don't have to study we will get you and Alphy. This might be a good time to spend the 13¢.

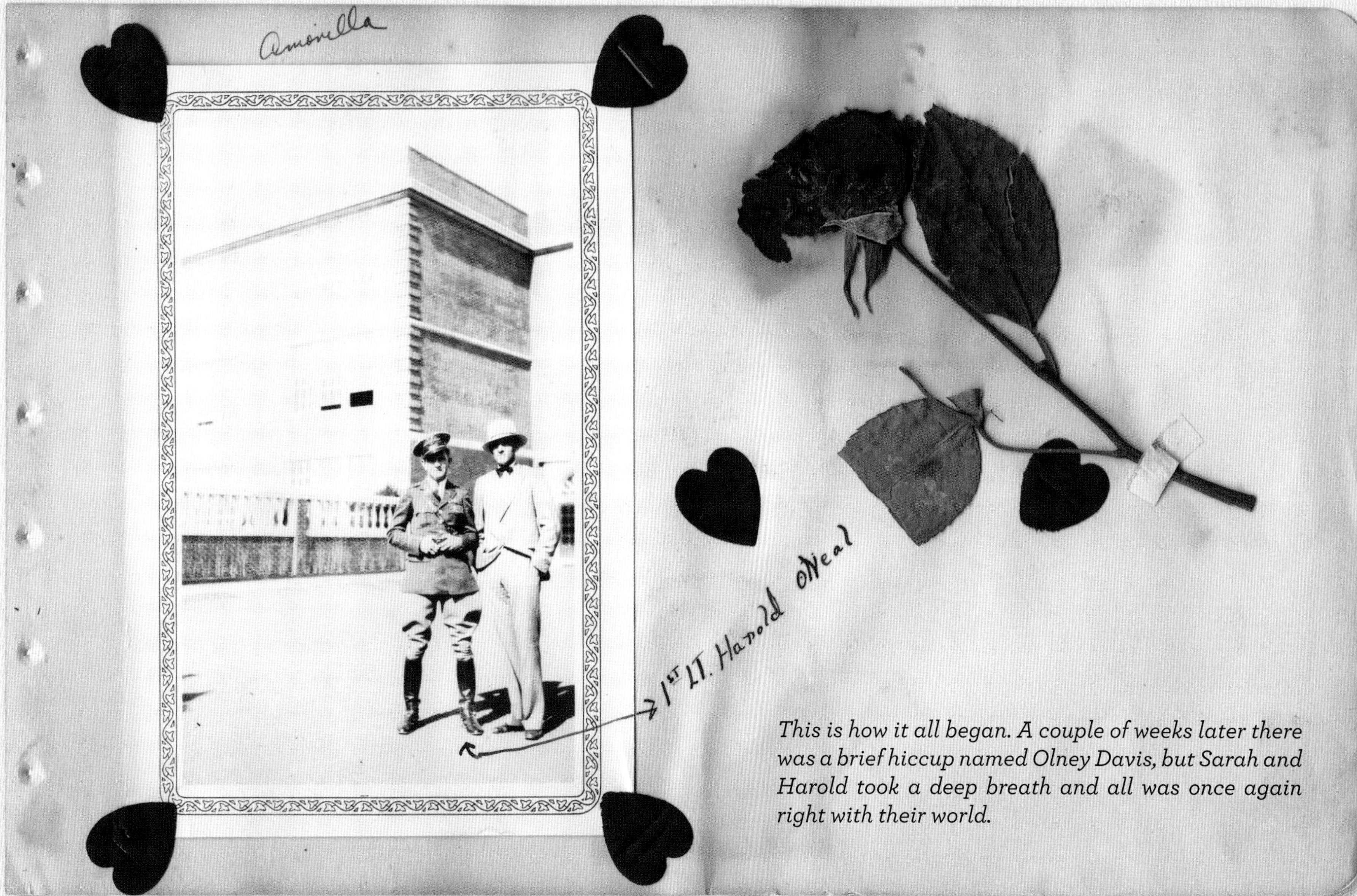


*This is how it all began. A couple of weeks later there was a brief hiccup named Olney Davis, but Sarah and Harold took a deep breath and all was once again right with their world.*

# My Class

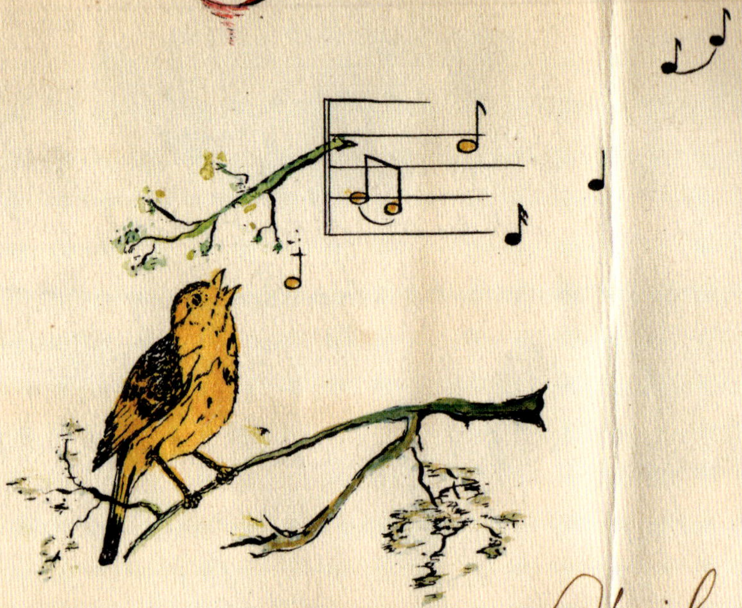

| 1932 | | | APRIL | | | 1932 |
|---|---|---|---|---|---|---|
| SUN | MON | TUES | WED | THUR | FRID | SAT |
| | | | | | 1 | 2 |
| 3 | 4 | 5 | 6 | 7 | 8 | 9 |
| 10 | 11 | 12 | 13 | 14 | 15 | 16 |
| 17 | 18 | 19 | 20 | 21 | 22 | 23 |
| 24 | 25 | 26 | 27 | 28 | 29 | 30 |

April 13, '32 - Wednesday

La Nelle had the club (Eliz C., Sunny N., Hazel P., Mary V. Kay, Jo Nell, Helen, Mary E. Nichols, & I.) over at her house. Olney danced with me then asked me to go get some gum with him. We went. Went to Drug Store Vances and came back. I didn't know what to think - then that night afterwards he talked to me lots

April 15, '32 - Friday —

Olney asked me to go over to Jack Hairstons to dance. Jack and Olney came after me. Jack's mother wasn't at home. Olney and I danced a lot, and we sat on the couch and talked a lot. We had given each other that date to show how nice we were. He was grand — "And when he holds my hand" —

April 20, '32 — Wednesday —

The club went out to Jack's country home. Olney had already asked me for a date — I had the most heavenly time. We watched the moon rise, walked in the woods, sat on the porch — Olney and I and talked. Jack gave Sunny a bracelet coming home. Oh gosh! I wore my little blue "jail" dress. Olney liked me.

Sunday, April 24, '32.

Olney came back from Hillsborough. He phoned me when he got in — asked if I didn't think my compact should come home — I did. He came and we went riding — Gee and "when he holds my hand" Il a dit à me que, il me aime et il m'embrasse mucho. Heavenly — Rode out Whitehouse highway.

Tuesday — April 26, '32 —

We were going to play but Olney had gone to Marshall to play tennis and didn't get back. Sent me telegram from Longview and got here and came over about 9:30. He had to take the cook home. Il me aime.

Wednesday, April 27, '32 —

I wore Martha's black dress and Olney came about 7:30. We had to go and see Mr. Nelson who's about to be fined. About 8:30 we went to the show to see "The Man Who Played God." Olney carri[ed] my coat and Gee we ha[d] [f]un.

TELEGRAMS CABLEGRAMS RADIOGRAMS

# Postal Telegraph

PAY NO CHARGES ON THIS MESSAGE UNLESS SHOWN ON DELIVERY SHEET

WILL ARRIVE ABOUT NINE WILL PHONE WHEN WE

OLNEY.

# My Class Picture.

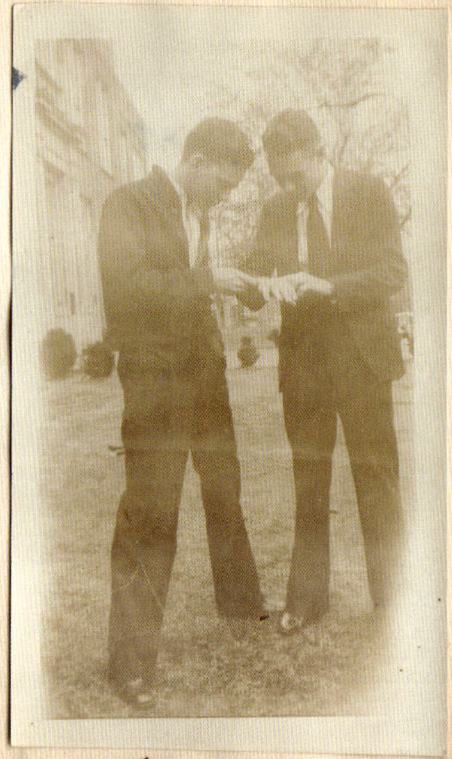

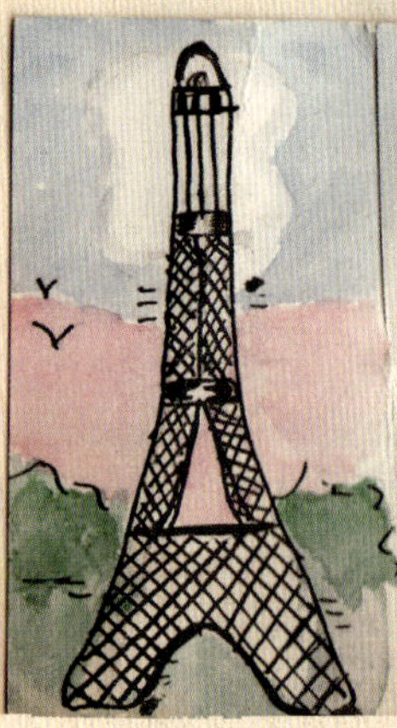

Olney Davis

French banquet with Olney

Night be-
for I left for
school, Sept 18.-
with
Harold-

Sat. Nite Nov. 26

Waco

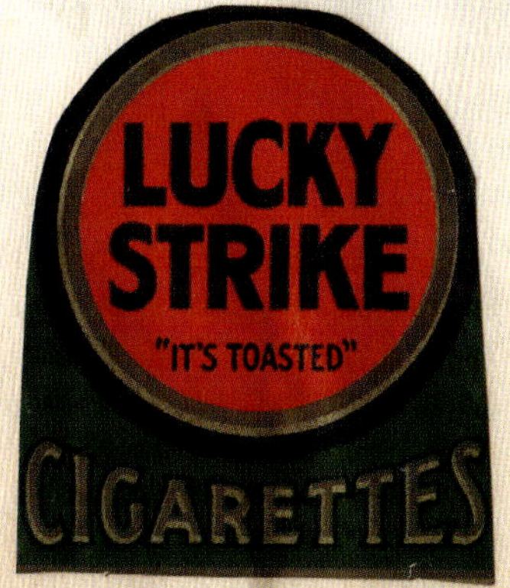

It was a time of the greatest upheaval of social systems in the United States since the Civil War, changes that are still being debated. It was the time of the rise of fascism in Europe and super nationalism in Japan, which would lead to World War II and, more than any other single factor, bring the United States out of the Great Depression. The war would ultimately cast the United States as the foremost actor on the world stage. It was the beginning of the atomic age, the Cold War and mutually assured destruction, but it was also the time that saw the rapid rise of white middle-class America, where millions and millions of people would achieve what a few sociologists had once called *The American Dream,* and it was now being trumpeted by hundreds if not thousands more would-be sociologists and social pundits. And so began the almost official quest to achieve it.

Perhaps the reason everything worked for Harold and Sarah is because they never called it *The American Dream* or even thought about it and certainly weren't on a quest for anything. Sarah used to say, "All things come to he who waits," and she waited with Harold and it all came true, but on that night and for many more over the next few days and weeks and months into years, such weighty matters never crossed their minds as they pursued one another and danced the night away listening to Bing Crosby, Russ Columbo, or Fred Astaire echo their thoughts with *Please, Prisoner of Love,* and *Night and Day.* And if they didn't dance the night away listening to the radio or a windup phonograph, or in a lakeside pavilion with real musicians playing the same songs, they could go to the picture show and see movie stars in love, Garbo and Barrymore heating up *Grand Hotel,* the doomed Helen Hayes and Gary Cooper in *A Farewell to Arms,* or the bubbling Jeanette and Maurice enjoying one another in *Love Me Tonight.* All slightly naughty Pre-Code masterpieces that were ideal for titillating young lovers in a theater balcony, even in a small city like Tyler or maybe Longview or Mineola.

Sarah was in school, an eighteen-year-old freshman at Baylor University in Waco, a long drive from Tyler and even longer from Amarillo, where Harold was phasing out of his ROTC teaching assignment. He tried to see Sarah as often as possible in Tyler, and took her to school in Waco in the fall, but it was clear that in order for him to be close to her, he had to make some changes. To keep the romance alive he had to see her more often than on holidays and occasional weekends. The change that was required was not made by him but by forces outside his control.

On November 7, 1932, the unemployment rate in the United States was slightly more than 23 percent, and on that day Franklin D. Roosevelt was still campaigning for the presidency against the incumbent president, Herbert Hoover. On November 8, Roosevelt won forty-two states; Hoover won six, all in the northeast. Harold voted for Roosevelt and his running mate, Texan James Nance Garner, an East Texas boy who'd made good. Since before the turn of the century Garner had been elected to various offices and was the Speaker of the House of Representatives. Sarah was only eighteen and too young to vote. It was the only time she didn't vote for Roosevelt, a man she idolized.

On November 9 the unemployment rate was still over 23 percent, but the election set in motion a series of events that led to the changes Harold was seeking. These changes would begin to take place early the following year, when Franklin D. Roosevelt was inaugurated the thirty-second president of the United States on March 4, 1933. Less than three weeks later, on March 21, he proposed the Emergency Conservation Work Act to a skeptical Congress, but despite this skepticism, it was passed by a voice vote on March 31, and the president signed it the same day. The act was put into practice by an executive order on April 5, one month and a day after his first day in office. One provision of the act was the creation of the Civilian Conservation Corps, which would prove to become the most popular of Roosevelt's many New Deal creations.

Reserve army officers were to be in charge of the CCC Camps. Harold was such an officer, hoping to find an

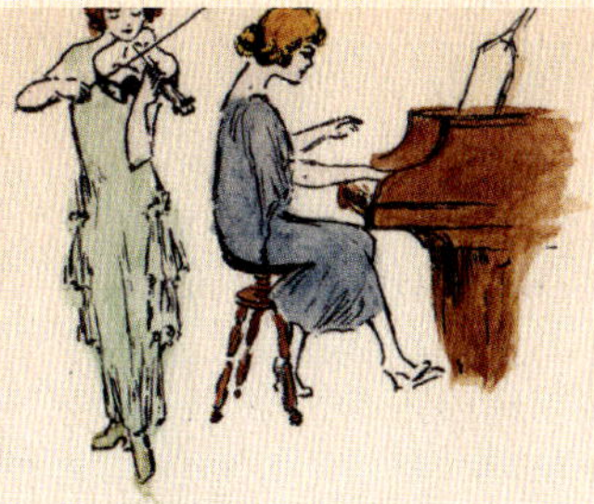

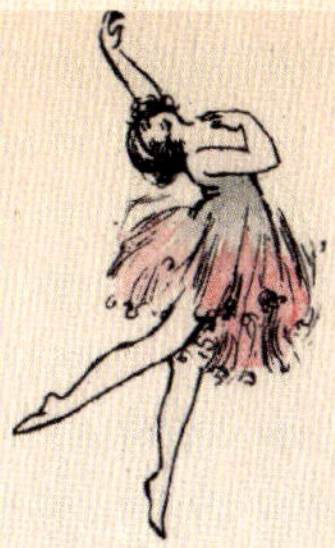

# My Ambitions.

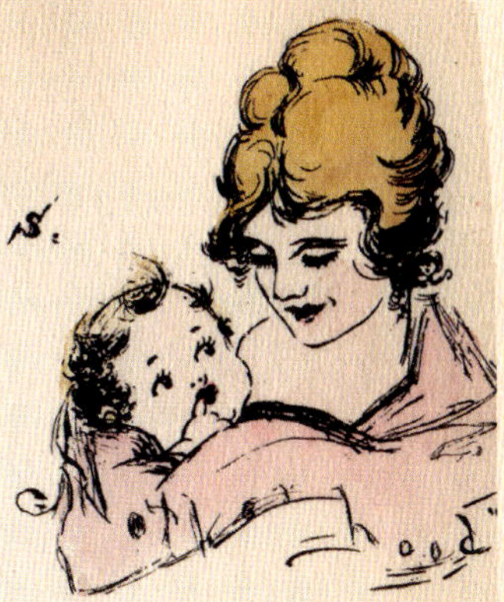

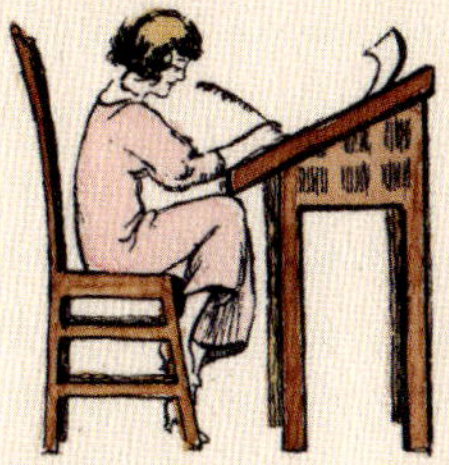

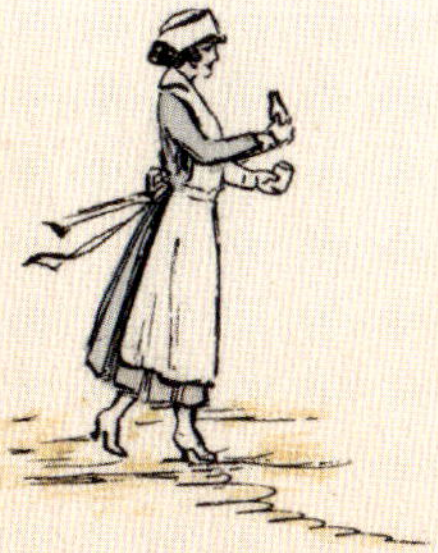

**BAYLOR UNIVERSITY**

OFFICE OF THE REGISTRAR

Waco, Texas

Report of Miss Sarah Beatrice Christian

for Quarter ending DEC 9 1932

| | Present | Absent | Grade | Passed | Not Passed | Chapel Demerits Current Qr. | Chapel Demerits Total |
|---|---|---|---|---|---|---|---|
| Ed. 245 | 59 | 1 | A | " | | 0 | 0 |
| Fren. 204 | 60 | 0 | B + | " | | | |
| Hist. 103 | 60 | 0 | A + | " | | | |
| Phys. Ed. 151 | 28 | 0 | B + | " | | | |

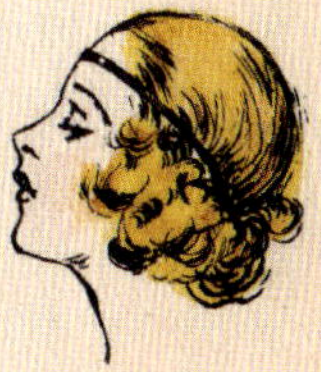

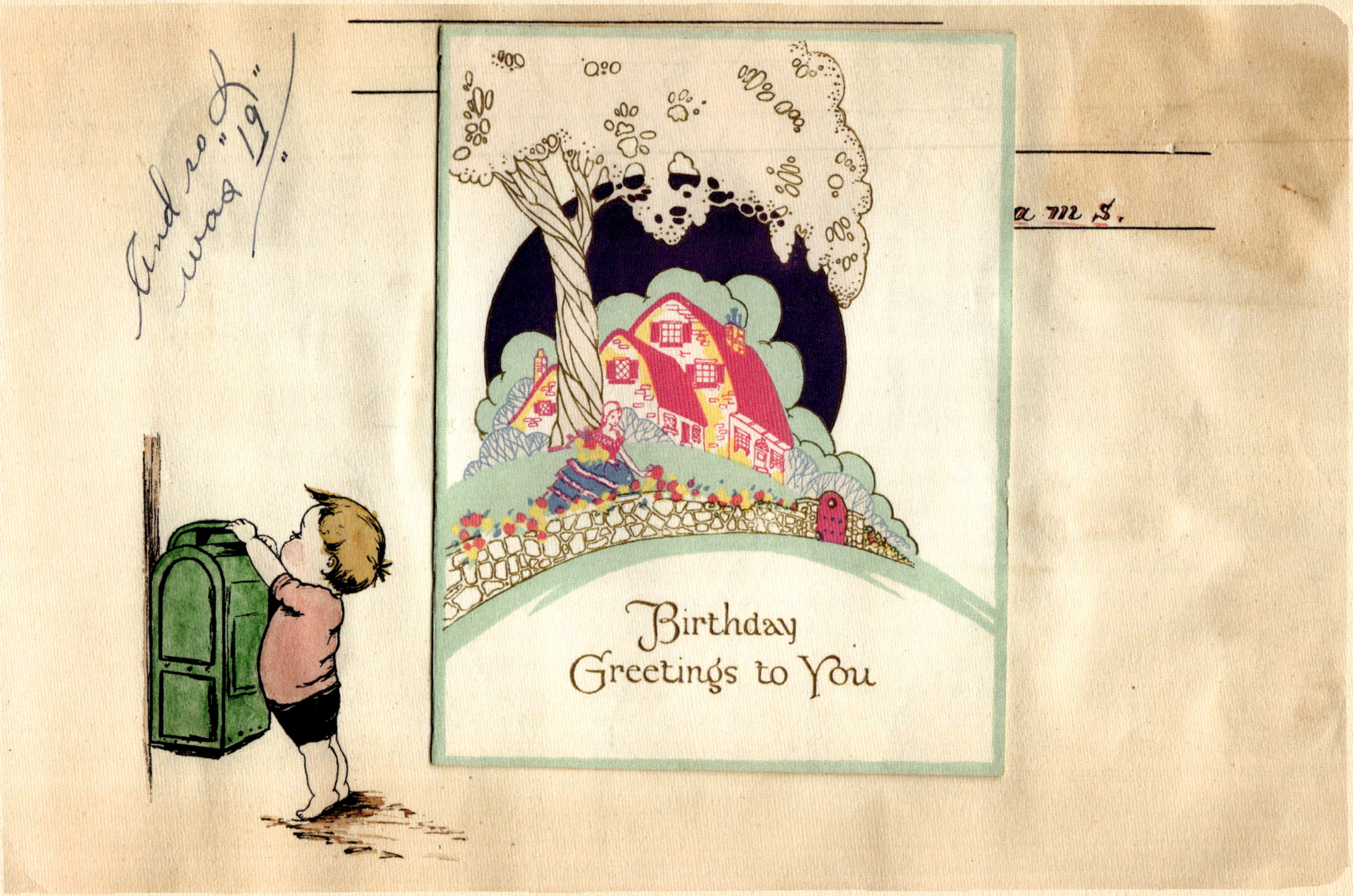
And so I was "19"
Birthday
Greetings to You

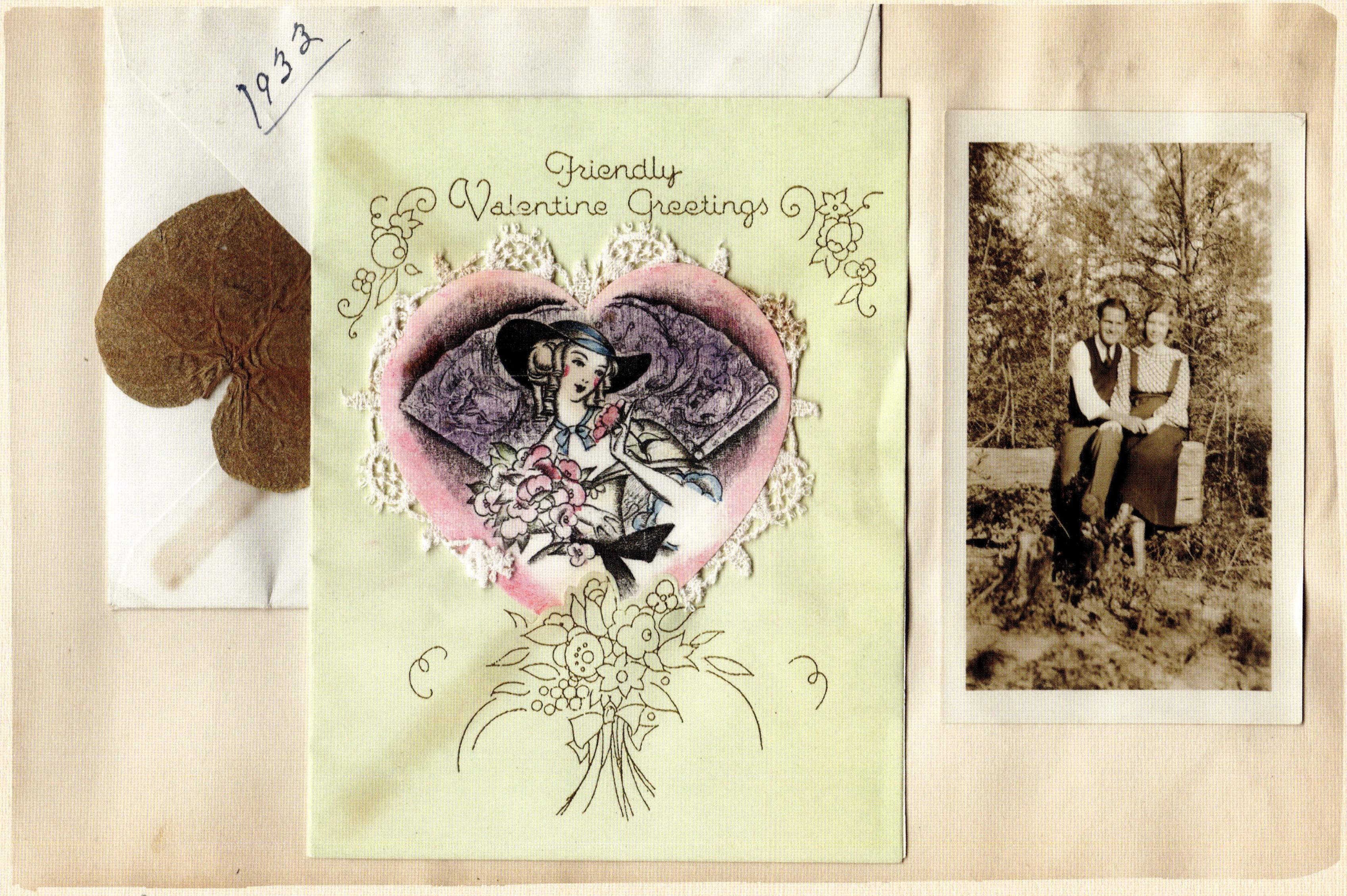
1932
Friendly
Valentine Greetings

Galvest

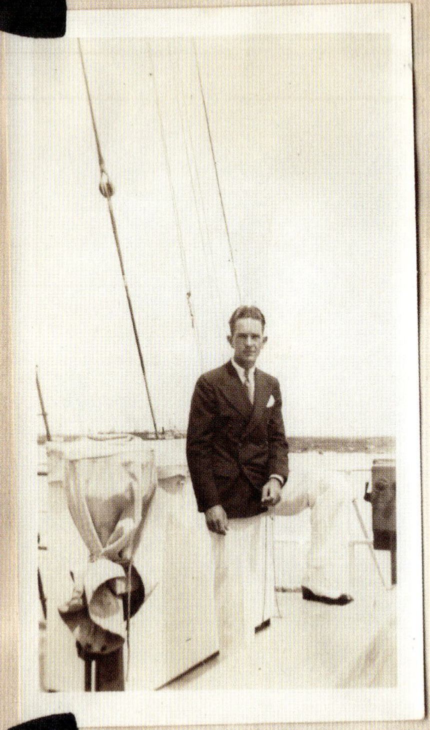

Waco – Oct 16 – Cameron Park –

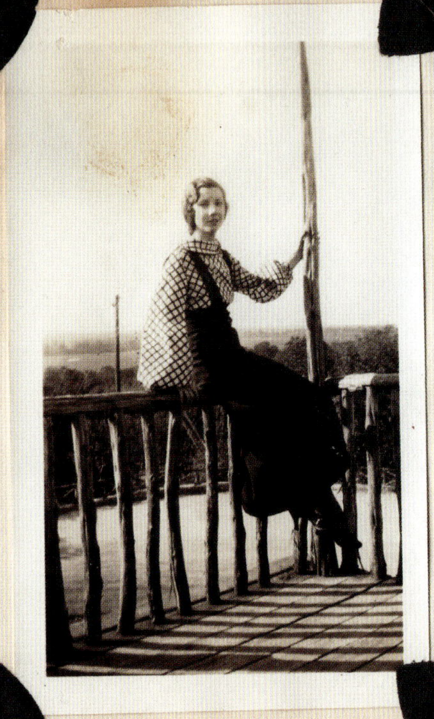

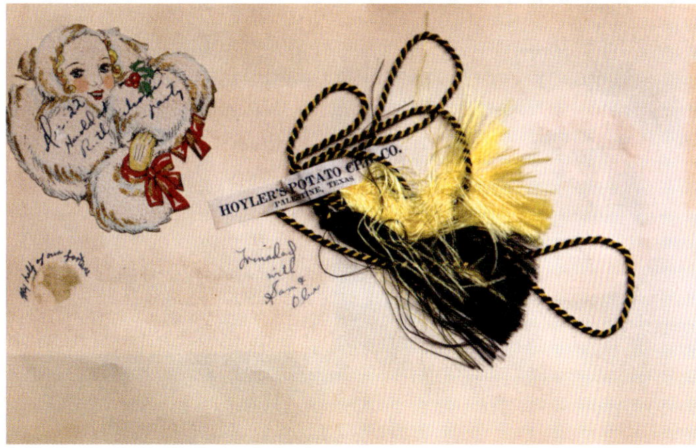


assignment in East Texas to be near Sarah. General Douglas MacArthur was put in charge of the program; ten years later Harold would once again be under MacArthur's command in the Pacific Theater during World War II. One unexpected result of the army's involvement with the CCC program was that young men with CCC training were better equipped than those without to integrate successfully into the armed forces after the Japanese attack on Pearl Harbor, and the many men with CCC experience helped considerably with war preparedness.

Three days after Roosevelt's Executive Order, on April 8, the first young man was enrolled in the CCC; the first CCC camp was established nine days later on April 17, and by July 1 there were 1,463 camps in existence with a quarter of a million young men enrolled in the program. It was all done very quickly, some thought too quickly, but the unemployment rate in the United States was at an all-time high in the summer of 1933, and people were hurting. Anything to ease this pain was a priority, and the CCC lessened the pain of a quarter million young Americans, and to some degree the pain of their families.

The majority of the young men who enrolled in the CCC came from rural families, and by some estimates nearly three-fourths of them arrived malnourished and poorly clothed. The educational levels ranged from illiterate to high school graduates, but most had only modest educational experiences, which made the educational component of the CCC important. The vast majority were not only poorly educated, but most had never been employed and had no workplace skills.

The young men who enrolled were usually eighteen to twenty-five years old, but as the CCC programs progressed these age limits were often extended to include men seventeen to twenty-eight. The men worked forty hours a week, five to six days a week, depending on the weather. They were enrolled for a minimum of six months, with options to serve as long as two years. Compensation was thirty dollars per month, but with as much as twenty-five dollars returned to their dependent families, depending on need. In addition to the work programs that were related to conservation, soil erosion, forestry—both culture and protection—and landscape and recreation, there was an educational component. Education was felt to be critical. Each camp also had trained medical personnel, as well as trained cooks to provide for the health and welfare of each enrollee.

Texas was very receptive to the CCC program, and almost a fifth of the enrollees nationwide were to be found in Texas. The state was divided into districts, and much of East Texas was included in the Tyler District. By 1936 there were fifteen CCC camps in the Tyler District involved in public works projects. Two of these camps, Winnsboro and Bogata, were for African American enrollees. All the camps were designated by a number; the African American camps were further designated with a (C) following the number.

Three of the camps in East Texas were primarily devoted to the construction of state parks: Caddo Lake near the town of Karnac; Daingerfield, two miles east of the small town of the same name; and Tyler State Park, north of that city. Inexplicably, the CCC Company that built Caddo Lake State Park was not included in the Tyler District but was considered to be part of the Oklahoma District.

Caddo Lake State Park was the first major CCC project undertaken in Texas, and construction began on June 5, 1933, just two months after the first volunteer had been enrolled on April 5. It was also the first CCC project in Texas to work in conjunction with the National Park Service. Initially, the project was under the command of Captain Walter K. Boggs, and since it was the first, it was designated State Park 1, or SP-1. Some of the land for the park had been donated by T. J. Taylor, later better known as the father of Claudia Alta Taylor, who was also later known as Lady Bird Johnson, the wife of Lyndon Johnson, the thirty-sixth president of the United States. Harold was not initially assigned to this project in 1933; he was nearly two hundred miles away in Denison, Texas, working on a park in that city that would later be known as Loy Park.

In October 1933 the city fathers of Denison, Texas, decided their community needed a recreational park with a small lake. They chose a site just outside town, purchased the land, and to save on construction costs, decided to take advantage of the newly created Civilian Conservation Corps. It is unclear if Denison's proximity to the birthplace of the new vice president had anything to do with the ease with which two hundred young men and their supervisors were allotted to this project.

In 2018 a historical marker at the entrance of the parks reads, in part:

*The county commissioners court purchased a site 2.5 miles southwest of Denison in October 1933 and secured the services of the Civilian Conservation Corps (CCC), a federal public works program, to construct the dam and build a recreational park. In early November, 200 men from Wisconsin who comprised CCC Company 857 arrived in Grayson County to begin construction. Many men returned home in April 1934 at the end of the six-month contract. Though it was unusual to employ CCC workers in their own areas, 48 Grayson County men were enlisted to replenish the supply of workers in Company 857. By 1934 the CCC men had created a recreation center with a lake, a roadway, 13 culvert bridges, six "battleship" picnic units, a baseball diamond, and a partially completed central tower of native stone. Initially called Grayson County Park, the facility was renamed Judge Jake L. Loy State Park in 1934 in an effort to secure state assistance in completing the park.*

The marker does not say that a twenty-three year old Harold O'Neal was one of the officers overseeing the creation of this park, but on October 12, 1934, the *Sherman Daily Democrat* did take notice. It wasn't front-page news but on page two, under a headline that read: *Grayson CCC Boys Leave Monday After Almost Completing A Beautiful Park.* A lengthy story tells of the work the "CCC Boys" had accomplished during the previous twelve months.

Part of the story reads:

*Before dawn breaks Monday, 222 men who form company 857 of the civilian conservation corps will be speeding away from Denison, entrained for their new assignment at Caddo Lake at Karnack in East Texas.*

*Behind them will be a year's work in the building of Grayson Park, "Loy's Park," and the closed and darkened barracks where they made their home.*

*Their train leaves at 2:55 a.m. and with them will go the last bit of their activity in the building of the park, unceasing until that time since Nov. 4 of last year. They leave the park almost complete but almost not quite.*

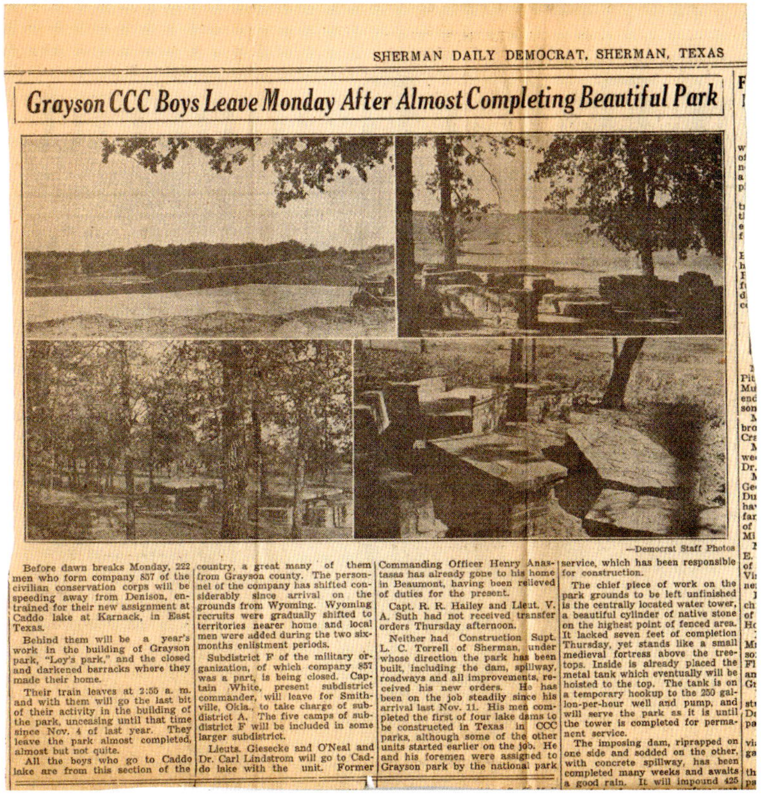

SHERMAN DAILY DEMOCRAT, SHERMAN, TEXAS

## Grayson CCC Boys Leave Monday After Almost Completing Beautiful Park

—Democrat Staff Photos

Before dawn breaks Monday, 222 men who form company 857 of the civilian conservation corps will be speeding away from Denison, entrained for their new assignment at Caddo lake at Karnack, in East Texas.

Behind them will be a year's work in the building of Grayson park, "Loy's park," and the closed and darkened barracks where they made their home.

Their train leaves at 2:55 a. m. and with them will go the last bit of their activity in the building of the park, unceasing until that time since Nov. 4 of last year. They leave the park almost completed, almost but not quite.

All the boys who go to Caddo lake are from this section of the country, a great many of them from Grayson county. The personnel of the company has shifted considerably since arrival on the grounds from Wyoming. Wyoming recruits were gradually shifted to territories nearer home and local men were added during the two six-months enlistment periods.

Subdistrict F of the military organization, of which company 857 was a part, is being closed. Captain White, present subdistrict commander, will leave for Smithville, Okla., to take charge of subdistrict A. The five camps of subdistrict F will be included in some larger subdistrict.

Lieuts. Giesecke and O'Neal and Dr. Carl Lindstrom will go to Caddo lake with the unit. Former Commanding Officer Henry Anastasas has already gone to his home in Beaumont, having been relieved of duties for the present.

Capt. R. R. Hailey and Lieut. V. A. Suth had not received transfer orders Thursday afternoon.

Neither had Construction Supt. L. C. Torrell of Sherman, under whose direction the park has been built, including the dam, spillway, roadways and all improvements, received his new orders. He has been on the job steadily since his arrival last Nov. 11. His men completed the first of four lake dams to be constructed in Texas in CCC parks, although some of the other units started earlier on the job. He and his foremen were assigned to Grayson park by the national park service, which has been responsible for construction.

The chief piece of work on the park grounds to be left unfinished is the centrally located water tower, a beautiful cylinder of native stone on the highest point of fenced area. It lacked seven feet of completion Thursday, yet stands like a small medieval fortress above the treetops. Inside is already placed the metal tank which eventually will be hoisted to the top. The tank is on a temporary hookup to the 250 gallon-per-hour well and pump, and will serve the park as it is until the tower is completed for permanent service.

The imposing dam, riprapped on one side and sodded on the other, with concrete spillway, has been completed many weeks and awaits a good rain. It will impound 425

Loy Park

*All the boys who go to Caddo Lake are from this section of the country, a great many of them from Grayson County. The personnel of the company has shifted considerably since the arrival on the grounds from Wyoming. Wyoming recruits were gradually shifted to territories nearer home and local men were added during the two six months enlistment periods. . . .*

*Lieuts. Giesecke and O'Neal and Dr. Carl Lindstrom will go to Caddo Lake with the unit. . . .*

Somehow the clipping from the eighty-three-year-old paper survived; perhaps Harold sent it to Sarah, and she kept it with her scrapbooks. It is the oldest of the clippings she saved that mentioned Harold. But no matter how it managed to survive, the two young lovers were thrilled. Karnack was at least two hours closer to Tyler.

Harold settled into his new assignment quickly. On November 16, 1934, a group photograph by E. L. Rothwell of the personnel at the camp pictured CCC Company 2891 and its 196 enrollees, 4 officers, and 7 cooks. A banner being held aloft reads *Civilian Conservation Corps Winners Oklahoma CCC District Award*. There is a caption on the photograph that reads *Outstanding Company Oklahoma District 3rd Enrollment Period*. The photograph also notes that twenty-three-year-old, soon to be twenty-four (less than a week later) First Lt. Harold O'Neal is second in command. His friend, A. H. Giesecke, is listed as camp commander, a position Harold would later assume.

The 8,253-acre park was completed in 1937 and has been modernized in many ways since that time, but the overall influence of the CCC Company's original work remains, and the park itself remains a major tourist destination in East Texas. Caddo Lake is the largest natural lake in the state, and it is possible to walk on the same trails, climb the same steps, and visit the same buildings that can be seen in the photographs taken in 1934 and 1935.

It is unclear if Sarah ever ventured north to Denison to meet Harold during the construction of Loy Park—there is no photo or written evidence—but with Karnack much closer to home, Sarah was in Karnack and in the park as often as possible while it was being constructed. She saved hundreds of photographs, some taken by her, some by Harold, some by their friends. All these photographs are in two scrapbooks, a visual record of their lives, as they became closer and closer. There were also words and sentimental souvenirs. These words, mostly love songs copied word for word by Sarah, or telegrams—the text messages of the day—arranging meetings and weekend rendezvous; all the yellowing but lovely photographs and sentimental holiday cards and tags from Christmas presents need no explanation.

Karvach 1934

HAROLD

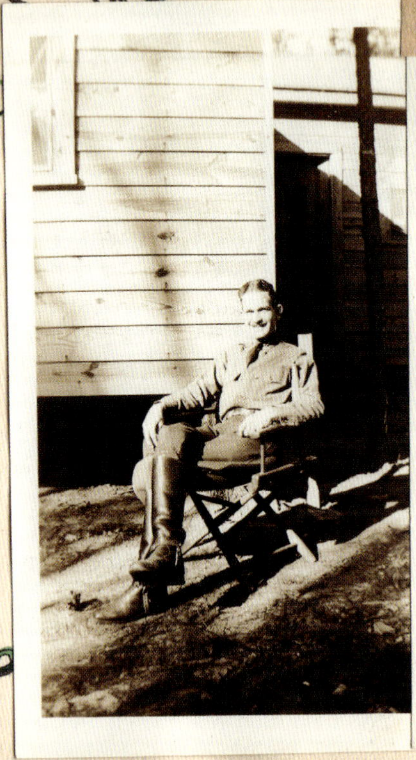

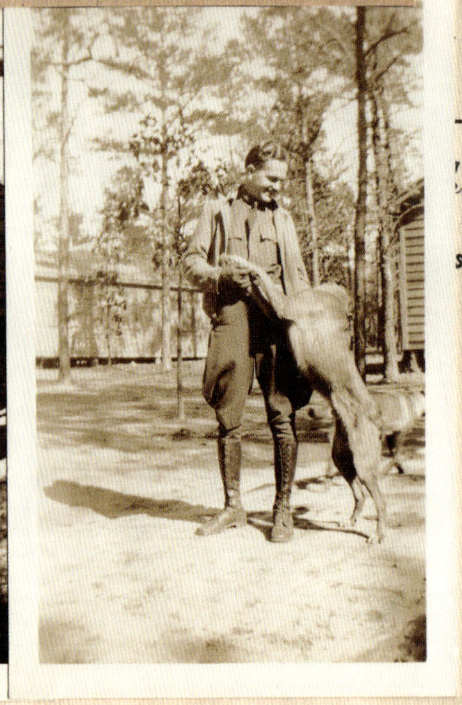

Book.

M. Owen.

strated

Kannach 1934

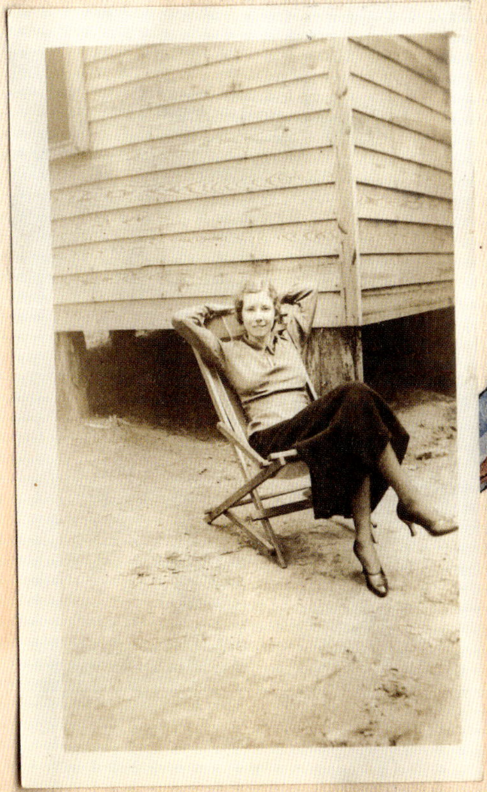

Kavach 1934

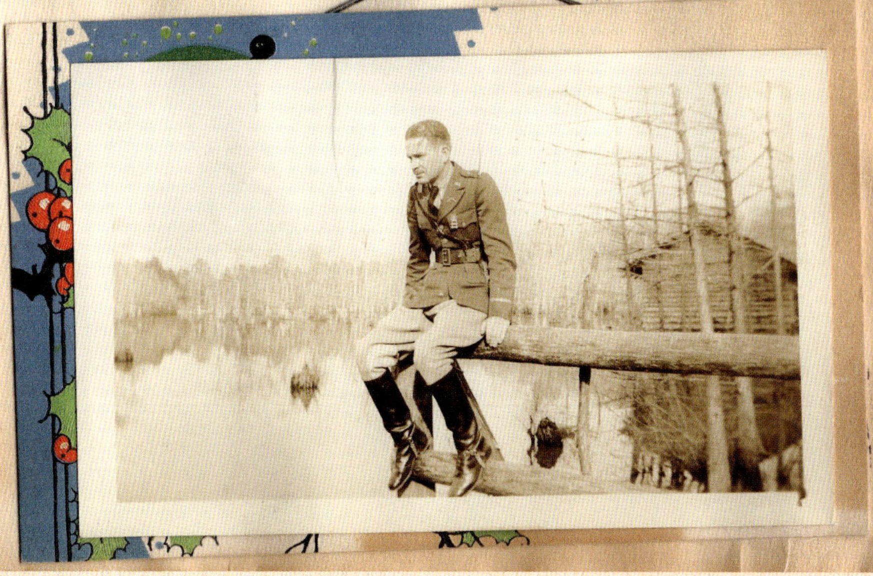

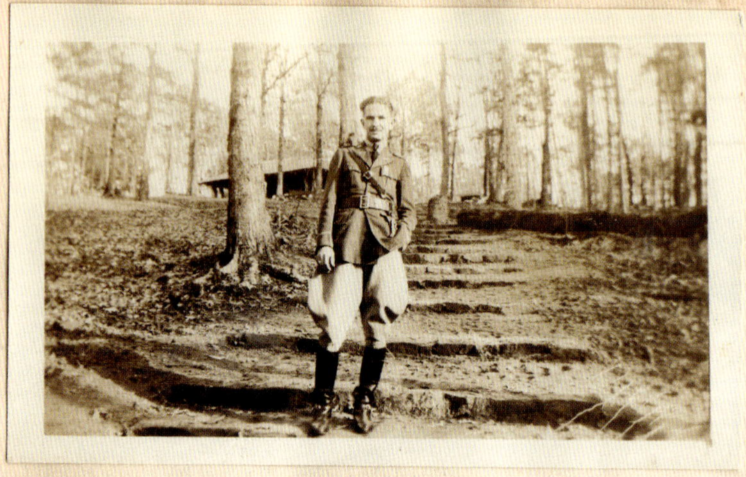

Cig. Case Nov. 22, 1934

Kavnach 1934

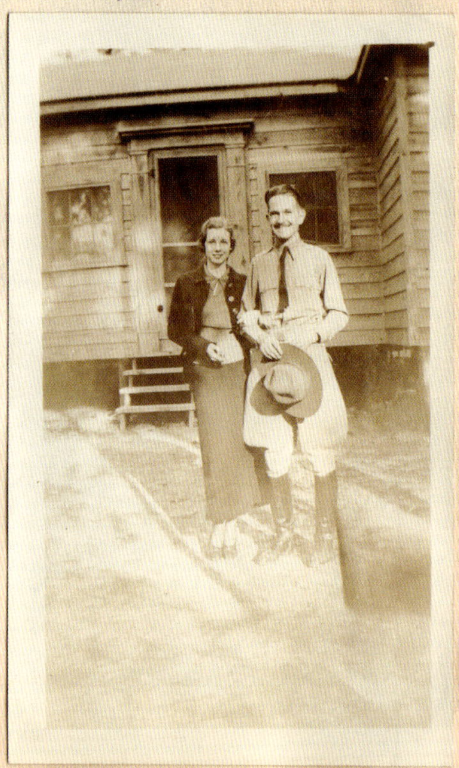

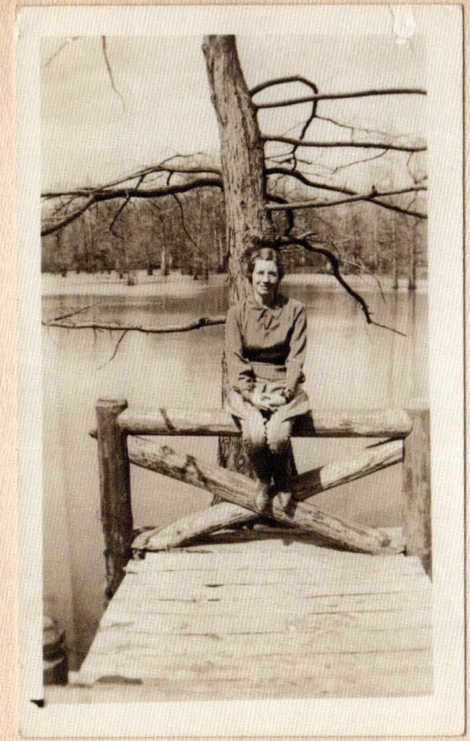

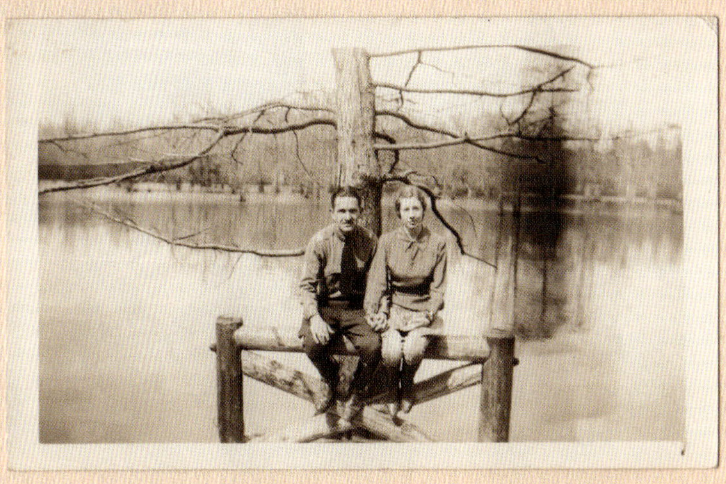

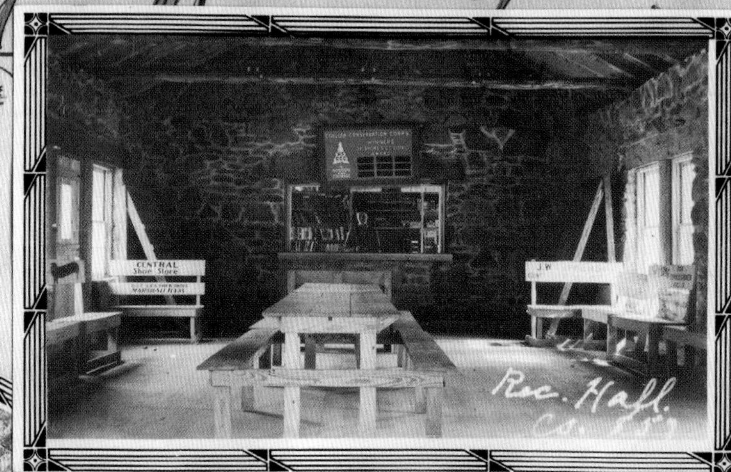

Rec. Hall.


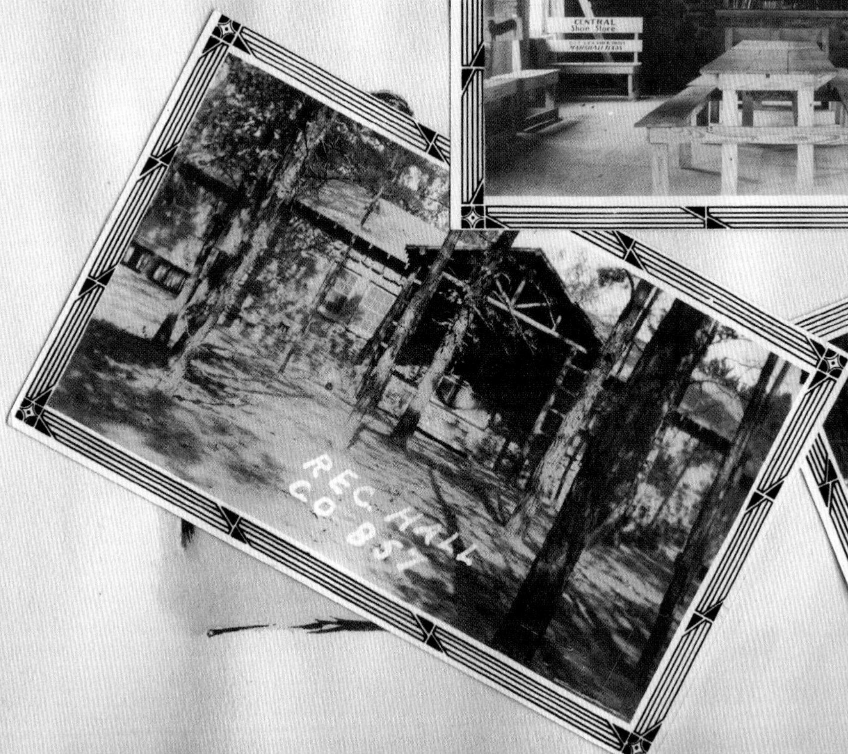

REC. HALL
CO. 857


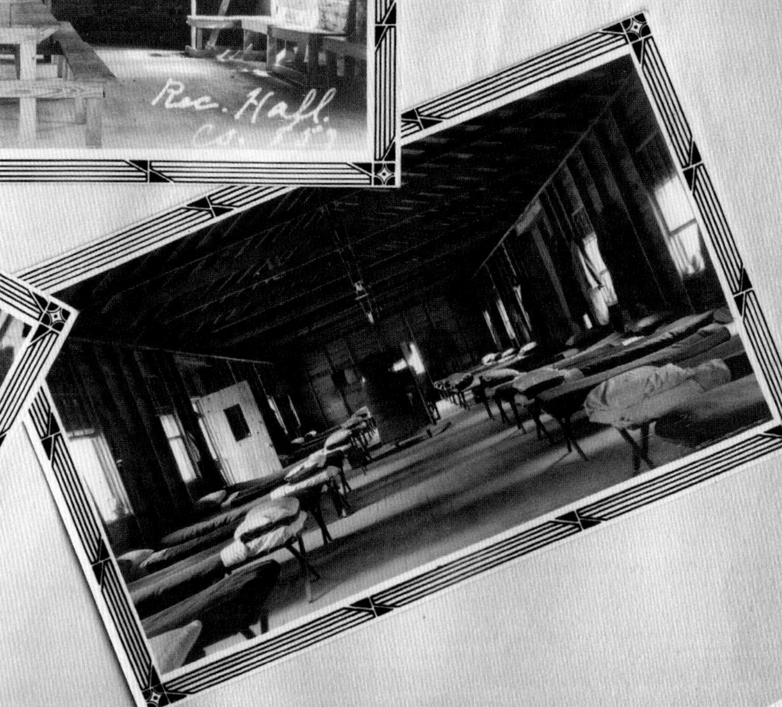

Dates -

March 19-1932-Met

January 7-1933-G. Ring

March 19-1933-B. E.

November 22-1934-D. Ring

~~December~~ September 11-1935-Got married.

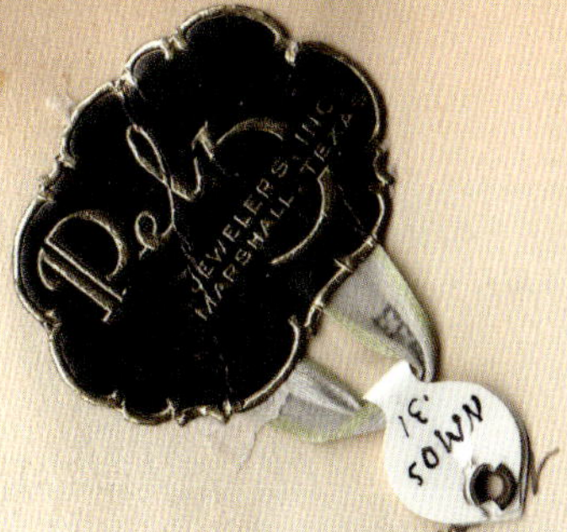


Engagement ring
Nov. 22, 1934

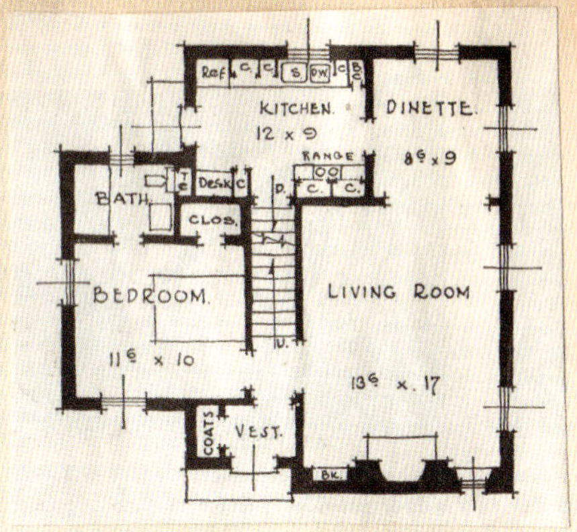


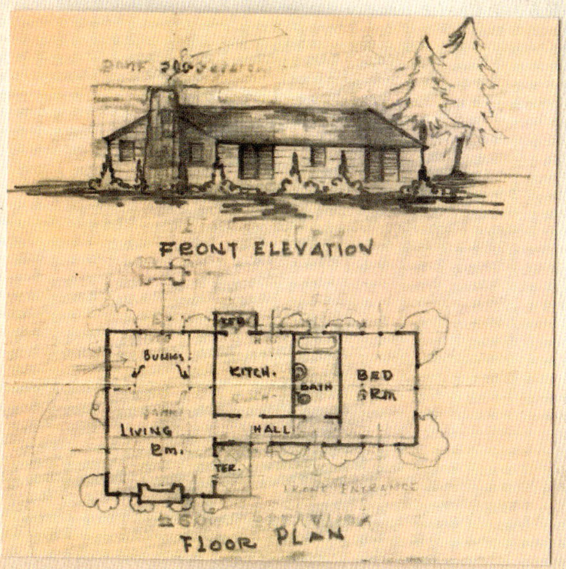


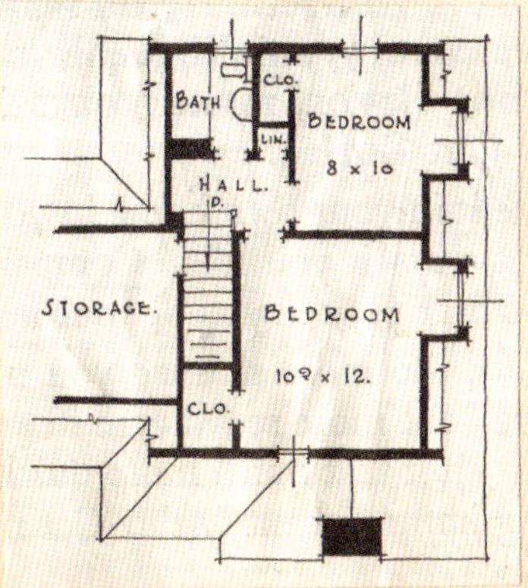

Christmas 1934

# JUDGE THE FLORIST

6 yellow chrysanthemums

Box of Martha Washington
Candy

Dec. 19, 1934

Also my crystal glasses — 36 pieces

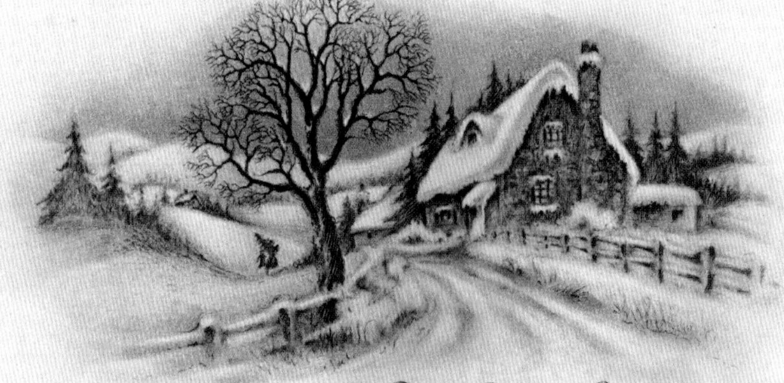

The Season's Greetings

C. C. Camp
Karnack
Dec. 1934

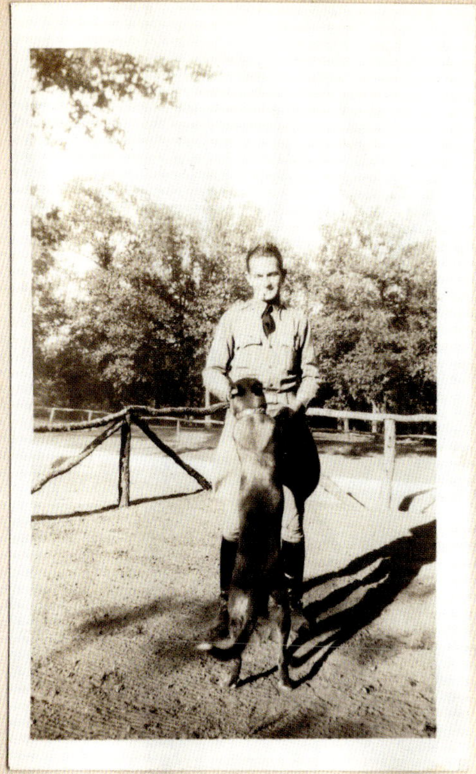

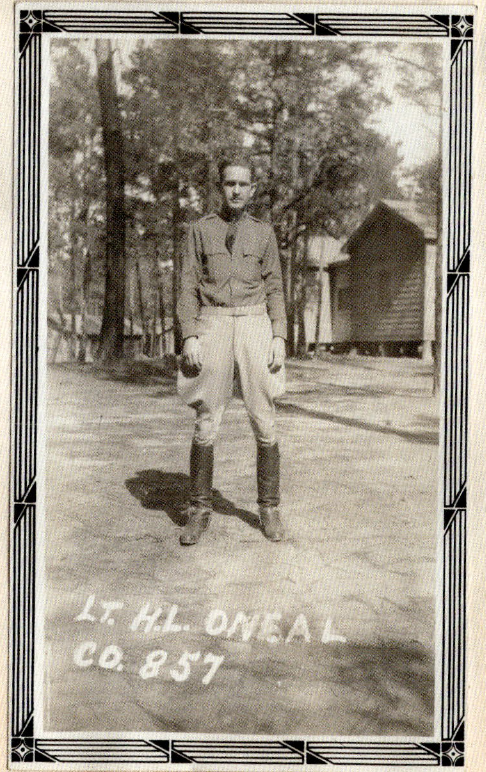


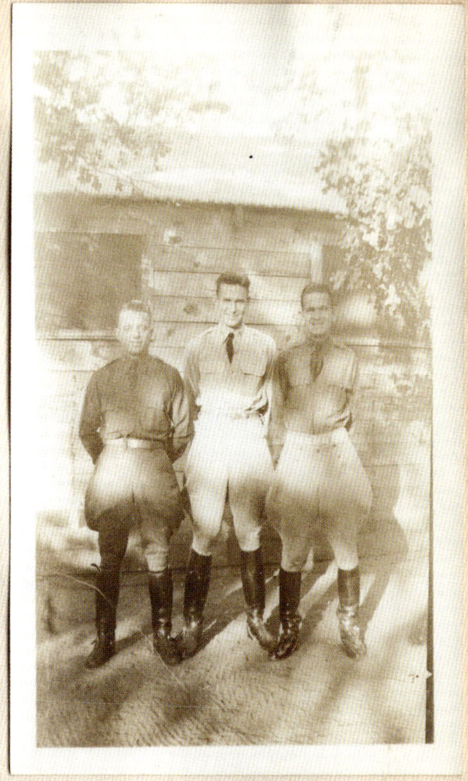

Harold
St Carl Linston
St Giesicke

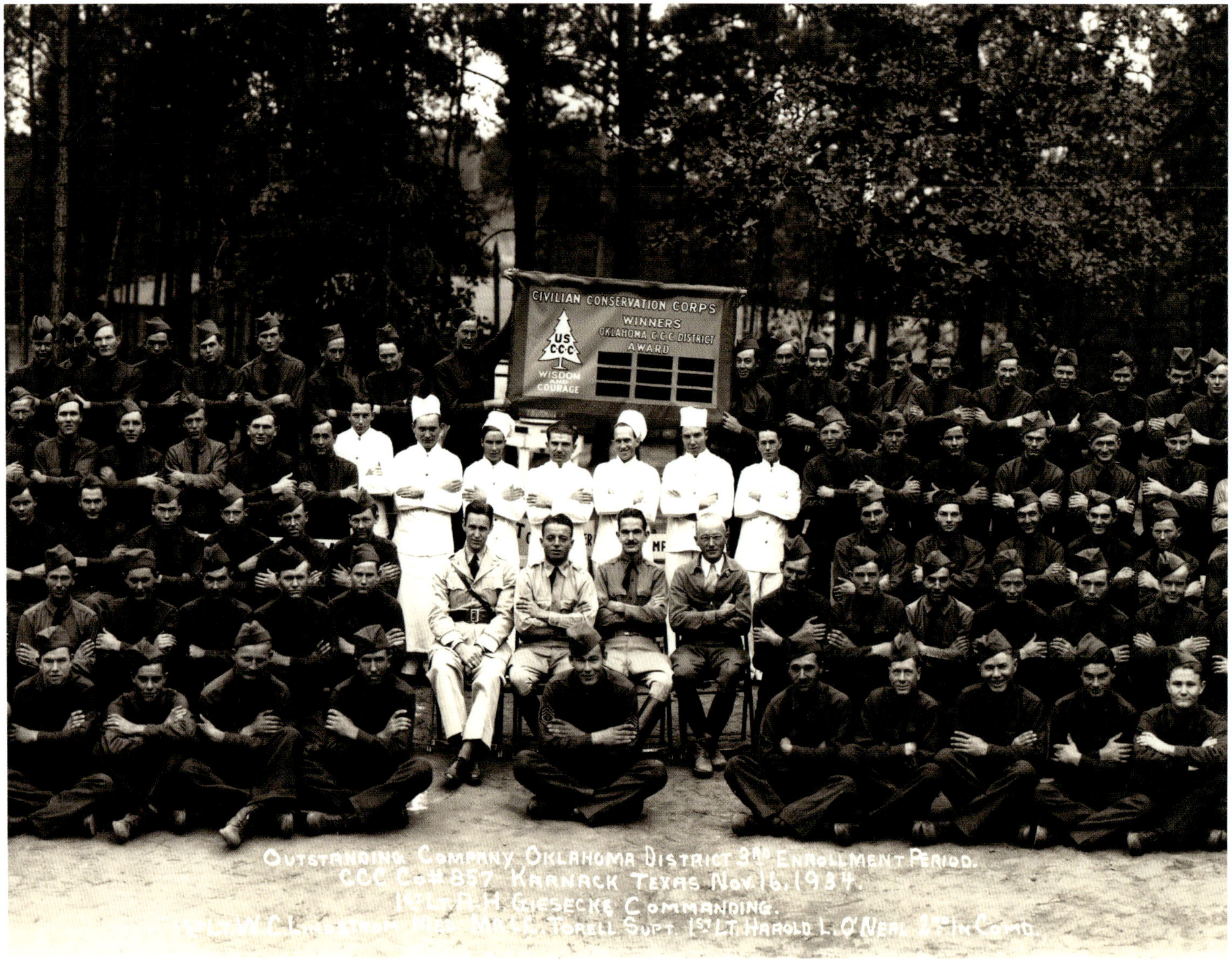


Caddo Lake CCC Company at Karnack

**1935**

Harold continued his work at Caddo Lake. Sarah was there with him more and more, and she was his best birthday present; they had been officially engaged on November 22, 1934, just after the group photo had been taken at Caddo Lake. They were together constantly, and as Harold's work at Caddo Lake was coming to an end in 1935, they took a holiday together, visiting Galveston and San Antonio. Just before the trip there was a headline in the June 9 edition of the Sunday *Houston Post*:

***CCC Unit Building State Park at Caddo Lake***

***Wilderness Will Become Beauty Spot***

***Work of Tree Army Will Revert to People***

*In the heart of a hunting, fishing and scenic paradise is Caddo Lake State Park near Karnack, one of the most beautiful state parks, and located on the banks of the largest natural lake in Texas.*

*Along the lake shore in the East Texas pinelands is Company 857, Civilian Conservation Corps, a camp that is second to none in beauty, permanence and completeness.*

*Placed on a high hill overlooking Big Cypress bayou, arm of Caddo Lake proper, the camp is surrounded by tall pines, stately oaks and beautiful flowering small trees. . . .*

*Close cooperation between national park officials and army officials is given full credit for the enviable progress in the works projects which the company has been engaged.*

*At the present time the personnel in charge of the camp includes First Lieutenant Harold L. O'Neal of Tyler, camp commander . . .*

It is unclear how Sarah managed to get a copy of the *Houston Post*—it seems unlikely this paper was widely distributed in Tyler—but somehow she did, and pasted the clipping in her scrapbook. Sarah's father had a sister who lived in Houston; perhaps she saw the article and saved it for her niece. But the article was somehow saved, and Sarah underlined the portion of the article that mentioned Harold and did the same where he was identified in the photograph that accompanied it.

Despite the modest publicity Harold and Sarah had much more on their minds. First was the romantic holiday in Galveston and San Antonio that would be followed shortly by a much more romantic encounter. Pasted on a page of Sarah's scrapbook, under the headline *Items of Interest*, is an innocuous piece of grey paper. A small piece of white lace is attached to the paper with a pin. Written on the paper are the words: *July 19, 1935 At 12 o'clock noon Benton, Louisiana Bossier Parish By Nat Tracy Dinner at Columbia Restaurant Shreveport. White gladiolas.* The lace is pinned beneath the words *white gladiolas*. This was a secret marriage that was later acknowledged but never explained. The official one would occur two months later.

The headline in the *Tyler Daily Courier Times* read: ***Sarah Christian and Lieut. O'Neal Wed***. The paper described the ceremony, noting that Reverend C. J. Youngblood had officiated, the same man who'd married Sarah's parents twenty-four years earlier. This is how the paper described Harold and Sarah:

*Lieutenant O'Neal is a member of one of the oldest families in the county which settled near Starrville in the early days. He attended high school in Dallas and received army training at San Antonio. He has been active in Reserve Army Training corps for some time and while a civilian was a leader in an R.O.T.C. class here. He formally was in command of the camp at Caddo Lake where he directed the construction of the state park and at present is supervising a similar camp at Daingerfield.*

*The bride has been popular with a large number of Tyler friends since childhood and is an accomplished pianist having appeared on many programs here. She has always taken an active part in social and club circles, particularly those of music groups. She attended Tyler High school and junior college and Baylor university.*

Caddo Lake State Park was large—8,253

1935

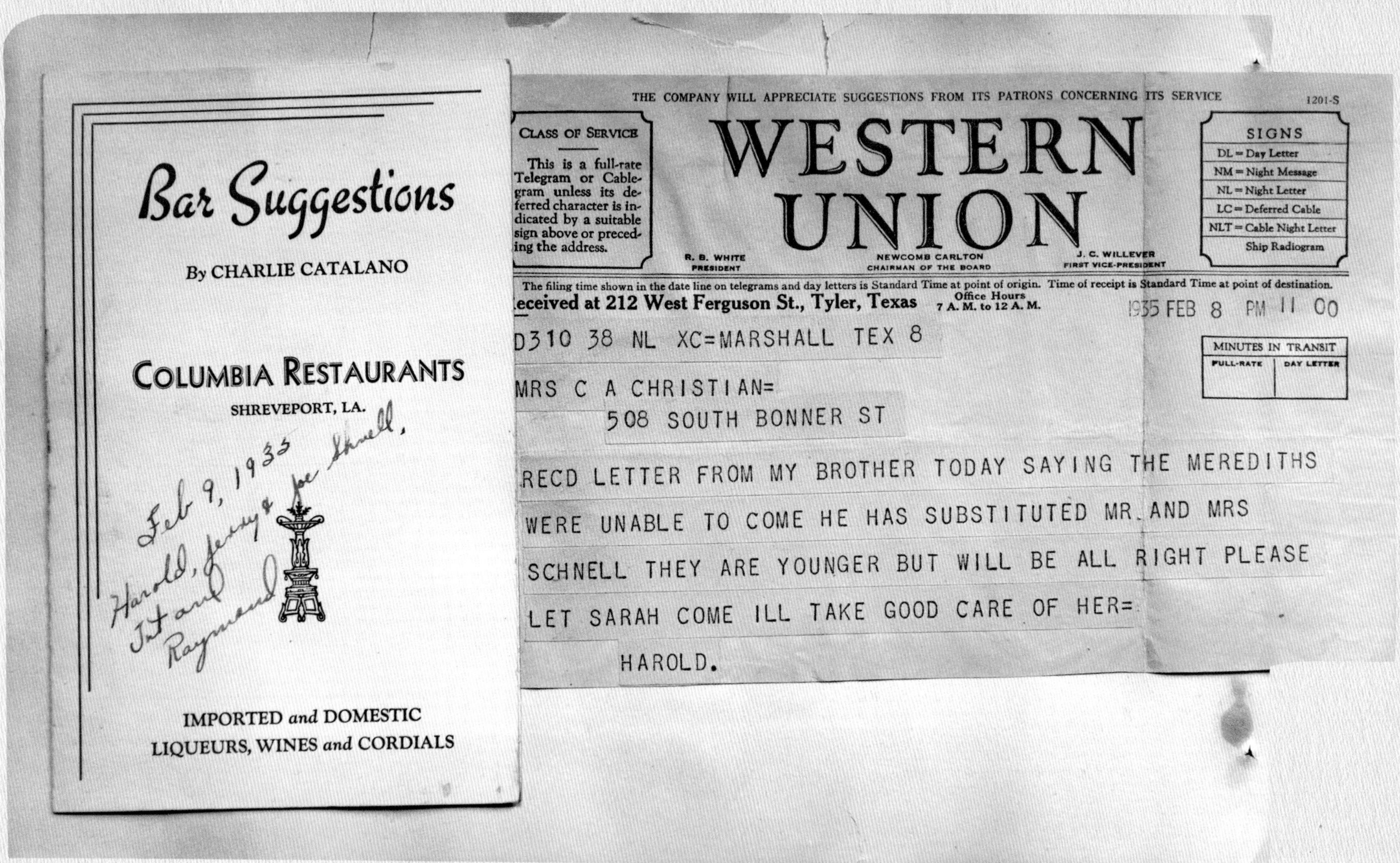

Bar Suggestions

By CHARLIE CATALANO

COLUMBIA RESTAURANTS

SHREVEPORT, LA.

Feb 9, 1935
Harold, Jerry & Joe Shnell, Jrt and Raymond

IMPORTED and DOMESTIC
LIQUEURS, WINES and CORDIALS

THE COMPANY WILL APPRECIATE SUGGESTIONS FROM ITS PATRONS CONCERNING ITS SERVICE 1201-S

CLASS OF SERVICE

This is a full-rate Telegram or Cablegram unless its deferred character is indicated by a suitable sign above or preceding the address.

WESTERN UNION

R. B. WHITE, PRESIDENT — NEWCOMB CARLTON, CHAIRMAN OF THE BOARD — J. C. WILLEVER, FIRST VICE-PRESIDENT

SIGNS
DL = Day Letter
NM = Night Message
NL = Night Letter
LC = Deferred Cable
NLT = Cable Night Letter
Ship Radiogram

The filing time shown in the date line on telegrams and day letters is Standard Time at point of origin. Time of receipt is Standard Time at point of destination.

Received at 212 West Ferguson St., Tyler, Texas — Office Hours 7 A. M. to 12 A. M. — 1935 FEB 8 PM 11 00

D310 38 NL XC=MARSHALL TEX 8

MINUTES IN TRANSIT — FULL-RATE — DAY LETTER

MRS C A CHRISTIAN=
508 SOUTH BONNER ST

RECD LETTER FROM MY BROTHER TODAY SAYING THE MEREDITHS WERE UNABLE TO COME HE HAS SUBSTITUTED MR. AND MRS SCHNELL THEY ARE YOUNGER BUT WILL BE ALL RIGHT PLEASE LET SARAH COME ILL TAKE GOOD CARE OF HER=

HAROLD.

Easter Greetings

Harald

Easter
~~1933~~
1934
Carnations

ROCKWELL'S
JEWELRY STORE
DENISON, TEXAS

Thursday

My Darling: I happened to be in town this afternoon and saw these. I hope you like them. Love
Harald

Salt & Pepper Shakers
October, 1934

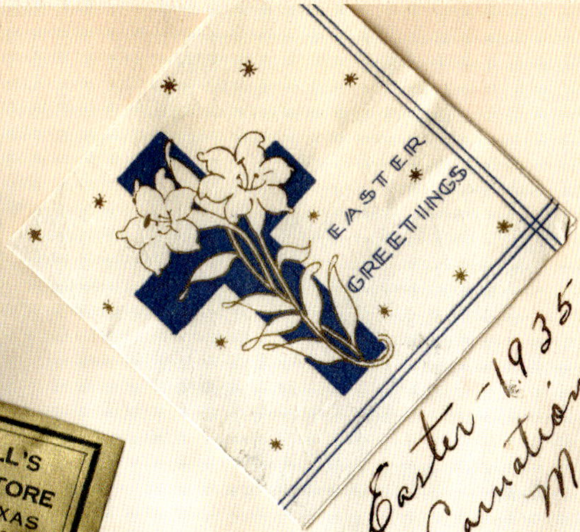


Easter-1935
Pink Carnations
from Marshall

Sports

and

Galveston

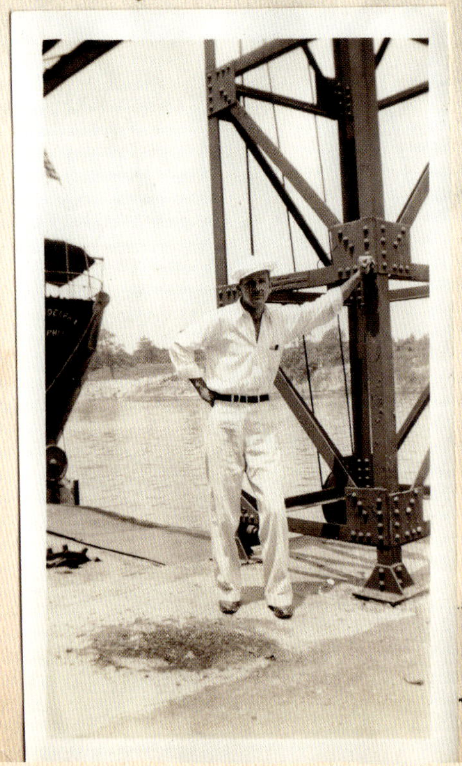

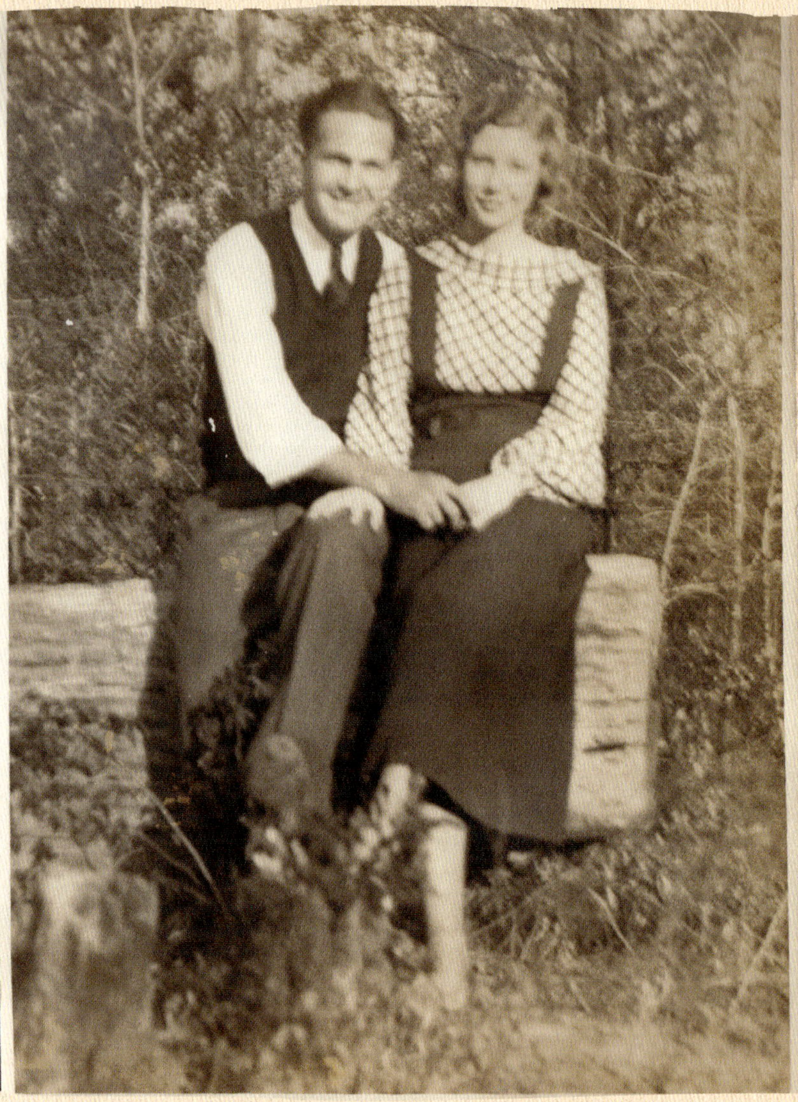

Galveston - June 12-13 1935 San Antonio - June 14-15-16

**EXCURSION BOAT GALVEZ, Inc.**

LEAVES PIER 22 AT 2:00 P. M. DAILY FOR 25-MILE SIGHT-SEEING HARBOR TRIP, INCLUDING 6 MILES INTO GULF SHOWING AND EXPLAINING ALL POINTS OF INTEREST. TWO AND ONE-HALF HOURS ON THE WATER. MUSIC ON BOARD.

**PRICE $1.00**
ROUND TRIP
(MINIMUM OF TEN PASSENGERS)

INSPECTED BY U. S. GOVERNMENT LOCAL INSPECTORS

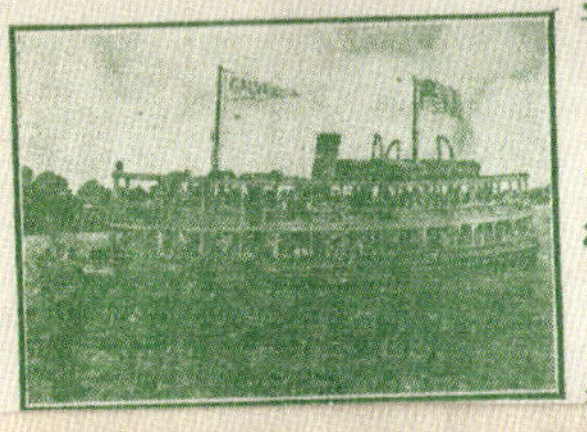

TO REACH BOAT TAKE ANY STREET CAR TO 22ND ST. AND AVE. C AND WALK TWO BLOCKS NORTH

**GUNTER 43**

NOT TRANSFERABLE

Harold & I danced on the roof garden at Gunter hotel June-15

THE COMPANY WILL APPRECIATE SUGGESTIONS FROM ITS PATRONS CONCERNING ITS SERVICE 1201-S

CLASS OF SERVICE

This is a full-rate Telegram or Cablegram unless its deferred character is indicated by a suitable sign above or preceding the address.

# WESTERN UNION (17).

R. B. WHITE, PRESIDENT — NEWCOMB CARLTON, CHAIRMAN OF THE BOARD — J. C. WILLEVER, FIRST VICE-PRESIDENT

SIGNS
DL = Day Letter
NM = Night Message
NL = Night Letter
LC = Deferred Cable
NLT = Cable Night Letter
Ship Radiogram

The filing time shown in the date line on telegrams and day letters is Standard Time at point of origin. Time of receipt is Standard Time at point of destination.

Received at 212 West Ferguson St., Tyler, Texas — Office Hours 7 A. M. to 12 A. M. — 1935 JUN 14 PM 8 21

MINUTES IN TRANSIT — FULL-RATE — DAY LETTER

D301 9=WUX SANANTONIO TEX 14 806P

C A CHRISTIAN=

CHRISTIAN PHARMACY TYLER TEX=

IN SANANTONIO NOW GOING STRONG HAVING LOTS OF FUN=

HAROLD & SARAH.

| Adm | .45 |
|---|---|
| Tax | .05 |
| Total | .50 |

A 081190

A 081191

MAJESTIC THEATRE
San Antonio, Texas

Saw Frederick March in - "Les Miserables"

MAGAZINE SECTION | SUNDAY, JUNE 9, 1935 | SUNDAY HOUSTON POST

# CCC Unit Building State Park at Caddo Lake

## Wilderness Will Become Beauty Spot

### Work of Tree Army Will Revert to People.

By H. GORDON DAVIS

IN THE heart of a hunting, fishing and scenic paradise is Caddo Lake State park near Karnack, one of the most beautiful of state parks, and located on the banks of the largest natural lake in Texas.

Along the lake shore in the East Texas pinelands, is Company 857, Civilian Conservation corps, a camp that is second to none in beauty, permanence and completeness.

Placed on a high hill overlooking Big Cypress bayou, arm of Caddo lake proper, the camp is surrounded by tall pines, stately oaks and beautiful flowering small trees.

**Buildings Permanent.**

By special arrangement between the army and the national park service the camp buildings were so constructed that most of them can be made a permanent part of the park. Altogether there are 28 buildings; nine of them will be improved during the next six months period by being veneered with heavy hewn log siding, ceiled and having stone footings substituted for the present log footings.

Seventeen of the camp buildings are barracks, ranging in size from log cabins holding six beds to two huge buildings each accommodating 40 men.

The main building at present houses kitchen, mess hall, recreation hall, canteen and supply room for the company. The central section is built of stone with a beautiful fireplace. The entire building is planned as the administration building of the park.

The smaller buildings will be available for public use when the park is turned over to the state by the National Park service, the governmental agency supervising the park development.

**Army Aids Work.**

Other buildings in the camp which will be utilized for the park include quarters for officers and national park supervisory force, infirmary, bathhouse, pumphouse and well. The sanitary facilities of the camp are complete in every detail.

The public generally does not realize that two distinct branches of the government are concerned in the work done by the Civilian Conservation corps, these being the army and a civilian work agency.

Commissioned officers of the United States army, selected almost exclusively from the reserve corps, are in charge of the feeding, housing, clothing and disciplining of the enrolled personnel.

Technically trained superintendents and foremen employed by branches of the department of agriculture or of the department of the interior direct the work and have complete charge of the men during the 40 working hours of the week.

In the case of Company 857 at Caddo Lake State park, and in park work generally, the national park service is the technical service.

**Officials Co-operate**

Close co-operation between national park officials and army officials is given full credit for the enviable progress in the work projects which the company has been engaged.

At the present time the personnel in charge of the camp includes First Lieutenant Harold L. O'Neal of Tyler, camp commander; First Lieutenant Homer Hagius of Terrell, mess officer, and Dr. B. R. Wolford, contract physician, camp surgeon.

For the park service: W. B. Edwards of Dallas, acting superintendent; Ted L. Edwards, Waco, engineer; Joe W. Westbrook of Dallas, landscape architect; Fred R. Carpenter, Marshall, architect; Will G. Stephens, Sherman; Allen W. Phillips, Woodville; W. P. Scott, Marshall, and Frank Jones of Texarkana, foremen.

Frank E. Davis of Houston, educational adviser, is a moving spirit of the camp welfare and recreational activities.

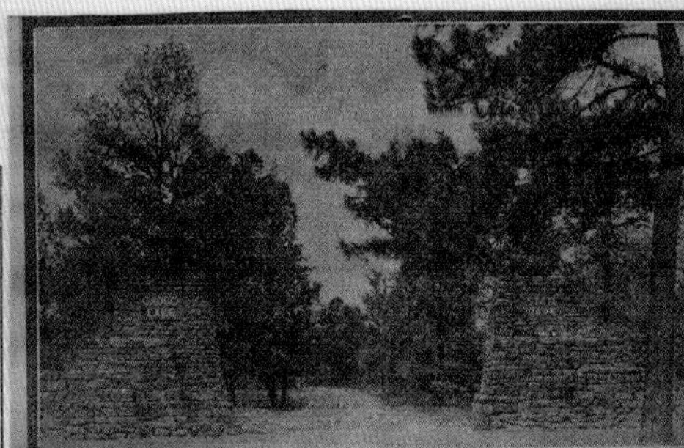

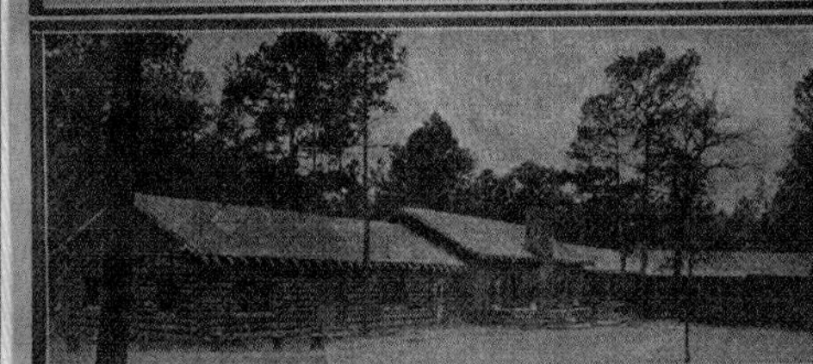

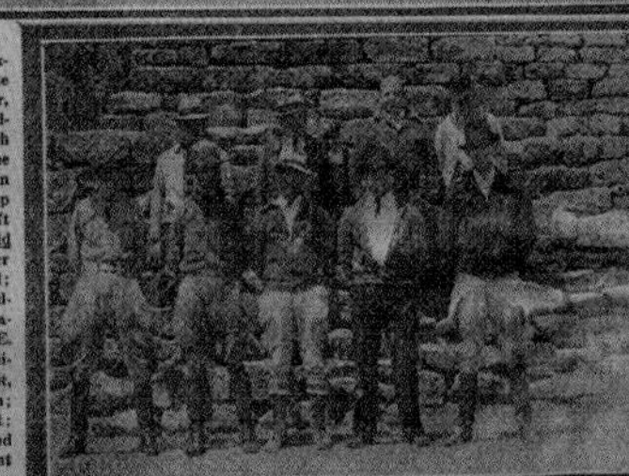

Top photo, the gates to Texas' newest and largest state park at Caddo lake. Center, the main administration building of CCC camp 857, which has furnished the labor for the construction of the park. In the lower photograph the camp staff is shown. Front row, left to right, Lieutenant Harold L. O'Neal, Lieutenant Homer L. Hague, second in command; W. B. Edwards, superintendent; Frank E. Davis, educational adviser, and Joe E. Westbrook, landscape architect. Back row, left to right, Dr. R. B. Wolford, physician; Fred Carpenter, architect; Frank Jones, foreman, and Allen W. Phillips, assistant foreman.

# Items of Interest.

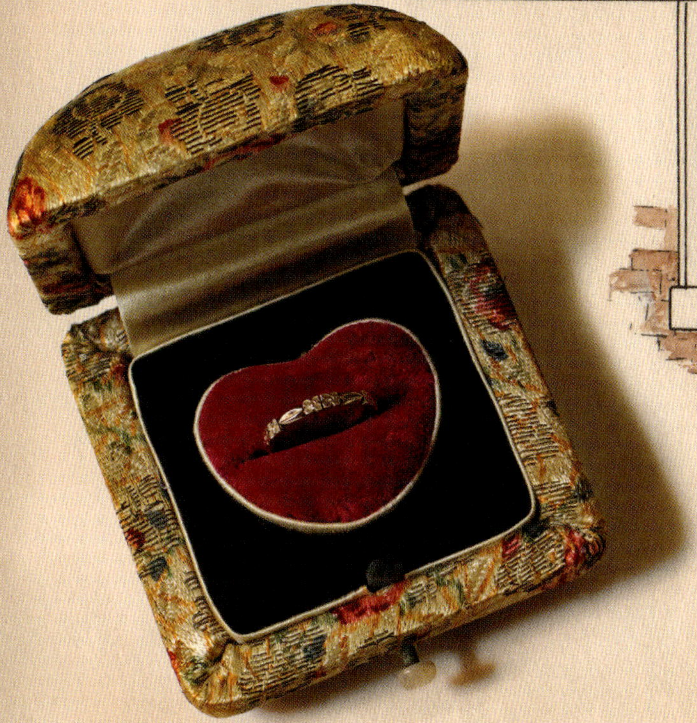

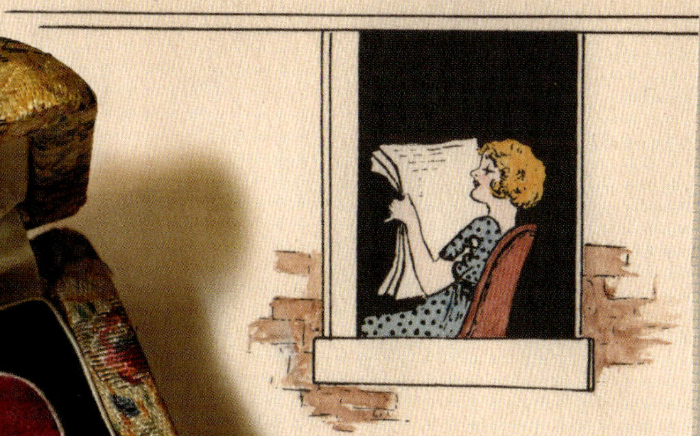

july 19, 1935
At 12 o'clock noon
Benton, Louisianna
Bossier Parish
By Nat Tracy

Dinner at
Columbia Resteraunt
Shreveport.
White gladiolas

Mr. and Mrs. C. A. Christian

announce the marriage of

their daughter

Sarah

to

Lieutenant Harold L. O'Neal

on Wednesday, September the eleventh

nineteen hundred and thirty-five

Tyler, Texas

At Home

Daingerfield, Texas

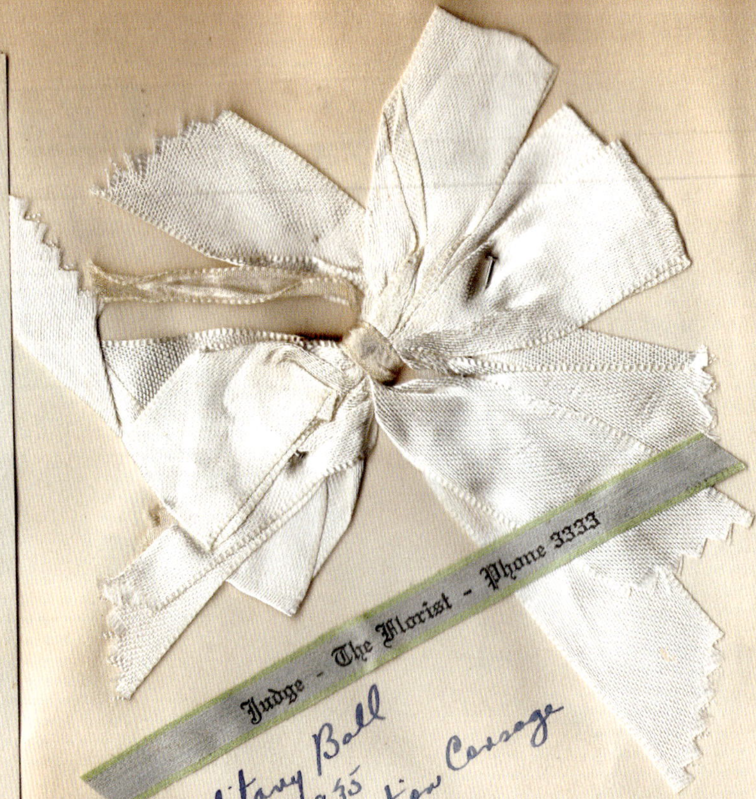


Military Ball
Oct 9, 1935
White Carnation Corsage

Sept. 11, 1935 10:30 · Married

White Carnations Corsage

# Sarah Christian and Lieut. O'Neal Wed

MISS SARAH CHRISTIAN, daughter of Mr. and Mrs. C. A. Christian, South Bonner avenue, and Lieut. Harol L. O'Neal of Tyler, were married Wednesday morning at 10:30 o'clock at the home of the bride's parents, with the Rev. C. J. Youngblood officiating. The same minister performed the marriage ceremony for the bride's parents.

There were no attendants and the ceremony was a very quiet one with only members of the family present. The couple left at once for Daingerfield where he is in command of one of the 18 CCC camps of the Tyler district.

Lieutenant O'Neal is a member of one of the oldest families in the county which settled near Starrville in the early days. He attended high school in Dallas ad receiving army training at San Antonio. He has been active in the Reserve Officers' Training corps for some time and while a civilian was a leader in an R. O. T. C. class here. He formerly was in command of the camp at Caddo lake where he directed construction of the state park and at present is supervising a similar camp at Daingerfield.

The bride has been popular with a large number of Tyler friends since childhood and is an accomplished pianist having appeared on many programs here. She has always taken an active part in social and club circles, particularly those of music groups. She attended Tyler High school and junior college and late Baylor university.

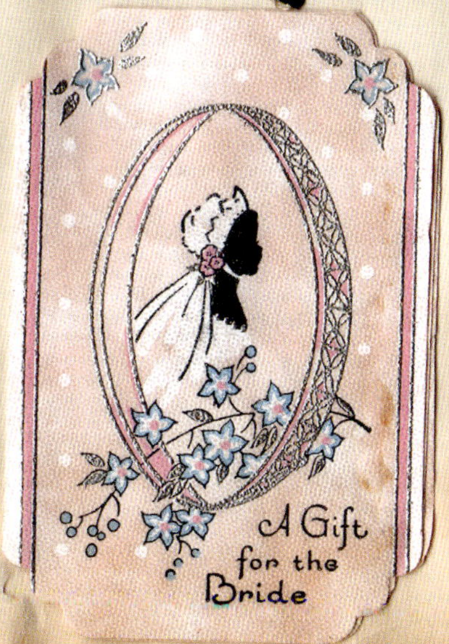


Something old -
Something new -
Something borrowed
Something blue

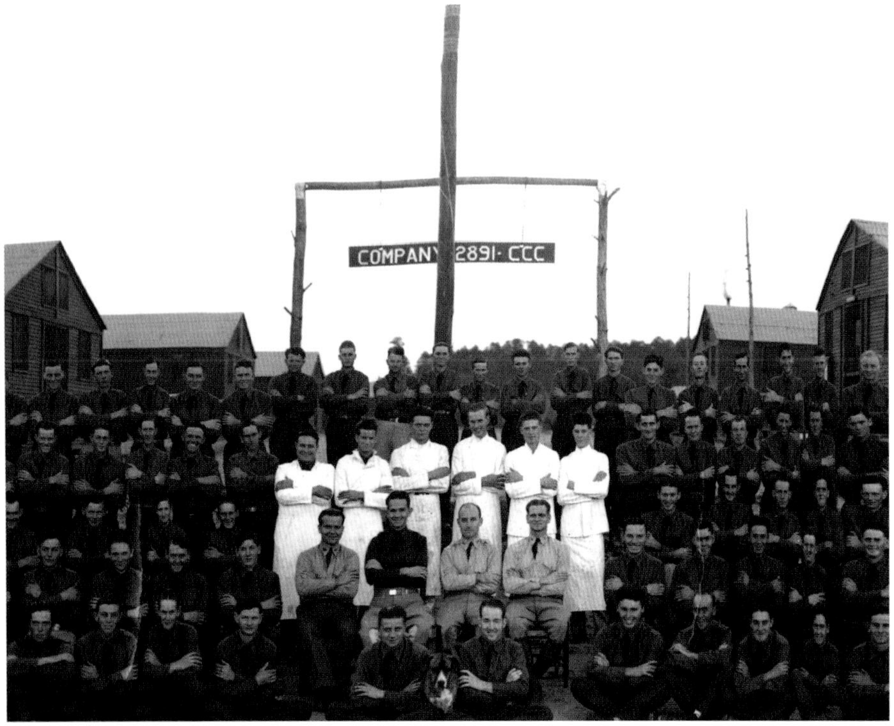


Daingerfield Company

acres. Harold's next assignment, to begin a month or two later, was smaller but more complicated. Daingerfield State Park began with only eighty acres; it was to grow to over five hundred, but the first chore was to build a lake that would be the centerpiece of the park. Caddo Lake was the largest in Texas; when Daingerfield State Park was begun there was no water in sight, only eighty donated acres that had to somehow be turned into a lake.

On November 7, 1935, another group photograph by E. L. Rothwell of the personnel at the camp pictured CCC Company 2891 and its 184 enrollees, 4 officers, 6 cooks, and 1 dog. The officer in command is First Lt. Harold O'Neal. On the same day, Rothwell also took a landscape picture of the park, showing the work done up to that point. A lot of earth had been moved around, a few buildings were under construction, but there was no lake yet, not even a puddle. This is how the work was described in the Tyler District Eighth Corps 1936 Civilian Conservation Corps Annual:

*Camp SP-49, Daingerfield Texas, was occupied August 20, 1935 by a cadre of 14 men, two from Company 857, Karnack, and the others from Company 1803, Ratcliff. The officers in charge were Lts. H. L. O'Neal and G. W. Greathouse. The new company, given the number 2891, attained full strength a week later with 213 names on the roll. Only two barracks were completed and ready for occupancy at the time, and the recreation hall was used for sleeping quarters for 60 men until the remaining two barracks could be finished. The conditioning period was barely sufficient for laying out walks and for cutting sprouts off the camp area.*

*The park superintendent, Ted L. Edwards, started the work of clearing stumps, brush, and trees from the basin of the park lake on September 9, 1935. On November 28, excavation was begun for the lake dam, which was carried to a depth of 30 feet. On January 28, 1936, the refill began, the clay for the purpose being taken from a hillside a half a mile from the lake basin. On October 1, 1936, the dam was 80 percent complete with a depth of 12 feet of water already in the lake. When the dam is completed about January 1, 1937, the lake will cover an area of approximately 80 acres. The foreman in charge of the work is Jack Smith.*

*Besides completing the dam, plans for future park work now include the building of a concession and bath house,*

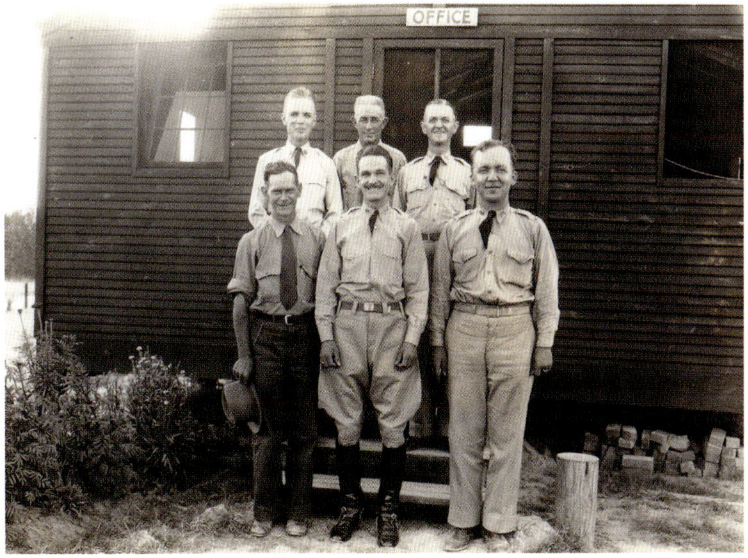


Harold and officers

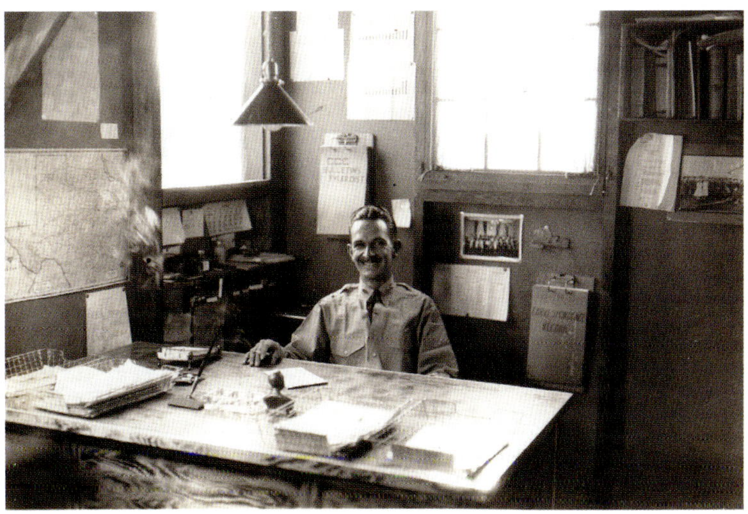

Harold in his office

*20 fireplaces at intervals over the park and placing 35 park tables near by, a boathouse, bathing beach, diving tower and beach shelters, finishing two miles of gravel road, the construction of a concrete underground storage tank with a capacity of 10,000 gallons to supply the park with water, the installing of a pump and pipeline system to distribute the water, installing the line to bring electric power from an outside source and stocking the lake with fish.*

The foregoing is a good description of how a group of 213 unemployed young men and a handful of officers and specialists could turn fallow unused land into a park. A park that not only offered modest employment to hundreds of men, but eventually provided enjoyment to thousands of their fellow citizens when everyone was suffering through hard times. Daingerfield State Park was just one of thousands that were built throughout the United States during the 1930s. It was completed in 1938, has been modernized and expanded to 507 acres over the years, and is enjoyed yearly by thousands of visitors.

One major difference between Harold's Daingerfield and Caddo assignments was that after they were married, Harold and Sarah lived in Daingerfield; their wedding announcement even said, *At Home in Daingerfield.* It gave no address, but it is unlikely they were living at the construction site. The life of a CCC commander was never easy, however. After a year of work and with the park at Daingerfield well underway, Harold was transferred to a new assignment in Bogata, Texas, in March 1936. Harold and Sarah would remain in that small city until November 1937.

Daingerfield was a metropolis of one thousand people. It even had a barely decade-old picture show, the Morris Theater on Lamar Street, where Harold and Sarah could enjoy first-run features without driving an hour. In 2018, the Morris Theater is still in business, still showing first-run features every evening at 6:30 and 9:00, perfect times for someone who has possibly spent the day at the park. But Bogata was a smaller town and didn't have a picture show, and the facility Harold was asked to build was not as impressive as a state park. It was an excellent learning experience for him nevertheless.

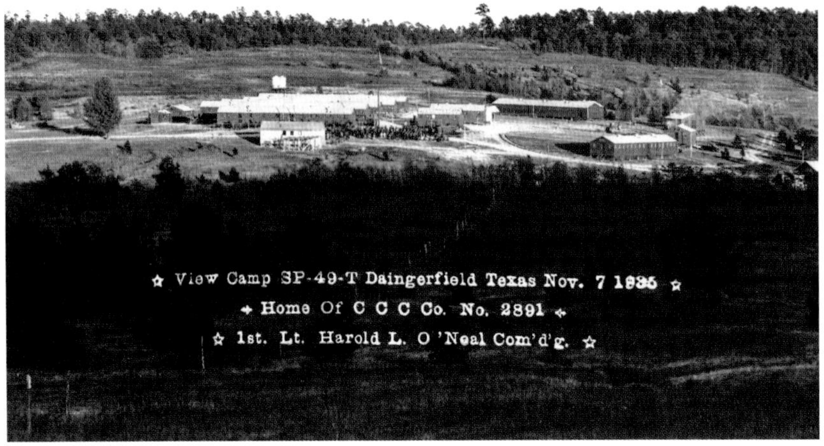
☆ View Camp SP-49-T Daingerfield Texas Nov. 7 1935 ☆
◆ Home Of C C C Co. No. 2891 ◆
☆ 1st. Lt. Harold L. O 'Neal Com'd'g. ☆

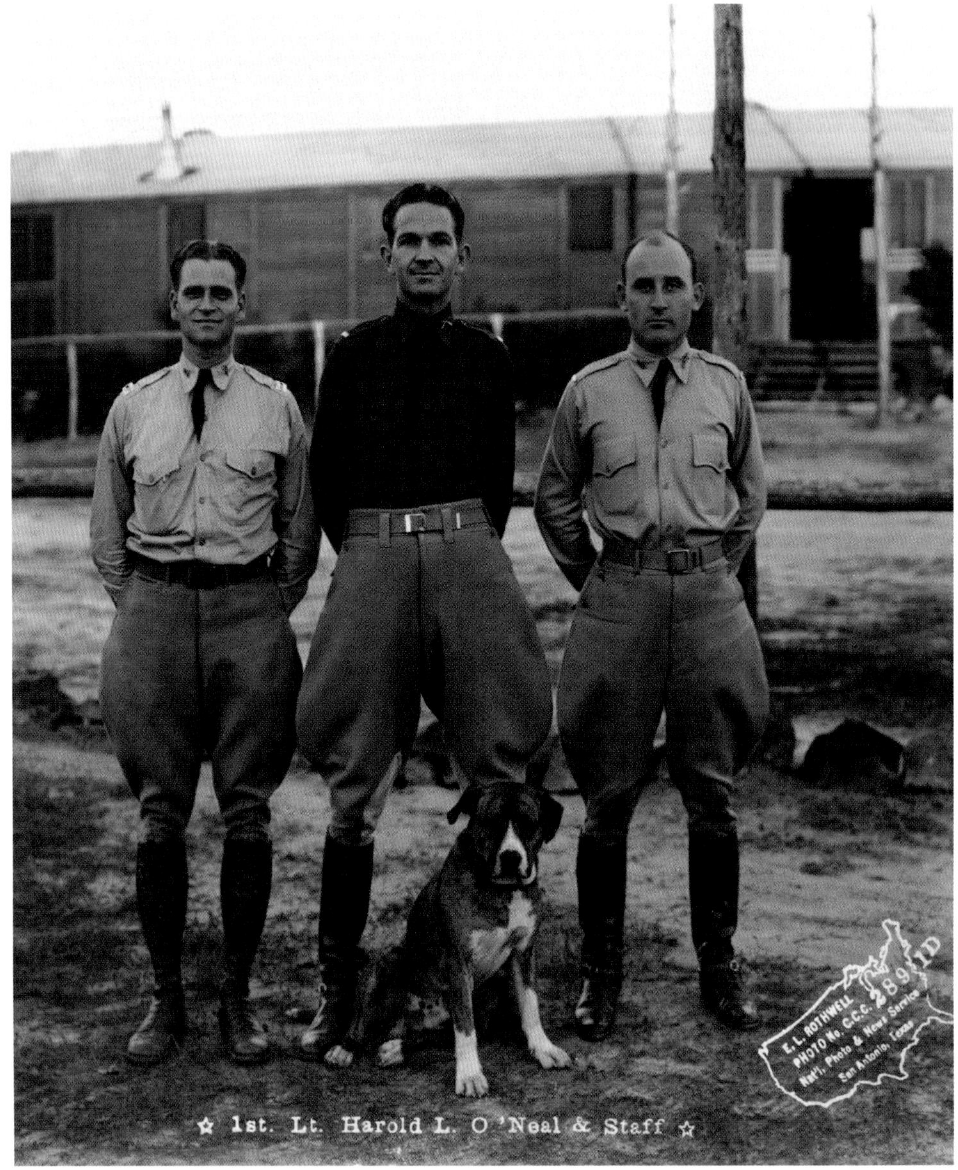
E. L. ROTHWELL
PHOTO No. C.C.C. 2891D
Nat'l Photo & News Service
San Antonio, Texas
☆ 1st. Lt. Harold L. O 'Neal & Staff ☆

**1936**

Harold was put in charge of Company 2889 (C) SCS-9-T. The Tyler District 8 Annual reported:

*One mile East of Bogata, in Red River country is situated Camp SCS-9-T Company 2889 (C). 1st Lt. Harold L. O'Neal, Inf.-Res. Of Tyler, Texas, is Commanding Officer, 1st Lt. Louis F. Benson, FA.-Res., Avery, Texas is 2nd in Command and Dr. Thomas M. Berry of Eldorado, Oklahoma is Camp Physician.... Organization took place August 20, 1935, Company strength was 228 colored enrollees with a cadre of 14 white juniors attached to give recruits an insight into the new life. The enrollees hailed from Red River, Lamar, Titus, Cameron, Delta, Gregg, Harrison and other nearby counties. During the first three weeks, the camp devoted itself to conditioning the men and improving the surroundings. The grounds were cleared of underbrush and leveled, sawdust walks were built, and a flagpole was erected with a park built around it.*

*Having transformed the little wilderness into a small community that teemed with the joys of life and comforts of civilization, Company 2889 (C) was ready to write a new page in its history. By September 10, 1935, the tools needed by the Technical Department arrived and... since then [it] has gone steadily forward in its soil conservation program. It has sodded pastures, built gully control and check dams, terraced fields and made outlet channels. Right along with this work the men have been schooled in the use of tools and machines. The success of these projects, that are praised by landowner and the tenant alike, for their utility and completeness, is indicative of the character and energy of the Project Superintendent and his staff of skilled technicians, engineers and foremen....*

*A school was organized and classes were instituted in Literacy, Elementary, High School and Vocational education. The school has proved to be of moral, spiritual and intellectual value to the company. It has striven to give the enrollees the right outlook on life, to encourage high ideals in them, and to discourage the wrong tendencies.*

*The company has a library equipped with easy chairs and divans where the men can browse and read good books, magazines and newspapers. In the recreation hall are tables for playing dominoes, cards and checkers; a pool table, a piano and an indoor tennis table.*

*Three Commanding Officers have served Camp SCS-9-T since its organization. Captain Carl Weber retired January 20, 1936, to be succeeded by Ensign Charles H. Clark, who served until Lt. Harold L. O'Neal, present commander, arrived March 15, 1936.*

*Lt. O'Neal had no trouble convincing the enrollees that he was an experienced and seasoned officer. After a few days in camp, an improvement program was organized, walks were raised out of the slush, and hard surfaced with white rock, the area was sodded with Bermuda grass and landscaped with evergreen trees, up to date furniture was placed in the recreation hall and library and the school was provided with better quarters and equipment.*

This was a different sort of assignment for Harold, one that didn't require building anything or creating a park. The "SCS" preface denoted that this CCC camp was part of the Soil Conservation Service. The (C) indicated the unit was "colored"; all the enrollees were African American.

President Franklin D. Roosevelt signed the Soil Conservation Act on April 27, 1935. In the words of the law, the mandate of the Soil Conservation Service was to "control floods, prevent impairment of reservoirs and maintain the navigability of rivers and harbors, protect public health, public lands and relieve unemployment."

The program had many components, but two were most important. One was to give farmers financial incentives to grow vegetables, grasses, or even trees rather than commercial crops like wheat, corn, and cotton that depleted soil far more rapidly. Another incentive was to supply farmers with manpower, supplies, and technical advice in order to implement conservation measures that might save their soil from further erosion and depletion. In 1936 the program was working sufficiently well that local conservation districts were established in some states. Texas was one of those states, and Bogata was in one of those districts. Harold and his staff and

Lt. and Mrs. Harold L. O'Neal left Friday for Monterrey and other points in Mexico for a vacation. They will return in time for Lt. O'Neal to report for duty July 30th at Fort Sam Houston in San Antonio.

Mexico
August 7, 8, 9, 10, 11, 12, 13
1936
With Harold
Captain and Mrs Van Houten

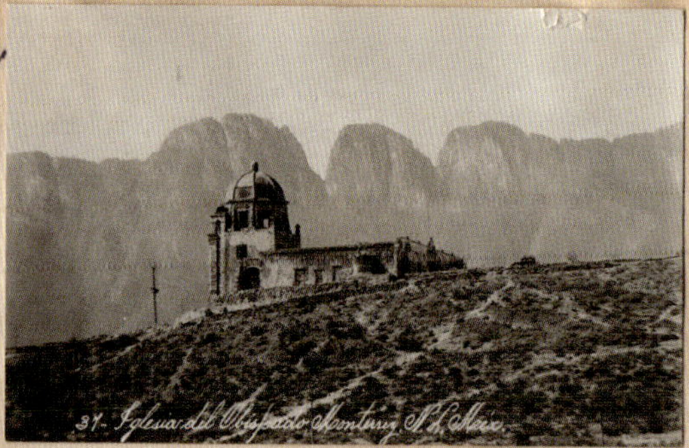


Night Club

JARDINES "TERPSICORE"
Monterrey's most Beautiful night Club
Teléfono 1687 · Bolivar 1375 · Apartado 173

BOLETO No. 13433 VALOR $ 1.00
DERECHO DE ASIENTO
(COVER CHARGE)

Mexico 1936

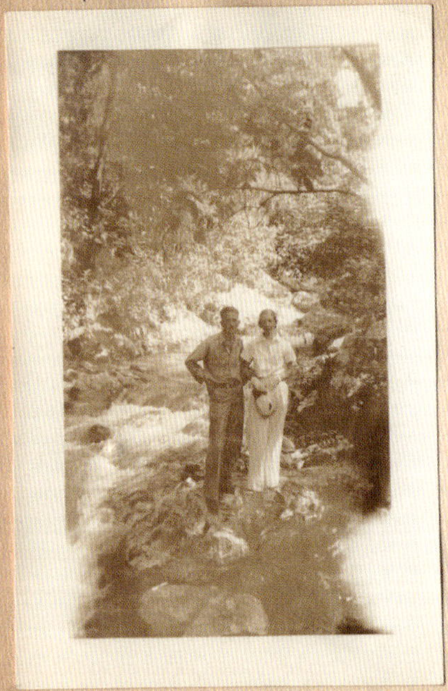

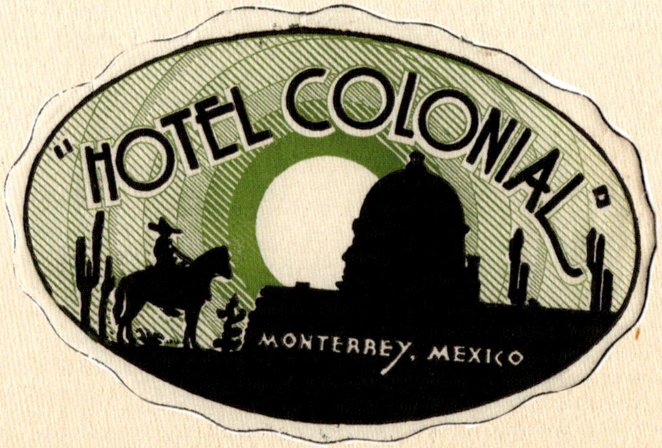

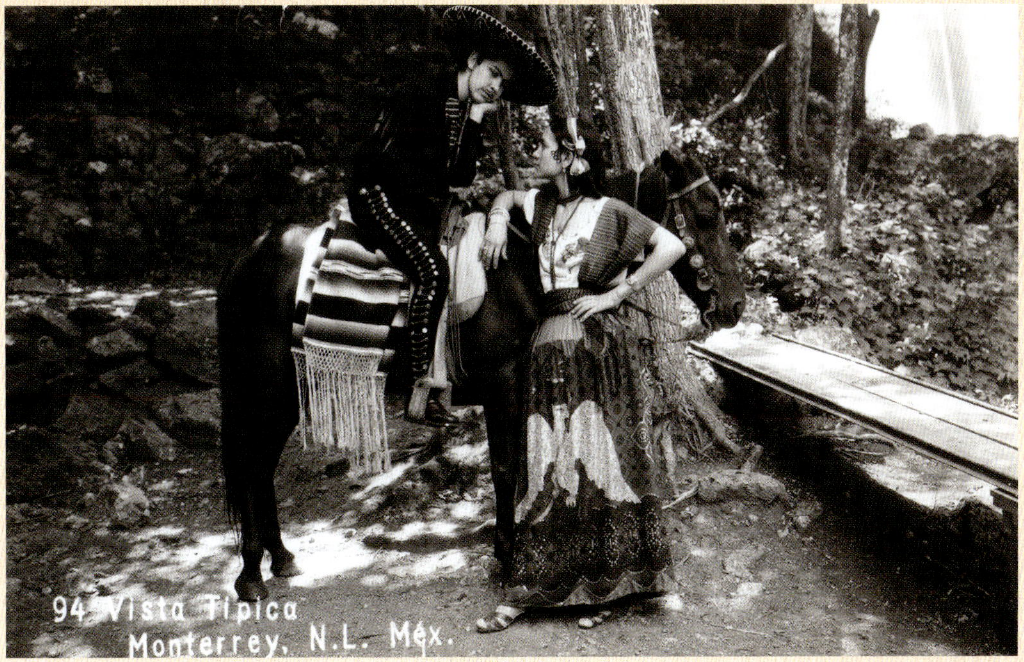


The Black Cat
El Gato Negro

Cordially invites you to sample our wide variety of genuine Mexican and imported liquors.

This card is good for a Black Cat Special Cocktail.

OUR PRICES ARE RIGHT

RIGHT IN FRONT OF MONTERREY HOTEL

over

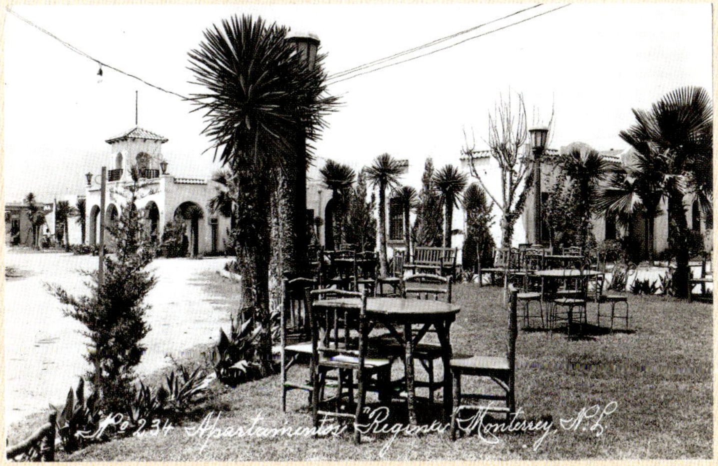


JARDINES "TERPSICORE"

Monterrey's most Beautiful night Club

Teléfono 1687 · Bolívar 1375 · Apartado 173

BOLETO No. 13434 VALOR **$ 1.00**

DERECHO DE ASIENTO

(COVER CHARGE)

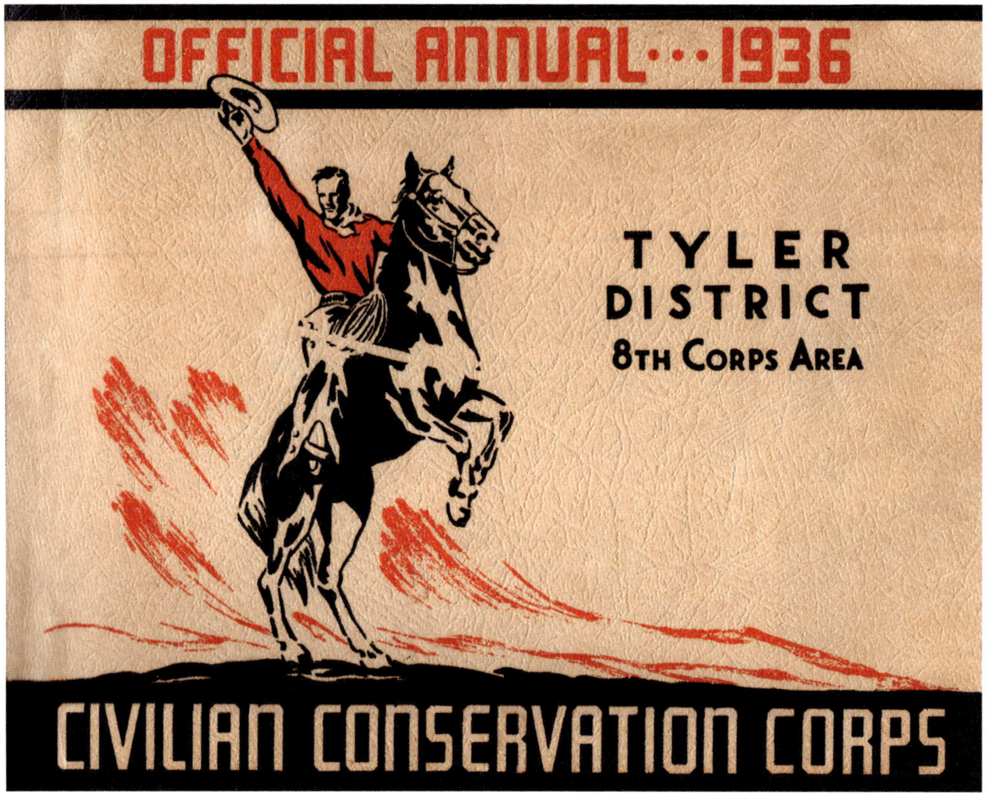


Tyler District, Official 1936 Annual

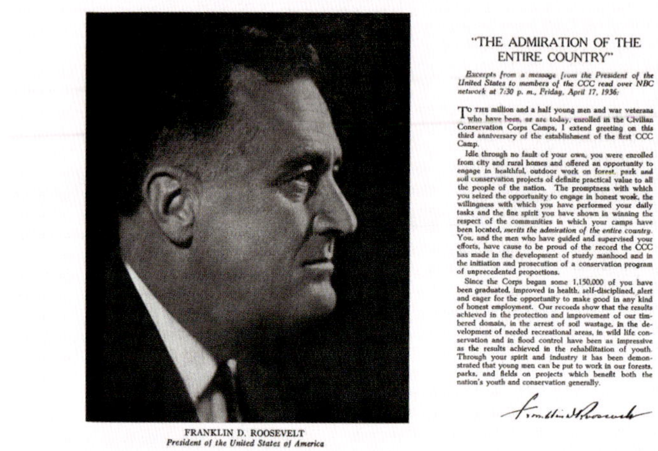

FRANKLIN D. ROOSEVELT
*President of the United States of America*

"THE ADMIRATION OF THE ENTIRE COUNTRY"

*Excerpts from a message from the President of the United States to members of the CCC read over NBC network at 7:30 p. m., Friday, April 17, 1936:*

TO THE million and a half young men and war veterans who have been, or are today, enrolled in the Civilian Conservation Corps Camps, I extend greeting on this third anniversary of the establishment of the first CCC Camp.

Idle through no fault of your own, you were enrolled from city and rural homes and offered an opportunity to engage in healthful, outdoor work on forest, park and soil conservation projects of definite practical value to all the people of the nation. The promptness with which you seized the opportunity to engage in honest work, the willingness with which you have performed your daily tasks and the fine spirit you have shown in winning the respect of the communities in which your camps have been located, *merits the admiration of the entire country.* You, and the men who have guided and supervised your efforts, have cause to be proud of the record the CCC has made in the development of sturdy manhood and in the initiation and prosecution of a conservation program of unprecedented proportions.

Since the Corps began some 1,150,000 of you have been graduated, improved in health, self-disciplined, alert and eager for the opportunity to make good in any kind of honest employment. Our records show that the results achieved in the protection and improvement of our timbered domain, in the arrest of soil wastage, in the development of needed recreational areas, in wild life conservation and in flood control have been as impressive as the results achieved in the rehabilitation of youth. Through your spirit and industry it has been demonstrated that young men can be put to work in our forests, parks, and fields on projects which benefit both the nation's youth and conservation generally.

President Franklin D. Roosevelt's message to CCC enrollees

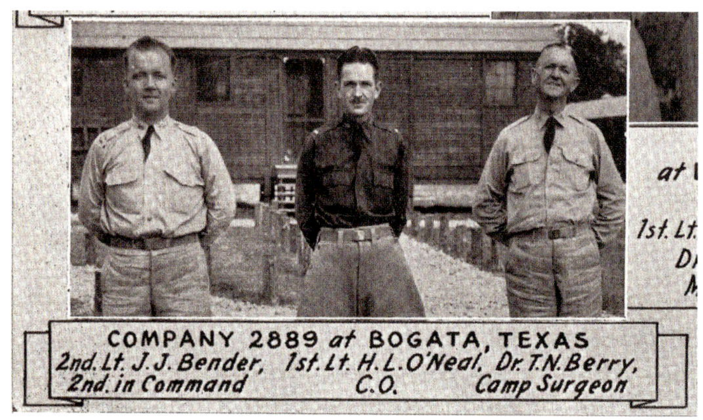


Officers at Bogata

## Bogata, 1936

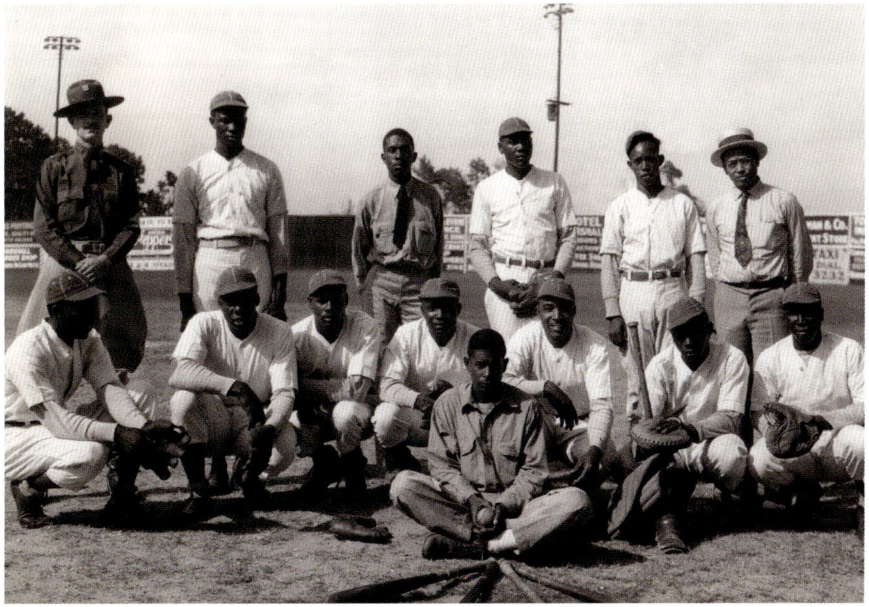

The Bogata baseball team

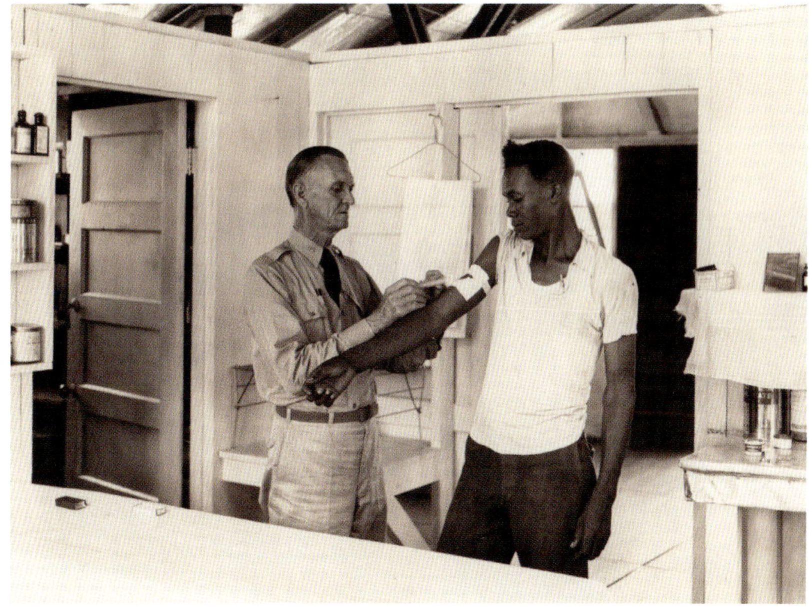

Medical care at Bogata

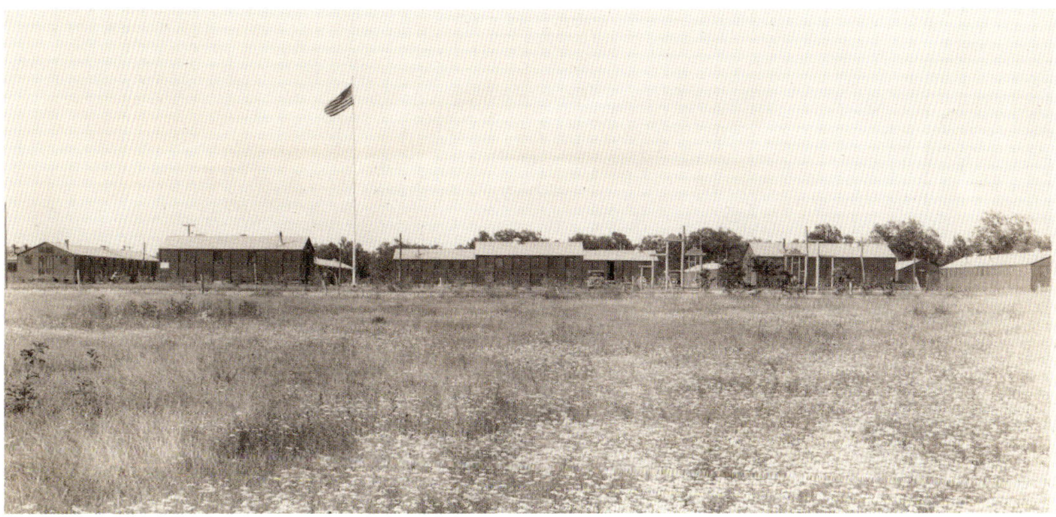

Bogata camp

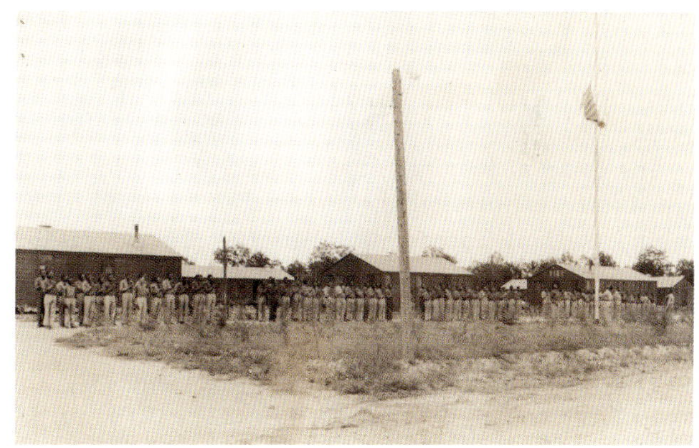

Bogata troops in formation

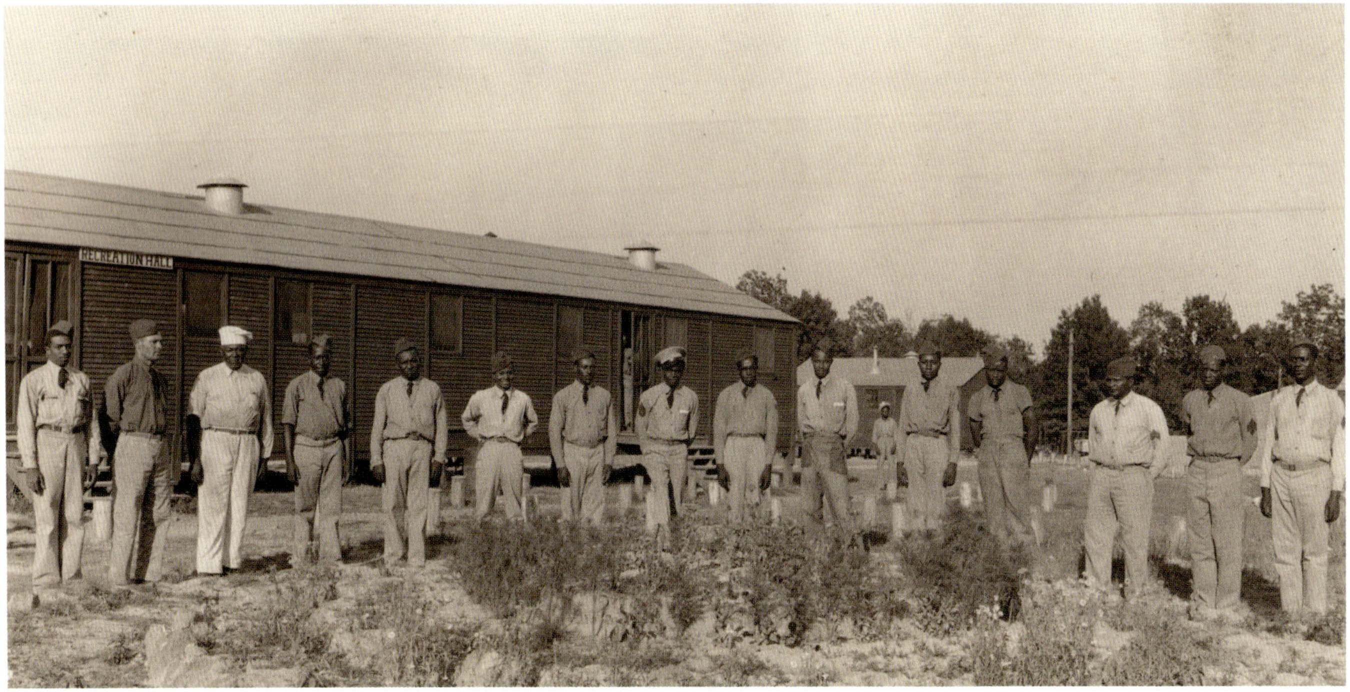


CCC enrollees outside Bogata recreation hall

men supplied the technical advice and labor.

The camp at Bogata was organized just a few months after the bill establishing the Soil Conservation Service. By the time Harold arrived in 1936 it had been functioning for almost a year. It was a learning experience for him and was the first time he was in charge of a CCC company composed entirely of African American enrollees. It was a positive experience that would prove important in the South Pacific during World War II and later when he was a school administrator.

Harold and Sarah remained in Bogata through the summer and into the fall. Harold was there long enough to field a baseball team that may or may not have been the best in Red River County, but they look as though they should have been.

At some point in his tenure as commandant at various CCC units in East Texas, Harold was involved with non-CCC military exercises in East Texas. The exact timing, location, and reason for these military maneuvers are not detailed in his papers, but there were many interesting photographs of these activities.

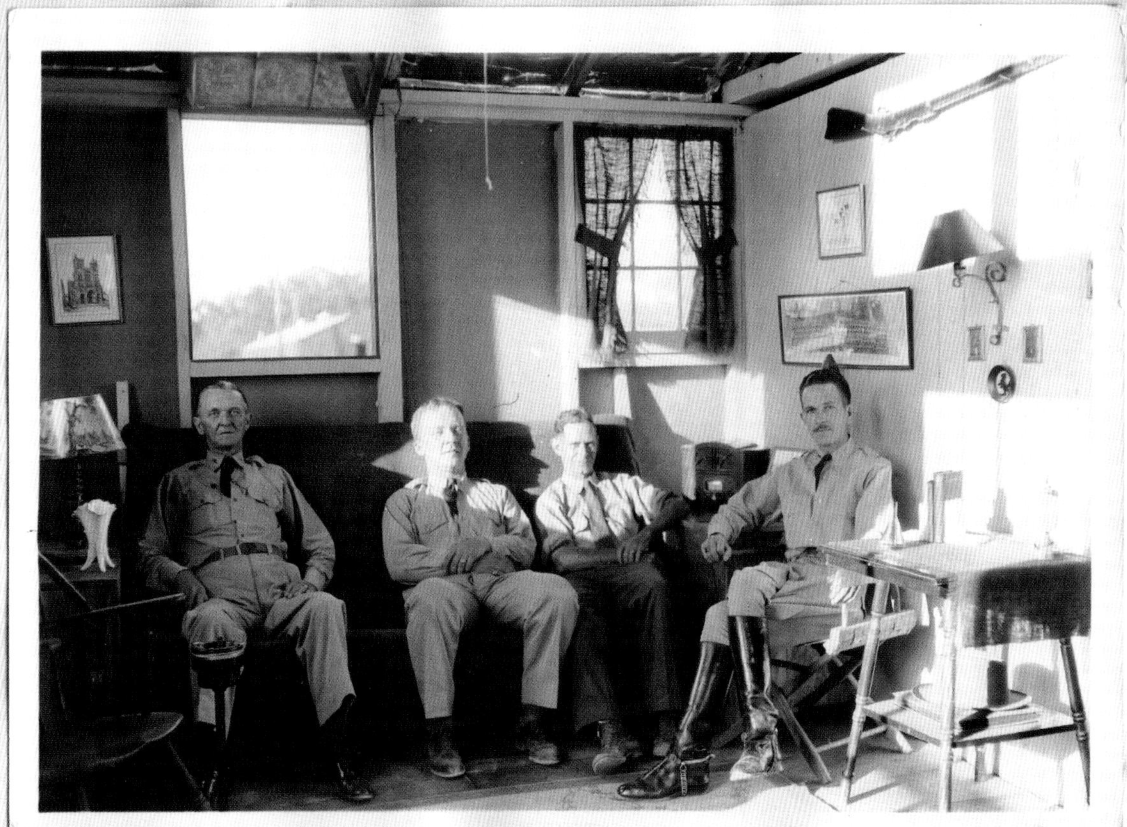

Bagoto - 1937

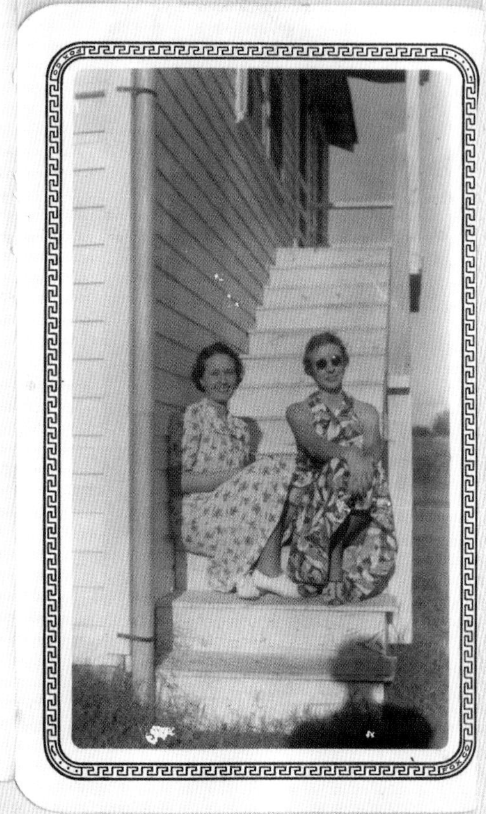

My penthouse

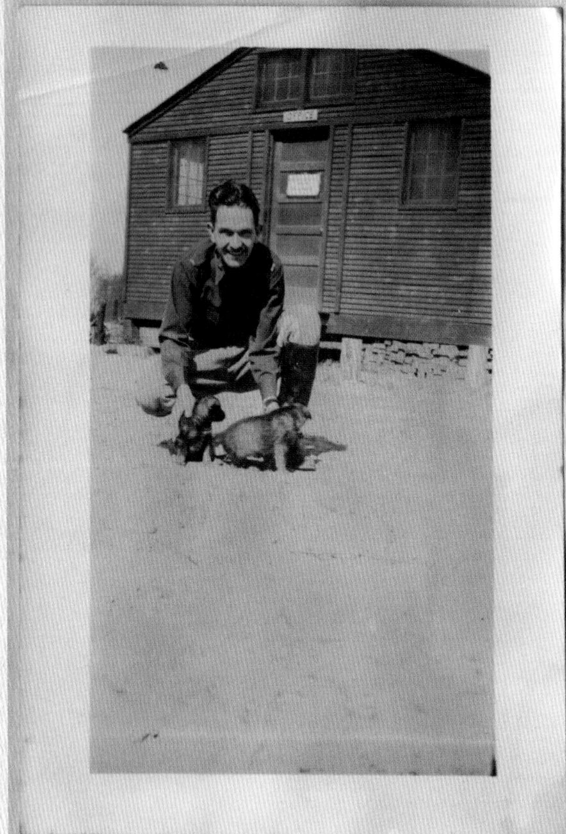

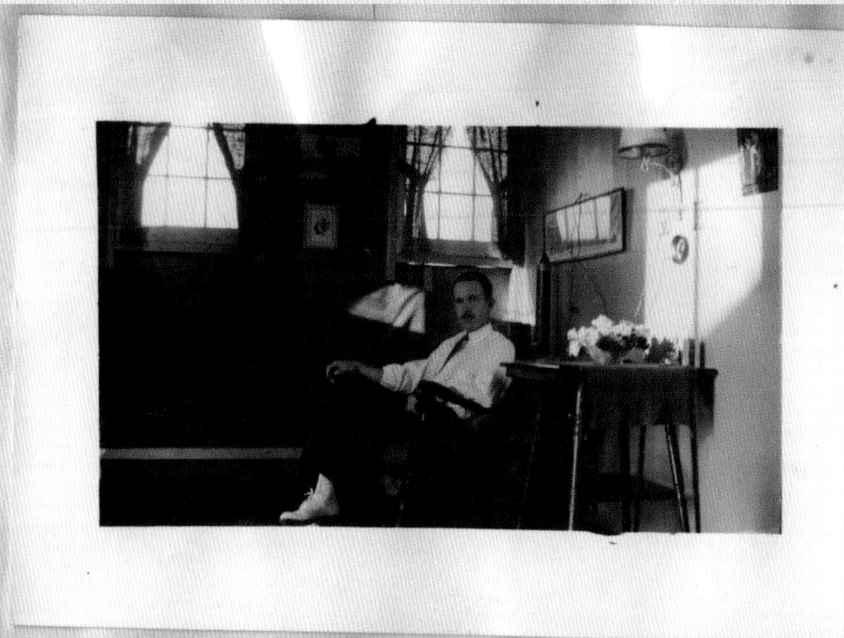

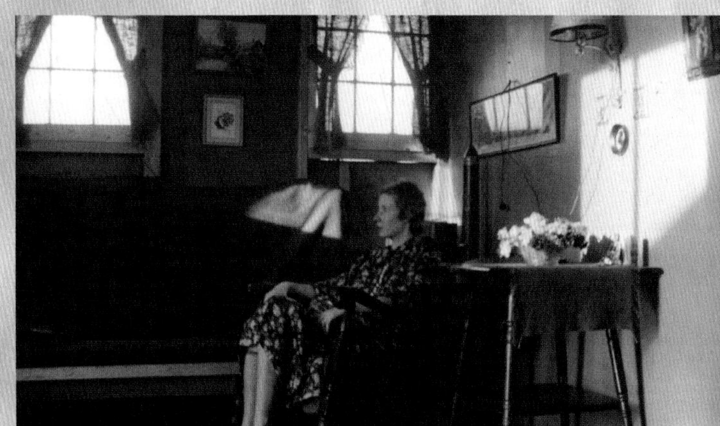

## Military Maneuvers in East Texas, 1936-37

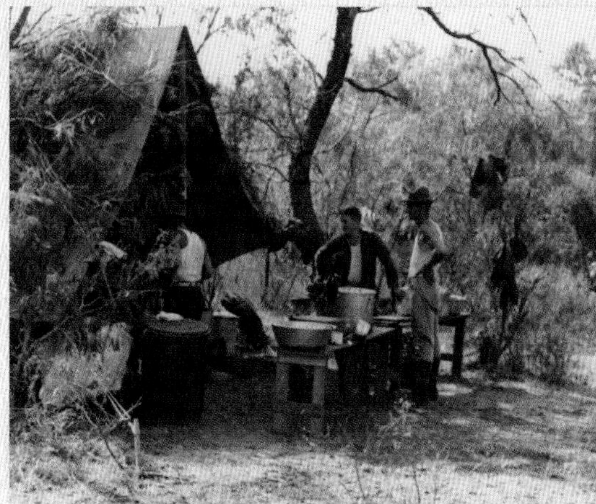

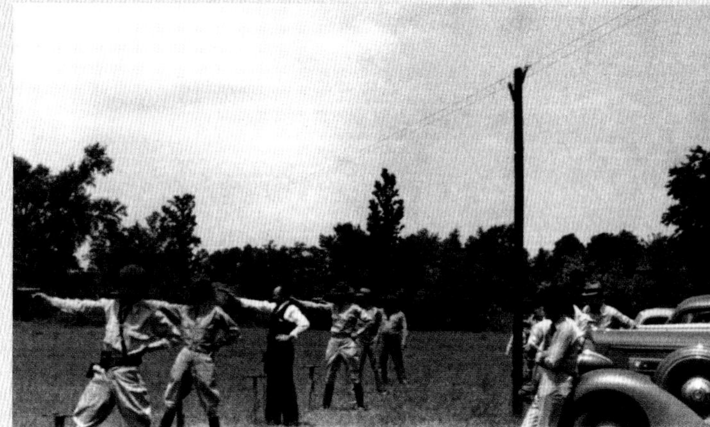

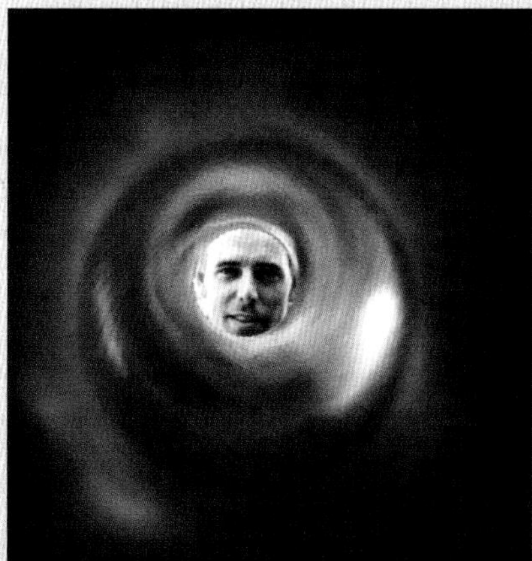

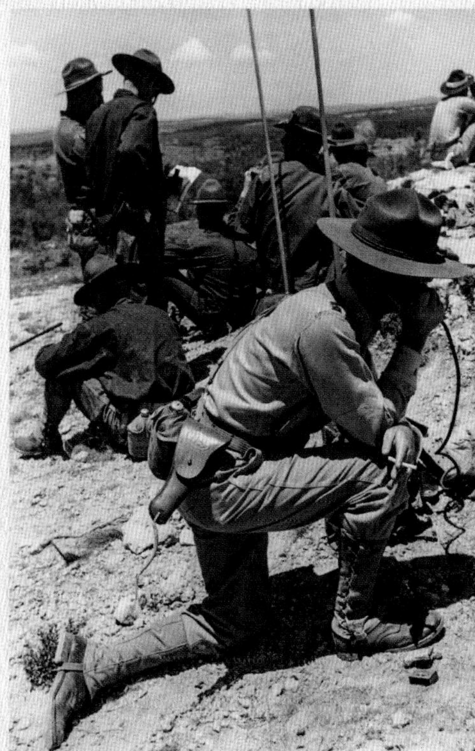

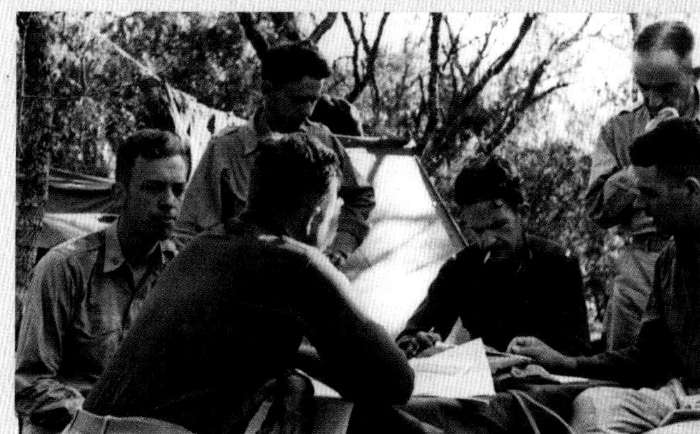

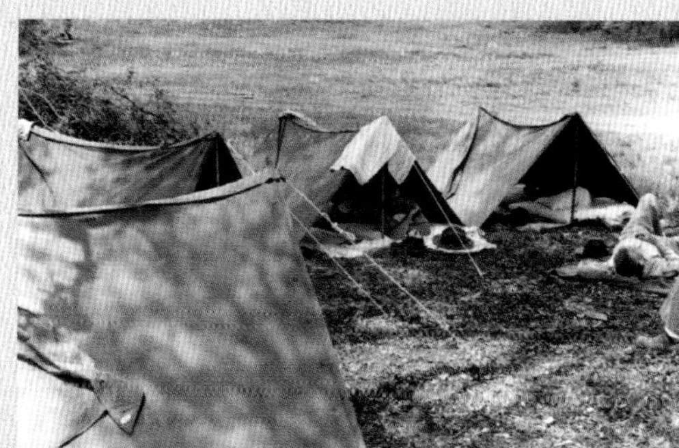

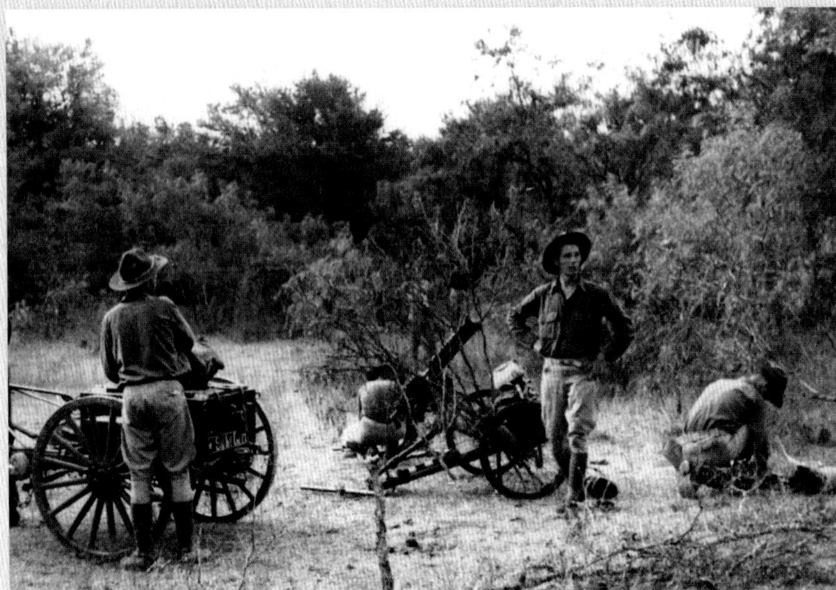
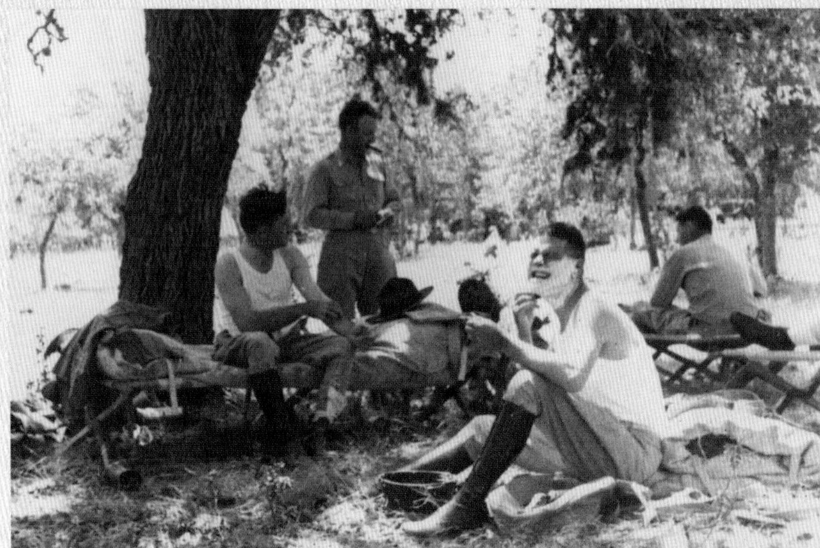
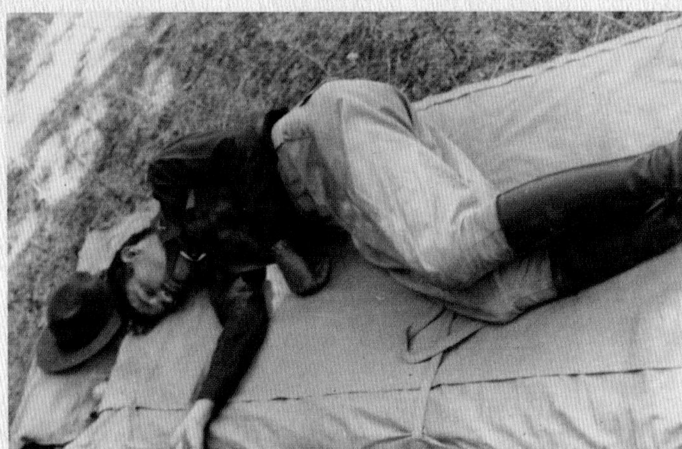
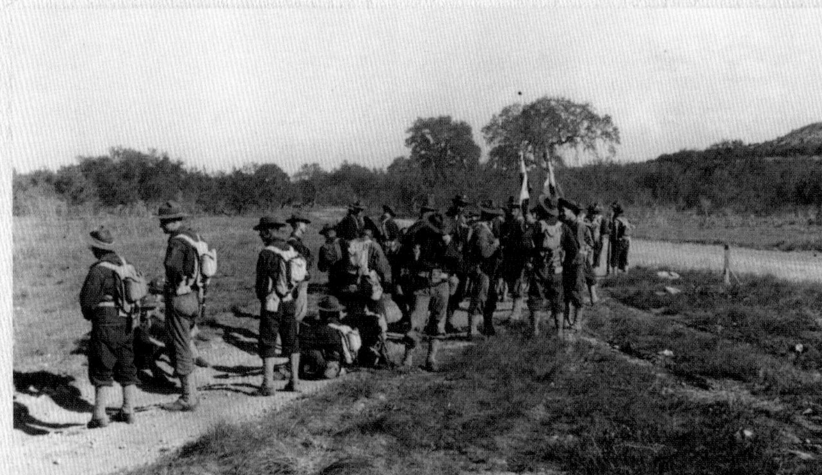

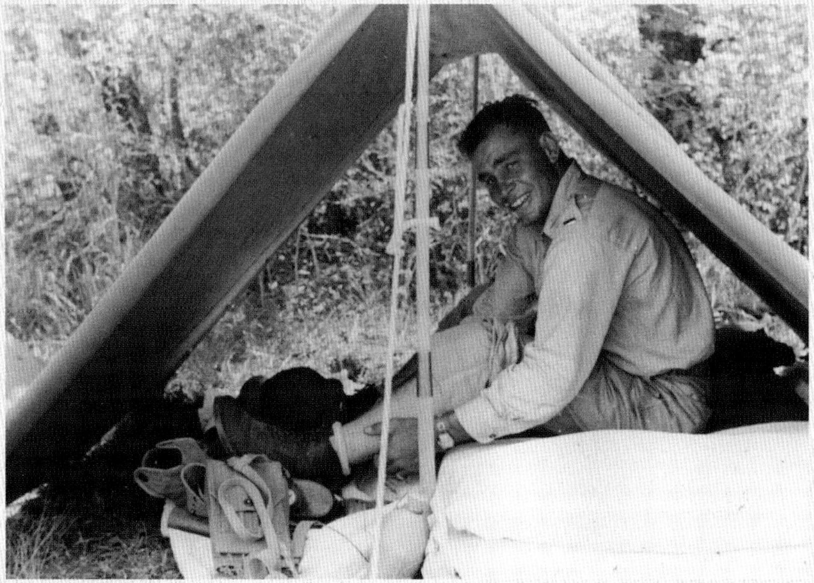

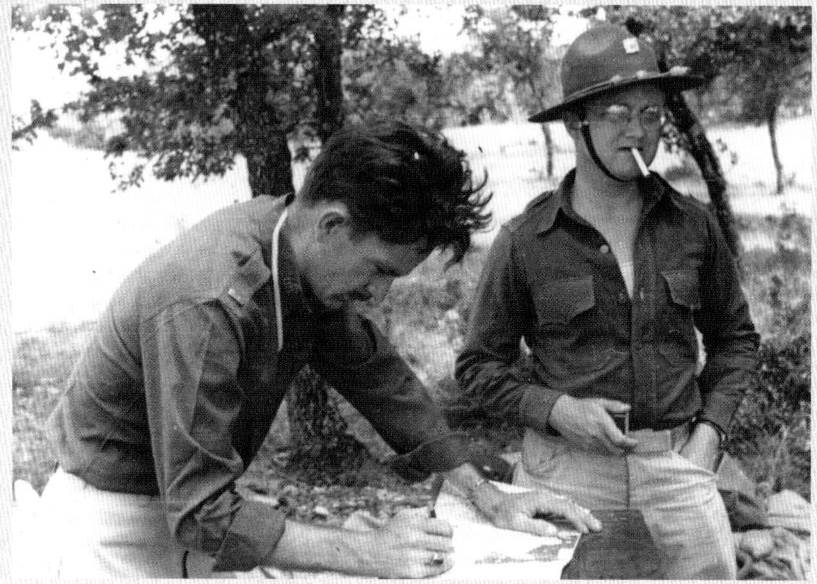

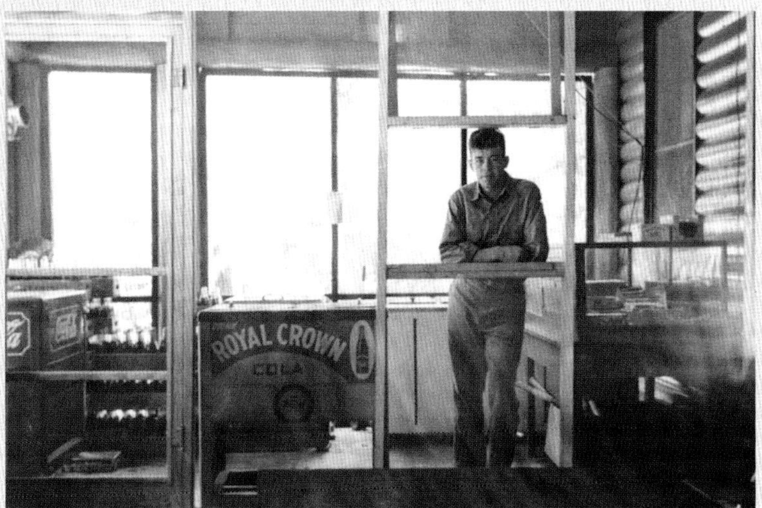
ROYAL CROWN
COLA

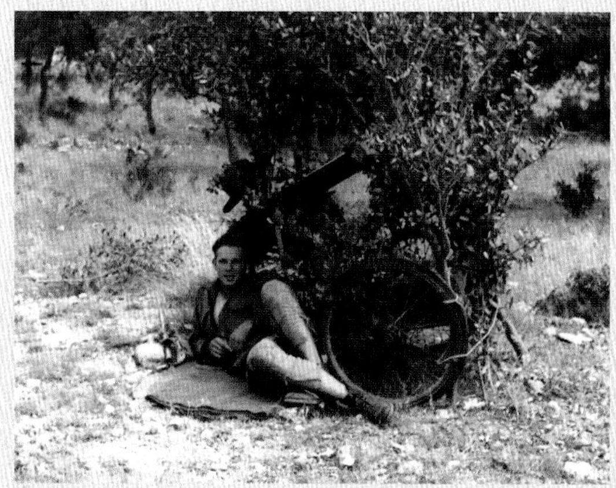

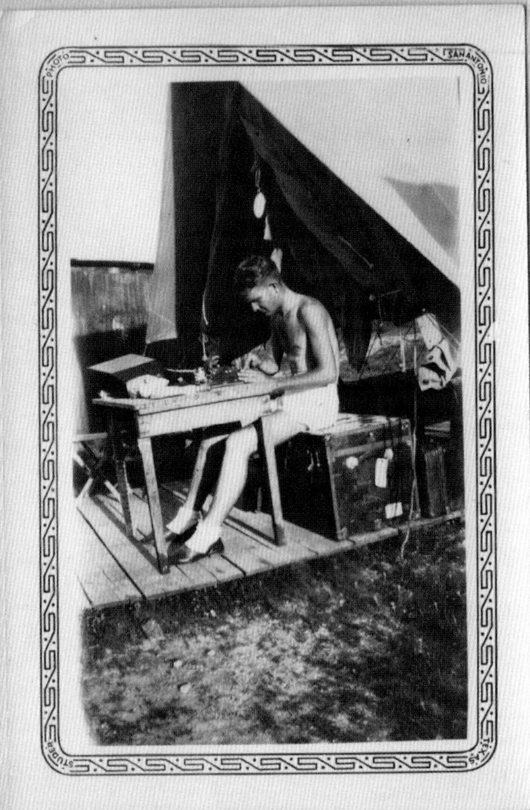

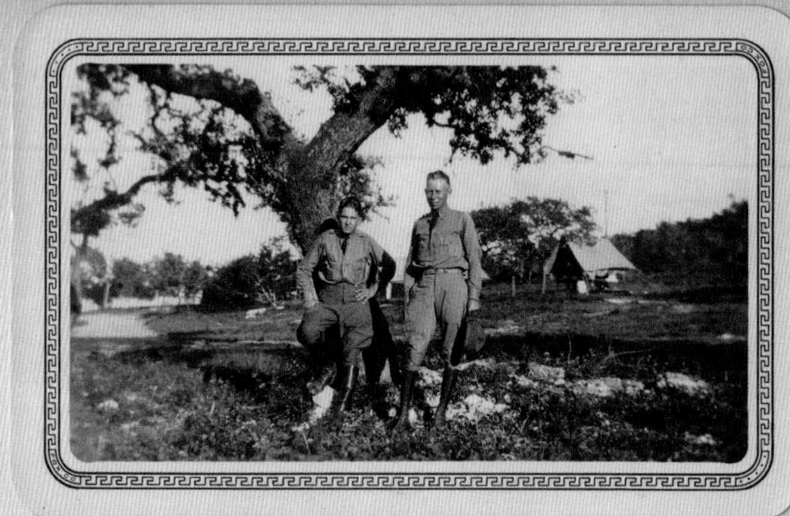

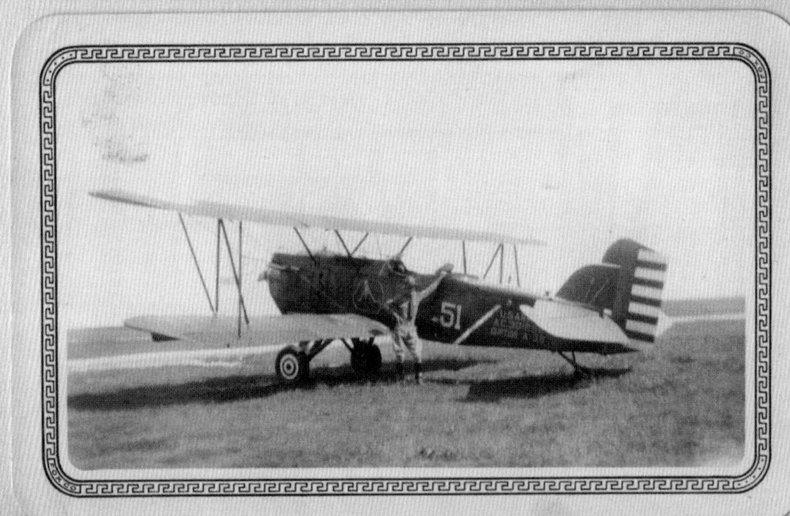
51

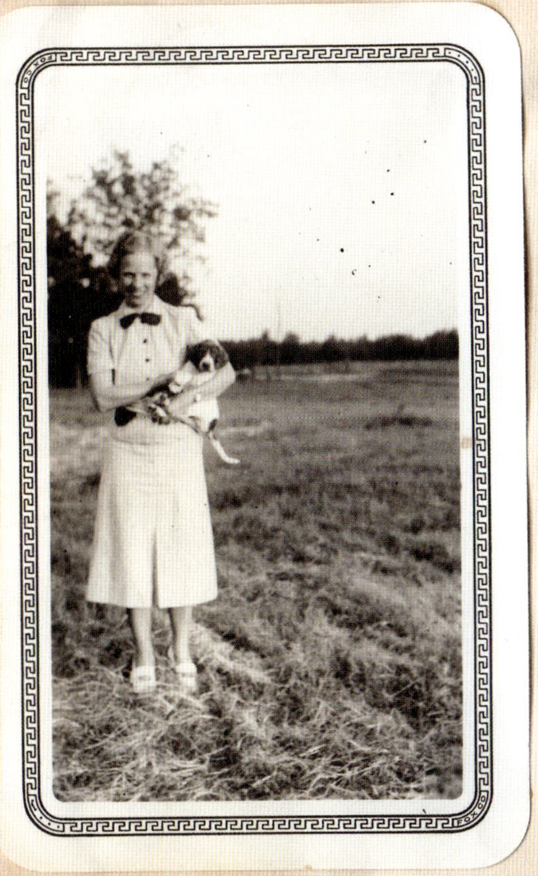

Waxahachie
Nov-Dec-1937

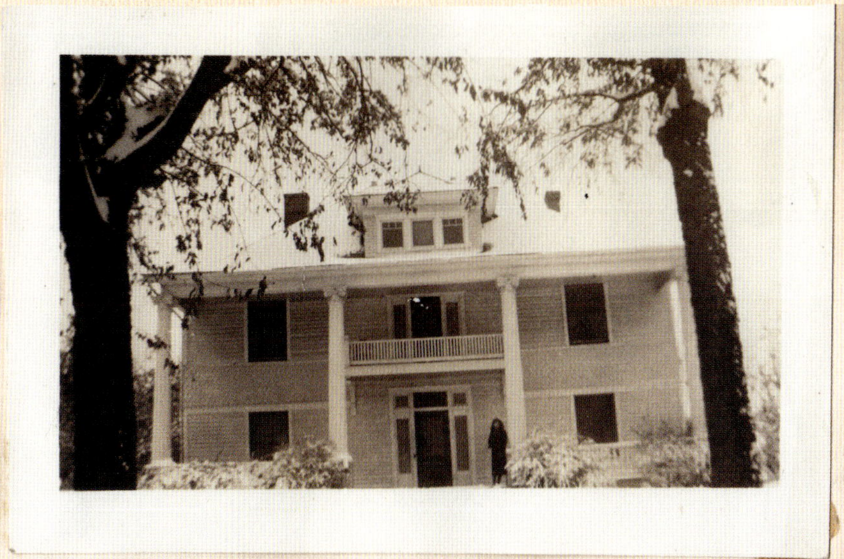

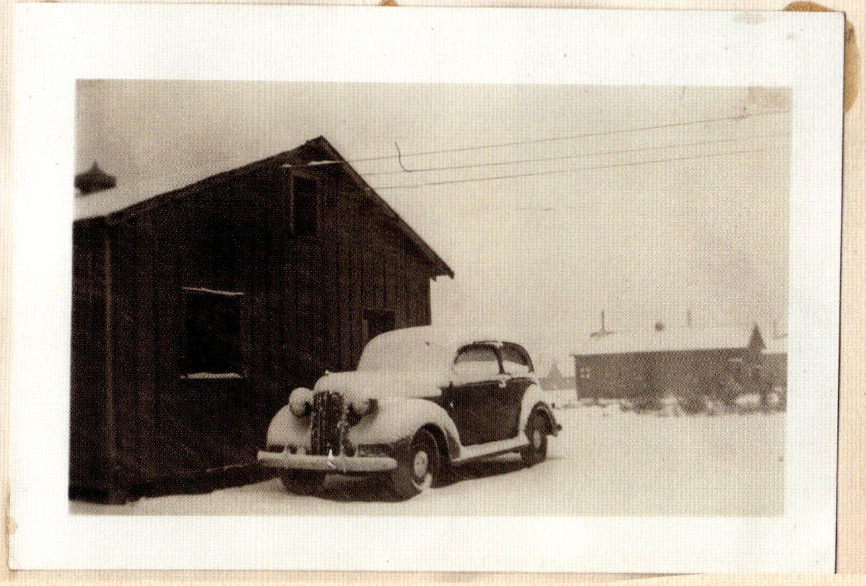

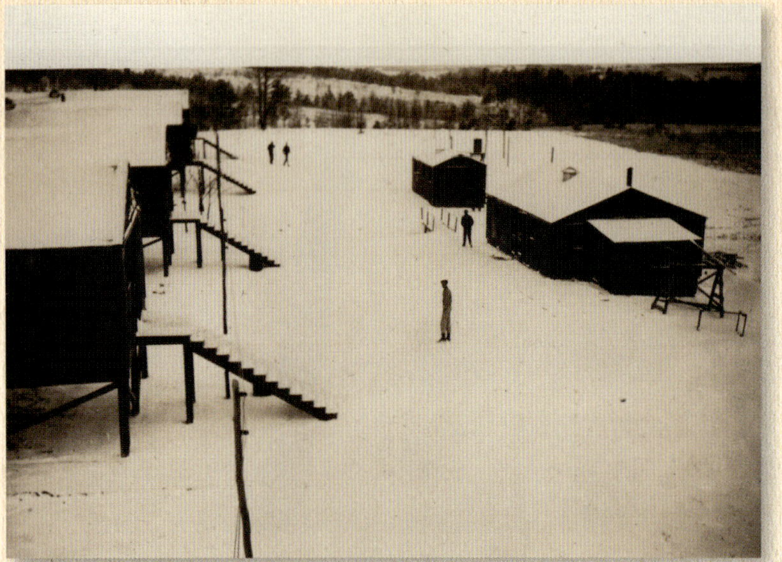

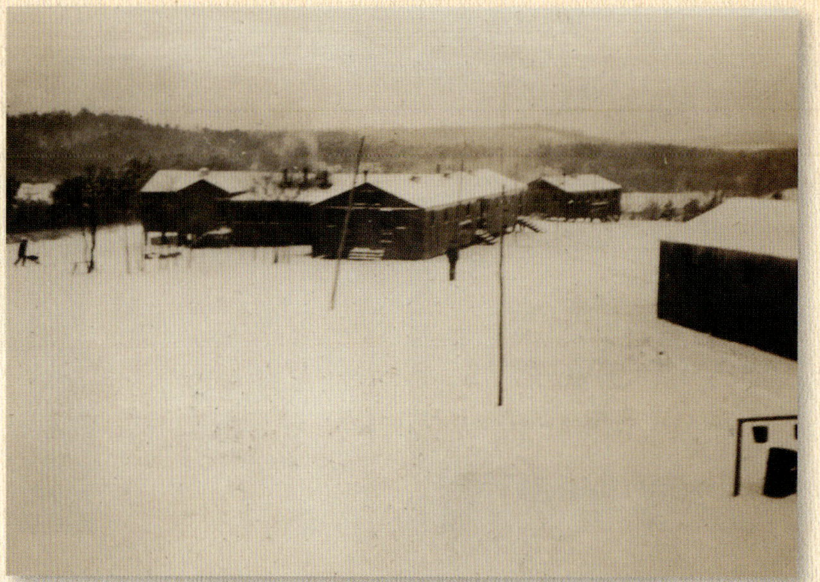

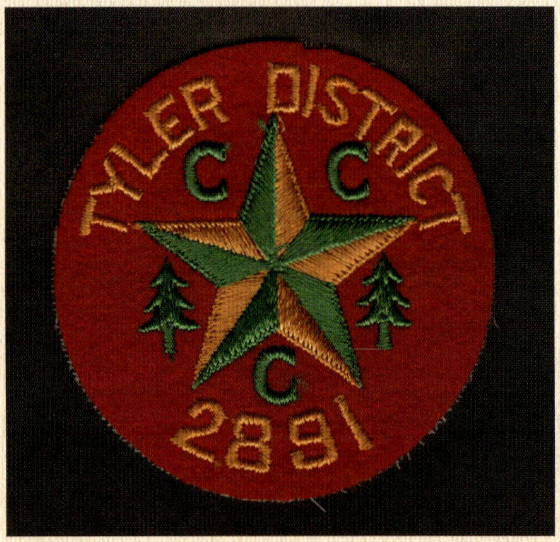
TYLER DISTRICT
C C C
2891

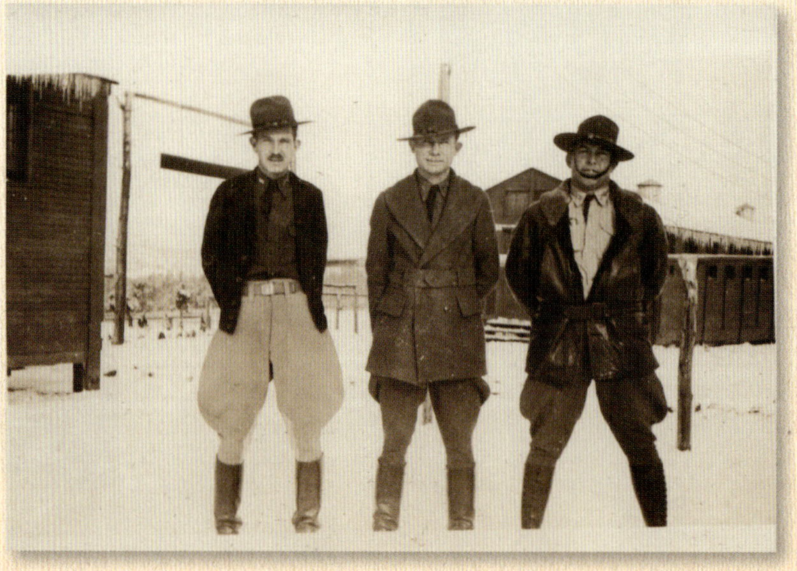

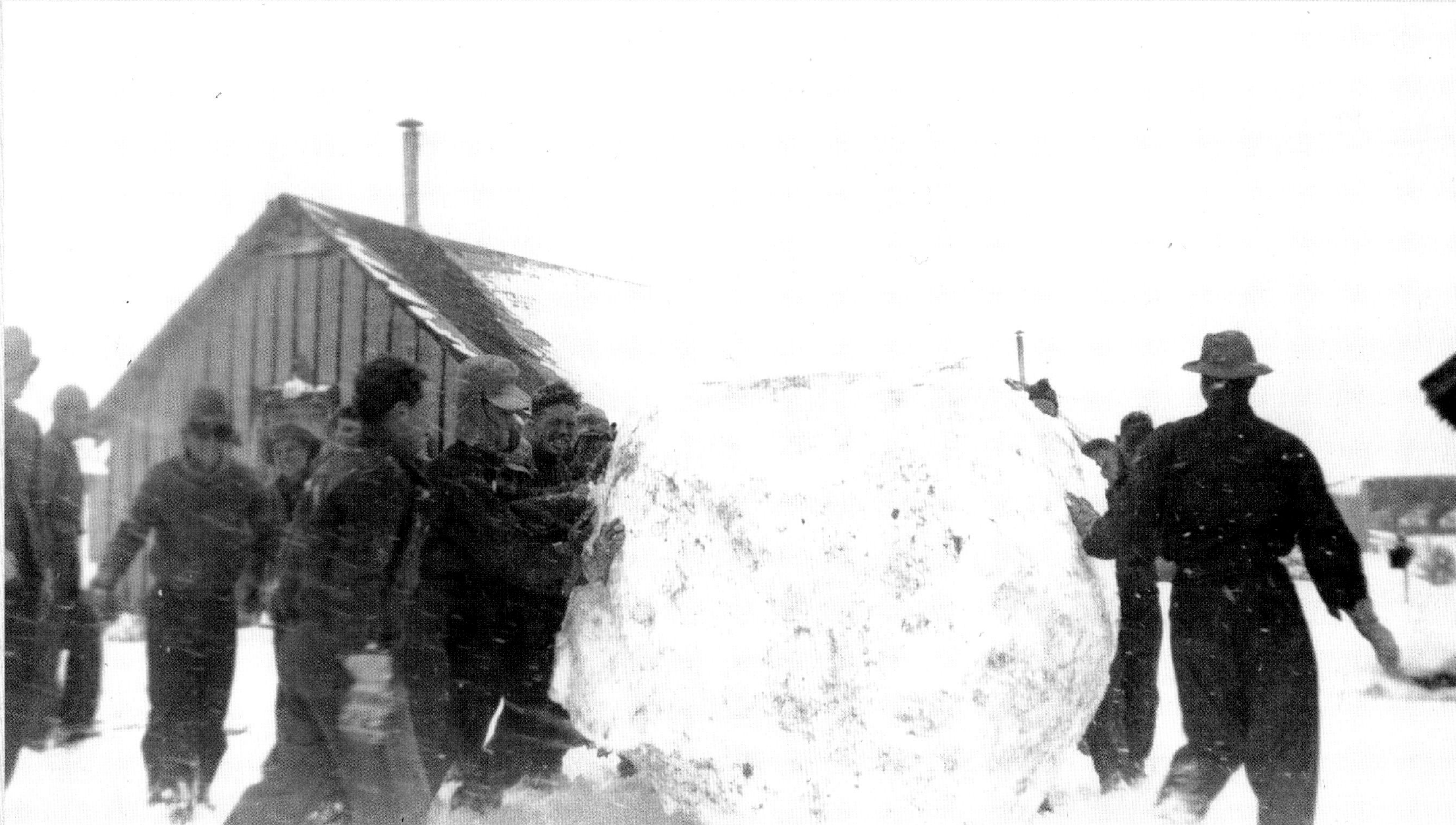

Xmas 1938

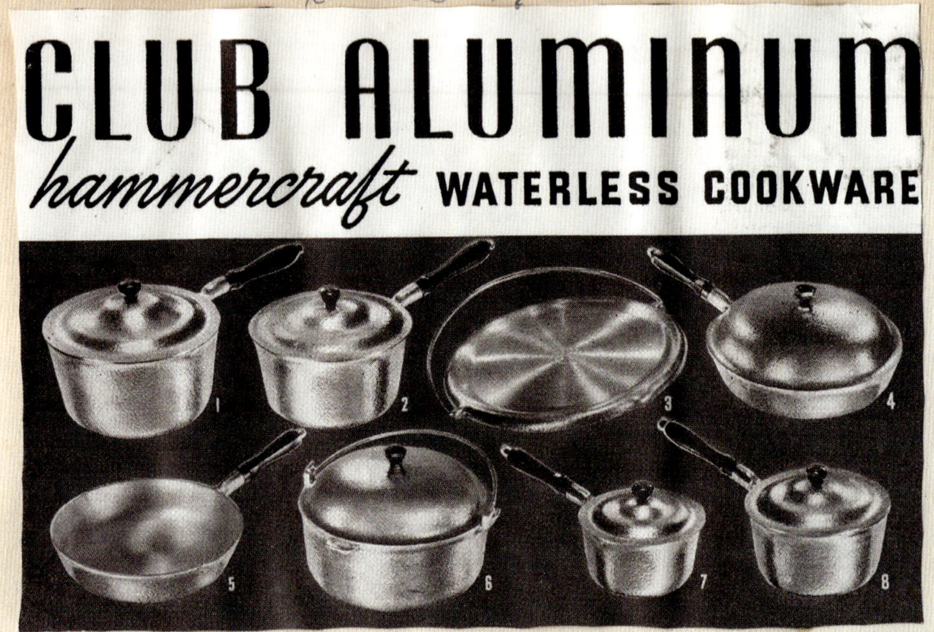


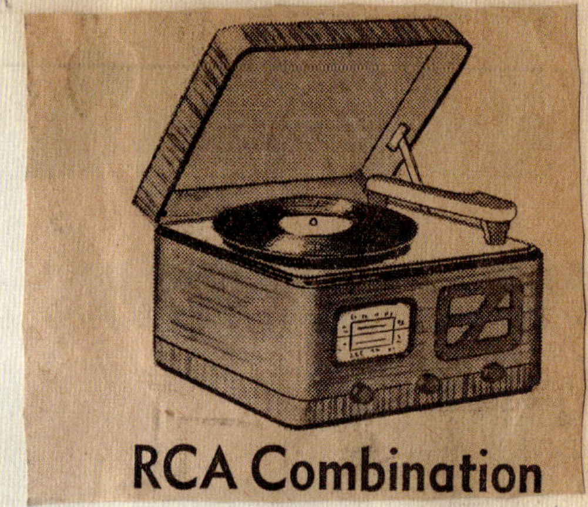


Harold's and my present

Birthday & Xmas present from Harold

Box candy - Zelma Patterson
Hose - "B" Hendricks
Po. Puffs - Mrs Ward
Talcum Po - Sue Thompson
Jello molds & cookie cutters - Harold
Cake decorator - Harold
Cream } Harriet
Po Base } Hibbard Ayer } Dad & Mom

Kleenex
Hand Lotion } Mom &
Cream } Dad
Measuring Cup } mom
Green pitcher }
Yellow blouse → Martha
Purse - Ray

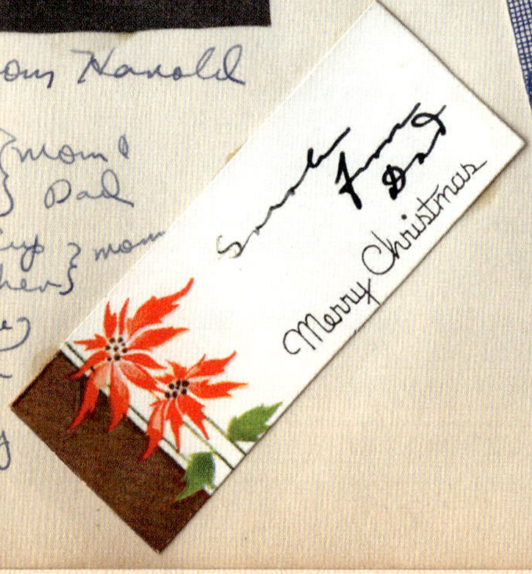


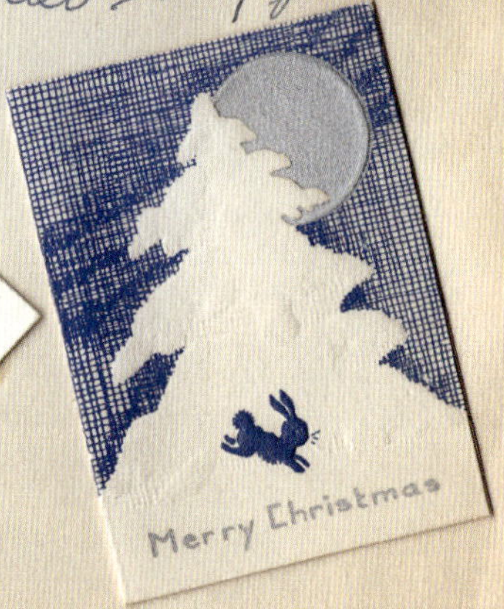

Jan 4, 1938 When Harold in Station Hospital

FORM 1529-GA

BUS WEDNESDAY MORNING A

D BRING YOUR NICE

E IF YOU

25¢
*for your selection of fixed texts*
35¢
*for 15 words of your own composition*

*for greeting messages* · FOR CHRISTMAS · NEW YEAR'S · VALENTINE'S DAY
EASTER · COMMENCEMENT · MOTHER'S DAY · FATHER'S DAY · THANKSGIVING ·
BIRTHDAYS · BON VOYAGE · · *on a special blank in special envelope*

TO ANY WESTERN UNION OFFICE IN THE UNITED STATES

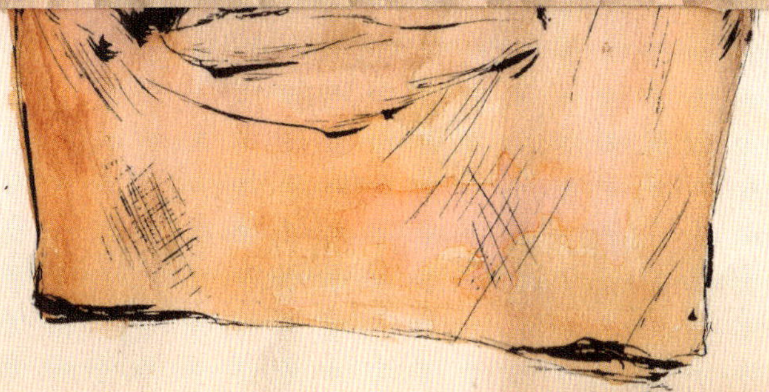

"Is it not good to have
in the background of one's
life a little walled-in
garden of memories,—where
one may go back, on rainy
days, and gather flowers!"

THE COMPANY WILL APPRECIATE SUGGESTIONS FROM ITS PATRONS CONCERNING ITS SERVICE 1201-S

CLASS OF SERVICE

This is a full-rate Telegram or Cablegram unless its deferred character is indicated by a suitable symbol above or preceding the address.

# WESTERN UNION

R. B. WHITE, PRESIDENT — NEWCOMB CARLTON, CHAIRMAN OF THE BOARD — J. C. WILLEVER, FIRST VICE-PRESIDENT

SYMBOLS

DL = Day Letter
NM = Night Message
NL = Night Letter
LC = Deferred Cable
NLT = Cable Night Letter
Ship Radiogram

The filing time shown in the date line on telegrams and day letters is STANDARD TIME at point of origin. Time of receipt is STANDARD TIME at point of destination.

**Received at 212 West Ferguson St., Tyler, Texas** Office Hours 7 A. M. to 12 A. M.

1938 JAN 4 AM 7 26

D26 40 NL=SANANTONIO TEX 3

MRS HAROLD L ONEAL=

508 SOUTH BANNER ST

CATCH THE 630 BUS WEDNESDAY MORNING AND COME DOWN CASH CHECK FOR WHAT YOU NEED BRING YOUR NICE DRESSES AS WE MIGHT HAVE TO MAKE SOME CALLS WIRE ME IF YOU ARE COMING AND ILL BE WAITING I LOVE YOU=

HAROLD.

630.

THERE IS NO DEPENDABLE SUBSTITUTE FOR WESTERN UNION TIME

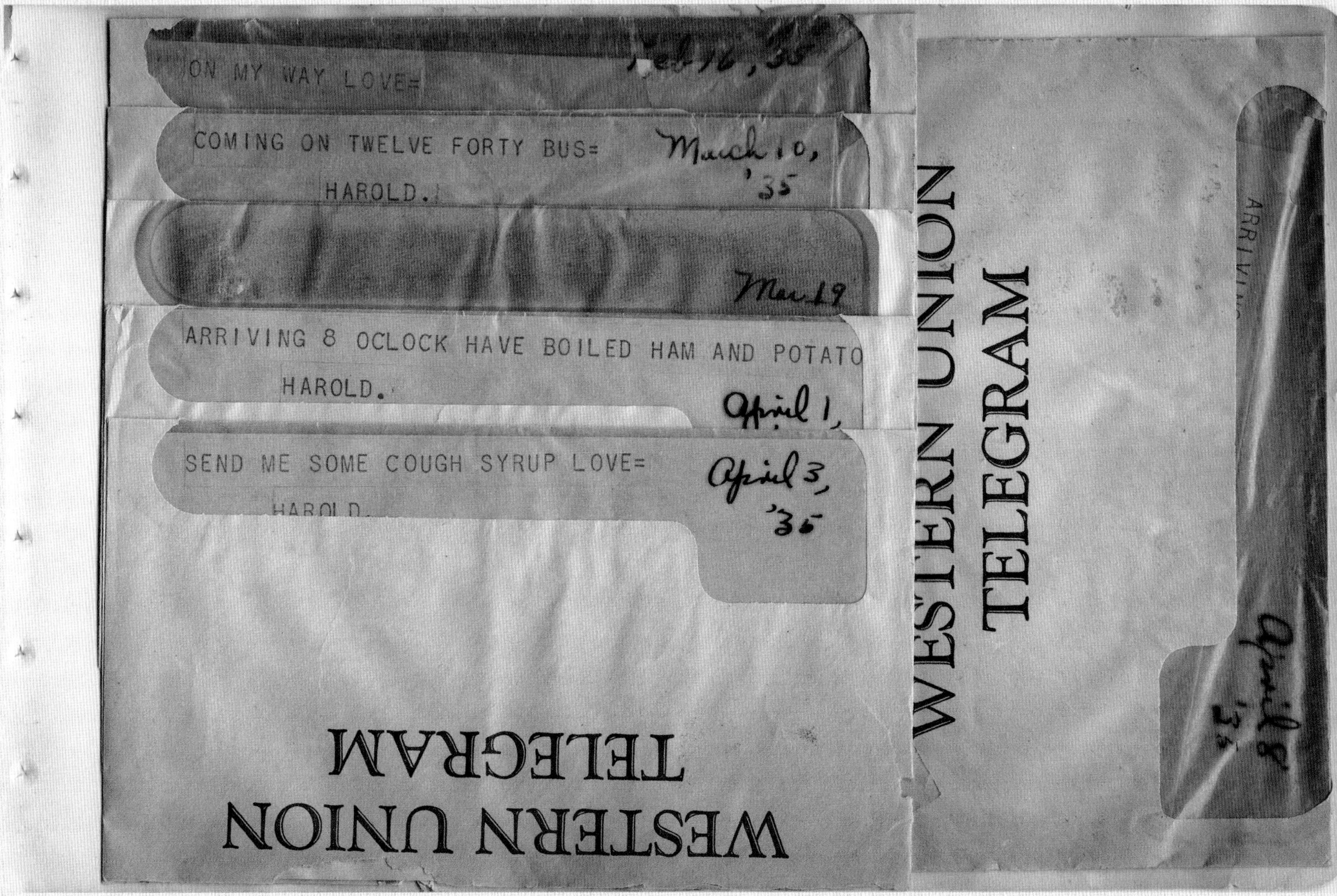
ON MY WAY LOVE=
COMING ON TWELVE FORTY BUS=
March 10, '35
HAROLD.
Mar 19
ARRIVING 8 OCLOCK HAVE BOILED HAM AND POTATO
HAROLD.
April 1,
SEND ME SOME COUGH SYRUP LOVE=
April 3, '35
HAROLD.
WESTERN UNION TELEGRAM
WESTERN UNION TELEGRAM
April 8 '35

**1937**

In November 1937 Harold was transferred to SCS—37, another Soil Conservation Service camp but this time near a town ten times as large as Bogata: Waxahachie. The work, however, was similar, except that this time Harold arrived at his new assignment in the dead of winter and managed to take a number of photographs of the snow-covered camps to prove it. There is no record of how he and his men conserved the snow-covered fields in and around Waxahachie.

As was the case in Bogata, the camp was built on private property, and the young white enrollees who worked to help repair the fields, string fences, clear brush, and even plant trees were not unlike the black enrollees at Bogata. Just young men who needed a job, even a modest job like working for the CCC. Their salary was still thirty dollars a month, of which they were allowed to keep as much as eight dollars or as little as five, depending on their family's need. But they earned more than that. Not only did the CCC often provide some education, it also instilled discipline and responsibility and provided the experience of working as part of a group, all of which would serve them well as the world marched closer to World War II.

This was Harold's last assignment with the CCC. What he assumed were minor health issues would sideline him in early 1938, but soon he was ready to return to duty, this time in a new capacity.

In a biographical statement written in the early 1950s he stated:

*At the termination of this CCC duty I was invited by the superintendent of schools, Kilgore, Texas, to take over the military department of the high school and junior college. In Kilgore, I served as Commandant of Cadets from 1938 until 1941. Duties, other than military, included being dean of boys in the high school for a year and sponsoring several extra-curricular activities.*

Harold and Sarah moved to Kilgore and entered a new and exciting part of their life together. Kilgore would be Harold's last assignment prior to the outbreak of World War II.

The CCC suspended its activities in Texas on July 13, 1942, but many of the young men who were enrolled in its programs and the officers who trained them were already taking an active role in the United States and overseas in Europe and the Pacific as World War II raged on.

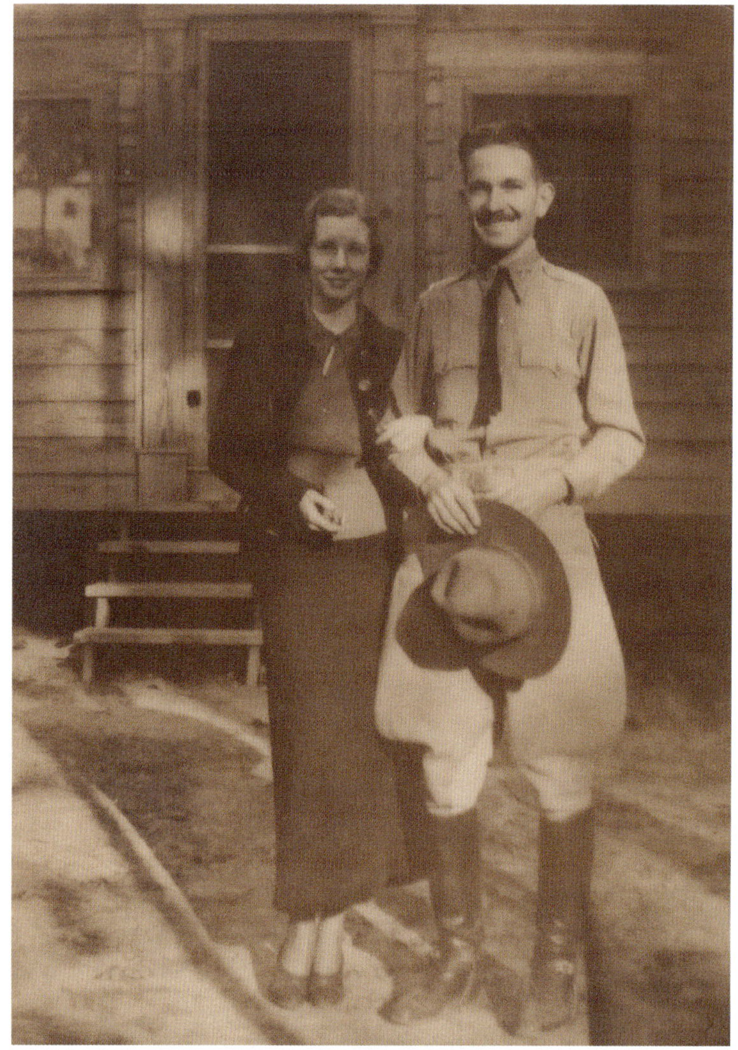

# Kilgore 1938

**IN 1938, THE KILGORE SUPERINTENDENT OF SCHOOLS ASKED HAROLD TO BECOME THE COMMANDANT OF CADETS AT THE THREE-YEAR-OLD KILGORE HIGH SCHOOL** and the newly constructed Kilgore Junior College. Harold and Sarah couldn't have been happier. Harold had five different assignments in five years, lived in small and even smaller towns for those years, and was never in one place for more than a year. Since their marriage in 1935, he and Sarah had lived together in Daingerfield, Tyler, Bogata, and Waxahachie. In 1938, Kilgore was a busy, bustling, prosperous metropolis compared to those cities.

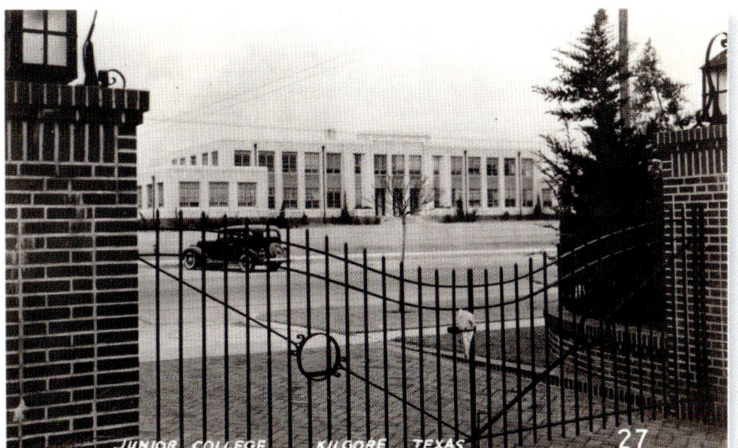


It was just the right time to be in Kilgore and become part of that city's school system. Kilgore wasn't the largest city in East Texas; Longview, Marshall, and Tyler had two, three, or four times as many residents, but the wealth Kilgore had derived from oil set it apart from the others in terms of what it could provide those who were part of this community.

In September 1930, before the oil came in, Kilgore had a population of five or six hundred, including some outsiders who'd been looking for oil for a decade; few paved streets, a substandard water supply, a barely adequate school system, a railroad line of modest proportions, a small picture show, a handful of churches, and a business district that could accommodate the basic needs of those who lived in town as well as the rural population outside the city. This changed overnight.

When the first well began gushing on October 5, Kilgore and many of the surrounding small towns like Overton, New London, and Gladewater were never quite the same, at least for two or three decades. They've settled down today, but within six months of the first well, 160,000 barrels of oil a day were being pulled out of the ground in and around Kilgore, and within three years there were thirteen thousand producing oil wells of varying sizes within the somewhat loosely defined borders of the oil patch. To put this in perspective, in 1940 there were almost twice as many oil wells in Kilgore—the estimate was about 1,100—and in many cases derricks to go with them, than there were people in the city a decade earlier. This kind of circumstance tends to create an unusual city, and it is into this East Texas town that Harold and Sarah settled. They timed it so that Harold could begin teaching basic military fundamentals to ROTC cadets at Kilgore High School in September 1938.

By this time Kilgore had a state-of-the art high school with oil wells on its grounds, a new junior college, public parks, a public pool, a newly built well-stocked library, and the finest movie theater in East Texas, one that could seat nearly one thousand people. There was a country club with a golf course, Mason-

COMPLETE SCHOOL COVERAGE

# THE MIRROR

GOAL—A BETTER HIGH SCHOOL

VOLUME 4 KILGORE, TEXAS, FRIDAY, OCTOBER 14, 1938 6 NUMBER 1

# Revised ROTC Program Is Introduced This Year

## DRILL CONTEST

Continued From Page 1

Cadet Captain Carl Cooper, adjutant.

Competitive drill will be the second section of the program, with a cup award for the best company. Company A will be under the command of Cadet 2nd Lieut. Norman Hurst; Company B under Cadet 1st. Lieut. Alonzo Robbins; and Company C under Cadet 1st. Lieut. Moultrie Coker. Each company will report to the judges and then drill for 10 full minutes.

The cup award is given annually by the Reserve Officers' Association, and members of the Association serve as judges. The winning ocmpany's name is inscribed on the cup.

The third division will be an "Old Grady" contest to determine the best drilled individual in any company. All cadets and cadet officers are eligible for this competition.

The final division will be the presentation of awards. Col. E. W. Chatterton of the Federal Tender Board will present the drill cup. Twenty-six other awards will be made by numerous individuals.

## Kilgore Cadets Will See Dallas Regiment Review

Lieut. Harold O'Neal, ROTC director in Kilgore, will accompany eleven officers of the high school unit to Dallas next week, to witness a regimental drill of the Woodrow Wilson High School ROTC cadets.

Lieut. O'Neal said he felt the trip would be well worth while, especially in view of the fact that during the next semester Kilgore cadets will devote more time to drill instead of class work. The Woodrow Wilson ROTC, he said, is the largest such unit in the United States.

O'Neal said cadets in Kilgore had advanced rapidly during the past few months, most of the work being done in the classroom. A few additional enrollments are expected.

Boys expected to make the Dallas trip include Cadet Major Wiley Oliver, Cadet Capt. Ardis Sanford, Capt. Bobby Cary, Capt. Carl Cooper, and Lieuts. Chas. Boyd, Billie Davis, Norman Hurst, Alonzo Robbins, Warren White, Hampton Cook and Bradley Knox.

## Enrollment Now At 115, Goal Is 180

Lieutenant Harold L. O'Neal is the new head of the R.O.T.C. unit in Kilgore this year. The subjects to be studied by the unit are: military courtesy and discipline, drill and command, extended order drill, map reading and conventional signs, scouting and patroling, interior guard duty, and musketry and military sanitation, hygiene, and first aid.

At present there are 115 enrolled for R.O.T.C., but Lt. O'Neal wants at least 180 enrolled for the course. R.O.T.C. this year will be quite different from that of last year. After it is well organized, there will be a battalion parade once a week. It will not be strictly drill every, but broken by frequent rest eriods, and group army games and mass formations. During Tuesday and Wednesday, A. Rosenberg, a representative of Saul-Frank Military Supply Company in San Antonio, Texas, was here measuring cadets for uniforms. This year the school is handling the uniforms, which are stocked in the supply room. Cadets may get them when necessary, no down payment, no C.O.D. to pay, and no long waiting for uniforms.

---

MONDAY, SEPT. 5, 1938

## HAROLD O'NEAL IS COMMANDANT

### He will Be in Charge of Cadets at Kilgore Junior College

First Lieut. Harold O'Neal, 9th infantry reserves of Tyler, has been appointed commandant of cadets at Kilgore Junior College and High school, according to an announcement.

Lieutenant O'Neal has already moved his family to Kilgore in preparation for assumption of his duties there about the middle of this month.

He succeeds Capt. William F. Cox, who has left Kilgore for California.

The new commandant recently returned from third army maneuvers at Camp Bullis, near San Antonio, where he spent three weeks of intensive military training. He also was in training there in June.

Since 1934 he has been engaged in military work of different kinds, being first commandant of cadets at Amarillo High school, and later commanding officer of several CCC camps in various parts of Texas.

During his last period at Camp Bullis, he was honored with a staff position with his battalion headquarters.

He is a member of the Tyler Reserve Officers association.

# Kilgore's R. O. T. C. Units Count More Than 120 Boys

By MACK ROBERTSON

"Sir. I need five buttons."

"Lieutenant, sir, may I get some practice targets?"

"Lieutenant, sir, I need two buttons."

"Lieutenant, sir . . ."

All day it goes on this way in the office of Lt. Harold L. O'Neal, commandant of the R.O.T.C. units at Kilgore High School and Kilgore Junior College.

Officially, the lieutenant signs his name Harold L. O'Neal, 1st. Lt. 9th Inf. RAA, Commandant of Cadets—which he vouches is the proper way to do it.

Recently he has moved his office to larger quarters in the basement of the Campus Ward wing of the high school, right next door to the unit's indoor target practice rang. The office looks something like those temporary army headquarters you see in the movies, including bare, unfinished walls, uncovered steel framework in the ceiling, and unpainted wooden steps leading from the basement to the outside.

But the room is large and provides a place where the boys can come around in the afternoon and talk things over among themselves and with the commandant. A little work, as Lt. O'Neal pointed out, will stop the water from seeping in, and in time the R.O.T.C. headquarters should be one of the most interesting places on the campus.

The High School unit has 120 members organized into three companies, each of which meets one hour a day. Lt. O'Neal is not satisfied with this enrollment and hopes to build it up to at least 180 for the second semester. As it stands, none is a full company, strictly speaking, a full company having at least 80 cadets.

Right now the boys are not drilling, but are receiving classroom instruction. Their calendar shows they will take to the field again the first of next semester.

The year's work has been divided into ten courses—drill and command, military courtesy and discipline, physical training, extended order drill, hygiene and first aid, map reading, conventional signs, musketry, scouting and patroling, and interior guard duty.

The college course is more advanced, and includes very little or no field work. Only 20 are enrolled, but since the unit works in the classroom, small enrollment is no problem. The college unit has only one officer. He is Cadet 2nd. Lt. Earl Calk, senior officer.

At the High School, each company has a staff of at least two officers, and there is a general staff for the unit.

Unit staff officers are Cadet Major Wylie Oliver, Cadet Capt. Ardis Sanford, Cadet Capt. Bobby Gory, and Cadet 2nd. Lt. Charles Boyd.

Company A officers are Cadet 2nd. Lt. Norman Hurst and Cadet 2nd. Lt. Billy Davis.

Company B officers are Cadet Capt. Carl Cooper, Cadet 2nd. Lt. Alonza Robbins, Cadet 2nd. Lt. Warren White, and Cadet 2nd. Lt. Hampton Cook.

Officers for Company C are Cadet 2nd. Lt. Moultree Coker, and Cadet 2nd. Lt. Bradley Knox.



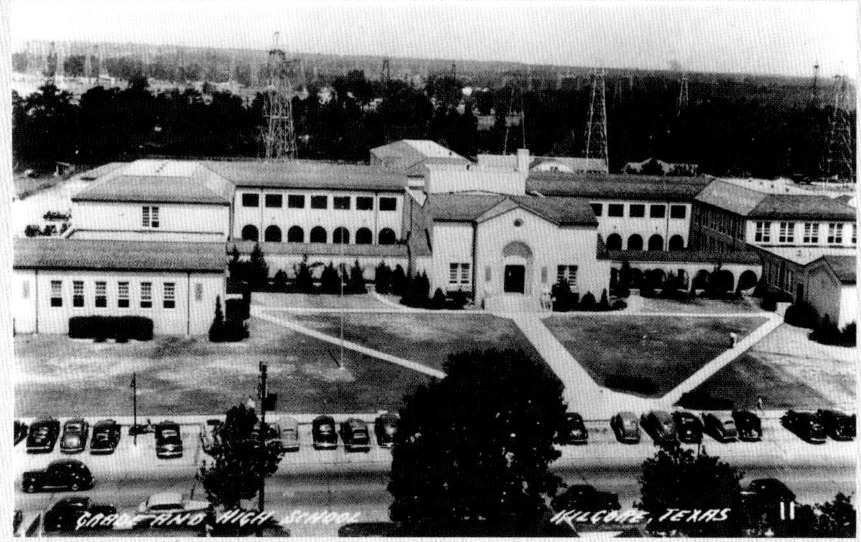


# MILITARY UNIT HERE WILL HOLD DRILL CONTEST

The Kilgore High School Military Training Department, under the direction of 1st. Lieut. Harold L. O'Neal, 9th Inf. RAA, Commandmant of Cadets, will present its first military competition at Kilgore Athletic Stadium Friday night at 7:30 o'clock, it was announced today by school officials. The public is invited to attend.

The competition will be presented in four divisions, the first of which will be the parade phase. In charge of this will be Cadet Major Wylie Oliver and

See DRILL CONTEST Page 8

ic Lodges (Harold joined the Danville Lodge), a dozen well-built churches that ranged from every Protestant denomination imaginable to Roman Catholic, some with producing wells on their grounds, and even a small synagogue. There were multiple banks, one of which had to move when oil was discovered underneath its lobby; road houses like Mattie's Ballroom on US 80 and Edna Matthews's Plantation Club on the Kilgore—Longview Highway, the Kilgore Boomers, who played their days away at Driller Park and won the 1939 East Texas League championship, and so much more, including municipal services that would rival a considerably larger city.

When *Gone With the Wind* premiered at the Crim Theater in early 1940, the owner of the theater, Liggett Crim, costumed people who appeared to have been transplanted from the days of Tara and the Civil War, decorated the theater with Spanish moss, and organized wonderful spectacles at the theater. Crim was one of the foremost citizens on Kilgore, not only deeply active in the oil business—the first well in Kilgore proper had come in in his mother's front yard—but a major philanthropist who enjoyed a good party. Later, in the fall of that year, when MGM released *Boom Town* staring Clark Gable and Spencer Tracy, Crim once again decorated the theater with elaborate graphic displays. Many residents of Kilgore saw a reflection of their own city in parts of this very successful motion picture.

By 1940 Kilgore was also the home of Gussie Nell Davis who, with the financial assistance of Mr. Crim, was in the process of creating the first and most famous college-level precision drill team in the United States, the Kilgore Rangerettes. On a different kind of playing field with eighty-eight black-and-white keys, a six-year-old Van Cliburn was being drilled just as hard as the Rangerettes by his piano-teaching mother, and was already on his way to becoming the most famous American-born classical pianist of the twentieth century.

Harold and Sarah would remain in Kilgore for three years, until Harold was called to active duty in September 1941. But this didn't mean they quite settled in. They had at least three different addresses: a post office box, 1209 Brook Drive, and what is described in a scrapbook as the "ROTC Camp." The post office box address was still in use for army purposes long after Harold left Kilgore, but the years in Kilgore were the longest they'd ever spent in one place. This was typical of army life and the life they would continue to lead until 1954.

It was still not time to consider moving into or even building a cottage that resembled those that filled pages in Sarah's scrapbook, but when the Kilgore school board assured Harold that they wanted him not only to maintain but grow the ROTC program, Sarah began to feel optimistic about a stable future. She had accumulated dishes, appliances, silverware, furniture, and other household items and was eager to assemble them in one location. She was also enthusiastic about improving their living conditions and, with that stability, possibly expanding the family as well.

**1939**

All throughout 1939 while he was developing the ROTC program at the high school, Harold was also watching events unfold in Europe and the Far East. There was much talk of war, particularly in Europe. As a military officer he knew that if things got out of control he might be called to active duty. When Germany invaded Poland on September 1, despite the promises of politicians and the strength of the isolationists, the war clouds darkened, and possibility of war involving the United States became more of a reality.

It is unclear how the prospect of war affected Harold and Sarah, but Sarah became pregnant in September. Was this because the couple felt sufficiently secure in his position at Kilgore High School to begin a family? Harold had, after all, just been asked not only to guide all the ROTC cadets, but to become the official adviser for all the boys in the school.

Or was it because if there was war, and Harold was called to active duty and sent to Europe, he felt it might be nice to know that he had a child waiting when he returned, or who might live on if he didn't? These possibilities may have been discussed in private, but never with me in later years. There was probably little

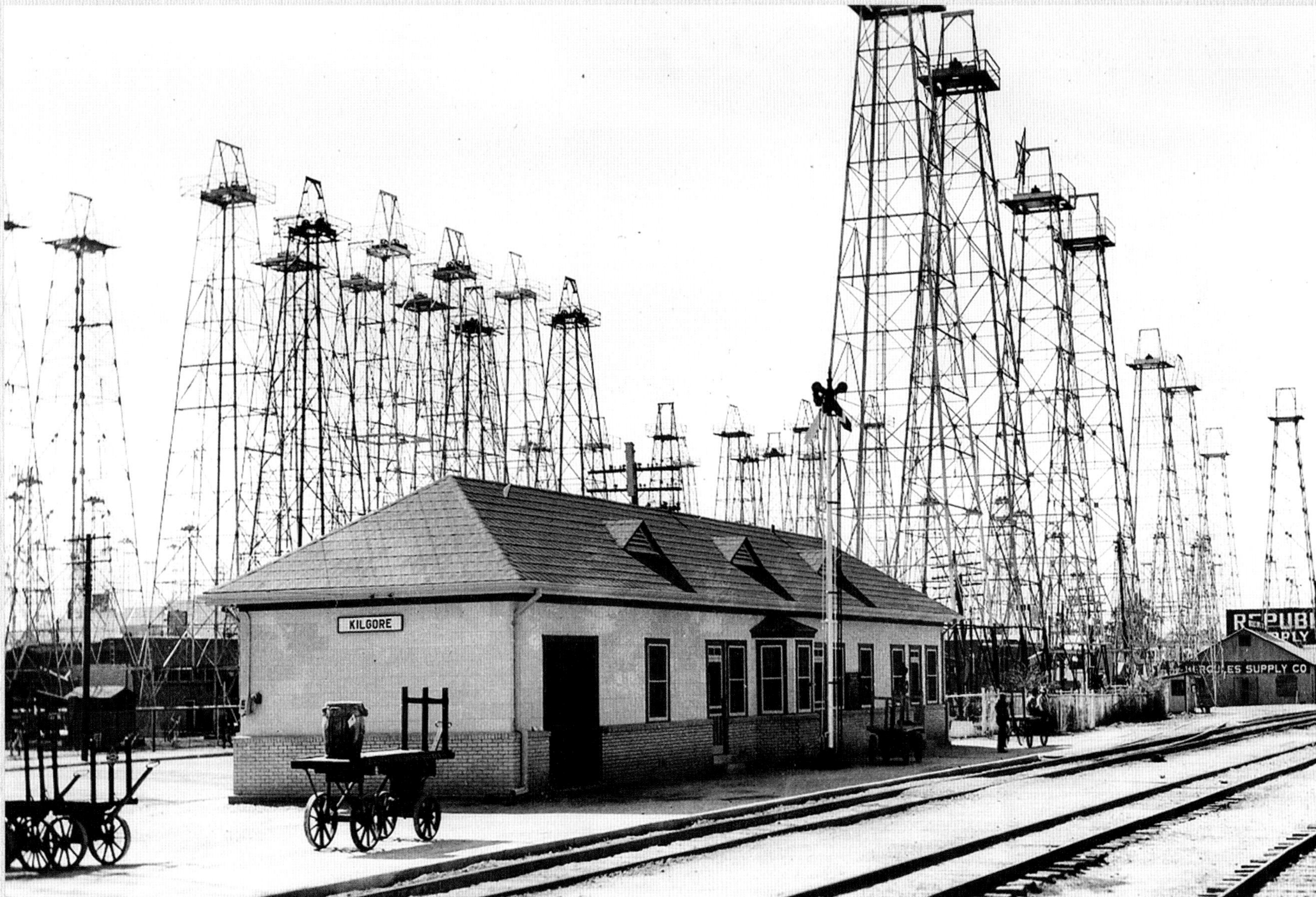
KILGORE
SUPPLY CO

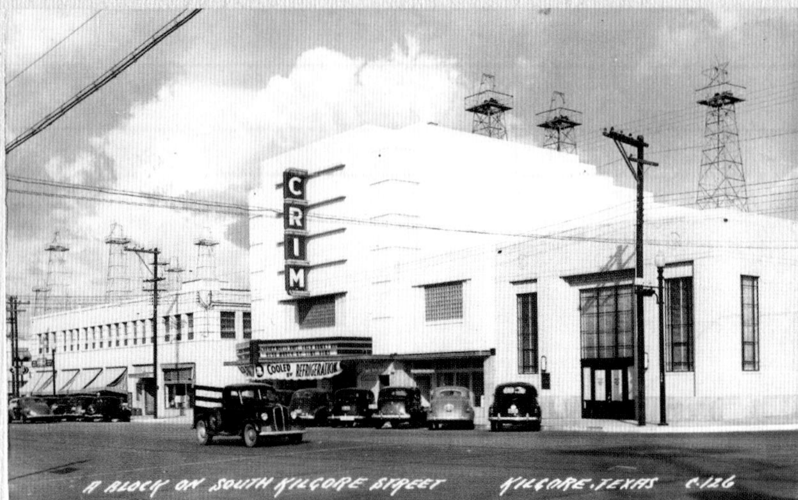
CRIM
A BLOCK ON SOUTH KILGORE STREET
KILGORE, TEXAS
C-126

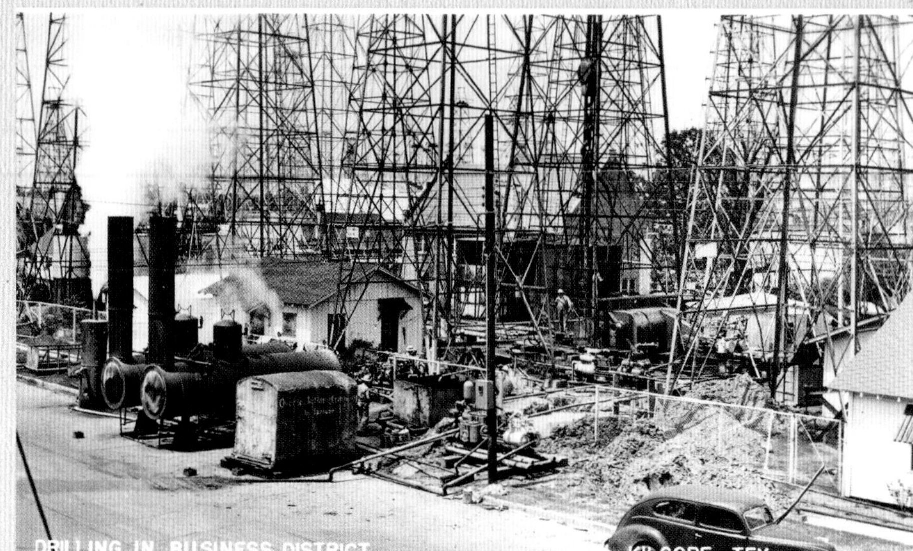
DRILLING IN BUSINESS DISTRICT

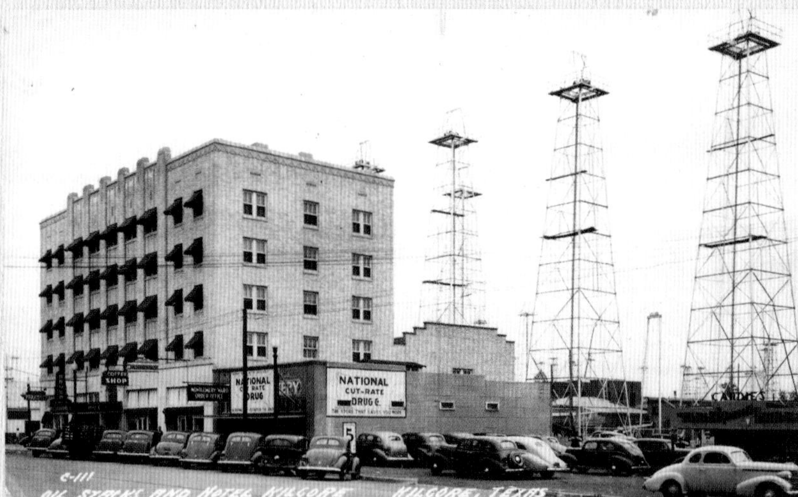
NATIONAL
CUT-RATE
DRUG
C-111
OIL STACKS AND HOTEL KILGORE
KILGORE, TEXAS

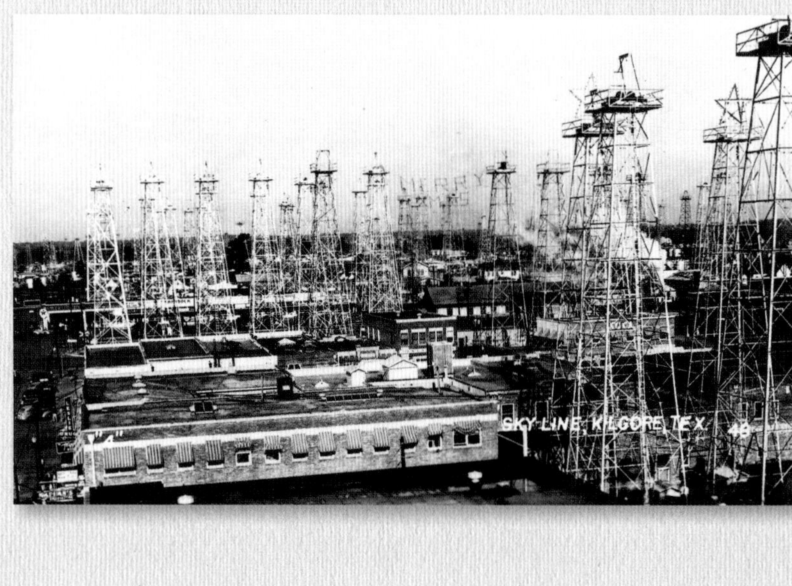
SKY LINE, KILGORE, TEX.
48

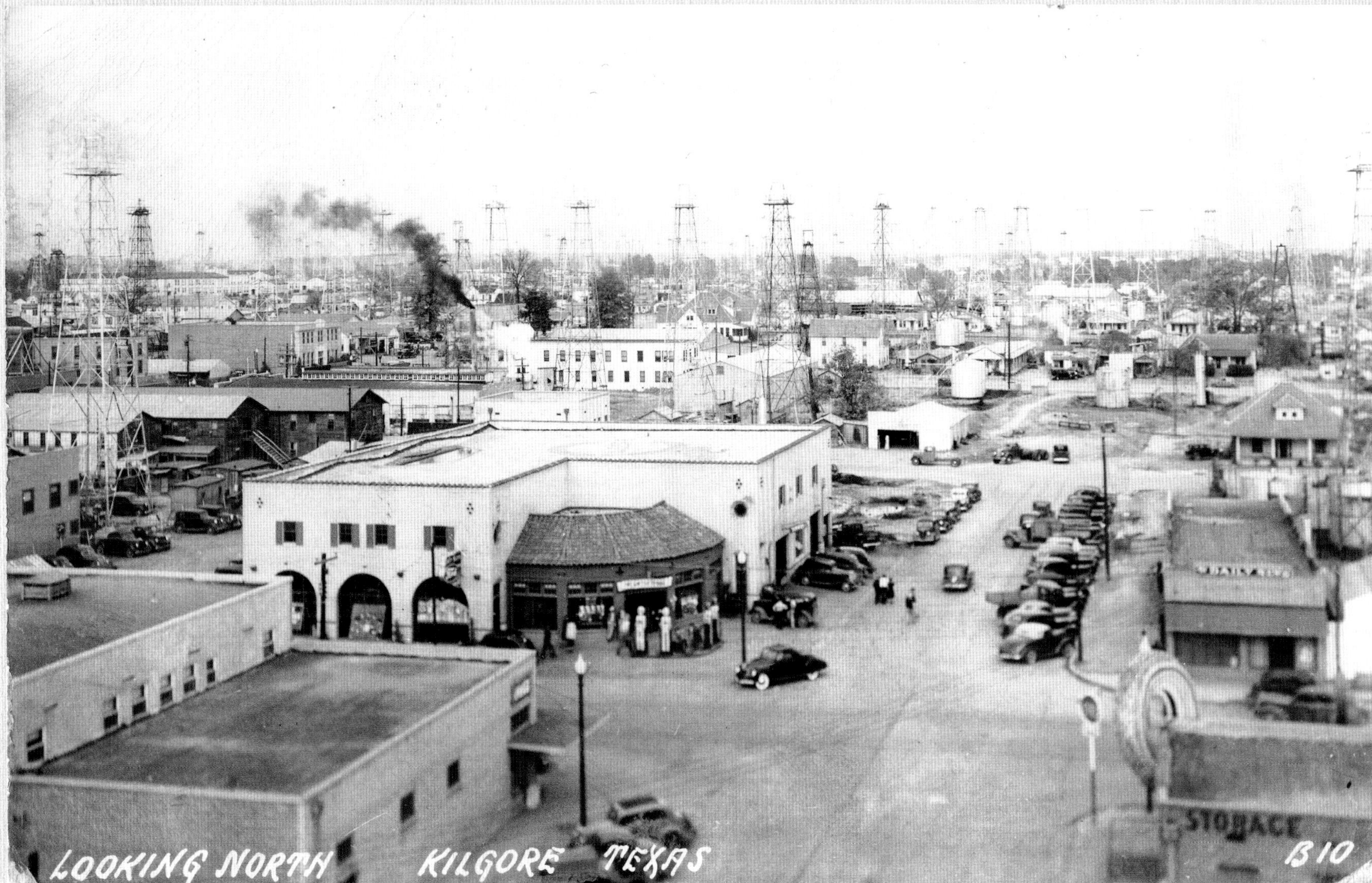
STORAGE
LOOKING NORTH KILGORE TEXAS
B10

thought given to Japanese aggression in the Far East. The headlines in the paper had to do with Europe, and they were only half right.

Kilgore High School was not a typical high school in 1938, not in Texas or perhaps anywhere else, and as Harold began his new assignment he found himself being interviewed by the editor of *The Mirror*, the school's in-house, student-managed newspaper. The newspaper had launched with the opening of the new school in 1935, and the first issue of Vol. 4 appeared on October 14. The front-page headline announced:

***Revised ROTC Program Is Introduced This Year***

***Enrollment Now At 115, Goal is 180***

*Lieutenant Harold L. O'Neal is the new head of the R.O.T.C. unit in Kilgore this year. The subjects to be studied by the unit are military courtesy and discipline, drill and command, extended order drill, map reading and conventional signs, scouting and patrolling, interior guard duty, musketry and military sanitation, hygiene, and first aid.*

*At Present there are 115 enrollees for R.O.T.C., but Lt. O'Neal wants at least 180 enrolled for the course. R.O.T.C. will be quite different from that of last year. After it is well organized there will be a battalion parade once a week. It will not be strictly drill every* [word missing], *but broken by frequent rest periods and group army games and mass formations. During Tuesday and Wednesday, A. Rosenberg, a representative of Saul-Frank Military Supply Company in San Antonio, Texas, was here measuring cadets for uniforms. This year the school is handling the uniforms, which are stocked in the supply room. Cadets may get them when necessary, no down payment, no C.O.D. to pay and no long waiting for uniforms.*

The program grew throughout 1939 and into 1940. Toward the end of 1939, as Sarah was becoming increasingly pregnant, Harold bought a better, more reliable car to transport his wife: a black Chrysler four-door sedan. Little did he know the car would be waiting for him when he returned from Japan, and he'd keep it for another seven years.

## ROTC Units Feted With Gala Dance

Complimenting the R. O. T. C. of the Kilgore High School, John T. Crim, Jr., entertained with a gala military ball at the Meadowbrook Country club Friday evening following the R. O. T. C. Drill competition in the Kilgore Athletic Stadium.

The club foyer was appointed with pennants on the wall and a clever Ferdinand the Bull scene arranged on a table at the entrance.

Receiving the guests were Mr. and Mrs. John T. Crim, Sr., Mrs. Crim lovely in a turquoise blue starched chiffon with purple accessories, Lt. and Mrs. Harold L. O'Neal, Mr. and Mrs. C. L. Newsome, and John T. Crim, Jr.

Music for dancing was furnished by Raymond Rhone and his orchestra from Tyler.

The club room was gaily decorated with red, white and blue balloons in the patriotic motif, repeated with American flags crossed over the lighting fixtures on the walls.

The R. O. T. C. colors were arranged on either side of the fireplace. Pennants and sabers marked other points of interest throughout the club rooms.

Twin refreshment tables were laid at either end of the club lounge with lace covers and centered with crystal punch bowls banked in summer blossoms.

Lounge tables held fragrant arrangements of Queen Anne's lace, roses, pink and blue cornflowers, and sweetpeas.

About three hundred guests, friends of the host from the sophomore, junior and senior classes of the high school, and the Kilgore College, formed the guest list.

## Kilgore Military Unit Is Praised By Army Colonel

Kilgore High School's trimly-uniformed R. O. T. C. unit passed in review before a United States Army colonel yesterday and heard that official warmly praise their division as "one of the best of its type I've seen."

In the reviewing stand as the cadets turned out were Colonel E. A. Keys, civilian components division, 8th Corps Area, U. S. A.; Lieutenant Harold L. O'Neal, 9th Infantry, R. A. A.; C. L. Newsome, high school principal; W. L. Dodson, school superintendent; and the Reverend Cecil Lang, pastor of the Presbyterian Church.

Col. Keys praised the school cadet system for both its concededly good influence on the development of youthful characters and its importance from the standpoint of national defense. He saw little to criticise in his review of the troops, although he did offer a few constructive suggestions to Lieutenant O'Neal.

"I think you have a very good unit," he told the Lieutenant. "You've done wonders when it is taken into account that you have had to work under some very unfavorable conditions and have been handicapped by lack of equipment. Your group is only one and one-half years old, but it is already making progress. You have the material for an A-1 unit."

## ROTC Unit Makes Step in Progress On Study Courses

A large step in progress has been taken by the Reserve Officers Training Corps of Kilgore College. Instead of the old "pavement pounding" unit, the organization has become a body of "book worms" in fine style. The college unit's aim is to become acquainted with the technical knowledege of a potential officer in the United States Army. The class has finished a course in extended order drill and is now dealing with personal hygiene, camp sanitation, and first aid. These courses will be finished in the near future. This type of instruction was introduced by Lt. O'Neal, the present commandant of the unit. His aim is to build a larger unit and with the present number enrolled only a technical

See ROTC, Page 3

The Editor's WASTEBASKET

**1940**

In the late spring of 1940, that year's edition of *The Reflector*, the high school yearbook, was released. It is a charming book, one in which a boy named Talmadge and a girl named Camie Dell were King and Queen. It was the first time Harold had been featured in a yearbook since the 1931 edition of *La Airosa* in Amarillo, and in this case he was over-featured, with so many pictures he probably got static from other instructors.

Harold's 1939-1940 ROTC program is pictured and described over nine pages. Perhaps the most interesting is one that shows the entire company on the grounds of the school with forty-one oil wells in the background, but another series of photographs under the heading *Summer Encampment* are far more charming and describe and picture an America that would soon be lost forever.

*Lucky boys who are members of the R.O.T.C find time each summer to take part in two weeks of life under the open skies. Living in tents, eating from army mess kits food prepared by an army mess sergeant, taking midnight hikes, shooting on the rifle ranges, and playing, provide so much to do that the days slip by too rapidly. Plans are underway to make a movie of this year's camp to show to the student body next fall.*

This idyllic description is followed by a picture of Harold, wearing nothing but a bathing suit, with a baseball bat in hand, ready to take a swing at anything thrown in his direction. It is captioned: *Smuck O'Neal demonstrates that old army stance for the boys as he prepares to get his pistol eye into good shape by socking the indoor ball at least fifty feet.*

Then, a few weeks later, Harold and Sarah's life was turned upside down when I arrived suddenly, during the 1940 Summer Encampment.

***OFFICIAL CAMP BULLETIN***

***Vol. I, No. 5 ******* June 6, 1940***

*General Harold L. O'Neal, Jr. made his appearance into this world yesterday afternoon at 3:18 o'clock at the Kilgore Memorial Hospital. He weighs eight pounds, two and a half ounces, and according to reliable sources, is a "chip off the old block." Mrs. O'Neal and the child are doing fine. According to Dr. Downs, he hasn't lost a father yet, so predicts that Lt. O'Neal will recover. Congratulations Lt. and Mrs. O'Neal.*

*****************

*Onions to Mr. Smith who cleaned up the headquarters in the absence of Lt. O'Neal.*

There was a modest announcement in the Tyler newspaper, but the notice in the *Kilgore News Herald* was much more fun. Under two owls and the words *Here's The Answer*, the headline read Soft Drinks followed by:

*THAT MAN YOU saw standing on the street corner last night babbling loudly in an unintelligible tongue was not a member of some new religious cult. He was Lt. Harold L. O'Neal, letting the world know he is the father of a son.*

*Harold L. O'Neal, Jr. was born yesterday afternoon at 3:21 at a local clinic. He weighed eight pounds, two and a half ounces. We wish we could describe the reception the R.O.T.C boys gave their commandant on his return to camp last night. The best we can do is give you the entry in the camp's journal of events.*

*"June 5, 1940, 5 o'clock: Cadets here at R.O.T.C summer encampment lined up and upon the arrival of Commandant Harold L. O'Neal fired six salutes with the cannon, celebrating the birth of his son, General Harold L. O'Neal, Jr. After the celebration, Lt. O'Neal treated all cadets to soft drinks.*

It was an exciting day for all concerned, but as the day wore on it became even more exciting in an unexpected way, and some of the ROTC students may have found out about what transpired later, but it wasn't common knowledge, though perhaps it should have been.

On the day of my birth, earlier in the day, Sarah's sister, Martha, had been married to her long-time sweetheart and musical companion/accompanist, Roy T. Will. It was just a coincidence that it took place on the day I was born. The wedding had been planned for many months.

The couple was looking forward to a brief honeymoon trip but were not scheduled to leave until the next day and had planned to spend the night in a hotel in Tyler. Hoping to make things easier for

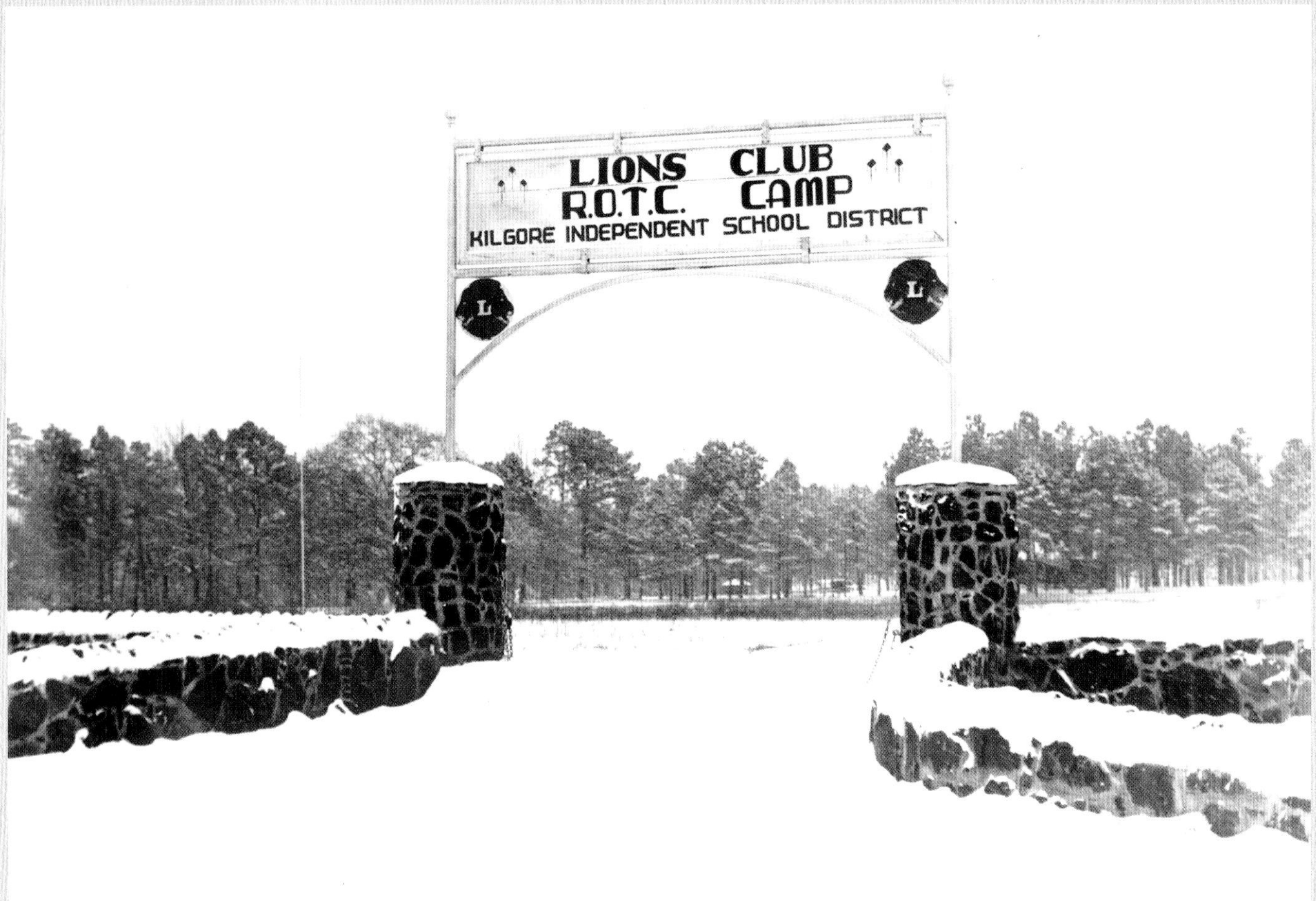


Entrance to summer camp in winter

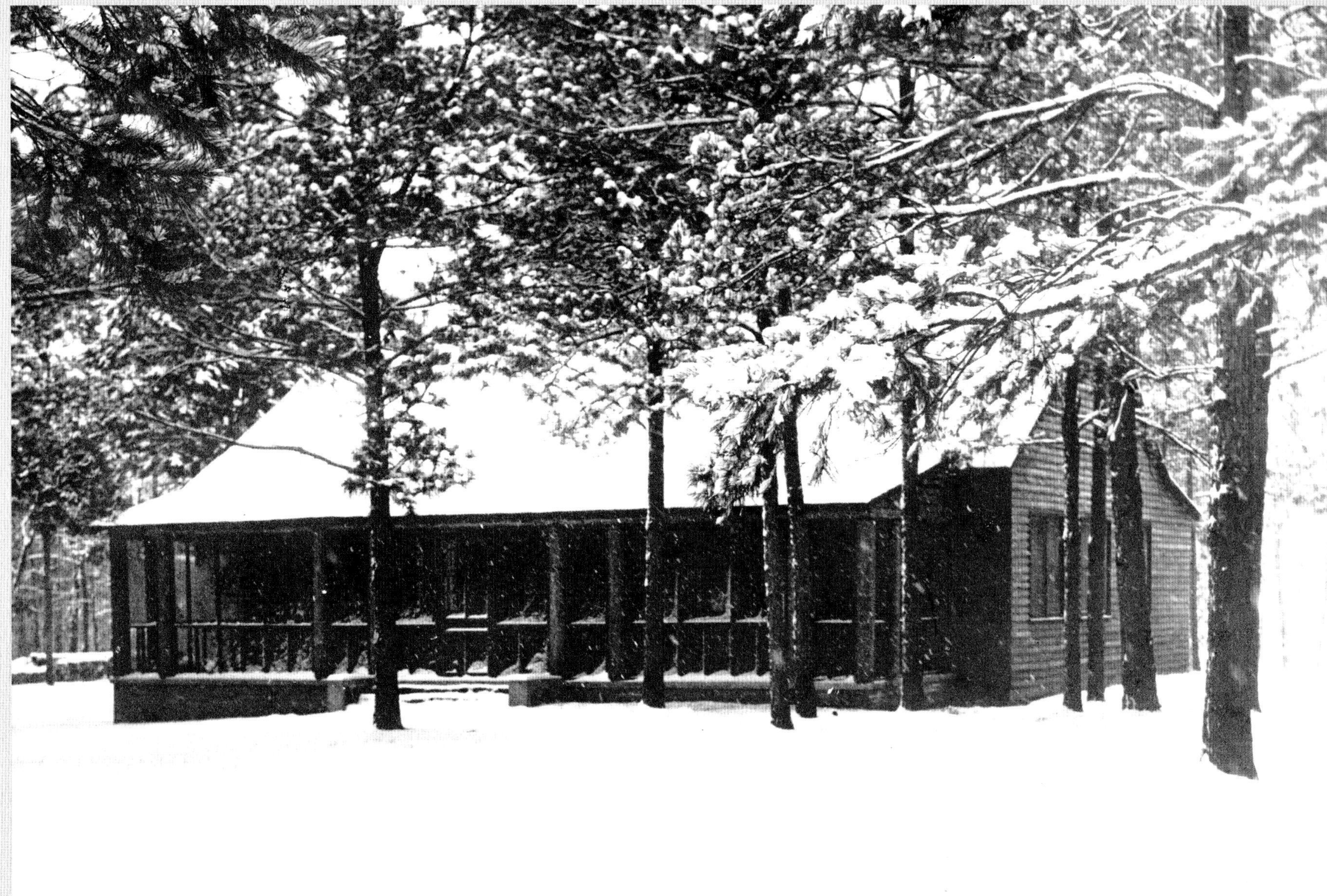

Encampment cabin in the winter

**Lieut. and Mrs. Harold O'Neal** will leave for their home in Kilgore today after a visit here with Mrs. O'Neal's parents, Mr. and Mrs. C. A. Christian. Lieutenant O'Neal has just returned from Fort Sam Houston, where he has been doing active duty training as a reserve officer. He is going to Kilgore to resume his duties as commandant of the Kilgore Junior college and Kilgore High school.

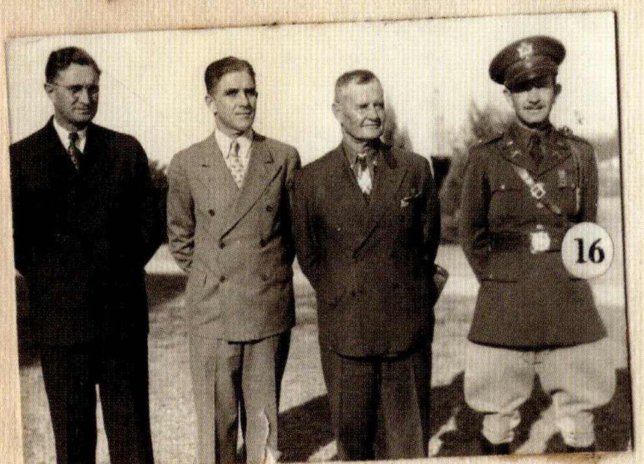


Kilgore, 1940

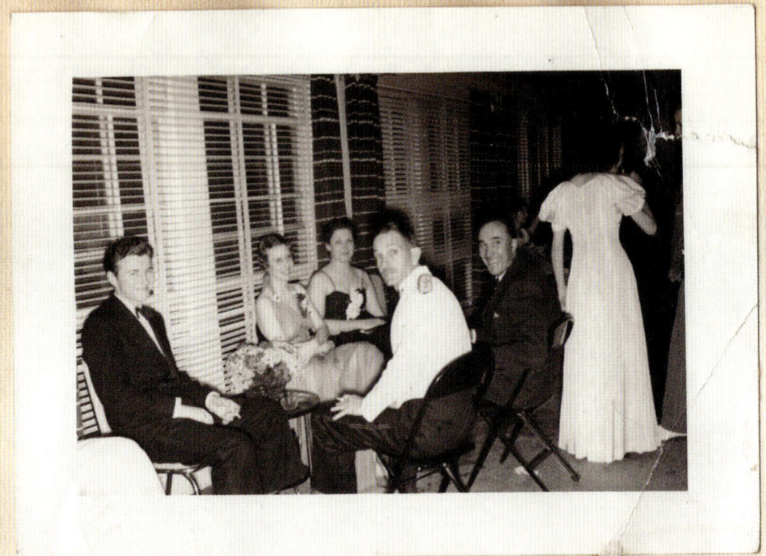

Kilgore, 1940
Military Ball, Country Club

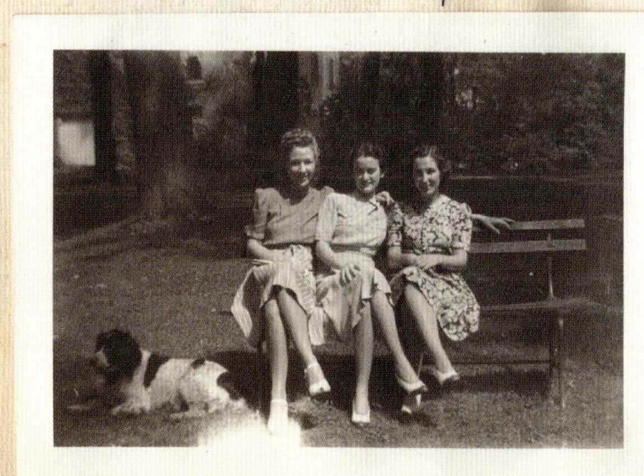

New York – 1939

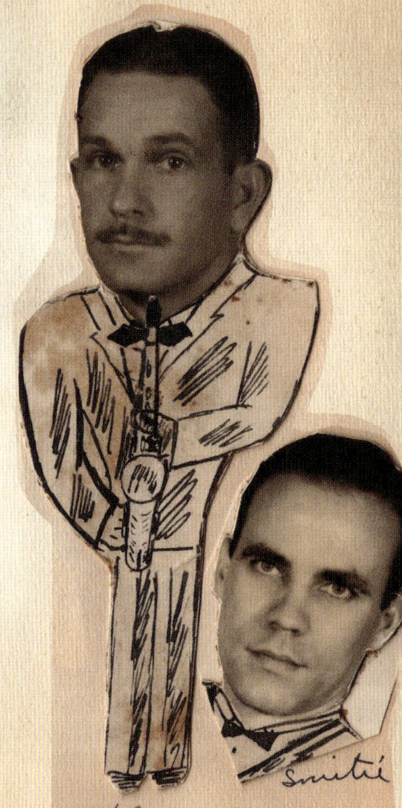


Kilgore 1938

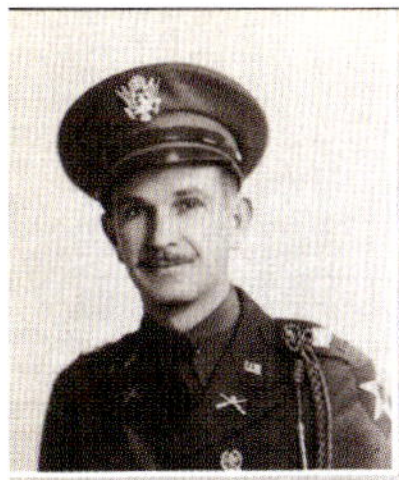

# R. O. T. C.

1st Lt. Harold L. O'Neal

COLORS

Sgts. Collum, Morehead, Pruett, and Hamilton.

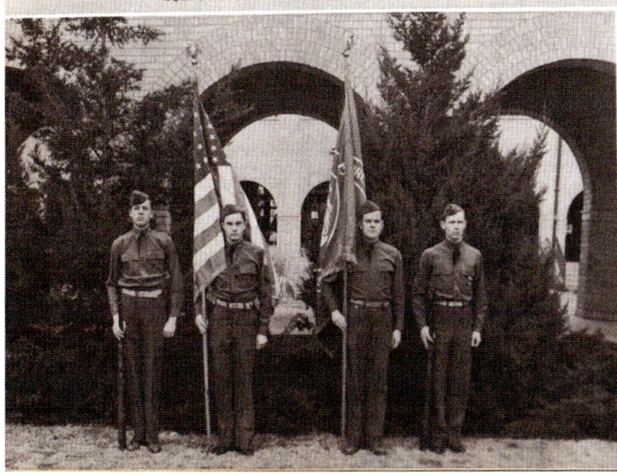

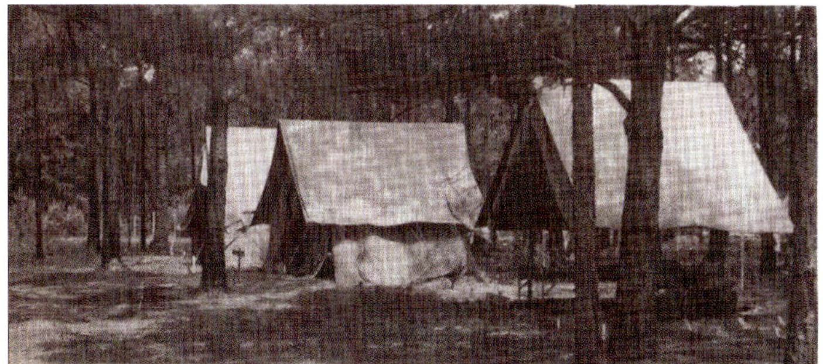

**Lucky boys** who are members of the R. O. T. C. find time each summer to take part in two weeks of life under the open skies. Living in tents, eating from army mess kits food prepared by an army mess sergeant, taking midnight hikes, shooting on the rifle ranges, and playing, provide so much to do that the days slip by far too rapidly. Plans are underway to make a movie of this year's camp to show to the student body next fall.

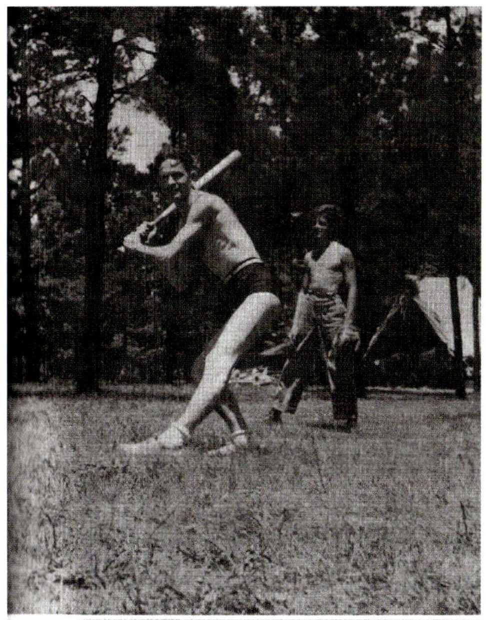

**Smuck O'Neal** demonstrates that old army stance for the boys as he prepares to get his pistol eye into good shape by socking the indoor ball at least fifty feet.

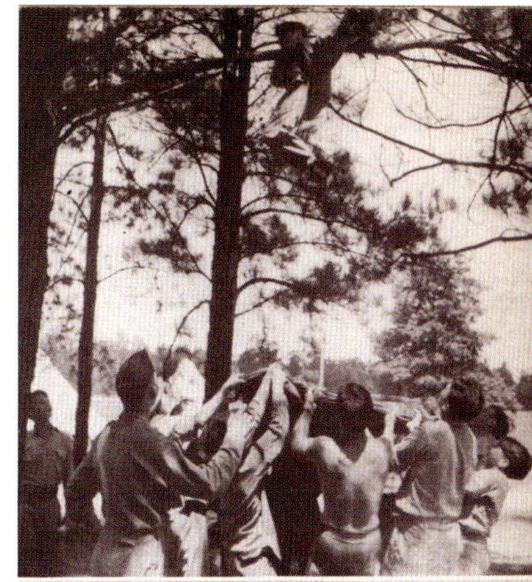

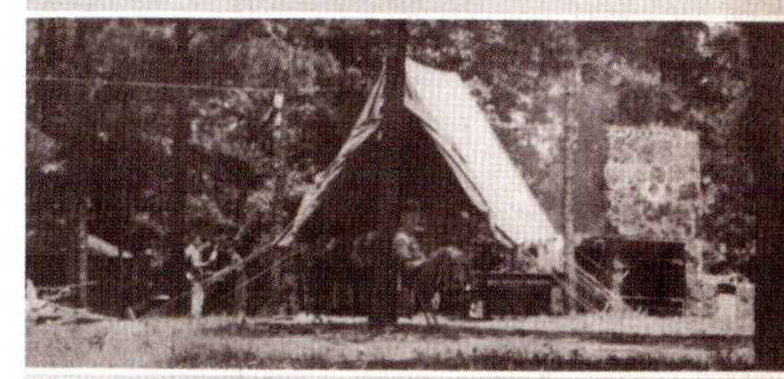

**Dillahunty** rides again (above) as the boys use a blanket to boost Buddy high enough to catch an overhanging limb. K. P. Daniels (below) would like to join the fun but must conserve his strength for potato peeling.

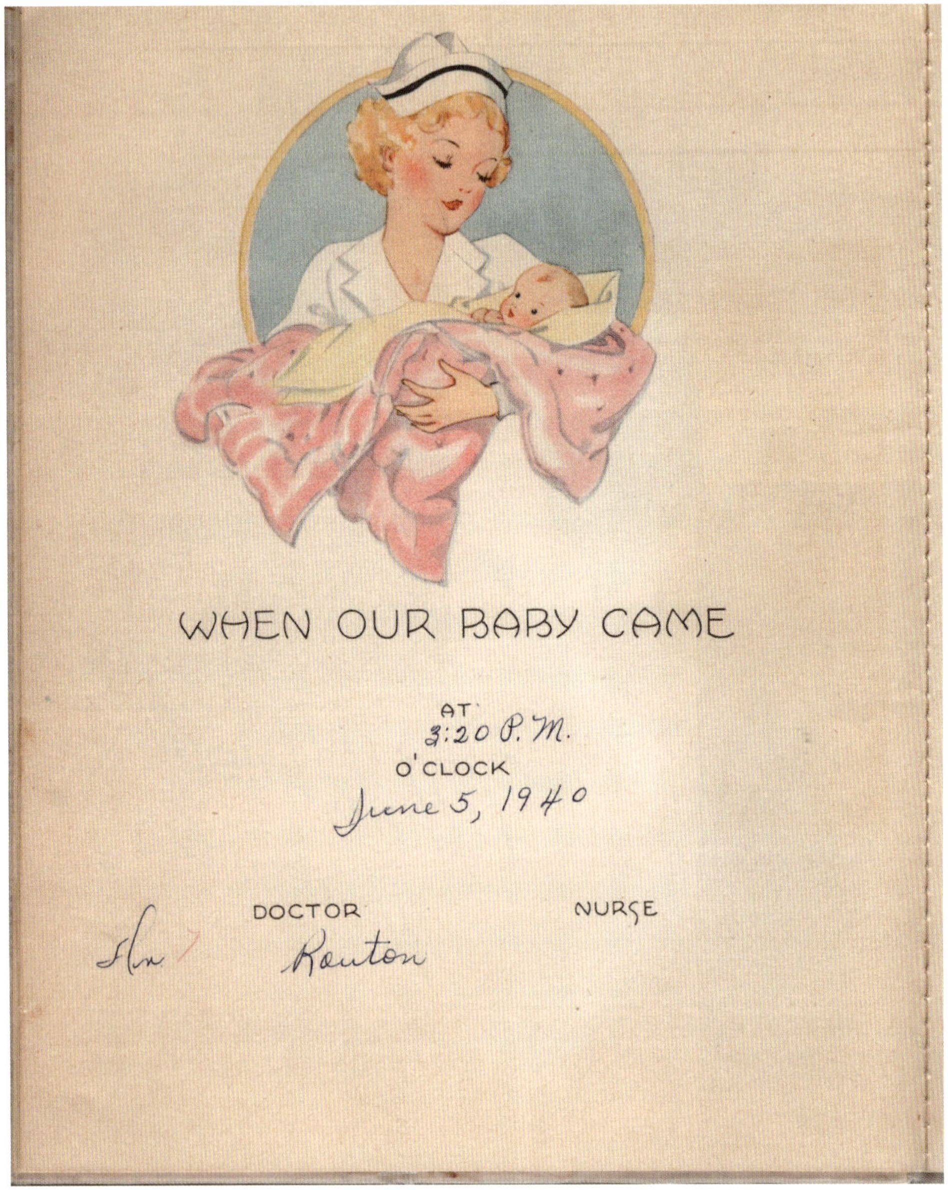

WHEN OUR BABY CAME

AT
3:20 P.M.
O'CLOCK
June 5, 1940

DOCTOR
Rauton

NURSE

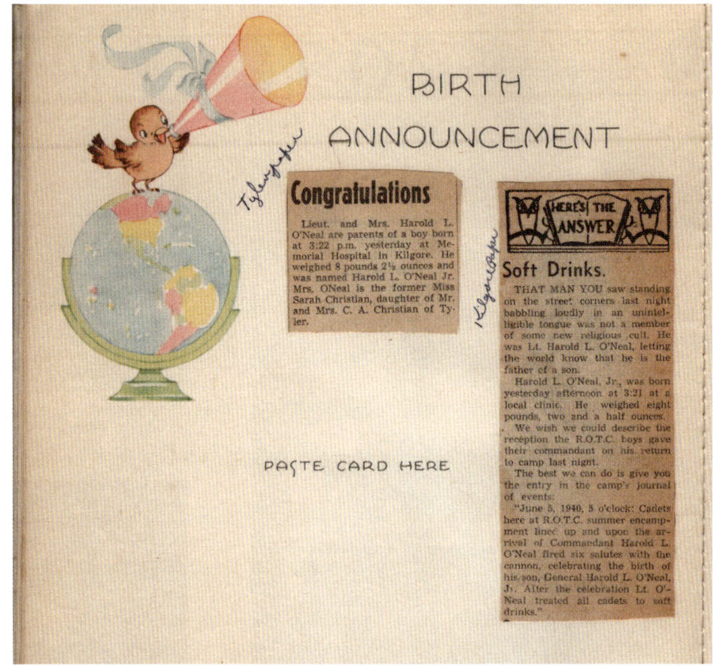

BIRTH
ANNOUNCEMENT

PASTE CARD HERE

Tyler paper

**Congratulations**

Lieut. and Mrs. Harold L. O'Neal are parents of a boy born at 3:22 p.m. yesterday at Memorial Hospital in Kilgore. He weighed 8 pounds 2½ ounces and was named Harold L. O'Neal Jr. Mrs. ONeal is the former Miss Sarah Christian, daughter of Mr. and Mrs. C. A. Christian of Tyler.

Kilgore Paper

HERE'S THE ANSWER

**Soft Drinks.**

THAT MAN YOU saw standing on the street corners last night babbling loudly in an unintelligible tongue was not a member of some new religious cult. He was Lt. Harold L. O'Neal, letting the world know that he is the father of a son.

Harold L. O'Neal, Jr., was born yesterday afternoon at 3:21 at a local clinic. He weighed eight pounds, two and a half ounces.

We wish we could describe the reception the R.O.T.C. boys gave their commandant on his return to camp last night.

The best we can do is give you the entry in the camp's journal of events:

"June 5, 1940, 5 o'clock: Cadets here at R.O.T.C. summer encampment lined up and upon the arrival of Commandant Harold L. O'Neal fired six salutes with the cannon, celebrating the birth of his son, General Harold L. O'Neal, Jr. After the celebration Lt. O'Neal treated all cadets to soft drinks."

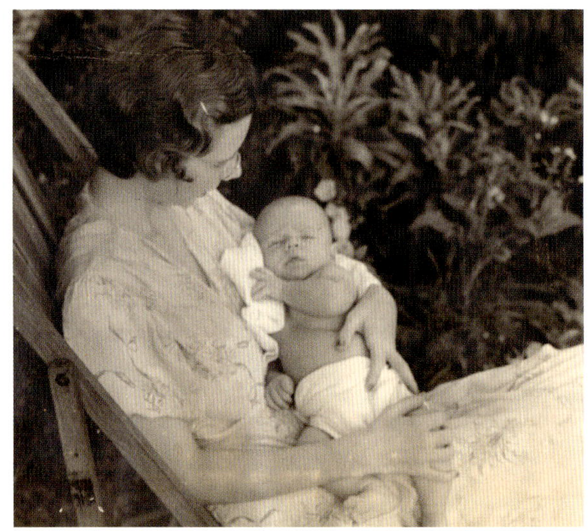

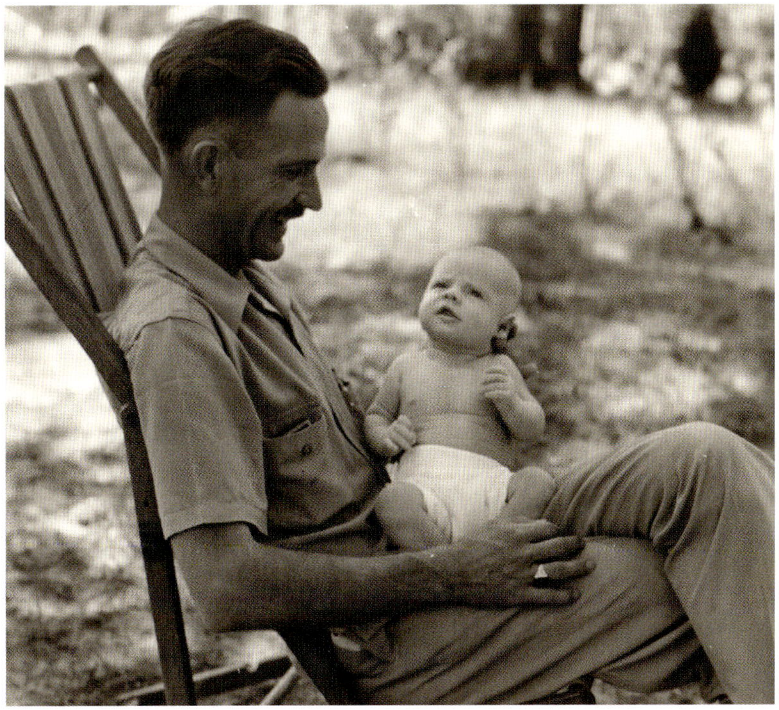

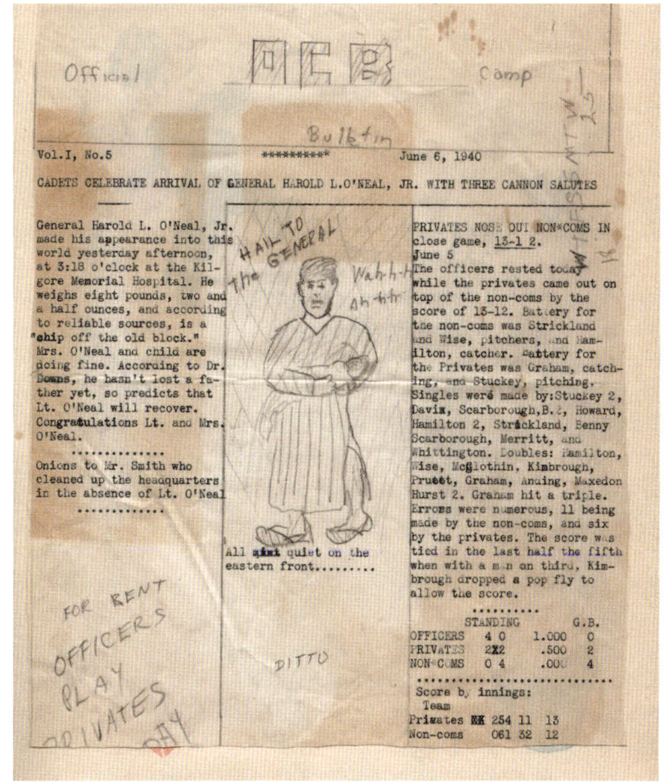

Official OCB Camp Bulletin

Vol.I, No.5 ********** June 6, 1940

CADETS CELEBRATE ARRIVAL OF GENERAL HAROLD L.O'NEAL, JR. WITH THREE CANNON SALUTES

General Harold L. O'Neal, Jr. made his appearance into this world yesterday afternoon, at 3:18 o'clock at the Kilgore Memorial Hospital. He weighs eight pounds, two and a half ounces, and according to reliable sources, is a "chip off the old block." Mrs. O'Neal and child are doing fine. According to Dr. Downs, he hasn't lost a father yet, so predicts that Lt. O'Neal will recover. Congratulations Lt. and Mrs. O'Neal.

...............

Onions to Mr. Smith who cleaned up the headquarters in the absence of Lt. O'Neal

.............



All quiet on the eastern front.........

DITTO

PRIVATES NOSE OUT NON-COMS IN close game, 13-12.

June 5

The officers rested today while the privates came out on top of the non-coms by the score of 13-12. Battery for the non-coms was Strickland and Wise, pitchers, and Hamilton, catcher. Battery for the Privates was Graham, catching, and Stuckey, pitching. Singles were made by: Stuckey 2, Davis, Scarborough, B. 2, Howard, Hamilton 2, Strickland, Benny Scarborough, Merritt, and Whittington. Doubles: Hamilton, Wise, McGlothin, Kimbrough, Pruett, Graham, Anding, Maxedon Hurst 2. Graham hit a triple. Errors were numerous, 11 being made by the non-coms, and six by the privates. The score was tied in the last half the fifth when with a man on third, Kimbrough dropped a pop fly to allow the score.

...........

| | STANDING | | G.B. |
|---|---|---|---|
| OFFICERS | 4 0 | 1.000 | 0 |
| PRIVATES | 2 2 | .500 | 2 |
| NON-COMS | 0 4 | .000 | 4 |

.............................

Score by innings:

| Team | | | |
|---|---|---|---|
| Privates | 254 | 11 | 13 |
| Non-coms | 061 | 32 | 12 |

FOR RENT

OFFICERS PLAY PRIVATES DAY

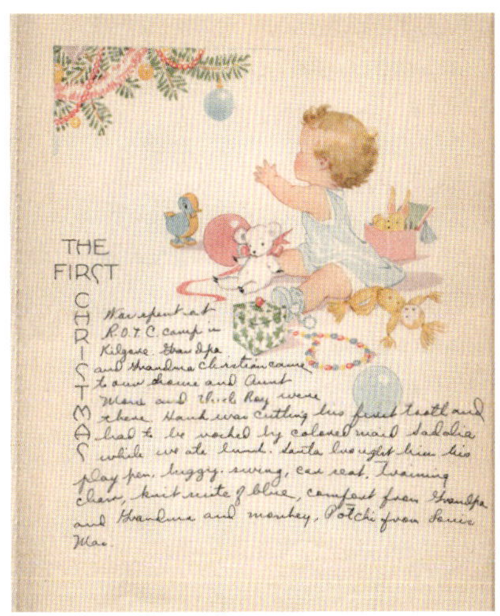

Martha and Roy, Harold suggested they spend their wedding night in his cabin at the summer encampment, and he'd find lodging elsewhere. Martha and Roy thought that was a fine idea, and they could save a few dollars in the process.

The ROTC students knew nothing of this arrangement. Later that night, possibly under the influence of something a bit more stimulating than soda pop, some of the cadets thought it would be fun to give Harold another salute. They dragged their cannon to his cabin, quietly positioned it outside the bedroom window and fired off a single round. This was not the kind of bang with which Martha and the super-sensitive Roy expected to begin their marriage. They jumped out of bed with the explosion and nothing was ever quite the same. They each had very successful careers in music and four children, but married one another twice and divorced twice as well. I don't know if this can be traced back to the cannon outside their bedroom window but it couldn't have helped.

The *Summer Encampment* ended about the same time as General O'Neal was arriving from the hospital to begin his life in a cabin on the ROTC camp on Stone Road. There were a dozen photographs in the yearbook that showed the camp and the young men who populated it for two weeks each year. Unhappily, there would not be many more of these carefree summer outings. Even the yearbook that was issued the following spring had an ominous tone. The Foreword read:

*These are indeed troubled times. Storm clouds of world-wide strife are beginning to gather on our own horizon. When school takes up again in the fall, some of our teachers will be absent, called for duty in the great national defense program. Few will be the families not represented in some phase of military service.*

*In the midst of the forebodings and preparations for almost inevitable conflict, we take time out to present this little book and its story of the happenings in Kilgore High School during the past year. We have tried to make this publication democratic in every page, editing and presenting it without the evils of dictatorship – a thing that could happen only in the United States of America.*

Further along in the yearbook is a description of ROTC duties that was subliminally ominous in 1941. The tip-off was the reference to .30 caliber rounds. Over twenty years later, when I was undergoing university-level ROTC training, we were still using rifles that fired .22 caliber rounds at targets that had a Necco wafer as a bull's eye. That Harold managed to get the larger rounds for his cadets indicates he understood where the world was headed. The entry read:

*The Reserve Officer Training Corps probably affects more students than any other organization on campus. Since its inception in 1938, the Corps has grown by leaps and bounds. It is the only unit in the Eighth Corps Area which fires the regulation .30 caliber round, most schools being limited to the .22 caliber. The purpose of*

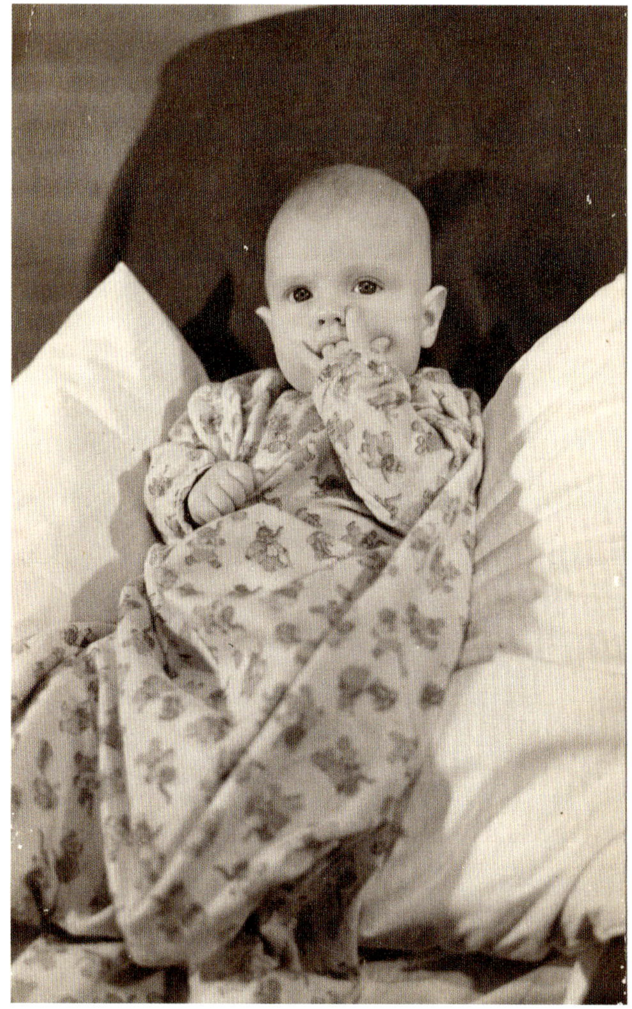

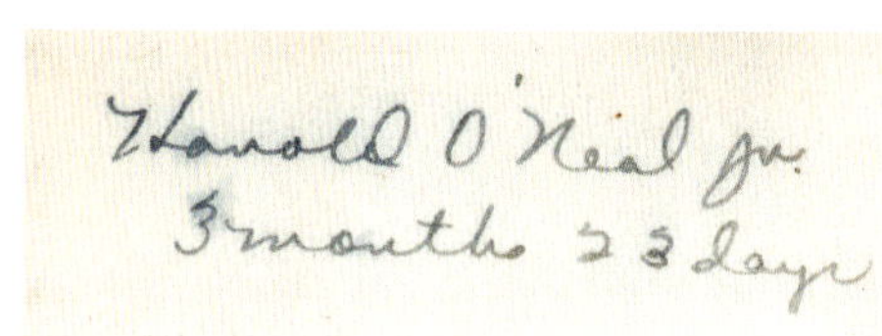

*the R.O.T.C. is often misrepresented. It is not primarily to furnish boys to the United States Army. A boy who enlists in the armed forces after having this training must begin at the bottom with the buck privates who never before saw a uniform. He does, however, have the advantage of having learned something about the cleaning and care of a rifle, marksmanship, drill, map reading, sanitation, and discipline that will enable him to seek advancement more rapidly than the less fortunate companion. Membership in the Corps is strictly voluntary and these boys are in it because that is what they desire.*

Clearly, the young men and women creating the yearbook for their classmates recognized what was going on in the world far more clearly than did many politicians who had their heads in the sand and those who supported the rabble-rousing groups like the America First Committee. What the editorial committee didn't realize was that one of the first men to be called up from their school would be Harold, but that was months away.

**1941**

The years 1940 and 1941 in Kilgore were exciting, a perfect time to work or be born in this East Texas city. The oil boom had subsided, the crazy parts of which might have been perfectly exciting for books and movie scripts, but were kind of rough on ordinary folks if you were living through them, particularly if you didn't have a couple of producing wells in your backyard. Wells were still being drilled, but at a far more leisurely pace, and it had been months if not years since a well had exploded and burned down buildings near it or even, in one case, an entire city block.

This was a time for Kilgore to step back for a moment and enjoy the schools and pools and movies and commerce and culture and recreation and Rangerettes the oil boom of the previous decade had made possible. And though it would be short-lived for them personally, Harold and Sarah and General O'Neal were able to take advantage of peace and prosperity for a while.

When a babysitter or a nurse could be found, Harold and Sarah could take a drive in their new car to attend a party at the Meadowbrook Country Club, catch the premier of a movie at the Crim Theater, drive to Edna Matthews's Plantation Club on the Longview Highway and take a few turns around the dance floor, or even travel as far as Dallas to hear the symphony or a great soloist like Jascha Heifetz or Fritz Kreisler. Mattie's Ballroom was still functioning in 1941, and there were famous big bands on the bandstand. For more civilized surroundings, but still filled with music and dancing, Leggett Crim loved to hire big bands for his special parties. Harold and Sarah were invited to these soirées. This may have had something to do with various Crim children, including his namesake, being cadets in Harold's ROTC program.

For a few short months, much of what they had been working toward seemed to be coming true. Time passed into 1941 and soon it was June and the annual ROTC *Summer Encampment* was underway, but this time with a twist. Since General O'Neal's first birthday coincided with the encampment, there were special celebrations that were captured with a series of cheerful photographs. There are no details of how Harold, Sarah, and General O'Neal spent the summer, but it was probably an anxious time as the prospects of American involvement in the war in Europe became more and more likely. Their days in Kilgore were numbered. Harold was called to active duty in September and would soon find himself in Brownwood, Texas, training a new company for eventual deployment to the Pacific Theater.

Harold's active-duty military activity was not restricted to Camp Bowie and the 208th Military Police Company. He had been promoted to Captain, took his company on maneuvers in Louisiana, and traveled as far as Vicksburg, Mississippi, with a complement of various vehicles, armed and unarmed, practicing traffic control and military vehicular movement. The highways of East Texas and Louisiana and the Civil War battlefields were not what they would later experience in Bougainville and the Philippines, but it served as useful basic training. Even though I had been demoted to the rank of Honorary First Lieutenant, I was still not allowed to accompany Harold on the Louisiana maneuvers.

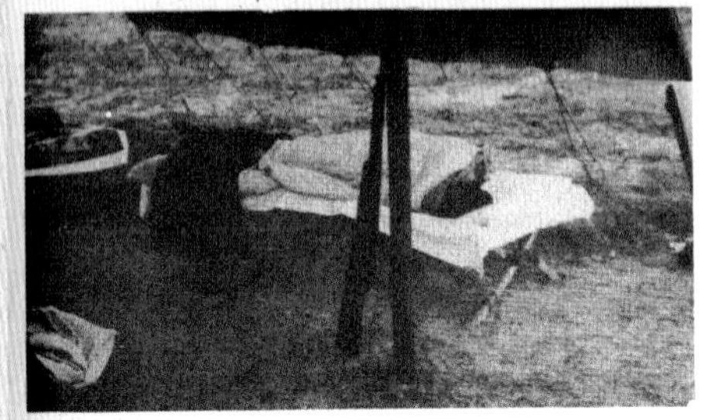

Even the sentry is asleep at 5:30 in the morning. Shoes and rifle are close at hand however and he will see that you sign the register before entering.

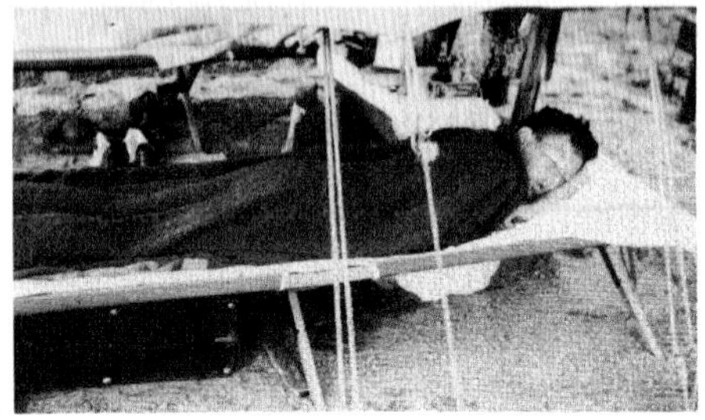

Captain Chandler gets that last forty winks before he has to leave his tent on Officer's Row. Each boy is responsible for cleanliness of his tent.

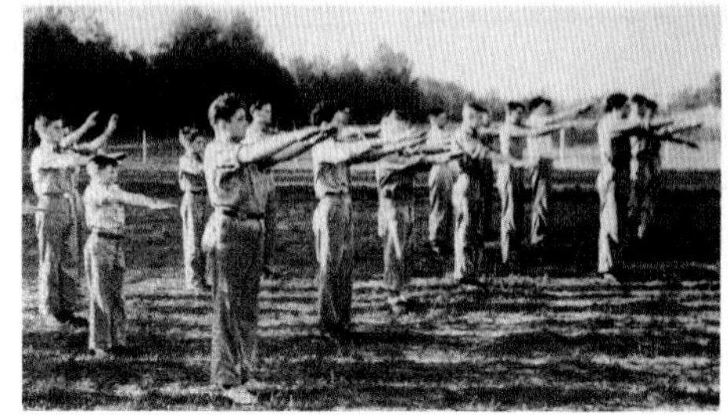

As the sun peeps over the tall pines, calisthenics serve to remove all vestiges of sleep and work up that appetite which comes with healthful living.

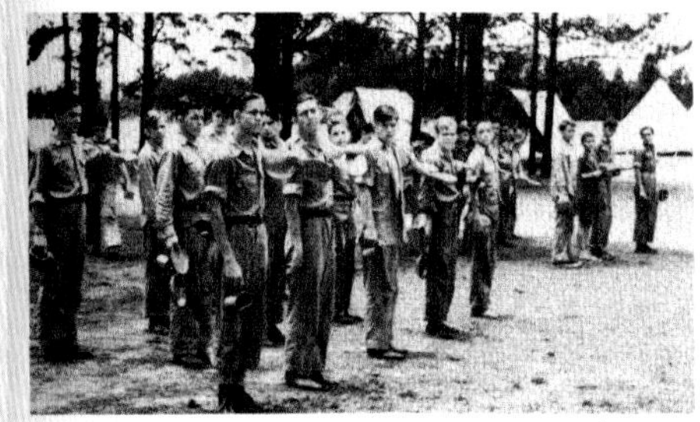

When the bugler blows "soupy," things begin to move fast. Here Companies A and B line up with all the tableware they will need to hold their food.

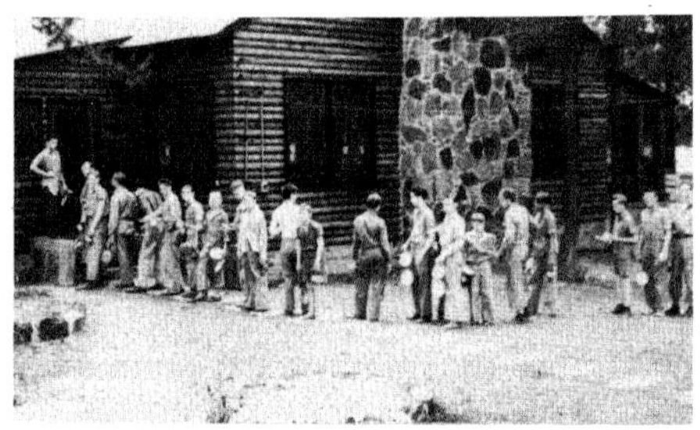

The line begins at the back door, except for visitors, who enter through the front portals. Parents and friends of the boys were present at nearly every meal.

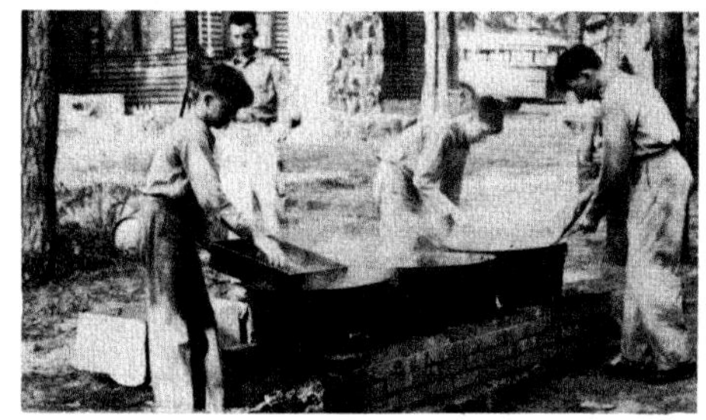

Captain Milam oversees the washing up of pans. Each boy must clean his own utensils, many of which bear souvenir marks obtained during the World War Number 1.

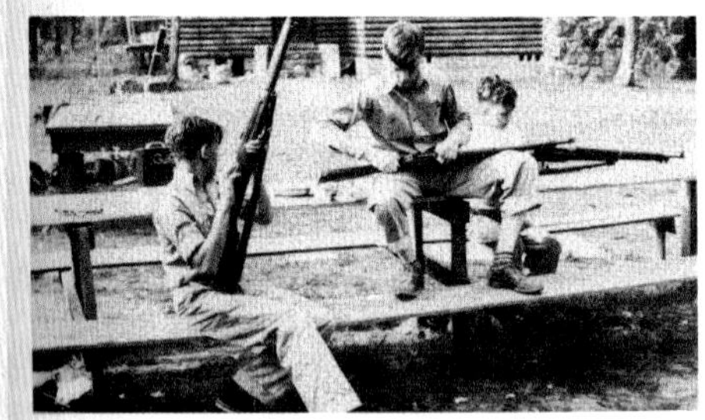

The rifle of each boy must pass inspection every day, so it is necessary to take time out after target practice to break down, clean, and reassemble the guns.

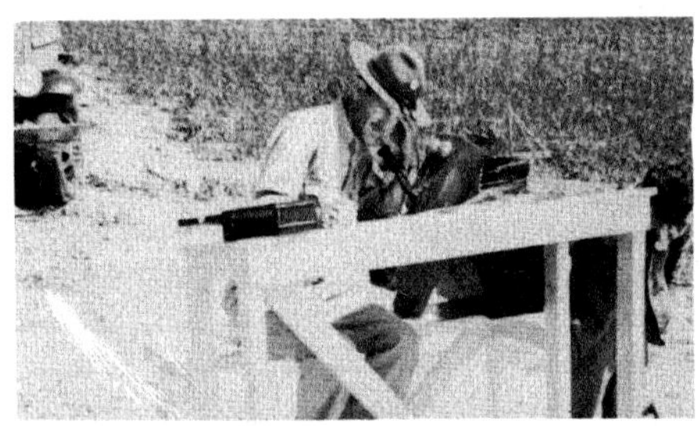

Telephones are used at the range to convey results from the pits. Ammunition is carefully checked by Lieut. O'Neal so there is absolutely no possibility of accidents.

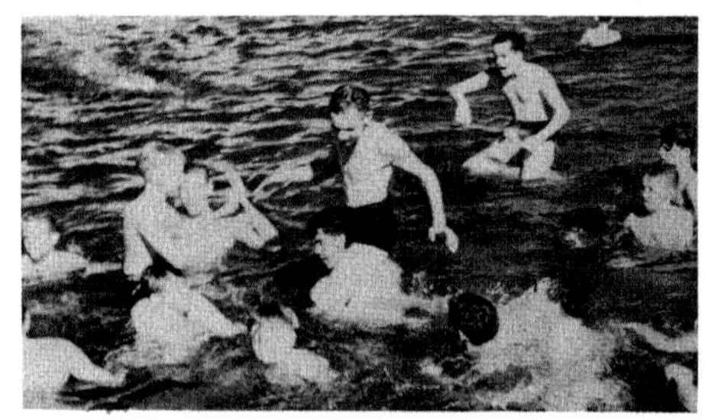

Time is taken out each day for a dip in the swimming pool and after a day full of activity, and still not ended, these boys enjoy indulging in a little horseplay.

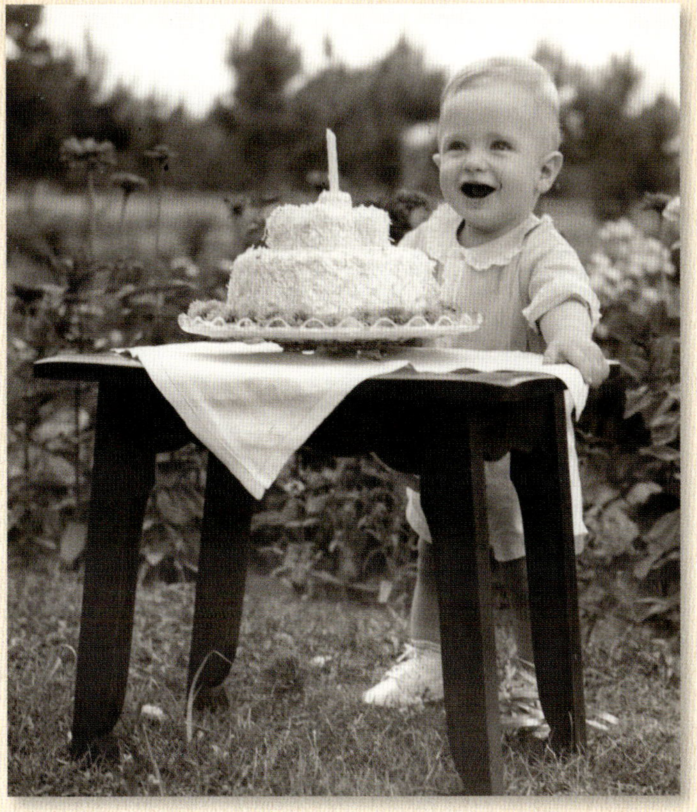

First birthday celebration
at summer encampment

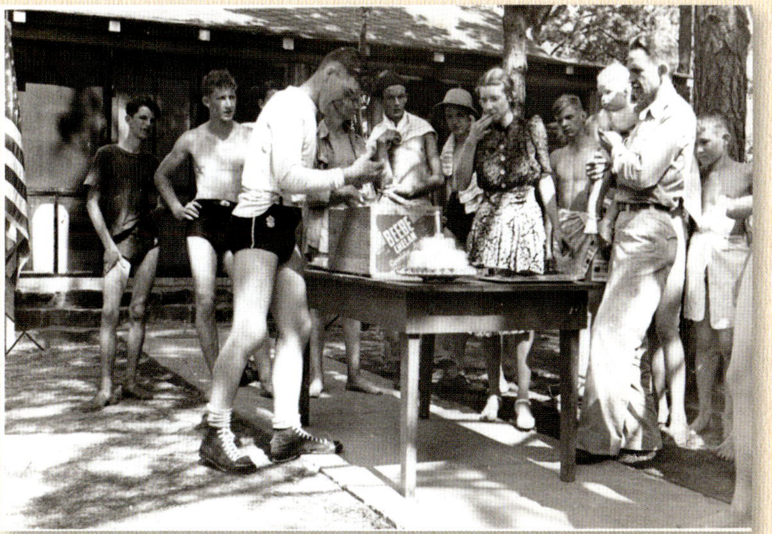

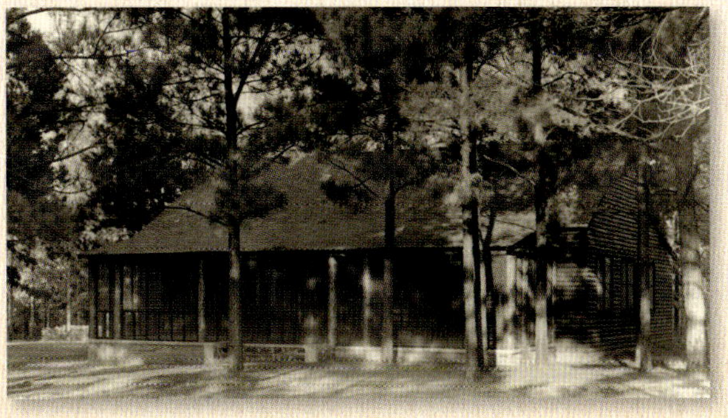

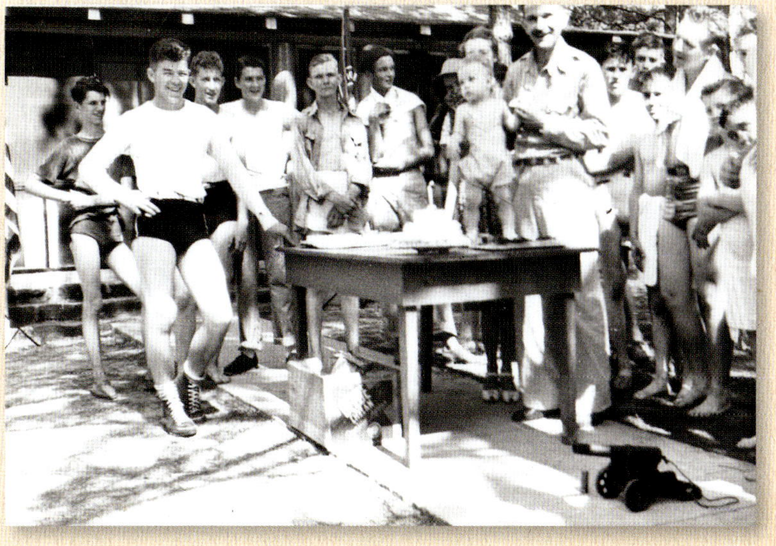

## Active duty, fall 1942

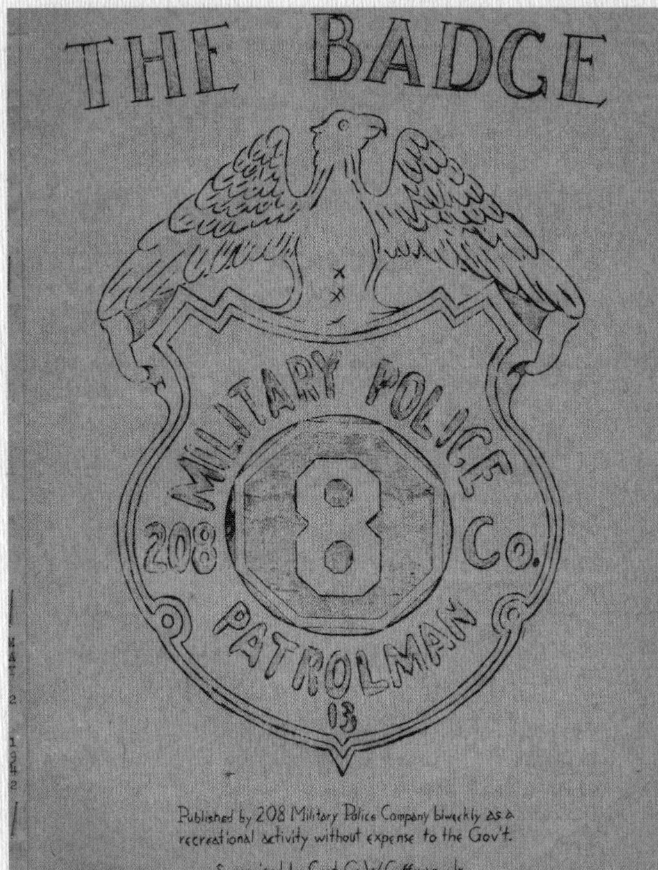


ALLAS MORNING NEV

***Promoted, Made Head Of Military Patrol***

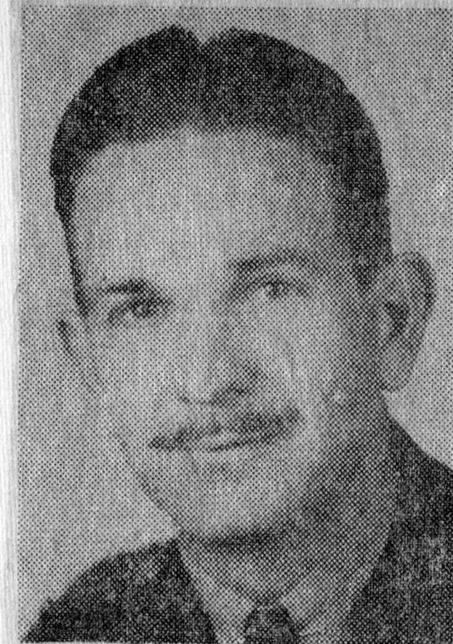

CAPT. HAROLD L. O'NEAL.

Promotion of Capt. Harold L. O'Neal and his assignment as assistant provost marshal of the VIII Army Corps has been announced by the War Department. O'Neal, graduate of old Bryan Street High School here and brother of R. J. O'Neal, 4710 Ross, will serve as ranking chief of the military patrol in the Texas and Louisiana maneuvers during August and September. He is headquartered at Mansfield, La. The patrol will police the entire area.

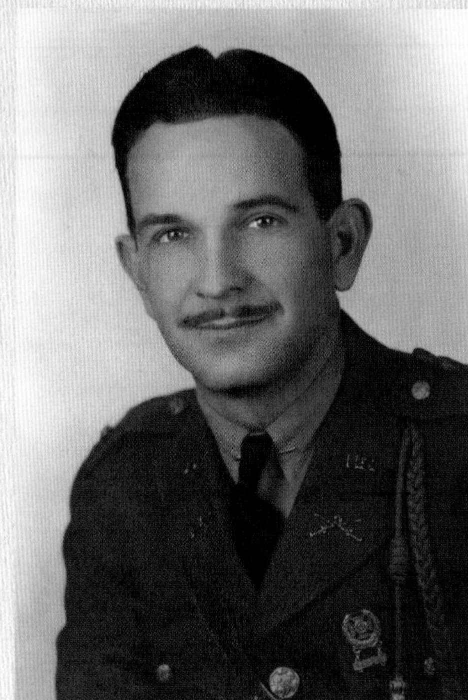

# The East Texas/Louisiana Maneuvers

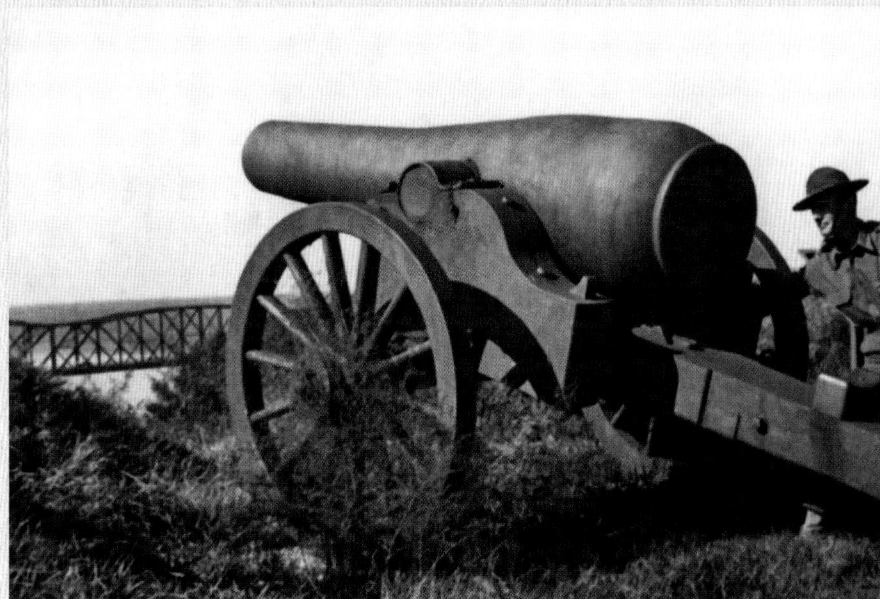

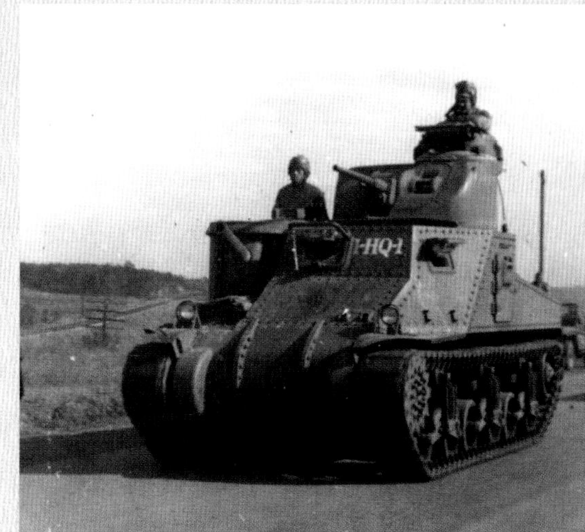

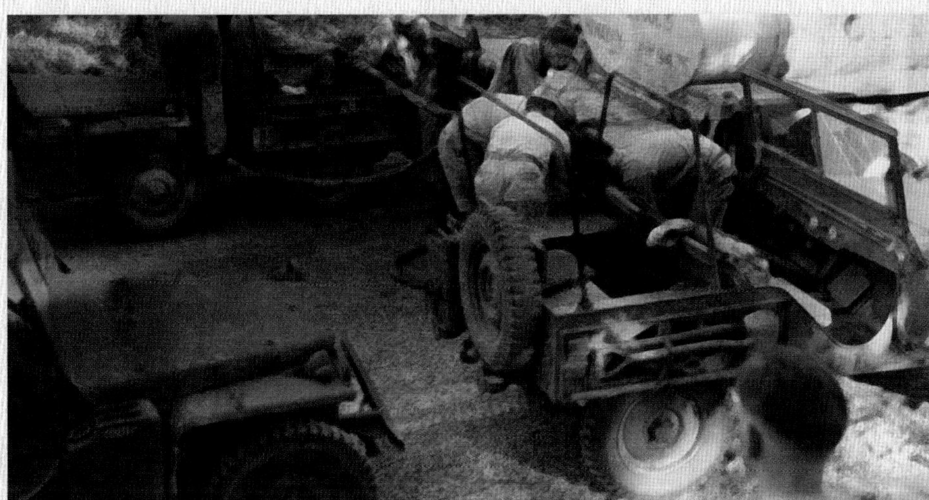

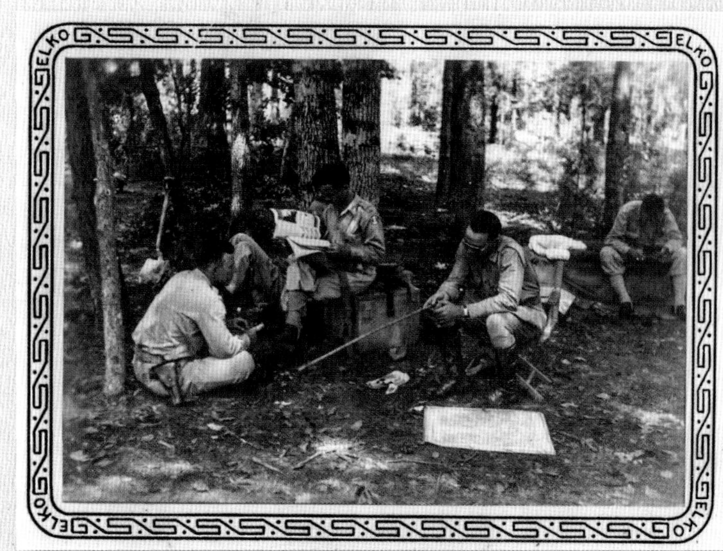

CIRCULATION

If your paper has not been received by 6:30 evenings or 7:30 a.m. Sunday, please call Western Union, No. 490, and request delivery.

# THE KILGORE NEWS HERALD

"PUBLISHED AT THE CAPITAL OF THE WORLD'S LARGEST OIL FIELD"

WEATHER

BY UNITED PRESS

EAST TEXAS: Fair Sunday and Monday; moderate to fresh southeast to south winds on the coast.

VOL. 11; NO. 210 EIGHTEEN PAGES KILGORE, TEXAS, SUNDAY, SEPTEMBER 7, 1941 UNITED PRESS PRICE 5c

# REPORT ON NAZIS STIRS SOUTH AMERICA

## GERMANS CHARGE GREER "ATTACKED FIRST"

### Kilgoround

MR. FLOYD WAGSTAFF, the high school football teacher, is no longer a very eligible bachelor He lost this status last August 29 at Houston when he was wedded to Miss Nell Renfrow, a very attractive reason for losing the rating. And now the Wagstaffs are at home on King Street. The bride hails from Corsicana.

**AND TAKE IT from Mr Wagstaff, Coach R. E. St. John is no longer the most eligible bachelor of the coaching department. Not since Mr. Harold (Nig) Neal joined up. Besides, says Wag, St. John has been around too long to claim such a title at the beginning of a school year. And just you wait, reports Wag, until the girls get a look at Nig Neal.**

THE GILLY DAVISES are back from a wedding trip which included a bit of sprawling on the beach in the sun along the Texas Gulf Coast and the Mexico Gulf Coast. They breezed in Friday night. They were married a week or so ago by Dr. Cecil H. Lang at Mineral Wells, you know. They were house hunting when last we saw them.

**PEOPLE AND THINGS: George Levinson, 716 Riverside Drive, reports that the Polish**

See KILGOROUND, Page 8

### HEART ATTACK PROVES FATAL

## *Big U. S.-Made Bombers Smash Reich Industries*

WAR GODS PEER DOWN

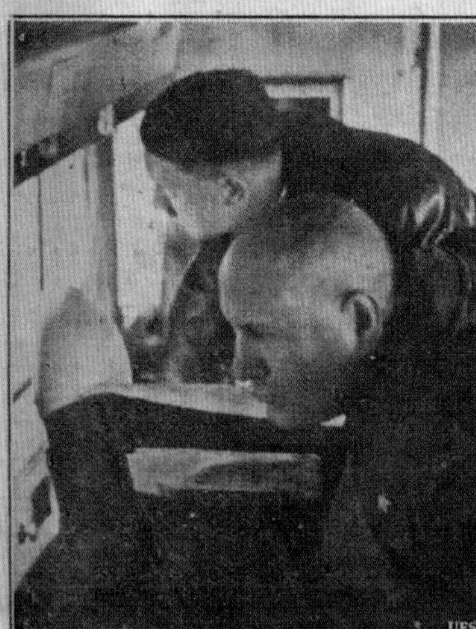

### Daylight Assaults Cause Damage Over Wide Area

LONDON, Sunday, Sept. 7 (UP)—Daylight assaults by American-built Flying Fortresses and Britain's new four-motor bombers have snarled German communications from Norway to France and heaped havoc on the heart of the Reich's war industries, the Air Ministry reported today.

A summary of the results of the stepped-up Royal Air Force offensive synchronized with Russia's stout resistance on the Eastern Front, came after a record-making attack by Flying Fortresses which sped nearly 500 miles across the North Sea Saturday morning and blasted shipping in Oslo harbor.

Oslo is 470 miles from the nearest point on the British coast and the press association said that it represents the longest flight so far undertaken by the huge American-built bombers serving in the RAF.

The Air Ministry said that the RAF's intensified attacks on shipping along the coasts of France, Belgium, Holland, Germany and Norway had become so destructive that business men were reluctant to send goods to Scandinavia by ships sailing from Dutch ports.

"And these business men complain that when they try alterna-

### FDR IS SEEKING "WAR INCIDENT" ASSERTS BERLIN

BY UNITED PRESS

The United States and Germany, brought to the verge of "shooting war," traded angry allegations and denials Saturday night in grave repercussions over the encounter between the U. S. destroyer Greer and a sea-roving Nazi submarine off Iceland on Thursday.

The German government said that the American warship was the aggressor and made the first attack under President Roosevelt's orders, after which the U-boat fired two torpedoes which went wide of their mark.

The President, it was alleged by the Nazis, hoped by means of the attack "to incite the American people to war against Germany," an allegation that has been the keynote of German attacks on this country during recent weeks.

**Navy Answers Charge.**

The Navy Department in Washington late Saturday night struck

See ATTACK, Page 8

### PREDICTS HOUSE WILL ACCEPT TAX BILL AMENDMENT

WASHINGTON, D. C., Sept. 6 (UP) — Chairman Walter F. George, (D., Ga.), of the Senate Finance Committee, predicted to-

GETS ARMY CALL

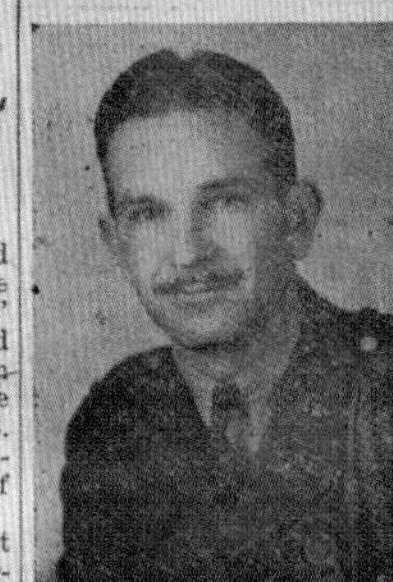

LIEUT. H. L. O'NEAL

### Kilgore ROTC Head Ordered To Army Duty

Lieutenant Harold L. O'Neal, for three years commandant of the ROTC in Kilgore schools, has been ordered to active duty by the War Department and will report to the Third Army Replacement Depot at Lake Charles, La., on Sept. 15.

Passing a physical examination Friday at Barksdale Field, Shreveport, Lieut. O'Neal has been assigned to the 208th military police company. Before he reports for active duty, Lieut. O'Neal will appear before an army board at Dallas for promotion to be a captain.

He was ordered originally to report for duty on Aug. 31, but obtained 15 days leave in order that

## 500,000 TROOPS ARE IN COUNTRY, SAYS COMMITTEE

### Demands For Ouster Of German Envoy To Argentina Made From All Sides

BUENOS AIRES, Sept. 6. (UP)—Strong demands for the ouster of Baron Edmund Von Thermann, German ambassador to Argentina, came from all sides tonight following allegations by a congressional committee that more than 500,000 Nazi storm troopers are strategically scattered throughout South America.

Raul Damonte Taborda, chairman of the congressional committee investigating anti-Argentine activities, asserted that the German storm troop "army" is organizing to "Nazify" the entire continent.

Taborda is directing a sweeping inquiry similar to that made by Rep. Martin Dies in the United States.

The newspaper Critica said editorially that, as result of the Taborda committee's revelations, the German ambassador "should be handed his passport."

Deputy Alejandro Gancedo, head of the anti-Personalist bloc in congress, said that the mask has been ripped "from the maneuvers of the German embassy, center of anti-Argentine movements" and that the Argentine people "feel a just antipathy for these acts which dishonor Germany."

**"Should Be Given Passport."**

"I don't believe the Argentine people will be able to stand much longer the presence of the German ambassador," Gancedo said. "The government must hand him his passport because he has ceased to be persona grata."

Deputy Reynaldo Pastor, head of the conservative wing in parliament, urged "repressive legisla-

### FDR To Make "Important" Talk Monday

HYDE PARK, N. Y., Sept. 6. (UP)—The temporary White House announced tonight that President Roosevelt will make an address of world-wide importance Monday night, Sept. 8.

The announcement climaxed a day of high tension engendered by German charges that the U. S. Destroyer Greer precipitated the attack on a Nazi submarine off Iceland.

Although the subject of Mr. Roosevelt's broadcast was not disclosed, it was considered significant that it should be announced so soon after the German allegations.

PAGE EIGHT

THE KILGORE NEWS H

# O'NEAL

(Continued From Page 1)
rected ROTC work in Amarillo schools for a time before being called to active army duty in 1934 at Fort Sam Houston, He came here from the camp in 1938.

Popular and well liked, Lieut. O'Neal has made a good record in his work here. He was the organizer and first president of the Gregg County Reserve Officers Association and named director of the association's school by the Chief of Staff. He helped with early organization work with the Texas Defense Guard unit here.

The local ROTC has become well known sinoe Lieut. O'Neal took over the reins. He introduced the latest type of military training, including all new drills.

Mrs. O'Neal plans to remain in Tyler with her parents for a time before joining her husband.

# SOUTH AMERICA

(Continued From Page 1)
leader of the Nazi network in South America, will be forced to leave Argentina as a result of the congressional investigation.

2. Nazi leaders have ordered "the establishment of bases in Brazil and the northern countries of South America."

3. The German embassy has a black list with the names of 3,000 Argentine residents unfriendly to the Nazi regime.

4. Germany "hopes to obtain political and economic control" of South America by use of "enormour sums of money to put Quislings in power through fomenting revolts."

**Seek To Gain Control.**

Taborda, whose committee has made two reports on alleged German activities here, said that Von Thermann was director of the Nazi campaign in all of South America and that 60,000 of the alleged storm troopers were concentrated at the base of the movement in Buenos Aires.

"Sixty thousand of them are in Argentina," Taborda said. "They are storm troopers, organized for a campaign to gain control of the South American countries. Strong groups have bases in the territory of Patagonia, adjacent to the German colony in Chile. Some are in the territory of Misiones, near the German colonies in Paraguay, in the Brazilian states of Rio Grande

**LI'L ABNER** **By Al Capp**

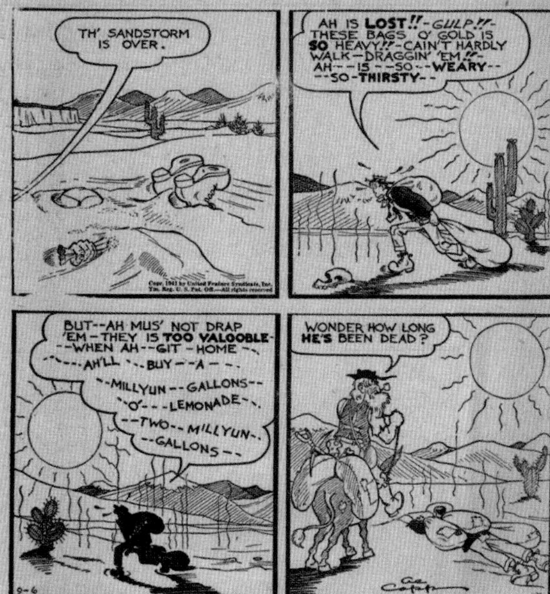


# U. S. BOMBERS

(Continued from Page 1)
railways are over-worked and cannot take their goods."

The Air Ministry said that photographs taken after the bombing of the German port and naval base of Emden by a Flying Fortress on July 26 revealed that at least four industrial buildings were completely demolished.

In an RAF attack on Bremen on July 4 several warehouses were completely destroyed and bombs crashed into a new factory building making Junker-87 bombers, destroying or damaging more than 20 of the new planes.

More than 100 workmen were killed in the Bremen attack, the Air Ministry added, and production was seriously set back.

Production of an iron and steel works north of the Dutch harbor of Ijmuiden was said to have been curtailed at least by one-third as a result of a daylight raid in which several large buildings were damaged badly as well as blast furnaces.

**home. While we're glad he's getting a better job, we regret to lose a good citizen . . . Miss Billie Grimmett, who has sold women's clothing here for nigh onto nine years, goes to work Monday at the Diane Shop . . Vincent V. Davis, the golden gloves prize fighter de luxe, is now at Mather Field, Calif., after graduating from the Air Corps mechanics school at Chanute Field recently. He's the son of Mrs. Elizabeth Davis, 1212 Oak Drive . . . And Wallace Gordon Daniels, son of Mr. and Mrs. D. W. Daniels, Kilgore, enlisted in the Coast Guard for three years the other day at Fort Worth.**

●

CONGRATS TO MR. C. R. Powers, who was the number two man in a Perkins Bros. sales contest recently. He was entertained at a company fishing party over toward Austin . . . . Understand Mr. Leo Haney has forgotten the answer to his red ink puzzle and unless he sends us the correct answer by Monday noon, he'll have to buy us all a root beer-

PAGE TWO

# The Kilgore News Herald

"PUBLISHED AT THE CAPITAL OF THE WORLD'S LARGEST OIL FIELD"

CHAS. K. DEVALL . . . . . . . Owner and Publisher
Published Sunday and Week Days Except Saturday
Special Weekly Edition Also Published on Friday Morning

Entered as Second Class Matter at the Kilgore, Texas, Post Office, Under the Act of Congress, March, 1879

Any erroneous reflection upon the character, standing or reputation of any person, firm or corporation that may appear in the columns of The Kilgore News Herald will be gladly and fully corrected upon being brought to the attention of the publisher.

**KEEP THE PRESS FREE**

A free press is that privilege of citizenship which makes government dictatorships impossible. Democracy cannot exist except through the maintenance of a channel through which information can flow freely from the center of the government to all of the people and through which praise and criticism can flow freely from the people to the center.

The News Herald is not responsible for copy omissions, typographical errors, or any unintentional errors that may occur in advertising other than to correct in next issue after it is brought to publisher's attention. All advertising orders are accepted on this basis only.

Subscription Rate: Daily by Mail, Year $7.00
Circulation Department . . . . . . . . . Phone 493-494

## America First To East Texas

An announcement that the America First Committee will conduct an anti-war drive in East Texas does not come as a surprise. A region which contains vast industries and resources of great value to national security seldom escapes the attention of those who would take part in controversies.

According to the announcement, which appeared in Friday press dispatches, A. V. Grant, Longview attorney, will head the East Texas America First Committee. Mr. Grant will be remembered as having made two unsuccessful attempts to become this district's congressman and having been a leader in organizing the bonus march on Washington in 1932.

While the News Herald unquestionably believes that Mr. Grant has the right to speak his piece any where he chooses, this newspaper cannot agree with the cause he has chosen to champion. About the only thing we can say for Grant and Burton K. Wheeler and Charles A. Lindbergh et al is that they are doubtless sincere in the doctrine they preach, for no axe-grinding man with a flare for public fancy would choose a cause so universally unpopular.

**1942**

I was not yet three years old, but just prior to his departure Harold and his friends took a series of pictures of me sitting in a Jeep like the big boy I wasn't, and, most tellingly, of me stuffed in Harold's duffle bag, with only my head sticking out. Just like he could pack me up and take me to the Pacific with him.

Kilgore was ablaze with Christmas lights on the evening of December 6, the day before the news of the Japanese attack at Pearl Harbor was broadcast nationwide. Harold and Sarah didn't see them unless they returned for a short visit. He'd been called to active duty and was busy at Camp Bowie in Brownwood, Texas. Their absence meant they missed out on all the excitement of another Kilgore-related story that had a crucial impact on the outcome of World War II, in which the United States now found itself embroiled.

In 1942 there was another oil boom of sorts in East Texas. Many of the ships that were sunk at Pearl Harbor were filled with fuel that had been created from East Texas crude and supplemented with product from California refineries. In the coming months German submarines sank other ships, including many oil tankers bound for ports on the east coast of the United States, or even headed towards the Panama Canal. Recognizing the need for a steady, uninterrupted supply of oil that could be refined into fuel to power aircraft, ships, and land vehicles, the decision was made to construct what would come to be known as the Big Inch Pipeline. Harold was at Camp Bowie when the construction of the pipeline began in August 1942, but he would indirectly benefit from the supplies it provided.

When the first wells came in in 1930, no one imagined that the oil underground would be the primary product that would fuel the largest and most efficient war machine ever assembled. Germany and Japan, the primary Axis powers in World War II, literally ran out of gas. It wasn't the only reason their war efforts failed, but it was an important element. Oil flowed uninterrupted from the East Texas fields until war's end. Some say oil from East Texas fueled 95 percent of the war effort in Europe, freeing up fuel from west coast refineries for the conflict in the Pacific. The ships on which Harold sailed to the South Pacific, the airplanes that flew him from one island to another, the ships that took him to the Philippines and Japan were at least partially fueled by East Texas crude.

The Big Inch was a twenty-four inch, 1,400-mile pipeline designed to transport crude oil from the East Texas oil fields to refineries in New York and New Jersey. It was the largest of its sort at the time. It had twenty-seven pumping stations: Station #1 was located in Longview, twenty short miles from Kilgore, and by the end of the war, 350 million barrels of East Texas crude had passed through the pipeline. But it was not without its detractors.

In the same front page of the *Kilgore News Herald* that announced Harold's call to active duty there was a story about this pipeline. The headline was South Texans Protesting Big Pipe Line. The story reads as follows:

*South Texas tonight harbored spreading rebellion against a proposed crude oil pipeline to relieve a purported gasoline shortage.*

*The press charged that the result, whether intended or not, would be to "by-pass" South Texas refineries. Oil that otherwise would be refined in the South would be sent to the East coast for processing, it was asserted.*

*The Port Arthur News expressed amazement that a crude oil instead of a gasoline pipeline was planned. It warned that any such line built under the guise of an emergency "will be in operation long after the emergency has passed."*

*Other newspapers wondered why Petroleum Coordinator Harold L. Ickes did not check up on existing transportation facilities, such as railroads and barges, before the pipeline project was launched.*

*Freely cited was testimony of J.J. Pelley, president of the American Association of Railroads before a special U.S. Senate investigating committee. Pelley contended that the carriers have 20,000 surplus tank cars which could replenish the East's gasoline supply within two weeks, He said, further, that Ickes and his staff never approached him on the subject.*

*Railroad Commissioner Jerry Sadler had said that 6,000 of the surplus cars were in Texas, many of them stored in yards in Houston for several years.*

The dispute was purely about economics in South Texas; there was no thought

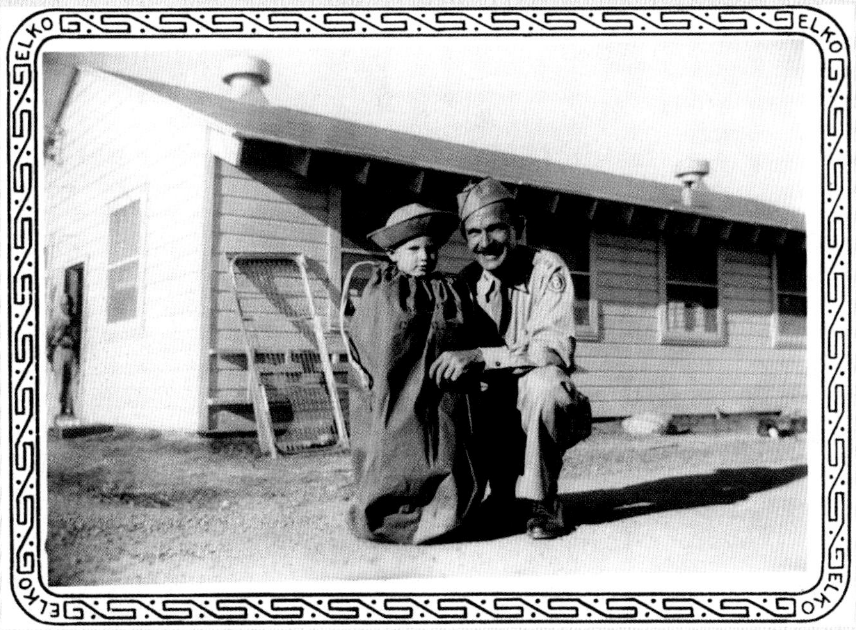

Hank

July 19, 1942

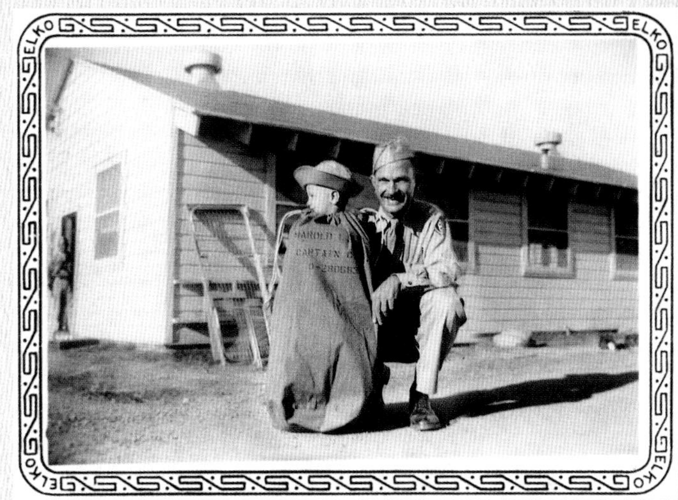

This is Harold's barrack bag he's in. & Harold's hat on him. They were playing at home in it & I Harold thought he looked so cute had to make his picture.

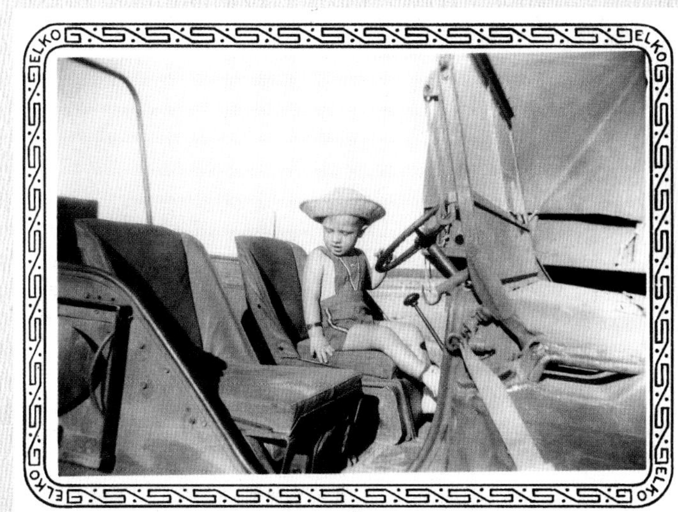

about what would be best for the war effort because officially the United States wasn't at war, and the thought of immediate financial benefit took priority. The Big Inch was built and was instrumental in the success of the Allied forces, particularly in Europe.

In the summer of 1942, probably a week or two after the annual June Summer Encampment, Harold was given a gift, the last of its sort he'd ever receive. It was a new publication created by the ROTC cadets at Kilgore High School. They now had their own yearbook, *The Cadet*, a fifty-page hardbound book, filled with hundreds of pictures that showed the military lives led by the 140 cadets during the 1941-42 school year. It is also filled with fifty tributes to Harold from the cadets in the program, including all but one of the female sponsors, just as it had been in Amarillo. It may have been one of the sponsors who rounded up all the signatures, and to see how the program had grown since 1938 was probably very gratifying. It was possibly his last interaction with the ROTC program in Kilgore, perhaps nearly the last with the city itself, because to the best of my knowledge, he never returned until many, many years after the end of World War II, possibly as much as two decades later. When the fine book, *Kilgore, Visions of Forgotten Streets*, was issued in 2007, Harold was listed as having been killed in action. Clearly he wasn't. When he returned in 1945, he still had the small silver locket Sarah had given him before he went overseas. It shows a lot of wear. Harold carried it with him throughout the war.

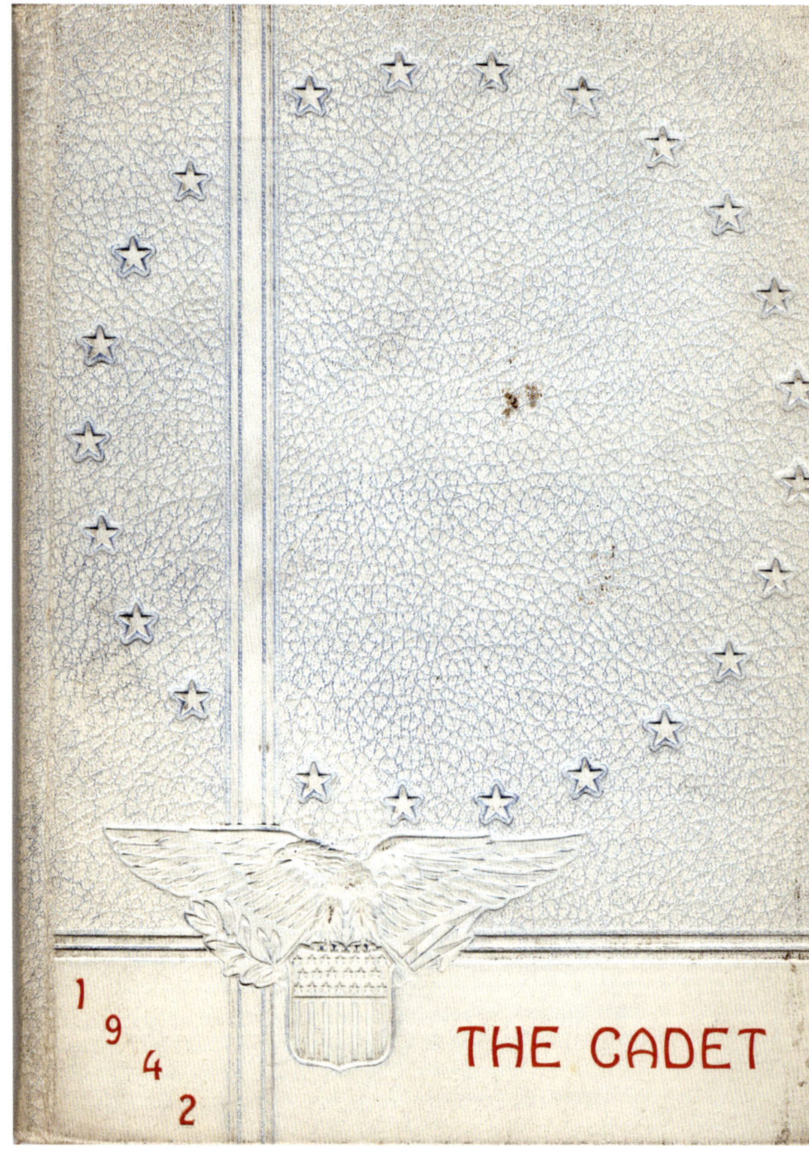

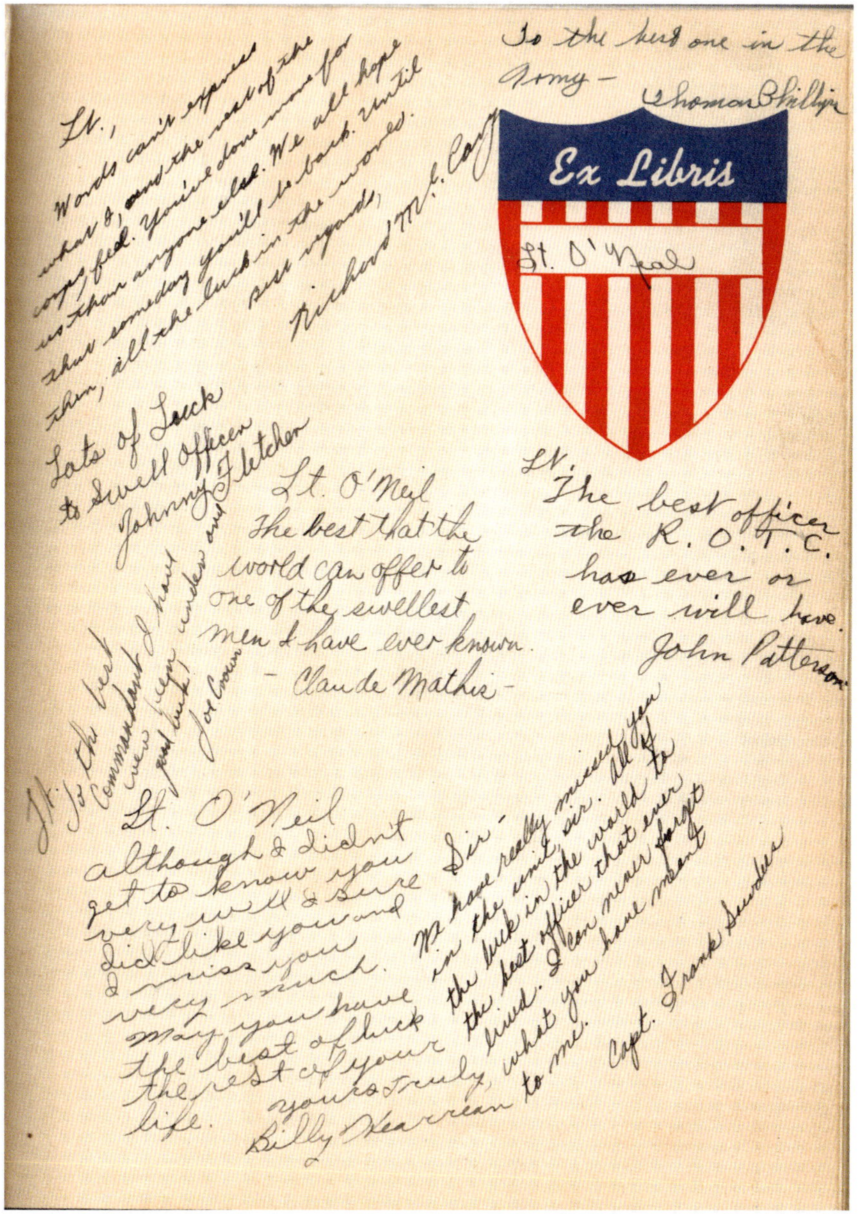

To the best one in the army — Thomas Phillips

Lt., Words can't express what I, and the rest of the company feel. You've done more for us than anyone else. We all hope that someday you'll be back. Until then, all the luck in the world. Best regards, Richard McCary

Ex Libris

Lt. O'Neal

Lots of Luck to Swell Officer Johnny Fletcher

Lt. O'Neil The best that the world can offer to one of the swellest men I have ever known. — Claude Mathis —

Lt. The best officer the R.O.T.C. has ever or ever will have. John Patterson

Lt. To the best Commandant I have ever been under and good luck! Joe Crown

Lt. O'Neil although I didn't get to know you very well I sure did like you and I miss you very much. May you have the best of luck the rest of your life. yours truly, Billy Kearrean

Sir — We have really missed you in the unit, sir. All of the luck in the world to the best officer that ever lived. I can never forget what you have meant to me. Capt. Frank Saunders

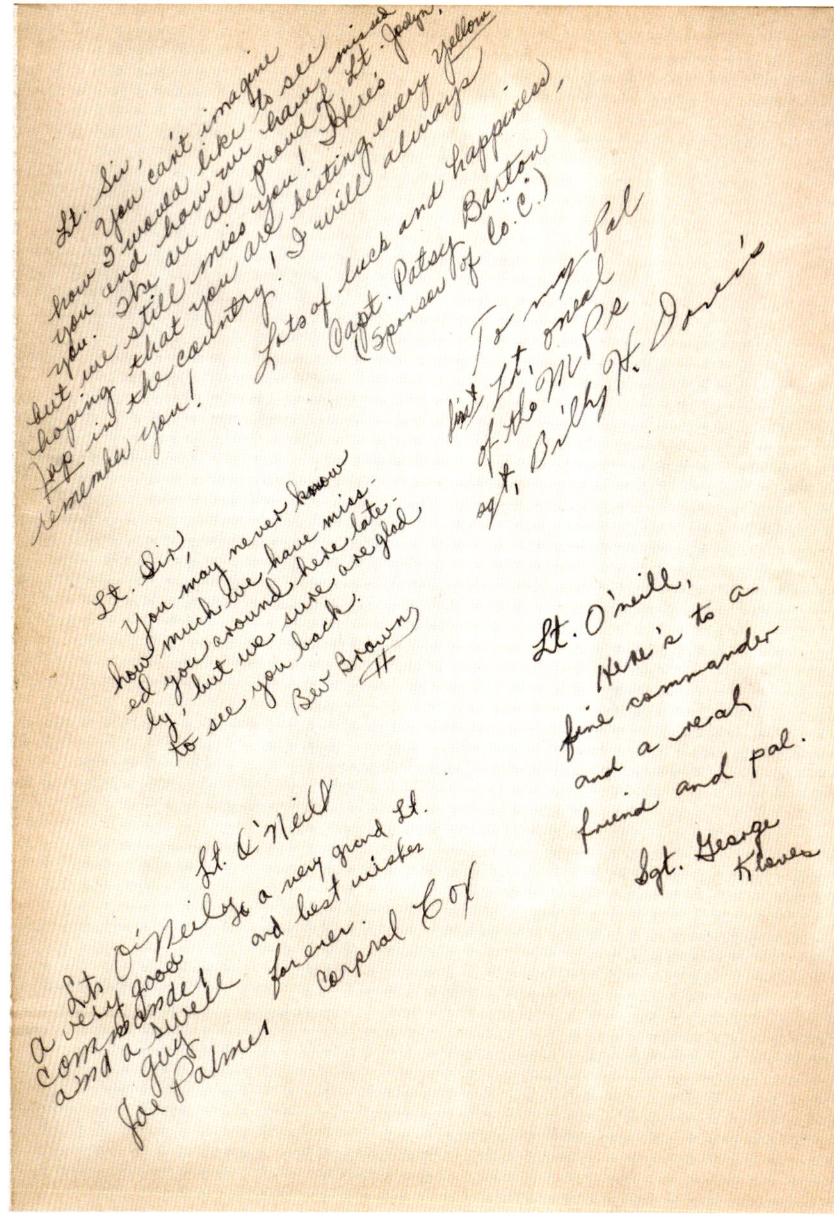

Lt. Sir, You can't imagine how I would like to see you and how we have missed you. We are all proud of Lt. Joslyn, but we still miss you! Here's hoping that you are beating every yellow Jap in the country! I will always remember you! Lots of luck and happiness, Capt. Patsy Barton (Sponsor of Co. C)

To my first Lt. oneal of the M.P.s pal Sgt. Billy H. Davis

Lt. Sir, You may never know how much we have missed you around here lately, but we sure are glad to see you back. Bev Brown

Lt. O'neill, Here's to a fine commander and a real friend and pal. Sgt. George Kleves

Lt. O'Neill To a very grand Lt. and best wishes forever. Corporal Cox

Lt. O'Neil a very good commander and a swell guy Joe Palmer

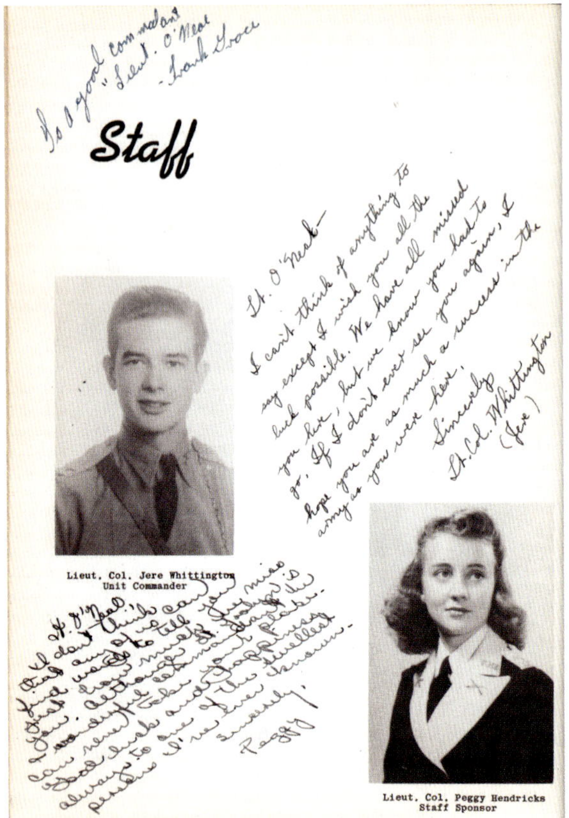

# Staff

Lt. O'Neal—
I can't think of anything to say except I wish you all the luck possible. We have all missed you here, but we know you had to go. If I don't ever see you again, I hope you are as much a success in the army as you were here.
Sincerely
Lt. Col. Whittington (Jere)

Lieut. Col. Jere Whittington
Unit Commander

Lieut. Col. Peggy Hendricks
Staff Sponsor

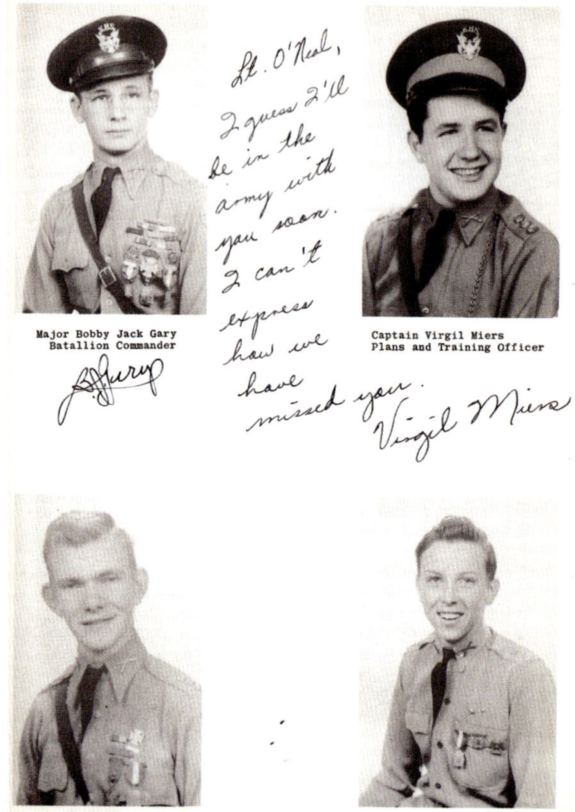

Major Bobby Jack Gary
Batallion Commander

B Gary

Lt. O'Neal,
I guess I'll be in the army with you soon. I can't express how we have missed you.
Virgil Miers

Captain Virgil Miers
Plans and Training Officer

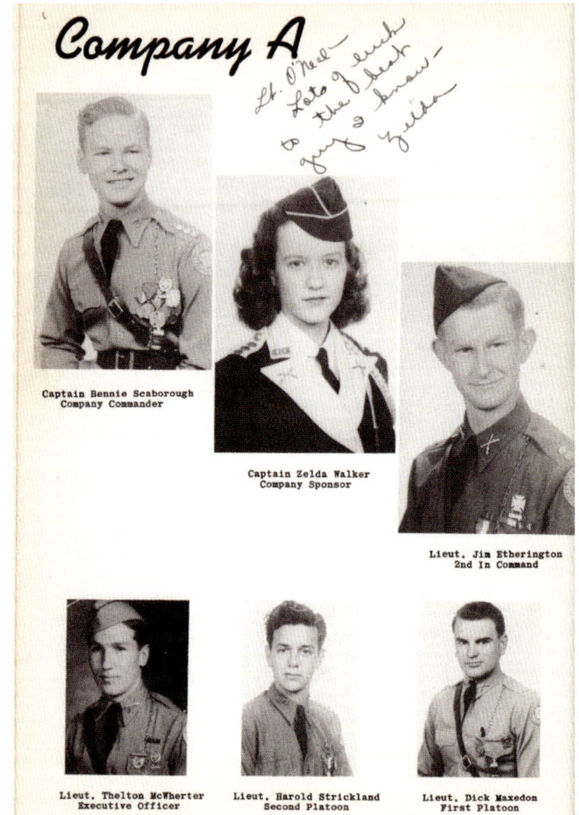

# Company A

Lt. O'Neal—
Lots of luck to the best guy I know—
Zelda

Captain Bennie Scaborough
Company Commander

Captain Zelda Walker
Company Sponsor

Lieut. Jim Etherington
2nd In Command

Lieut. Thelton McWherter
Executive Officer

Lieut. Harold Strickland
Second Platoon

Lieut. Dick Maxedon
First Platoon

# The Dream Deferred

## December 7, 1941

WW II

**THE INEVITABLE MARCH TO WORLD WAR II WAS A RAGTAG AFFAIR. NOT ALL THE COUNTRIES LINED UP AT THE SAME TIME.** Nor did they line up willingly. Many people pinpoint the start as the day on which Germany invaded Poland in 1939, September 1 to be exact. In the United States in 1941, as well as in 2018, most Americans believe the war began on December 7, 1941, when the Japanese attacked the US Fleet at Pearl Harbor. But actual on-the-ground hostilities had begun a decade earlier in 1931, when the Japanese invaded Manchuria and set up the puppet state they called Manchukuo.

Italy was the next bad actor; it invaded Ethiopia and other states in Africa in 1935. In 1936 there was a proxy war in Spain where the Germans tried out their new airplanes, and the following year Japan invaded China. In 1938 the Germans annexed Austria and Sudetenland, part of Czechoslovakia, and in 1939 they decided to take the rest.

In August 1939 Germany and the Soviet Union signed a nonaggression pact and hatched plans to divide up Eastern Europe between them, leaving the door open for Germany to invade Poland in September, and then the war was really on. Germany moved into Denmark and Norway in April 1940, France, Belgium, the Netherlands, and Luxembourg in May, followed by Italy invading France in June. The Battle of Britain began in July 1940, even though Germany had bombed British ships in Scotland in March. Italy invaded Greece in October, but the Greeks beat them soundly.

In early 1941 the Germans joined their Italian partners in North Africa and the Afrika Corps was in place by late February. Two months later, in April, Germany invaded both Greece and Yugoslavia, and each country surrendered within days. Two months after this success the Germans tore up the nonaggression pact signed by Molotov and Ribbentrop and invaded the Soviet Union—a move that essentially doomed Germany, even though they didn't know it at the time.

On December 7, 1941, Japan attacked the US Fleet at Pearl Harbor, and the United States declared war on Japan the following day. The day after that, December 9, Germany declared war on the United States, and for the next forty-two months there was all-out war in the European Theater until Germany surrendered on May 7, 1945. The war continued for four more months in the Pacific Theater until Japan did the same on August 15, and then formally surrendered on September 2.

In East Texas there had been some military preparedness, encouraged by those who were confident war in Europe was likely, but there were other people, notably the followers of the isolationist America First Committee, who were openly opposed to preparedness, including helping our longtime allies in Europe, notably Great Britain. They and others even opposed the Lend-Lease Act that was instrumental in preventing Germany from overwhelming that country. But these isolationists were in a distinct minority, and four days after the attack on Pearl Harbor, the America First Committee disbanded itself, and the men and women who had championed this cause quickly vanished and remained in the shadows until the end of the war. In recent days others trumpeting "America First" can be heard throughout land. For many years American isolation has been the cause of much mischief.

Despite the pacifists and isolationists there were many in government who were convinced that the United States could not remain on the sidelines and observe the carnage in Europe from a safe distance, and these leaders took steps to insure that the United States was on a modestly secure military footing. This included activating reserve officers who for the previous decade had commanded CCC units and overseen Reserve Officer Training Corps programs in high schools and universities. The aim was to have 1.5 million men in uniform by mid-1941. This goal was met as more and more men enlisted. Then on two Sundays three months apart, each on the 7th, there were events that determined how Harold and Sarah's lives would be lived until 1968 and 1972. The first Sunday fell on September 7.

There are also no records or remembrances of what Harold and Sarah did on Saturday evening, September 6, but they woke up the following morning and saw the front page of the *Kilgore News Herald* filled with headlines that proclaimed: ***REPORT ON NAZIS STIRS SOUTH AMERICA; 500,000 TROOPS ARE IN COUNTRY; FDR To Make "Important" Talk Monday; Big U. S.-Made Bombers Smash Reich Industries; HELD AS SPY; SOVIETS SMASH ENEMY LINES; South Texans Protesting Big Pipe Line.***

The inside pages listed the movies, *Meet John Doe* at The Texan, *Devil Dogs of the Air* at the Crim, and *Tillie The Toiler* at the Strand. The funny papers included *Lil' Abner, Nancy, Bronco Bill, Tailspin Tommy, Ella Cinders, Spunkie, Abbie an' Slats,* and *Hap Hopper, Washington Correspondent.* There were ads for doctors, clothing stores, and a beauty salon; even a crossword puzzle.

The editorial on page two had a headline ***America First to East Texas***, and after voicing its opinion that these misguided souls had every right to speak out, concluded by saying:

*But we doubt if the accomplishments of the America First Committee in East Texas will warrant its expenditures. The citizens of this region are sound in principle and are not the type to be misled by those upon whom the Nazis look with favor. Moreover, we are a people who have had occasion to learn when to put our tongues in our cheeks and sprinkle the salt.*

On a lighter note, on the back page was a story about Mrs. Ingrid Vallo of Brooklyn who, when she did not win the Mrs. America contest in Palisades, New Jersey, felt the judge, Walter Thornton, had done her wrong and "started out by throwing a punch at Thornton. Then pulling his hair. Finally she threw him down." After recovering, Thornton said he would be on hand to judge the finals the following week.

But for Harold and Sarah, the most important headline in the paper that Sunday morning read:

***GETS ARMY CALL***

***Kilgore ROTC Head Ordered To Army Duty***

*Lieutenant Harold L. O'Neal, for three years commandant of ROTC in Kilgore schools, has been ordered to active duty by the War Department and will report to the Third Army Replacement Depot at Lake Charles, La. on Sept. 15.*

*Passing a physical examination at Barksdale Field, Shreveport, Lieut. O'Neal has been assigned to the 208th military police company. Before he reports for active duty Lieut. O'Neal will appear before the army board at Dallas for promotion to be a captain.*

*He was ordered originally to report for duty on Aug. 31, but obtained 15 days leave in order that he might help his successor start off the new school year. Lieut. E. J. Joslyn of Fort Sam Houston, a veteran army officer will replace Lieut. O'Neal.*

*A native of Dallas, Lieut. O'Neal joined the army in 1930. He directed ROTC work in Amarillo schools for a time before being called to active duty in 1934 at Fort Sam Houston. He came here from the camp in 1938. Popular and well liked, Lieut. O'Neal has made a good record in his work here. He was the organizer and first president of the Gregg County Reserve Officers Association and named director of the association's school by the chief of staff. He helped with the early organization work with the Texas Defense Guard unit here.*

*The local ROTC has become well known since Lieut. O'Neal took over the reins. He introduced the latest type of military training, including all new drills.*

*Mrs. O'Neal plans to remain in Tyler with her parents for a time before joining her husband.*

And so it was in East Texas and throughout the state and the rest of the nation. Young men enlisted, the reserves and National Guard were ordered to active duty, and this mobilization was ongoing when the second Sunday the 7th occurred, this time in December, when the Japanese attacked Pearl Harbor and brought the United States into World War II. The Sunday morning surprise in Hawaii was the defining moment in the lives of most of these men who were called to arms, and it was the defining moment in the lives of their families as well. Harold and Sarah were no longer in Kilgore when the attacked occurred; they were living in nearby Brownwood, where Harold was training his company of military policemen at nearby Camp Bowie.

In 1958, in a short biographical sketch, Harold described his wartime experience as follows:

*At the close of the school year in 1941, I was recalled to active duty with the Army and remained on such duty until September 1946. During this period I initially trained a company of military police, as Captain, and took them overseas (South Pacific) in February 1943, as a separate organization. My first assignment overseas was that of Provost Marshall of the harbor facilities and Japanese prisoner of war stockades at Noumea, New Caledonia. In September of that same year I was separated from my command and flown to the battle area in the Solomon Islands to be trained as Headquarters Commandant of the XIV Corps, for the invasion of Bougainville. In 1945, I was appointed Provost Marshall of the XIV Corps during the campaign of Luzon, in the Philippines, and promoted to the rank of Major. Shortly after this, I was decorated for service in the Philippines, and was among the initial troops to land in Japan for the occupation.*

*. . . Extended travel, at Government expense in the Pacific to include New Caledonia, Guadalcanal, Rendova, Munda, Vella LaVella, Kolambangara, Bougainville, New Guinea, the Philippines, and Japan.*

It was far more complicated than is offered in this brief description. Harold carried a small red notebook throughout his time in the Pacific. On one page he has listed the dates of his arrival at various locations:

3/21/43 – 10/15/43
New Caledonia (Noumea)
10/15/43 – 10/17/43
Guadalcanal
10/17/43
Munda, New Guinea
10/27/43
Kolambangara
11/19/43
Vella Lavella
11/19/43
Adonga
11/24/43
Guadalcanal
12/7/43
At Sea
12/10/43
Bougainville
11/20/44
Finchhaven, New Guinea*
11/21/44
Ora Bay, New Guinea*
12/7/44
Finschafeb, New Guinea*
12/15/44
Bougainville*
12/15/44
At Sea
12/20/44 – 12/31/44
Mannua?
1/16/45
Off Leyte
1/7/45
Luzon, The Philippines

His last entry was the beginning of the Luzon campaign. He then created a monthly calendar of three months per page where he marked off the days. The last page has July, August, and September. The last day crossed off is August 29; presumably this was his final day in action in the Philippines, after which he was transported to Sendai, Japan, with his company, where he would remain until he was sent back to the United States two months later.

Harold saved an oversized four-page souvenir pamphlet that describes the activities of the XIV Corps during the twenty-one months he spent with them in Bougainville and the Philippines. There was a primitive mimeographed version in his 201 file. The pamphlet is described

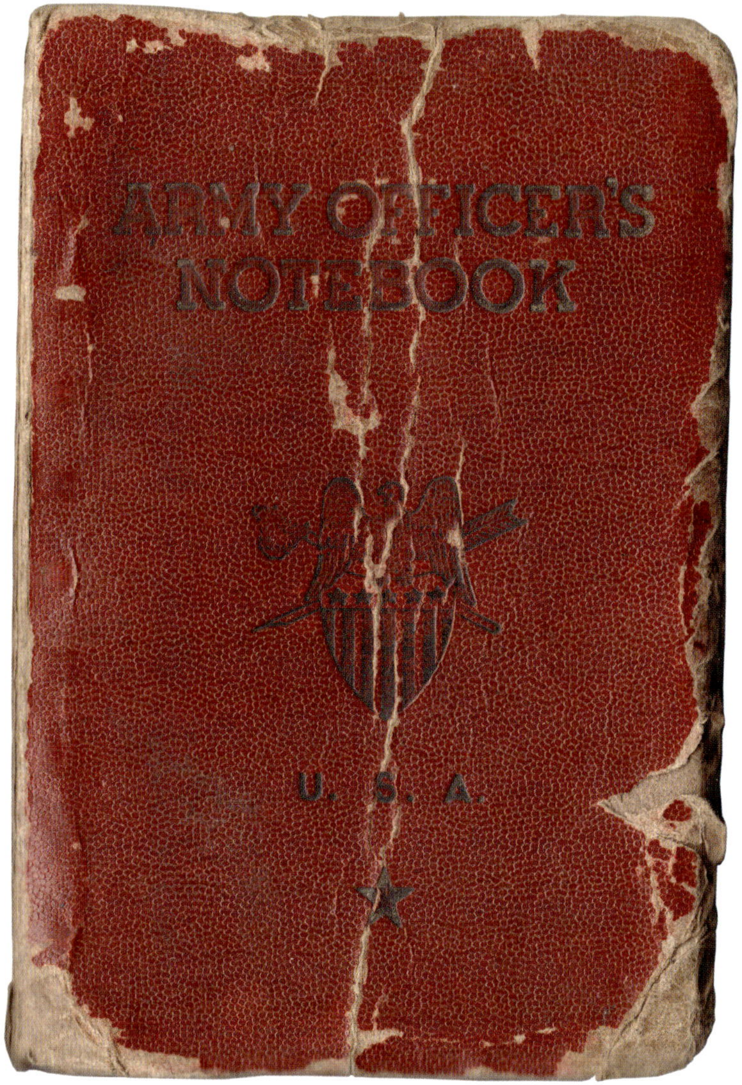


The notebook

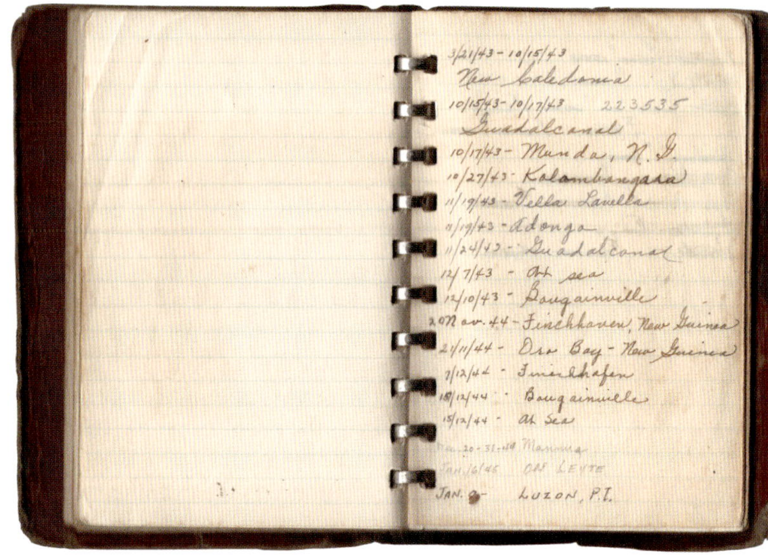


Arrivals and Departures

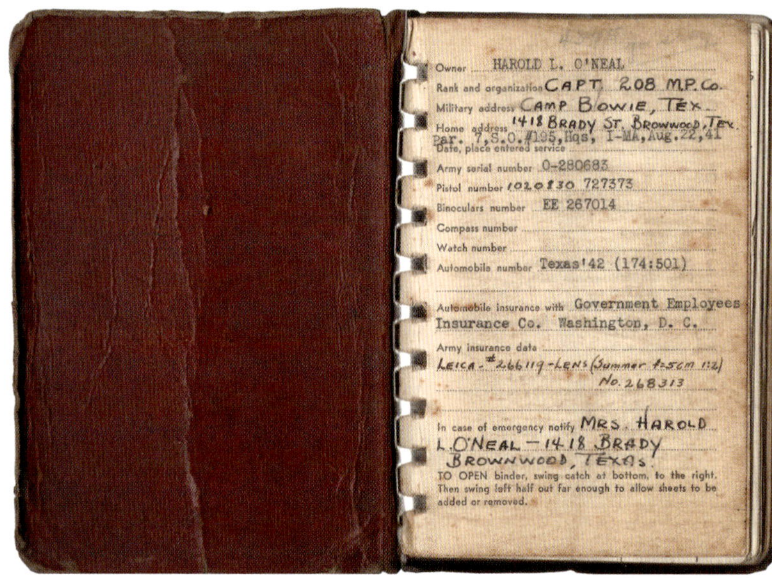


Personal ID

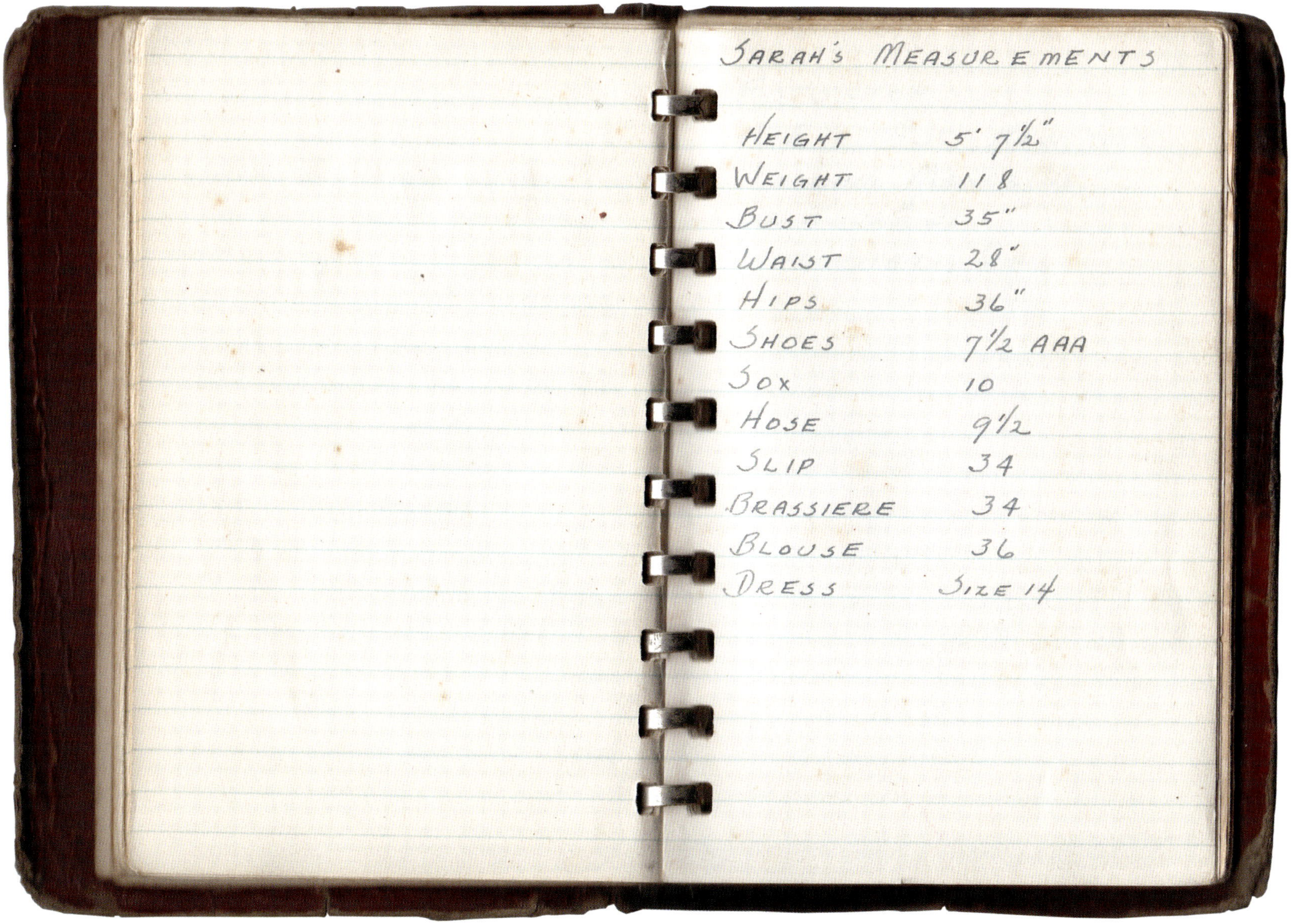


Sarah's Measurements

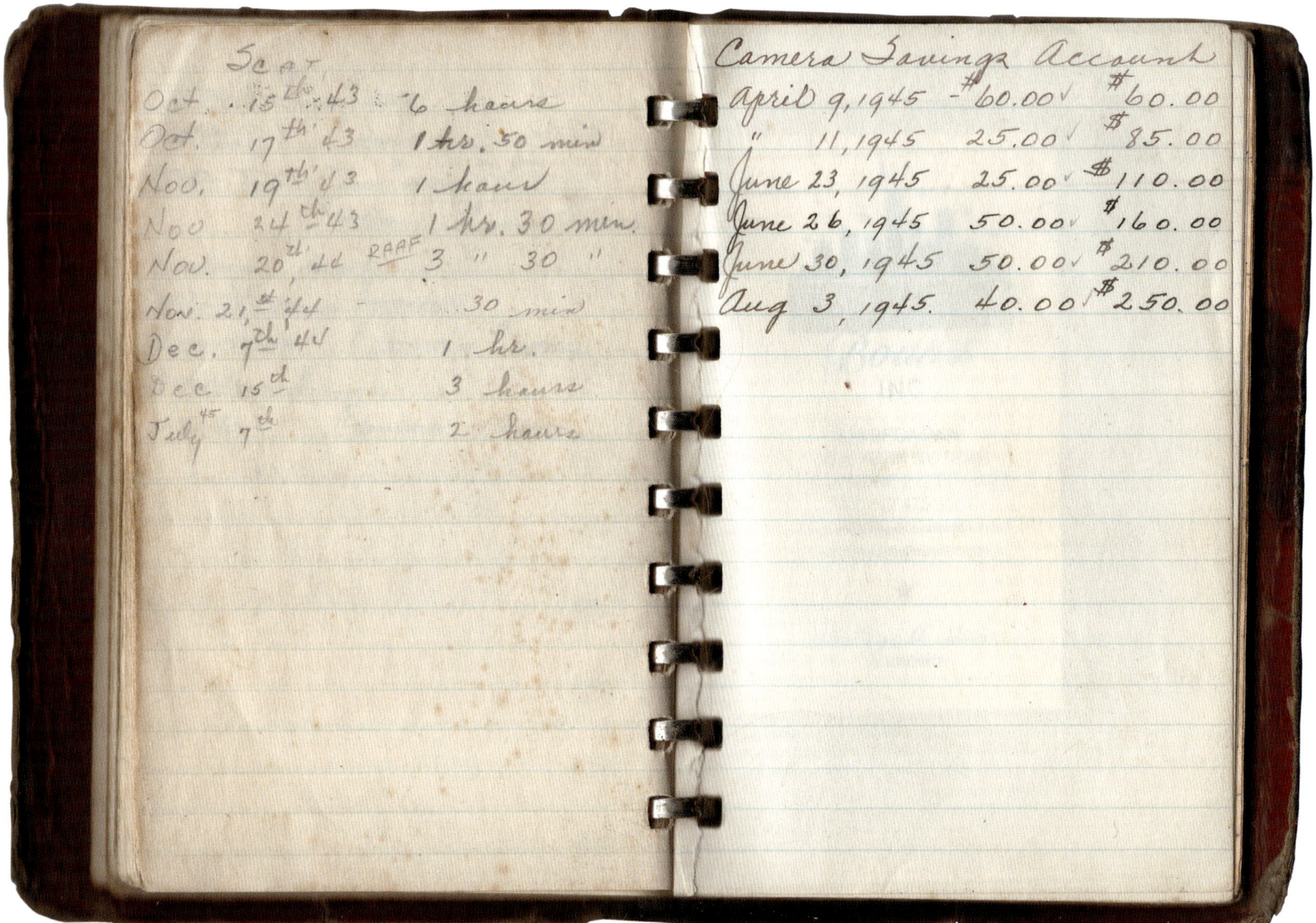

SCAT

| | |
|---|---|
| Oct. 15th '43 | 6 hours |
| Oct. 17th '43 | 1 hr. 50 min |
| Nov. 19th '43 | 1 hour |
| Nov 24th '43 | 1 hr. 30 min. |
| Nov. 20th '44 RAAF | 3 " 30 " |
| Nov. 21st '44 | 30 min |
| Dec. 7th '44 | 1 hr. |
| Dec 15th | 3 hours |
| July 45 7th | 2 hours |

Camera Savings Account

| | | |
|---|---|---|
| April 9, 1945 | $60.00 | $60.00 |
| " 11, 1945 | 25.00 | $85.00 |
| June 23, 1945 | 25.00 | $110.00 |
| June 26, 1945 | 50.00 | $160.00 |
| June 30, 1945 | 50.00 | $210.00 |
| Aug 3, 1945. | 40.00 | $250.00 |

SCAT flights and camera account

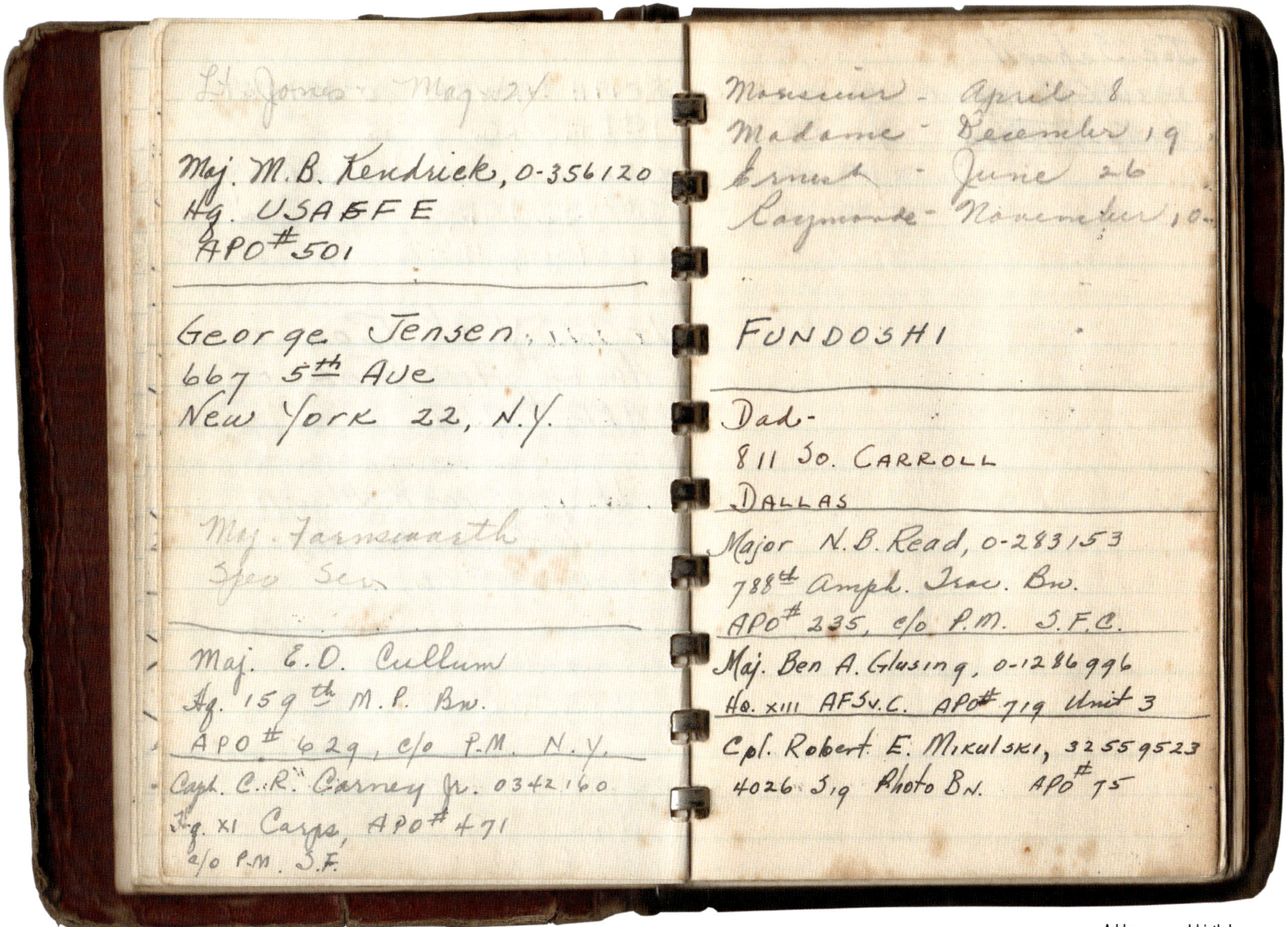

Addresses and birthdays

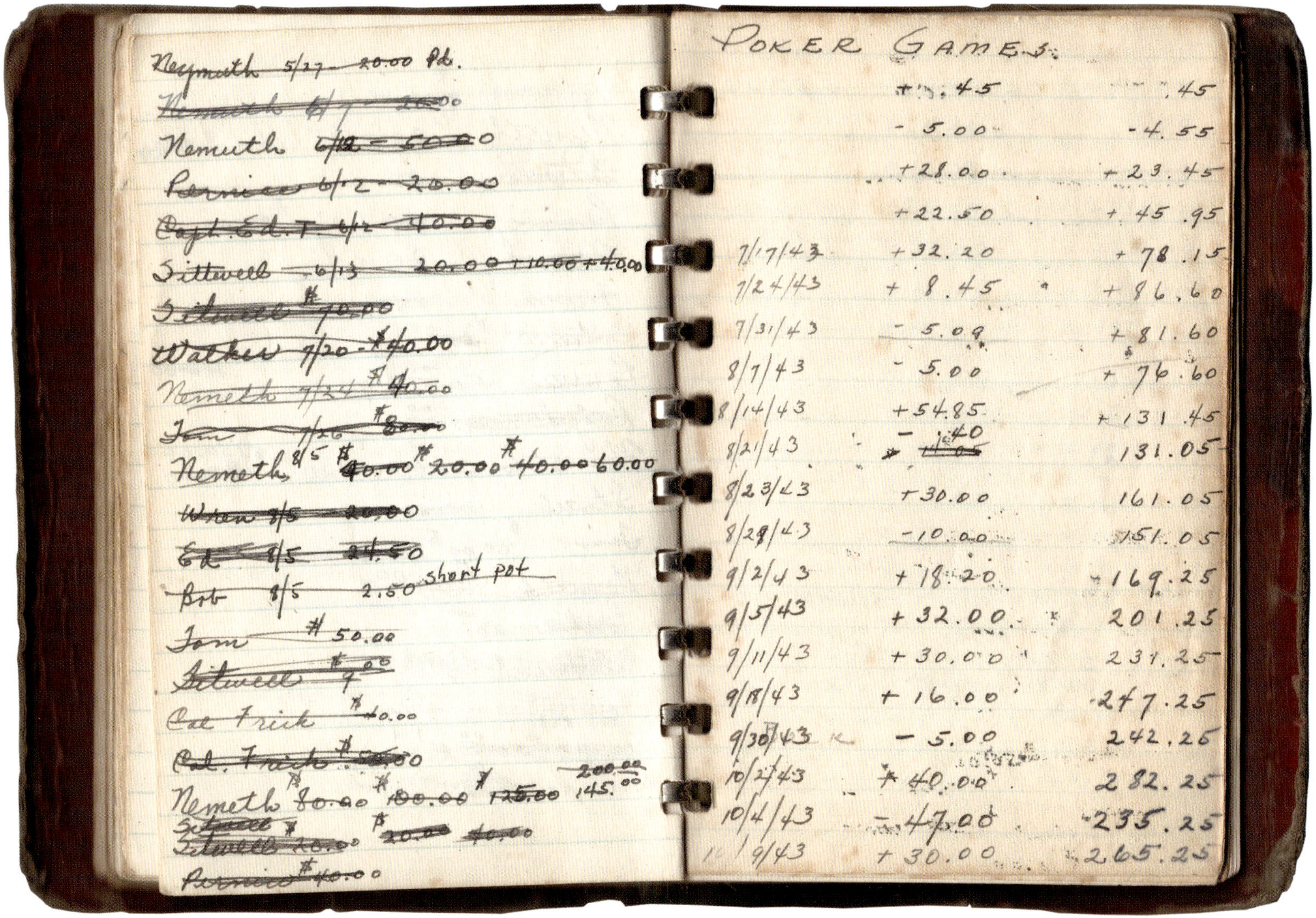


Poker games

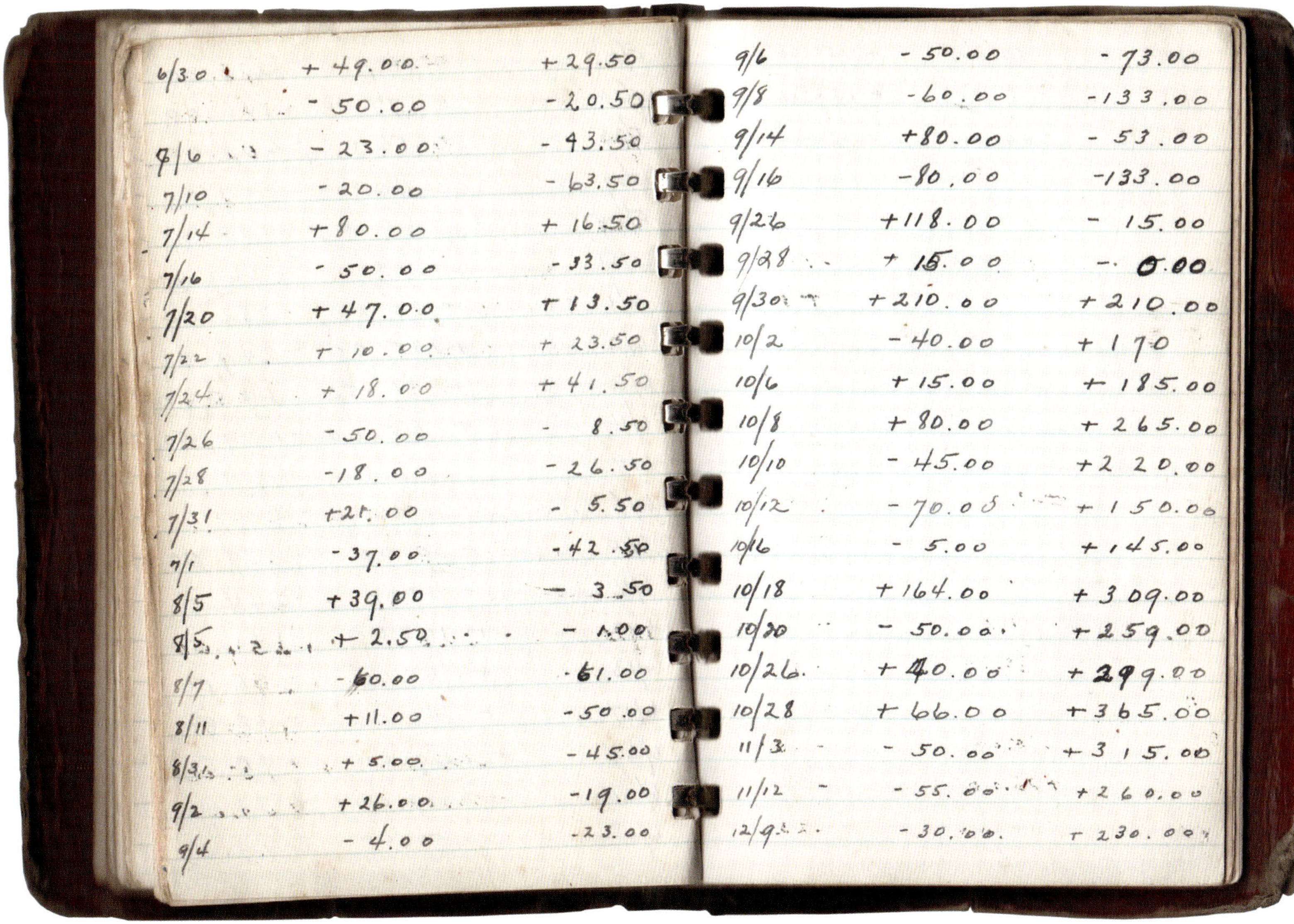


Running balance

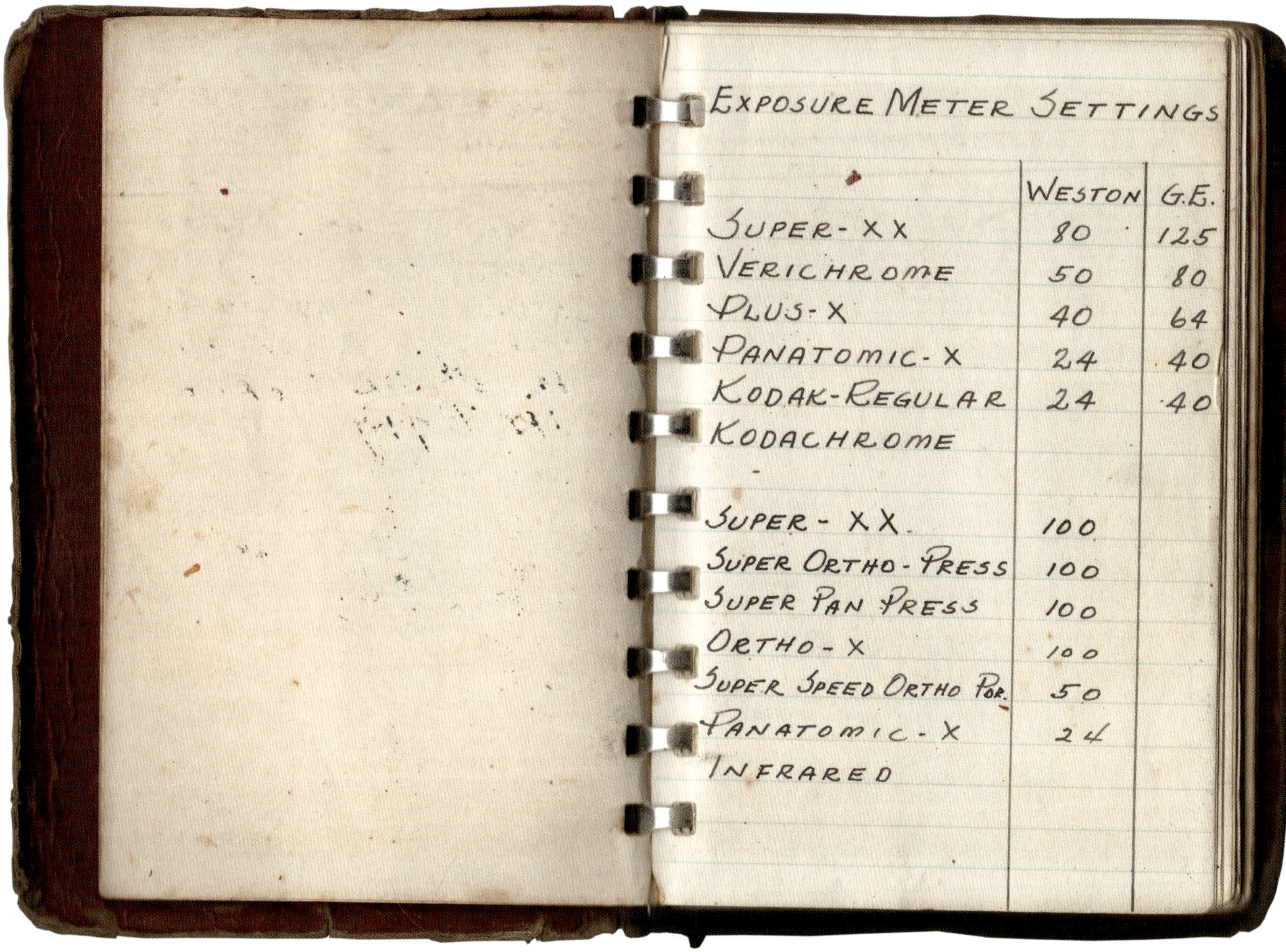


Exposure Meter Settings

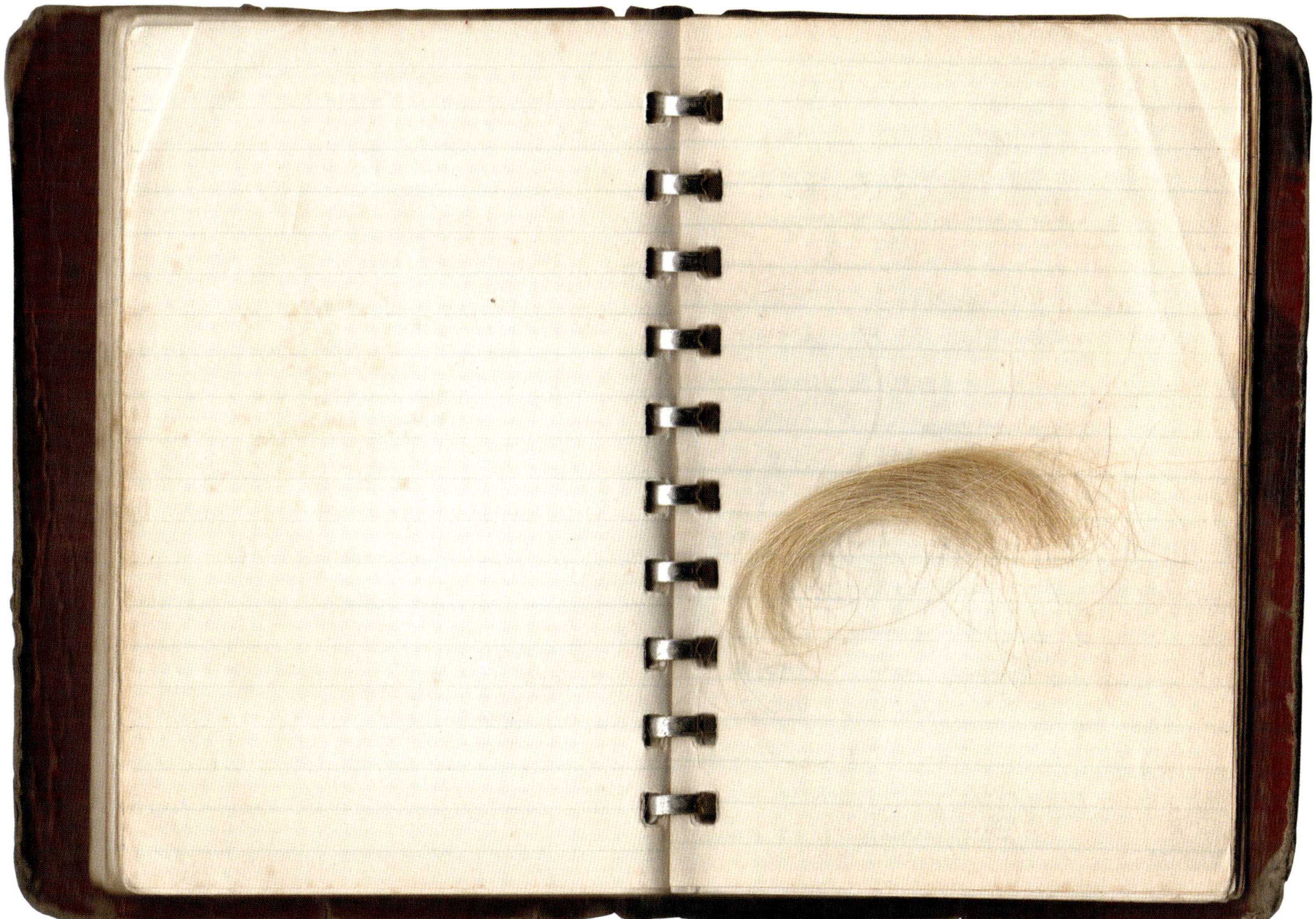

Hank's hair

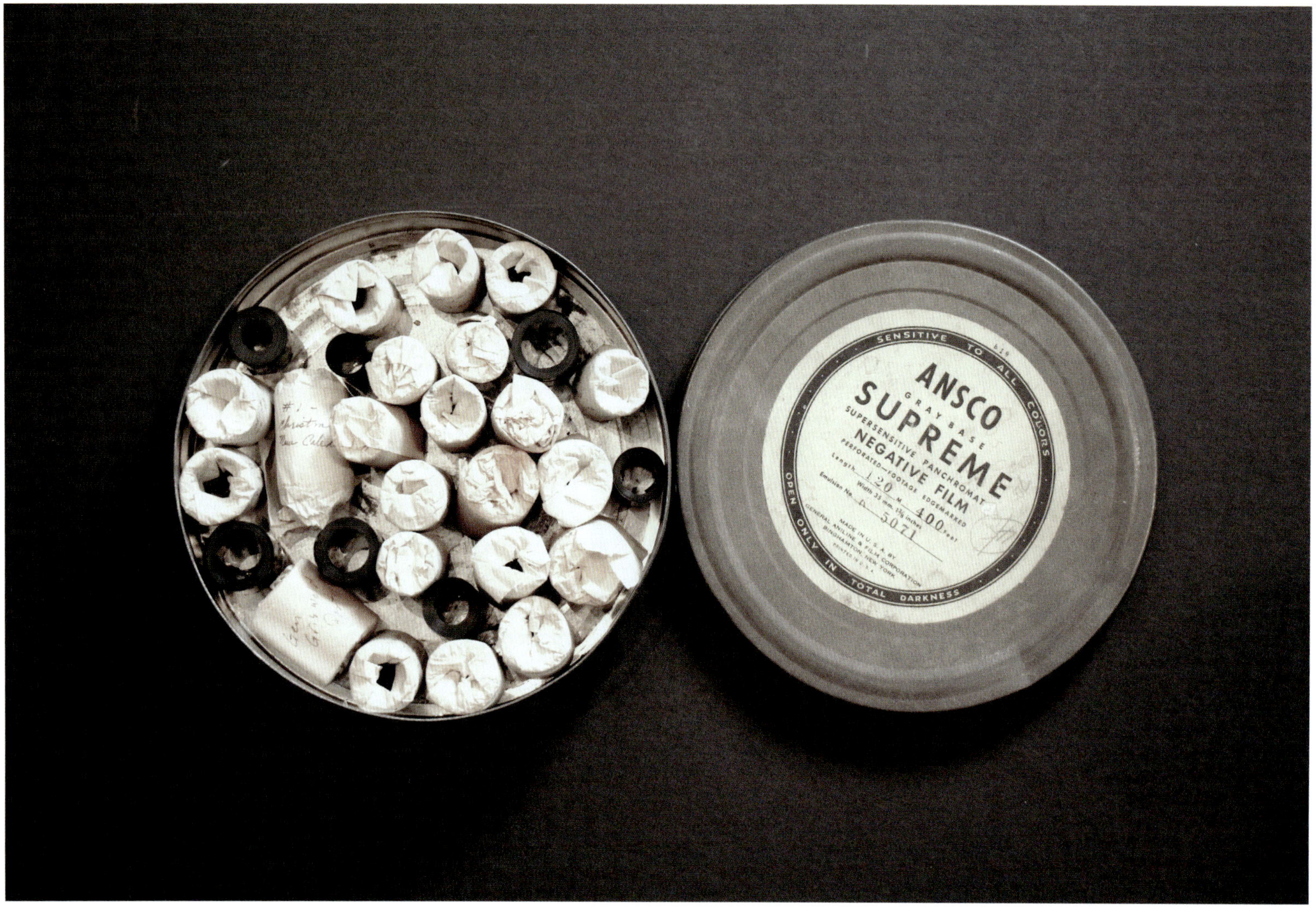


Thirty rolls of film

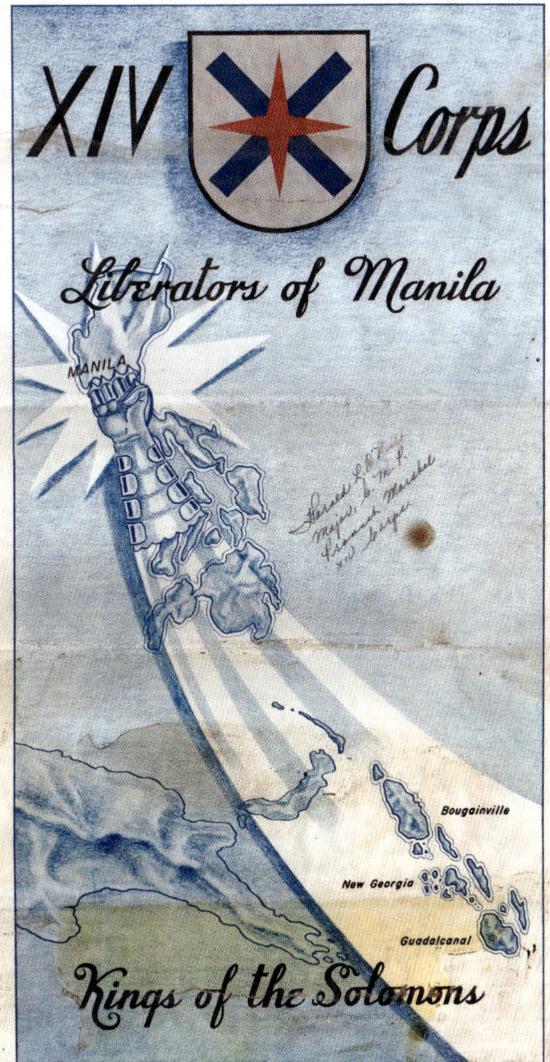


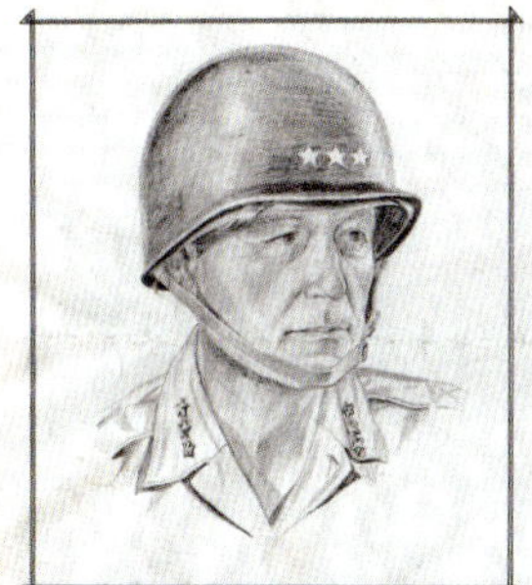

Lieutenant General O. W. Griswold

## KINGS OF THE SOLOMONS

The history of the XIV Army Corps in World War II dates from December, 1942. Under Lieut. Gen. (then Maj. Gen.) Alexander M. Patch, the XIV Army Corps directed the Americal and 25th (Tropic Lightning) Army Infantry Divisions, the 2nd Marine Division and the 147th Separate Infantry Regiment in the final drive which expelled the Japanese from Guadalcanal early in February, 1943. From air fields here guarded by the XIV Army Corps, Allied aircraft began the neutralization of the enemy's vital Munda airfields on New Georgia.

Lieut. Gen. (then Maj. Gen.) O. W. Griswold succeeded General Patch as XIV Corps commander April 26, 1943. In a lightning campaign which began June 30, 1943 with the invasion of Rendova Islands, General Griswold's forces which included the 43rd (New England) and the 37th (Buckeye) Infantry Divisions with elements of the 25th Division, seized New Georgia and the important Munda airfield Aug. 6. Mopping up of the adjacent islands was completed and the New Georgia campaign ended Oct. 6, 1943. American and New Zealand aircraft operating from the Munda field began the neutralization of Kahili and other enemy airfields in Bougainville.

In one of the most decisive defeats in the history of the Japanese military, the XIV Corps in Bougainville in March, 1944, slew more more than 9,000 Japanese in 18 days of violent fighting. Virtually annihilated was a once fine 17th Imperial Japanese army. Part of this army was the Sixth Imperial Infantry Division, considered Japan's best division in the early Chinese campaigns. It played a major part in the Rape of the Chinese city of Nanking in 1937.

General Griswold's forces racked up an impressive ratio of more than 30 Japanese slain for each American killed in this Second Battle of Bougainville. The 37th and Americal Divisions and two Battalions of the Fiji Military Forces were principal combat units of the XIV Corps for this operation. Elements of the 93rd (Negro) Army Infantry Division arrived after the peak of the battle and assisted in harassing retreating Japanese troops. The three airfields in the Bougainville perimeter were used as bases for allied aircraft which reduced the once mighty Japanese air and naval base of Rabaul, New Britain, to an impotent outpost of the enemy's island empire. The first raid on Truk, big Japanese air and naval base in the Central Pacific was staged through Bougainville by Liberators of the 13th Army Air Force.

From the Solomon's campaigns the XIV Army Corps gained the nickname, "Kings of the Solomons."

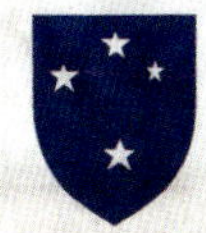

Americal Division

6th Division

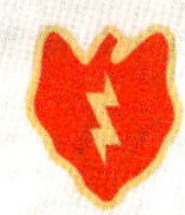

25th Division

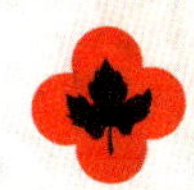

43rd Division

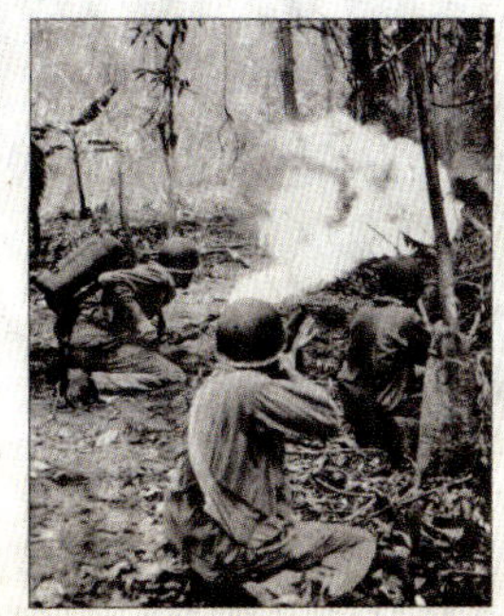

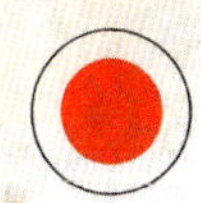

37th Division

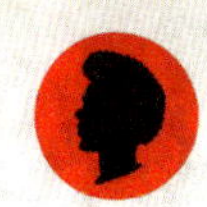

Fiji Military Forces

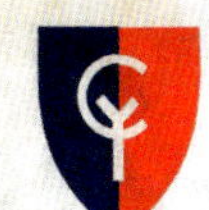

38th Division

# LIBERATORS OF MANILA

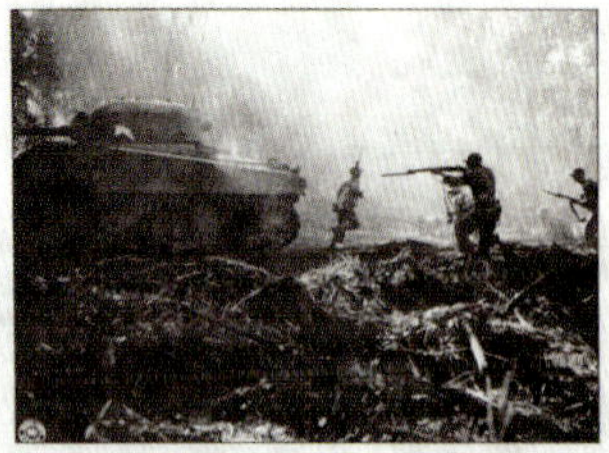

The XIV Army Corps with its initial divisions, the 37th and the 40th (Sunshine), Infantry Divisions, landed on the shores of Lingayen Gulf, Luzon, Philippine Archipelago, S-Day which was Jan. 9, 1945. The landing was made without ground opposition as the Japanese garrison completely surprised, fled three days before S-Day at the start of an intensive naval and aerial bombardment.

Meeting spasmodic resistance the corps drove rapidly south towards Manila, capturing successively Binmaley, San Carlos, Malasiqui and Tarlac. At Bamban the enemy was strongly entrenched in the 40th's sector in the foothills of the Zambales Mountains. Attacking abreast the 37th and 40th sufficiently reduced the resistance to allow the 37th to continue on to Manila. The 40th was left to contain and exterminate the stubbornly resisting Japanese.

The 1st Cavalry Division from Guimba began a drive to Manila overrunning the towns of Cabantuan, Santa Rosa and Gapan, and by Feb. 1, 1945, the 37th and the 1st Cavalry were poised north of Manila ready for the battle for the Philippines' capital city.

Elements of the 11th Airborne Division made a para-troop, amphibious invasion of Nasugbu on the west coast of Batangas Province, 32 miles southwest of the former American naval base of Cavite, Feb. 2. This move was to seal off the Japanese forces south of Manila. The 11th, passing to XIV Corps control, began a push toward a junction with columns of the 37th and 1st Cavalry.

Feb. 3 the 1st Cavalry entered Manila liberating 3,700 American internees at Santo Tomas and the next day doughboys of the 37th marched into Bilibid Prison freeing 800 American civilians and soldiers captured on Bataan and Corregidor in 1941.

Resistance was quickly reduced north of the Pasig River but the Japanese fought ferociously in Southern Manila. Forces of the 37th, 1st Cavalry and the 11th Airborne joined up in Manila Feb. 13. Meanwhile the 6th (Red Star) Infantry Division joined the XIV Corps Feb. 17 and attacked well fortified enemy forces in the Shimbu Line east of Manila. In a brilliantly executed amphibious, air, para-troop, ground assault, elements of the 11th Airborne Division aided by elements of XIV Corps Special Troops, freed 2,100 American internees from the Los Banos Prison Camp, Feb. 23.

Main enemy resistance collapsed with the taking of the ancient walled city (Intramuros) Feb. 24 by the 37th Division. Mopping up was completed in three public buildings which had been fortified by the Japanese and in Manila Bay where Japanese had set up desperation defenses in hulks of sunken ships.

The cleanup of Southern Luzon with the 1st Cavalry and 11th Airborne comprising major corps units was begun March 15, and by May 20 the area was declared free of Japanese organized resistance. Then the corps with the 6th, 32nd (Red Arrow), 37th and the 38th (Cyclone) Divisions began the cleanup of Northern Luzon, July 1.

In the Solomon Islands the XIV Corps had slain more than 21,000 Japanese and in Central and Southern Luzon killed more than 41,000 enemy, 17,173 of which were exterminated in the Manila area. To its sobriquet of "Kings of the Solomons" the XIV Army Corps had added "Liberators of Manila."

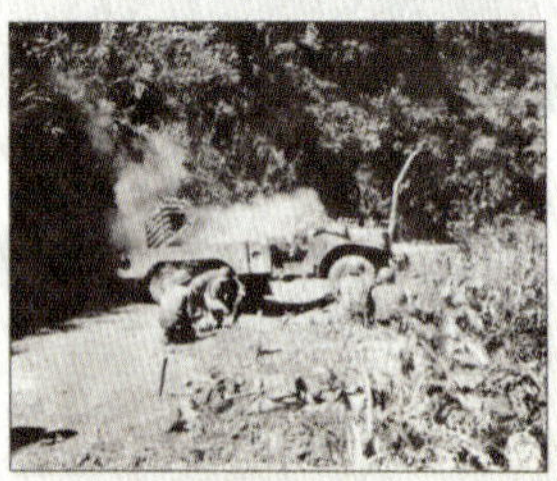

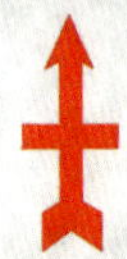

32nd Division

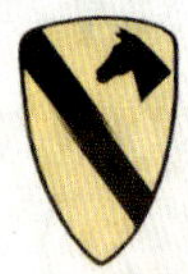

1st Cavalry Division

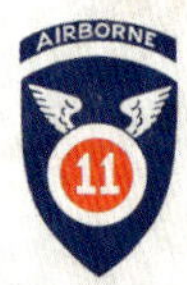


11th Airborne Division

2nd Marine Division

40th Division

93rd Division

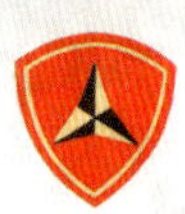

3rd Marine Division

ALL PHOTOS

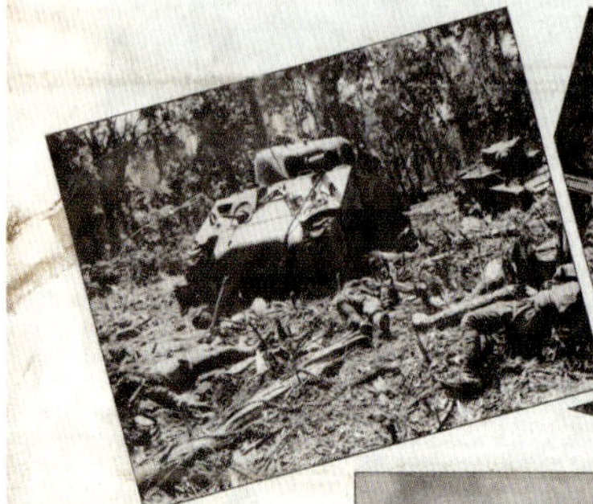

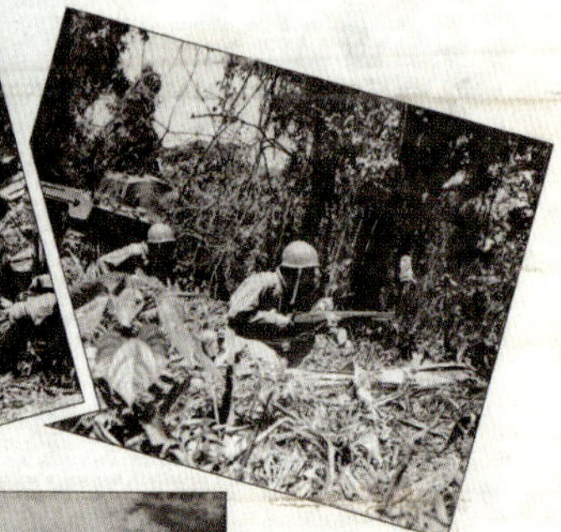

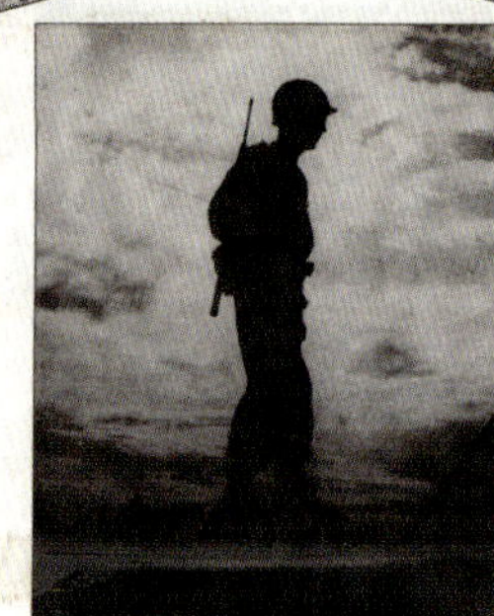

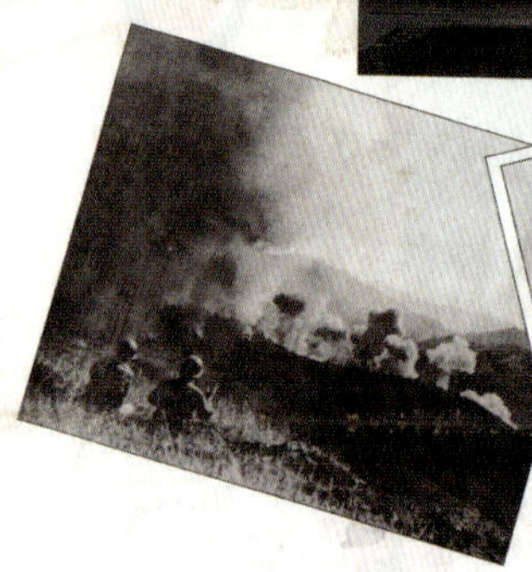

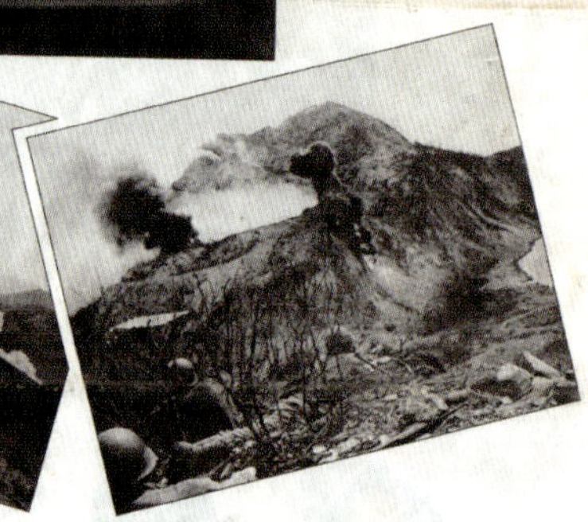

This pictorial history has been prepared and reproduced by the 670th Engr. Top. Co. under supervision of XIV Corps Public Relations Office. It has been approved for mailing by the XIV Corps Base Censor.

as follows: *This pictorial history has been prepared and reproduced by the 670th Engr. Top. Co. under the supervision of XIV Corps Public Relations Office. It has been approved for mailing by the XIV Corps Base Censor.* Harold signed the front of the pamphlet followed by the notation: *Major, C.M.P. Provost Marshall XIV Corps.*

***Kings of the Solomons***

*The history of XIV Army Corps in World War II dates from December, 1942. Under Lieutenant General (then Maj. Gen.) Alexander M. Patch, the XIV Army Corps directed the Americal and 25th (Tropic lightning) Army Infantry Division, the 2nd Marine Division, and the 147th Separate Infantry Regiment in the final drive which expelled the Japanese from Guadalcanal early in February, 1943. From airfields here guarded by the XIV Army Corps, Allied aircraft began the neutralization of the enemy's vital Munda airfields on New Georgia.*

*Lieutenant General, (then Maj. Gen.) O.W. Griswold succeeded General Patch as XIV Corps commander April 26, 1943. In a lightning campaign which began June 30, 1943 with the invasion of Rendova Islands, General Griswold's forces which included the 43rd (New England) and the 37th (Buckeye) Infantry Divisions with elements of the 25th Division, seized New Georgia and the important Munda airfield on August 6th. Mopping up of the adjacent islands was completed and the New Georgia campaign ended October 6, 1943. American and New Zealand aircraft operating from the Munda field began the neutralization of Kahili and other enemy airfields in Bougainville.*

*In one of the most decisive defeats in the history of the Japanese military, the XIV Corps in Bougainville in March, 1944 slew more than 9,000 Japanese in 18 days of violent fighting. Virtually annihilated was a once fine 17th Imperial Japanese Army. Part of this army was the Sixth Imperial Infantry Division, considered Japan's best division in the early Chinese campaigns. It played a major part in the Rape of the Chinese city of Nanking in 1937.*

*General Griswold's forces racked up an impressive ratio of more than 30 Japanese slain for each American killed in this Second Battle of Bougainville. The 37th and Americal Divisions and two battalions of the Fiji military forces were principal combat units of the XIV Corps for this operation. Elements of the 93rd (Negro) Infantry Division arrived after the peak of the battle and assisted in harassing retreating Japanese troops. The three airfields in the Bougainville perimeter were used as bases for allied aircraft which reduced the once mighty Japanese air and naval base of Rabaul, New Britain, to an impotent outpost of the enemy's island empire. The first raid of Truk, a large Japanese air and naval base in the Central Pacific, was staged through Bougainville by Liberators of the 13th Army Air Force. From the Solomon's campaigns the XIV Army Corps gained the nickname, Kings of the Solomons.*

***Liberators of Manila***

*The XIV Army Corps with its initial divisions, the 37th and the 40th (Sunshine) Infantry Division, landed on the shores of Lingayen Gulf, Luzon, Philippines, S-Day which was January 9, 1945. The landing was made without ground opposition as the Japanese garrison completely surprised, fled three days before S-Day at the start of an intensive naval and aerial bombardment.*

*Meeting spasmodic resistance the corps drove rapidly south towards Manila, capturing successively Binmaley, San Carlos, Malasiqui and Tarlac. At Bamban the enemy was strongly entrenched in the 40th's sector in the foothills of the Zambales Mountains. Attacking abreast, the 37th and 40th sufficiently reduced the resistance to allow the 37th to continue on to Manila. The 40th was left to contain and exterminate the stubbornly resisting Japanese.*

*The 1st Cavalry Division from Guimba began a drive to Manila overrunning the towns of Cabanatuan, Santa Rosa and Garapan, and by February 1, 1945, the 37th and the 1st Cavalry were poised north of Manila ready for the battle for the Philippines' capital city.*

*Elements of the 11th Airborne Division made a paratroop, amphibious invasion of Nasugbu on the west coast of Batangas Province, 32 miles southwest of the former American naval base of Cavite, February 2. This move was to seal off the Japanese forces south of Manila. The 11th, passing to XIV Corps control, began a push toward a conjunction with columns of the 27th and 1st Cavalry.*

*February 3 the 1st Cavalry entered Manila liberating 3,700 American internees at Santo Tomas and the next day soldiers of the 37th marched into Bilibid Prison freeing 800 American civilians and soldiers captured on Bataan and Corregidor in 1941.*

*Resistance was quickly reduced north of the Pasig River but the Japanese fought ferociously in Southern Manila. Forces of the 37th, 1st Cavalry and 11th Airborne joined up in Manila February 13. Meanwhile the 6th (Red Star) Infantry Division joined XIV Corps February 17 and attacked well fortified enemy forces in the Shimbu Line east of Manila. In an amphibious, air, para-troop, ground assault, elements of the 11th Airborne Division aided by elements of XIV Corps Special Troops, freed 2,100 American internees from Los Banos Prison Camp, February 23.*

*Main enemy resistance collapsed with the taking of the ancient walled city of Intramuros on February 24 by the 37th Division. Mopping up was completed in three public buildings which had been fortified by the Japanese and in Manila Bay where the Japanese had set up defenses in the hulks of sunken ships.*

*The cleanup of Southern Luzon with the 1st Cavalry and the 11th Airborne comprising major corps units was begun March 15, and by May 20 the area was declared free of Japanese organized resistance. Then the corps with the 6th, 32nd (Red Arrow), 37th and 38th (Cyclone) Division began the cleanup of Northern Luzon, July 1.*

*In the Solomon Islands the XIV Corps had slain more than 21,000 Japanese and in Central and Southern Luzon killed more than 41,000 enemy, 17,173 of which were exterminated in the Manila area. To its sobriquet "Kings of the Solomons" the XIV Army Corps had added "Liberators of Manila."*

Harold's notebook listed service in twelve different locations; in some instances, such as Guadalcanal and New Caledonia, service on more than one occasion. The shortest stay was one day in Vella Lavella; the longest was eleven months in Bougainville. He also spent seven months in New Caledonia, eight in the Philippines, and two in Japan, from which he returned to the United States. Most of photographs in his *War Odyssey* are from the four locations where he spent most of his time.

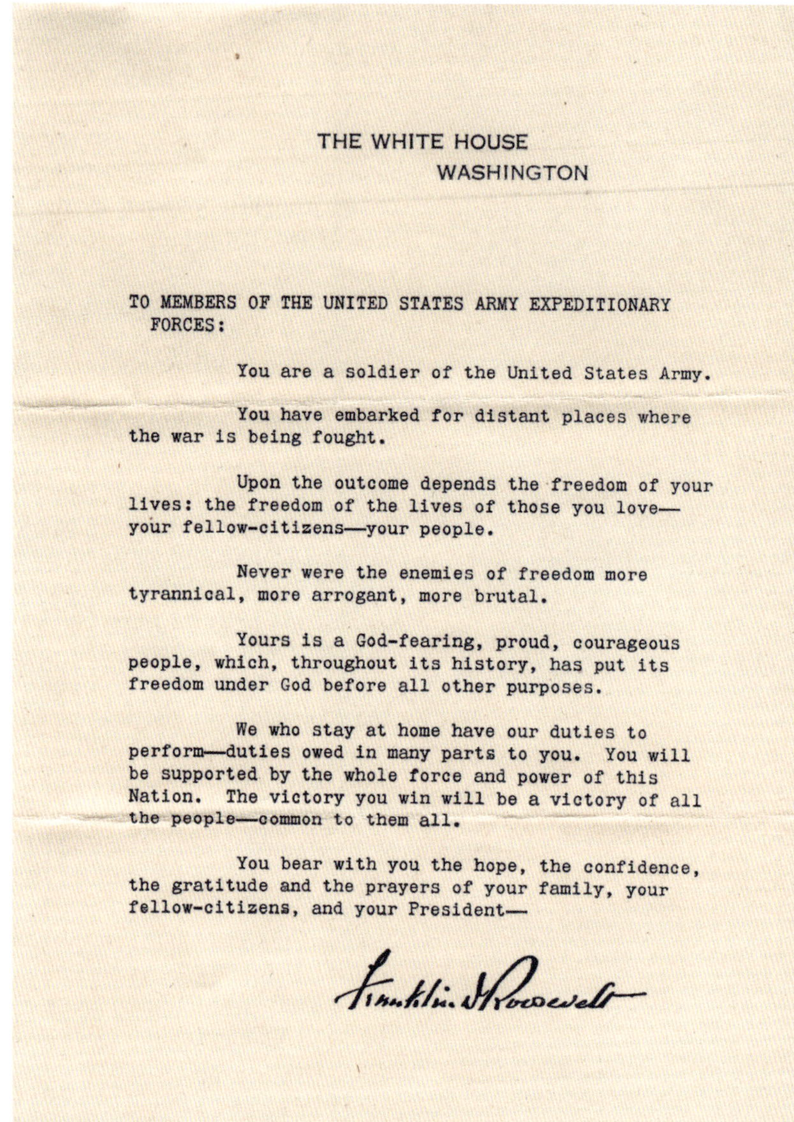

THE WHITE HOUSE
WASHINGTON

TO MEMBERS OF THE UNITED STATES ARMY EXPEDITIONARY FORCES:

You are a soldier of the United States Army.

You have embarked for distant places where the war is being fought.

Upon the outcome depends the freedom of your lives: the freedom of the lives of those you love—your fellow-citizens—your people.

Never were the enemies of freedom more tyrannical, more arrogant, more brutal.

Yours is a God-fearing, proud, courageous people, which, throughout its history, has put its freedom under God before all other purposes.

We who stay at home have our duties to perform—duties owed in many parts to you. You will be supported by the whole force and power of this Nation. The victory you win will be a victory of all the people—common to them all.

You bear with you the hope, the confidence, the gratitude and the prayers of your family, your fellow-citizens, and your President—

Franklin D Roosevelt

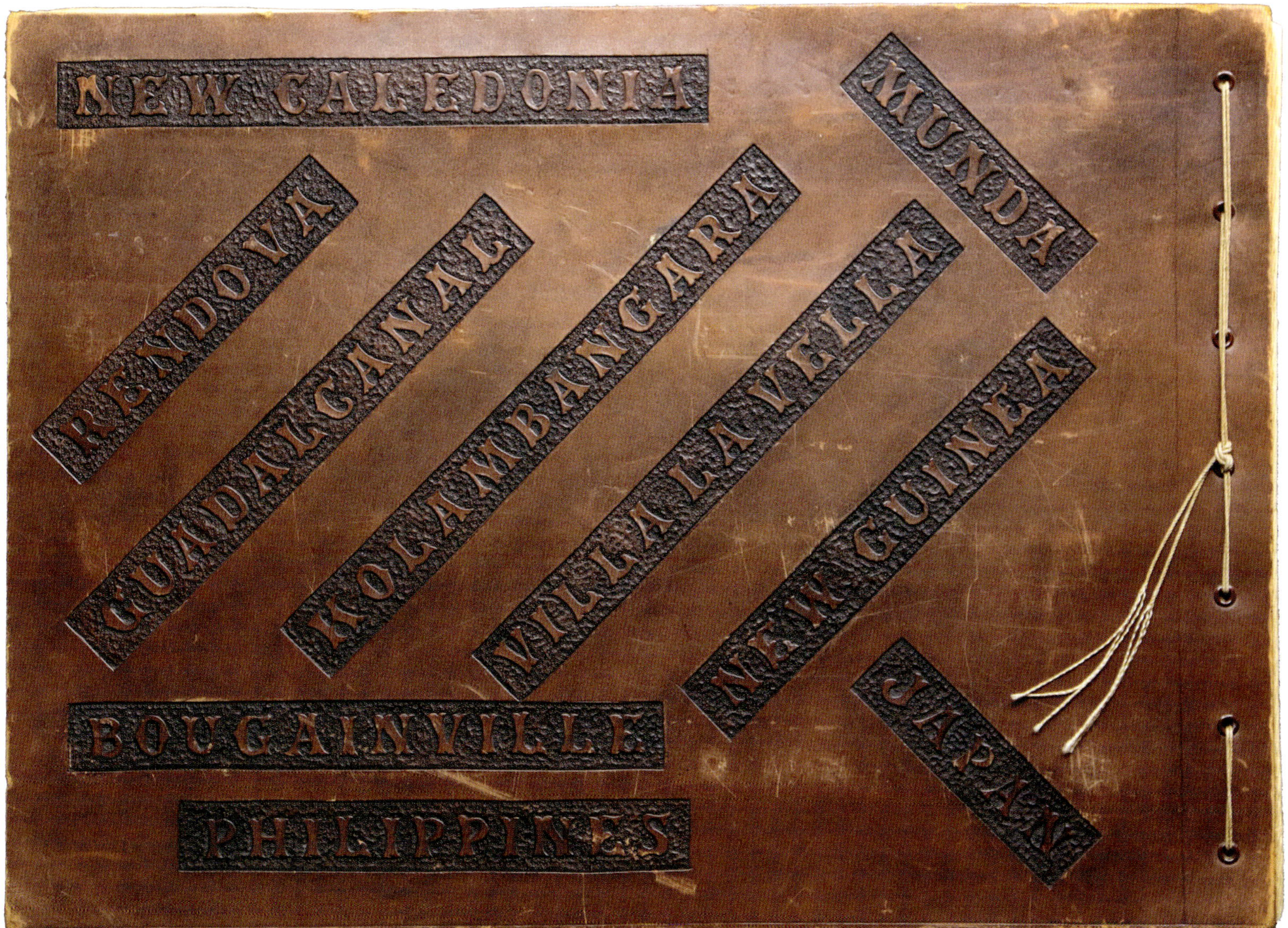


Harold's War Odyssey

**MUNDA**
**October 17-27, 1943**

The US Third Marine Division landed at Torokina on the northern side of Empress Augusta Bay on November 1, 1943. They secured the beachhead and then were relieved by the XIV Corps on November 15. Harold's note indicates he and his company arrived on December 10. There was heavy fighting, and in March 1944 the Japanese launched a full-scale offensive against the American positions but were repulsed. The Americans did not extend their perimeter farther and were in the same positions when the Australian II Corps under the command of Lieutenant General Stanley Savige took command in December 1944. There were still many Japanese troops on the island, some of whom could still offer significant resistance.

**BOUGAINVILLE**
**December 12, 1943—December 15, 1944**

Harold's year in Bougainville offered many different opportunities for taking photographs in a variety of circumstances and in some cases even appearing in photographs with visiting celebrities. But one of the celebrities happened to be leading a division of troops from Fiji, men Harold considered the finest jungle fighters he had ever witnessed in action. Their commander was Edward T. Cakobau, later Sir Edward, an Oxford-trained intellectual cricketer and sometime political figure who was also a direct descendant of the last King of Fiji. Harold and Edward were only two years apart in age and became good friends. Harold enjoyed taking portraits of his wartime friends, and his portrait of an injured Cakobau wearing a traditional sulu as well as his service pistol is one of his best. He also photographed the Fiji soldiers on numerous occasions, and Harold was even photographed wearing a sulu, given to him by Cakobau, who probably also took the photograph.

By mid-summer 1944 Japanese resistance on Bougainville was modest, despite their numbers; they had been deprived of normal rations of food for months, and their supplies with which to wage war were seriously depleted. They were still very dangerous, but as starvation set in their ability to fight was diminished. By August hostilities were so infrequent it was decided this would be a good time for a series of USO tours to be presented on the island.

The first Hollywood stars to arrive were in a show featuring Randolph Scott and Joe E. Brown. This was shortly followed by a more elaborate presentation featuring Bob Hope, Jerry Colonna, Frances Langford, Tony Romano, and Peggy Alexander. Harold was at the airfield when the planes arrived bringing this group; he took photographs in color, and there are photos of him standing by an airplane with Hope and Langford and talking to Colonna that were taken by others. There are also pictures of Hope and his troupe in performance and clowning with native islanders and troops from Fiji.

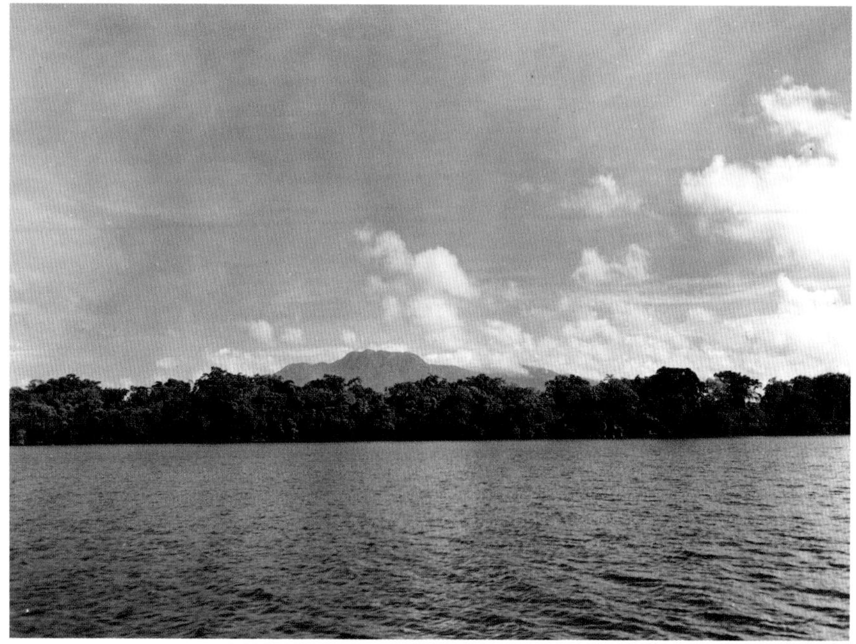

Kolambangara: "I had the living hell scared out of me on this island."

Bob Hope actually did a radio show from Bougainville on August 12 that was broadcast throughout the United States. Portions of it survive, and it is possible that Sarah heard the broadcast in Fort Worth. It is unknown if this particular show was in front of an audience that included Harold, but it is nice to think it might have been and that Sarah had heard it. Hope was an NBC artist, but at the end of the show he announces the show has been transmitted courtesy of the *Mosquito Network*. Someone else had suggested that these large open-air shows were being presented at "Loew's Bougainville," after the theater chain.

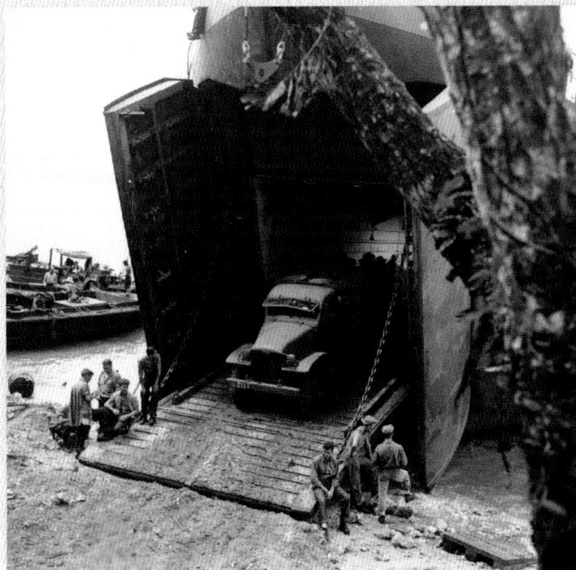

Unloading a long, slow target at Munda

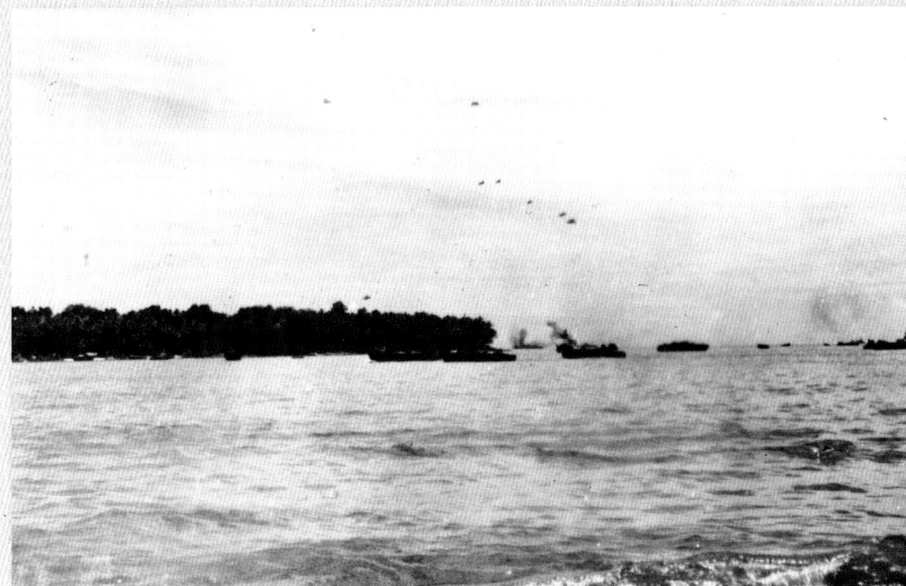

The landing at Munda under fire

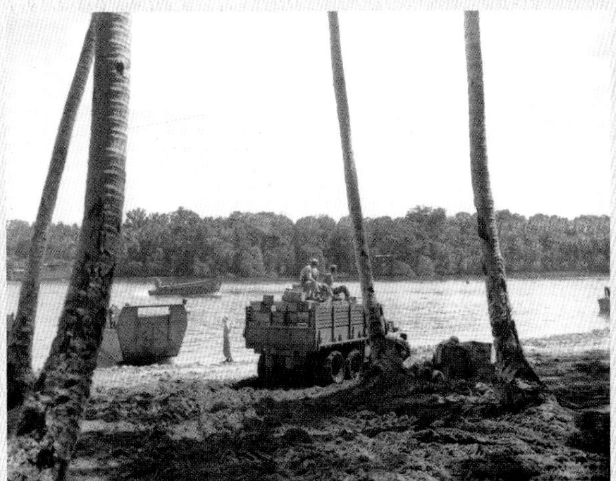

Loading supplies on shore at Munda

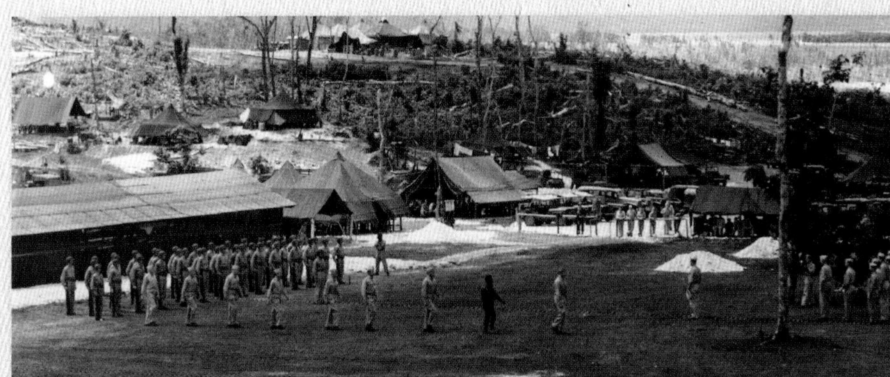

Munda, Rendova in the background

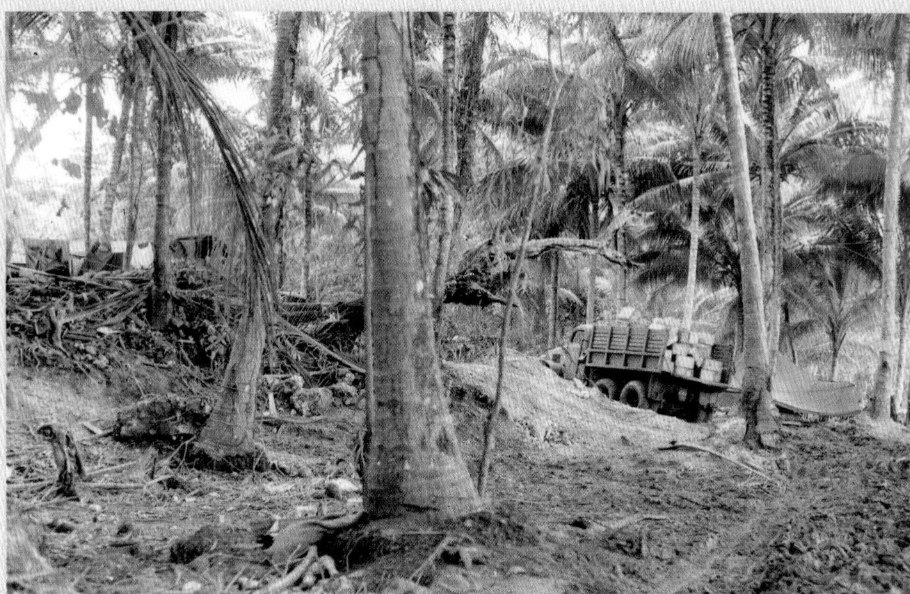

Delivery supplies on a muddy road

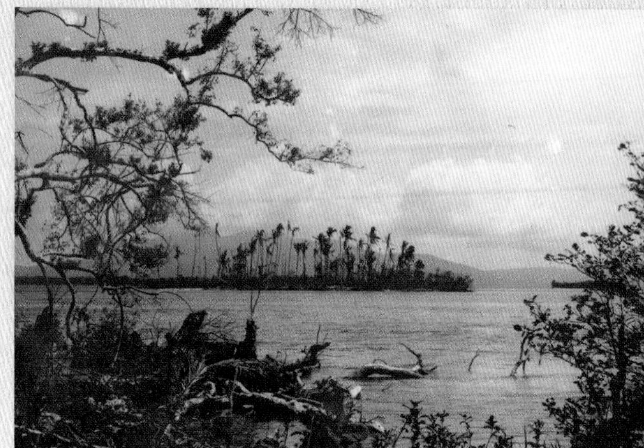

Rendova: "The Island of Mud" as seen from the end of the Munda strip

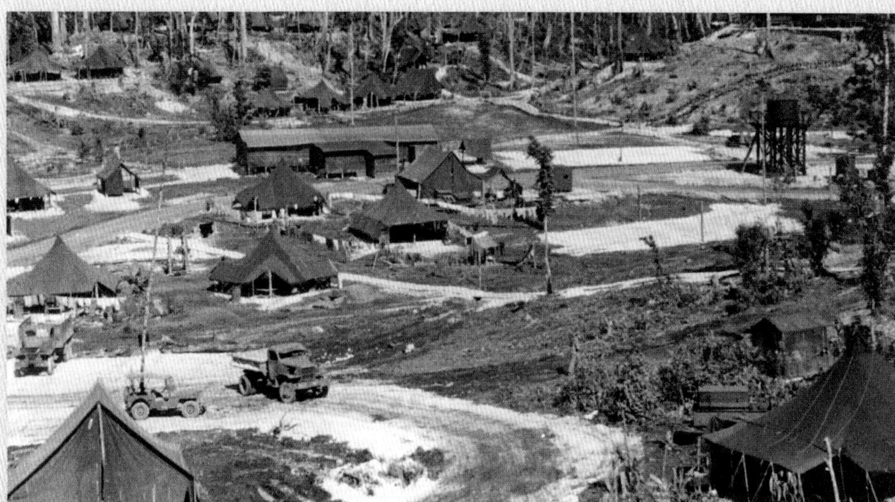

XIV Corps. Command Post, Munda

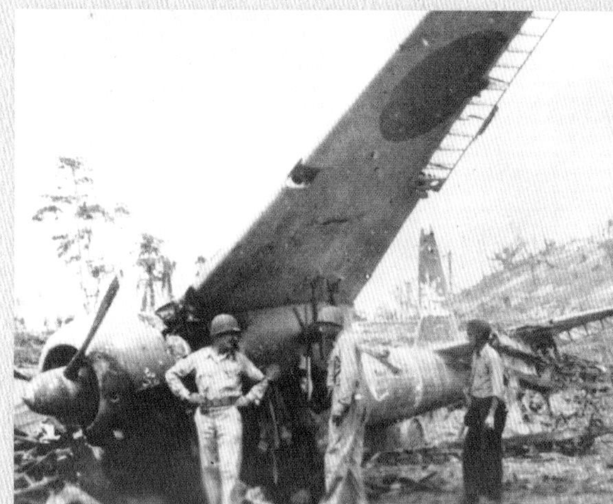

Me on left with crashed Jap airplane, Munda

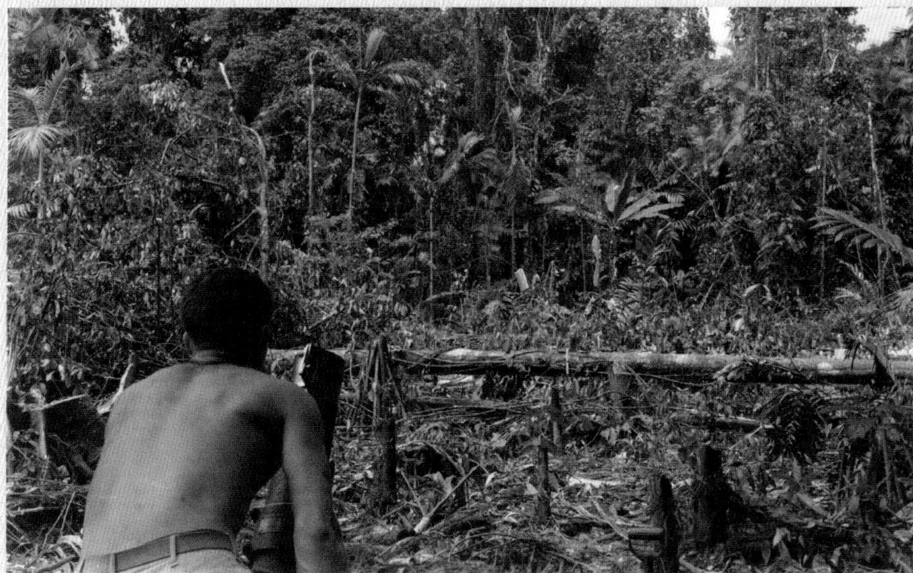

Mortar position for firing on Bougainville

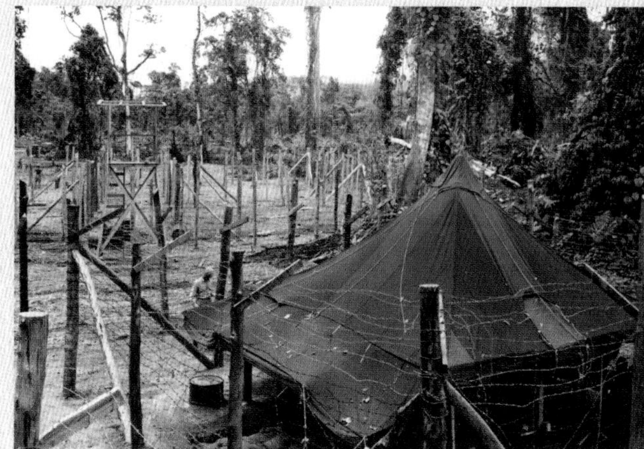

New Japanese prisoner of war stockade being constructed. Unnecessary as only eighty-eight prisoners were taken on Bougainville. All the rest were killed.

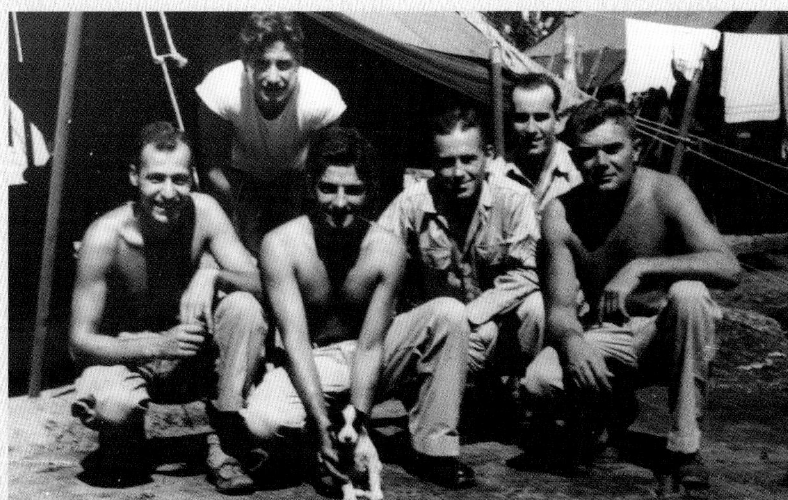

A dog will always be found

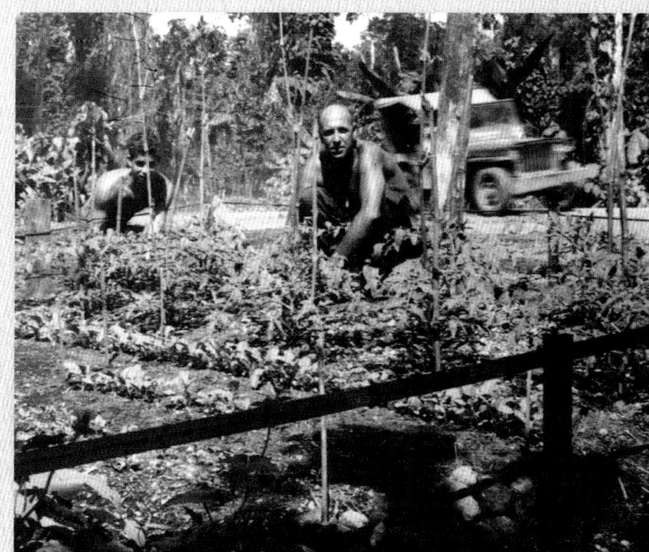

Backyard garden with zinnias and cucumbers and Toth with his tomatoes

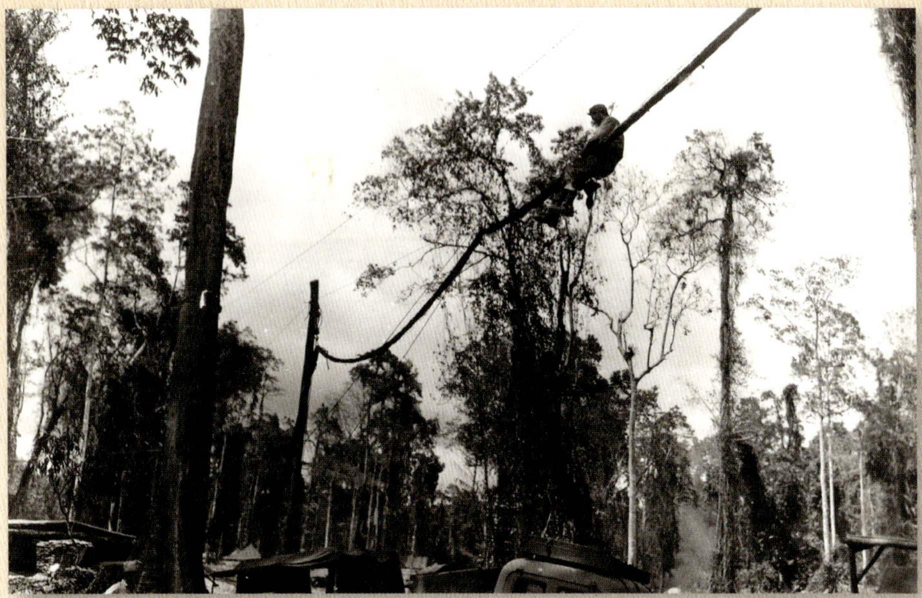

Signal construction set up by the XIV Corps signal organization on Bougainville

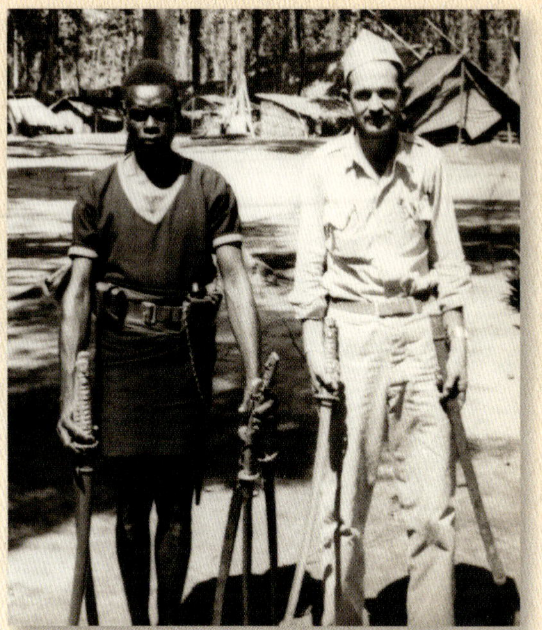

Captured Japanese swords on display

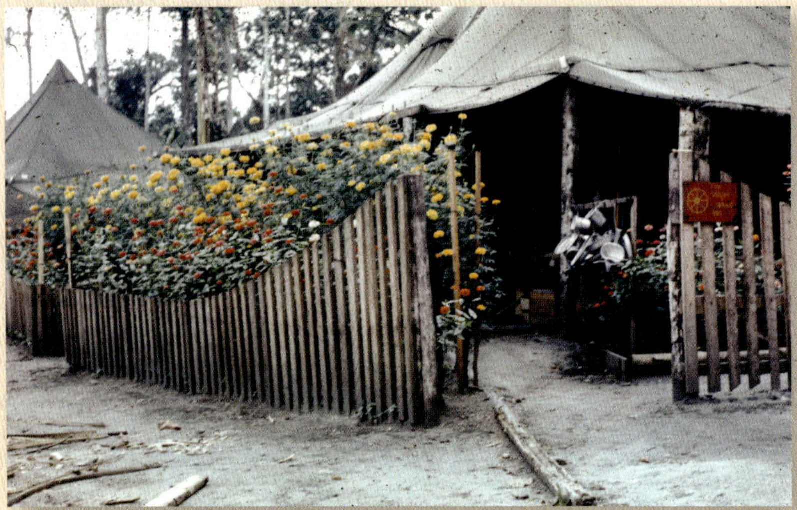

Flowers and tents in compound on Bougainville

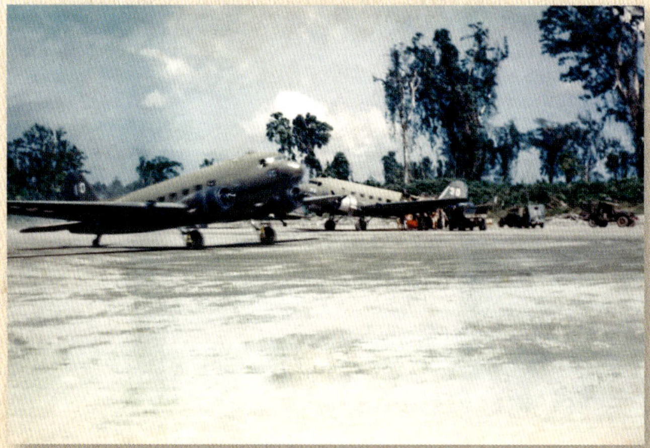

DC-3s on Bougainville

## Edward T. Cakobau and His Fiji Troops

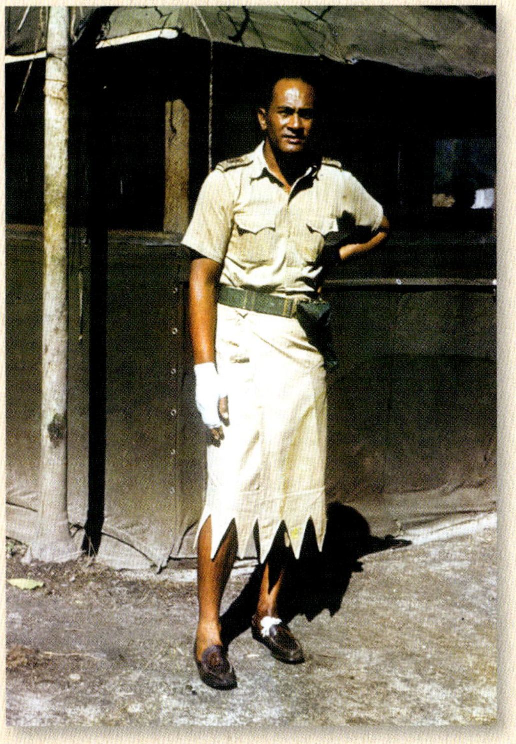

Edward T. Cakobau

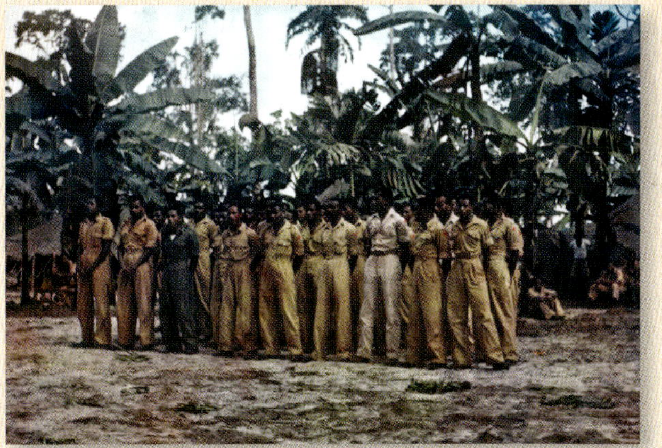

Fiji Troops at Parade Rest

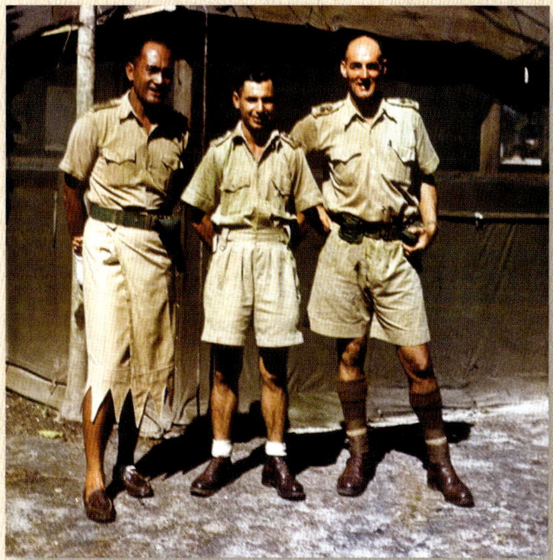

Cakobau with Australian officers

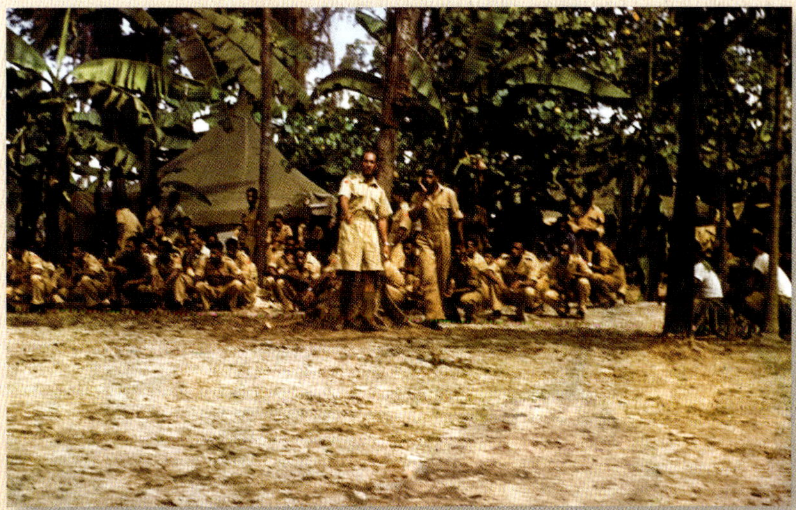

Edward T. Cakobau and his Fiji troops at rest

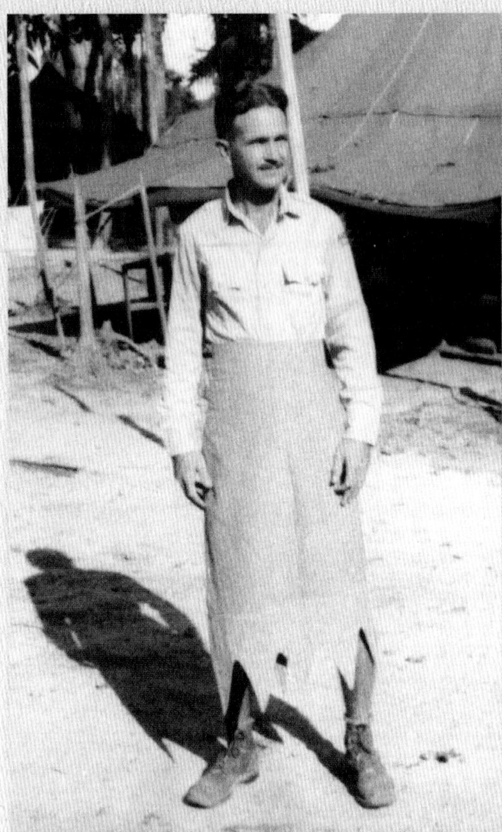

Harold in Ed Cakobau's sulu

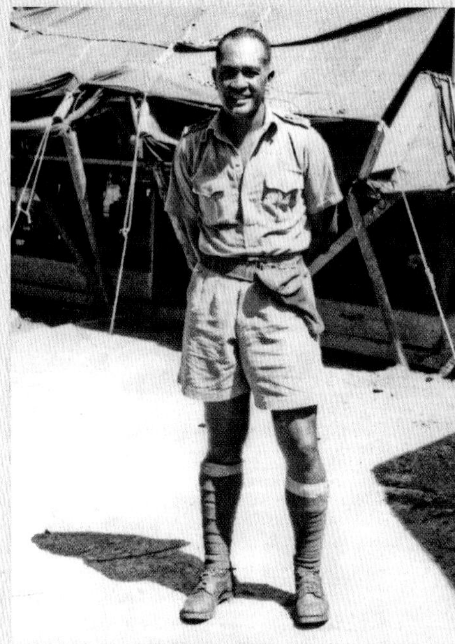

Edward T. Cakobau

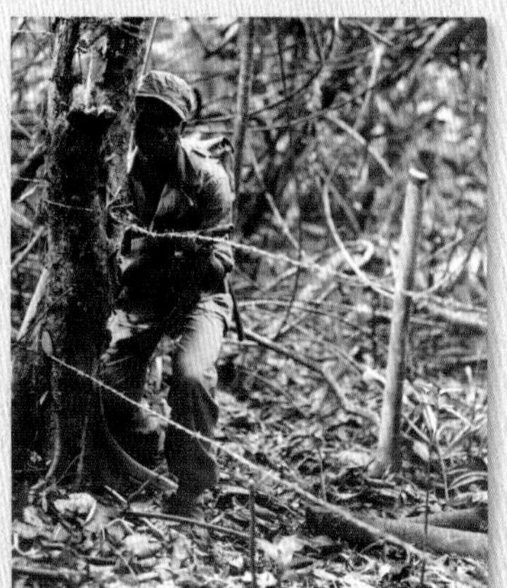

Fiji soldier in action

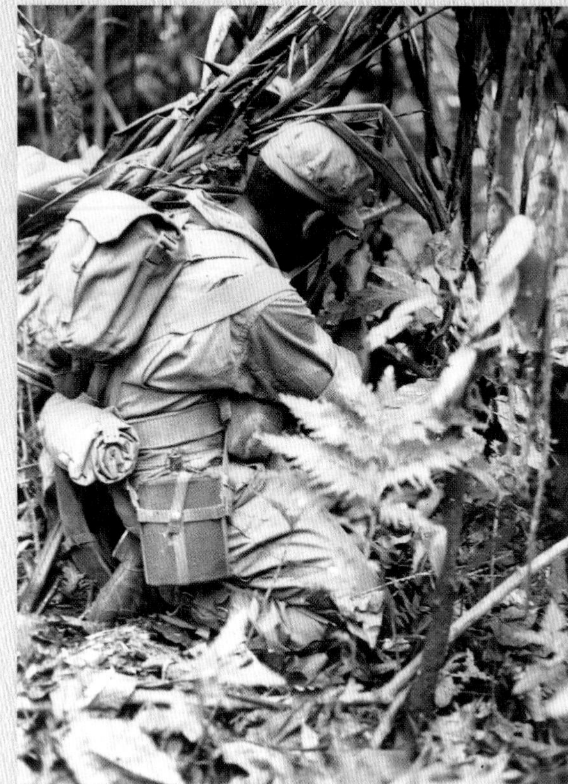

Fiji soldier in action

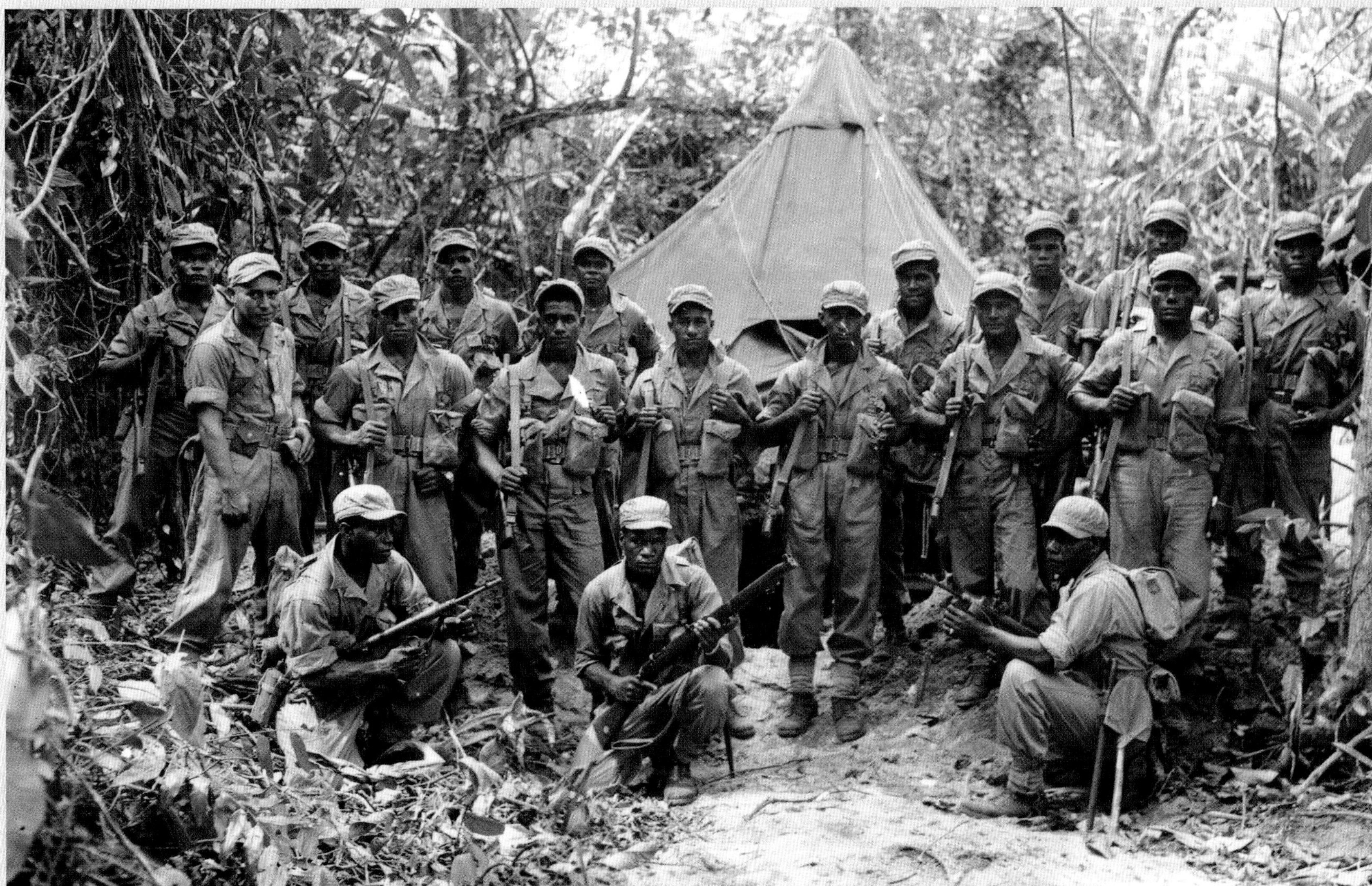

Fiji unit returned from action against Japanese

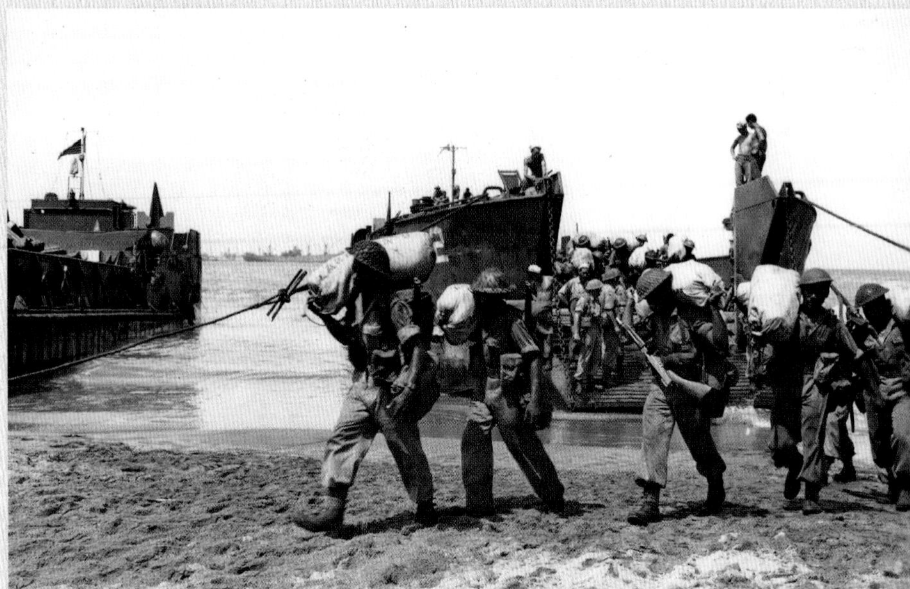

Fiji troops come ashore

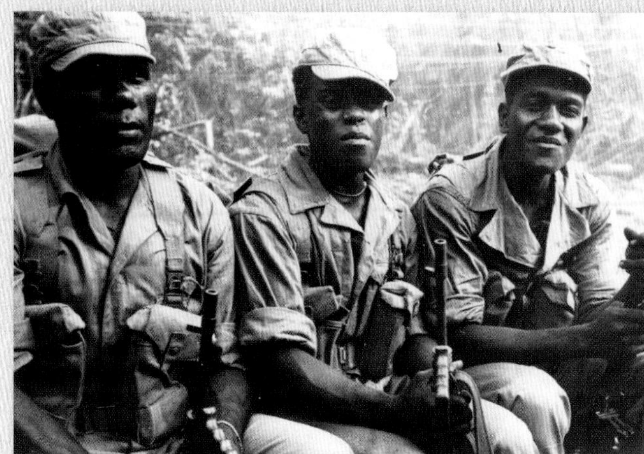

Three Fiji soldiers ready for action

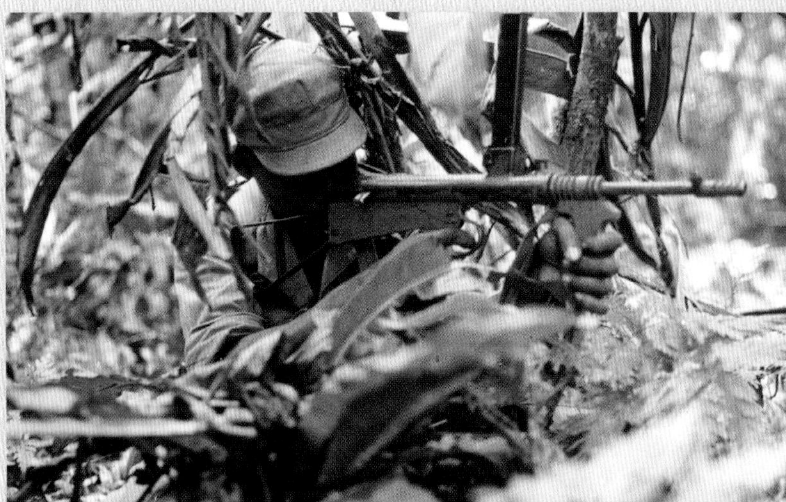

Fiji soldier in jungle cover

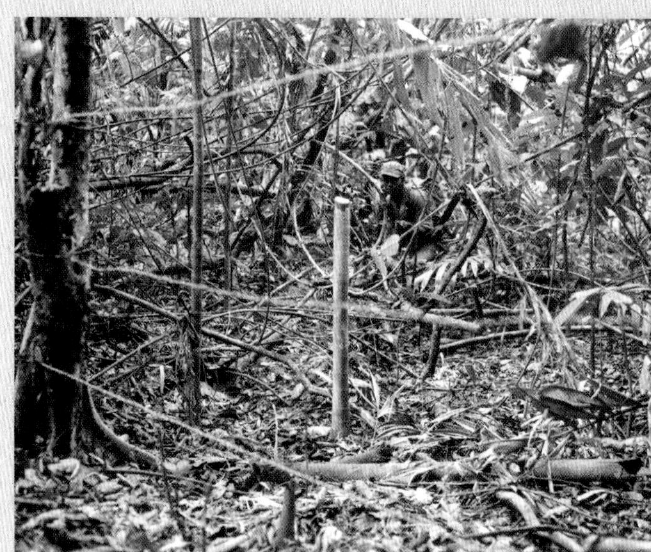

Fiji soldier in dense jungle

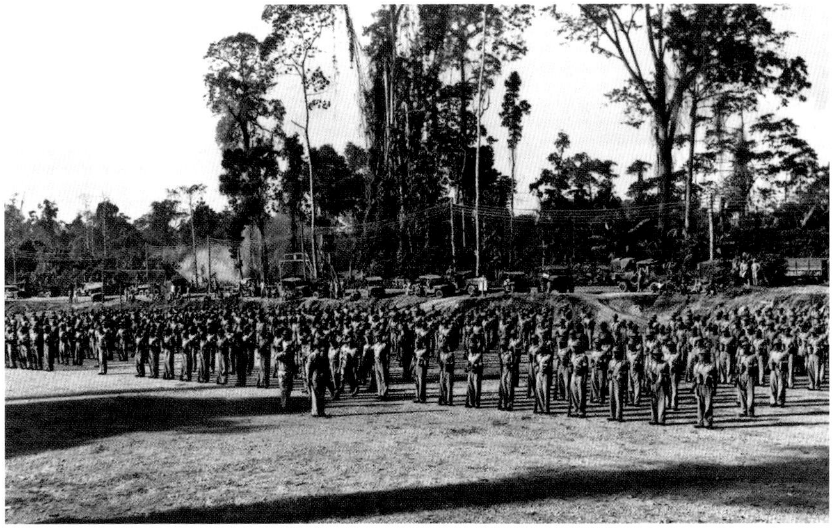

Fiji battalion in formation

The final touring group Harold saw in August was one headlined by Jack Benny that also included Carole Landis, Larry Adler, Martha Tilton, and Jane Bruner. This group also put on a show that was broadcast in the United States, but again it is not known if this was the one Sarah could have heard. What is known, however, is that Harold managed to take some photographs of Benny and Landis having coffee and doughnuts with some of his men.

After the last USO group departed, Harold and his company spent three months preparing for their next assignment, the invasion of the Philippines, at the same time working with Australian forces that would take over the US positions on Bougainville. There were still many Japanese troops on the island: estimates ranged from a low of 10,000 (US estimates) to 25,000 (Australian estimates), but in fact there were over 40,000, down from the 65,000 on the island when the US invaded. Approximately 23,500 Japanese soldiers surrendered to the Australians in September 1945.

### The Philippines

Harold and his company departed Bougainville on December 15 aboard the USS *Pinkney*. The ship was sturdy but slow, and it reached Lingayen Gulf on January 7, 1945. There was a short wait before he and his company clambered into the waiting landing craft and headed toward the beach on January 9. They first set foot in the Philippines on Binmaley Beach, then headed into the town of Binmaley itself. From there and for the next eight months he led his company in a generally southern direction until they reached San Jose on June 21. They were headquartered in San Jose until they shipped out to Japan on September 4.

Harold's papers included a detailed log of the day he reached a certain city, how long he remained there, and when he arrived in the next. He passed through many small towns and cities in Luzon, but remained only in Binmaley, Manila, Canlubang, and San Jose for more than two or three days. He managed to take a handful of photographs during his landing in Binmaley and photographed other Americans who landed later. It appears resistance was light.

Over the next nine months he would travel south and sometimes southeast to:

| | |
|---|---|
| Binmaley | January 9 -18 |
| San Carlos | January 18 – 22 |
| Camiling | January 22 – 23 |
| San Miguel | January 23 – 28 |
| Conception | January 28 – February 1 |
| Angeles | February 1 – 1 |
| San Fernando | February 2 – 4 |
| Santa Isabel | February 4 – 6 |
| North Manila | February 6 – March 15 |
| Canlubang | March 15 – April 3 |
| Santa Thomas | April 3 – May 12 |
| Canlubang | May 12 – June 21 |
| San Jose | June 21 – September 3 |

In 2018 most people rely on computer printouts, GPS systems, or even talking smartphones to guide them from one place to the next. Harold and his MP company were not so lucky; in 1945 they had a paper map. Had there not been a war raging it would have been given to tourists who wanted to navigate the Philippines on their own by car. In Harold's papers is a folded map that measures about twenty-four by thirty-six inches fully opened. In the upper right hand corner appear the words **Mobilgas** *1942 Road Map of the Philippines (Island of Luzon)*. It is moderately annotated with routes taken, one name, Major Orton, the word Fireball 27, and "Base M" near the town of San Fernando. It is unclear if this was the only map Harold had at his disposal, but if it was, it would seem he was lucky to have made his way to so many cities on this

# USO Tours - The Bob Hope Troupe

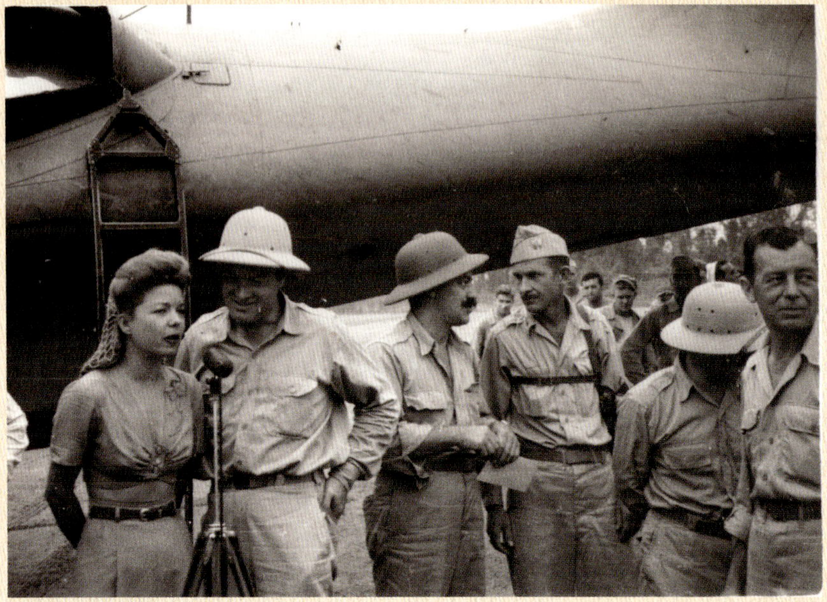

Francis Langford, Bob Hope, Jerry Colonna, Harold

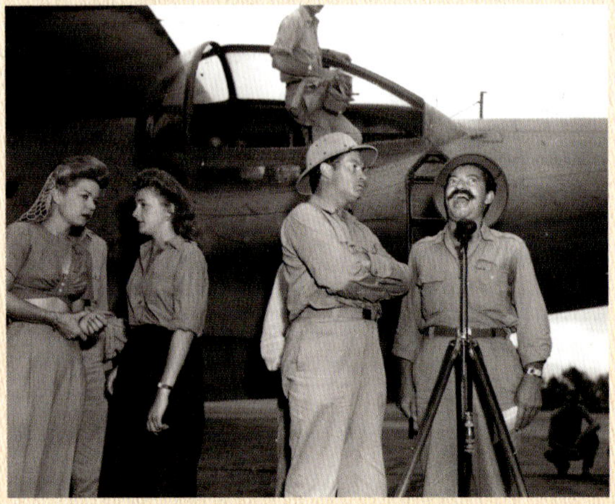

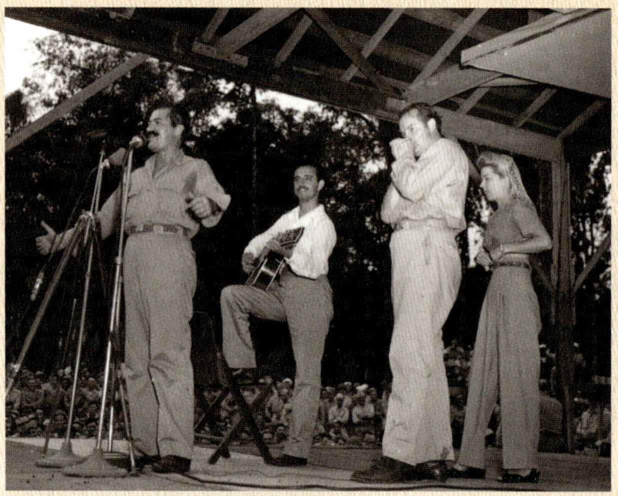

Jerry Colonna, Tony Romano, Bob Hope, Francis Langford

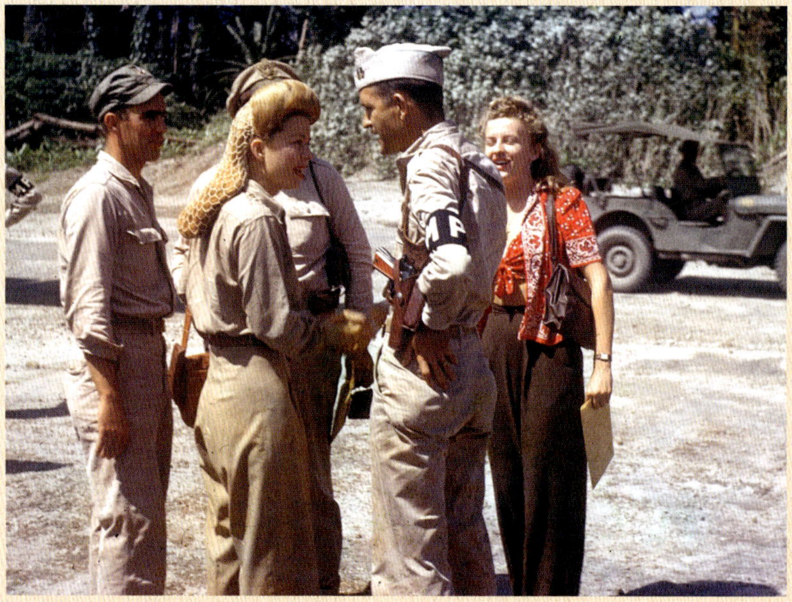

Francis Langford, Harold, and others at airfield

# USO Tours - The Jack Benny Troupe

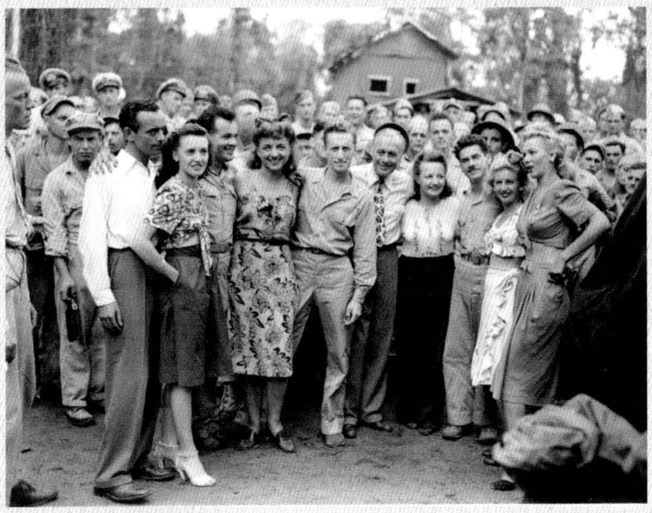

Jack Benny Troupe (Benny is fifth from right) with soldiers

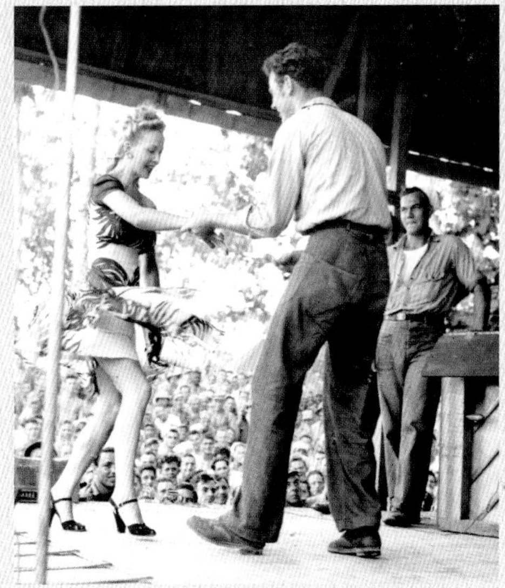

Carole Landis' jitter bugs with a sailor

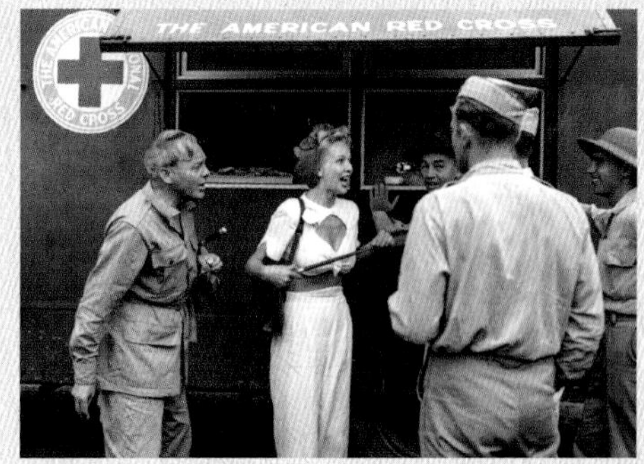


HAROLD L. O'NEAL, Captain, C.M.P.

Jack Benny & Carole Landis

First mail for them since they left the states.

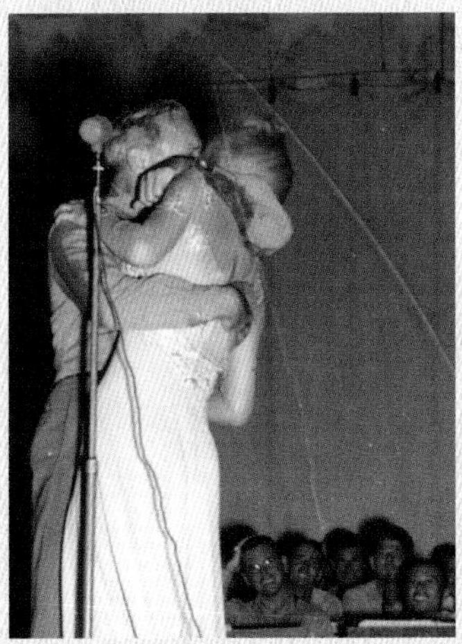

Jack Benny and Carole Landis

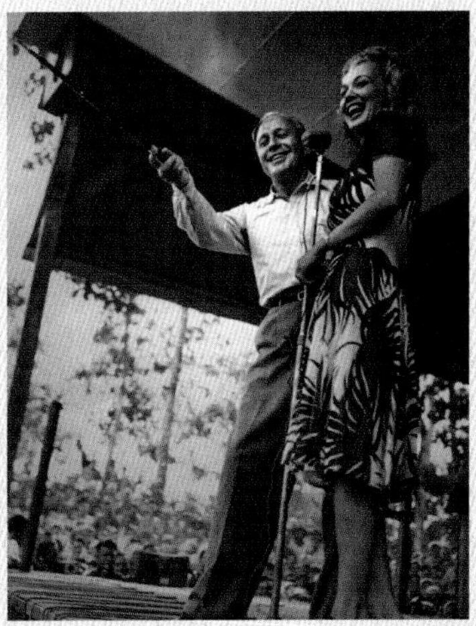

Jack Benny and Carole Landis

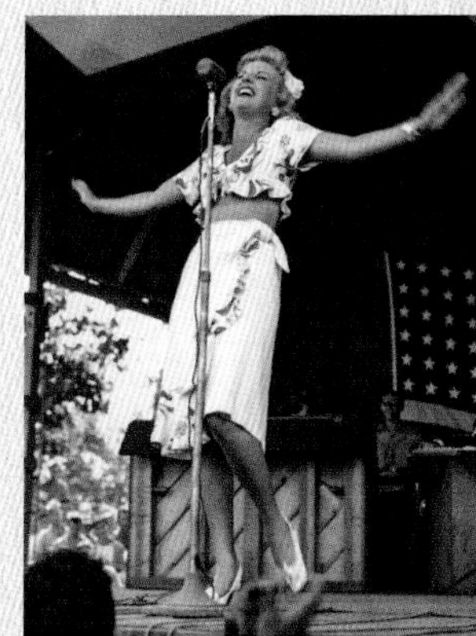

Martha Tilton

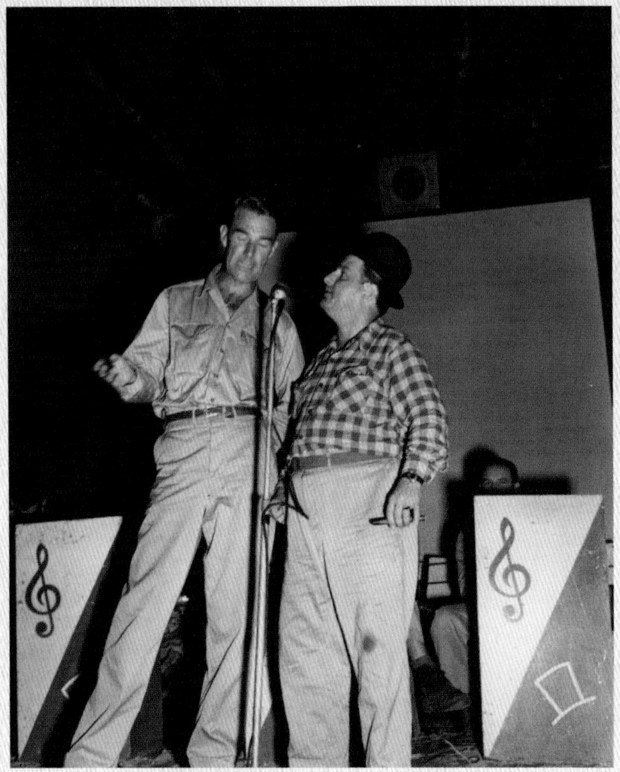

Randy Scott

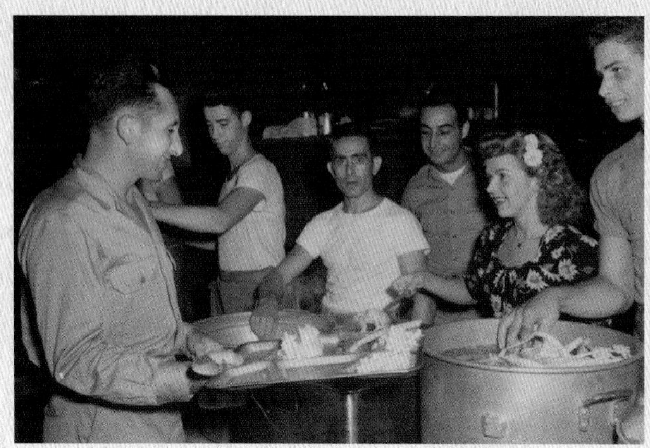

Peggy Alexander—U.S.O.
serves chow in my
kitchen.

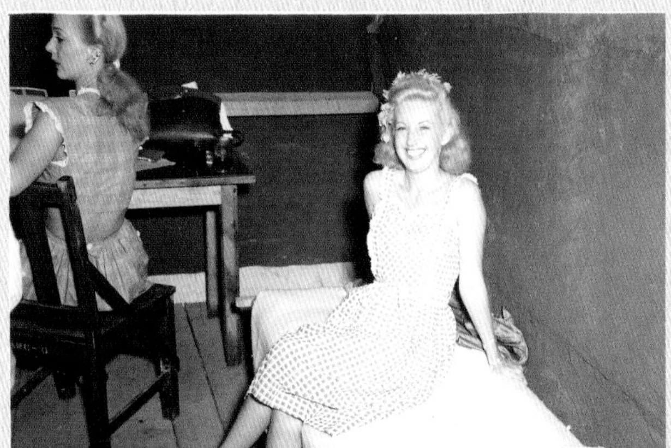

Carole & Martha

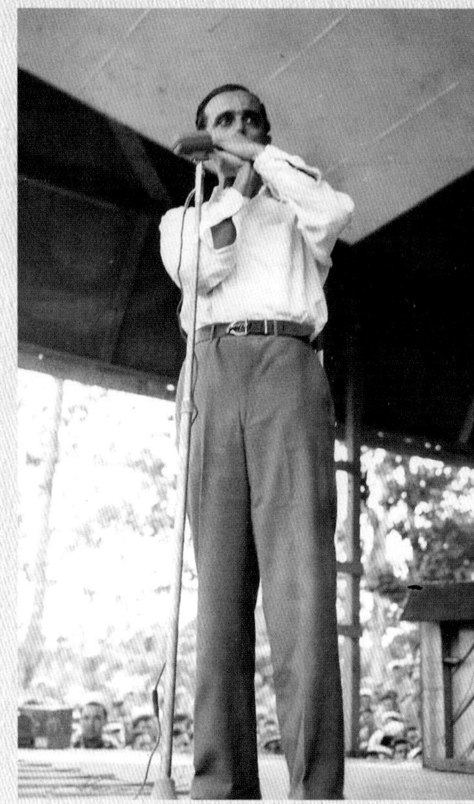

Larry Adler

## Harold and Men Relaxing

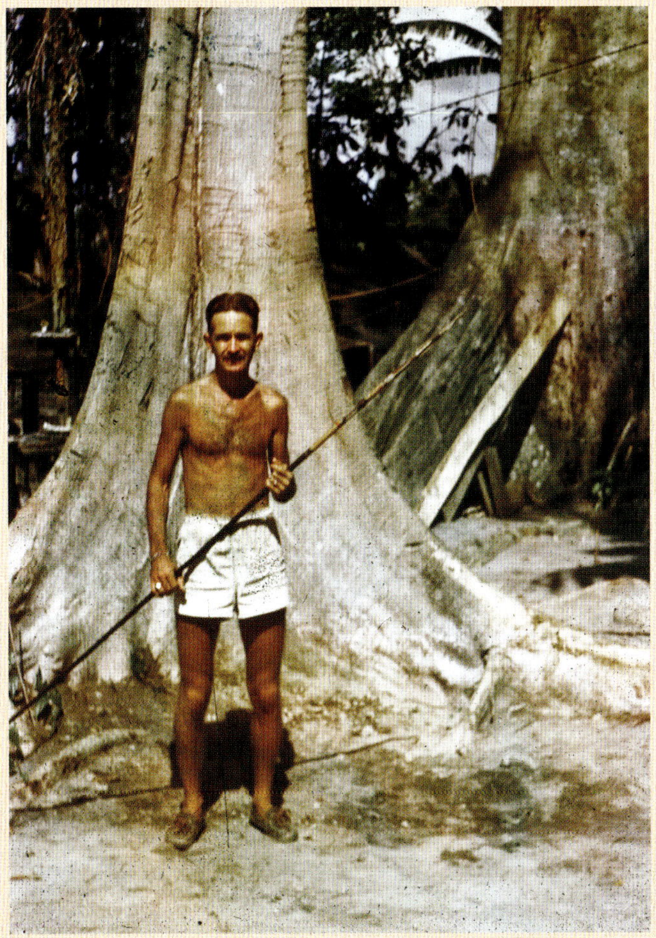

Armed with a spear

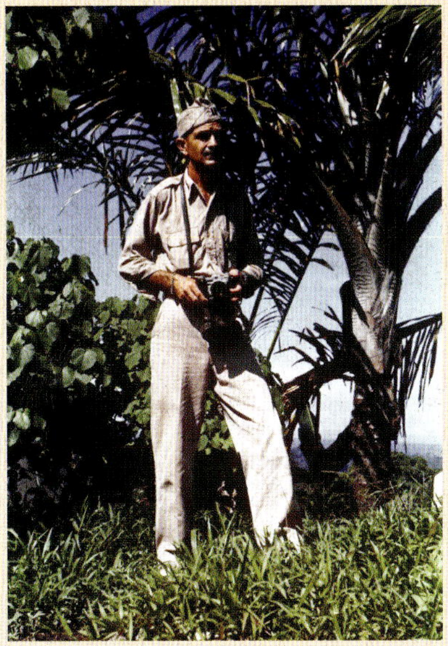

Armed with a Leica

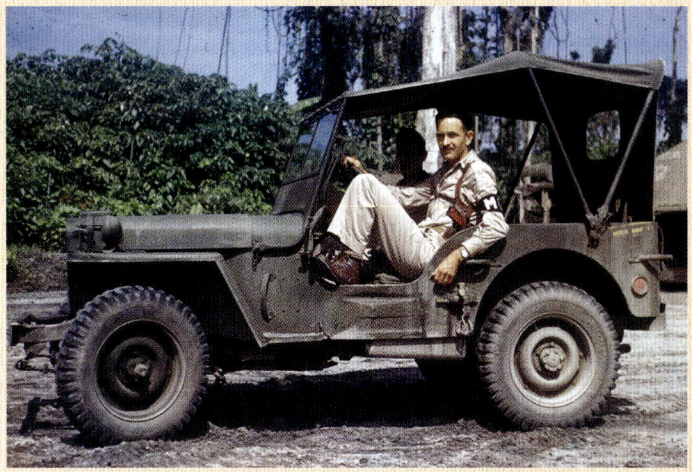

Armed with a Jeep

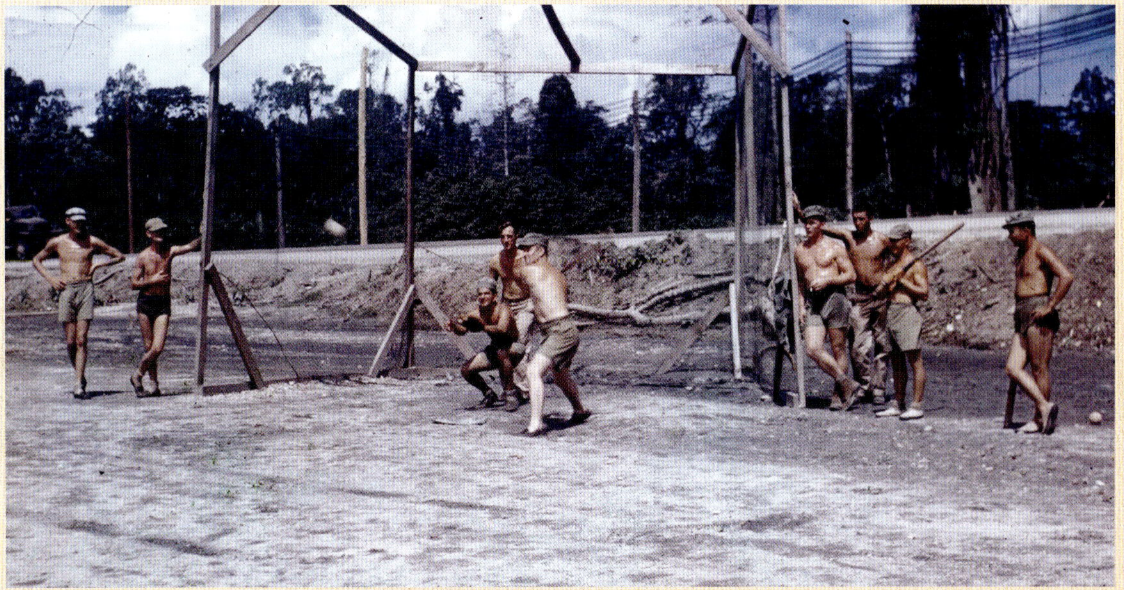

Softball game

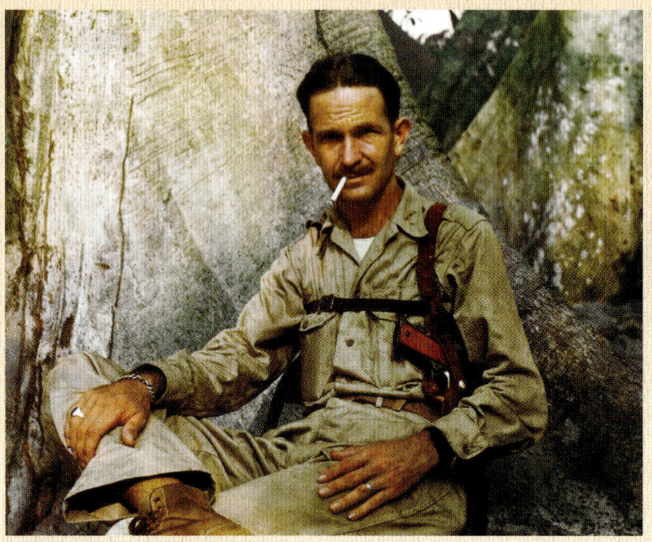

Armed with a Lucky Strike and a .45

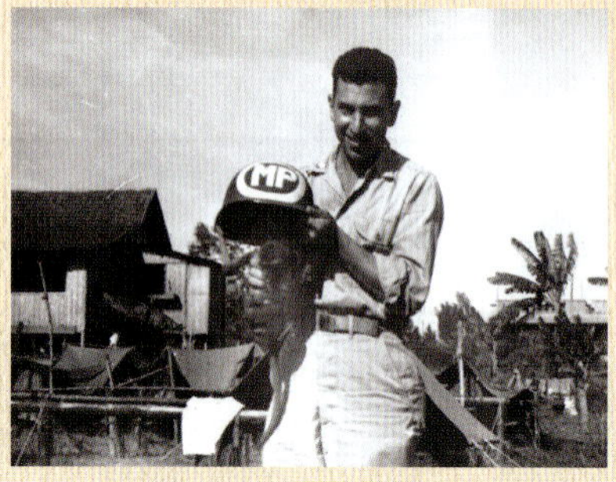


MP monkey and keeper

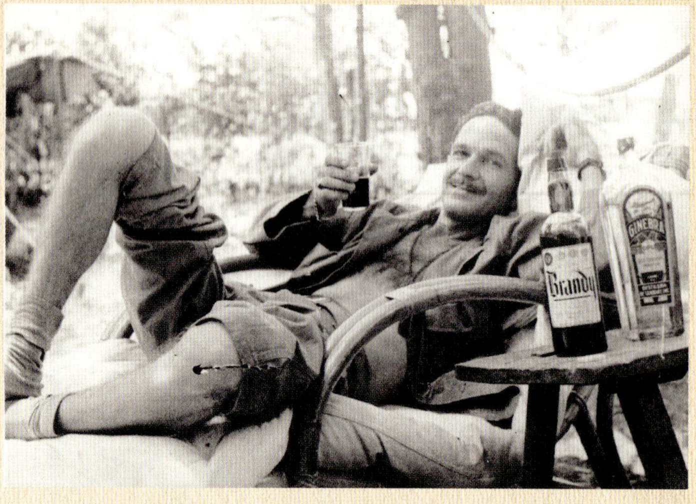


Harold and two friendly bottles

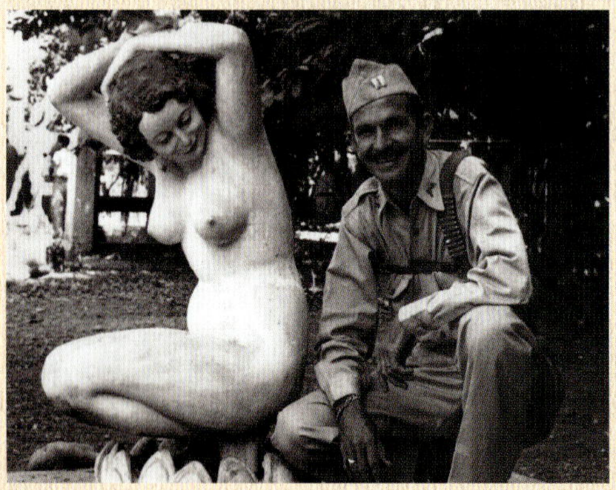

Harold's blind date

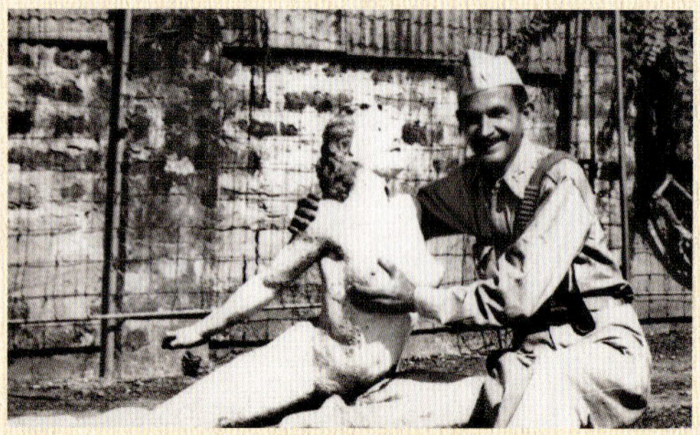

This is a bit too firm

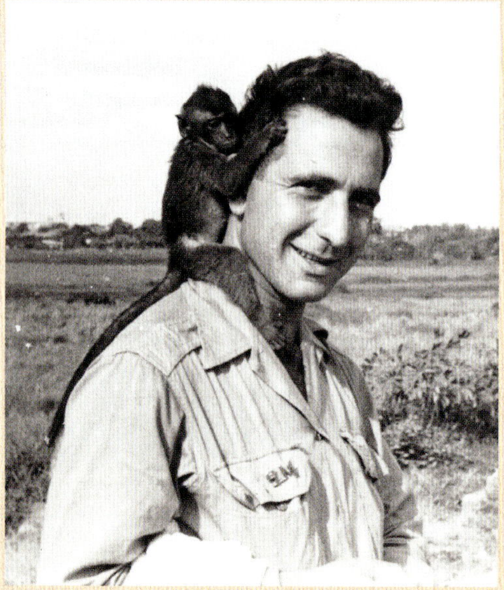

I'll stick with my monkey

battle-ravaged island. In later years he would teach me how to read a map, and I remain grateful.

Harold took many photographs in the Philippines, but since he was on the road so much, few of them have been printed. He did slow down long enough in Manila, where there was apparently reliable postal service, to contact Fotoshop, a camera store on Forty-Second Street in New York City, to order a Leica manual and a few rolls of film. On the same day he subscribed to *Minicam Magazine*, the precursor of *Modern Photography*. But the most important development while he was based in Manila is that he was appointed the Provost Marshall of the XIV Corps, replacing Col. John Frick. Three months later, on June 28, he became Major Harold L. O'Neal, a rank that was more appropriate for his responsibilities.

According to his records, Harold remained in San Jose until early September. Earlier in the year he had created a handmade calendar in his personal notebook. It begins with January 1, 1945. He then marked off the days until August 29, 1945. There are codes in the marking; one date is circled in red, January 9, the day he landed in the Philippines. But it was clear he was becoming war weary. His health was failing, and in the photographs of him from the Philippines it is clear his weight had plummeted, reflecting a condition that would cause his earlier-than-expected evacuation from Japan

His 201 files, however, provide a lot of details about what was happening as the war wound down. There was incredible activity and new orders and notices as the XIV Corps, including Harold's Military Police, were transitioned into the Eighth Army in preparation for their eventual assignment to Japan.

There is no mention in any of the paperwork about the atomic bombs on August 6 and August 9. The August 11 EXTRA edition of the *XIV Corps News* says simply that Secretary of State Byrnes had not received a formal notice that the Japanese were prepared to accept the unconditional surrender terms of the Potsdam Ultimatum. At the bottom of the EXTRA edition was a sentence that read:

**XIV Corps News**

***IN THE EVENT OF JAPAN'S SURRENDER IT IS URGENTLY REQUESTED THAT TROOPS REFRAIN FROM FIRING THEIR ARMS.***

The August 15 EXTRA EXTRA edition of the mimeographed XIV Corps News headline reads ***JAPAN QUITS! (FROM STATION KJEX SAN FRANCISCO) PRESIDENT TRUMAN HAS ANNOUNCED THAT JAPAN HAS ACCEPTED THE ALLIED TERMS OF UNCONDITIONAL SURRENDER***.

**Eichelberger Letter**

On August 17, General R. L. Eichelberger wrote to all the Commanders of Eighth Army Units.

*Eighth Army has been given the important mission of the unopposed occupation of Tokyo and Northern Honshu Island in Japan. With such a mission, the standards of conduct and dress which have developed during the long tedious months of jungle warfare are no longer applicable. From the moment the first American sets foot on the Japanese homeland, each soldier becomes an ambassador of the United States. His conduct and appearance will form the basis on which an outstandingly austere and repressed people will judge all Americans.*

*Ours is a happy but very difficult task. It will be made easier if each of us conducts himself with dignity and observes the highest standards of military courtesy, discipline, uniform and military appearance.*

*It will be necessary, from time to time, to promulgate certain curfew and "off limits" regulations. Such regulations will be kept to a minimum, but troops must be impressed with the importance of such rules to the maintenance of civil order. They must be obeyed.*

*Nothing is more important to a Japanese as "face." His leaders have lost prestige because we have proven ourselves to be better combat soldiers than they. We must not lose "face" by misconduct or slovenliness now that hostilities are over.*

*I have every confidence that my commanders will thoroughly indoctrinate the officers and men of subordinate units with*

## Wartime Supplies

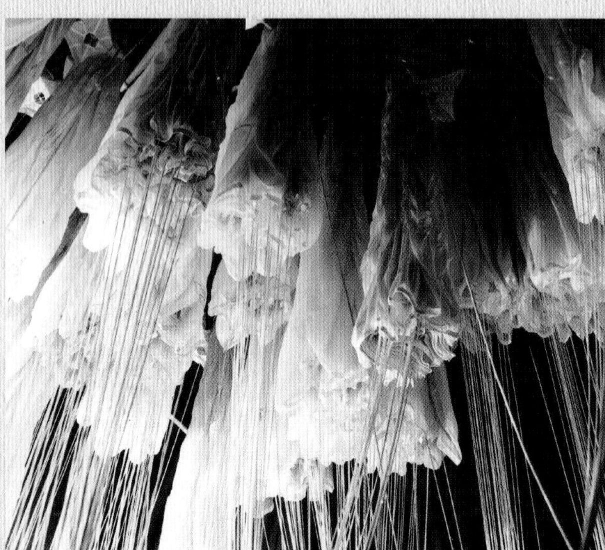

Parachutes

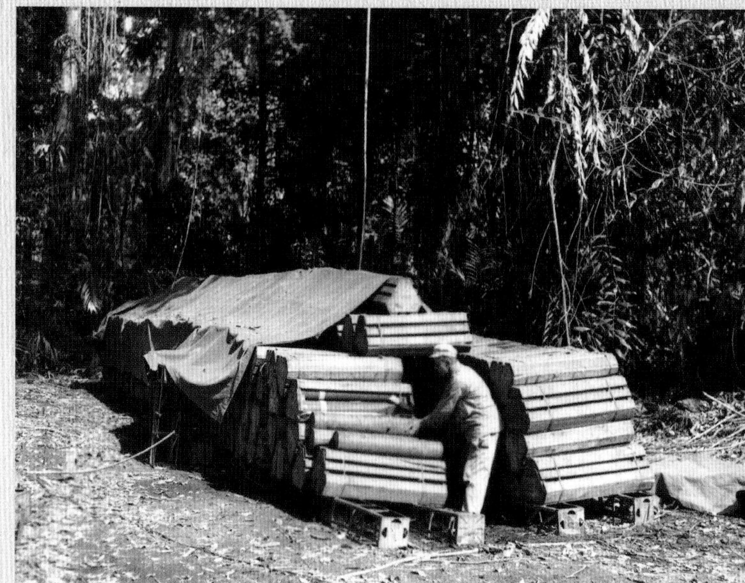

Ordnance dump

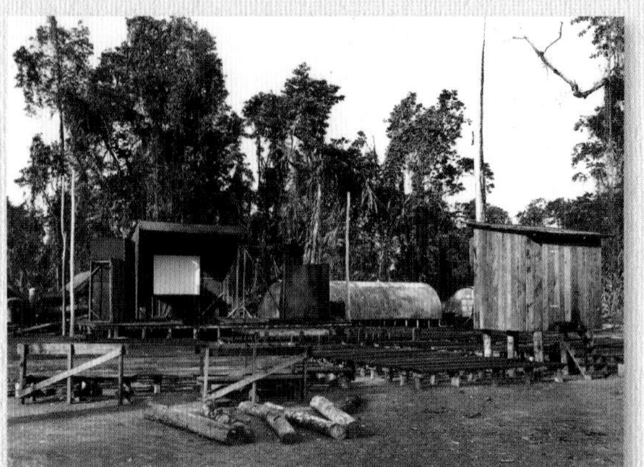

Outdoor movie theater

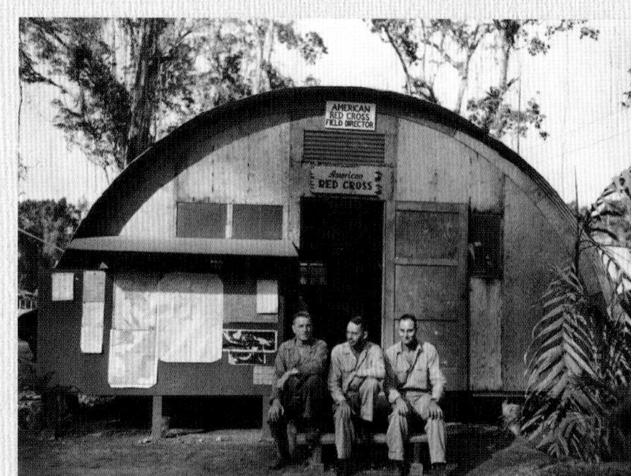


American Red Cross

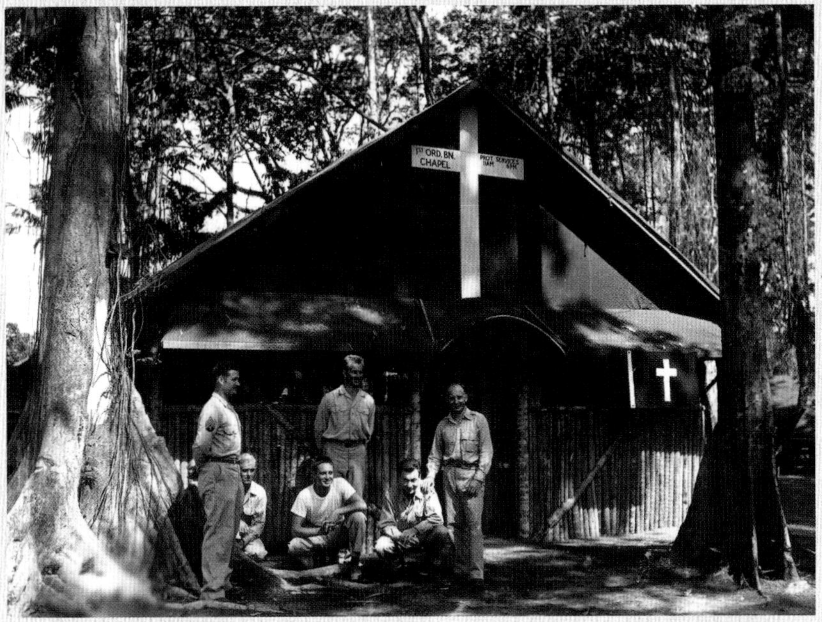


The Chapel

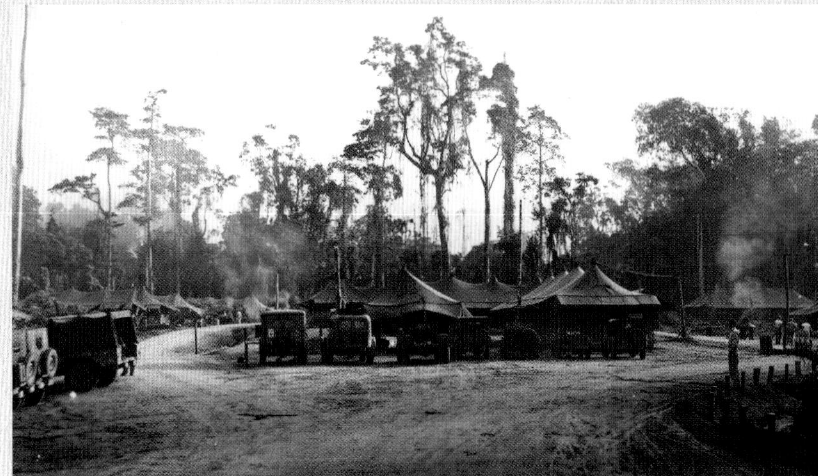

Hospital and Ambulances

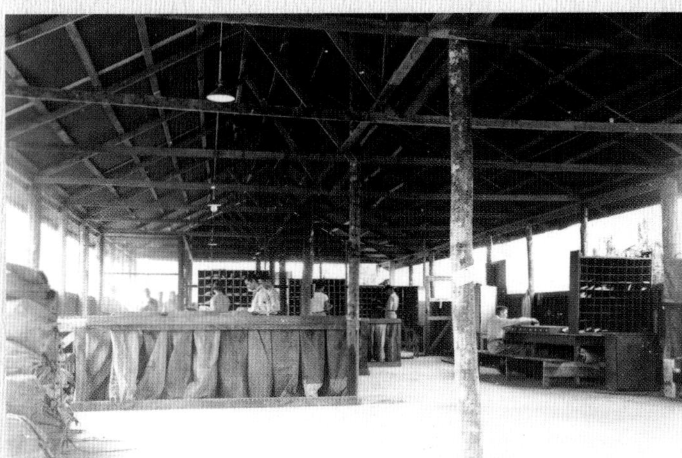

XIV Corps Post Office

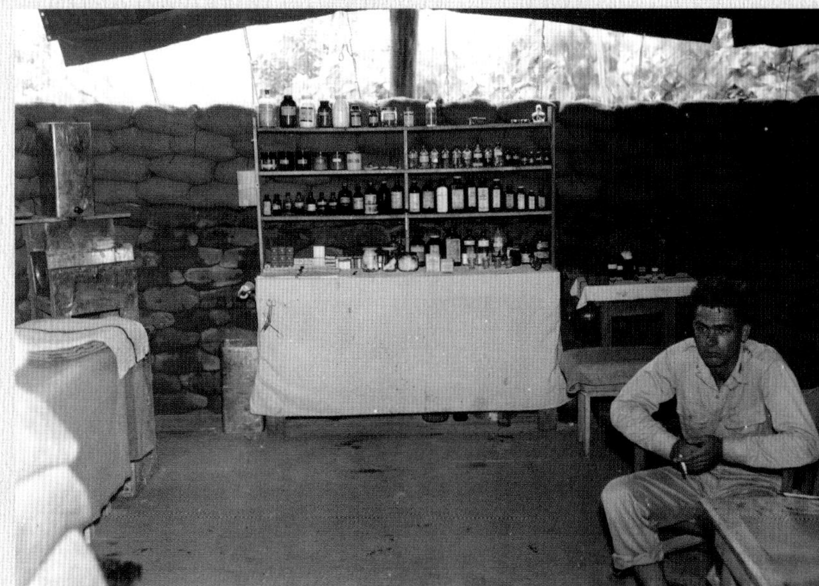

Infirmary

## Indigenous People

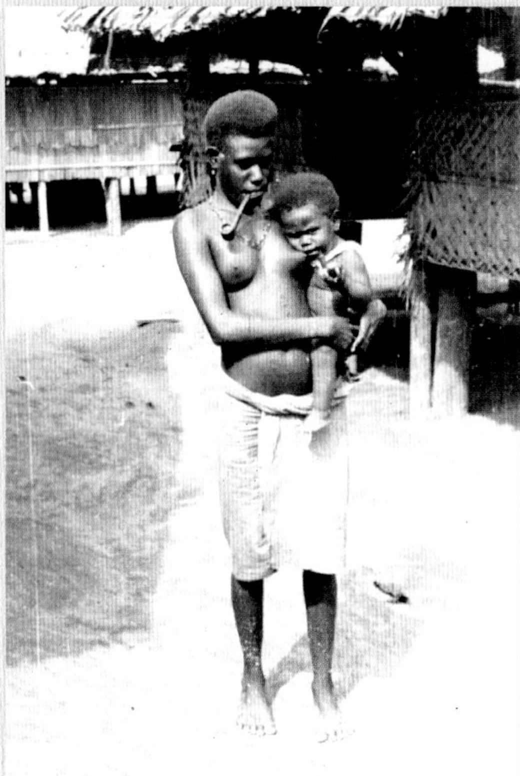

Mother and child

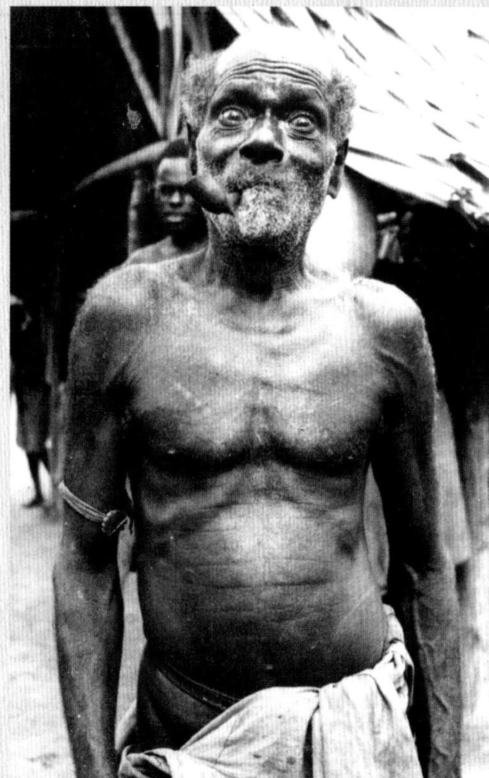

The oldest man–in his late 40s

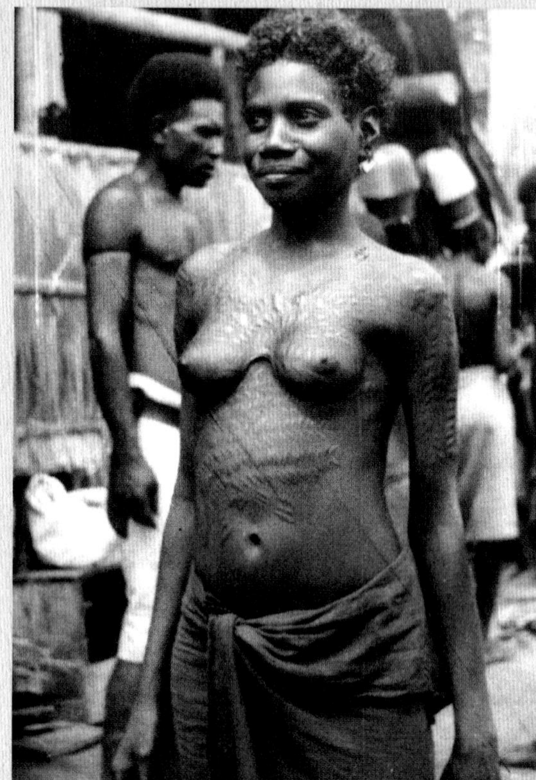

Most ceremonial scarring

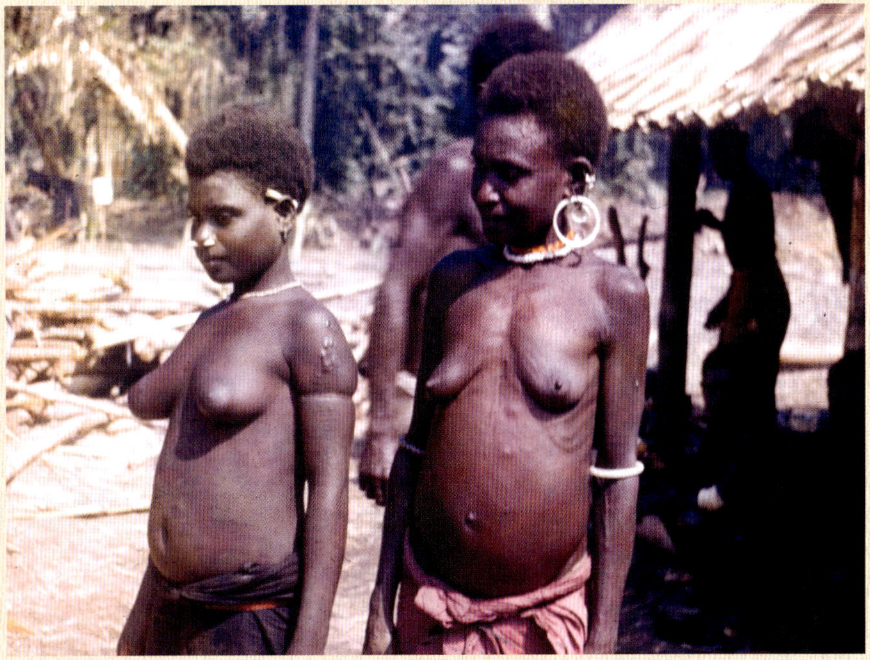

Mother and daughter

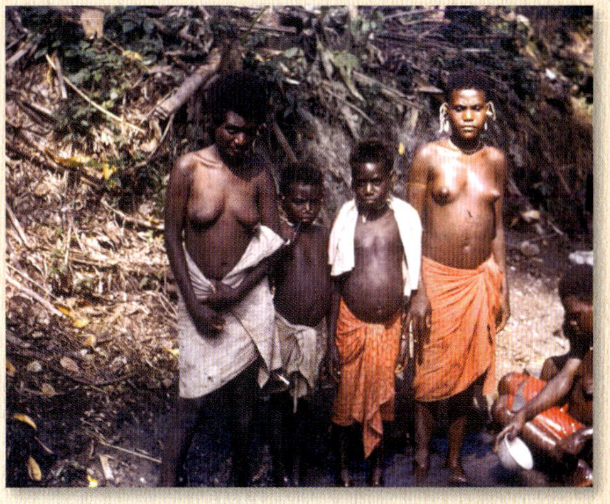

Women and children in stream

## The Philippines

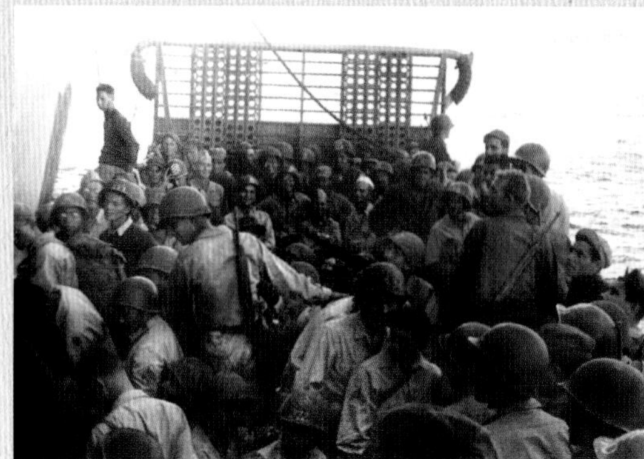

Landing craft filled with soldiers

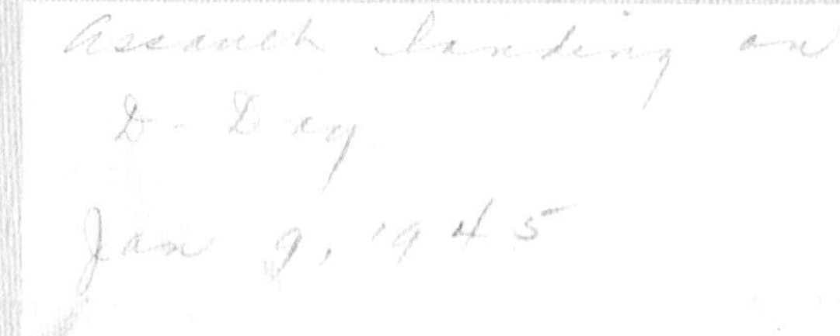


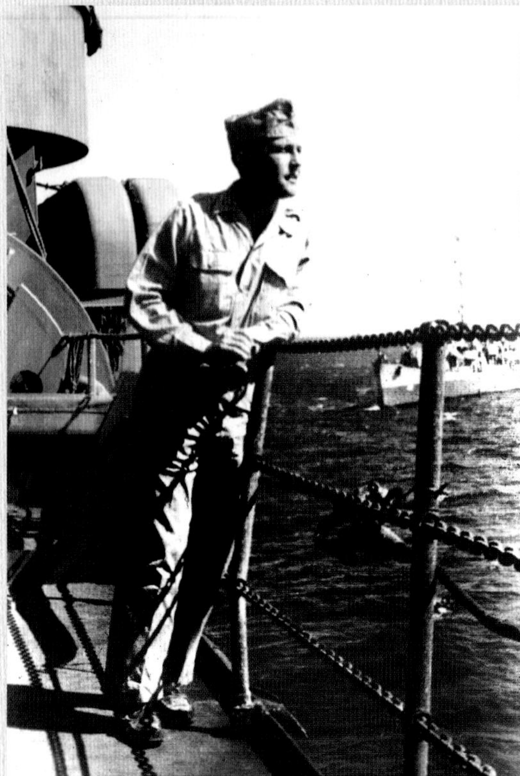

On board the USS *Pinkney* prior to invasion

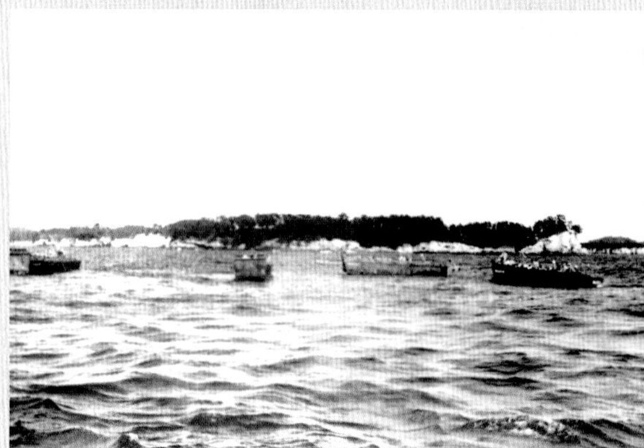

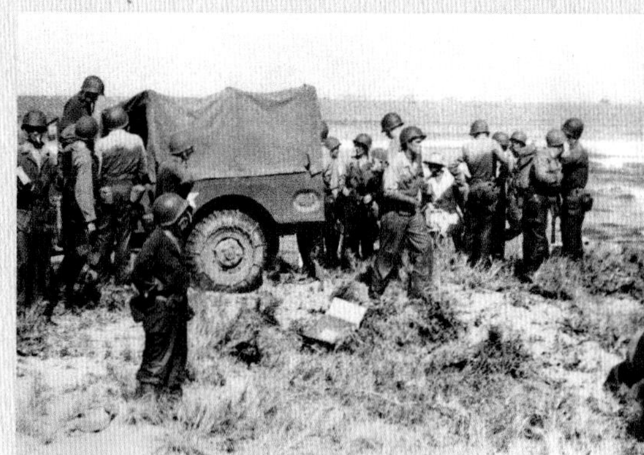

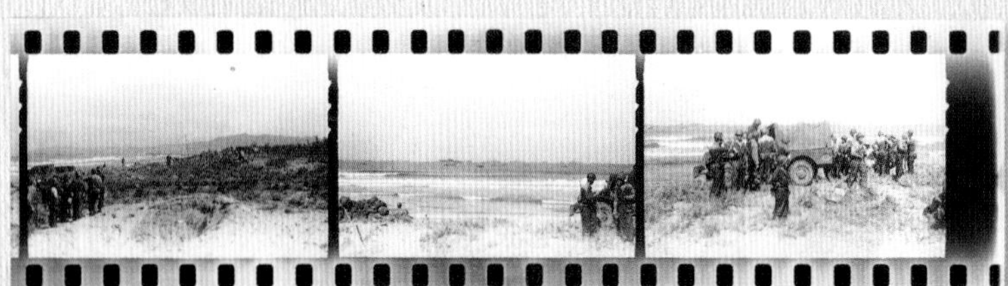

On the beach

# The Philippines

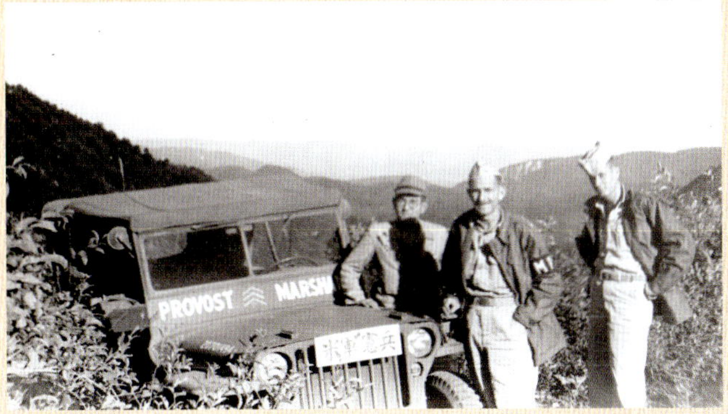


On the road

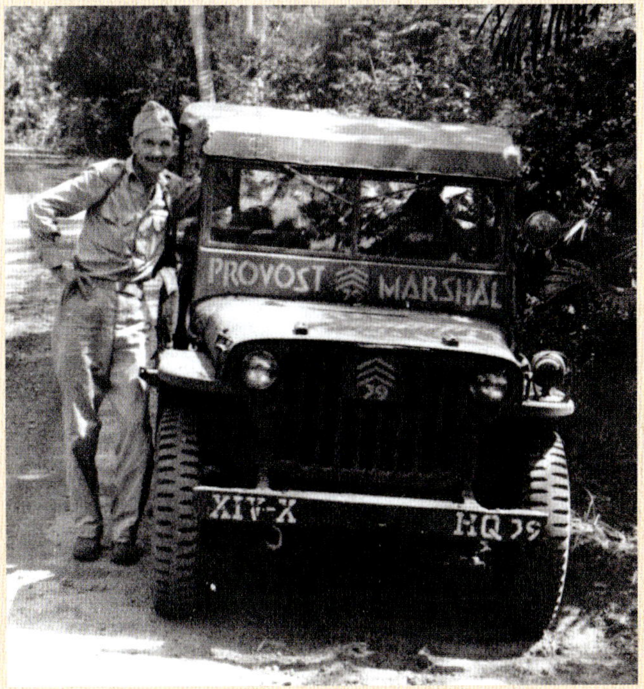


Harold and his Jeep

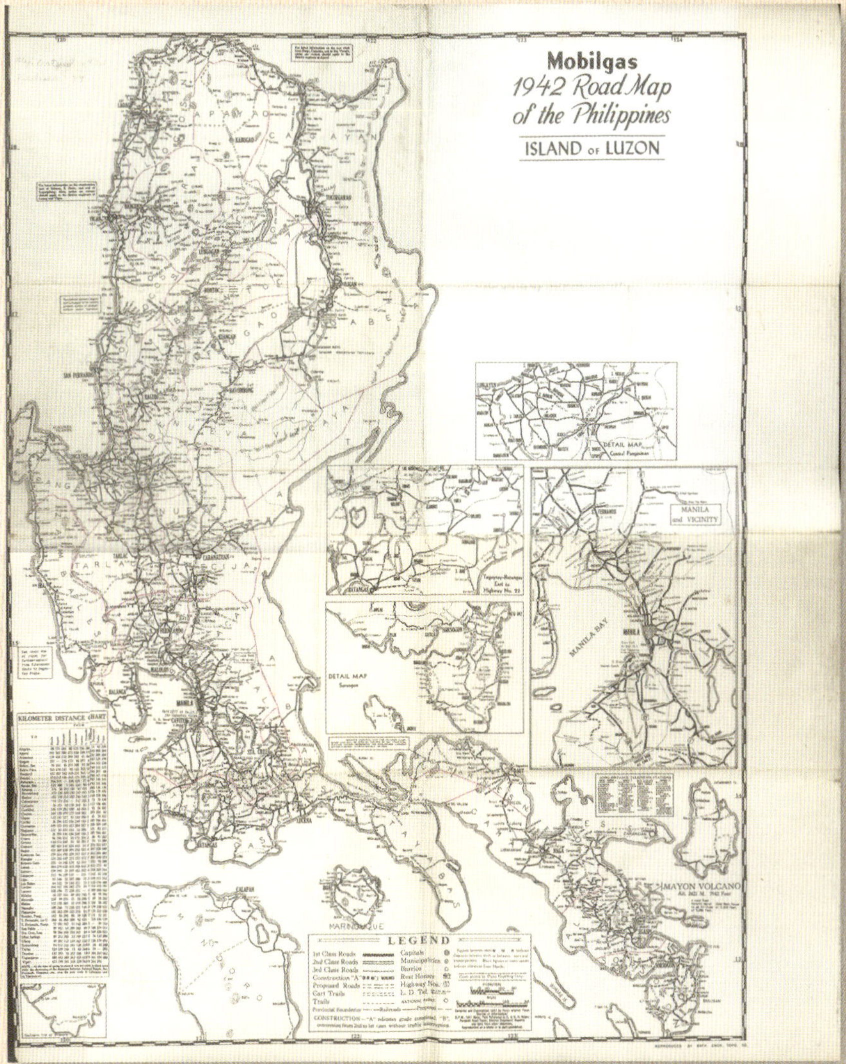


Harold's road map

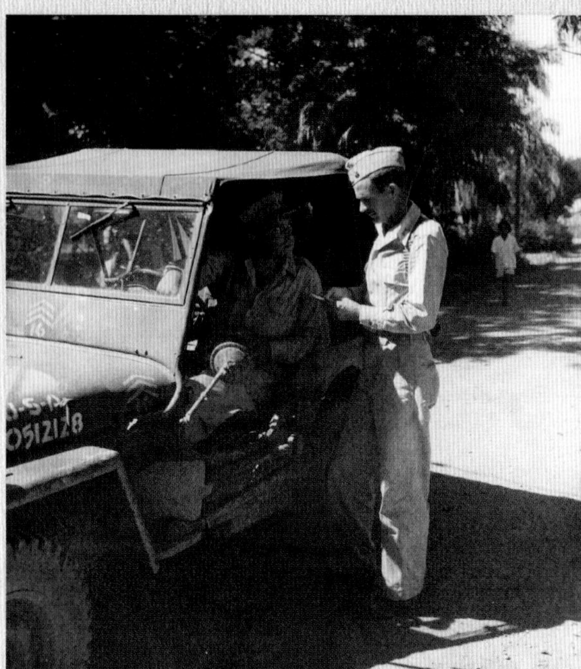

SWPA-51-C-45-[illegible] 27 July 45

With the XIV Army Corps in (Luzon, P.I.), speeding laws are enforced even in the combat areas. Maj. Harold L. O'Neal, (right), [illegible], Texas, demonstrates how it's done with the cooperation of Maj. Frank J. Vidlak, [illegible] Marcy Street, Omaha, Nebraska at the wheel.

Photo: Parry

APPROVED FOR MAILING
PHOTO SERVICE 27

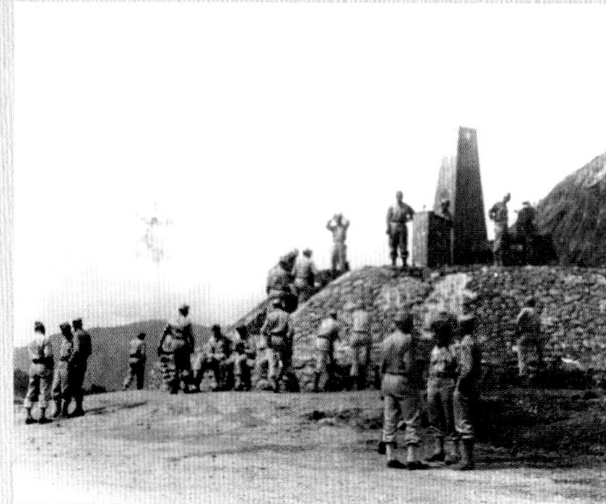

Memorial to the dead at Balete Pass.

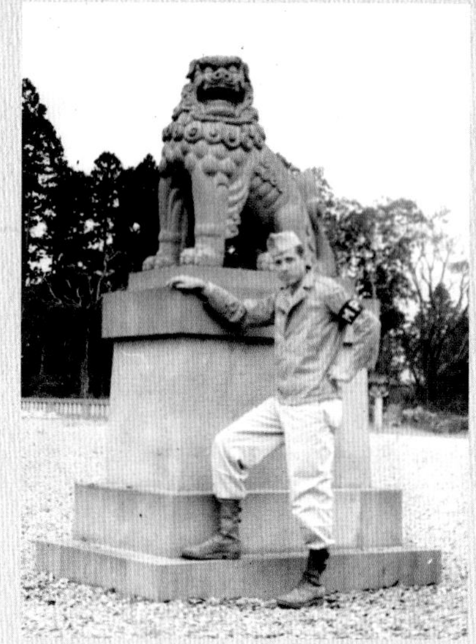

MP with statue

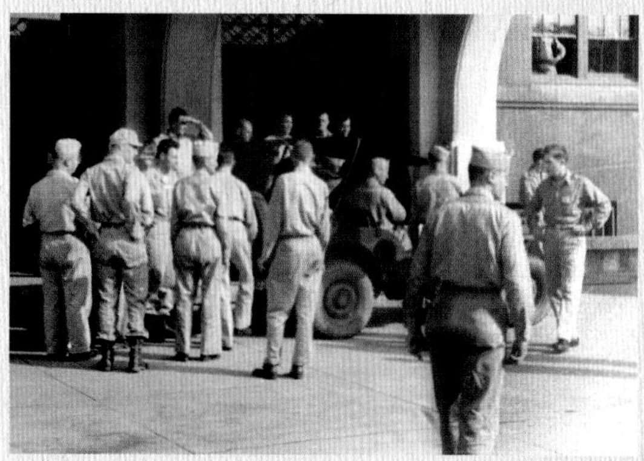

XIV Corps headquarters, summer 1945

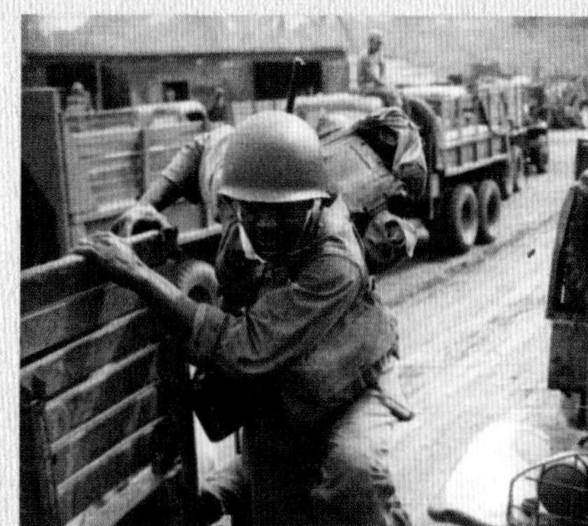

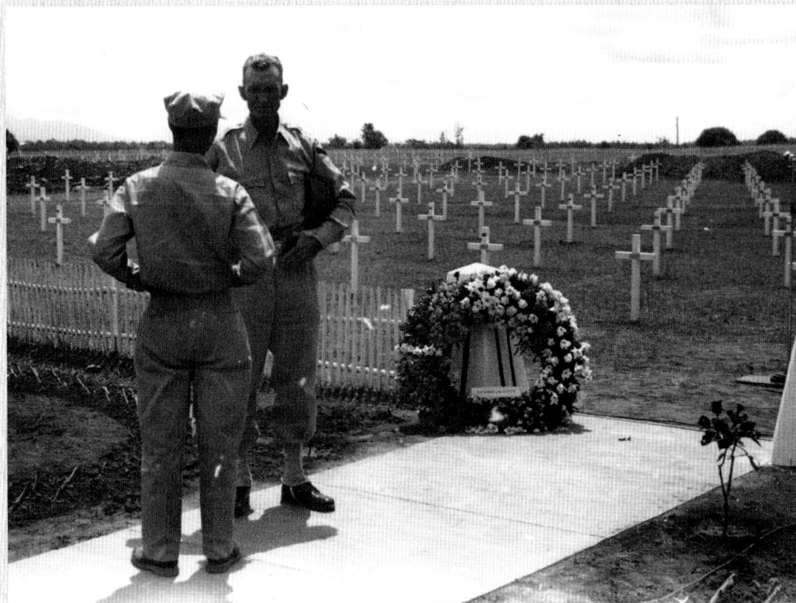

USAF Cemetery, Batangas

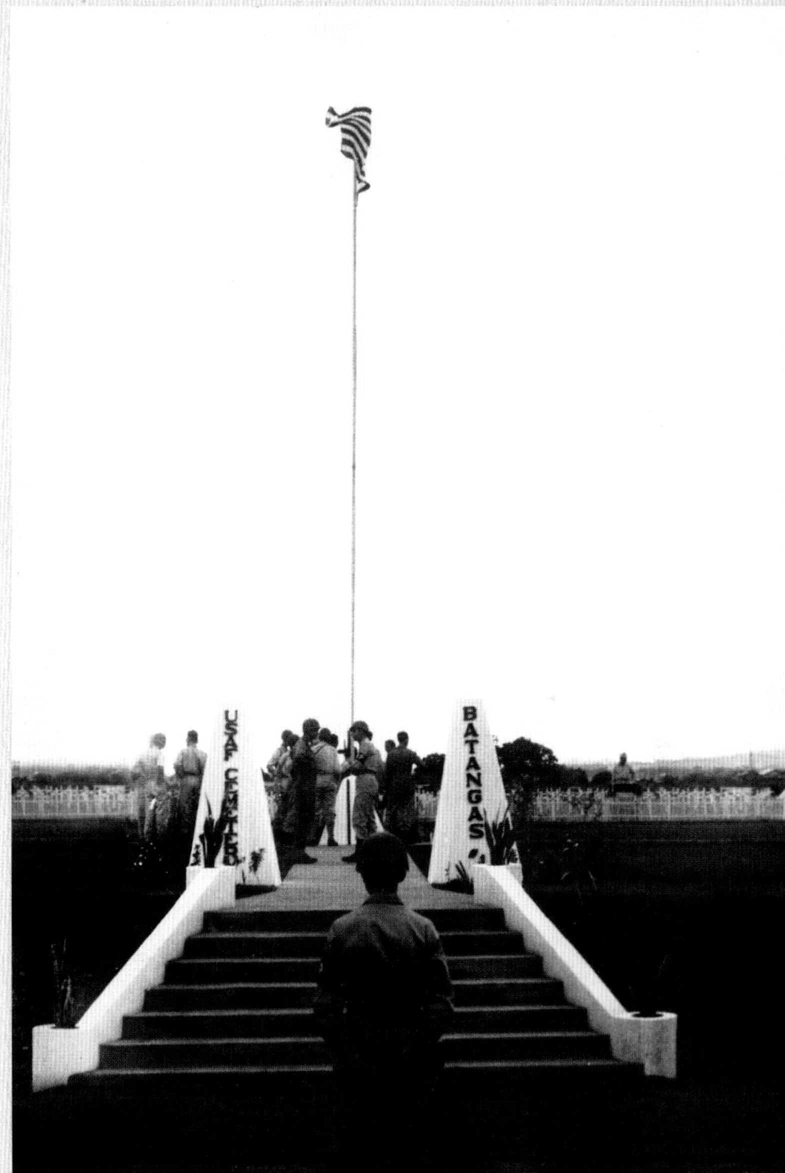


USAF Cemetery, Batangas

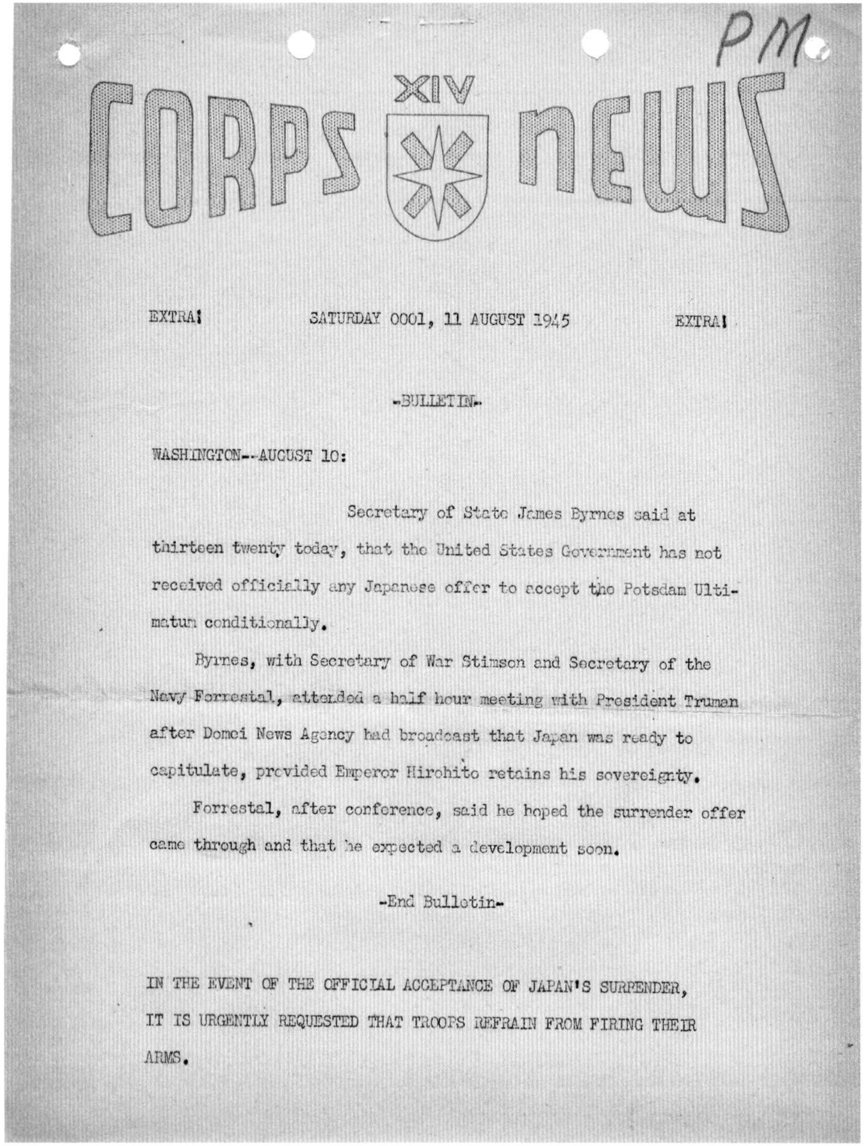

PM

# CORPS XIV NEWS

EXTRA! SATURDAY 0001, 11 AUGUST 1945 EXTRA!

-BULLETIN-

WASHINGTON--AUGUST 10:

Secretary of State James Byrnes said at thirteen twenty today, that the United States Government has not received officially any Japanese offer to accept the Potsdam Ultimatum conditionally.

Byrnes, with Secretary of War Stimson and Secretary of the Navy Forrestal, attended a half hour meeting with President Truman after Domei News Agency had broadcast that Japan was ready to capitulate, provided Emperor Hirohito retains his sovereignty.

Forrestal, after conference, said he hoped the surrender offer came through and that he expected a development soon.

-End Bulletin-

IN THE EVENT OF THE OFFICIAL ACCEPTANCE OF JAPAN'S SURRENDER, IT IS URGENTLY REQUESTED THAT TROOPS REFRAIN FROM FIRING THEIR ARMS.

XIV Corps News, August 11, 1945

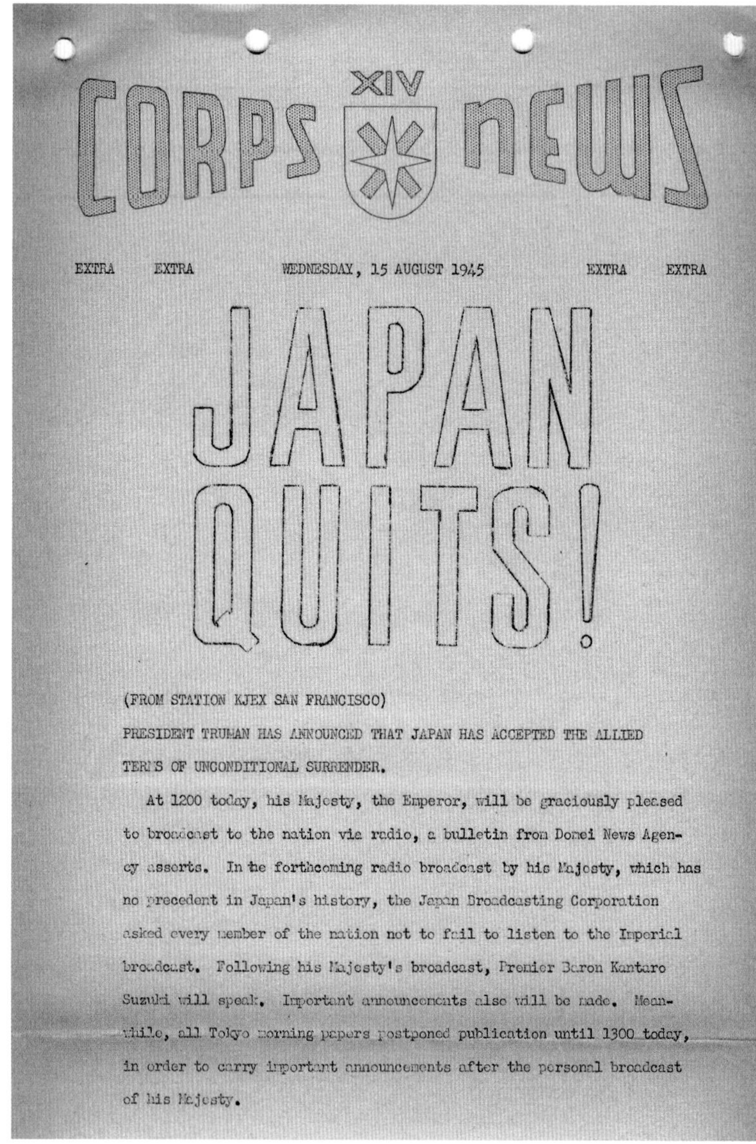

# CORPS XIV NEWS

EXTRA EXTRA WEDNESDAY, 15 AUGUST 1945 EXTRA EXTRA

# JAPAN QUITS!

(FROM STATION KJEX SAN FRANCISCO)

PRESIDENT TRUMAN HAS ANNOUNCED THAT JAPAN HAS ACCEPTED THE ALLIED TERMS OF UNCONDITIONAL SURRENDER.

At 1200 today, his Majesty, the Emperor, will be graciously pleased to broadcast to the nation via radio, a bulletin from Domei News Agency asserts. In the forthcoming radio broadcast by his Majesty, which has no precedent in Japan's history, the Japan Broadcasting Corporation asked every member of the nation not to fail to listen to the Imperial broadcast. Following his Majesty's broadcast, Premier Baron Kantaro Suzuki will speak. Important announcements also will be made. Meanwhile, all Tokyo morning papers postponed publication until 1300 today, in order to carry important announcements after the personal broadcast of his Majesty.

XIV Corps News, August 15, 1945

*the importance of these matters. We have proven we are the best in combat – now let us show we are the best in victory.*

**Griswold Letter**

The following day, August 19, General Griswold issued General Orders Number 64.

*At this last stage of my duties in connection with operations on Luzon, I wish to acknowledge my profound gratitude to the men and officers of all units of XIV Corps for the splendid achievements of this campaign.*

*The combat units deserve the greatest credit in the attainment of the goal for which we have striven so long. Their superb courage, determination and skill have defeated a stubborn and fanatical enemy in severe and savage fighting. . . . This campaign has been an affair of "beans, bullets and bridges" throughout the length of Luzon. To our comrades in arms, the service units, I extend my heartfelt thanks and appreciation for a difficult job well done. . . .*

*The outstanding ability and aggressive leadership of division and other combat commanders is brightly reflected in the brilliant accomplishments of their units.*

*To the courageous and determined men and officers of the Philippines Forces, I extend my sincere appreciation for the invaluable aid they have given with the limited resources at their disposal. . . .*

*We give humble and reverent homage to our comrades whose white crosses mark the long, hard course of our triumphal march. May the sacrifice they have made steel us all in the firm determination that this peace for which they have sacrificed so much shall not be denied them, nor we, nor those who will follow us.*

Then, on August 20, Harold responded to General Griswold in a letter that offered a description of what the men under his command had accomplished in the Luzon Campaign. These comments could apply equally to the actions these men had taken in New Caledonia and Bougainville.

*Subject: Military Police Activities Northern Luzon Operation.*

*To: Commanding General, XIC Corps, APO 453*

*Military Police activities encountered during the Northern Luzon operation were: Traffic control; Handling Prisoners of War, Collaborators, and Enemy Aliens and evacuating them to the Island Enclosure; Police of towns; Apprehension of A. W.O.L's.; Enforcing curfew regulations; Investigations of crimes and accidents involving military personnel; Confiscation of Government property from civilians; Placing establishments "Off Limits" for insanitary conditions.*

*a. The control of traffic was relatively easy due to the nature of the supply route. Highway #5 from the Corps C.P. extending north for 244 miles was divided into Division zones and controlled by same. Due to excessive distance from one C.P. to another few vehicles were on the road unless absolutely necessary. Thru the mountainous area frequent land slides occurred during rainy weather causing the road to be blocked until cleared away with bulldozers.*

*b. A marked increase in Prisoners of War has been noticed since the beginning of the present operation. During the month of July 1046 prisoners were cleared thru the XIV Corps stockade, and a total of 1726 for the period. This number includes prisoners and voluntarily surrenders and is entirely out of proportions to previous operations.*

*c. Police of towns within the sector presented little trouble as there were none of any size and most had been destroyed by bombing. A curfew was established for civilians and in most instances streets were cleared of soldiers at an early hour. It was noticed that the misappropriation of Government vehicles had been practically non-existent in this area.*

*d. Personnel report absent without leave from their organization was less than for any other like period.*

*e. Incidents involving civilians were confined mostly to pilfering charges. Attempts were constantly being made to pilfer Class I, II, & III supplies from a large army supply point servicing the Corps. In some instances there was evidence of organized planning but in most cases the plans were frustrated. Close cooperation was maintained with local civil authorities and offenders were rapidly tried and convicted.*

*f. A Corps medical officer accompanied by Military Policemen inspected all establishments dispensing food, placing "Off Limits" the ones not meeting necessary sanitary conditions.*

On September 4 Harold and the men under his command boarded the USS *San Saba* for a ten-day journey of about two thousand miles. The USS *Saba* was

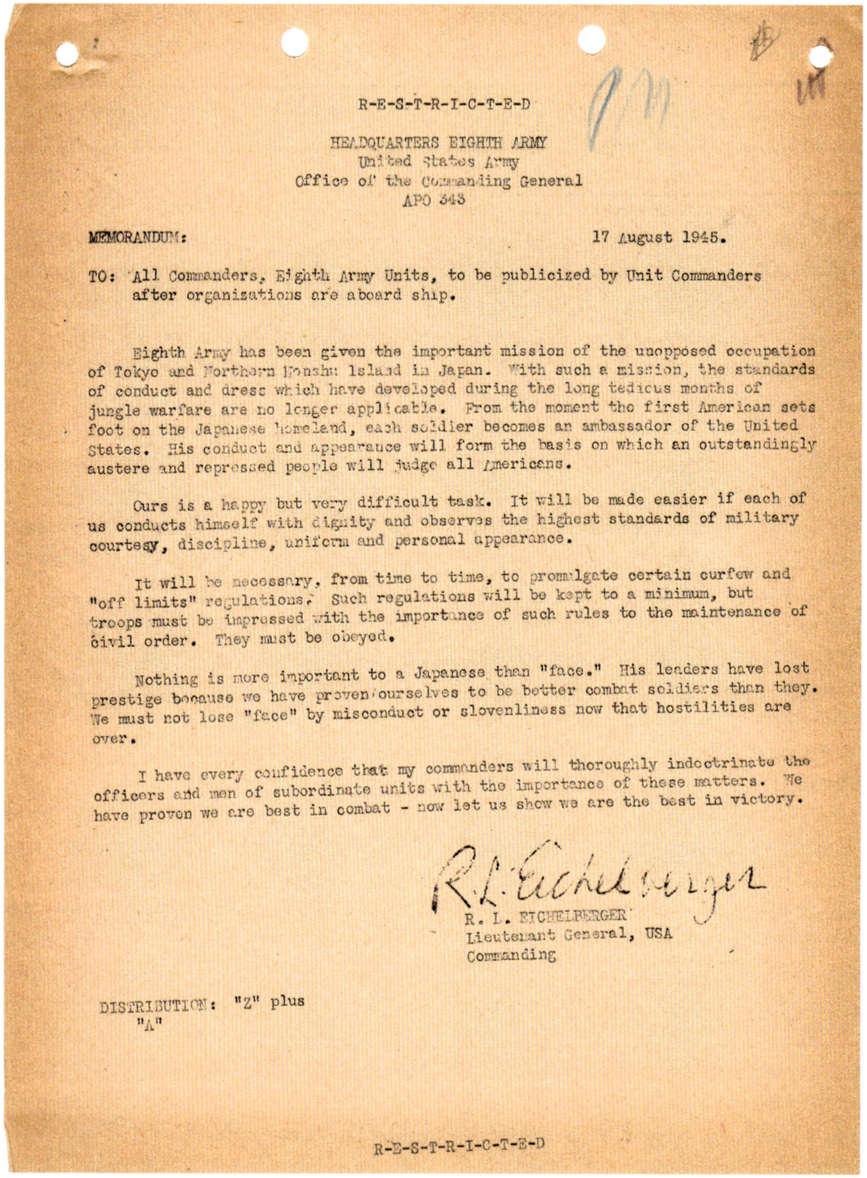

R-E-S-T-R-I-C-T-E-D

HEADQUARTERS EIGHTH ARMY
United States Army
Office of the Commanding General
APO 343

MEMORANDUM: 17 August 1945.

TO: All Commanders, Eighth Army Units, to be publicized by Unit Commanders after organizations are aboard ship.

Eighth Army has been given the important mission of the unopposed occupation of Tokyo and Northern Honshu Island in Japan. With such a mission, the standards of conduct and dress which have developed during the long tedious months of jungle warfare are no longer applicable. From the moment the first American sets foot on the Japanese homeland, each soldier becomes an ambassador of the United States. His conduct and appearance will form the basis on which an outstandingly austere and repressed people will judge all Americans.

Ours is a happy but very difficult task. It will be made easier if each of us conducts himself with dignity and observes the highest standards of military courtesy, discipline, uniform and personal appearance.

It will be necessary, from time to time, to promulgate certain curfew and "off limits" regulations. Such regulations will be kept to a minimum, but troops must be impressed with the importance of such rules to the maintenance of civil order. They must be obeyed.

Nothing is more important to a Japanese than "face." His leaders have lost prestige because we have proven ourselves to be better combat soldiers than they. We must not lose "face" by misconduct or slovenliness now that hostilities are over.

I have every confidence that my commanders will thoroughly indoctrinate the officers and men of subordinate units with the importance of these matters. We have proven we are best in combat - now let us show we are the best in victory.

R. L. Eichelberger
R. L. EICHELBERGER
Lieutenant General, USA
Commanding

DISTRIBUTION: "Z" plus "A"

R-E-S-T-R-I-C-T-E-D

Eichelberger Letter, August 17, 1945

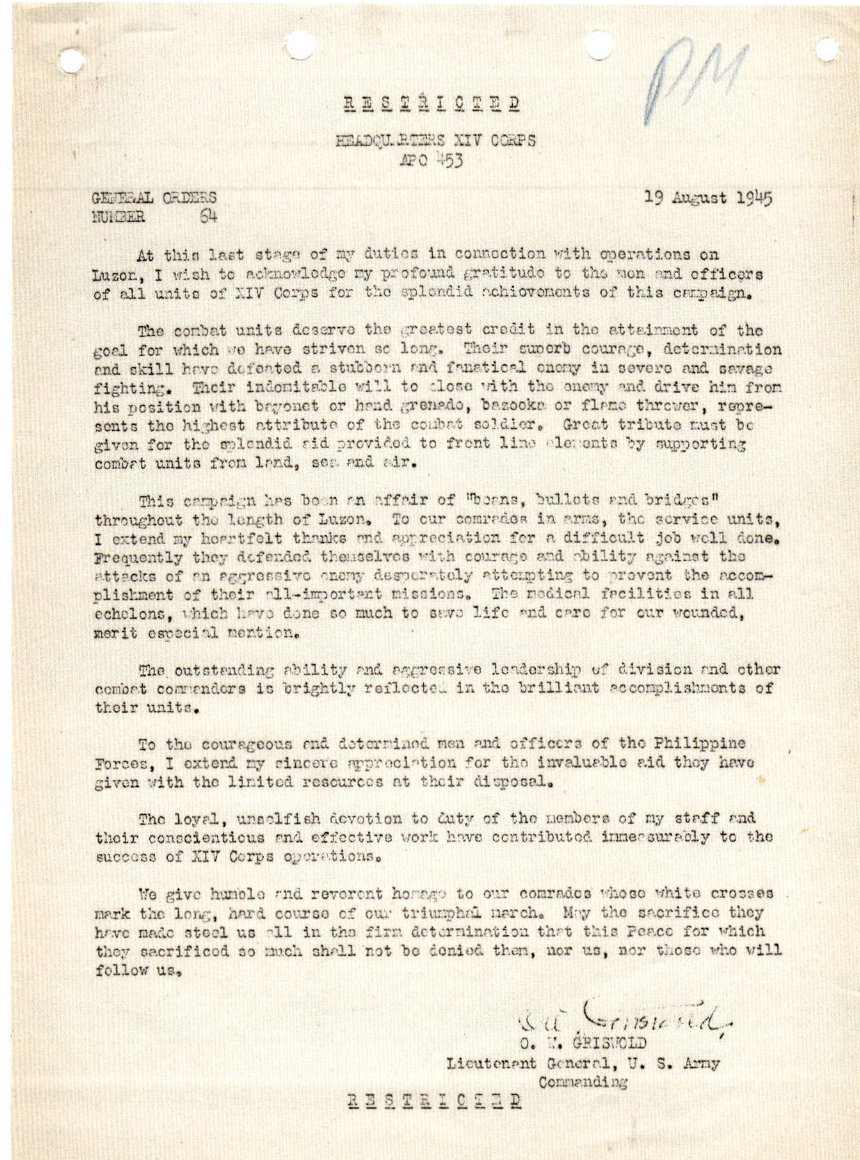

RESTRICTED

HEADQUARTERS XIV CORPS
APO 453

GENERAL ORDERS
NUMBER 64

19 August 1945

At this last stage of my duties in connection with operations on Luzon, I wish to acknowledge my profound gratitude to the men and officers of all units of XIV Corps for the splendid achievements of this campaign.

The combat units deserve the greatest credit in the attainment of the goal for which we have striven so long. Their superb courage, determination and skill have defeated a stubborn and fanatical enemy in severe and savage fighting. Their indomitable will to close with the enemy and drive him from his position with bayonet or hand grenade, bazooka or flame thrower, represents the highest attribute of the combat soldier. Great tribute must be given for the splendid aid provided to front line elements by supporting combat units from land, sea and air.

This campaign has been an affair of "beans, bullets and bridges" throughout the length of Luzon. To our comrades in arms, the service units, I extend my heartfelt thanks and appreciation for a difficult job well done. Frequently they defended themselves with courage and ability against the attacks of an aggressive enemy desperately attempting to prevent the accomplishment of their all-important missions. The medical facilities in all echelons, which have done so much to save life and care for our wounded, merit especial mention.

The outstanding ability and aggressive leadership of division and other combat commanders is brightly reflected in the brilliant accomplishments of their units.

To the courageous and determined men and officers of the Philippine Forces, I extend my sincere appreciation for the invaluable aid they have given with the limited resources at their disposal.

The loyal, unselfish devotion to duty of the members of my staff and their conscientious and effective work have contributed immeasurably to the success of XIV Corps operations.

We give humble and reverent homage to our comrades whose white crosses mark the long, hard course of our triumphal march. May the sacrifice they have made steel us all in the firm determination that this Peace for which they sacrificed so much shall not be denied them, nor us, nor those who will follow us.

O. W. Griswold
O. W. GRISWOLD
Lieutenant General, U. S. Army
Commanding

RESTRICTED

Griswold Letter, August 17, 1945

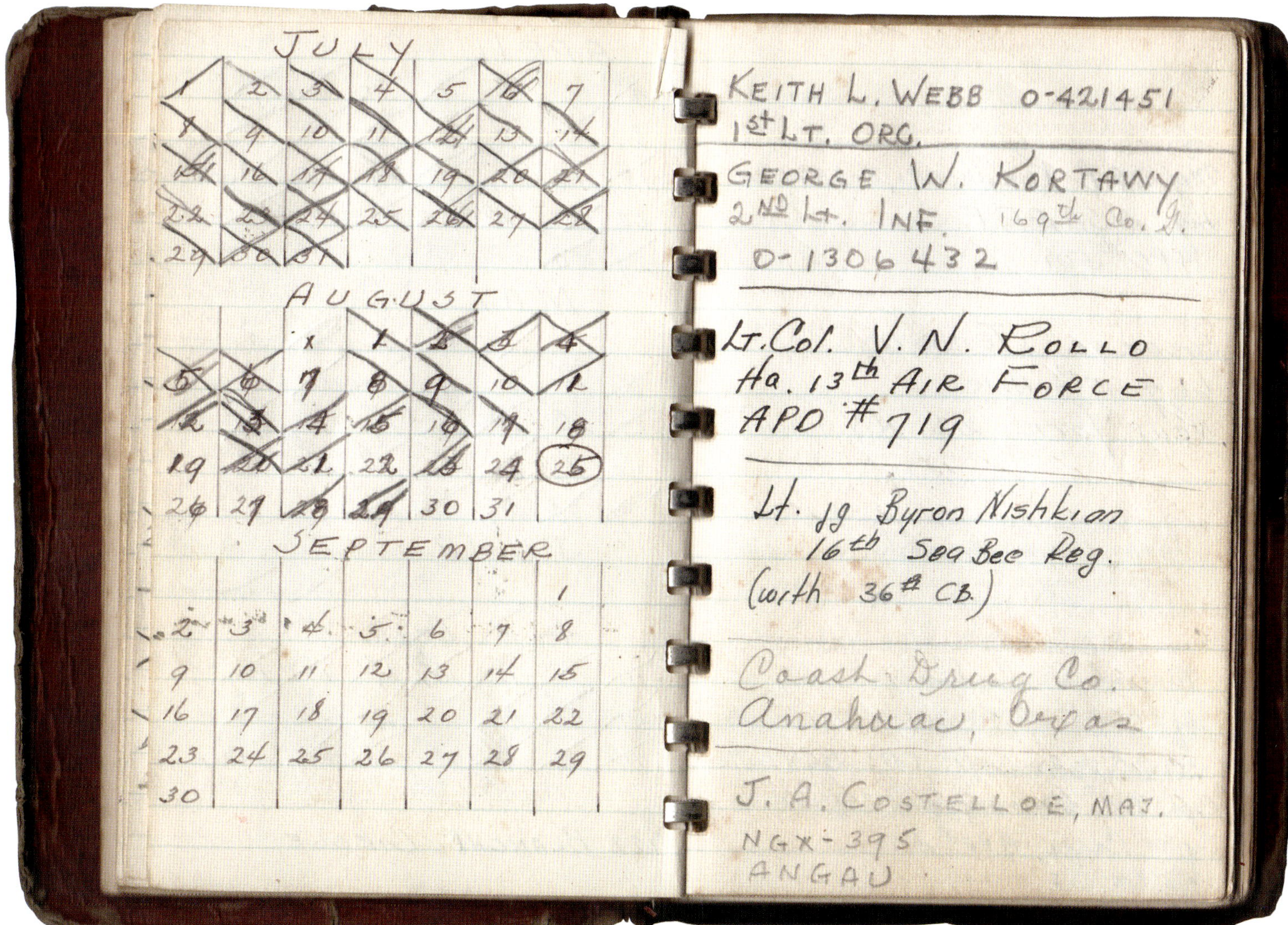

Last calendar entries

HEADQUARTERS XIV CORPS
Office of the Provost Marshal
APO 453

20 August 1945

SUBJECT: Military Police Activities Northern Luzon Operation.

TO : Commanding General, XIV Corps, APO 453.

1. Military Police activities encountered during the Northern Luzon operation were: Traffic control; Handling Prisoners of War, Collaborators, and Enemy Aliens and evacuating them to the Island Inclosure; Police of towns; Apprehension of A.W.O.L's; Enforcing curfew regulations; Investigations of crimes and accidents involving military personnel; Confiscation of Government property from civilians; Placing establishments "Off Limits" for insanitary conditions.

a. The control of traffic was relatively easy due to the nature of the supply route. Highway #5 from the Corps C.P. extending north for 244 miles was divided into Division zones and controlled by same. Due to excessive distance from one C.P. to another few vehicles were on the road unless absolutely necessary. Thru the mountainous area frequent land slides occured during rainy weather causing the road to be blocked until cleared away with bull dozers.

b. A marked increase in Prisoners of War has been noticed since the beginning of the present operation. During the month of July 1046 prisoners were cleared thru the XIV Corps stockade, and a total of ~~1718~~ 1726 for the period. This number includes prisoners who voluntarily surrendered and is entirely out of proportions to previous operations.

c. Police of towns within the sector presented little trouble as there were none of any size and most had been destroyed by bombing. A curfew was established for civilians and in most instances streets were cleared of soldiers at an early hour. It was noticed that the misappropriation of Government vehicles has been practically non-existant in this area.

d. Personnel reported absent without leave from their organization was less than for any other like period.

e. Incidents involving civilians were confined mostly to pilfering charges. Attempts were constantly being made to pilfer Class I, II, & III supplies from a large army supply point servicing the Corps. In some instances there was evidence of organized planning but in most cases the plans were frustrated. Close cooperation was maintained with local civil authorities and offenders were rapidly tried and convicted.

f. A Corps medical officer accompanied by Military Policemen inspected all establishments dispensing food, placing "Off Limits" the ones not meeting necessary sanitary conditions.

HAROLD L. O'NEAL,
Major, C. M. P.,
Provost Marshal.

Harold's Letter, August 20, 1945

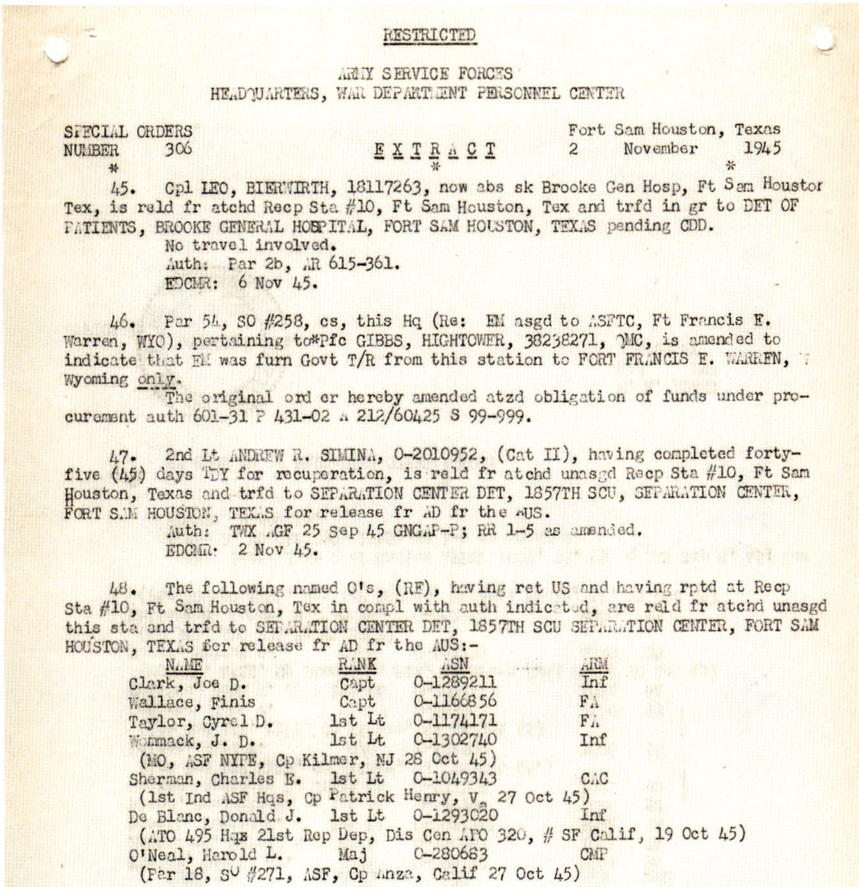

RESTRICTED

ARMY SERVICE FORCES
HEADQUARTERS, WAR DEPARTMENT PERSONNEL CENTER

SPECIAL ORDERS NUMBER 306 — EXTRACT — Fort Sam Houston, Texas, 2 November 1945

*   *   *

45. Cpl LEO, BIERWIRTH, 18117263, now abs sk Brooke Gen Hosp, Ft Sam Houston Tex, is reld fr atchd Recp Sta #10, Ft Sam Houston, Tex and trfd in gr to DET OF PATIENTS, BROOKE GENERAL HOSPITAL, FORT SAM HOUSTON, TEXAS pending CDD.
No travel involved.
Auth: Par 2b, AR 615-361.
EDCMR: 6 Nov 45.

46. Par 54, SO #258, cs, this Hq (Re: EM asgd to ASFTC, Ft Francis E. Warren, WYO), pertaining to*Pfc GIBBS, HIGHTOWER, 38238271, QMC, is amended to indicate that EM was furn Govt T/R from this station to FORT FRANCIS E. WARREN, Wyoming only.
The original order hereby amended atzd obligation of funds under procurement auth 601-31 P 431-02 A 212/60425 S 99-999.

47. 2nd Lt ANDREW R. SIMINA, 0-2010952, (Cat II), having completed forty-five (45) days TDY for recuperation, is reld fr atchd unasgd Recp Sta #10, Ft Sam Houston, Texas and trfd to SEPARATION CENTER DET, 1857TH SCU, SEPARATION CENTER, FORT SAM HOUSTON, TEXAS for release fr AD fr the AUS.
Auth: TWX AGF 25 Sep 45 GNGAP-P; RR 1-5 as amended.
EDCMR: 2 Nov 45.

48. The following named O's, (RF), having ret US and having rptd at Recp Sta #10, Ft Sam Houston, Tex in compl with auth indicated, are reld fr atchd unasgd this sta and trfd to SEPARATION CENTER DET, 1857TH SCU SEPARATION CENTER, FORT SAM HOUSTON, TEXAS for release fr AD fr the AUS:-

| NAME | RANK | ASN | ARM |
|---|---|---|---|
| Clark, Joe D. | Capt | 0-1289211 | Inf |
| Wallace, Finis | Capt | 0-1166856 | FA |
| Taylor, Cyrel D. | 1st Lt | 0-1174171 | FA |
| Wommack, J. D. | 1st Lt | 0-1302740 | Inf |
| (MO, ASF NYPE, Cp Kilmer, NJ 28 Oct 45) | | | |
| Sherman, Charles E. | 1st Lt | 0-1049343 | CAC |
| (1st Ind ASF Hqs, Cp Patrick Henry, Va 27 Oct 45) | | | |
| De Blanc, Donald J. | 1st Lt | 0-1293020 | Inf |
| (ATO 495 Hqs 21st Rep Dep, Dis Cen APO 320, # SF Calif, 19 Oct 45) | | | |
| O'Neal, Harold L. | Maj | 0-280683 | CMP |
| (Par 18, SO #271, ASF, Cp Anza, Calif 27 Oct 45) | | | |

a newly commissioned attack transport ship that was named after a county in Central Texas. It was ironic that he was traveling on a ship that was named after a county and town in Texas that was about 150 miles due north of the hospital bed that would be waiting for him when he returned to the United States.

The ship headed to Sendai, a city about two hundred miles north of Tokyo on Honshu. Much of the city had been destroyed in a bombing raid in July 1945, and this is evident in many of Harold's photographs. The city had seen much better days; so had Harold. It is unclear when the medical officers attached to the XIV Corps. noticed that he was unwell, and it is equally clear he had not been at "fighting weight" for some time; he was always thin, but he appears gaunt in photographs taken in the Philippines in mid-1945. But someone noticed and he was examined, possibly before his departure for Japan or possibly after he arrived in Sendai.

Within a week of his arrival in Japan he was given a memorandum with the title **WHAT YOU SHOULD KNOW REGARDING THE RULES AND REGULATIONS RELATIVE TO YOUR RE-ENTRY INTO THE UNITED STATES**. On September 28 a list of the names of all the officers and their home addresses was circulated, and at the end of the list it was noted:

*This morning Capt Joe Verde, First Lieut. Franklin Grupe, Warrant Officers "Corky" Gordon and Ralph Baker and 75 enlisted men of the Headquarters Company left Sendai headed for home.*

*The group, largest to leave the XIV Corps on reployment or readjustment, was addressed by General Griswold yesterday afternoon. He complimented the officers and men upon their contributions to the teamwork which has gained for the XIV Corps an enviable record in World War II. General Griswold cautioned the group that it would meet some problems in the eventual readjustment from military to civil life routines.*

*Since Captain Verde and his men are attached to the 43rd (New England) Infantry Division for transportation back to the states, there is a probability the XIV Corps contingent may put through the Panama and dock in New York Harbor.*

Later in the same day it was announced there would be a **GALA PARTY TO BE GIVEN FOR DEPARTING OFFICERS** on September 29. Also announced was an **All Japanese Floor Show Including Fifteen Girls; Beer and Possibly Whiskey**.

*Captain Charles L. "Cowboy " Sims, the sturdy gent. from the Oklahoma panhandle, acting as chairman has procured an all-Japanese floor show including 15 girls through the good offices and connections of Maj. Raymond O. Reichard, the pipe smoking engineer. . . .*

*There will be iced beer from a reliable brewery and Maj. Harold L. "The Sheriff" O'Neal is working on a deal to procure some whiskey which may be consumed with safety.*

The day after the gala farewell party Harold found his name on Special Order 203 and was advised to await further orders to proceed to the USA for readjustment. There is no paperwork to indicate exactly when he departed Sendai. In his papers there are business cards and photographs of the Japanese officers he interacted with in both Sendai and Fukishima, but there is no other paperwork. One handwritten card in perfect Japanese by H. Kosaki, the Chief of Police in Fukishima, states that Harold should be extended every courtesy, so it is clear he continued with his duties until he departed.

On October 10, Harold and 1,400 other officers and men boarded the USS *Hansford* (APO 106), a newly (1944) commissioned Bayfield-class attack transport. Like the USS *Saba*, it was also named after a county in Texas, a remote, lightly populated county in the Texas panhandle. The county seat, Spearman, had a population slightly less than that of the USS *Hansford*. The trip from Sendai to San Francisco was part of *Operation Magic Carpet*, and took slightly more than two weeks. When Harold and his fellow passengers arrived, he was greeted by a rubber stamp that applied the following words to the bottom of his orders: *Transportation completed. You were subsisted in the Wardroom Mess of this vessel, without cost from October 11 – 26, 1945.*

Harold was then transported to the hospital at Fort Sam Houston, arriving on November 2. He would be in and out of the hospital for the next eighteen months, worrying about how he would handle re-adjustment and an uncertain future. He'd just traveled 6,500 miles and was too tired to dream about much of anything.

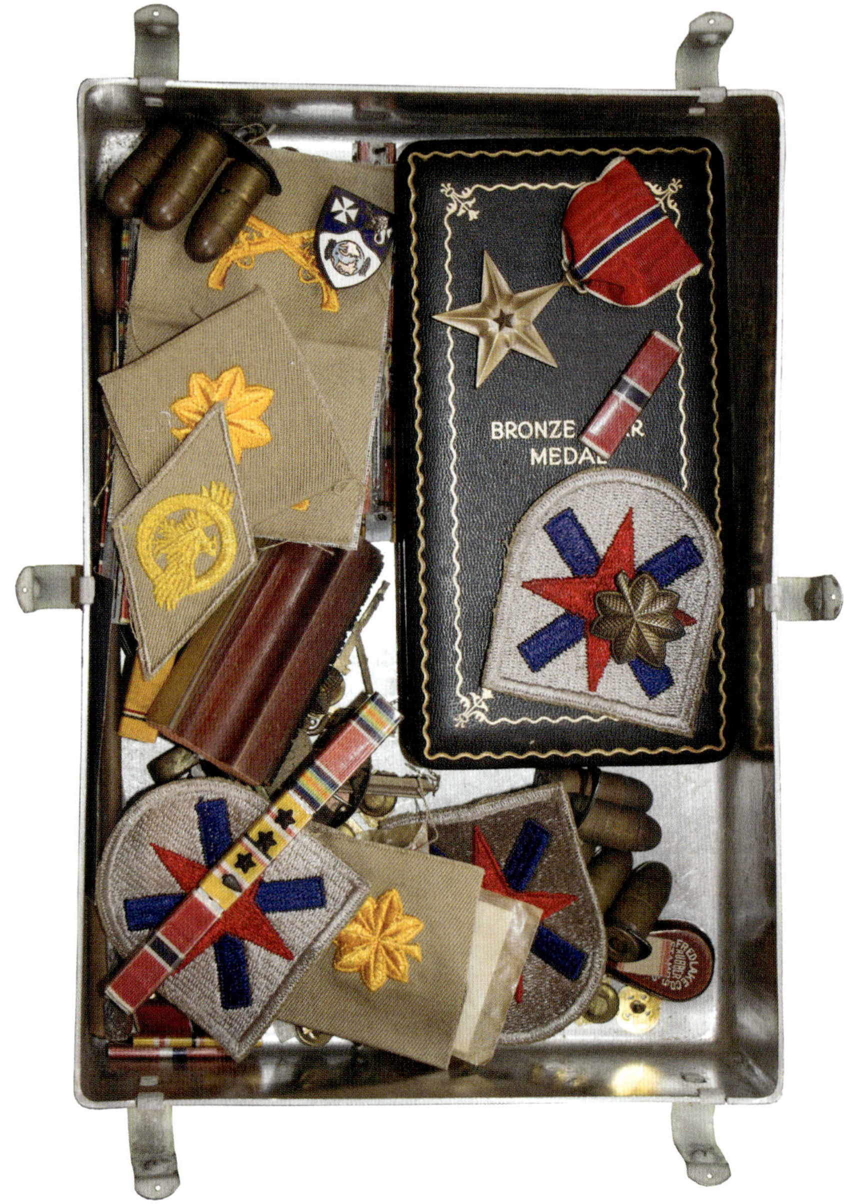

# Home Front
## 1943 - 1945

**HAROLD WAS CALLED TO ACTIVE DUTY ON SEPTEMBER 7, 1941**. After a few weeks in Louisiana and Dallas he was assigned to the newly constructed Camp Bowie, near Brownwood, Texas, where he began training a company of MPs for eventual deployment to the Pacific theater. The *Kilgore News Herald* said "Mrs. O'Neal plans to remain in Tyler with her parents for a time before joining her husband," which is what she did until Harold found accommodations in Brownwood, an upstairs apartment just a short distance from Camp Bowie. They remained at 1418 Brady Avenue throughout 1942 and into January 1943, when Harold and his men were sent overseas.

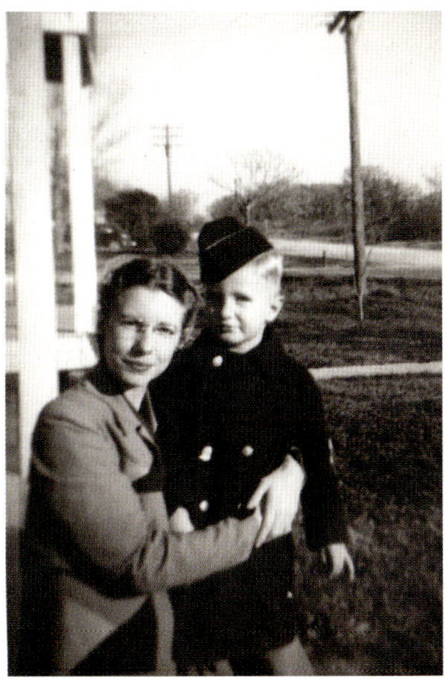

Sarah and Hank, Brownwood, 1943

After he departed, Sarah loaded the old Chrysler, and she and I headed to Denton, Texas, to live for a short while with her sister, Martha. The car was crammed with everything she thought she might need to start again, and somehow there was room in the car for the scrapbooks and family pictures. There was not room for a small baseball bat I seem to recall I treasured, and I've always worried about it being left behind.

Harold arrived in New Caledonia on March 21, 1943. A little more than one month later he sent a letter to me dated Easter Sunday (April 25).

Sometime later, before he left "the island," he managed to acquire a forty-inch-long perfectly scaled outrigger canoe and send it back to the United States. It arrived safely, complete with hand-carved wooden oars and a funny little device that could be used to bail out unwanted water. The little canoe proved itself to be seaworthy in a stream on Bougainville, but was never tested in Fort Worth or any place else after it arrived, remaining in permanent dry dock.

In short order the families of both Sarah and Martha moved to Wildwood Road in Fort Worth and opened a personal home front to aid the war effort in that city. Martha's husband, Roy T. Will, was ill-suited for military service but was able to be one of more than thirty thousand men and women working at the Consolidated plant building B-24 aircraft. Sarah wanted to do the same, but her weak eyes prevented her from doing so. Martha was busy with a new baby and the two families—two sisters, one husband, two children, and a baby on the way—lived together for most of 1943, long enough to plant and harvest a backyard Victory Garden, blow up a pressure cooker in a vain attempt to can vegetables for the winter, raise a coop full of chickens, gather their eggs successfully but sometimes not, and not get in one another's way too much.

World War II experts estimate there were somewhere between twenty million to twenty-five million Victory Gardens and home canners during the war years. Everyone who had an unused patch of land was encouraged to plant a garden. The government and private companies created cookbooks, posters, balanced vegetarian-based and meat-substitute diets, and guides on how to put up vegetables with titles like *Can All You Can* and *Grow Your Own Can Your Own*. The exploding pressure cooker seems to indicate that despite good intentions, part of the advice in these "how to" books went unheeded.

But by the end of the year with the new baby, the bungalow at 3801 Wildwood Road became overcrowded, and when a similar bungalow across the street

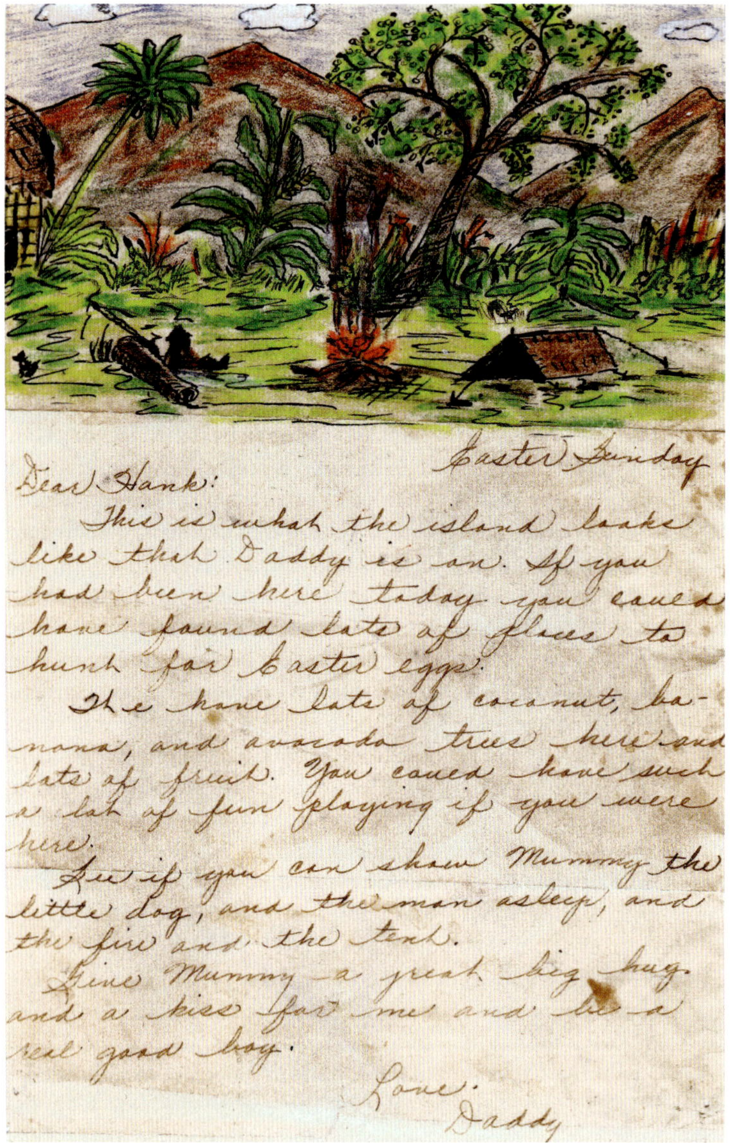

Easter Sunday

Dear Hank:

This is what the island looks like that Daddy is on. If you had been here today you could have found lots of places to hunt for Easter eggs.

We have lots of coconut, banana, and avocado trees here and lots of fruit. You could have such a lot of fun playing if you were here.

See if you can show Mummy the little dog, and the man asleep, and the fire and the tent.

Give Mummy a great big hug and a kiss for me and be a real good boy.

Love:
Daddy

Easter letter from New Caledonia

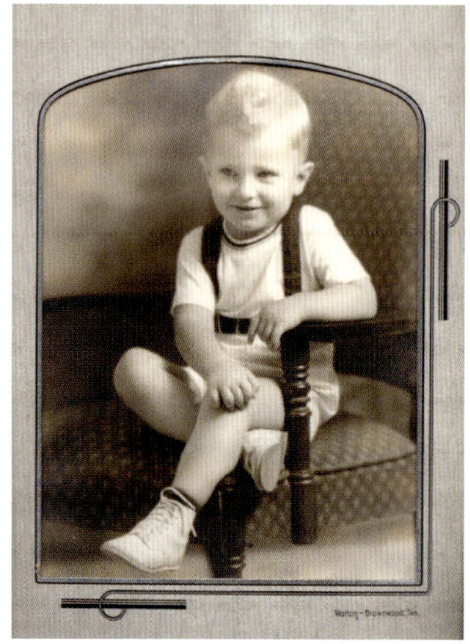

Brownwood, 1943

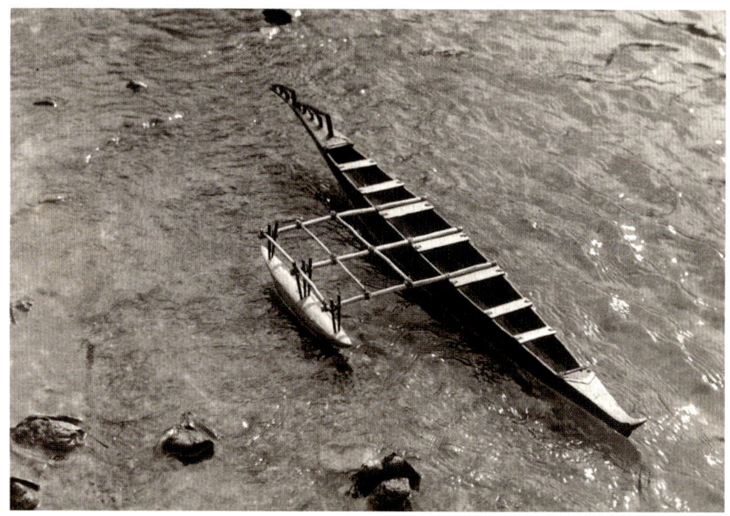

Water-worthy outrigger canoe

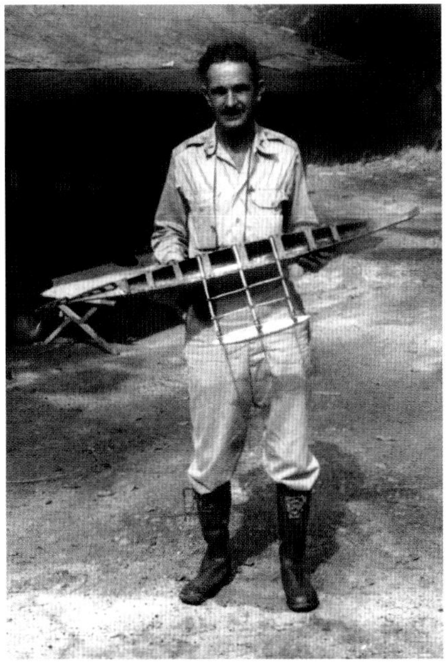

Harold with outrigger canoe

at 3800 became available, Sarah rented it and opened her own home front. The only thing she didn't do was plant a backyard garden because there was no backyard. The extra property was in the front of the house. At some point she even made a drawing of the house and the yard and the sidewalk, with me on my tricycle. It seems likely the owner of the property was not keen on digging up the front yard for a garden. Backyard patriotism is one thing; the front yard is something else. But this was not always the case. For at least one season we had an okra patch in front of the new apartment Sarah prepared for Harold's eventual homecoming.

One wartime letter from Harold to Sarah survives. It was written just about the time the Victory Garden was beginning to yield a bountiful harvest and before the pressure cooker exploded. It is dated July 3, 1943.

*My Darling:*

*Another Saturday night. Nowhere to go but plenty to do right here and it's all work.*

*Tomorrow is the 4th of July. I wonder what you and little Hank will be doing. Usually we didn't do so much on the 4th but it would be so nice for us to be together. At times honey, like right now, I just get so damned lonesome for you I don't know what to do. That's just the catch, there's nothing I can do. If I could just wrap myself up in your arms everything would be perfect. I've been away from you 5 months now and that is just too long.*

*Am so proud of you being such a busy little lady in the kitchen. At the rate you're going you'll soon have more canned goods than you'll know what to do with. Just keep on canning more and more. They'll come in mighty handy next winter when they'll be so hard to get. My but they sound so good. Bet they would sure be good eating. However when I come back it'll be a long time before I'll even want to see anything canned. Let alone eat it. I'm so fed up on canned goods that I can't look one in the face. My pet gripes are beans, spam, butter, bacon, eggs and the Australian carrots. My, my I shouldn't get started. This could go on for hours.*

*Good old oatmeal cookies. How I would like to have a nice batch of them. By the way this reminds me. Please get a good recipe book on cookies and send it to me for M. Raymande. I told them a couple of weeks ago I would write you for one but I suppose I forgot it. Monsieur Gauchet built a big French oven in one of his sheds and every day they bake a lot of cookies to sell to the soldiers. I think they've already made enough money to buy a Jeep when the war is over. That's slightly exaggerated but that's what they are doing with the money.*

*All of my new men are running me nuts. They were casuals and this is the first home they've had since being in the army. They've been knocked around quite a bit and the short time they've been on the island have been allowed to write only one letter home a week. Since they've been here with me I've let them write as many as they want. Boy oh boy, I believe it's all they do all day long, just write letters. Seems to me there's hundreds of letters. All I do is censor and stamp mail.*

*They can also ask quite a few questions. That takes up quite a bit of more time. In their mail the main topic is how good and how much they are being fed. It makes me very happy. I take my own mess for granted but I know it is far superior to many of the messes on the island.*

*I received the reel and fishing stuff from Raymond a couple of weeks ago. Haven't had a chance to use it yet, but maybe I can pretty soon.*

*I'm very proud of "Sally" but haven't had much of a chance to get out in her. To date have only been out one time. Maybe things will slack up pretty soon and I can go out some more. As it is I get to go aboard enough boats of all kinds.*

*Got such a kick out of Hank's observance on the Camel package. He's a mighty smart little boy. Must try to send the little scamp more pictures. Have meant to write him again but it seems that I've been so busy or so tired that I just keep putting it off. Tell him that Daddy thinks about him a whole lot and that I will try to write him a letter about something pretty soon.*

*Do I remember those heavenly nights at the Castle Courts?, the piney woods?, Daingerfield, Tyler, Kilgore and all the rest? It's what my dreams are made of. All about you.*

*Have to leave. Will close as I don't know what time I'll get back.*

*I love you darling.*

*Yours only Harold*

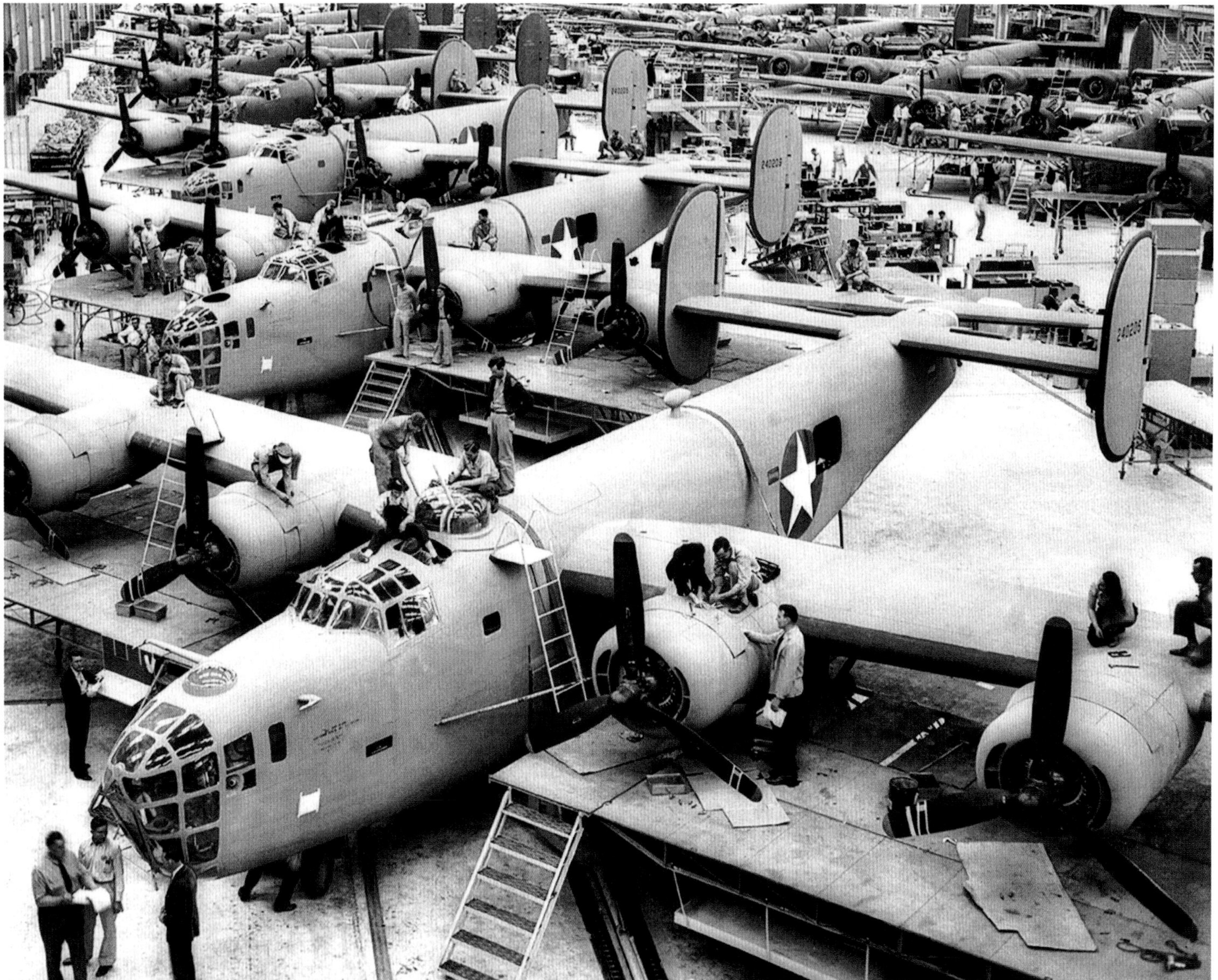

Consolidated B-24 plant

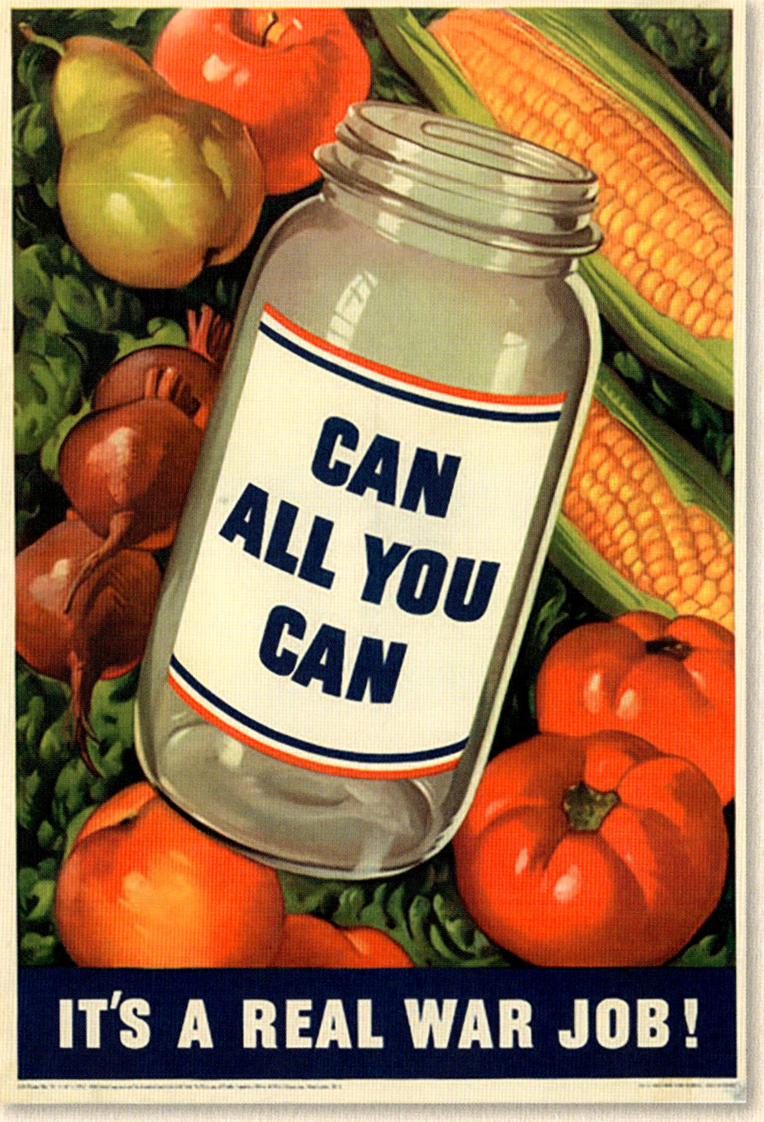
CAN
ALL YOU
CAN
IT'S A REAL WAR JOB!

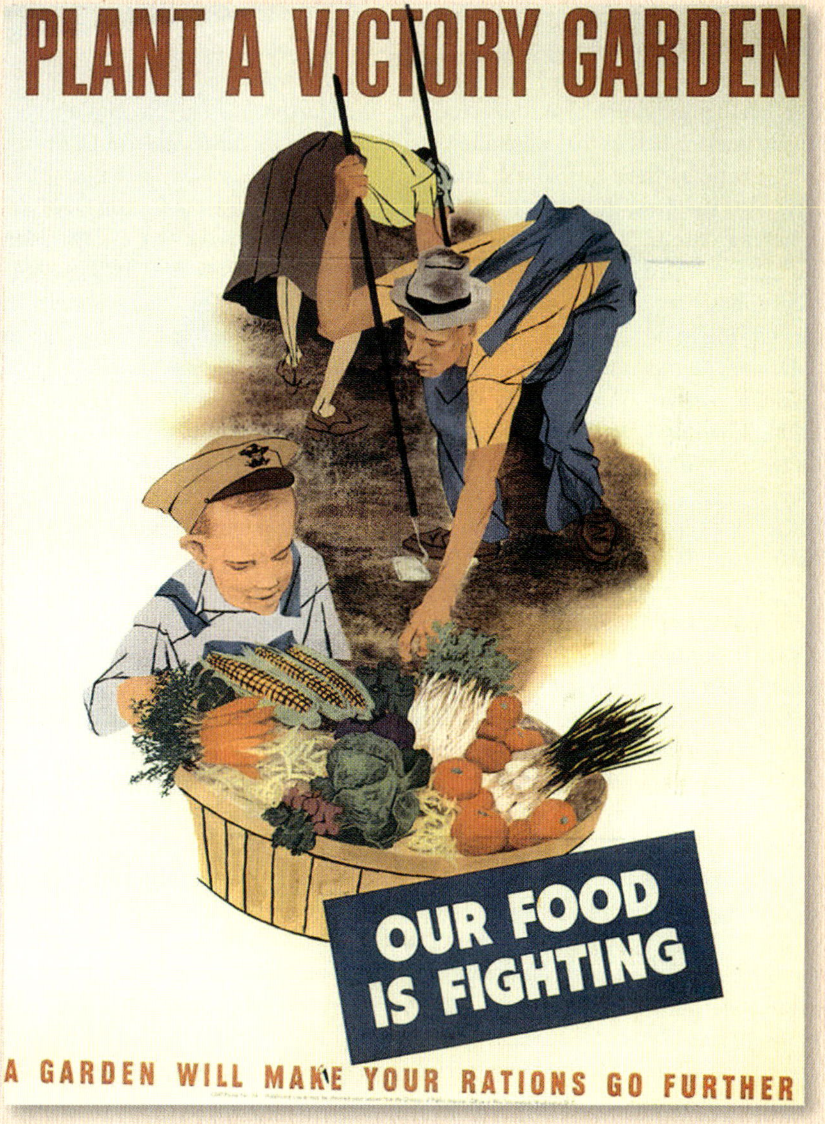
PLANT A VICTORY GARDEN
OUR FOOD
IS FIGHTING
A GARDEN WILL MAKE YOUR RATIONS GO FURTHER

It was tough on the men overseas in terms of danger as well as physical, mental, and emotional strain. The women they left behind were also subjected to private interior battles that were often just as traumatic as their husband's. Another letter also survives, this time from Sarah to her parents in Tyler. Precisely dated and time stamped: October 7, 1943, 9:45. It describes how she is coping and what she is trying to do for Harold.

*Dearest Mother and Daddy,*

*Roy is reading, Martha is ironing him a shirt, Chris and Hank are snoozing and I have just finished writing Harold and wrapping up a Corny coffee pot for him which is measured to the 16th of inch to get inside the 36 in limit. Its what he has been dying to have and up until today I have been unable to find one that would come anywhere within 36 inches. At that I am having to send it in two separate packages. Harold has electricity in his tent and I have sent him a hot plate, an electric toaster and now this. He is really fixed comfortably. He has an iron cot with springs, his tent is screened and walled, his carpenter built him a chest of drawers and he made himself an easy chair out of a weapons carrier so he is really fixed up. Their summer is just now starting and he is so glad because he much prefers warm weather and too his troops had no clothes for the cool weather they have just had and he got awfully chilly at times. He has a new French teacher as his other one died. I have to write French letters occasionally to a French family, the Gouchets who have him to dinner every Wednesday and incidentally have a Victrola and lots of classical records. They have written me a couple of letters.*

*Martha has been feeling a little under the weather lately and the Doctor told her Monday to just stay in bed for a few days. So Miss Sarah has been chief cook and bottle washer for the last 4 days. Martha is feeling a lot better now but has been trying to do too much so I will probably continue to be chief maid of all work. Roy washes and dries the supper dishes and puts Chris to bed so that helps a lot. I'm so glad I'm here to help tho' as negroes to help are just impossible to find and so high if you do find one. Chris and Hank have been so good and Martha and I really enjoyed resting and reading.*

*Hope you all have solved your problems about where to live and are happy with what you have. Hope you get settled before the winter winds start blowing in earnest. Hope you can have butane heat or if you have wood it isn't as high as it is here. Roy wanted to get a little wood to burn in the fireplace but it is $15 a cord delivered. Bet we don't get any I'll tell you.*

*Hank is getting so big. I bought him some overalls about 3 weeks ago and today I put them on him and decided they were just too tight and when I first bought them they weren't too tight at all. They are size 5 so I guess I'll have to get size 6. He is eating more now that it is cool and it makes me very happy. At lunch the other day he was so cute. He had been wanting his lunch for about 15 minutes or more so when we finally got it on the table and got sat down he was really anxious. I asked him to return thanks, so we bowed our heads and just as fast as he could rattle he said "God is great, God is good, and we thank him for this food" and instead of the customary "Amen," he said "wake up" and immediately started devouring his food. He has so much life since I've been giving him an iron tonic that Dr. Weir prescribed that I can barely keep up with him.*

*Must run to bed as I am a busy woman from daylight to dark and must get my good old sleep. I love you two so very much and be sweet to each other.*

*Lots of love*

*Sarah & Hank*

Sarah wasn't physically strong, but even though she slept with a loaded pistol under her bed while Harold was away, she wasn't a coward. She was twenty-seven when Harold was called to active duty, twenty-eight when he left Camp Bowie for the war in the Pacific, thirty-one when he returned. She had never lived alone, managed a house or even an apartment by herself, was not a good driver, and was ill-prepared for the life of a single mother. One decision that she made early on was that it would be good to have a man around the house other than a three-year-old, a man who could help her and who she could help as well. This man was Lieutenant FNU W. Hulsey of the Army Air Corps. He was stationed at the Fort Worth Army Airfield.

In those years, at least in Fort Worth, anyone with an extra room in their home was encouraged to donate it to a married

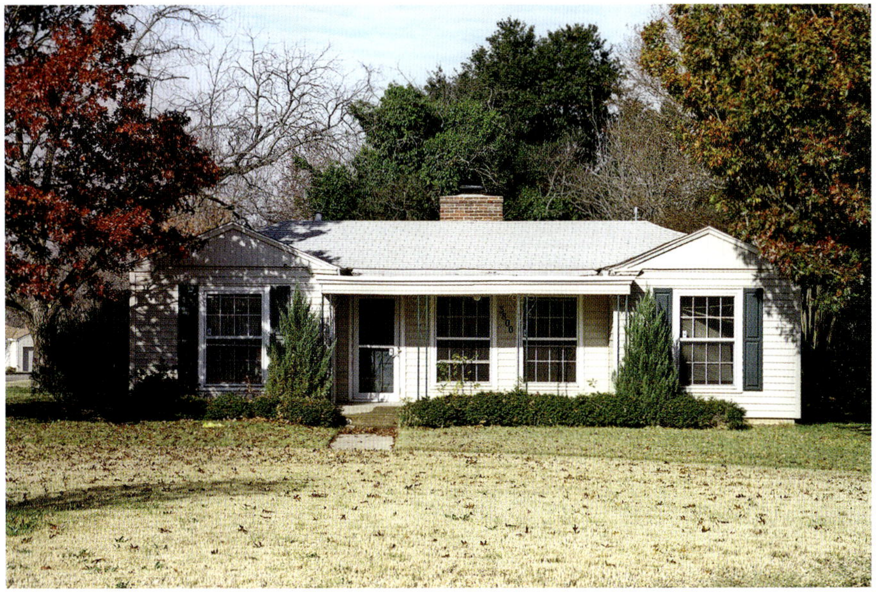

3800 Wildwood Road in 2008

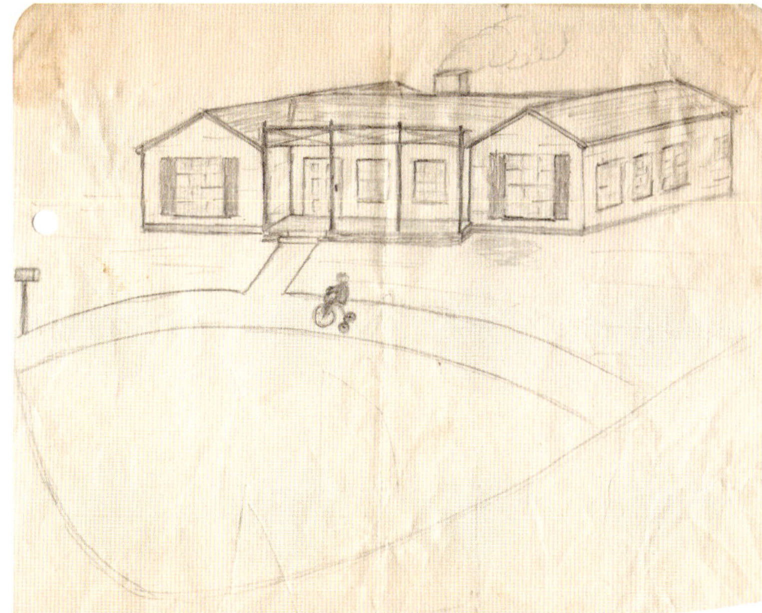

Sarah's drawing of 3800 Wildwood Road in 1944

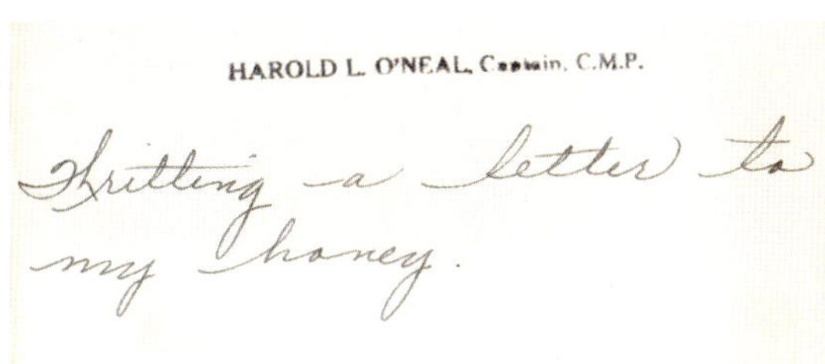

HAROLD L. O'NEAL, Captain, C.M.P.

Writting a letter to my honey.

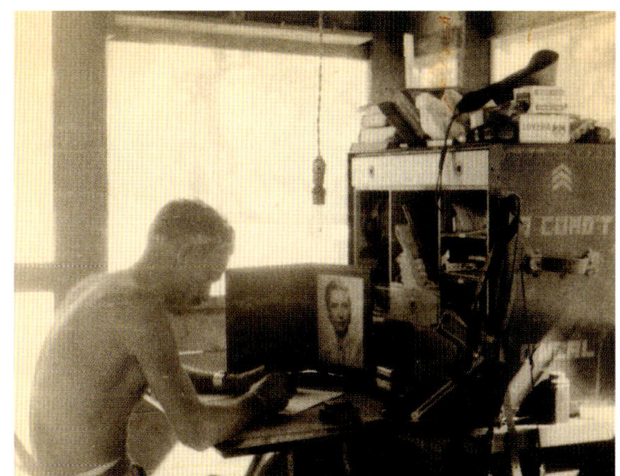

# Harold's letter

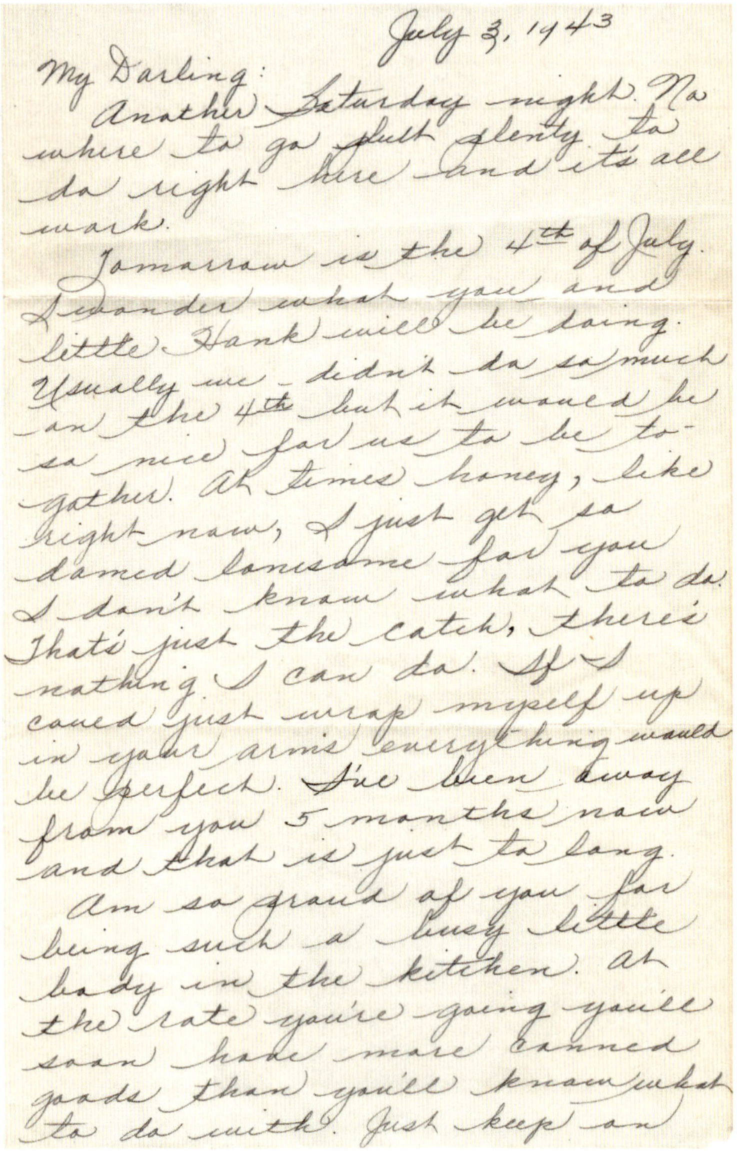

July 3, 1943

My Darling:

Another Saturday night. No where to go but plenty to do right here and it's all work.

Tomorrow is the 4th of July. I wonder what you and little Hank will be doing. Usually we didn't do so much on the 4th but it would be so nice for us to be together. At times honey, like right now, I just get so darned lonesome for you I don't know what to do. That's just the catch, there's nothing I can do. If I could just wrap myself up in your arms everything would be perfect. I've been away from you 5 months now and that is just to long.

Am so proud of you for being such a busy little body in the kitchen. At the rate you're going you'll soon have more canned goods than you'll know what to do with. Just keep on

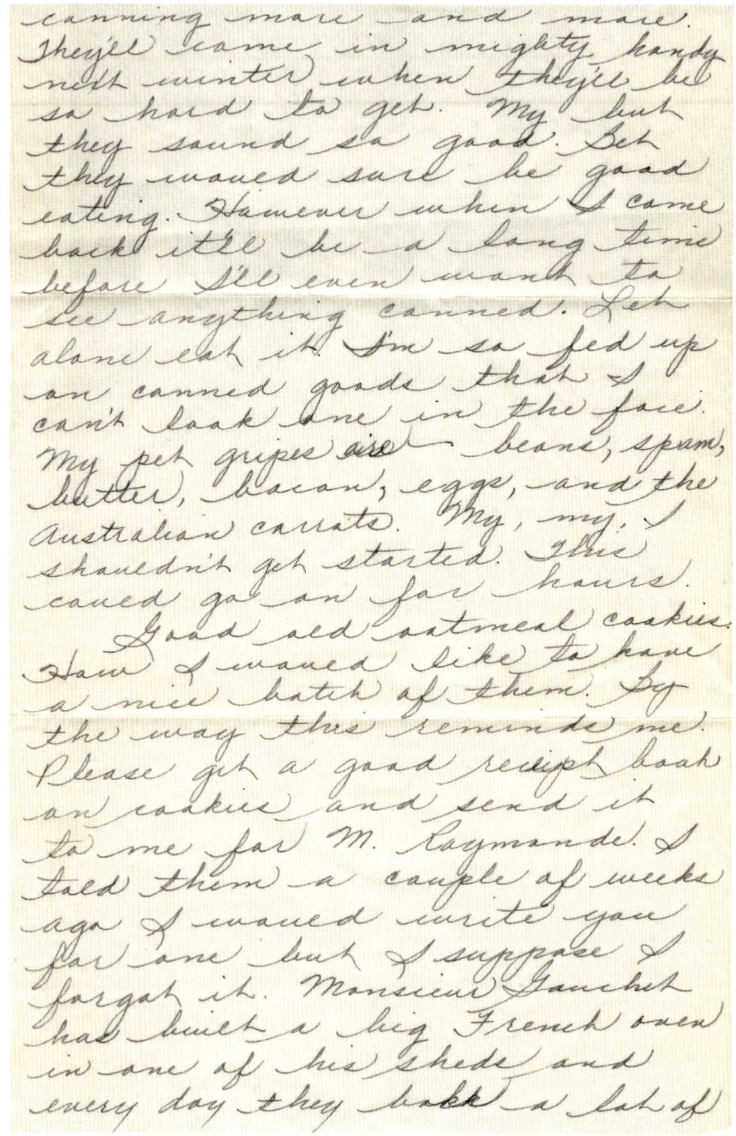

canning more and more. They'll come in mighty handy next winter when they'll be so hard to get. My but they sound so good. Bet they would sure be good eating. However when I come back it'll be a long time before I'll even want to see anything canned. Let alone eat it. I'm so fed up on canned goods that I can't look one in the face. My pet gripes are beans, spam, butter, bacon, eggs, and the Australian carrots. My, my, I shouldn't get started. This could go on for hours.

Good old oatmeal cookies. How I would like to have a nice batch of them. By the way this reminds me. Please get a good receipt book on cookies and send it to me for M. Raymonde. I told them a couple of weeks ago I would write you for one but I suppose I forgot it. Monsieur Gauchet has built a big French oven in one of his sheds and every day they bake a lot of cookies to sell to the soldiers. I think they're already made enough money to buy a Jeep when the war's over. That's slightly exagerated (?) but that's what they are doing with the money.

All of my new men are running me nuts. They were casuals and this is the first home they've had since being in the army. They've been knocked around quite a bit and the short time they've been on the island have been allowed to write only one letter home a week. Since they've been here with me I've let them write as many as they want to. Boy, oh boy, I believe it's all they do all day long, just write letters. Seems to me there's hundreds of letters. All I do is censor and stamp mail.

They can also ask quite a few questions. That takes up quite a bit more time. In their mail the main topic is how good and how much they're being fed. It makes me very happy. I take my own mess for granted but I know its far superior to many of the messes on the island.

I received the reel and fishing stuff from Raymond a couple of weeks ago. Haven't had a chance to use it yet, but maybe I can pretty soon.

I'm very proud of "Lacy" but haven't had much chance to get out in her. To date have only been out one time. Maybe things will slack up pretty soon and I can go out some more. As it is I get go aboard enough boats of all kinds.

Got such a kick out of Hank's observance on the Camel package. He is a mighty smart little boy. Must try to send the little scamp more pictures. Have meant to write him again but it seems that I've been so busy or so tired that I just keep putting it off. Tell him that Daddy thinks about him a whole lot and that I will try to write him a letter about something pretty soon.

Do I remember those heavenly nights at Castle Courts?, the piney woods?, Daingerfield, Tyler, Kilgore and all the rest? It's what my dreams are made of. All about you.

Have to leave. Will close as I don't know what time I'll get back.

I love you darling.

Yours only

Harold

## Sarah's letter

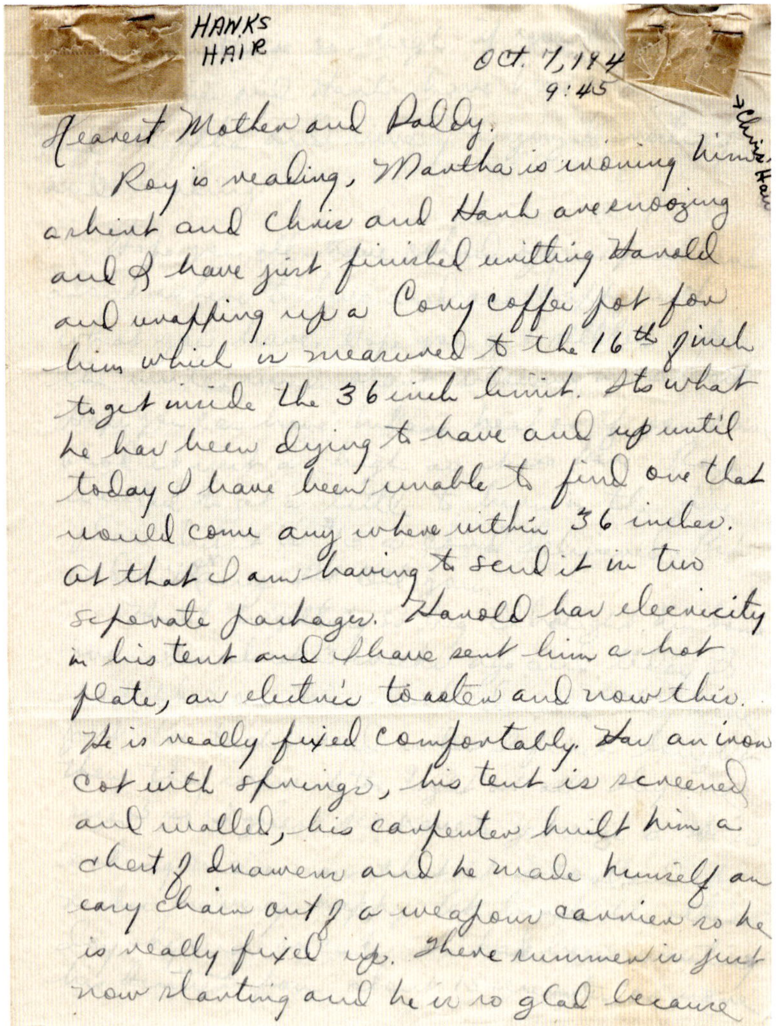

HANKS HAIR

Oct. 7, 1944
9:45

→Chris' Hair

Dearest Mother and Daddy,

Roy is reading, Martha is ironing him a shirt and Chris and Hank are snoozing and I have just finished writing Harold and wrapping up a Cory coffee pot for him which is measured to the 16th inch to get inside the 36 inch limit. Its what he has been dying to have and up until today I have been unable to find one that would come anywhere within 36 inches. At that I am having to send it in two seperate packages. Harold has electricity in his tent and I have sent him a hot plate, an electric toaster and now this. He is really fixed comfortably. Has an iron cot with springs, his tent is screened and walled, his carpenter built him a chest of drawers and he made himself an easy chair out of a weapons carrier so he is really fixed up. There summer is just now starting and he is so glad because

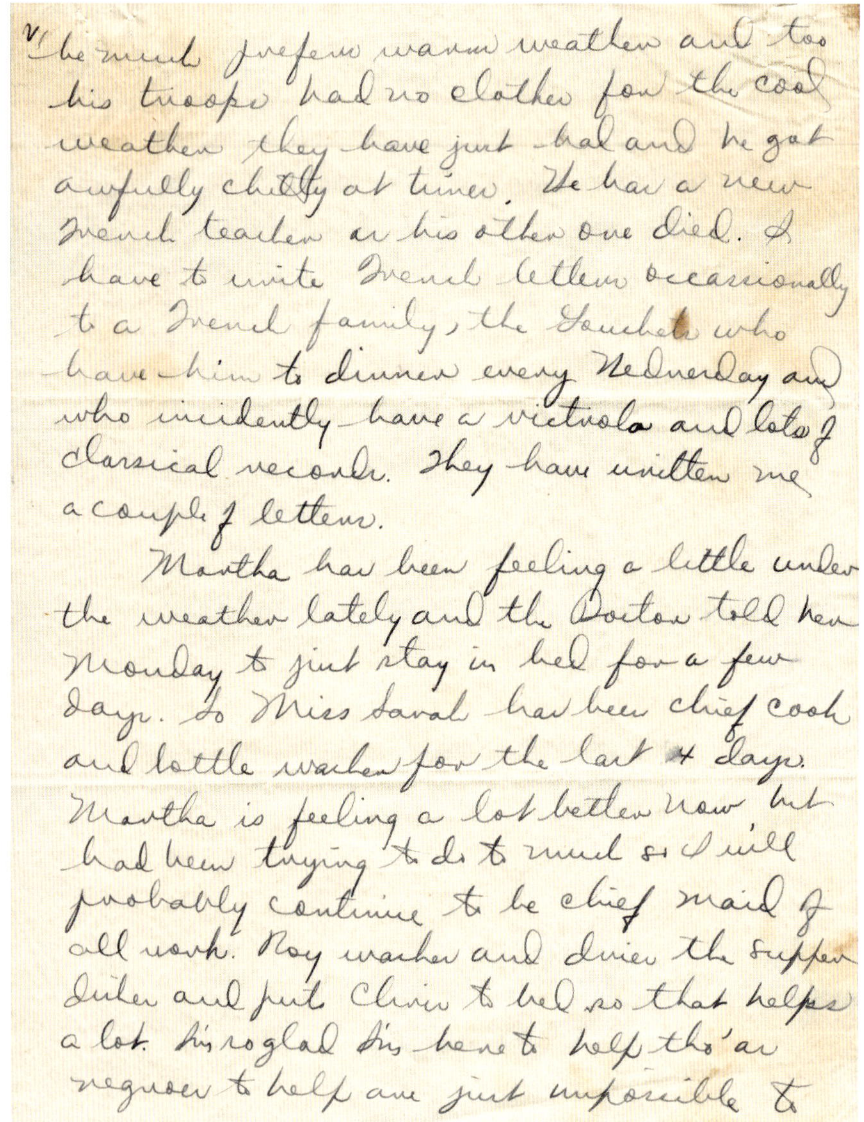

2

he much prefers warm weather and too his troops had no clothes for the cool weather they have just had and he got awfully chilly at times. He has a new French teacher as his other one died. I have to write French letters occasionally to a French family, the Gauchets who have him to dinner every Wednesday and who incidently have a victrola and lots of classical records. They have written me a couple of letters.

Martha has been feeling a little under the weather lately and the Doctor told her Monday to just stay in bed for a few days. So Miss Sarah has been chief cook and bottle washer for the last 4 days. Martha is feeling a lot better now, but had been trying to do to much so I will probably continue to be chief maid of all work. Roy washes and dries the supper dishes and puts Chris to bed so that helps a lot. I'm so glad Sis here to help tho' as negroes to help are just impossible to to find and are so high if you do find one. Chris and Hank have been so good and Martha and I surely enjoyed resting and reading.

Hope you all have solved your problem about where to live and are happy with what you have. Hope you get settled before the winter winds start blowing in earnest. Hope you can have butane heat or if you have wood it isn't as high as it is here. Roy wanted to get a little to burn in the fire place but it is $15. a cord delivered. But we don't get any I'll tell you.

Hank is getting so big. I bought him some overalls about 3 weeks ago and today I put them on him and decided they were just too tight and when I first bought them they weren't too tight at all. They are size 5 so I guess I'll have to get size 6. He is eating more now that it is cool and it makes me very happy. At lunch the other day he was so cute. He had been wanting his lunch for about 15 minutes or more and so when we finally got it on the table and got sat down he was really anxious. I asked him to return thanks, so we bowed our heads and just as fast as he could rattle he said "God is great, God is good, And we thank him, For this food" and instead of the customary "Amen", he said "wake up" and immediately started devouring his food. He has so much life since I've been giving him an iron tonic that Dr. Stein prescribed that I can hardly keep up with him.

Must run to bed as I am a busy woman from daylight to dark and must get my good old sleep. I love you two so very much and be sweet to each other.

Lots of love
Sarah & Hank.

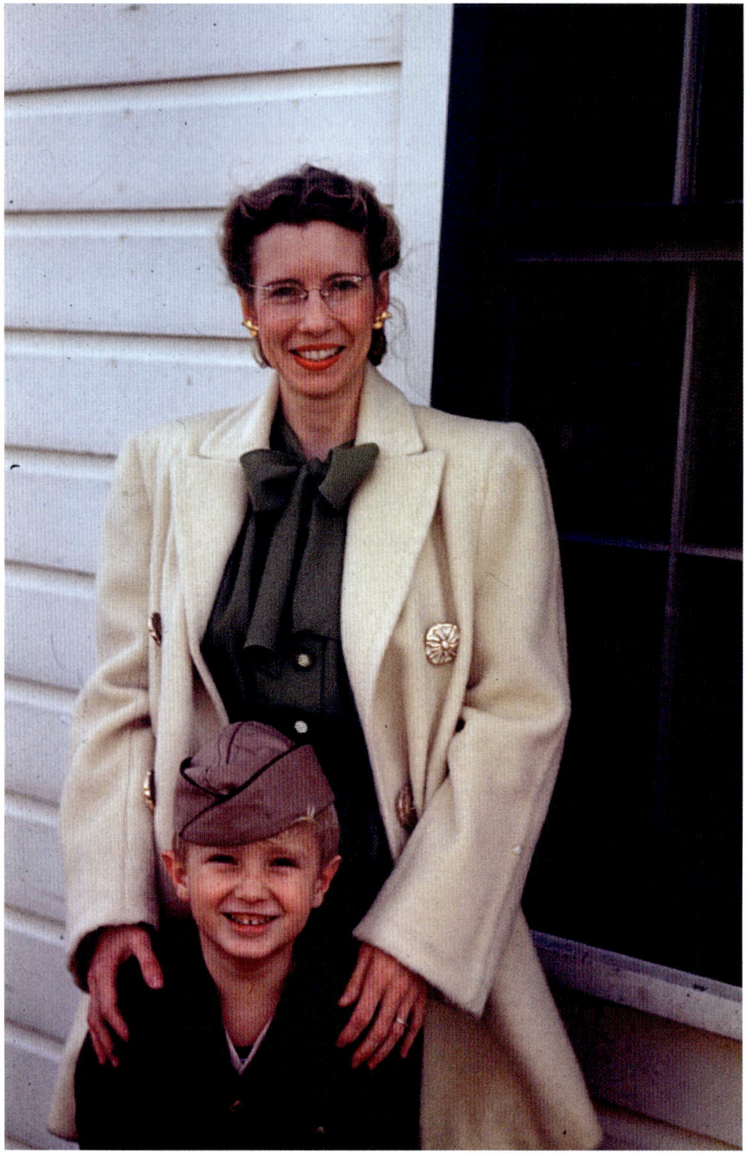

Sarah with Hank in uniform, 3800 Wildwood Road

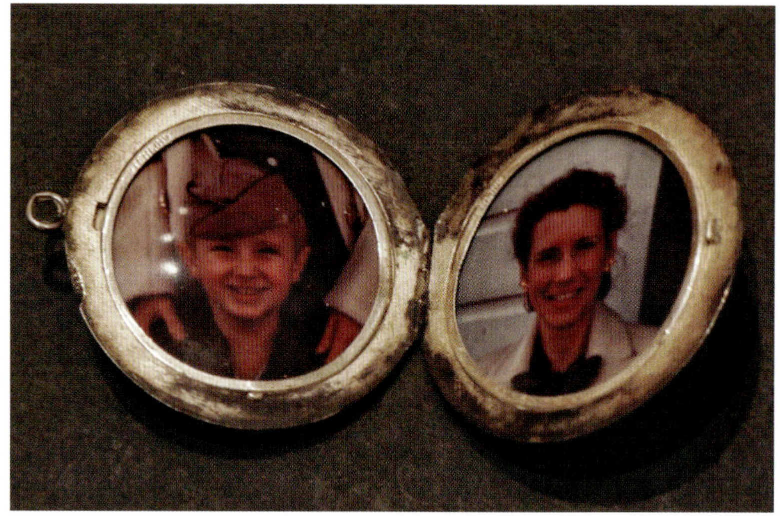

From Brownwood to Japan and back again.

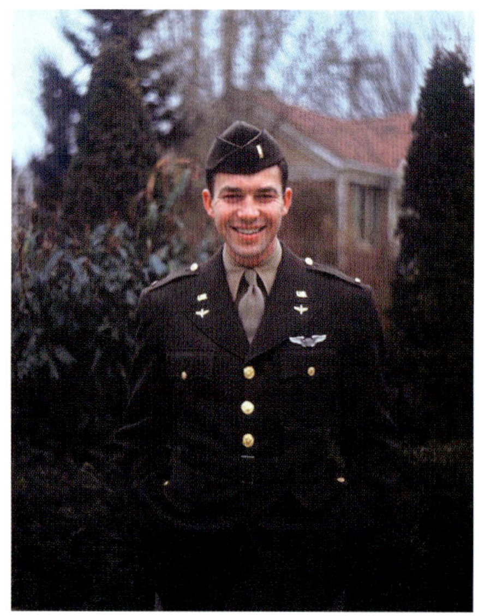

Lieutenant Hulsey, 1944

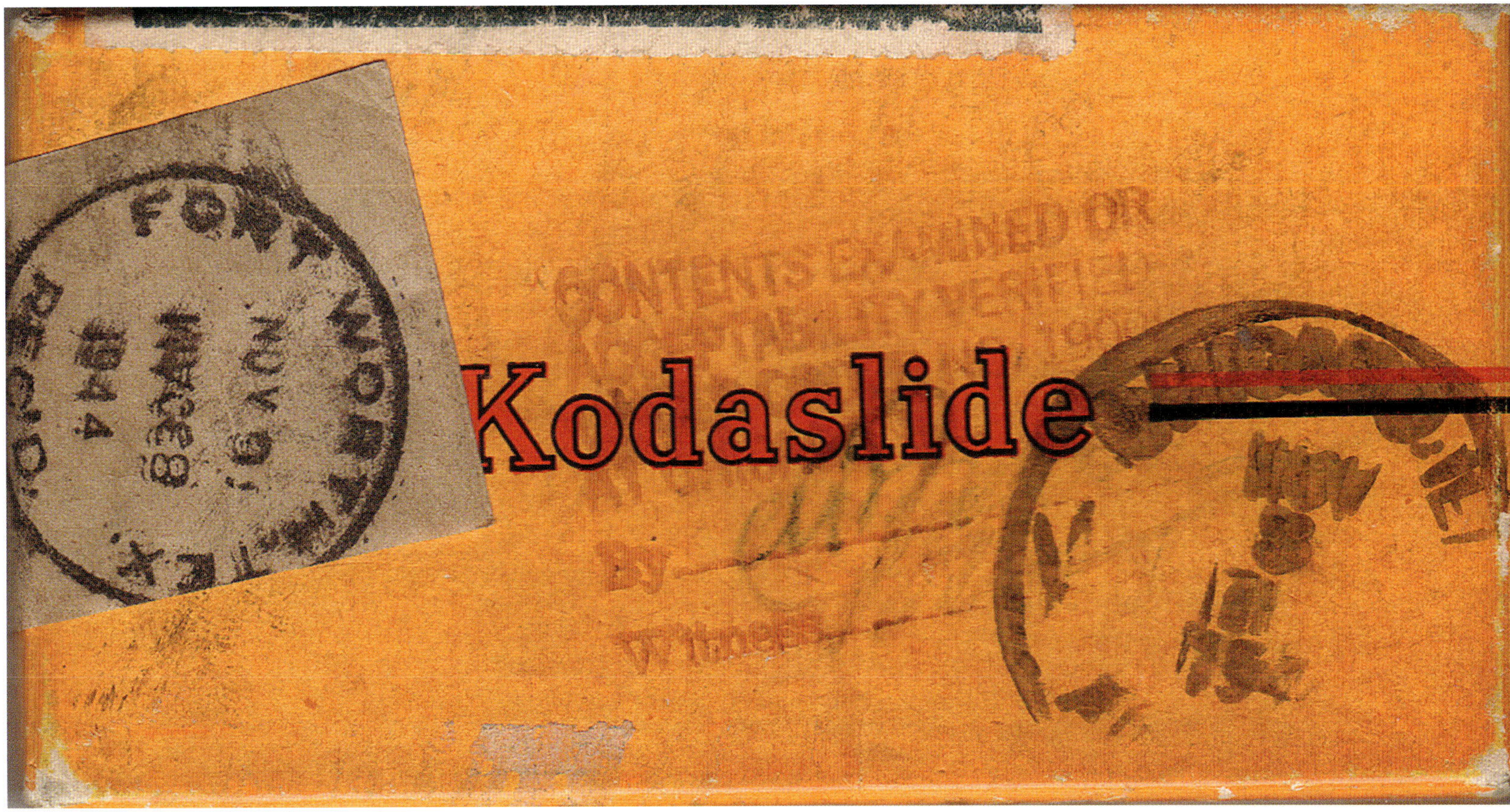


Kodak box

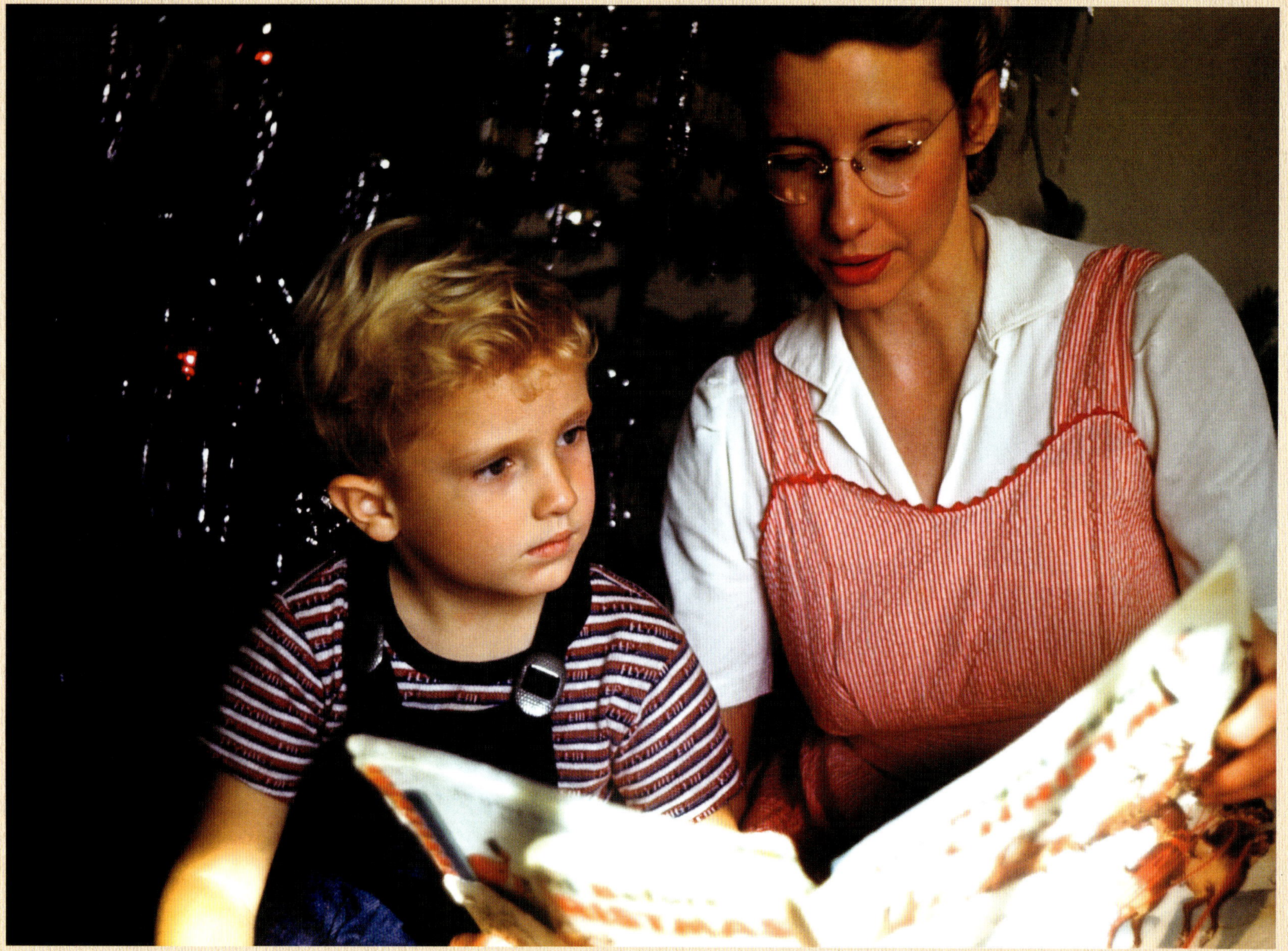

Sarah and Hank, Christmas 1944

soldier, so he could be with his wife as long as possible before shipping out to wherever. Lieutenant Hulsey was with us until at least November 9, 1944; there is a box of Kodachromes with that date with part of his name surviving on the address, and I distinctly remember that this young soldier took me out on Halloween a week or so earlier, possibly my first excursion into the land of trick or treating. I was probably terrified, dressed up in some kind of dreadful costume, but I could play like I was brave if he was with me in his uniform.

My only other memory of Lieutenant Hulsey is from the day he and his wife arrived at 3800 Wildwood. The little bungalow had a living room, kitchen, dining alcove, and three small bedrooms, two on the south side of the house and one on the north that was being used as a storeroom. Lieutenant Hulsey was in charge of cleaning out the room for him and his wife in the hope of turning it into a modest bedroom. For some reason Sarah had stored two large tires in the room, tires much too large for our Chrysler. I have no idea where she got them or why she had them, other than to perhaps trade for tires that would fit our car. New tires, like new cars, were almost nonexistent in those days.

In the spring of 1945, a 1940 Chrysler in good condition with four functioning tires was a valuable commodity. There had been no new cars since 1942; automobile dealers either went out of business or became used car showrooms, as Ford, General Motors, and Chrysler went into wartime production mode. The same was true of tires: there were no new ones available for ordinary civilian use. These were the days when many tractors on farms had metal "tires."

I must have decided I wanted to help clean the room, and in doing so got in everyone's way. At one point Lieutenant Hulsey decided to have some fun and convinced me to get inside one of the large tires. By getting inside, I mean I curled up and took the place of a rim, and then he rolled me out into the living room. Sarah was horrified and possibly suspected Lieutenant Hulsey and his wife might not be the best choice for roommates. I thought he was great and have never forgotten him. How many kids get rolled around in a tire? All that remains of Lieutenant Hulsey and those times are a Kodachrome slide showing a smiling young Lieutenant, a present he gave me for some unremembered reason, real silver Army Air Force wings, just like the ones he is wearing in the picture, and bombardier wings, which he isn't. I often thought about him and hope he made it.

A few short weeks later it was the Christmas season. Christmas 1944 was the last one Harold and Sarah would be apart for a quarter of a century, but on this Christmas the war still raged all over Europe and throughout the Pacific. In Europe the Germans were mounting their last great offensive to try and halt the Allied advance into Germany. The battle that ensued, popularly known as the Battle of the Bulge, was launched by the Germans on December 16 in the Ardennes forest, where the borders of Belgium, Luxembourg, and France converged.

The Allied forces, primarily Americans, were caught completely off guard by a German army of 450,000 men and thousands of tanks, artillery, and supporting aircraft. The Allies in the area numbered 600,000 men, and although the Germans would not be completely stopped and forced to retreat until the end of January, the Allied forces mounted a counteroffensive on December 23, and the tide began to turn by Christmas Day. The German casualties for the five weeks of fighting were close to 125,000 killed and wounded. Nearly 90,000 Allied troops were killed and wounded. It was perhaps the most costly European battle in terms of lives lost, and it was reported December 25 was the coldest Christmas Day in recent recorded history.

Half a world away, Harold and his company were on the USS *Pinkney*, an evacuation transport ship in the midst of a 2,600-mile journey from Port Oro, Papua, New Guinea, to a beachhead in Lingayen Gulf, to take part in the Allied invasion of that part of the Philippines.

Sarah had not heard from Harold for many weeks, but she read the *Fort Worth Star-Telegram* and listened to the radio. On Christmas Eve she listened to President Roosevelt's address. He said:

*It is not easy to say Merry Christmas to you my fellow Americans in this time of destructive war nor can I say Merry Christmas lightly tonight to our armed forces at their battle stations all over the world. . . .*

There was a Christmas tree displayed in the bungalow's living room, decorated with a few lights, a smattering of fake tinsel icicles, and some fragile glass ornaments left over from the days before the war. Much of the material used to decorate Christmas trees, like tinfoil, were scarce commodities. Tinfoil saved from cigarette packs, candy bars, and even chewing gum was an integral part of scrap drives.

Scrap drives were crucial. Any kind of metal scrap was important. Early in the war, in 1942, President Roosevelt made an urgent plea for scrap of all kinds, all the way from metal to rags to newspapers and even old kitchen grease. It's hard to imagine today that people saved grease, a bottle of which could be traded in for ration stamps. Why grease? You could make glycerin from fat, and processed properly this was an ingredient of nitroglycerin, which was an important part of bombs and explosives. I remember glass jars of cooking grease saved on the kitchen counter. Maybe some of those jars of grease led to enough stamps to get a pound of bacon that made a breakfast on the weekend much more fun, so it was a tragedy the day one got knocked off the counter and spilled all over the kitchen floor.

Everything was saved. I still remember my mother and I separating the paper and tinfoil from sticks of chewing gum. I was lucky no one took my tin soldiers or tricycle; many children's toys went into the scrap drives. So did old silk and nylon stockings that were used for parachutes.

That year there were some presents, perhaps a few tin soldiers from the dime store and maybe a Buck Rogers ray gun or a Rudolph the Red-Nosed Reindeer storybook. But celebrations were modest. Sarah was terrified and not in a mood to celebrate too joyously. She hadn't heard from Harold in many weeks and didn't even know where he was. Even if he could write, he couldn't tell her his location or anything about what he was doing. Harold knew this only too well, since he was in charge of censoring all the mail sent by the men of his company.

Young Lieutenant Hulsey, if he hadn't already been deployed, was more than likely soon dispatched to Europe to fly a B-24, on which he'd been trained in Fort Worth. There were still hundreds if not thousands of targets in Germany that needed to be destroyed. If he was a bombardier, as the insignia he gave me would seem to indicate, it would be his job to drop the bombs and destroy those targets.

Six thousand miles away Harold was at sea on Christmas Day, and didn't have radio broadcasts or a newspaper to deliver the news, but he did have the *Pinkney News*, a mimeographed daily news report published and distributed on board the USS *Pinkney* to keep the men up to date on the war in Europe and the Pacific, as well as to provide basketball scores and a little gossip. The news contained information that ranged all the way from the horrific to the mundane with a smatter-

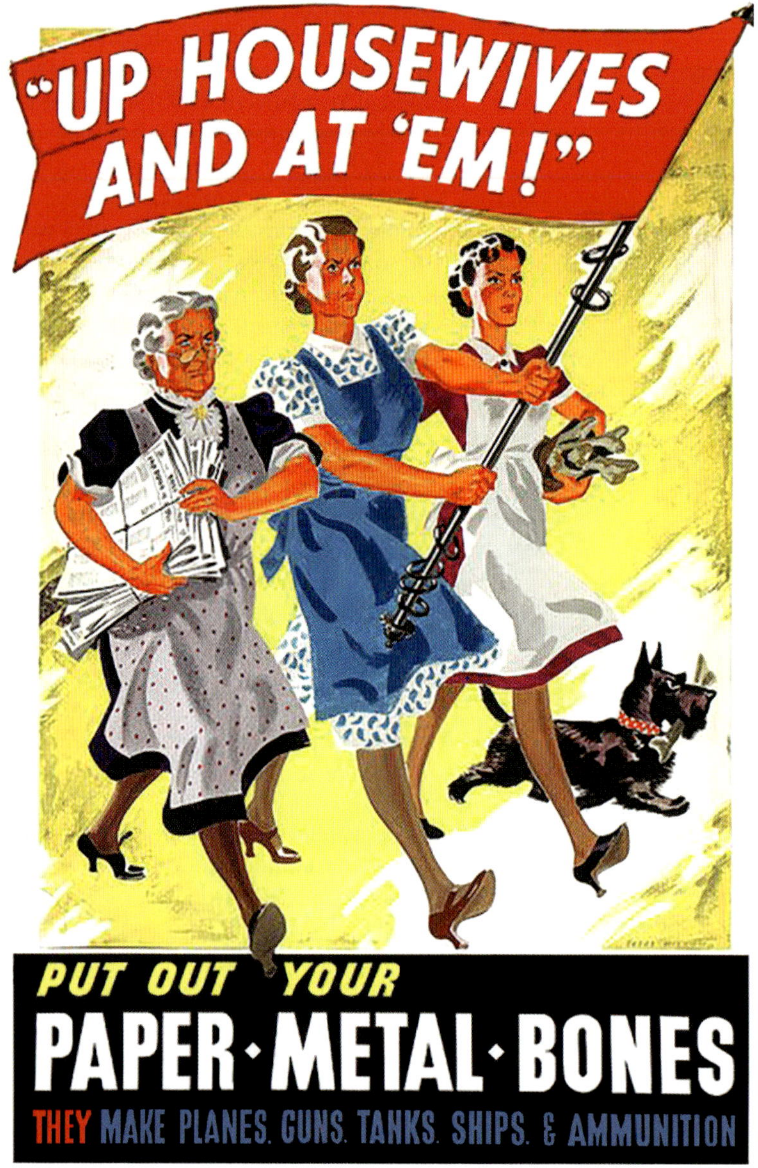

ing of the ridiculous, all presented with no particular priority. Harold saved three issues: December 24, 25, and 26, so, like Sarah, he knew a little about the Battle of the Bulge.

**December 24th**

*PARIS: The German winter offensive lost a great deal of its momentum Friday after grinding 40 miles across Belgium in seven days, a front dispatch said as the U.S. First Army rallied to a call from General Eisenhower to turn this great gamble into the German's worst defeat. . . . It would be premature to say Field Marshal Von Rundstedt's scheme had failed if he hopes to sweep across the Meuse River some 65 miles west of the Belgian border as some quarters believe. . . .*

*LEYTE ISLAND, PHILIPPINES: Publication of a newspaper for isolated Japanese troops was started by the American Psychological Warfare Branch. A weekly two page illustrated tabloid will be delivered from air and by artillery. It is printed in Japanese with pictures illustrating the good treatment accorded the Japanese on American occupied Saipan. The purpose is to break enemy morale by disclosing the truth. . . .*

*LONDON: The Polish government in exile said Friday the Germans had massacred twenty thousand Jews in a forced labor camp at Plaszov near Cracow. A spokesman quoted a report from underground channels which said the Germans also liquidated Jewish forced laborers at camps at Skarsvsk, Starachowice, Pionki and Ostrowwiek.*

*(T'was the night before Christmas and all through the house . . .)*

*MERRY CHRISTMAS FELLOWS*

**December 25th**

*BEVERLY HILLS: The body of Lupe Valez was on its way by train for burial in Mexico City . . .There was a dramatic moment before the service when Harold Raymond, handsome Austrian-born actor, walked into the chapel, stood silently before the casket making the sign of the cross and walked out. Raymond was named by Lupe as the father of her unborn child in a note she left when she ended her life last week.*

*PARIS: The first German spies captured in American uniforms during the Nazi counter-offensive were executed Saturday, Supreme headquarters announced one officer candidate and two non-commissioned officers were put to death by a firing squad. . . .*

*LONDON: American relief columns swinging up through Luxembourg and southeast Belgium have dented the Southern Flank of the German offensive which has now reached Libramont, twenty-three miles Northeast of Sedan. Meanwhile skies cleared and Allied planes smashed at German flying sorties, shooting down at least 175 planes. Headquarters lifted a forty-eight hour time lag on front news and disclosed the Americans had dented the Nazi flank north of the city of Luxembourg. . . .*

**December 26th**

*TO THE MEN AND WOMEN OF THE ARMED FORCES:*

*On behalf of a grateful nation I send to the men and women of the armed forces everywhere warm and confident good wishes this fourth Christmas of the war. On Christmas Day more than on any other day we remember you with pride and with humility and anguish and with joy we shall keep remembering you all the days of our lives.*

*It is therefore with solemn pride that I salute those who stand in the foreground of the struggle to bring back to a suffering world the way of life symbolized by the spirit of Christmas.*

*FRANKLIN D. ROOSEVELT*

*COMMANDER IN CHIEF*

*PARIS: The German winter offensive ground almost to a halt yesterday and its deep (sic) Wednesday in Belgium and Luxembourg were pounded from the ground today by a hurricane of destruction turned loose by the mightiest air force ever massed in war. A record of two thousand United States heavy bombers with one thousand fighter escorts roared out from Britain in one wave hundreds of medium bombers and fighters bombers sailed into the attack from continental bases and it appeared the total force would exceed even the thirteen thousand which flew on D Day.*

BASKETBALL SCORES: Kentucky beat Ohio State, Yale beat Dartmouth and 26 other teams won or lost.

*WASHINGTON: Fishing and hunting are precisely what the doctor ordered for the frayed nerves of homecoming war Veterans and Congressional groups intend that they get plenty of both. A House committee has just completed a two year study*

LARGEST CIRCULATION IN TEXAS
OVER 175,000 DAILY

# FORT WORTH STAR-TELEGRAM

MORNING
★★★★★

(CTS)—Chicago Tribune Service • (CDN)—Chicago Daily News
(NANA)—North American Newspaper Alliance.

A Fort Worth Owned Newspaper

(INS)—International News Service • (NYT)—New York Times
(AP)—Associated Press (Four Wires).

SIXTY-FIFTH YEAR. NO. 72. . FORT WORTH, TEXAS *** Where the West Begins *** FRIDAY, APRIL 13, 1945. EIGHTEEN PAGES PRICE FIVE CENTS

# President Roosevelt Dies at Warm Springs Of Cerebral Hemorrhage; Truman Is Sworn In

## U. S. 1st, 3rd Storm Gates Of Leipzig

### 2nd Armored Division Awaits Orders for Dash To Berlin, Possibly Today

PARIS, Friday April 13 (AP). — U. S. 9th Army tanks smashed across the Elbe River on a six-mile front just 57 miles from Berlin Thursday and the U. S. 1st and 3rd Armies in sweeps of nearly 50 miles thundered at the gates of the great city of Leipzig, 75 miles southwest of the capital.

A field dispatch said only orders from Lt. Gen. William H. Simpson were needed to send the 2nd Armored Division dashing on into Berlin, which could possibly be reached Friday. Wholly unconfirmed French reports said Allied parachute troops had been dropped at Bradenburg, barely 20 miles from greater Berlin.

The electrifying crossing of the Elbe—last big river barrier before the devastated capital—came with such speed that supreme headquarters was unable to confirm it, a spokesman saying that SHEAF was ompletely out of touch with 9th

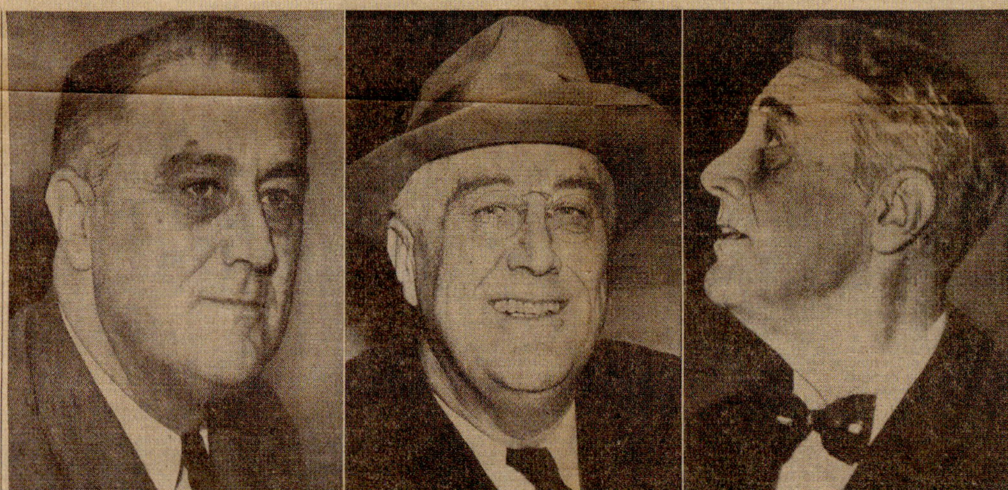

1933 1940 1945

## Executive Is Stricken Sitting at Fireplace

BY D. HAROLD OLIVER.

WARM SPRINGS, Ga., April 12 (AP).—President Franklin D. Roosevelt died Thursday at 4:35 p. m. (EWT) of a cerebral hemorrhage.

In Washington at 7:09 p. m., Vice President Harry S. Truman took the oath as the nation's 32nd chief executive.

Roosevelt's last words were:

"I have a terrific headache."

He spoke them to Cmdr. Harold Bruenn, Naval physician.

Roosevelt, 63, was sitting in front of a fireplace in the Little White House here atop Pine Mountain when the attack struck him.

Bruenn described it as a massive cerebral hemorrhage.

The President's Negro valet, Arthur Prettyman, and a Filipino messboy carried him to his bedroom. He was unconscious at the end. It came without pain.

Roosevelt, in the third month of his fourth term as President, came here three weeks ago to rest.

The President's wife was flown from Washington in an Army plane and was taken immediately to the Warm Springs Foundation.

It was made known that the funeral train would start for Washington during the day, arriving Saturday for the funeral at 4 p. m., in the East Room of the White House.

**He slept away Thursday afternoon, she told them. He did his job to the end, as he would want to do. Bless you all and all our love. She**

consultant to the Navy surgeon general.

Paullin was present when Bruenn gave the statement of the cause of death to reporters of the three national news services.

In response to a question, Dr. Bruenn said the President died without pain.

News of the President's death spread quickly and caused many a tear among the 125 infantile paralysis patients at the foundation here.

Mayor Frank W. Allcorn of Warm Springs was giving a barbecue at his mountain cabin Thursday afternoon for the President and about 50 other guests. Allcorn was awaiting the President's arrival when reporters got word through the Army Signal Corps radio telephone and Summer White House telephone communication to rush to the foundation.

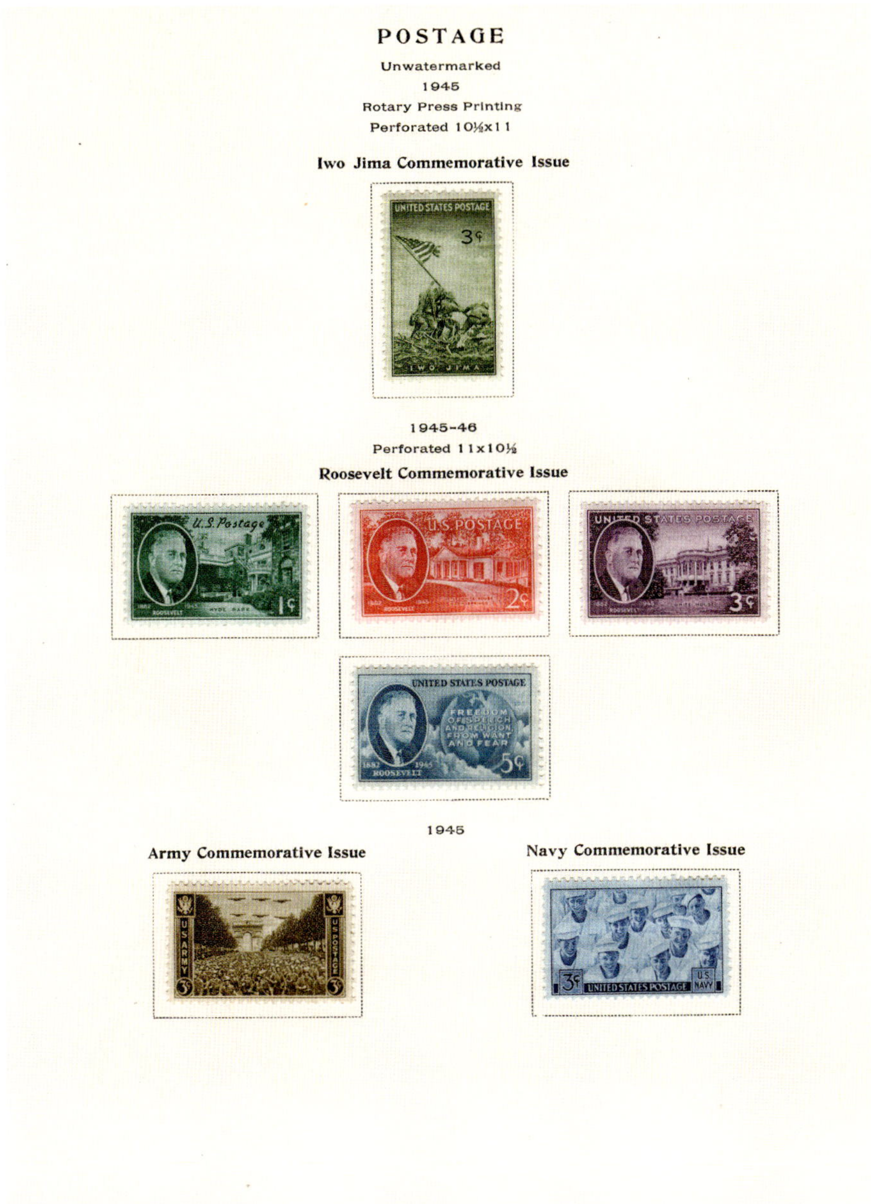


*on the subject and will introduce legislation in January.*

*WASHINGTON: Pres. Roosevelt in a Christmas broadcast voiced a prayer Sunday that with Victory will come a New Day of peace on earth in which all the Nations of the world will join together for all time. He said we cannot yet say when our Victory will come. Our enemies still fight fanatically. They still have reserves of men and military power. But they themselves know that they and their evil works are doomed. We may hasten the day of their doom if we here at home continue to do our full share.*

*HAPPY NEW YEAR AND MANY MORE IN PEACE.*

Sarah continued to do her full share for the next nine months. At some point that spring she moved from the Wildwood bungalow to a two-floor apartment two miles away at 122 Blanch Circle, where she'd put in the okra patch next to the front porch. It probably had to do with finances: an apartment in a new development surrounded by other apartment buildings, open fields, and automobile dealerships stocked with used cars cost less than a tidy bungalow in a residential neighborhood. It also had to do with rationing and the black 1940 Chrysler.

There were no stores of any kind within walking distance of the house on Wildwood; there were a few close to Blanch Circle. Another plus was the new apartment would be one mile closer to everything: the stores, the church, even the washeteria. In an era when everything was rationed, from gasoline to soapsuds, saving a mile here and there made a difference. There was nothing to tie Sarah to the house; her sister had moved away, and Crestwood, the school where she planned to enroll me in kindergarten in September, was less than a mile from Wildwood and Blanch Circle—just in opposite directions.

In the midst of this there was a death in the family. In the eyes of Sarah and probably Harold as well, the man who had the greatest impact on of their lives was President Roosevelt. His death on April 12, 1945, was probably not a surprise to many of those in government who undoubtedly knew how sick he was when he was elected to his fourth term in November 1944. His health had continued to deteriorate, but this was not well known by the general public. With the willing cooperation of the media, his infirmities had been well hidden from the country.

Harold was still in the Philippines in April 1945, and I was just a child, approaching my fifth birthday, and much of what I remember is undoubtedly in retrospect, but Roosevelt's death impacted my mother very much. I don't remember seeing her clip the papers, but she saved the front page of the April 13 issue of the *Fort Worth Star-Telegram,* and over the next few days clipped stories and photographs from the inside pages of the paper while weeping over them. She carefully preserved all these clipping, with her scrapbooks and memorabilia, and when she died many years later, Harold made sure they were saved as well.

Such was Sarah's admiration for Roosevelt that she encouraged me to collect stamps as he did, to use them to learn geography and the names of the countries of the world, world leaders, presidents of the United States, and most importantly, the history of our country. She made certain I had all the stamps that featured his portrait, whether they were US stamps or from other countries. She did this until I was a teenager and my interest in baseball and girls replaced my interest in postage stamps, but she continued to buy commemorative stamps until the early 1960s, especially if Roosevelt was featured. The last pages in my childhood stamp album are from 1962, when a first class letter cost five cents, and she made certain all the pages were filled up to that time.

Roosevelt's first New Deal program had made an incredible difference in her life, but at the time of his death, she had no idea that the last New Deal program, the Serviceman's Readjustment Act, would have an equally great impact, one that would enable so many of her dreams to come true. One can only imagine what might have been possible if Roosevelt's economic plans as outlined in his "Second Bill of Rights" speech could have been implemented, but there was a war to be won, his health was failing, and there was considerable resistance to this plan from conservatives in both the House and Senate.

Sarah had no idea when the war would be over or when Harold would come home, or indeed if he'd come home at all. As she fixed up the new apartment this was always on her mind, and for many months she carried on just as she had for the past three years. Weekly trips to the washeteria, Sunday school, sometimes downtown for this and that, and the grocery store, either the little one close by on University Drive that we could both walk to through the vacant lots behind the apartment building across the street, or the bigger store, the semi-supermarket on Camp Bowie Boulevard. It was a mundane waiting game that I didn't understand, and Sarah didn't either.

Then it all ended with a flash, actually two flashes: one over Hiroshima and then over Nagasaki. Within a few weeks Sarah was less terrified and suddenly filled with some measure of hope. In the Philippines Harold stopped crossing off the days in his notebook, sailed for Japan, was suddenly exchanging business cards with Japanese police officials, planning farewell-to-the-war in the Pacific parties with his fellow officers, parties that would feature Japanese entertainers (real girls!), cold beer, extra portions of Spam, and maybe whiskey. All to be followed by a long trip home on the USS *Hansford*, with Sarah counting the days.

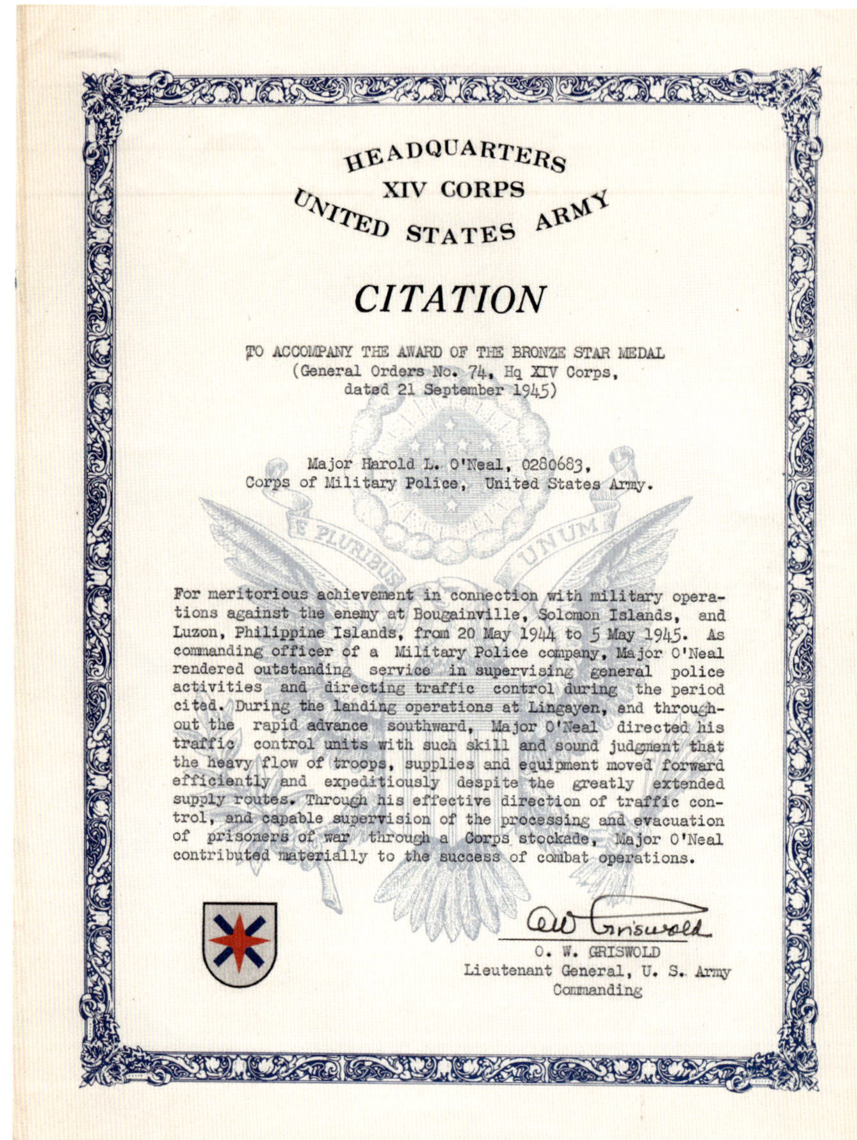
HEADQUARTERS
XIV CORPS
UNITED STATES ARMY

CITATION

TO ACCOMPANY THE AWARD OF THE BRONZE STAR MEDAL
(General Orders No. 74, Hq XIV Corps,
dated 21 September 1945)

Major Harold L. O'Neal, 0280683,
Corps of Military Police, United States Army.

For meritorious achievement in connection with military operations against the enemy at Bougainville, Solomon Islands, and Luzon, Philippine Islands, from 20 May 1944 to 5 May 1945. As commanding officer of a Military Police company, Major O'Neal rendered outstanding service in supervising general police activities and directing traffic control during the period cited. During the landing operations at Lingayen, and throughout the rapid advance southward, Major O'Neal directed his traffic control units with such skill and sound judgment that the heavy flow of troops, supplies and equipment moved forward efficiently and expeditiously despite the greatly extended supply routes. Through his effective direction of traffic control, and capable supervision of the processing and evacuation of prisoners of war through a Corps stockade, Major O'Neal contributed materially to the success of combat operations.

O. W. GRISWOLD
Lieutenant General, U. S. Army
Commanding

# Back on Track
## 1945 - 1950

**HAROLD RETURNED TO THE UNITED STATES AND DISEMBARKED IN SAN FRANCISCO ON OCTOBER 27,** but didn't have much time to enjoy the city, leaving quickly for his final destination in Texas. He arrived at Fort Sam Houston for medical treatment on November 2, and the next day, November 3, received two official documents. The first, Special Order 307, was filled with confusing abbreviations and typos and stated:

*DP each of the fol named officers are granted terminal lv as indicated of 4 November 1945. WP their homes or unit rendezvous as shown so as to arrive thereat not later than dates indicated at which time officers are reld fr atchd unasgd Separation Center this Hg and fr further AD, and revert ti inactive status not by reason of physical disability.*

A few lines down were the orders that applied to Harold: He was given four months of terminal leave to begin getting his life back on track. Later that same day another document, the subject of which was *Appointment under Section 37 National Defense Act, as amended* stated:

*The Secretary of War has directed me to inform you that by direction of the President, you are appointed in the Army of the United States Officers' Reserve Corps. Effective this date, in the grade and section shown after A. above (Major, CMP). Your serial number is shown after B. above. You will not perform the duties of an officer under this appointment until specifically called to active duty by competent orders.*

After three years Harold was no longer on active duty; he would receive ongoing medical treatment as a reserve officer. He left Fort Sam Houston and arrived in Fort Worth on Sunday, November 4. This was the first time Sarah had seen him in nearly three years and, of course, I'm sure I didn't really recognize him, not because he was thin and sick but because I was only two when he left. He may have been ill but he was up for an interview with a reporter from the *Fort Worth Star-Telegram*.

In later years, Harold often told friends in a joking manner that his last job was "chief of police of Tokyo." This was his little joke; he was actually carrying out those duties in Sendai, a city 150 miles north of Tokyo, where he'd arrived on September 15. He didn't remain at his job very long, because he was seriously ill. Nearly three years in the jungles of New Guinea and the Philippines and all the islands in between had taken their toll.

In his prime, Harold was 5'10" and weighed over 140 pounds. He was still the same height but weighed about 116 pounds. He was plagued with what he called "jungle rot" all over his legs, and what his doctors called "tropical sprue," which, given his symptoms, may have been an accurate assessment. Not only had he lost one fifth of his weight, he was often so tired and weak it was difficult to function. When he arrived at Fort Sam Houston, he hoped military doctors might properly diagnose his illness and cure him so he could return to active duty and get his life back on track. He had no idea his time in the hospital would be his last military assignment.

Harold was in and out of military hospitals for the next eighteen months and, despite everyone's best efforts, there was no medical solution then available to treat

WD PERSONNEL CENTER
SEPARATION CENTER
FORT SAM HOUSTON, TEXAS

In Reply
Refer to

SUBJECT: Appointment under Section 37 National Defense Act, as amended

DATE: 3 NOVEMBER 1945

TO: HAROLD LEE O'NEAL

A Major, C M P

B 0-280 683

1. The Secretary of War has directed me to inform you that by direction of the President, you are appointed in the Army of the United States Officers' Reserve Corps, effective this date, in the grade and section shown after A above. Your serial number is shown after B above.

2. You will not perform the duties of an officer under this appointment until specifically called to active duty by competent orders.

3. Upon receipt in the War Department of the Oath of Office which was properly executed at the Separation Center, a commission evidencing your appointment will be sent to you.

4. Whenever your permanent address is changed, it is important that you notify the Adjutant General, Washington 25, D.C. and not this Center, using the inclosed Personal Report Form.

BY COMMAND OF BRIGADIER GENERAL FOX:

L. L. STEWART
Major, A G D
Officer in Charge
Separation Center

Inclosures:
Personal Report Form

DATE OF ACCEPTANCE
3 NOVEMBER 1945

---

2. Under auth contained in Radio 8th Army, D 71843 DC, 2 Oct 45, the following Off, atchd unasgd 272d RC this RD, reld fur dy in this Theatre & WP by first available water T to a Reception Station in the US to be named by indorsement to this order by the CG of the US port at which Off is debarked. ASRS indicated is based on recomputation as of 2 Sep 45.

| RANK | NAME | ASN | MOS | BRANCH | ASRS | RECEPTION STATION |
|---|---|---|---|---|---|---|
| Maj | O'NEAL, HAROLD L<br>122 Blanch Circle, Ft. Worth, Tex. | 0280683 | 9101 | CMP | 110 | 10 |

3. Off will be custodian of own records during movement to US and will be under control of the CG, ASF from time of departure from this sta until released by proper auth in the US.

4. TCN. TCNT. 212/60425 65-216 P431-02.

BY ORDER OF COLONEL ARNY:

A. H. DEAN, Jr.
Capt, AGD
Asst Adj General

DISTRIBUTION:
"T"

-1-
RESTRICTED

RECEIVED FOR TRANSPORTATION
OCT 11 1945
U.S.S. HANSFORD

Endorsement.
U.S.S. HANSFORD (APA-106)
1. Transportation completed. You were subsisted in the Wardroom Mess of this vessel, without cost, from Oct. 11-26, 1945

TRANSPORATION COMPLETED
26 Oct. 1945

---

RESTRICTED
ARMY SERVICE FORCES
HEADQUARTERS WAR DEPARTMENT PERSONNEL CENTER

Book 4 85/325

SPECIAL ORDER NO. - 307

Fort Sam Houston, Texas.
3 November 1945

EXTRACT

*  *  *

19. DP each of the fol-named officers are granted terminal lv as indicated eff 4 November 1945, WP their homes or unit rendezvous as shown so as to arrive thereat not later than dates indicated at which time officers are reld fr atchd unasgd Separation Center this Hq and fr further AD, and revert to inactive status not by reason of physical disability. AUS appointments held continue in force during the present emergency plus six months unless sooner terminated DP. AUS-AC appointments terminate in compliance Public Law 455 77th Congress. Officers entitled to WD AGO Form 53-98 which will be completed prior departure terminal lv and distributed at expiration thereof as required Cir 472, WD, 16 Dec 44. PCS. TDN. TPA. 601-32 P 431-02-03-07 A 212/60425 S 99-999.

| NAME | TERM LV GRANTED | HOME OR UNIT RENDEZVOUS | DATE RELD FROM AD |
|---|---|---|---|
| CAPT EUGENE J KLEIN<br>0-299 618, AC | 3 months & 10 days | Laredo, Tex | 15 Feb 46 |

Mailing Address: 430 Avant Ave, San Antonio 3, Texas.
Auth: DP; RR 1-5; Part 1 or 2 of Radios AFPMP 1097, 1098, 1099, Hq AAF, 8 Sep 45.

| NAME | TERM LV GRANTED | HOME OR UNIT RENDEZVOUS | DATE RELD FROM AD |
|---|---|---|---|
| MAJ JOHN V OSBORNE<br>0-563 967, AC | 3 months & 5 days | Pampa, Tex | 12 Feb 46 |

Mailing Address: 1122 Mary Ellen Street, Pampa, Texas.
Auth: DP; Parts 1 or 2 of Radios AFPMP 1097, 98, 99 Hq AAF Sep 8. 45; Par 6 Sec 2, WD Cir 290, 1945; RR 1-5 as amended.

| NAME | TERM LV GRANTED | HOME OR UNIT RENDEZVOUS | DATE RELD FROM AD |
|---|---|---|---|
| MAJ HAROLD L O'NEAL<br>0-280 683, CMP | 4 months | Kilgore, Tex | 5 Mar 46 |

Mailing Address: Kilgore, Texas.
Auth: DP; TWX AGF 25 Sep 45 GNGAP-P; RR 1-5 as amended.

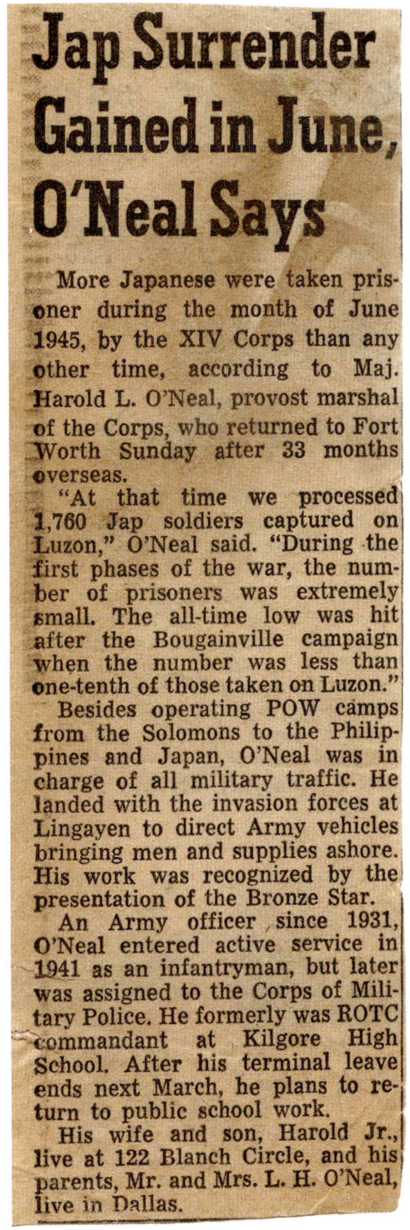

# Jap Surrender Gained in June, O'Neal Says

More Japanese were taken prisoner during the month of June 1945, by the XIV Corps than any other time, according to Maj. Harold L. O'Neal, provost marshal of the Corps, who returned to Fort Worth Sunday after 33 months overseas.

"At that time we processed 1,760 Jap soldiers captured on Luzon," O'Neal said. "During the first phases of the war, the number of prisoners was extremely small. The all-time low was hit after the Bougainville campaign when the number was less than one-tenth of those taken on Luzon."

Besides operating POW camps from the Solomons to the Philippines and Japan, O'Neal was in charge of all military traffic. He landed with the invasion forces at Lingayen to direct Army vehicles bringing men and supplies ashore. His work was recognized by the presentation of the Bronze Star.

An Army officer since 1931, O'Neal entered active service in 1941 as an infantryman, but later was assigned to the Corps of Military Police. He formerly was ROTC commandant at Kilgore High School. After his terminal leave ends next March, he plans to return to public school work.

His wife and son, Harold Jr., live at 122 Blanch Circle, and his parents, Mr. and Mrs. L. H. O'Neal, live in Dallas.

his problems. It became apparent he could no longer serve as an active duty officer or even in the active reserve. When further treatment was deemed fruitless, he was discharged with a permanent medical disability, a status that provided him with a modest pension. To put this into perspective, the Individual Income Tax Return for income earned by the O'Neal family (i.e. Harold, since Sarah didn't work, and I was six), was $3,177.08, and after exemptions and deductions the tax owed was $4.00.

Now in his thirty-seventh year, Harold had been an officer in the US Army in various capacities since 1929, but had only a high school education. He needed a job to support his family, but couldn't consider any kind of employment that required physical exertion. It was time to make some hard decisions, decisions that would alter his life and the lives of his family forever. He considered many possibilities.

When Harold was called to active duty on September 7, 1941, the life he envisioned for Sarah and his son was put on hold for four years, as it was for millions of other Americans. His and their dreams were put off for a day when it might be possible to dream again. Now it was that day, and he and Sarah could think about the bungalow and new furniture and listening to music and reading books and other things they had wanted for many years. They wanted these things, but they were not things either of them thought they *deserved*, as if they were some kind of peculiar American birthright.

A bungalow filled with simple amenities was a thing of daydreams, but after three years away from the peaceful, civilized, and mannered world of East Texas, Harold fully understood that for dreams to come true he would have to start over, work hard at a new enterprise, be flexible and moderate in both beliefs and actions, and be prepared to take advantage of any and all opportunities that might come his way. One such opportunity was provided in the same way it had been offered in 1933.

Just as the first New Deal act had created the Civilian Conservation Corps and a job, the last New Deal act, the Serviceman's Readjustment Act of 1944, better known today, as well as then, as the GI Bill, provided qualified returning military personnel with an opportunity to undertake various kinds of educational training, all the way from developing vocational skills to obtaining degrees at the finest colleges and universities throughout the United States. Harold already had great vocational skills: he was an exceptional carpenter/woodworker, but this was not a skill he wanted to use at that time, nor could he if he wanted to. But he believed in and understood the importance of education.

The Serviceman's Readjustment Act was perhaps the most important element in making it possible for millions of women and men like Harold to return from the war and not only adjust to civilian life, but to begin their own pursuit of the American Dream—in the process helping

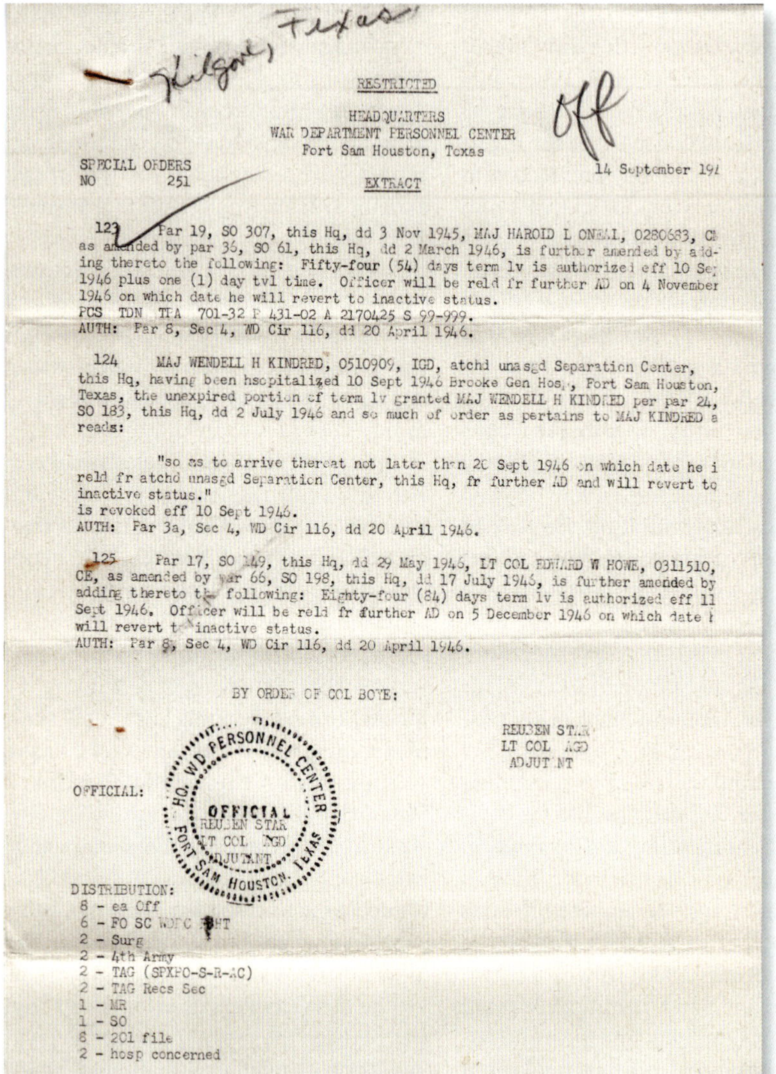

Kilgore, Texas

RESTRICTED

HEADQUARTERS
WAR DEPARTMENT PERSONNEL CENTER
Fort Sam Houston, Texas

SPECIAL ORDERS
NO 251

14 September 194

Off

EXTRACT

123 Par 19, SO 307, this Hq, dd 3 Nov 1945, MAJ HAROLD L ONEAL, 0280683, CE as amended by par 36, SO 61, this Hq, dd 2 March 1946, is further amended by adding thereto the following: Fifty-four (54) days term lv is authorized eff 10 Sep 1946 plus one (1) day tvl time. Officer will be reld fr further AD on 4 November 1946 on which date he will revert to inactive status.
PCS TDN TFA 701-32 P 431-02 A 2170425 S 99-999.
AUTH: Par 8, Sec 4, WD Cir 116, dd 20 April 1946.

124 MAJ WENDELL H KINDRED, 0510909, IGD, atchd unasgd Separation Center, this Hq, having been hsopitalized 10 Sept 1946 Brooke Gen Hosp, Fort Sam Houston, Texas, the unexpired portion of term lv granted MAJ WENDELL H KINDRED per par 24, SO 183, this Hq, dd 2 July 1946 and so much of order as pertains to MAJ KINDRED a reads:

"so as to arrive thereat not later than 20 Sept 1946 on which date he i reld fr atchd unasgd Separation Center, this Hq, fr further AD and will revert to inactive status."
is revoked eff 10 Sept 1946.
AUTH: Par 3a, Sec 4, WD Cir 116, dd 20 April 1946.

125 Par 17, SO 149, this Hq, dd 29 May 1946, LT COL EDWARD W HOWE, 0311510, CE, as amended by par 66, SO 198, this Hq, dd 17 July 1946, is further amended by adding thereto the following: Eighty-four (84) days term lv is authorized eff 11 Sept 1946. Officer will be reld fr further AD on 5 December 1946 on which date he will revert to inactive status.
AUTH: Par 8, Sec 4, WD Cir 116, dd 20 April 1946.

BY ORDER OF COL BOYE:

REUBEN STAR
LT COL AGD
ADJUTANT

OFFICIAL:

HQ. WD PERSONNEL CENTER
FORT SAM HOUSTON, TEXAS
OFFICIAL
REUBEN STAR
LT COL AGD
ADJUTANT

DISTRIBUTION:
8 - ea Off
6 - FO SC WDPC BHT
2 - Surg
2 - 4th Army
2 - TAG (SPXPO-S-R-AC)
2 - TAG Recs Sec
1 - MR
1 - SO
8 - 201 file
2 - hosp concerned

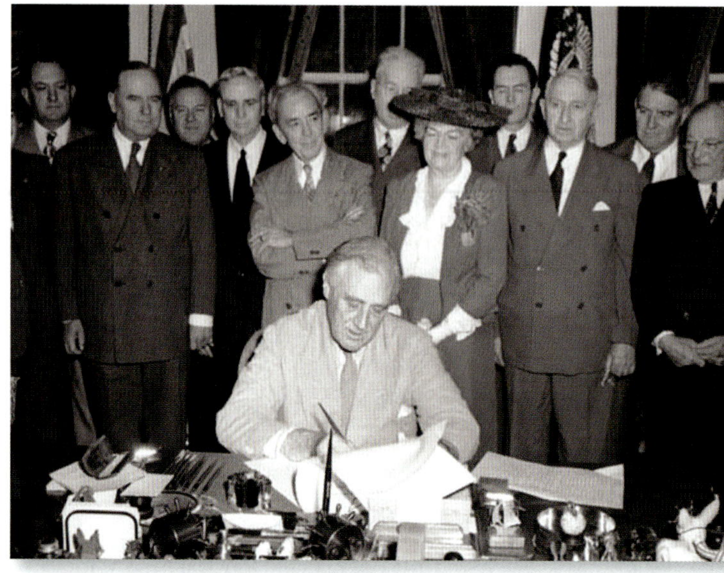

President Roosevelt signs the GI Bill on June 22, 1944

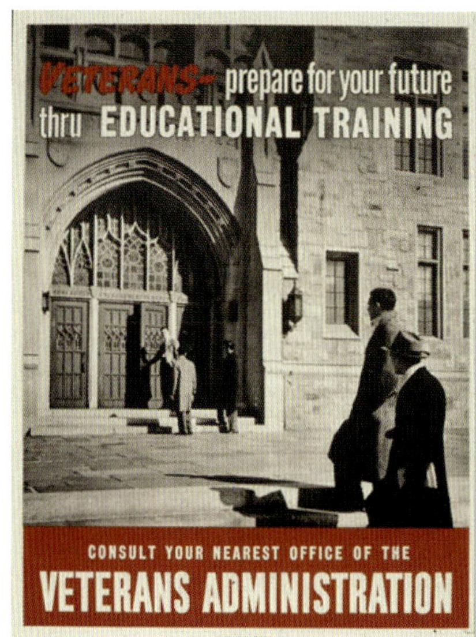

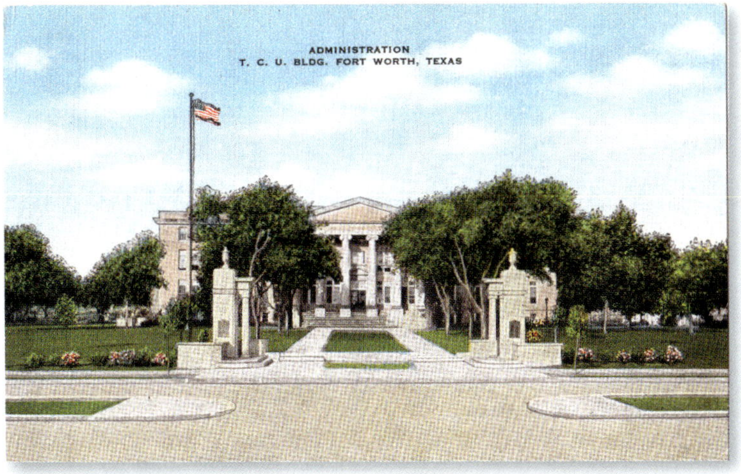


to make America into the industrial and military colossus it became in the 1950s. If President Roosevelt's original ideas had been implemented, the program would have also benefited needy and destitute Americans, but this was more than conservative Republicans and veterans' groups could tolerate, and it was never seriously considered.

What became known informally as the GI Bill was a law that provided a range of benefits for returning veterans. The best-known programs provided funds for tuition and living expenses for veterans who wanted to attend high school or college or even get vocational training. The only stipulation was that the veteran had to have been on active duty for at least one hundred and twenty days and be honorably discharged. By the mid-1950s, 2.2 million veterans had taken advantage of the program to attend various colleges and universities, and 5.6 million more had used the program to complete high school or receive other kinds of training. Still more had taken advantage of programs that helped young entrepreneurs start new businesses or assisted would-be homeowners with low-cost mortgages.

If there was a flaw in the program, it was that the GI Bill was not colorblind and primarily helped white Americans achieve their dreams. Since white veterans groups such as the American Legion and the Veterans of Foreign Wars directed many of the programs at the local level, the result was that large numbers of African American veterans were routinely denied benefits to which they were entitled. Of the first 67,000 low-cost mortgages, only one hundred were given to African Americans, and only about twenty thousand of the first one hundred thousand men to apply for educational assistance were registered in a college or university. Fewer still graduated.

But for those aided by the GI Bill, it was transformational. It jump-started dreams that had been on hold for four years. It didn't happen overnight, and much hard work and many sacrifices were required, but when it worked it worked remarkably well. The bill and the people it assisted were a crucial element in the economic recovery following World War II and the expansion of this recovery into the 1950s and beyond. The benefits in human terms are incalculable.

Harold had taught ROTC at the high school or junior college level since 1929, but he no longer wanted to be a teacher. He had just finished three years of active duty in World War II, commanding hundreds of men under severe conditions, and was certain he could lead men and women in peacetime in the field of education. He also knew how to read a map, and the map showed him he lived one block from University Drive, a street that led directly to the campus of Texas Christian University. This highly regarded educational institution was just two miles south of the Blanch Circle apartment.

Somehow Harold learned TCU's School of Education was highly regarded and that the university welcomed returning GIs. He was more than qualified to take advantage of the GI Bill, was accepted to TCU as a thirty-six-year-old freshman in 1946, and got to work, competing with teenagers in the freshman class who were half his age. He told Sarah she could now begin thinking again of the dream house, sketches and plans for which had filled her scrapbook in the previous decade.

The idea of the "dream house" was so ingrained in each of them, as well as in many other young couples in America, that a year or so later, in 1948, when Cary Grant and Myrna Loy were featured in *Mr. Blandings Builds His Dream House*, they were standing in line when the movie opened at the Worth Theater in July. Fort Worth was also one of the cities where the studio (RKO) and the distributor (David O. Selznick) decided to build promotional "dream houses" just like the one in the movie, and raffle off the rights to buy them. The other Texas cities where "dream houses" were built were well known to Harold and Sarah: places like Dallas, Amarillo, Houston, and Austin, cities where other couples could dream.

Well in advance of the opening of the film, publicity for the house filled the *Fort Worth Star-Telegram* and the *Fort Worth Press*. The construction company, concrete suppliers, flooring companies, electricians, Fake's & Company (a major department store), title companies, Frank Kent's Ford (using Goodyear tires exclusively), planning mills, plumbers—everyone wanted to get in on the dream house and took out ads in the paper. The actual Fort Worth house at 3801 Arundel Avenue was sold to one Dr. Val Scroggie, who lived in it until he died in 1961. In 2018 it is someone else's dream house. Sarah had wished for a dream house for two decades, as did millions of others. This is why the movie and the marketing plans were so successful.

The house was just a few blocks south of the TCU campus, and Harold and Sarah visited it on more than one occasion. They probably took me along for the ride, but I don't remember anything if they did. Much of America was dreaming in those years, and such was the mood of the country that this piece of motion picture fluff resonated with enough people that Cary Grant appeared as Jim Blandings on radio for the next three years in adaptations of the movie, and in 1951 with his real wife, Betsy Drake, as Mr. and Mrs. Blandings on an NBC radio series. I not only saw the house and movie in Fort Worth with my parents, but later heard it on the radio on Sunday afternoons in Indiana.

While Harold adjusted to life as possibly the oldest member of the freshman class at TCU, Sarah continued in her role running the house, looking after me, balancing a budget based on a meager medical disability pension supplemented by her husband's wartime poker winnings, and supporting Harold, who struggled with illness, adjusted to sleeping in a real bed with both eyes shut, and worrying about freshman English, history, and basic educational theory. In the first year he got mainly Bs and Cs. He wasn't used to a classroom or the civilized, peaceful life that surrounded him.

His grades improved as he adjusted to civilian life, and everything ultimately worked. No one at 122 Blanch Circle ever missed a meal; the old Chrysler never ran out of gas; balding tires were replaced with retreads or new ones as they became available; there was a Christmas tree each year; there were no raggedy clothes; and the radio played every day, seemingly all day, especially on Sunday evenings. They even saved $35 and invested it in a battered upright piano so Sarah could play songs she remembered and Harold could try to pick out his favorite classical melodies. *Mon cœve s'ouvre à ta voix* from Saint-Saens *Samson et Dalila,* which he'd heard in a concert in Tyler before the war, was his favorite, and despite lessons

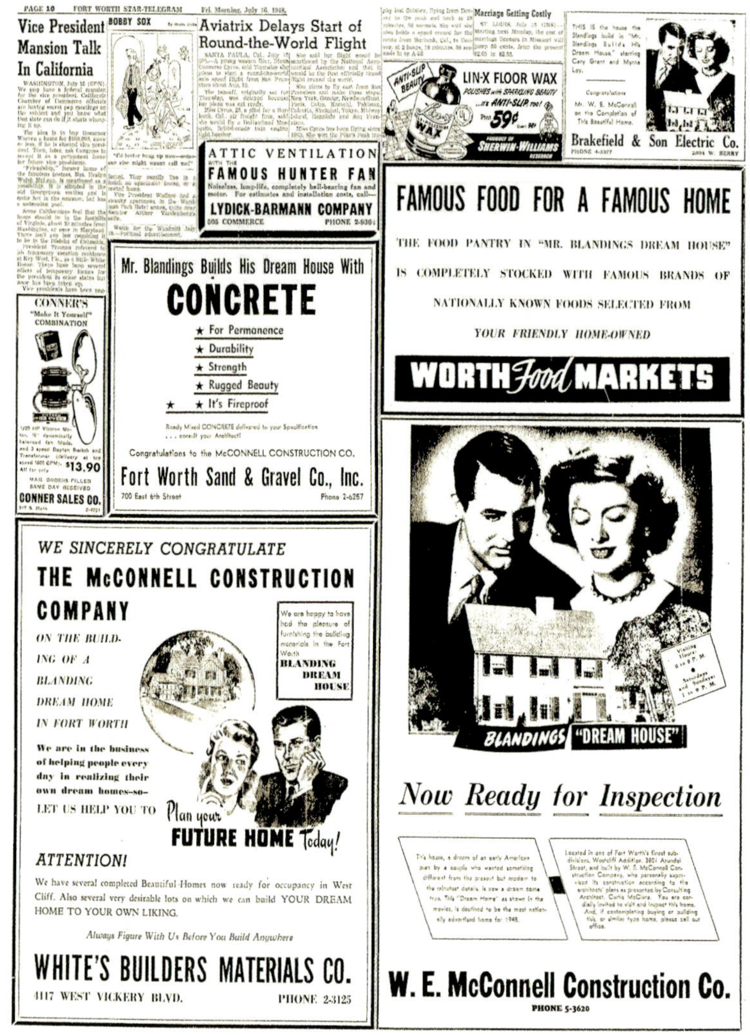
PAGE 10 FORT WORTH STAR-TELEGRAM Fri. Morning, July 16, 1948.

Vice President Mansion Talk In California

BOBBY SOX

Aviatrix Delays Start of Round-the-World Flight

Marriage Getting Costly

ATTIC VENTILATION WITH THE FAMOUS HUNTER FAN
Noiseless, long-life, completely ball-bearing fan and motor. For estimates and installation costs, call—
LYDICK-BARMANN COMPANY
505 COMMERCE PHONE 2-9301

LIN-X FLOOR WAX
POLISHES with SPARKLING BEAUTY ...it's ANTI-SLIP, too!
ANTI-SLIP BEAUTY
Pint 59¢
SHERWIN-WILLIAMS

THIS IS the house the Blandings build in "Mr. Blandings Builds His Dream House," starring Cary Grant and Myrna Loy.
Congratulations Mr. W. E. McConnell on the Completion of This Beautiful Home.
Brakefield & Son Electric Co.
PHONE 4-3377 2404 W. BERRY

CONNER'S "Make It Yourself" COMBINATION
$13.90
MAIL ORDERS FILLED SAME DAY RECEIVED
CONNER SALES CO.

Mr. Blandings Builds His Dream House With
CONCRETE
★ For Permanence
★ Durability
★ Strength
★ Rugged Beauty
★ It's Fireproof
Ready Mixed CONCRETE delivered to your Specification . . . consult your Architect!
Congratulations to the McCONNELL CONSTRUCTION CO.
Fort Worth Sand & Gravel Co., Inc.
700 East 6th Street Phone 2-6257

FAMOUS FOOD FOR A FAMOUS HOME
THE FOOD PANTRY IN "MR. BLANDINGS DREAM HOUSE" IS COMPLETELY STOCKED WITH FAMOUS BRANDS OF NATIONALLY KNOWN FOODS SELECTED FROM YOUR FRIENDLY HOME-OWNED
WORTH Food MARKETS

WE SINCERELY CONGRATULATE
THE McCONNELL CONSTRUCTION COMPANY
ON THE BUILDING OF A BLANDING DREAM HOME IN FORT WORTH
We are happy to have had the pleasure of furnishing the building materials in the Fort Worth BLANDING DREAM HOUSE
We are in the business of helping people every day in realizing their own dream homes—so—
LET US HELP YOU TO Plan your FUTURE HOME Today!
ATTENTION!
We have several completed Beautiful Homes now ready for occupancy in West Cliff. Also several very desirable lots on which we can build YOUR DREAM HOME TO YOUR OWN LIKING.
Always Figure With Us Before You Build Anywhere
WHITE'S BUILDERS MATERIALS CO.
4117 WEST VICKERY BLVD. PHONE 2-3125

BLANDINGS "DREAM HOUSE"
Now Ready for Inspection
W. E. McConnell Construction Co.
PHONE 5-3620

I would be forced to prove over and over again I had no musical talent whatsoever.

There were occasional movies downtown or on Saturdays at the Bowie, a local theater on Camp Bowie Boulevard, but when funds were scarce there were free movies at the big public library downtown. Harold and Sarah relived their past and gave me fun-filled presents with great silent films like *The Thief of Bagdad* or comedies with Buster Keaton and Harold Lloyd. They taught me early on that free was not only good but was often better than things you had to pay for; that old is sometimes better than new, and places where books were available were good places to be, whether in the children's department of the library or in the pushcarts that were rolled in the aisle of my third-grade classroom in a prefab building built next to Crestwood Elementary School on White Settlement Road.

There were also adventures at Crestwood School. As Harold adjusted to civilian life he occasionally found time to take photographs with the new camera; he'd swapped his wartime Leica for a Speed Graphic. One day he set up his camera on a tripod and took pictures of me on the steps of the school. About the same time, he and Sarah were surprised to see another picture of me on the steps of the school. It had been taken in early March 1947.

In Fort Worth in those days there was a special dress up day at Crestwood, in fact at most schools city-wide, and on Ranch Day all the children in the school were encouraged to dress up as little gun-slinging cowboys and cowgirls and celebrate their wild western heritage. A reporter and photographer from the *Fort Worth Star-Telegram* arrived at the school; seven suitably western-attired children were selected and posed, some with cap pistols at the ready (including me); and the photograph ran in the paper on March 6 with the caption *RANCH DAY PARTICIPANTS – These Crestwood School pupils are among those who participated in the Ranch Day program at 10:30 a.m. Wednesday.* The paper identified all seven students. I am standing next to Carolyn Sue Jackson, a really cute girl who lived across the street on Blanch Circle. I was probably selected because I was wearing special chaps, super elegant hand-made chaps that Harold had made for me while he was in recovery at Fort Sam Houston. He had also made my hand-tooled gun belt and holsters.

But there's something else about this story. This is probably the first time I ever appeared in a non-family-oriented photograph, one taken by Harold, Sarah, or a relative. It must have gone out on a wire service, because in Sarah's papers there is not only a clipping from the Fort Worth paper, but another from St. Louis, on the back of which someone has written *Do you happen to know these Blanch Circle children?* There is also an Atlas Chick Co. ad for assorted chicks, no cripples, no culls at $6.90 per one hundred, or you could save fifty cents by purchasing one thousand for $68.50.

On the back of the Fort Worth clipping there's a headline that reads: *2 GIs Found Guilty of Defrauding Japs. SENDAI, Japan, March 6 (AP) – Two American privates who posed as "Capt. Buck Jones" and "Staff Sgt. Tom Mix" have been convicted by a 9th Corps court-martial of assuming false names and fraudulently obtaining about $250 worth of rubber from a Japanese factory.* If Harold hadn't been sent home for health reasons and remained in Sendai, his men might have arrested these two.

Sarah was in charge of all non-military, non-medical activity, and she held it all together; about the only change Harold instituted was that the wartime Broadway Baptist Church was replaced by the First Methodist. This wasn't a monumental change; *Jesus loves me yes I know* sounds pretty much the same in Baptist or Methodeeze. Both churches maintained the same decent core values, and I wasn't old enough to tell any difference if there was one. The only thing I really remember is that most of the time when Sarah took me to Sunday school, if she was told I did well with my Bible verses and wasn't unruly, I would be treated to a lime or orange sherbet cone on the way home.

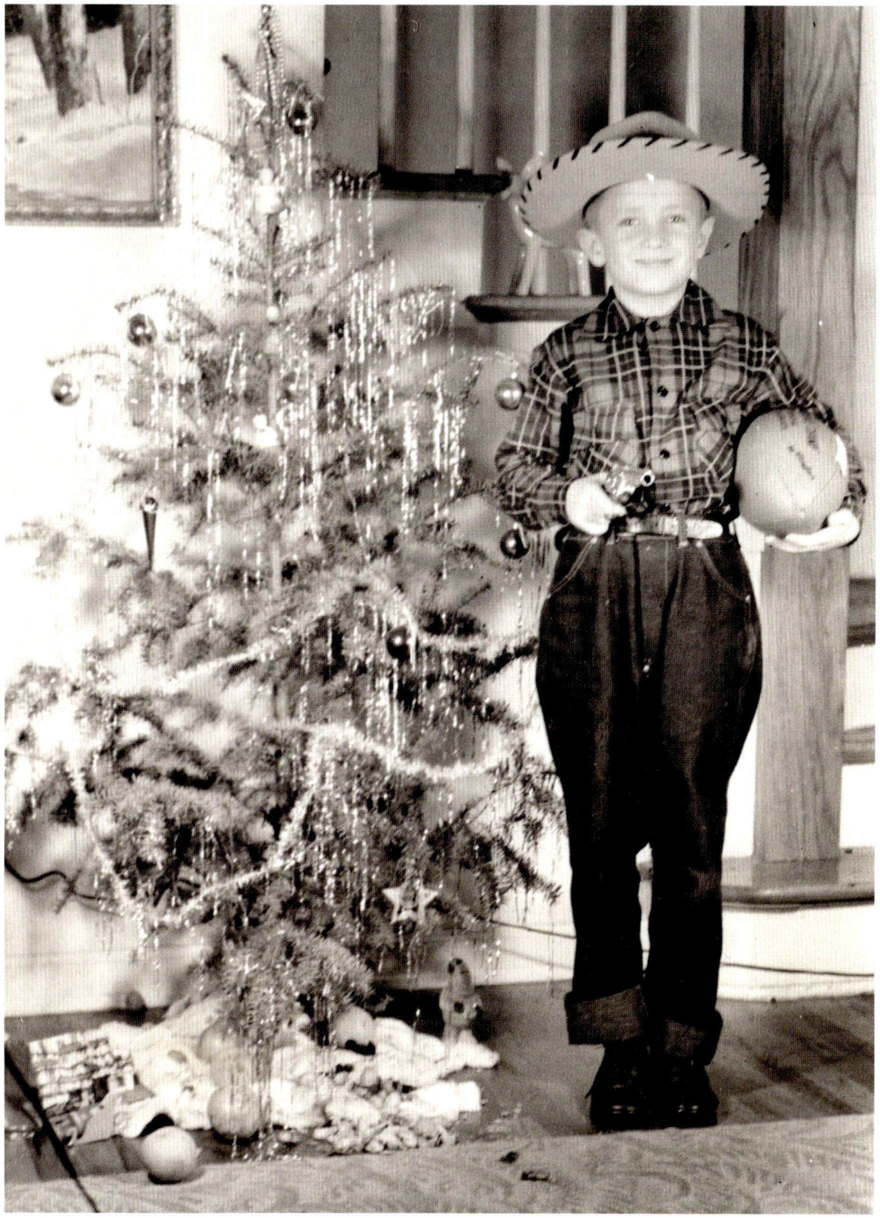

Christmas, 1947

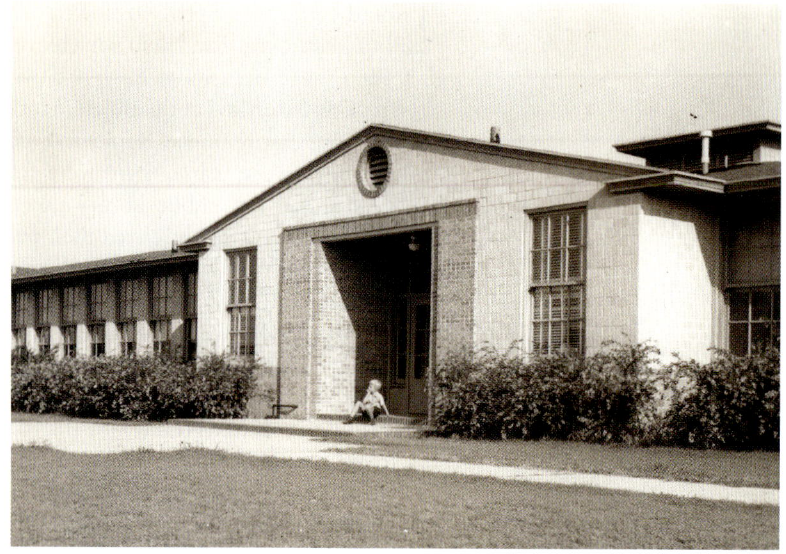

Crestwood School, 1947

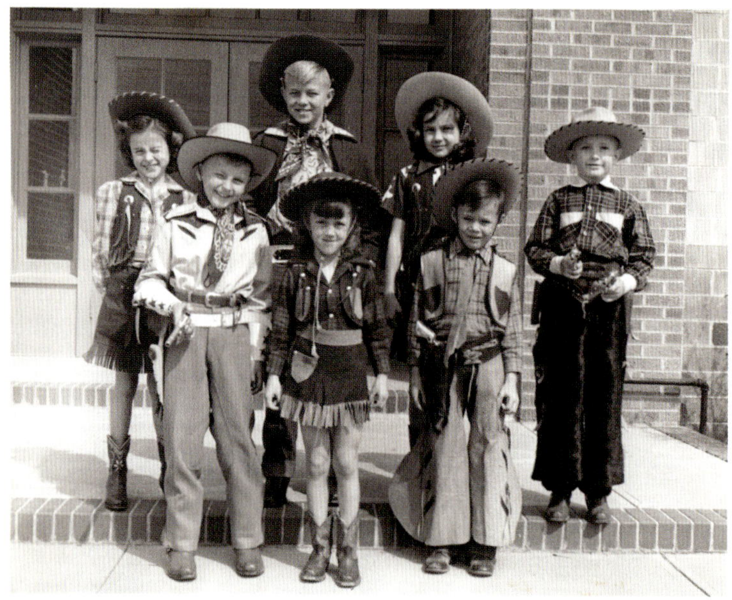

Ranch Day, 1947

Thurs. Eve., March 6, 1947. 32—FORT WORTH STAR-TELEGRAM

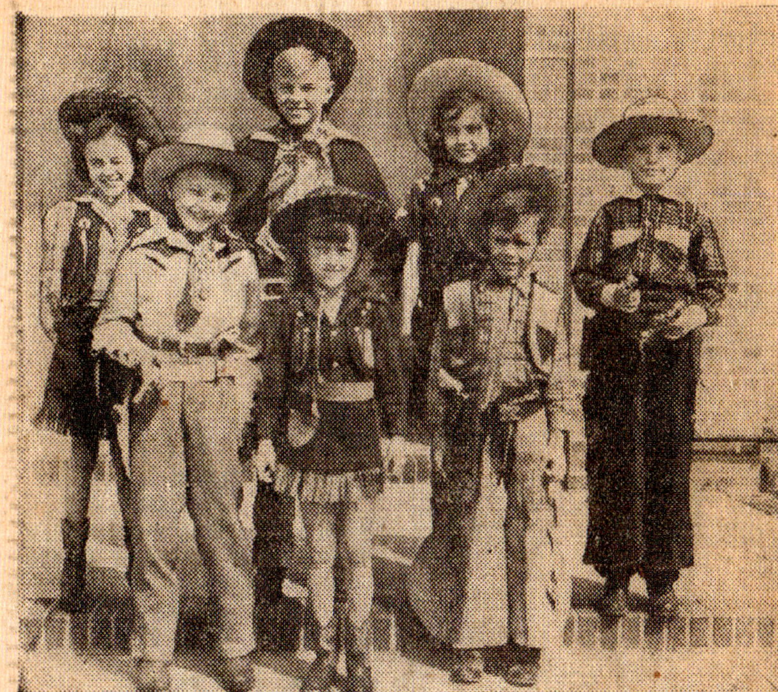

**RANCH DAY PARTICIPANTS** — These Crestwood School pupils are among those who participated in the school's Ranch Day program at 10:30 a. m. Wednesday. Left to right the pupils are, front row, Tommy Nichols, son of Mr. and Mrs. Nick Nichols, 3210 Wingate; Marcia Panter, daughter of Mr. and Mrs. Jack Panter, 200 Crestwood Dr.; Jimmy Lynaugh, son of Mr. and Mrs. J. A. Lynaugh, 400 Lindenwood; back row, Terry Dale Smith,, son of Mr. and Mrs. Rolein Smith, 3225 Wingate; Harry Ryan, son of Mr. and Mrs. Ray Ryan, 632 Westwood; Carolyn Sue Jackson, daughter of Mr. and Mrs. Thomas Jackson, 123 Blanch Circle, and Hank O'Neal, son of Mr. and Mrs. Harold O'Neal, 122 Blanch Circle.



Do you happen to know these Blanch Circle Children?

Harold L. O'Neal 1

Edward T. Cakobau

When it's dark one can easily become lost in the jungle. It happened to Ed who wandered into my bivouac area one night, hailing us at a safe distance so as not to be discovered as a stranger in our midst. Upon invitation he entered the tent where some of us were playing cards to pass the time, and by uniform was recognized as a captain of the Fijians.

The Fijians were new arrivals on the little island of Bougainville which lies five degrees south of the equator. They were something new and thereby interesting to us. Here was one in our presence for close observation and from the viewpoint of appearance he would be able to pass any muster. Introductions revealed him to be Captain Edward T. Cakobau, Company C, 3rd. Battalion, of the Fijian Military Forces.

Ed was outstanding in appearance being tall, about six foot three, with the necessary weight to go with that height and was about thirty-five years old. His color was dark, not black as the majority of Melanesians but more similar to our own Indians. We afterwards discovered that Ed was actually half Melanesian and half Polynesian, a combination of Fijian and Tonganese.

He declined our invitation to join the game by asking for a rain check. Thereafter, for the balance of the evening, he was perfectly content in "sweating out" our hands and joining frequently in our line of chatter. At the same time he was sizing each of us up for some future game. I must admit that he did this remarkably well. By the end of the evening he was no longer a stranger from a strange land but just one of the fellows. After he had left for his own area I had the desire, and I'm sure the others did too, to know him better.

During the next few weeks we became good friends. Our areas were not too

Harold L. O'Neal 2

far apart and we got into the habit of droping in to see each other. It was a novelty for him to join me in coffee whereas the same held true when I joined him in tea. Naturally this association gave me ample time to observe and pick up bits of information relative to his background which I found deeply interesting.

He was an Oxford graduate and had traveled extensively. But best of all he was a gifted conversationalist. At our request he would spend hours telling stories and relating the folklore of the Fijians. I shall never forget two such stories he told relating to the sea turtles and the rising of the worms. When at certain times of the year the callers stand on a high cliff overlooking the Pacific and at their call the giant sea turtles rise to the surface and swim to the beach, unexplained, yet a fact. The sea worms at a known period of the year in a definate location mysteriously arise from the depth of the coral crevices of the sea by the millions and cover the entire surface of the area. They are eagerly awaited by the people who consider them a great delicacy. Ed had an abundant supply of such stories and with his ability in relating them you clearly visualized each happening in your minds eye making you wish countless times for the opportunity of visiting Fiji in order to see things for yourself.

There was a difference between Ed and the other Fijians. From the very first time I was in his area I was conscious of this but it was something I couldn't grasp. More or less, it was a undercurrent of excitement that one could hardly put his finger on. To my observations it was evident mostly through the attitude towards him of the men in his command, including the three white Australian officers who were his brother officers. Not until weeks later did I leard the cause. Ed was, Edward T. Cakobau, Captain in his Majesties Service, and also, the King of Fiji.

## Texas Christian University

Harold was in a hurry, and despite the occasional movie or local baseball or football games, there was little time for extracurricular activities, social clubs, or the normal activities one might expect a college freshman to enjoy. He'd been a career soldier for almost two decades and expected to remain in that capacity for years to come, but since that was impossible, he set about developing other skills that would enable him to earn a decent living in another line of work.

Even though he was still undergoing medical treatment, commuting to and from San Antonio, he was also taking English 311a and a host of other classes at TCU and, on occasion, writing papers that related to his recent wartime experience. He handed in what was possibly his first essay on October 3, 1946. It was about one of his wartime buddies, Edward T. Cakobau. It was only two pages long, and though his professor found three or four errors in it it was still an A- effort with the notation *A very good story, very neat*.

This is the only one of his early college papers that survived, probably because it was filed with his military papers instead of college transcripts. I was later to learn Captain Edward T. Cakobau was not the King of Fiji; he was merely a prince. It was his great-grandfather who had been the king and in later years, despite his royal lineage, he never rose higher than Deputy Prime Minister because he was so occupied with other matters of state. Of course, he was also Fiji's most noted cricketer in his younger days, which only added to his stature. In 2011 I met his son, Ratu Epeli Nailatikau, and we exchanged stories about our fathers. At the time Ratu Epeli was the president of Fiji, a position he'd maintain until 2015. I was once the president of my homeroom class in 1957. Despite this, or perhaps because of it, we have remained friends.

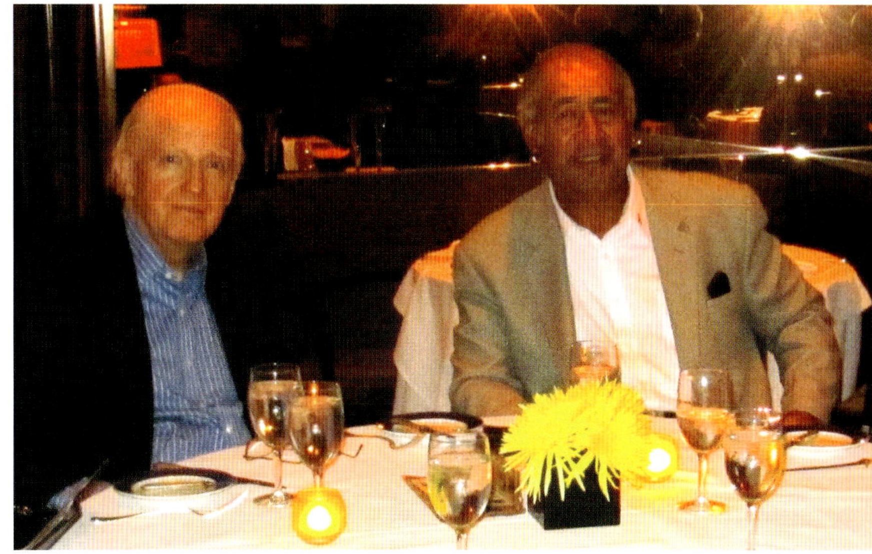

Hank on the left; Ratu Epeli Nailatikau on the right

Harold's only extracurricular activities were Sarah and me. She understood how busy he was; I was too young to understand. But even though he didn't have time to play baseball in the backyard, some of his classmates did. In the old TCU yearbook from 1946 there are two faces I recognize and names I remember from the baseball team, two teenage Jims: Nolan and Busby. They also played for a semi-pro team called Turf Bar. I don't know the dynamics of the relationship. Harold was almost twice the age of his classmates, but perhaps because he was a no-nonsense grownup home from the war with a child who loved baseball they took an interest in me and I wound up with a bat, ball, and glove, and an occasional game of catch in the backyard. If I was lucky, it might even be tossing a ball back and forth before a Turf Bar ball game at Rockwood Park down by the Trinity River, or at one of the other city parks where they played. Jim Busby, an outfielder, was a college star and was playing for the Chicago White Sox by

1950 and would have a fine major league career. Jim Nolan, a third baseman, was not quite as good and never played higher than the Double-A New Orleans Pelicans, but of the two he was my hero, because he signed his name on the baseball he gave me.

Harold and Sarah were very protective of me. They had many reasons to be protective, but overly protective as far as I was concerned. I was their only child and much of what Harold was working towards and Sarah was supporting was focused on my well-being and future.

During the years after the war the scourge of polio was real in Fort Worth. I had a friend who lived and died a few doors down the street. It was the disease that had crippled the man who in their minds had made their life together up to that point possible. It was also a disease that no one understood; no one knew where it came from or what caused it. This uncertainty meant doing things that seemed irrational, and in my case this meant if it was sunny and hot I was not allowed to be outdoors between the hours of twelve noon and 3:00 p.m. I may have chafed a little, but not too much. I was also frightened, especially after the little girl down the street died. But there was plenty of time for play when it wasn't too hot, often in the great big empty field in back of our apartment. We played like we were soldiers or cowboys or even baseball players on a makeshift Yankee Stadium we created with big rocks for bases. Some of my friends and I wanted to

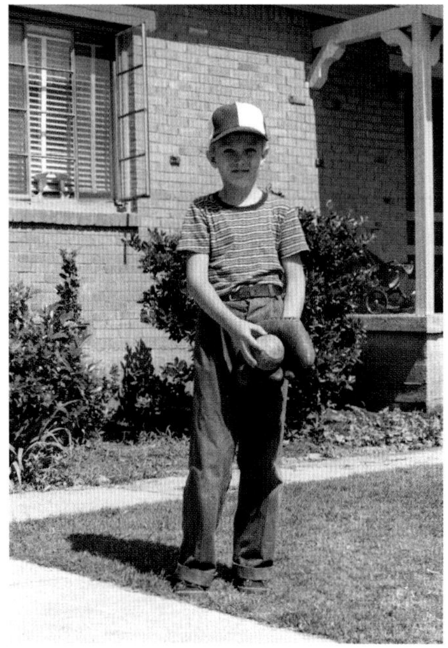

build a "fort" that might withstand attacks from some kids from around the corner on Wingate Street. Always supportive, Harold suggested we use big pieces of cardboard, which he found somewhere, and then arm ourselves with water pistols. Ever resourceful, I wanted to have a secret weapon if we were attacked, and I convinced Sarah to empty the eggs she cooked for breakfast using a small hole in the top of the egg, shaking out the contents and saving the shell, which I then filled with water.

At some point we were attacked and fought like crazy with water pistols blazing and an eggshell filled with by-then

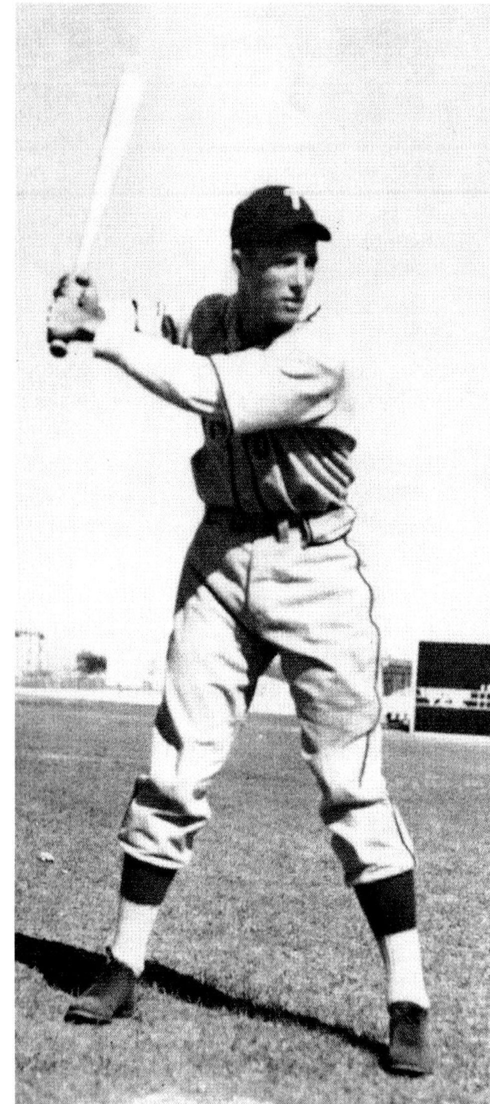

**• Outfielder Jim Busby**

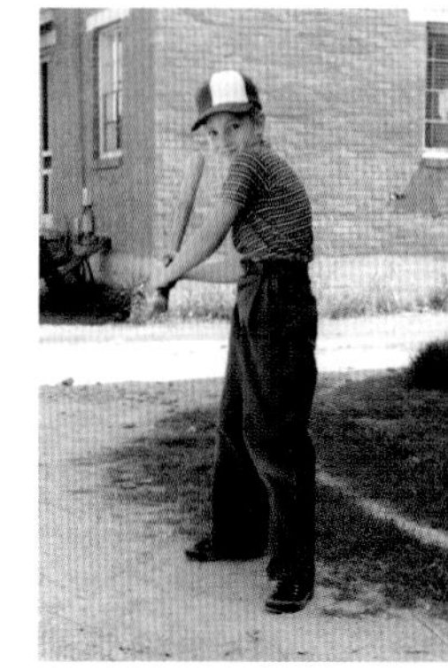

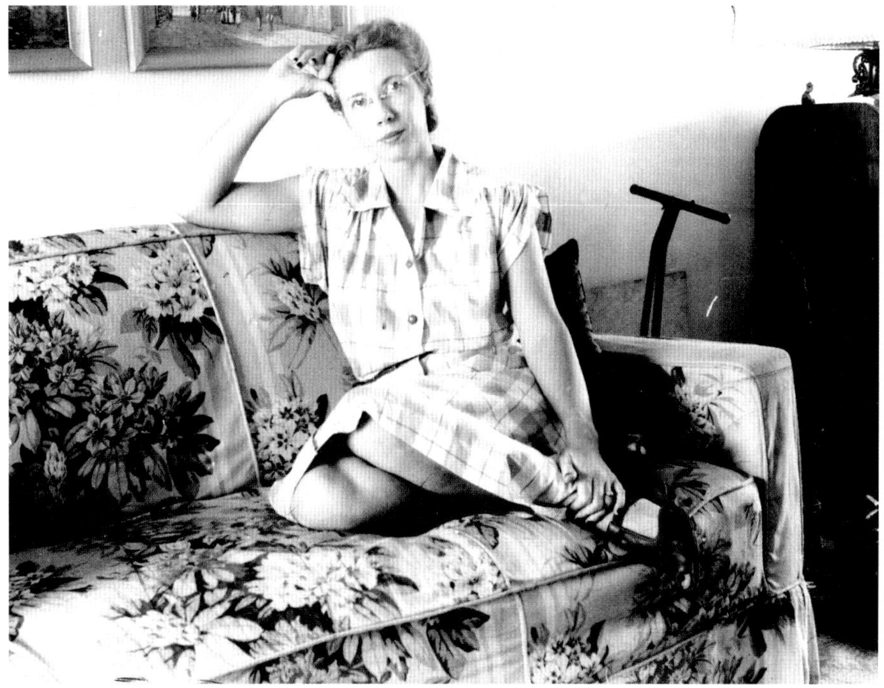

Sarah, 122 Blanch Circle, 1946-7

rancid water, and the bad guys were repelled, after which I probably had to be peaceful for the rest of the day to keep polio at bay.

The old-wives-tale type wisdom was that strenuous exercise was to be avoided, as were crowds in public places. For example, I was not allowed to go to a public swimming pool, but most of them were closed anyway because the city fathers had shut them down. I was never in water, other than a bathtub, except for an occasional dip in a creek during an East Texas holiday or on one trip to Galveston. It was my first time at the seashore and my first time in the water for a year or so. But it worked, in their minds. When Jonas Salk and his team came up with the vaccine I was polio free, and didn't even get a shot.

And so three years passed and it was 1949. I was nearing the end of the third grade, Harold was completing his coursework for his bachelor of arts in education, but for a moment the game was delayed because of rain.

I might have been outside on the evening of May 16, 1949, when the rain started to fall, but if I was, I probably didn't stay very long because this rain was different. It was strong and unrelenting, the kind of rain that stings you when it hits, rain so strong you can't keep your eyes open because there's just too much water on your face, and the thunder and lightning were scary. I probably ran out for a minute and ran right back inside, dried off, and then just watched the storm from the front porch in amazement. I probably even forgot about the evening radio shows I listened to with Sarah and with Harold, if he wasn't studying. Maybe they listened to the radio and fought their way through the static caused by the lightning while I listened to the storm. I'd never seen anything like it. It's nearly sixty years later and I still haven't.

Nothing seemed unusual when I woke up the next morning. It was still raining lightly, but it stopped after awhile. I didn't sense that anything was wrong until my mother told me I shouldn't get ready for school, that she thought there wouldn't be any school that day. Harold had been listening to the radio and thought he should go down to the end of the block and see what it looked like. Our street was a little higher that those to the north, as the ground sloped down toward the Clear Fork of the Trinity River.

I asked if I could tag along, and he nodded. We walked east on Blanch Circle to Wingate Street and headed north. I had a friend who lived on Wingate; I used to visit him on the sly because he was one of three people I knew whose family had a television. I wasn't allowed to watch tele-

## Backyard squirt gun battle

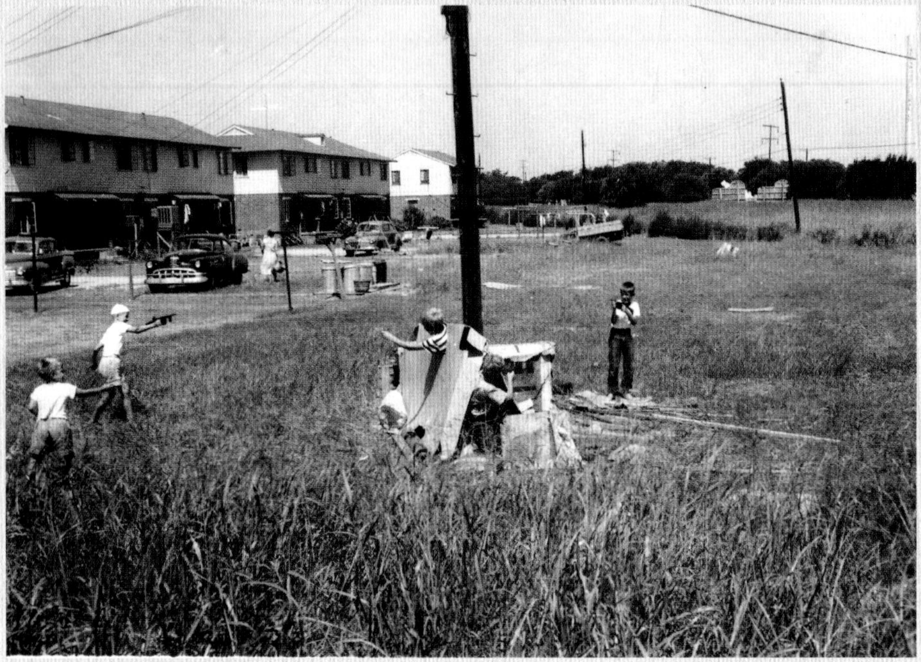

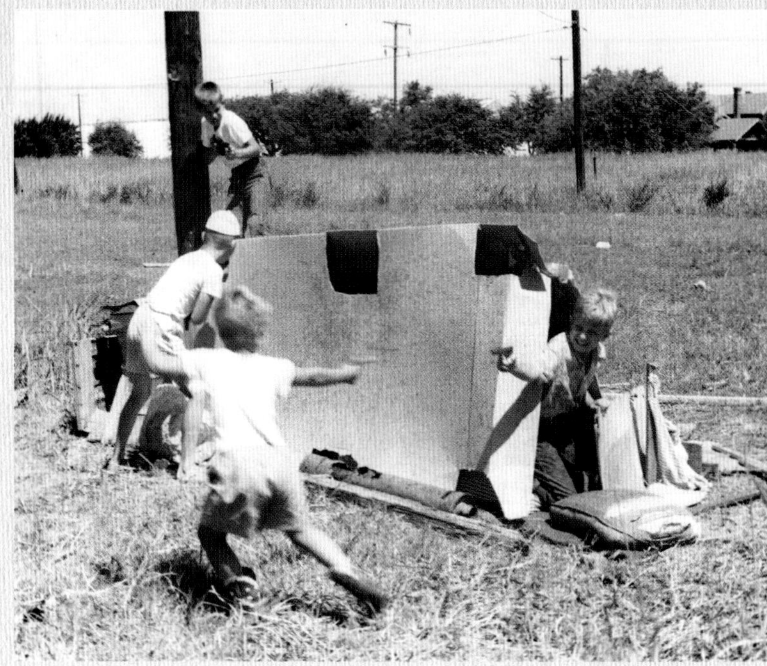

Here you can
see Hank
pretty well
sticking his
head out at
the enemy.

vision, except at a neighbor's house close by, where my mother could keep her eye on me. But the house on Wingate, all of three or four blocks away, would have been off-limits. I would never have been allowed to watch Gorgeous George and all the other wrestlers with silly names, so I had to sneak off to see them.

We hadn't even reached University Drive when Harold saw all he needed to see, something that terrified me. Just down the street, the roof was all I could see of my friend's house; all the houses surrounding it were also under water, and it looked as though the water was heading in our direction. He grabbed me by the hand and we ran back toward our apartment. He went inside, told Sarah what was happening, that he was going to take the car to higher ground and hope for the best. He said we should start moving anything we could from the first floor to the second, and he'd be back as soon as possible to help.

The old 1940 Chrysler was the only thing we owned that was worth anything except for the $35 piano. Harold drove off and parked somewhere a few blocks away. He probably got away just in time, because the water just kept coming. It didn't come up the street; it seemed to come from across the street, from the direction of the submerged houses.

I didn't know what was happening, what had happened. I didn't know anything except there had been a rainstorm and now there was water everywhere. It wasn't raining now, but I later learned almost a foot of rain had been dumped in and around Fort Worth that night, the most since records had been kept. I didn't know the levees had been blown up and breached in a vain attempt to save the waterworks. I didn't know that it hadn't worked, that not only was the water coming, but there was none to drink because the waterworks were flooded.

Sarah and I carried whatever we could upstairs. I was just a kid and she was just a soft, ordinary-sized woman. We carried assorted stuff, things water would ruin. Books, magazines, the family scrapbooks and pictures, records, the small radio, a Victrola, pillows, food from the kitchen, my baseball gear, a bat and a glove I'd probably used the day before, before it started to rain. I may have even carried Harold's camera and film processing equipment upstairs. Then I coaxed Mickey, my cocker spaniel, upstairs and made sure he stayed.

Harold came back in time to move some of the bigger things—some chairs, a small table, other things Sarah and I couldn't carry. The water kept coming. Somehow we'd forgotten to think about ourselves. The plan was to put us on the second floor and hope for the best, because the water was now covering the front yard.

I don't remember any sense of panic or despair. Harold had spent three years in the Pacific under much more extreme conditions. Water lapping at the bottom porch step and extending as far as we could see was complicated, but not nearly as hazardous as directing amphibious landing craft or riding on one. I wasn't old enough to understand, but maybe his cool reaction to the difficulties at hand made an impression on me that eventually served me well.

We were lucky in a way. Our apartment wasn't at ground level. It was built up on a cement foundation that was about three or four feet high. This meant it took longer for the water to reach the first floor, but it kept rising higher and higher, and about the time it reached the front porch, the rescue boat arrived. With Harold holding Mickey, wrapped in a large towel, just as he had a year earlier when he'd brought him home as a puppy, the three of us stepped off the porch into a small boat of some kind and were saved. We were taken to higher ground, possibly close to our car, and we made our way to a friend's house where we waited for the flood to subside. It eventually did. Typhoid fever shots really hurt but kept disease at bay, the ground dried out so baseball was possible, and then on August 28 Harold and forty-five of his fellow students in the School of Education received their BS in education.

This was a milestone, but his career in education was just getting started. Less than a year later, on May 31, 1950, Harold put on his robes again and appeared at another TCU commencement ceremony, this time to receive an MS in Education. Some of his instructors must have put out the word that an overqualified, mature man was graduating, because within a few

TEXAS CHRISTIAN UNIVERSITY
FORT WORTH, TEXAS

Office of
Dean of Students

March 18, 1950

Mr. Harold L. O'Neal
122 Blanch Circle
Fort Worth, Texas

Dear Mr. O'Neal:

I have just been checking through the fall semester grade reports, and I noticed that you made an outstanding record. My personal congratulations to you!

Frequently we become so involved in the problems of those who are in difficulty that we fail to express our appreciation for those who are doing their work as we hoped that they would do.

My sincerest congratulations and best wishes are meant in this informal letter. I hope to be able to know you personally.

Yours very truly,

Thos. F. Richardson

Thos. F. Richardson,
Dean of Students.

TFR/ap

TEXAS CHRISTIAN UNIVERSITY
FORT WORTH, TEXAS

May 3, 1950

Mr. Harold L. O'Neal
2122 Blanch Circle
Fort Worth, Texas

Dear Mr. O'Neal

By reason of the satisfactory type of work you have done in pursuance of your Master's Degree, this is to state that by action of the Dean of the Graduate School and the faculty of the School of Education, we are exempting you from the oral examination usually required for this degree.

Sincerely

Raymond A. Smith

Raymond A. Smith, Dean
School of Education

RAS:hj

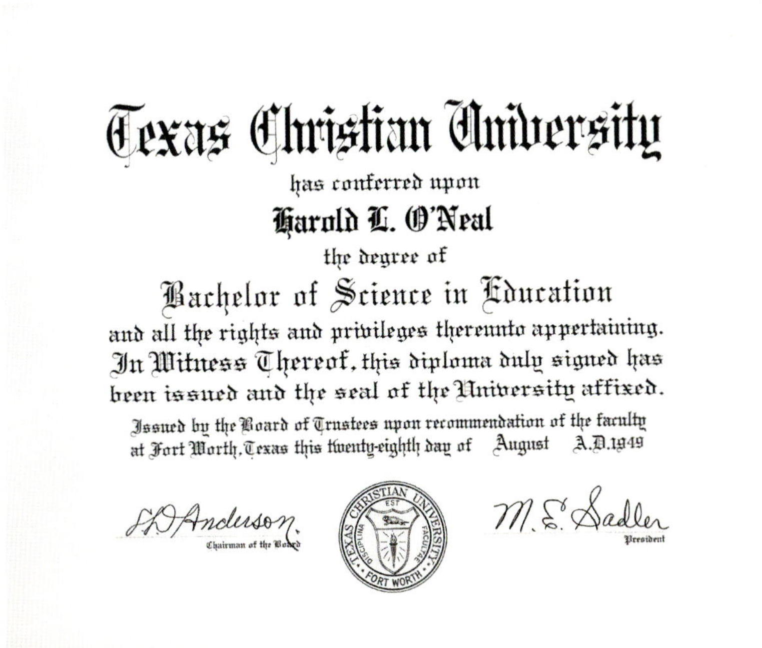

Texas Christian University
has conferred upon
Harold L. O'Neal
the degree of
Bachelor of Science in Education
and all the rights and privileges thereunto appertaining.
In Witness Thereof, this diploma duly signed has been issued and the seal of the University affixed.
Issued by the Board of Trustees upon recommendation of the faculty at Fort Worth, Texas this twenty-eighth day of August A.D. 1949

L.D. Anderson, Chairman of the Board
M. E. Sadler, President

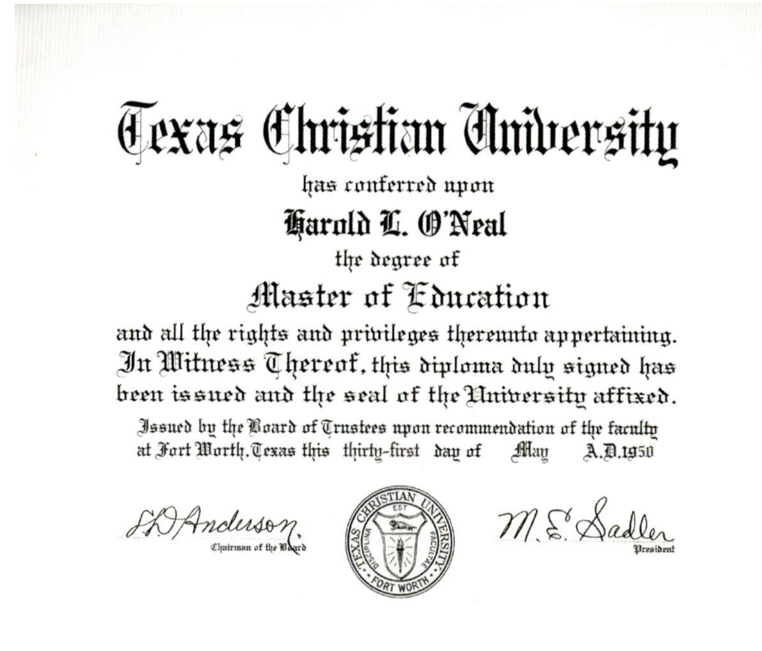

Texas Christian University
has conferred upon
Harold L. O'Neal
the degree of
Master of Education
and all the rights and privileges thereunto appertaining.
In Witness Thereof, this diploma duly signed has been issued and the seal of the University affixed.
Issued by the Board of Trustees upon recommendation of the faculty at Fort Worth, Texas this thirty-first day of May A.D. 1950

L.D. Anderson, Chairman of the Board
M. E. Sadler, President

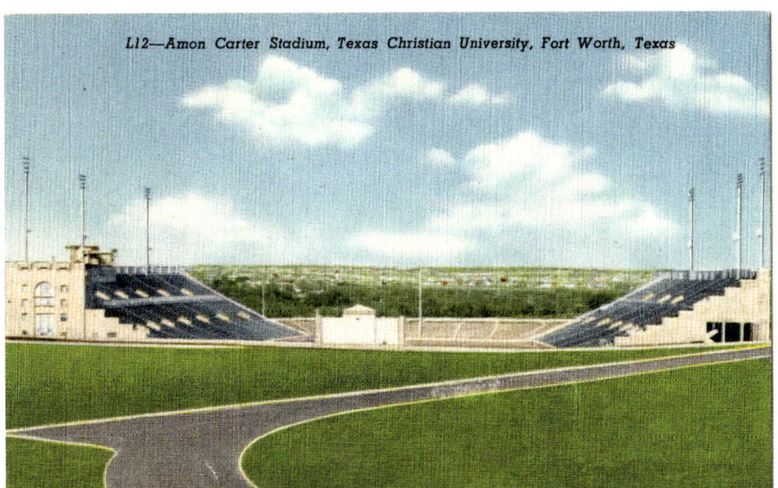


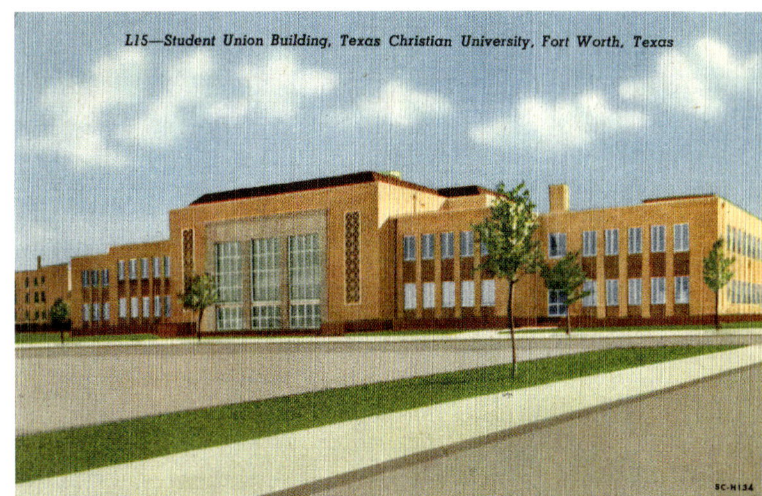

birthright, no generational access to the company store, were not even aware of what sociologists would later call the American Dream. They instinctively realized that if things were going to work out, if their dreams were to be fulfilled, they had to be willing to move around, break family ties, not take the first job that came along, leave home as well as friends and family, take chances, and possibly fail once or twice. They had to get an education and not settle for what was first and easy, not live safely without too much effort on the same block forever until you moved into a cemetery down the street. Many people didn't see it that way. Harold wasn't like those people, and Sarah backed him all the way. I was perhaps the major recipient of this decision.

Harold had been weighing his options through the spring of 1950 and after he saw the grass growing in the cracks of the steps of the school before his job interview, he made up his mind to tough it out a little longer. He had been accepted to pursue an advanced degree at another university, one far away from Texas. He had not only been accepted, but the GI Bill would cover his tuition and he still had modest monthly disability payments, so it was worth taking the chance. It would be at least two years of hard work, maybe more, living in modest circumstances with few creature comforts. He had sailed through the coursework for his master's degree at TCU, and he was certain he could do the same at Indiana University, where he'd been accepted into a program for a doctorate in education. To make things a bit easier, Sarah had worked it out so the family could live in a spare bedroom in a log cabin owned by her sister Martha and her husband, in Brown County, Indiana, just a few short miles from the university campus in Bloomington.

In August 1950, Harold rented a trailer, hitched it to the back of the old Chrysler, filled it up with everything he felt to be essential to begin a life far away from Fort Worth, including all the scrapbooks, family pictures, and other items used to create *Preserving Lives,* and headed north to a faraway place called Indiana.

My personal recollections of the trip are but three. The first was a trip to the bank where Harold closed down his account. He withdrew the full amount, $2,000.50. He asked for two one-thousand-dollar bills and a fifty-cent piece. Out of sight of prying eyes he put a thousand-dollar bill in each shoe. He gave me the fifty-cent piece, probably the first I'd ever had.

The second memory is of stopping at a firecracker stand somewhere in the Ozarks, where we probably spent our first night on the road in an inexpensive tourist court. I spent most of my fifty-cent piece in the Ozarks. It was for a box of cherry bombs, firecrackers I exploded very sparingly for the next two or three years. The box was red; so were the cherry bombs, and they were loud.

The last memory is of St. Louis, the only city I'd ever been in that had a major league baseball team—and it actually had two: the Cardinals, who were not much good that year but were better than the usually-in-last-place Browns. I was already in love with baseball and how I wanted to see a game! But all I really remember is that it seemed hotter in St. Louis than it had been in Texas. Years later, when I read Fielding Dawson's memorable *The Greatest Story Ever Told,* part of which involves a game at Sportsman Park that was played a year before I passed through St Louis, and which ends with the words *. . . as Slaughter slammed a liner into right and Musial scored,* I could still recall how hot it was driving through the not-so-very-nice parts of that city on the Mississippi. And that we couldn't stop to see a ball game.

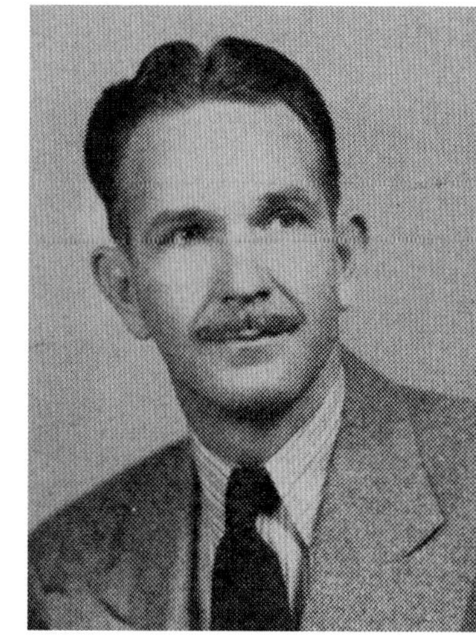

# The Last Lap

## The American Dream in the 1950s PART I

**ONCE WE REACHED SOUTHERN INDIANA IN THE LATE SUMMER OF 1950, FIRST NASHVILLE AND THEN BLOOMINGTON, THERE WAS NO TURNING BACK.** The safety of family in Fort Worth and East Texas, a modest but comfortable place to live, and the low-key atmosphere of Texas Christian University was a thing of the past. Harold had struggled since the end of World War II, and Sarah had struggled along with him, but now each was faced with new challenges. All the while, I was largely oblivious to any difficulties, just along for the ride. My primary concerns were wondering about what school would be like in Indiana, protecting my best pal, Mickey the cocker spaniel, while also guarding the stash of cherry bombs I'd bought at the firecracker stand in the Ozarks.

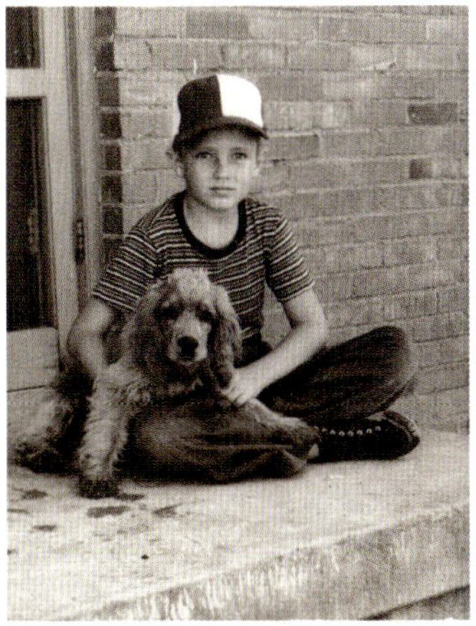

Harold and Sarah saw how life had worked out for Martha and her husband. They could see it firsthand because we were living with them in a spare bedroom that contained a modest double bed and a tiny cot-like bed for me in the corner. It was a large log cabin on three levels, surrounded by woods at the end of a gravelly, often muddy driveway pitched close to a ravine that ran alongside Yellowwood Lake Road. The log cabin was about twenty-five miles from the Indiana University campus and about the same distance from Nashville, the small town to which I'd be bused to attend the fifth grade in a room that was shared with the sixth.

The bedroom I shared with my parents was on the middle level, close to a bathroom, which was not the best place to be on a cold morning when the furnace had conked out. There were three other children in residence—my younger cousins—and we all got along well together. There were eight places at the dinner table, and Martha and Roy wanted at least one more child. This was the first time I had lived with anyone other than my parents since the short stay on Wildwood in Fort Worth, and probably the first time Harold and Sarah had since they were married, and my guess is that while they were grateful, it wasn't what they wanted to do. They had their eyes set on married student housing closer to the university. Things were cordial enough in the log cabin, but they wanted their own place, however humble it might prove to be. Each knew they were now on the last lap.

The Indiana sojourn began in the summer of 1950 and ended in the summer of 1953. It was perhaps the hardest struggle of all. Harold and Sarah were uprooted from friends and family, living in a bedroom along a dirt road in Brown County, Indiana, twenty-five miles from a real grocery store or much of anything else except pretty countryside. Harold was commuting to his classes every morning, I was doing the same in the other direction in a yellow school bus, but Sarah had it the hardest, as she would for the next three years. No friends—and despite the company of her sister and four young children, she had little to do but wait. There wasn't even a church close by; this was the first time in my life there wasn't regular church on Sunday morning. But there were fields full of corn, and at the age of ten I actually got to drive a tractor in one of those fields. I survived.

But this didn't last very long because

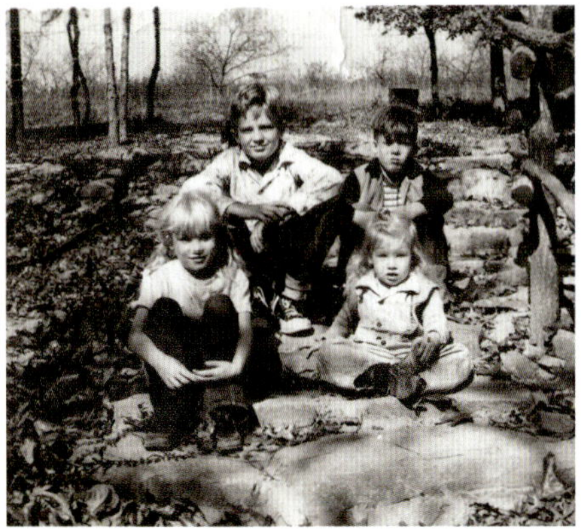

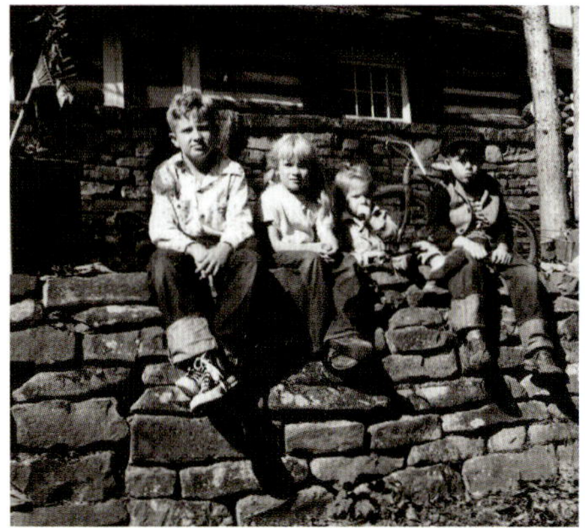

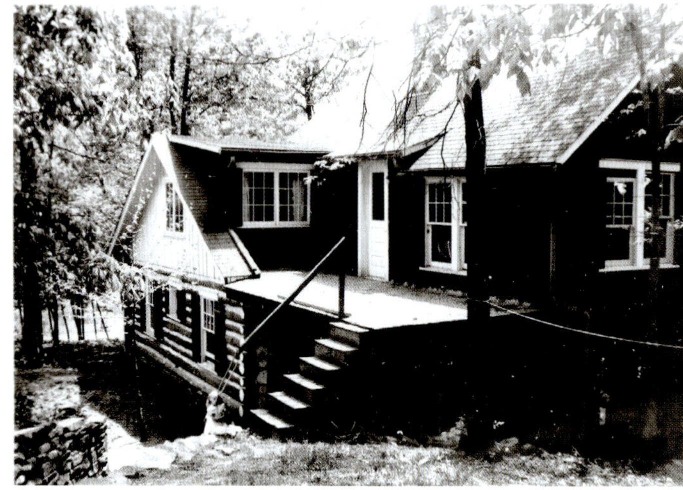

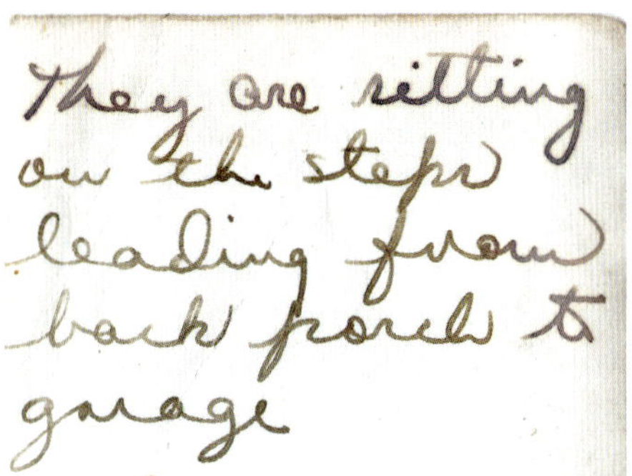


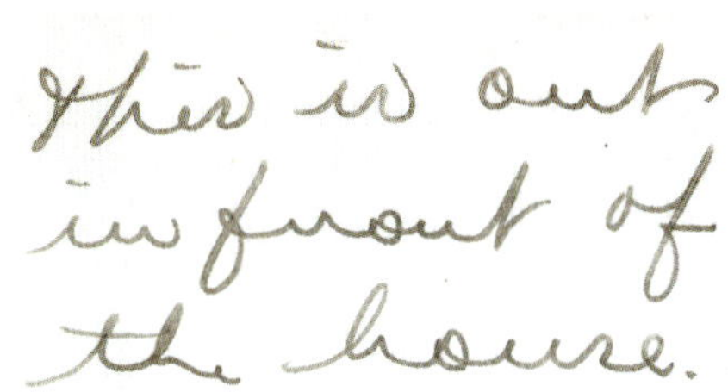


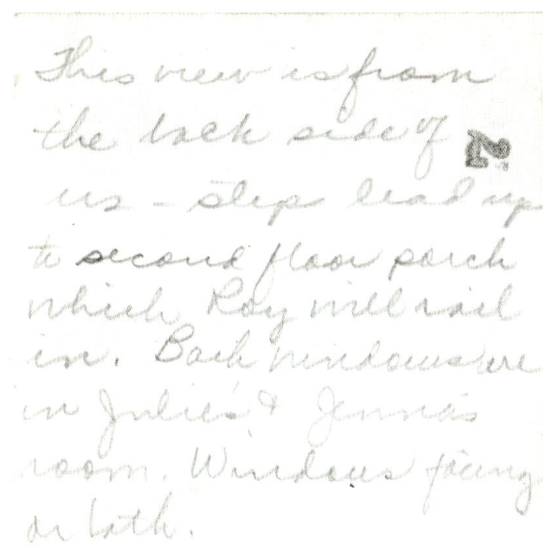


Harold and Sarah didn't like living in one room in a log cabin on a dirt road in Brown County, and they were waiting and waiting for an apartment to free up at a place called Hoosier Courts in Bloomington that was close to the University and close to a real school where kids learned to read and write and spell, where there was a regular school year. In Nashville kids got out early in May to put in the crops and didn't get to go back until the corn was picked and shucked. I got to be on corn-picking duty on more than one occasion, but while quaint and charming Nashville and surrounding Brown County was the home of dozens of exceptional regional artists, it produced few scholars in the seven and one-half months a year school was in session.

Then there was a break. An apartment near the university became available and we moved quickly. Perhaps somebody moved, or maybe they died or just flunked out of school or they looked at the place and hated it, but suddenly we were moving from hillbilly heavenly Brown County

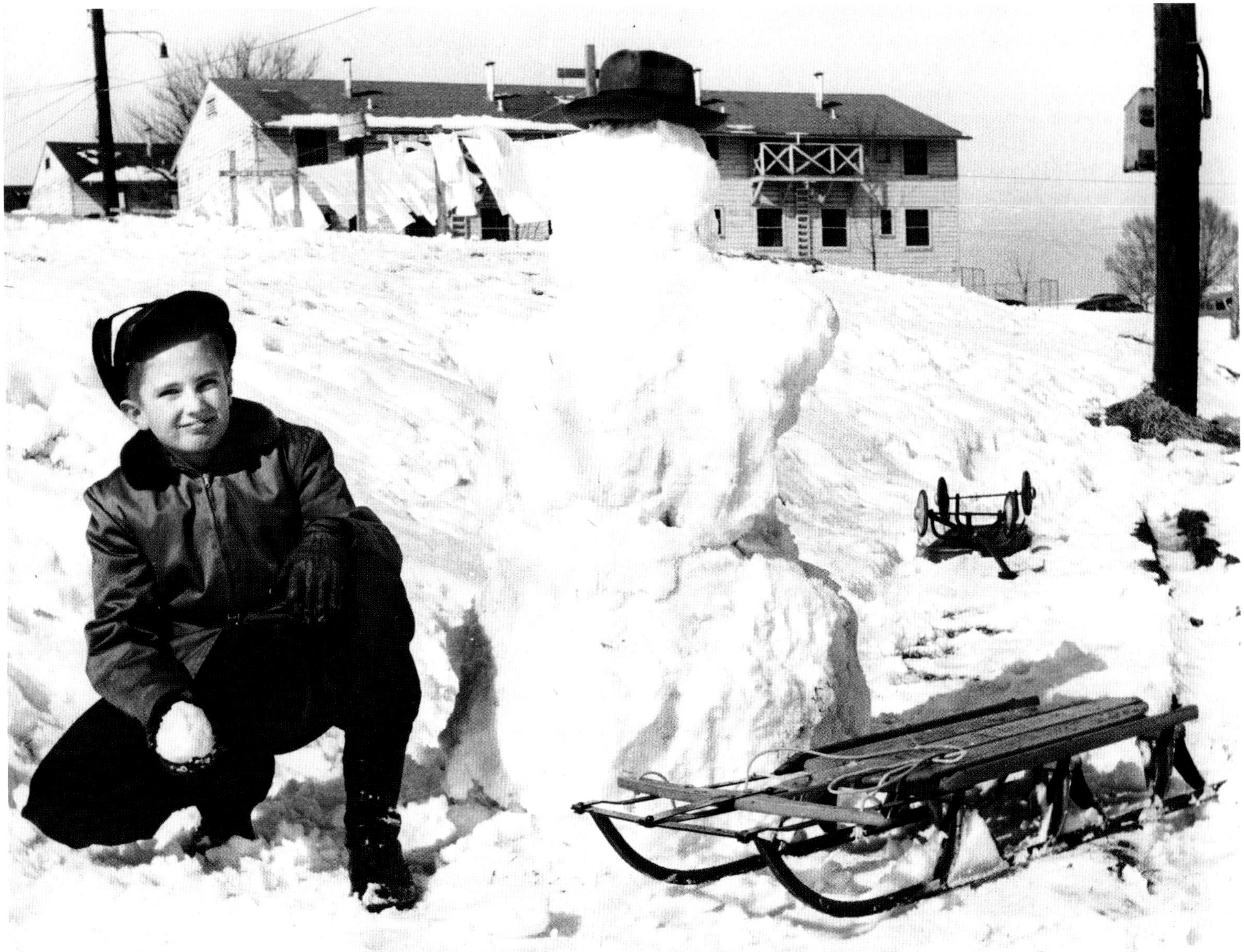

Hoosier Courts on a snowy day

to our very own place. Not that I didn't like the log cabin in the woods, because I did. The only thing that was hard on me was the school, but only because it wasn't very good; the fifth and sixth grades were in the same room. The shared bedroom was far too cold: I woke one morning and a bottle of ink was frozen next to my cot. Everything else was pretty good except when Uncle Roy messed up, which was almost every night at dinner because he insisted on serving everyone and passing out plates of food and he usually forgot to save any for himself, and since he was naturally unhealthy, not eating properly didn't help.

He was always getting sick, and that often made life complicated. During the years we were in Indiana he got pneumonia at least once a year, had a bout with polio that didn't affect much of anything, and almost died of the mumps. I was there when the mumps grabbed him, and he had to be evacuated in an ambulance that came in from goodness knows where by the back way from the north because Salt Creek had flooded and Yellowwood Lake Road was impassable from the south. Somebody said the ambulance came all the way from Indianapolis, but that seemed unlikely. It probably just came in from Bloomington over the back roads but I don't really know. I only know that he had a fever of about a zillion, looked like he was dead when they loaded him into the ambulance, but managed to survive. The mumps didn't ruin him either, because Martha gave birth to another little girl a year or so later. He lived another forty years or so and had plenty of time to cause trouble and come out of his bisexual closet and surprise all his children and grandchildren and maybe even my mom's sister.

And so we moved to Hoosier Courts. We didn't wait until the school year or even the semester ended because I was smart and already knew how to read and write, but we had to go in a hurry since the small, soon-to-be-cluttered apartment to which we were moving was available then and might not ever be available again—or if it was, goodness knows when. I remember two things. One was wonderful and the other perhaps the most awful thing that had ever happened to me up until then. The good thing was that Hoosier Courts looked like paradise, like going to heaven, surrounded by fields of fresh snow. This apartment was far from elegant but would be home for only two and a half years, although that was almost forever to me because those two and a half years were a quarter of the life I'd lived so far.

Hoosier Courts was inexpensive housing for married students attending Indiana University. The apartments were really for a family of four, but somehow Harold managed to convince someone to let us move in with three. The housing complex was on the north side of the tracks, outside the Bloomington city limits; had been completed in 1946, and was made up of thirty-five World War II Army surplus barracks that were converted into

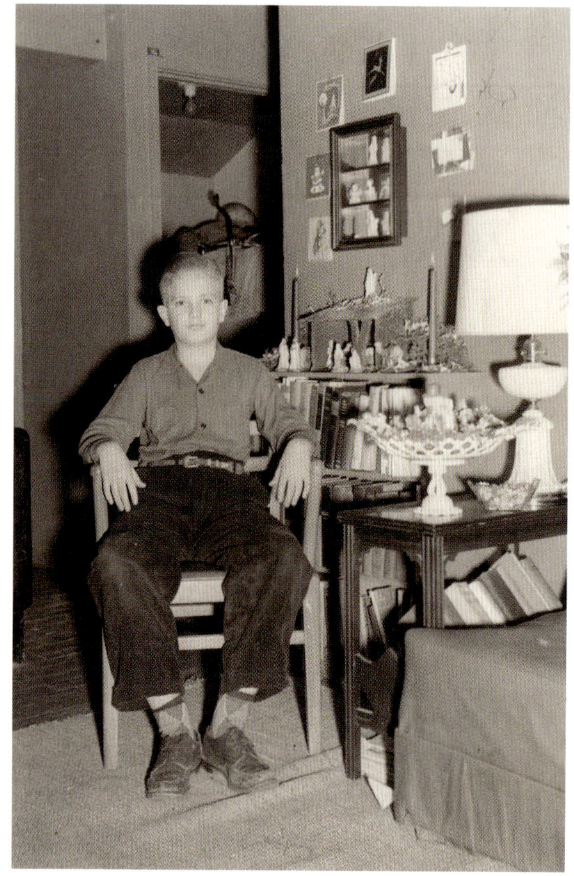

Hoosier Courts living room at Christmas

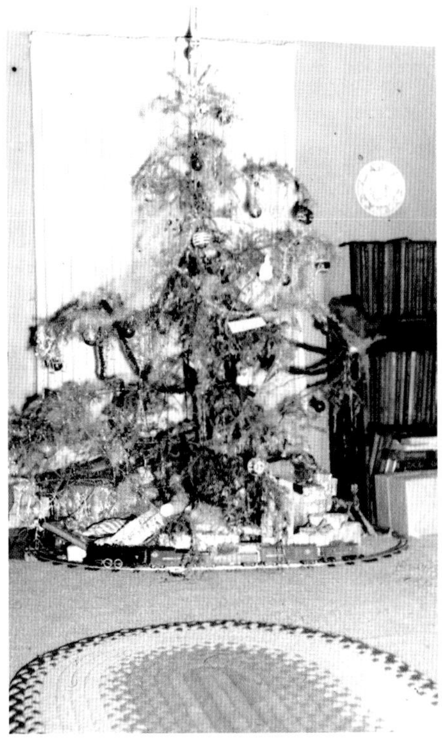

A new train set under the tree

housing units with eight apartments. We were assigned to Building 21, Apartment 4. Better known as 21-4. It was on the second floor.

This is what our new home was like. Harold and Sarah probably didn't pay too much attention; they were happy to finally be alone together and have a bedroom they could call their own. But I can still remember almost everything. You reached it by climbing up sturdy but creaky unpainted wooden stairs. At the top there was a pay phone that cost a nickel. It didn't ring very often, and I don't remember ever using it to call anyone. Our door was on the right. I don't remember ever arriving to find it locked, but this may be because Sarah was always home. I know I didn't have a key, but maybe there was a lock to discourage dishonest Hoosiers from stealing what we didn't have anyway.

Inside. A large room, a living, dining, sitting, family room all rolled into one. There was an inexpensive, straight-from-a-thrift-shop white-painted wooden table just inside the door to the right. It was against the wall so there were but three chairs, which was plenty, because I don't remember anyone but the three of us at the table. And why do I remember it was white, cheap, shiny white? It was because I ruined it with the iodine crystals my grandfather had sent me when I started to get interested in science. He sent me little bottles of chemicals that would supplement my Gilbert No. 1 chemistry set, and one day I spilled the iodine crystals all over the table and didn't clean them up immediately and they left nasty brown spots.

The room was spare, and until my father took up making rugs as a hobby, the floor was nothing but an expanse of wood from wall to undecorated wall—and that isn't a joke, because sometime in 1951 or 1952 Harold thought it would be relaxing to take a break from his studies to make rugs out of scrap wool that could be bought in strips for a few cents a pound from a local mill. He would braid the strips together and ultimately make a circle and weave the ends together, then make a larger circle and sew it to the previous one, and on and on he went until he had a braided rug that covered part of the floor and created an illusion that was less spare.

This was the only touch of luxury in the room, with the possible exception of the wonderful RCA radio-record player console that had made the journey from Texas to Indiana and survived to once again spin old 78 rpm records and invite Jack Benny, Fred Allen, and soaps and serials and baseball games into 21-4. Harold also made rugs for the two bedrooms and maybe made them for friends, but as late as the 1970s I was using two of these rugs in various locations. Harold made long-lasting rugs.

Stand by the white table and look to the left. There was an open area that housed a tiny kitchen that was made up of a counter, a small four-burner stove with an oven that could hold a chicken or a pot roast, open shelves for pots and pans with dishes and glasses above them, and perhaps a drawer or two for knives and forks and spoons and more shelves for canned goods, cereal, and baking supplies, and a small sink in which to wash up after dinner. There was no refrigerator, just an icebox into which ice was put every so often to keep food cool but wasn't good for anything that had to be kept really cold, so there was no frozen food or even food that had to be kept cold to avoid spoilage.

This meant shopping every day in the summer. Late fall, winter, and early spring were better because the window that led to the wooden fire escape was open, and anything that needed to be cold was just left outside. But sometime in 1952, maybe about the time my father traded in the old 1940 Chrysler and bought the grey 1952 Nash, he found himself with an extra $75 and bought a small Norge refrigerator. The icebox was sent to wherever circa 1920 kitchen appliances were sent in those days, and it is unlikely it was an antique store.

Back to the living-dining-sitting room. Just past the kitchen opening was a large, noisy space heater used to heat the entire apartment. It was fired by natural gas and probably violated every fire code known to man because the converted wooden barracks were just that, converted wooden barracks that would burn to the ground in about a second, but the heater worked. No inkbottles froze at 21-4.

Standing at the heater looking west was a bookcase crammed with Harold's textbooks, school supplies, and projects on which he was working. If it was holiday time and there is a photograph when it was, a small nativity scene is displayed, with an inexpensive Jesus, Mary, Joseph, wise men, donkeys, little lambs lying down, a few angels and other usual suspects, with Christmas cards stuck on the wall surrounding a small shadowbox my mother filled with porcelain figures. Next comes another smaller bookcase filled with my father's photo books, on top of which is a reading lamp, one of two in the room use to augment the bare bulb in the ceiling, and next to the lamp is one of Sarah's treasures, a milk glass server filled with holiday treats. The nativity scene, milk glass server, and photo books have survived.

Then there was a thrift-shop foldaway couch just in case there was a visitor who needed a bed, but I don't remember it ever being used; then a wooden cabinet with two shelves and a drawer Harold made sometime before the war in which he kept his classical record albums. The drawer was filled with old letters, assorted treasures, and record catalogs that were wish lists of records Harold wanted to buy and someday play on his elegant RCA radio-record player console.

The console only played 78 rpm discs, even though LPs had been available for five years, and the radio on the right folded out and had multiple bands, even though we only had local AM and were glad to get it. Next came Harold's easy chair, which he was happy to get into now and again and listen to a record, and then it was the end of the room except for the window in the middle that looked out onto another converted army barracks that looked just like Building 21 except it was Building 22 or perhaps 23.

Harold's handmade cabinet survives and is still in use, and the record albums they once held are stored away, rarely played but recalled in dreams fondly, because these were the first recordings I ever heard and there's one 78 album of Stokowski conducting what he called a "Symphonic Synthesis" of *Tristan and Isolde* that's as good as I ever heard, and has never been reissued anywhere and is only available on four Columbia twelve-inch 78 rpm discs hidden away in hundreds of attics all over the world.

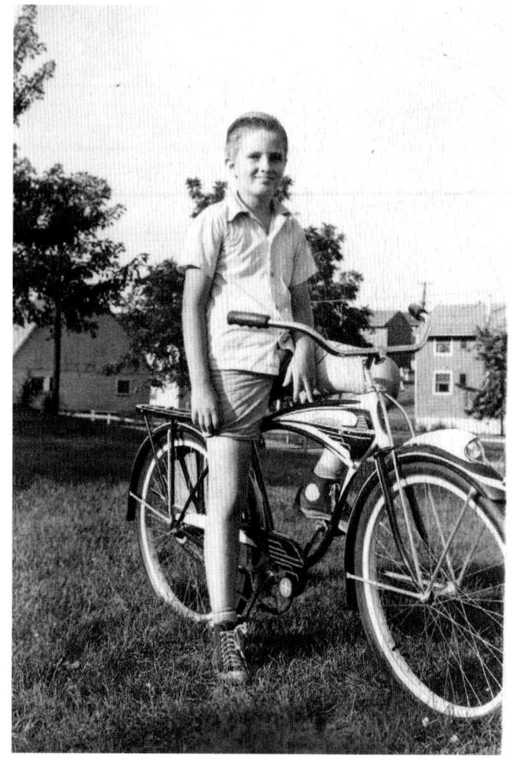

The new Schwinn bicycle

The eastern wall was less crowded: a couple of chairs, a three-section wooden bookcase with glass doors that folded up and slid into the top, a good idea because it kept dust off the books that my father had accumulated in the 1930s and 1940s mainly from book clubs, many of which I still have like *The Seven Pillars of Wisdom*, *Wind Sand and Stars*, *The Croquet Player*, *Gone With the Wind,* and whatever else the Book of the Month Club or Literary Guild was offering just before he went to war.

Those books were about the only part of the dream that didn't come true. After Harold came back from the war he had other books to read, to try and make up for lost time and get educated. Until the end of his days he always said he was going to read all the books he'd accumulated but they were read by me instead, which was part of the legacy Harold and Sarah passed along to me: exposure to Lawrence of Arabia and St. Exupery, H.G. Wells and many others, and not just comics or whatever was handed out in school for a fifth-grader or even a sixth to read.

That's about all there was in that room except for the television with a tiny screen that didn't show up until sometime in the winter of 1953 because it wasn't nearly as important as the Norge or the Nash or even a new Schwinn bicycle for me, and besides there was only one channel that the crude rabbit ears could pick up. The one and only was a locally owned station, WTTV, which did a lot of local programming and, when it could, had various network affiliations. On some days, if the weather was right, it was possible to get a wavy, jumping, static-filled signal from Indianapolis, but on WTTV all I can remember is *Dangerous Assignment*, *Ding Dong School* and local shows and basketball games and, somehow, baseball games from Cincinnati. The games were courtesy of the Burger Beer Broadcasting Network and featured commentary by old-time New York Yankees pitcher turned broadcaster, Waite Hoyt, and it was possible to watch fuzzy images of Ted Kluszewski, a local boy who'd made good, knock baseballs over the fence at Crosley Field. When the TV arrived my father's chair was moved around and set by the window, but Harold and Sarah watched it infrequently because there were other more important matters to attend to.

The bathroom should have been called the shower room because it had no bathtub, only a stall shower, a toilet, and a sink, all lit by the light bulb in the ceiling and maybe another bulb over the mirror behind which might have been a medicine cabinet. I don't remember if there was one because I wasn't taking any medicine in those days, and didn't use anything else that might have lived there except maybe toothpaste that was left out on the sink. Maybe it was just a mirror, possibly the only one in the apartment. I don't remember one anywhere else except in Sarah's handbag, where she kept a small mirror she used to powder her nose or put on lipstick.

Then came my tiny bedroom that consisted of a double bunk bed where I slept on the bottom, and after the Schwinn arrived, courtesy of my father who rode it all the way home from the bicycle shop where he bought it, the bike was stored on top. I still have a memory of seeing him riding it up the hill toward 21-4.

My bedroom also had an indoor basketball court, one with a "basket" I had fashioned out of a Maxwell House Coffee can that I nailed above the bedroom door through which I tried to toss a tennis ball with modest success. It was noisy when I tossed the ball around or played with a friend, but Harold and Sarah never complained.

There was also a four-by-eight piece of plywood with a tacked-down train track upon which to run my little Marx train I'd brought from Texas, but which was soon forgotten when I was given an American Flyer that ran on a two-rail track instead of three, which didn't look real. It was the least expensive set the A.C. Gilbert Company produced; it was only $14.95 and had a 4-4-2 Atlantic engine, a red boxcar, a red gondola, and a red caboose. The engine had a little light in the front. About the same time there was a raffle at the Harris Grand movie for a complete American Flyer train set with a big engine that smoked and whistled, lots of cars, little buildings and switches, and a fancy layout, but I didn't win, so I made do with my tiny Atlantic engine on the floor because I never took the three rail tracks off the plywood, I just turned them to the wall and used the other side to keep track of how many hits I'd made playing baseball or touchdowns I'd scored in the big green pasture across the street where we played baseball all spring and summer

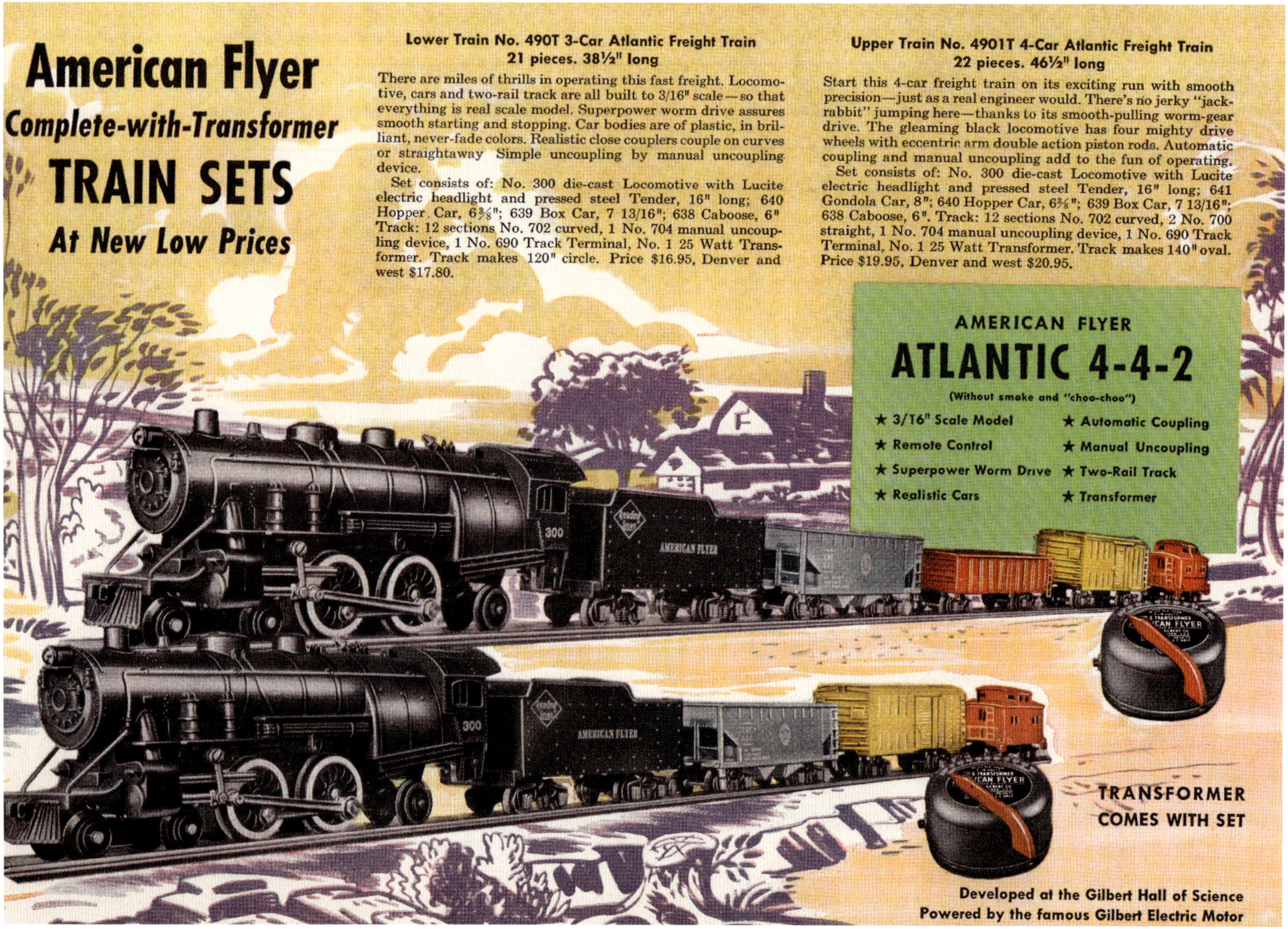
American Flyer
Complete-with-Transformer
TRAIN SETS
At New Low Prices
Lower Train No. 490T 3-Car Atlantic Freight Train
21 pieces. 38½" long
There are miles of thrills in operating this fast freight. Locomotive, cars and two-rail track are all built to 3/16" scale—so that everything is real scale model. Superpower worm drive assures smooth starting and stopping. Car bodies are of plastic, in brilliant, never-fade colors. Realistic close couplers couple on curves or straightaway. Simple uncoupling by manual uncoupling device.
Set consists of: No. 300 die-cast Locomotive with Lucite electric headlight and pressed steel Tender, 16" long; 640 Hopper Car, 6⅜"; 639 Box Car, 7 13/16"; 638 Caboose, 6" Track: 12 sections No. 702 curved, 1 No. 704 manual uncoupling device, 1 No. 690 Track Terminal, No. 1 25 Watt Transformer. Track makes 120" circle. Price $16.95, Denver and west $17.80.
Upper Train No. 4901T 4-Car Atlantic Freight Train
22 pieces. 46½" long
Start this 4-car freight train on its exciting run with smooth precision—just as a real engineer would. There's no jerky "jack-rabbit" jumping here—thanks to its smooth-pulling worm-gear drive. The gleaming black locomotive has four mighty drive wheels with eccentric arm double action piston rods. Automatic coupling and manual uncoupling add to the fun of operating.
Set consists of: No. 300 die-cast Locomotive with Lucite electric headlight and pressed steel Tender, 16" long; 641 Gondola Car, 8"; 640 Hopper Car, 6⅜"; 639 Box Car, 7 13/16"; 638 Caboose, 6". Track: 12 sections No. 702 curved, 2 No. 700 straight, 1 No. 704 manual uncoupling device, 1 No. 690 Track Terminal, No. 1 25 Watt Transformer. Track makes 140" oval. Price $19.95, Denver and west $20.95.
AMERICAN FLYER
ATLANTIC 4-4-2
(Without smoke and "choo-choo")
★ 3/16" Scale Model
★ Automatic Coupling
★ Remote Control
★ Manual Uncoupling
★ Superpower Worm Drive
★ Two-Rail Track
★ Realistic Cars
★ Transformer
300
AMERICAN FLYER
TRANSFORMER
COMES WITH SET
Developed at the Gilbert Hall of Science
Powered by the famous Gilbert Electric Motor

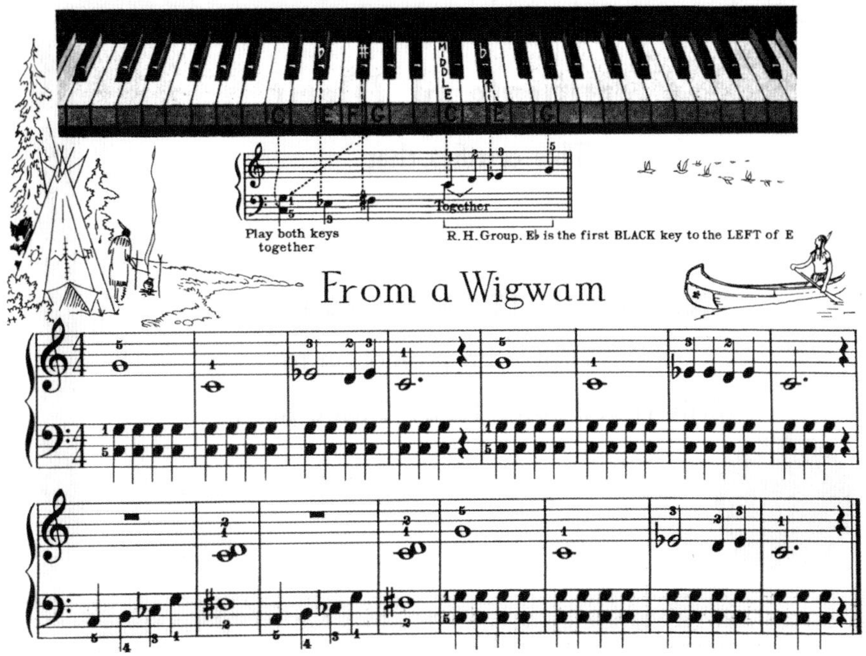


and football all fall and winter, unless it was raining or snowing.

Across the hall was my mother's and father's bedroom where I wasn't welcome except when it was time to practice the piano which they insisted I do once a day ever since they spent another $25 for another old, never-to-be-tuned upright. I don't remember anything about that room except the piano, and I also remember the day it left the room. My parents were very smart most of the time and worked hard to make sure I was never lacking in anything important, but one thing they didn't recognize for many years was that my talents as a piano player lay on the baseball field. After I'd spent two years trying to get through the John Thomson 2nd Grade book without success they got the point, and the piano was sold, probably at a loss. It was moved from the bedroom, and I was called upon to help push and shove it out the door and down the stairs and into a waiting truck where it was probably delivered to someone else who had even less talent than I did. I never went into their bedroom again, but I was encouraged to study hard and even to play baseball. My untalented fingers never tried to play *From a Wigwam* again, or anything else.

I have no idea where the boxes of family photographs and scrapbooks were kept. There were no closets or storage areas in this small apartment, but somehow all the treasures and photographs and memorabilia from the 1920s, 1930s, and 1940s that have been used as the raw material for this book lived somewhere in those three rooms. Perhaps they were under Harold and Sarah's bed. I don't remember seeing any of these items until many years later.

And all this cost $35 a month, or about $1.00 a day, and the two and a half years there were probably the happiest, most carefree times of my ten-year-old life or maybe forever, where hundreds of other families all with kids just like me lived in identical circumstances. While the living conditions would seem dreary to someone looking in on us, they seemed pretty good to me, because nobody was looking out for anything but another ball game, and no one starved.

Those years were not the best for Harold and Sarah, however. Harold was working hard to obtain his doctorate, traveling the state preparing educational reports, acting as a teaching assistant, and finally writing his dissertation entitled *Adequacy and Changes Associated with Conducting Selected Cooperative School Building Surveys*. Later he had it bound, and today it still sits on a shelf. I've never read it. It sounds very complicated. I only managed to take Education 101 in college, and I'm sure it would make about as much sense to me as reading Ovid in Latin.

Sarah's job was to comfort Harold and tend to me. They had no social life. I can

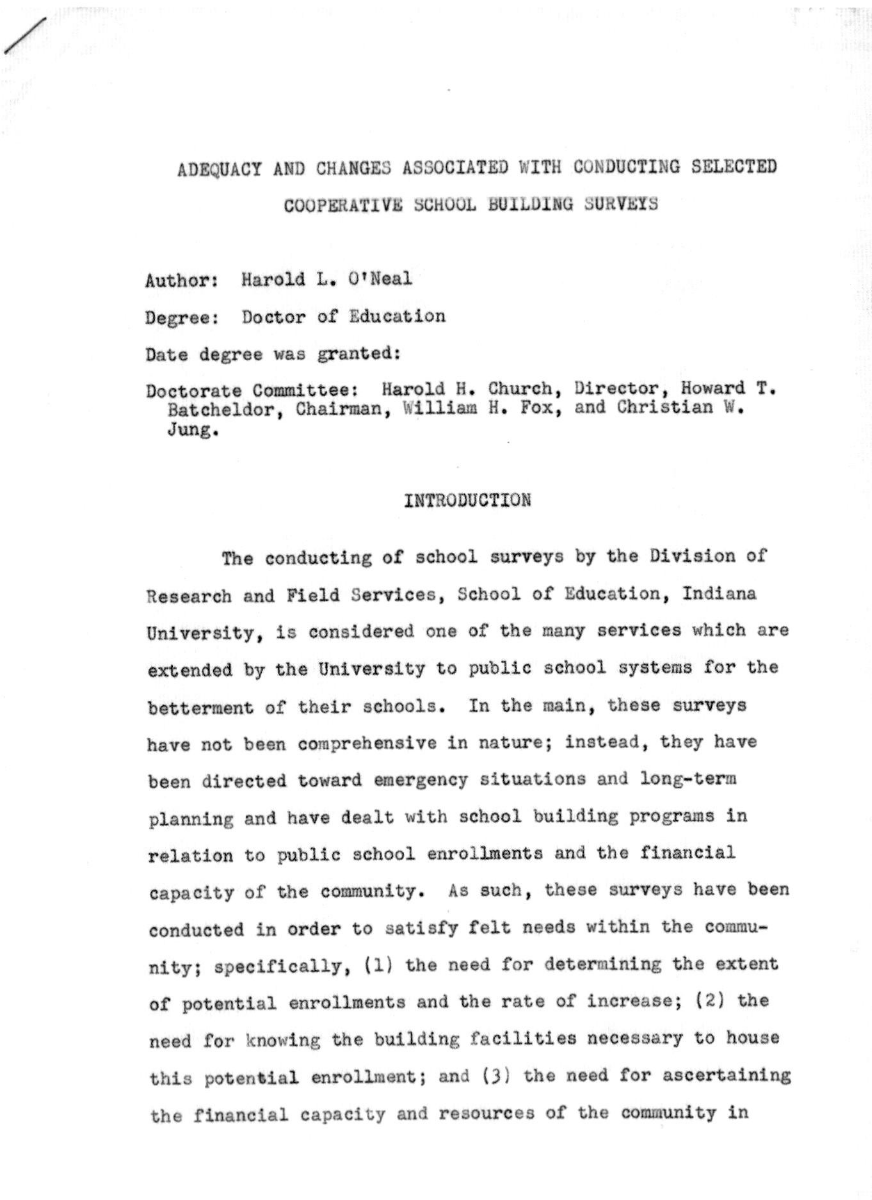

ADEQUACY AND CHANGES ASSOCIATED WITH CONDUCTING SELECTED COOPERATIVE SCHOOL BUILDING SURVEYS

Author: Harold L. O'Neal

Degree: Doctor of Education

Date degree was granted:

Doctorate Committee: Harold H. Church, Director, Howard T. Batcheldor, Chairman, William H. Fox, and Christian W. Jung.

INTRODUCTION

The conducting of school surveys by the Division of Research and Field Services, School of Education, Indiana University, is considered one of the many services which are extended by the University to public school systems for the betterment of their schools. In the main, these surveys have not been comprehensive in nature; instead, they have been directed toward emergency situations and long-term planning and have dealt with school building programs in relation to public school enrollments and the financial capacity of the community. As such, these surveys have been conducted in order to satisfy felt needs within the community; specifically, (1) the need for determining the extent of potential enrollments and the rate of increase; (2) the need for knowing the building facilities necessary to house this potential enrollment; and (3) the need for ascertaining the financial capacity and resources of the community in

remember one or two times we went as a family to the movies or took an occasional trip to a state park for a picnic. There was even a trip to Indianapolis, a big city all of fifty miles away. We went to the movies in the enormous Avenue Theater and saw an MGM action thriller, *Scaramouche.* It was the summer of 1952, and I really remember the newsreel more than the movie because it was the first time I'd ever seen a boxing match on a big movie screen. The newsreel featured highlights of Sugar Ray Robinson trying to become a world champion in three weight classes, this time Light Heavyweight, but Joey Maxim wouldn't give up his crown, and Sugar Ray couldn't answer the bell for the fifteenth round. Time passed, and it was the winter of 1952, and Harold and Sarah couldn't have been more proud: I made my operatic debut.

In November 1952 I became one of four midshipmen in the American premier of Benjamin Britten's very new opera, *Billy Budd*, a premier that was a big deal with a cast of a hundred singers, a seventy-piece orchestra, sets and scenery, and even a good luck telegram from Britten himself tacked to a backstage bulletin board. I had been in the choir at McCalla School and picked up where I'd left off when enrolled at University High School in the fall. Someone associated with the opera told the choirmaster they needed four children who could sing in tune, and I was chosen.

We rehearsed a lot, probably for two or three weeks before the December 7th

INDIANA UNIVERSITY
SCHOOL OF MUSIC
Thirty-Fifth Season—Nineteenth Program
1952-53

presents

THE AMERICAN STAGE PREMIERE OF

# BILLY BUDD

An Opera in Four Acts

Libretto by E. M. Forster and Eric Crozier

after the story by Herman Melville

Music by

BENJAMIN BRITTEN

**December 7, 1952** **3:00 P.M.**

**Indiana University Auditorium**

## CHORUS

OFFICERS OF THE QUARTER-DECK: Donald Balser, Garth Conley, William Lohmeyer, Jack Mason, Wendell Mertz, Jerry Miller, Gus Pancol, Herbert Parks; MARINES OF THE QUARTER-DECK: Gene Carsten, Richard Eskeli, Robert Harter, James Matthews, James Sandifer, Stanley Sheets; MAIN DECK: Ronald Alley, William Barnard, Ronald Carter, James Dartnall, Maurice Laymond, Melvin Maudlin, Anthony Meyer, William Powell, Mack Rowe, Robert Sanders, James Scott, Melvin Sunderman, Robert Thompson, Edward Williams; GUNNERS: Charles Greenwood, Lee Lacy, Donald Leffel, Norman Rappe, William Stoner, John Woods; SEAMEN: David Kishline, Albert Lucas, Peter Salm, Earl Stahl, Thomas Brodheckr, Richard Cumberland, Robert George, W. Eugene Henry; AFTER-GUARDSMEN: Norman Bishea, Sheldon Breskow, Barry Davis, James Jeffrey, Richard Sowash; MARINES: Max Capestany, Lynn Ernest, Richard Klemeyer, Phillip Knoepple, Robert Koenemann, Robert Lau, Thomas Rea, Albert Rullman; MIDSHIPMEN: Thomas Hensley, Harold O'Neal, Chris Young, Billy Youngs.

Robert Koenemann, Robert Lau, Thomas Rea, Albert Rullman; MIDSHIPMEN: Thomas Hensley, Harold O'Neal, Chris Young, Billy Youngs.

Pearl Harbor Day premiere, and it was terrific fun because we actually got to sing a little, and I remember some of the words our raggedy little quartet sang. *Toplights down there, and scrub! Scrub!* I had no idea what "toplights" referred to and still don't, but we sang this and our other two or three lines bravely, hoped for the best, and after the last dress rehearsal my mother came and picked me up at the theater. I was all of twelve and still looked after carefully by my parents, even on the safe streets of Bloomington, Indiana. I was in costume and smeared with makeup to look as though I was the gamiest of urchins, fresh from battle and a hard day of carrying buckets of gunpowder. As we headed home, my mother casually announced she'd gone by the grocery store and there was a notice that announced I'd won a prize. This was the first and only time I'd ever won any sort of a prize in a drawing or lottery. I begged her to go by the store, but she felt I looked too awful to be seen in public, so I had to get my prize the next day after school. The prize turned out to be a Brownie Hawkeye camera, and so my career in photography and my love of opera pretty much began at the same time. I have since seen *Billy Budd* at the Met and listened to it lots and taken many, many pictures that aren't too bad, but my dueling debuts, my probably badly sung debut on stage, and my shaky debut with my very own camera, at least based on the few snapshots that survive, were equally awful. But I still have the camera on a shelf in the country, and fifteen tickets for the upcoming season when I will not see *Billy Budd.*

I wasn't even a teenager, I was ten or eleven or twelve in Indiana, and it was a wonderful time to be in Bloomington and Hoosier Courts and McCalla and University High School, as well as the Harris Grande, where first-run movies played, and the Roxy, where the B movies with Hopalong Cassidy and Lash LaRue and Tex Ritter and Bob Steele held forth, or the Indiana, which showed even fancier movies than the old Harris Grand ever presented.

There were lots of things to do that were free. Just like during the war, there were still scrap drives, and Harold and Sarah encouraged me to collect as much as I could, usually old newspapers but occasionally soda pop bottles. I'd collect the papers, then pile them into the back seat and trunk of the car, and Sarah would take me to a scrap dealer who would weigh them and I might earn a dollar or two, which went for bubblegum cards.

Another activity encouraged by both of them was the local garden club. The university sponsored the club and gave all the children who signed up, mostly from Hoosier Courts, a ten by ten foot plot of land, seeds, fertilizer, and garden tools, as well as instruction. It wasn't exactly a Victory Garden but it was good training, and I got to take home everything I grew, which turned out to be a lot, and it was a welcome addition to the dinner table. I was good at onions, radishes, beans, tomatoes, and even corn. I won a prize for

*May 5, 1952*

DAILY HERALD-TELEPHONE BLOOMINGTON INDIANA

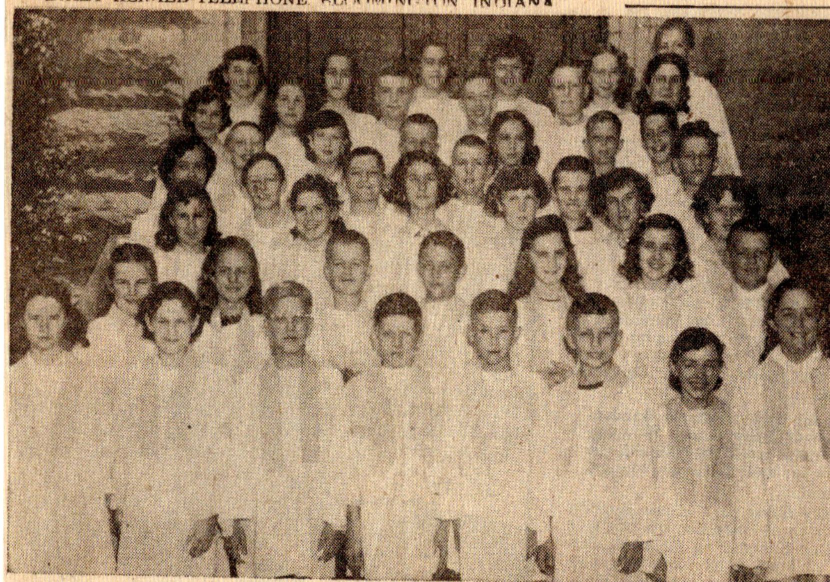

**McCALLA CHILDRENS' CHOIR** entertained with several selections at luncheon of Bloomington Council of Church Women. Choir includes, left to right: Front row — Judy Rogers, Jennie VanEtten, David Hall, Howard Bruce, Terry Miller, Ronnie Williamson, Catherine Hinkle, and Nancy Thompson; Second row — Mary Jo Hilt, Heather Hall, George Stanger, Jerry Martin, Judy Arnett, Sandra Blair, Kenny Nikirk; Third row — Darla Sylvester, Judy Cook, Judy Barrow, Nancy Arnett, Beverly Shields, Karen Hamilton; Fourth row — Suzanne Graves, Larry Clark, Jerry Steel, Jim Baldwin, Jackie Lemon, Michael Douglas; Fifth row — Delmar Haywood, Linda Hankins, Sonny Baugh, Linda Gigli, Joe Deckard, Mike Roark; Sixth row — Judy Carlisle, Carolyn Snoddy, Billy Deckard, Richard Cohee, Donald Baker, Harold O'-Neal; Seventh row — Connie Biedenkopf, Patricia Crandall, Wyoma Smith, Karen Stevens, Linda French, and Arbutus Wilson.

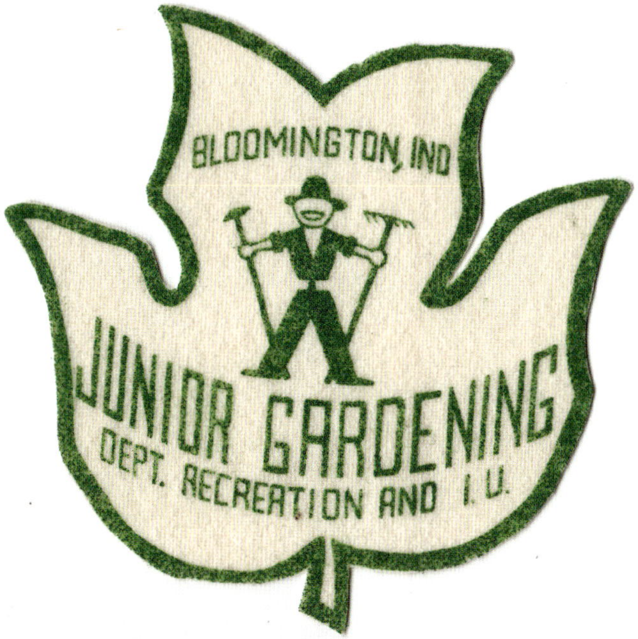


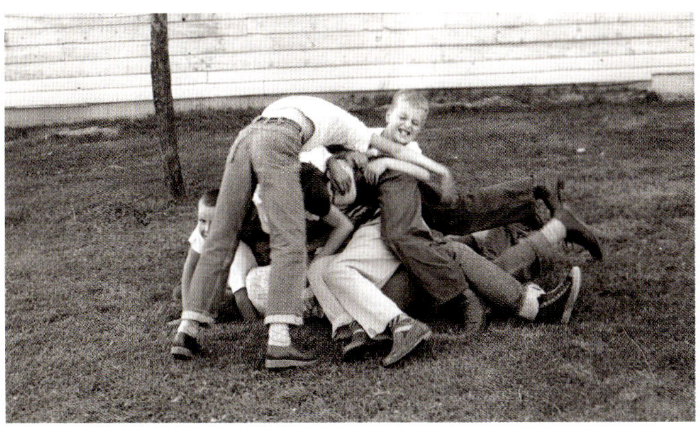

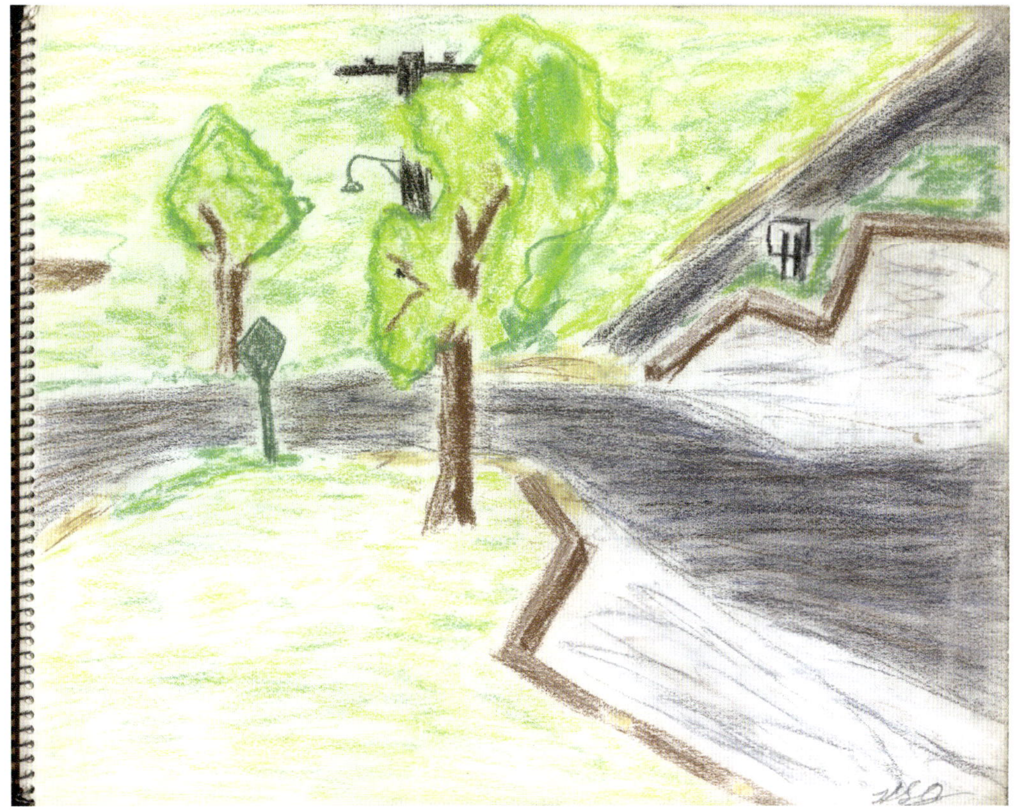

View from bedroom window

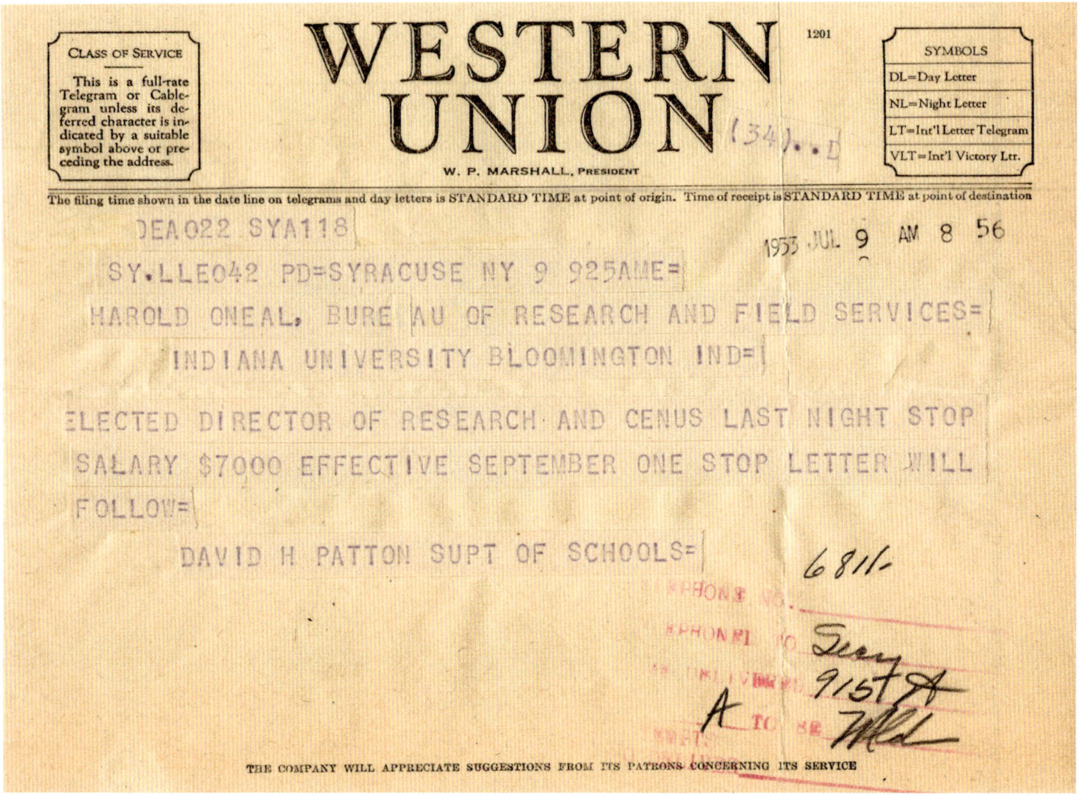

CLASS OF SERVICE

This is a full-rate Telegram or Cablegram unless its deferred character is indicated by a suitable symbol above or preceding the address.

WESTERN UNION

W. P. MARSHALL, PRESIDENT

1201

SYMBOLS

DL=Day Letter

NL=Night Letter

LT=Int'l Letter Telegram

VLT=Int'l Victory Ltr.

(34)..D

The filing time shown in the date line on telegrams and day letters is STANDARD TIME at point of origin. Time of receipt is STANDARD TIME at point of destination

DEA022 SYA118

1953 JUL 9 AM 8 56

SY.LLE042 PD=SYRACUSE NY 9 925AME=

HAROLD ONEAL, BUREAU OF RESEARCH AND FIELD SERVICES=

INDIANA UNIVERSITY BLOOMINGTON IND=

ELECTED DIRECTOR OF RESEARCH AND CENUS LAST NIGHT STOP SALARY $7000 EFFECTIVE SEPTEMBER ONE STOP LETTER WILL FOLLOW=

DAVID H PATTON SUPT OF SCHOOLS=

6811-

THE COMPANY WILL APPRECIATE SUGGESTIONS FROM ITS PATRONS CONCERNING ITS SERVICE

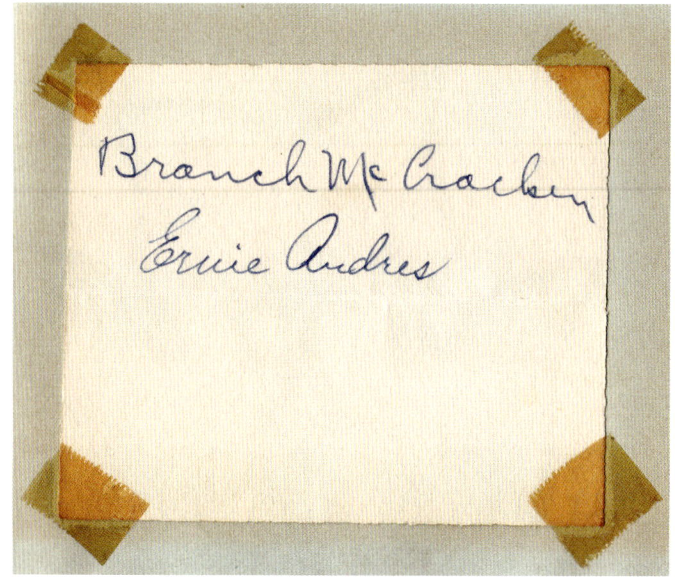

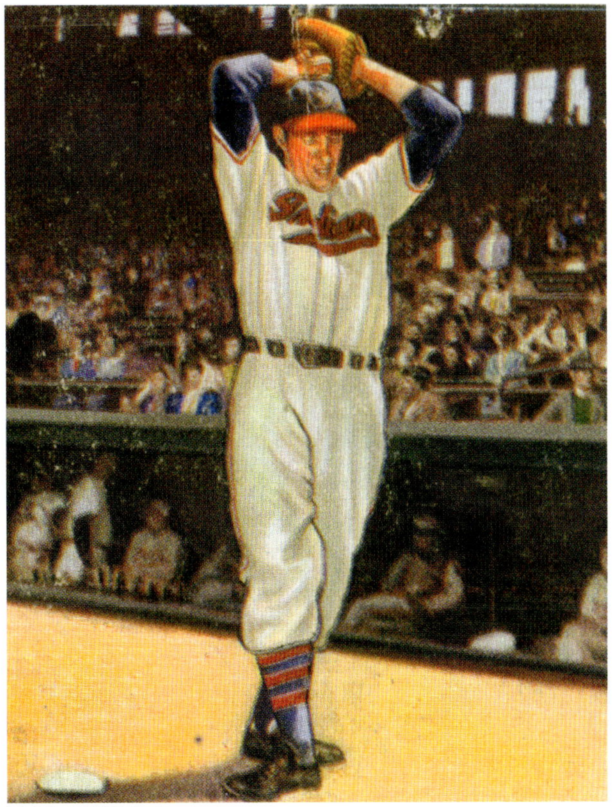

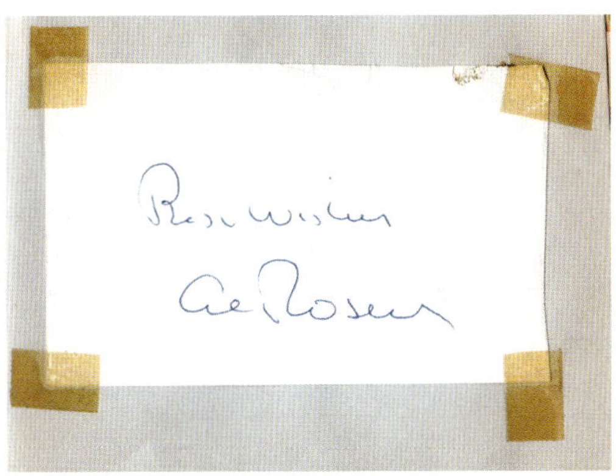

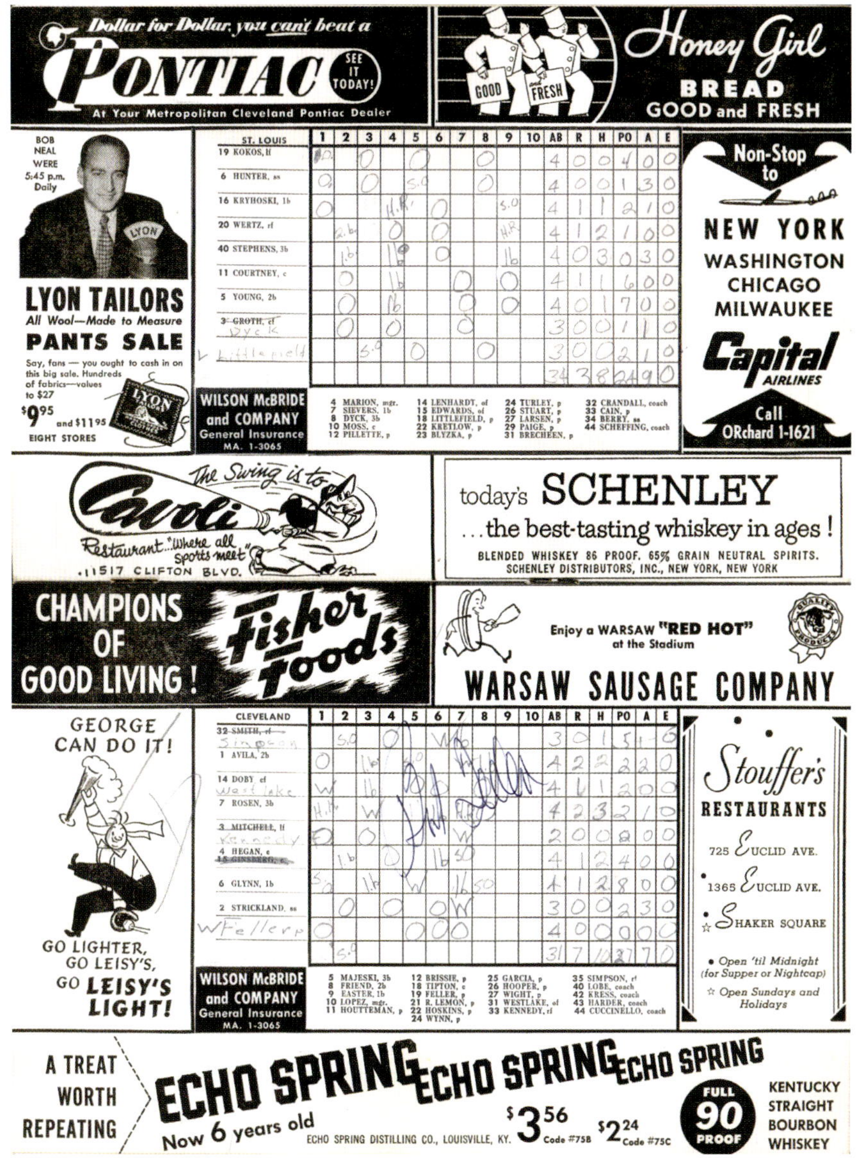
Dollar for Dollar, you can't beat a
PONTIAC
SEE IT TODAY!
At Your Metropolitan Cleveland Pontiac Dealer
GOOD and FRESH
Honey Girl
BREAD
GOOD and FRESH
BOB NEAL WERE 5:45 p.m. Daily
LYON
LYON TAILORS
All Wool—Made to Measure
PANTS SALE
Say, fans — you ought to cash in on this big sale. Hundreds of fabrics—values to $27
$9.95 and $11.95
EIGHT STORES
ST. LOUIS
19 KOKOS, lf
6 HUNTER, ss
16 KRYHOSKI, 1b
20 WERTZ, rf
40 STEPHENS, 3b
11 COURTNEY, c
5 YOUNG, 2b
3 GROTH, cf
1 2 3 4 5 6 7 8 9 10 AB R H PO A E
WILSON McBRIDE and COMPANY
General Insurance
MA. 1-3065
4 MARION, mgr. 7 SIEVERS, 1b 8 DYCK, 3b 10 MOSS, c 12 PILLETTE, p
14 LENHARDT, of 15 EDWARDS, of 18 LITTLEFIELD, p 22 KRETLOW, p 23 BLYZKA, p
24 TURLEY, p 26 STUART, p 27 LARSEN, p 29 PAIGE, p 31 BRECHEEN, p
32 CRANDALL, coach 33 CAIN, p 34 BERRY, ss 44 SCHEFFING, coach
Non-Stop to
NEW YORK
WASHINGTON
CHICAGO
MILWAUKEE
Capital AIRLINES
Call ORchard 1-1621
The Swing is to Cavoli
Restaurant "Where all sports meet"
11517 CLIFTON BLVD.
today's SCHENLEY
...the best-tasting whiskey in ages!
BLENDED WHISKEY 86 PROOF. 65% GRAIN NEUTRAL SPIRITS.
SCHENLEY DISTRIBUTORS, INC., NEW YORK, NEW YORK
CHAMPIONS OF GOOD LIVING!
Fisher Foods
Enjoy a WARSAW "RED HOT" at the Stadium
WARSAW SAUSAGE COMPANY
GEORGE CAN DO IT!
GO LIGHTER, GO LEISY'S, GO LEISY'S LIGHT!
CLEVELAND
32 SMITH, rf
1 AVILA, 2b
14 DOBY, cf
7 ROSEN, 3b
3 MITCHELL, lf
4 HEGAN, c
6 GLYNN, 1b
2 STRICKLAND, ss
1 2 3 4 5 6 7 8 9 10 AB R H PO A E
WILSON McBRIDE and COMPANY
General Insurance
MA. 1-3065
5 MAJESKI, 3b 8 FRIEND, 2b 9 EASTER, 1b 10 LOPEZ, mgr. 11 HOUTTEMAN, p
12 BRISSIE, p 18 TIPTON, c 19 FELLER, p 21 R. LEMON, p 22 HOSKINS, p 24 WYNN, p
25 GARCIA, p 26 HOOPER, p 27 WIGHT, p 31 WESTLAKE, of 33 KENNEDY, rf
35 SIMPSON, rf 40 LOBE, coach 42 KRESS, coach 43 HARDER, coach 44 CUCCINELLO, coach
Stouffer's
RESTAURANTS
725 EUCLID AVE.
1365 EUCLID AVE.
SHAKER SQUARE
• Open 'til Midnight (for Supper or Nightcap)
☆ Open Sundays and Holidays
A TREAT WORTH REPEATING
ECHO SPRING ECHO SPRING ECHO SPRING
Now 6 years old
ECHO SPRING DISTILLING CO., LOUISVILLE, KY.
$3.56 Code #758 $2.24 Code #75C
FULL 90 PROOF
KENTUCKY STRAIGHT BOURBON WHISKEY

the biggest cauliflower. But I failed with carrots and spinach.

The university had the best basketball team in the land if not the world, a bicycle race on its way to glory and a feature film, a great school, and wonderful teachers. Fred Mills, an Ohio State footballer, was not only the football coach but also an art teacher. I had a modest career in a real opera, a new camera, a church where nobody yelled at me or told me or anyone else they were a wicked sinner, role models devoid of prejudice, a hundred friends who all pretty much wanted to do the same things, a modest place to live, enough food to eat, and sometimes as much as a quarter in my pocket, but almost always a nickel, which is what a pack of 1952 Topps baseball cards cost.

Bloomington is where I learned to play basketball and that I was pretty good at it. This was a perfect time and place to learn about basketball, because kids named Dick Farley, Bob Leonard, Charlie Kraak, Jim Schooley, and the most famous of all, All-American Don Schlundt, kids just five or six or seven years older than me, were the best players in the land and beat Kansas in 1953 by one point in the NCAA finals to prove it, and the campus paper ran a headline that read *We Dood It*. I still have a copy of it in a drawer in the dining room in the country. Harold often got tickets and took me to the games. These may have been the last basketball games he ever attended, and they were certainly the most exciting I'd ever seen. He even got me close enough to the action to get autographs from the legendary coach Branch McCracken and his assistant Ernie Andres.

It all changed very quickly. For Harold and Sarah it was like a quick glimpse of dreamland, for me it was less certain. One day in the late spring of 1953, just when I was getting into the new set of Topps baseball cards, Harold came home with the news that he was not only a Doctor of Education but he was to be an employed Doctor of Education, that he was to have his first job since he'd been put out of the Army because of his wartime diseases and medical disability, and we'd soon be packing up and heading toward a place called Syracuse, somewhere I'd never heard of, but as it turned out, it was a place where dreams came true. Maybe not everyone's dreams, but they came true for Harold and Sarah. The official telegram came in on July 9 from David H. Patton, the Superintendent of Schools in Syracuse. Harold's official job title was Director of Research and Census. The salary was $7,000 per year.

I was a little bit frightened. I had many friends, loved my school, and loved the big green field where I played baseball and football and the gym where I tossed the basketball better and better. I had just turned thirteen and was growing up. But then Harold told me that when we moved to Syracuse we would spend the first night on the road in a town called Cleveland which I had heard of because they had a baseball team called the Indians, and they were my favorite because I really liked their star pitcher, Bob Feller. I had a bubble gum card of him in action tacked on my bedroom wall. On the day we were going to be in Cleveland they would be playing the lowly St. Louis Browns, who were probably glad to get out of the heat of St. Louis to play on the cool shores of Lake Erie, and Harold promised to take me out to the ballgame, so I started packing that night and wasn't afraid of anything other than that it might rain the day we were in town.

It worked out. It was a twilight-night double header. Bob Feller pitched and won his game; Al Rosen hit three home runs; the legendary Satchel Paige was in the bullpen for St. Loo, sitting on his rocking chair. I didn't get to see him pitch, but I got to see him rock.

# The Finish Line

## The American Dream in the 1950s PART II

**IN THE SUMMER OF 1953 HAROLD AND SARAH ARRIVED IN SYRACUSE, NEW YORK,** a town slightly smaller than Fort Worth but substantially larger than Bloomington, Indiana. It was the perfect time to arrive in Syracuse for many reasons, and not just because it was Harold's first job and the beginning of a new life for his family, but because Syracuse was at its peak and would continue to be a vigorous city for over a decade until it fell into a slow decline, which continues to this day. In 1953 its population was about 225,000; in 2018 it is barely half that.

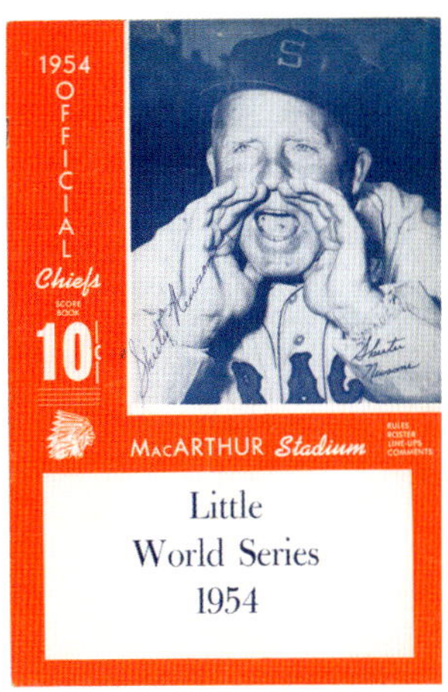


Imagine the excitement felt by a thirteen-year-old who loved sports, mainly baseball and now basketball, even more than studies and music. Syracuse was the home of an NBA basketball team, the Syracuse Nationals, one that not only had a player from the 1953 Indiana NCAA championship team (Dick Farley), but one that would win the NBA playoffs in the first full season after we arrived. The Nationals were a major league team in a tiny minor league city.

The Syracuse Chiefs were a Triple-A baseball team in the International League, a team filled with former and soon-to-be major league stars. They were a Philadelphia Phillies farm team; in 1954 they would be International League champions, and even though they lost the Little World Series to Louisville, they were heroes to me. It turned out that when Harold found a place for us to live, one of the players, Benny Zientara, lived three doors away. He was a good guy, a grizzled veteran at thirty-three, and he convinced Harold and Sarah to let me go to McArthur Field by myself.

Then there was the Syracuse University football team. The legendary Jimmy Brown, easily the greatest natural athlete (in almost any sport) I saw in action, or maybe anybody ever saw in action, was to begin his career in Syracuse in 1954, and this normally ordinary college team has been vaguely professional ever since.

But while that was exciting to me, Harold and Sarah had more mundane matters to attend to, like finding a place to live, which initially was something called a "tourist home," a 1953 version of today's Airbnb, a bedroom in a private home on West Genesee Street, "with kitchen privileges." They felt it was better to stay in the city than in a "tourist court" or motel outside the city. It was to be a short stay.

There was no housing crisis in Syracuse that summer, and Harold found a permanent home for us within the week, a modest apartment on the north side of town that was within walking distance of Grant Junior High School, where I would go to school. This was convenient, but it was also within walking distance of McArthur Stadium, where the Syracuse Chiefs battled opponents from other cities in New York State like Rochester and Buffalo, but also distant cities in foreign lands like Montreal and Havana.

Our new home was a simple apartment, just like in Fort Worth, with two bedrooms up and a living area down with a kitchen, dining, and living room. It also had a working refrigerator and a novelty, at least to me: a basement. It was one of forty-two identical apartments located at the corner of Lemoyne and Kenwood Avenues. It was unclear how old they were in 1953, but the eleven red-brick apartment buildings are still there in 2018, now sixty-five years older. We were there for less than a year, but it was a remarkable year.

Harold and Sarah were not planning their future now: they were beginning to live it. Harold no longer had to go to school all day and study all night and teach undergraduates when he wasn't studying or attending class or traveling all over the state of Indiana gathering statistics of all sorts about public schools and the children that attended them. His new job, officially titled Director of Research and Census, provided a decent salary, which meant he could purchase a few creature comforts, like a new television that filled the living room with new sights and sounds every evening.

When Harold came home from work, after a meal together which was always preceded by a short thanksgiving prayer, there was time to enjoy *Death Valley Days* or *Dragnet* or *I Love Lucy*, but especially the shows that featured what Harold thought was good music. *The Voice of Firestone* was a favorite, and even the half-hour show in which the always fawning Liberace played for the grandmothers of America, a one-man Lawrence Welk Show without the overhead. But strangely enough, when Liberace had used up his saccharine, he really could play, and if he kept his mouth shut, the music was pretty good. I could tell that as a thirteen-year-old, but I also knew the good music on the television and other relaxing shows replaced listening to the old prewar 78 rpm classical albums Harold had enjoyed in Fort Worth and Bloomington. I missed those symphonies and concertos. A year or so later I was allowed to handle those old records on my own, but not quite yet.

Harold and Sarah knew the finish line was just a few months or maybe a year or two away, so they were happy to make do at the Lemoyne Arms. It was just a temporary stop on the way to better things. But it was a monumental year for many reasons, for them and for me. Harold's no-nonsense attitude and maturity stood out with his superiors in the Syracuse school system, and he was quickly given increased responsibilities. Since I was no longer a child, Sarah was also able to venture out more, joining civic and church groups; sometimes she wouldn't be home when I returned from school. But she was still at the mercy of others to fetch her, or of the Syracuse bus system, which stopped a couple blocks away. We were not a two-car family, but even if we had been, she didn't like to drive.

On the other hand it was tough for me at school because I was an outsider, soon to be upgraded to outcast, a kid who'd been thrust into a group of teenagers who had grown up together. In September 1953 the student population of Grant Junior High School was about 98 percent Italian, and many of the teachers were as strict as the nuns at the Franciscan nunnery across the street from the school,

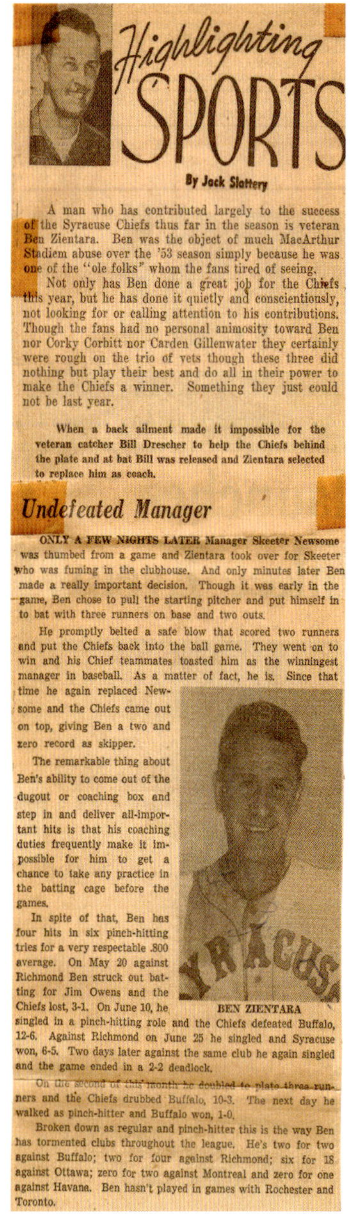
Highlighting SPORTS

By Jack Slattery

A man who has contributed largely to the success of the Syracuse Chiefs thus far in the season is veteran Ben Zientara. Ben was the object of much MacArthur Stadiem abuse over the '53 season simply because he was one of the "ole folks" whom the fans tired of seeing.

Not only has Ben done a great job for the Chiefs this year, but he has done it quietly and conscientiously, not looking for or calling attention to his contributions. Though the fans had no personal animosity toward Ben nor Corky Corbitt nor Carden Gillenwater they certainly were rough on the trio of vets though these three did nothing but play their best and do all in their power to make the Chiefs a winner. Something they just could not be last year.

**When a back ailment made it impossible for the veteran catcher Bill Drescher to help the Chiefs behind the plate and at bat Bill was released and Zientara selected to replace him as coach.**

**Undefeated Manager**

ONLY A FEW NIGHTS LATER Manager Skeeter Newsome was thumbed from a game and Zientara took over for Skeeter who was fuming in the clubhouse. And only minutes later Ben made a really important decision. Though it was early in the game, Ben chose to pull the starting pitcher and put himself in to bat with three runners on base and two outs.

He promptly belted a safe blow that scored two runners and put the Chiefs back into the ball game. They went on to win and his Chief teammates toasted him as the winningest manager in baseball. As a matter of fact, he is. Since that time he again replaced Newsome and the Chiefs came out on top, giving Ben a two and zero record as skipper.

The remarkable thing about Ben's ability to come out of the dugout or coaching box and step in and deliver all-important hits is that his coaching duties frequently make it impossible for him to get a chance to take any practice in the batting cage before the games.

BEN ZIENTARA

In spite of that, Ben has four hits in six pinch-hitting tries for a very respectable .800 average. On May 20 against Richmond Ben struck out batting for Jim Owens and the Chiefs lost, 3-1. On June 10, he singled in a pinch-hitting role and the Chiefs defeated Buffalo, 12-6. Against Richmond on June 25 he singled and Syracuse won, 6-5. Two days later against the same club he again singled and the game ended in a 2-2 deadlock.

On the second of this month he doubled to plate three runners and the Chiefs drubbed Buffalo, 10-3. The next day he walked as pinch-hitter and Buffalo won, 1-0.

Broken down as regular and pinch-hitter this is the way Ben has tormented clubs throughout the league. He's two for two against Buffalo; two for four against Richmond; six for 18 against Ottawa; zero for two against Montreal and zero for one against Havana. Ben hasn't played in games with Rochester and Toronto.

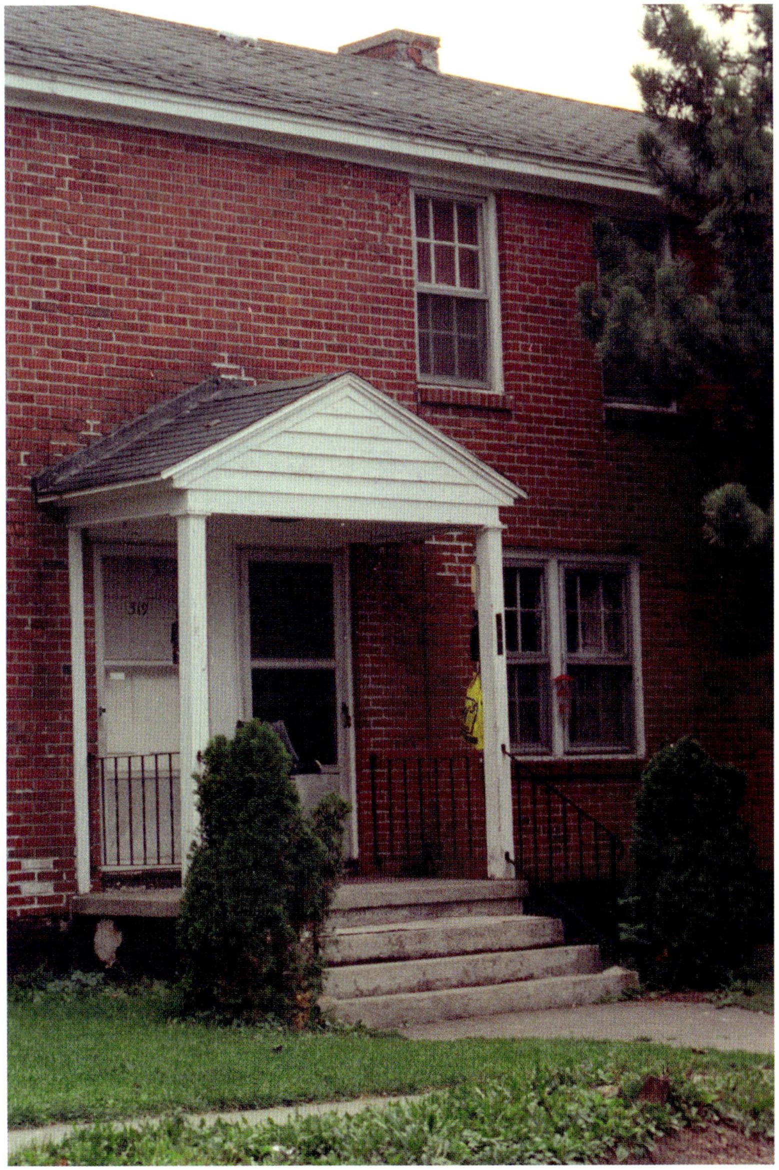

321 Kenwood Avenue

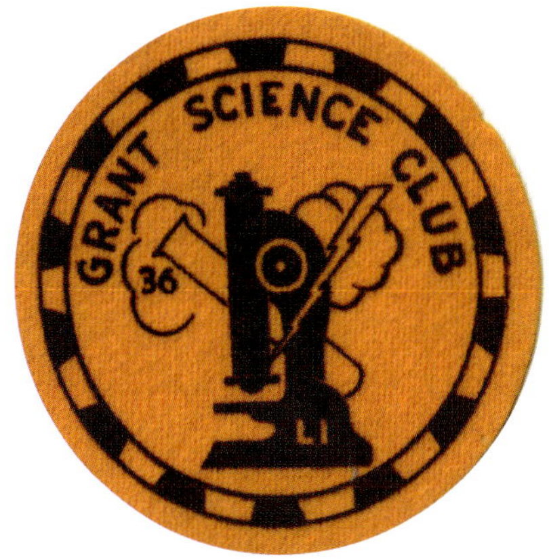


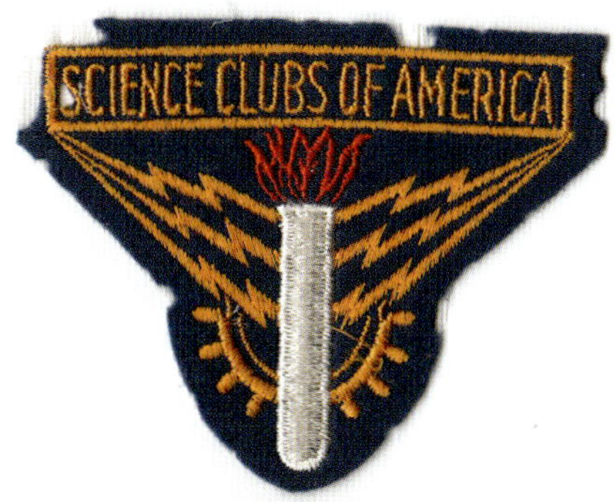


where I suspected some of the teachers took nastiness lessons. The kids were used to that; they were all Roman Catholics. I was not. I was also very naïve and knew nothing about the Catholic Church.

On the first day of school Miss Hanley, the homeroom teacher, announced that every Wednesday afternoon the school would shut down for something called "released education." This was a program where the students would be "released" to head off to the church of their choice for religious education. This was usually the church closest to their home. I listened as Miss Hanley read off the names of the churches that were part of the program, and there didn't seem to be anything with the name "Methodist" in it, so I opted for the next best thing: St. John the Baptist.

Later that day at dinner, probably after Harold had said grace, I told them I was going to be receiving religious education every Wednesday at St. John the Baptist. They suggested I would not be spending Wednesday afternoons in church, and with one telephone call from Harold to Mr. Renwick Peet (yes, that was the name of the principal in charge of the school), it was arranged that I would be allowed to sit by myself in Charles Gardner's science laboratory, probably because he may have been the only teacher on duty, or maybe he wasn't a Catholic. I was the only student in the school who didn't participate in the religious education program and was regarded as a leper or worse.

Of course this was good luck for me. Charles Gardner took a liking to me, gave me science books to read, and encouraged me to read them carefully and expand the little chemistry lab I'd set up in the basement of our apartment. He also suggested I get a project, develop it, and enter the Central New York State science contest. I didn't have a clue about such things or how to undertake a scientific project, but he wouldn't take no for answer. He said he'd help me and suggested I ask someone in my family to buy a red cabbage. Sarah was puzzled, but did as I asked, and from that point on I worked with various red cabbages for the next few months, entered the contest, and suitably terrified standing before an auditorium full of other students and teachers and a panel of judges, managed to make a coherent presentation and wound up coming in second place. The first, third, and fourth-place winners were high school seniors. There was even a picture of the winners in the paper and I look like a very young nerd.

Once again I was an outsider, but it made Harold and Sarah proud; they were so happy I was on the right track and was clearly not a moron. At the altar of St. John the Baptist maybe the wine turned into the blood of Christ, but in my experiments the cabbage juice turned bright red or green or blue depending on whether I put in vinegar or baking soda. So academics were working out.

By this time I had also won over the older kids in my class. By older I mean they were two or three years older than I was because they were far more adept at stealing hubcaps than opening a book and had been put back a couple of times. This is how it happened. In those years at the junior-high level there were no organized sports where one school played another, so those who wanted to play basketball would be organized into a handful of intramural teams. I loved basketball and wanted to play, but as a nerdy, studying-all-the-time, non-Catholic thirteen-year-old whose father could tell Renwick Peet what to do, I was never selected to play and warmed the bench game after game.

My team was on its way to winning the school championship, but the team fell apart in the last game, and we were getting thoroughly thumped. Then something funny happened. We got in foul trouble, and suddenly there was no one left to send in, so it was either send me in or play with a four-man team. So I came in, used all the skills I could remember from my basketball-for-real days in southern Indiana, and we won by a few points. I went from nerd to hero in a few minutes. No one wanted to beat me up in the locker room any longer. One guy offered me his younger sister as a prize; another tossed me a pack of cigarettes and said to keep it.

One of the older guys said he'd watch out for me, and maybe he did for a minute; a couple of years later his head was cut off in a gruesome automobile accident. Nobody was watching out for him that night. I was much too terrified to even consider the sister prize and I'd never smoked a cigarette, so the pack of Camels was useless to me. But it was fun not to get bullied any longer.

The point of all this is that with the new job, the better place to live, and the beginnings of some upward mobility, the thing that was probably the priority in the lives of both Harold and Sarah was me. It wasn't that I might have a better lifestyle when I was their age, but that I seemed to be turning out okay. I could throw a ball through a hoop under pressure, win a prize in a science contest, develop my own pictures in the basement, and if pressed, talk about chemistry or American history or even the McCarthy hearings that were all the rage about the time I was winning the science contest. In other words, there was some indication that I was on the right track and might grow up to be a sensible person who could find a job and be something of a success. That I would turn out okay was far more important to them than other trappings of the American Dream.

This little working-class neighborhood on the north side of town was just perfect for me. I could walk to the baseball games by myself, I could begin taking photographs and develop and print them in the basement, and I could do scientific experiments when not developing and printing pictures.

The big reveal occurred in the early summer. Harold and Sarah had hurriedly rented the apartment near the junior high school knowing I had to be enrolled in a few weeks, but a home, a real home that would be the culmination of a journey that had begun twenty-plus years earlier was another matter.

Harold had saved enough to make a down payment on a modest home, but it had to be right, and from their standpoint right meant it was in a school district that would enable me to go to the best high school in the city, and he knew which one that had to be. In 1954 that was William Nottingham High School, where over 90 percent of the graduates went on

## The Junior Science Contest

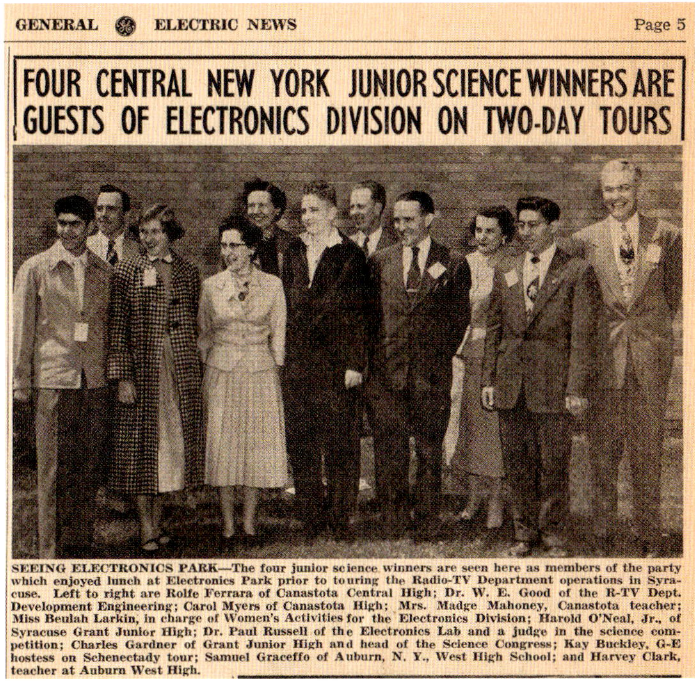

GENERAL ELECTRIC NEWS Page 5

# FOUR CENTRAL NEW YORK JUNIOR SCIENCE WINNERS ARE GUESTS OF ELECTRONICS DIVISION ON TWO-DAY TOURS

**SEEING ELECTRONICS PARK**—The four junior science winners are seen here as members of the party which enjoyed lunch at Electronics Park prior to touring the Radio-TV Department operations in Syracuse. Left to right are Rolfe Ferrara of Canastota Central High; Dr. W. E. Good of the R-TV Dept. Development Engineering; Carol Myers of Canastota High; Mrs. Madge Mahoney, Canastota teacher; Miss Beulah Larkin, in charge of Women's Activities for the Electronics Division; Harold O'Neal, Jr., of Syracuse Grant Junior High; Dr. Paul Russell of the Electronics Lab and a judge in the science competition; Charles Gardner of Grant Junior High and head of the Science Congress; Kay Buckley, G-E hostess on Schenectady tour; Samuel Graceffo of Auburn, N. Y., West High School; and Harvey Clark, teacher at Auburn West High.

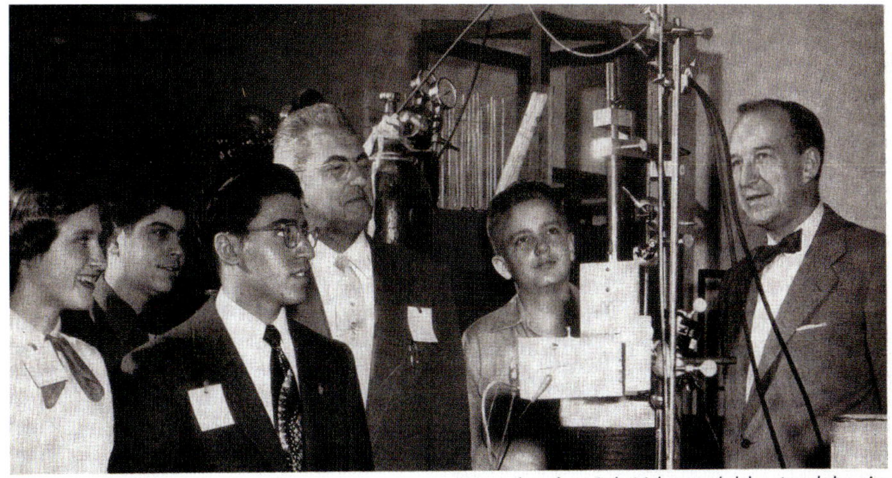

A tour through an industrial research laboratory helps give these young people first-hand knowledge of modern industry.

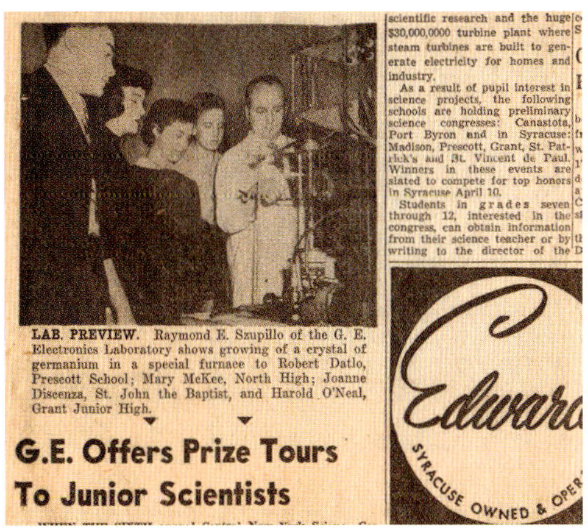

**LAB. PREVIEW.** Raymond E. Szupillo of the G. E. Electronics Laboratory shows growing of a crystal of germanium in a special furnace to Robert Datlo, Prescott School; Mary McKee, North High; Joanne Discenza, St. John the Baptist, and Harold O'Neal, Grant Junior High.

### G.E. Offers Prize Tours To Junior Scientists

scientific research and the huge $30,000,0000 turbine plant where steam turbines are built to generate electricity for homes and industry.

As a result of pupil interest in science projects, the following schools are holding preliminary science congresses: Canastota, Port Byron and in Syracuse: Madison, Prescott, Grant, St. Patrick's and St. Vincent de Paul. Winners in these events are slated to compete for top honors in Syracuse April 10.

Students in grades seven through 12, interested in the congress, can obtain information from their science teacher or by writing to the director of the



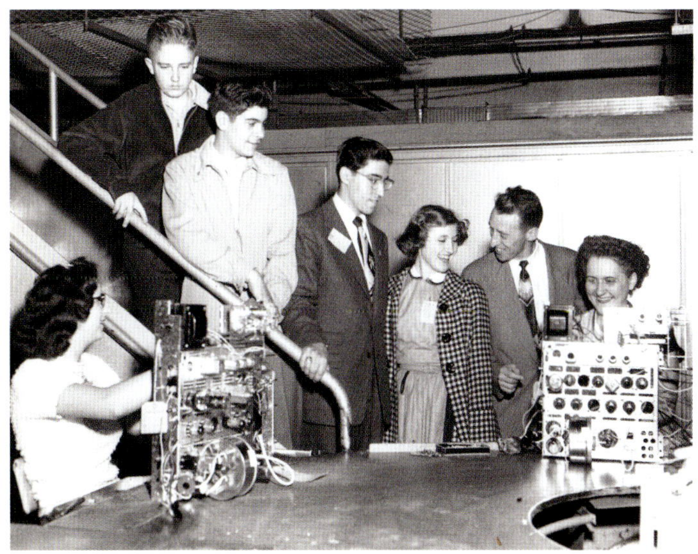

**MEMO**

**HAROLD L. O'NEAL**

**Date** Feb. 27, 1954

**To** Mom

**Subject** Chemicals

$.30 worth of Hydrochloric acid, either 90cc's 35% U.S.P. or 270cc's 10% U.S.P.

$.16 1 quart of ammonia

$.46

Balance $1.10
Bought .46
Balance $.64
35
29

over →

$.30 There is a large bottol of a chemical right above the center at the end the closist to the door. I don't know what it is but it is a phosphate. they have a small bottol. If it does not cost over $.30, buy it.

$.26 Red and Blue litmus paper

$.9 Small bottle of Iodine

$1.11

## Halloween playmates

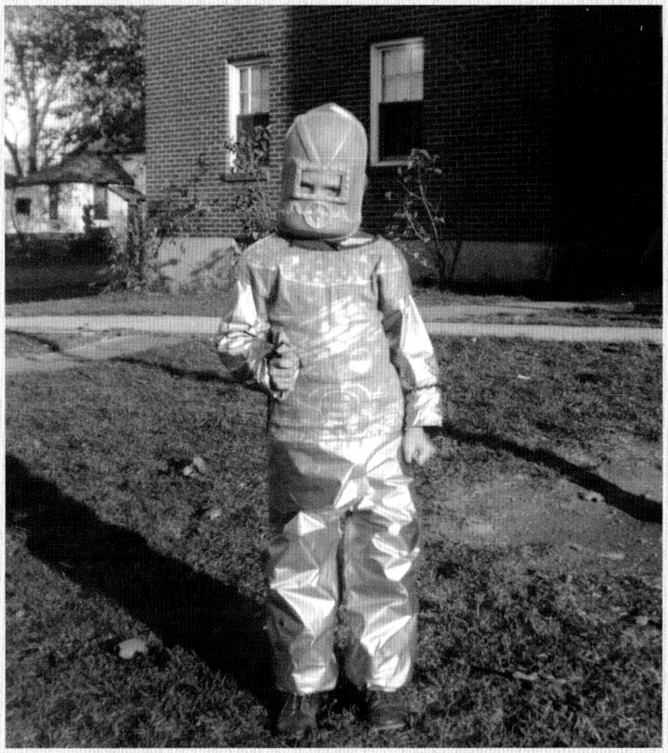

Little Space Boy

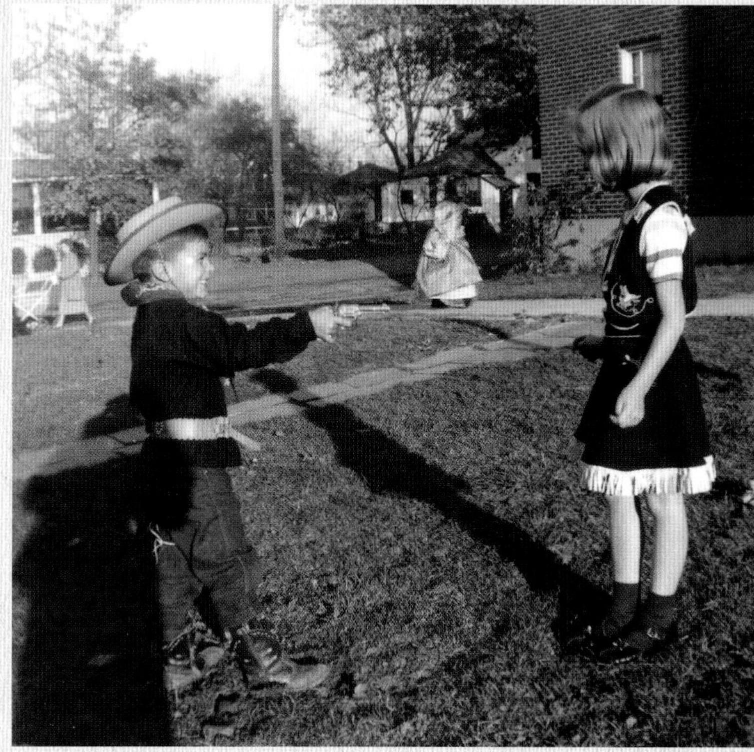

Cowboy and cowgirl

## The Syracuse Chiefs

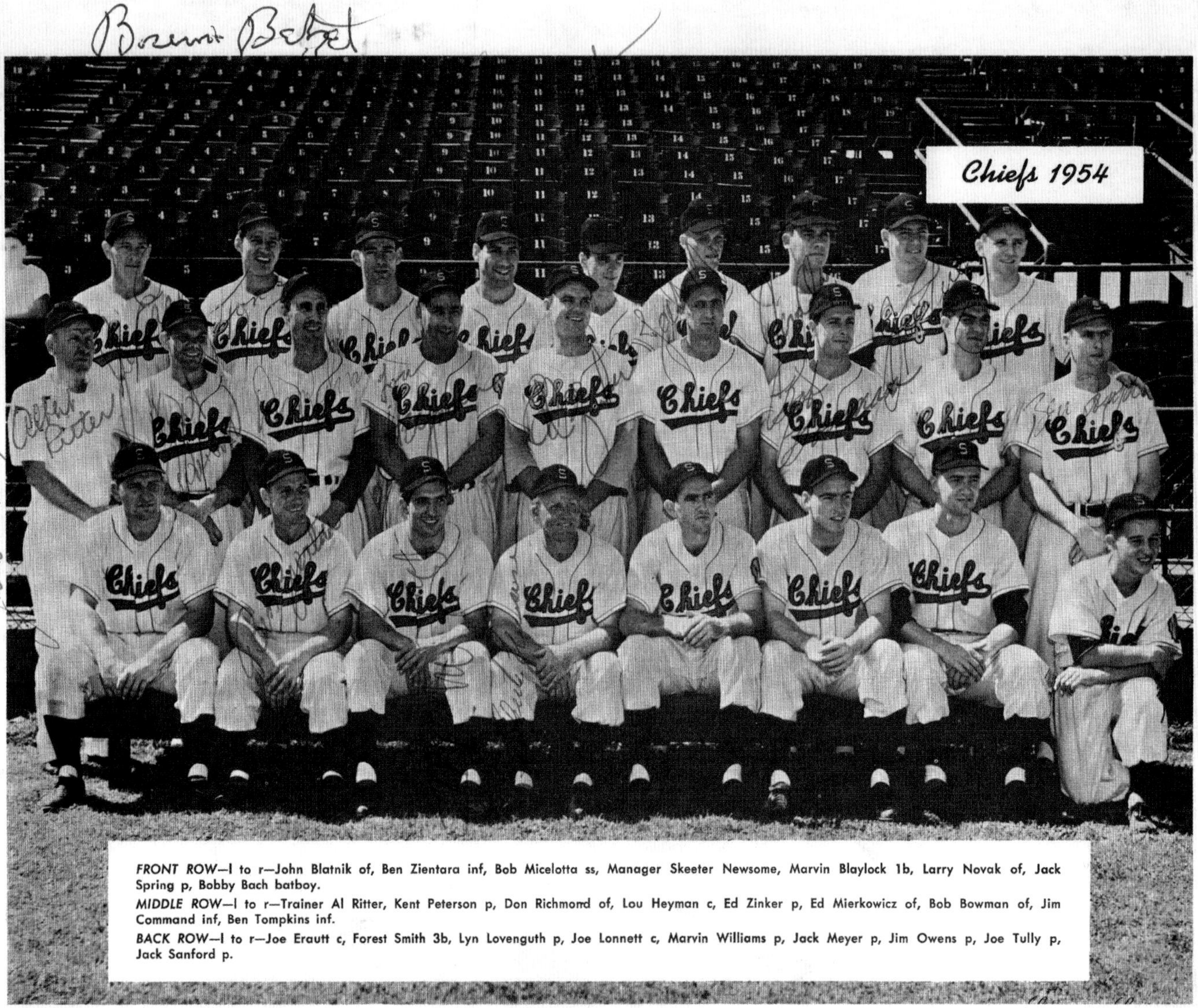


*FRONT ROW*—l to r—John Blatnik of, Ben Zientara inf, Bob Micelotta ss, Manager Skeeter Newsome, Marvin Blaylock 1b, Larry Novak of, Jack Spring p, Bobby Bach batboy.

*MIDDLE ROW*—l to r—Trainer Al Ritter, Kent Peterson p, Don Richmond of, Lou Heyman c, Ed Zinker p, Ed Mierkowicz of, Bob Bowman of, Jim Command inf, Ben Tompkins inf.

*BACK ROW*—l to r—Joe Erautt c, Forest Smith 3b, Lyn Lovenguth p, Joe Lonnett c, Marvin Williams p, Jack Meyer p, Jim Owens p, Joe Tully p, Jack Sanford p.

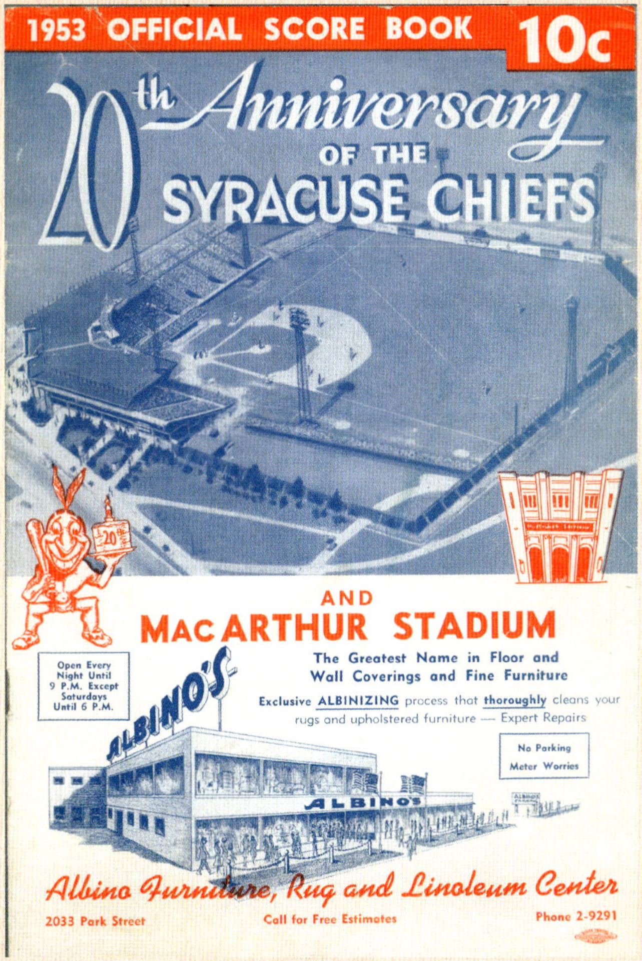


Grant Junior High School

wishes to inform you that

Harold O'Neal

has for the term ending

June 1954

attained the Scholastic Requirements

necessary for recognition as a

High Honor Student

H. Renwick Peet

PRINCIPAL

to the college of their choice. And so in the summer of 1954, Harold signed the paperwork and paid nearly $18,000 to secure a two-story 1920s home at 219 Kensington Road. It was within walking distance to the high school (fifteen blocks); Erwin Methodist Church (four blocks), where we rarely missed a Sunday for four years; Syracuse University (eight blocks), where I would have summer jobs and go to football games; Thornton Park (six blocks), where I'd play my baseball games once I made the high school team; and even the local picture show on Westcott Street (eight blocks). There was a small neighborhood grocery, a drugstore (with a five-seat soda fountain), a barbershop across the street, and a cleaner that finally burned down destroying my tacky striped blazer. All a minute away.

In Sarah's scrapbook from the 1930s there was a poem she'd saved entitled *Prayer For a Bride's House* by Christie Lund. The last lines read: *And this is her first house—what what 'er you do Let everything about it, Lord be . . . new.* The house wasn't new, but it was in a nice neighborhood, had its own driveway, a parking place out back, and a garage across the street; two enormous one-hundred-year-old elm trees that offered shade; a screened-in porch, kitchen, separate living, dining, and breakfast rooms downstairs; three bedrooms and a bath upstairs; a full basement that would soon have a washing machine and would eventually be partially finished with a recreation room on one side and a chemistry lab-darkroom on the other, as well as a bank of grow lights so Harold could culture African violets and other flowers from seed that would be transplanted to the backyard as soon as the ground thawed.

Harold and Sarah were more or less a couple of feet from the finish line. There would be other milestones and achievements along the way: promotions and educational accolades for Harold; more social activities for Sarah; no financial distress because their goals had always been modest; decent health for at least a decade, which was remarkable considering the starting point for Harold; creature comforts as they were needed; golf every so often in the summer, and yes, Harold had a hole in one which was celebrated in the newspaper and later turned into a remarkable plaque by a master woodworker named Giuseppe Eduardo Filipelli, better know to jazz fans as Flip Phillips.

The house on Kensington Road was not Mr. Blanding's Dream House, nor was it even close to most of the plans Sarah had sketched and Harold had finished in the 1930s, but it was a lovely home, one they could afford. It wasn't a starter home; Harold and Sarah were not a starter husband and wife. The house was it, as were they. Almost all of their dreams were in place. Only one remained: me.

In time there was a new car, a black and white four-door 1955 Oldsmobile; a new television (still black and white, just like the Oldsmobile); a small record player in a suitcase that arrived as a Christmas

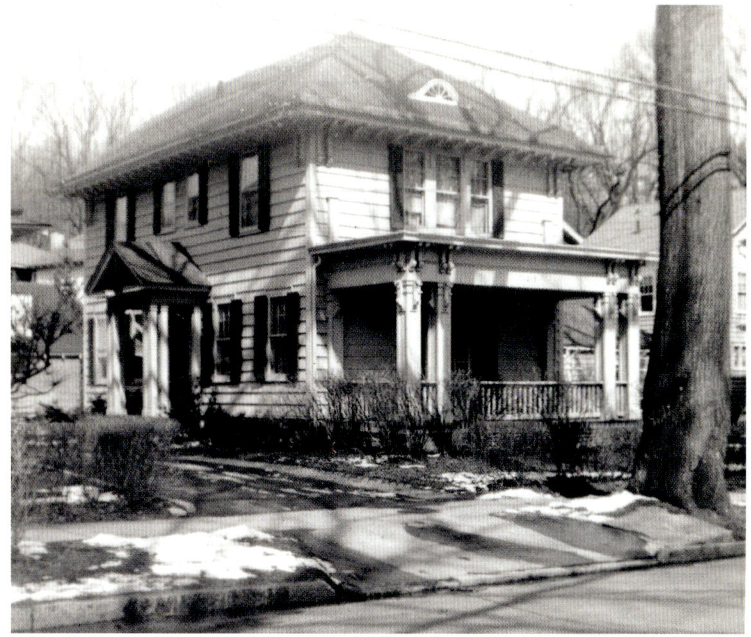

219 Kensington Road

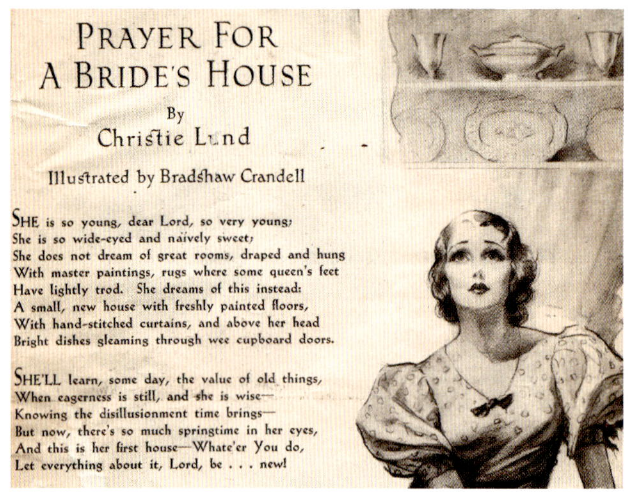

PRAYER FOR
A BRIDE'S HOUSE

By
Christie Lund

Illustrated by Bradshaw Crandell

SHE is so young, dear Lord, so very young;
She is so wide-eyed and naïvely sweet;
She does not dream of great rooms, draped and hung
With master paintings, rugs where some queen's feet
Have lightly trod. She dreams of this instead:
A small, new house with freshly painted floors,
With hand-stitched curtains, and above her head
Bright dishes gleaming through wee cupboard doors.

SHE'LL learn, some day, the value of old things,
When eagerness is still, and she is wise—
Knowing the disillusionment time brings—
But now, there's so much springtime in her eyes,
And this is her first house—Whate'er You do,
Let everything about it, Lord, be . . . new!

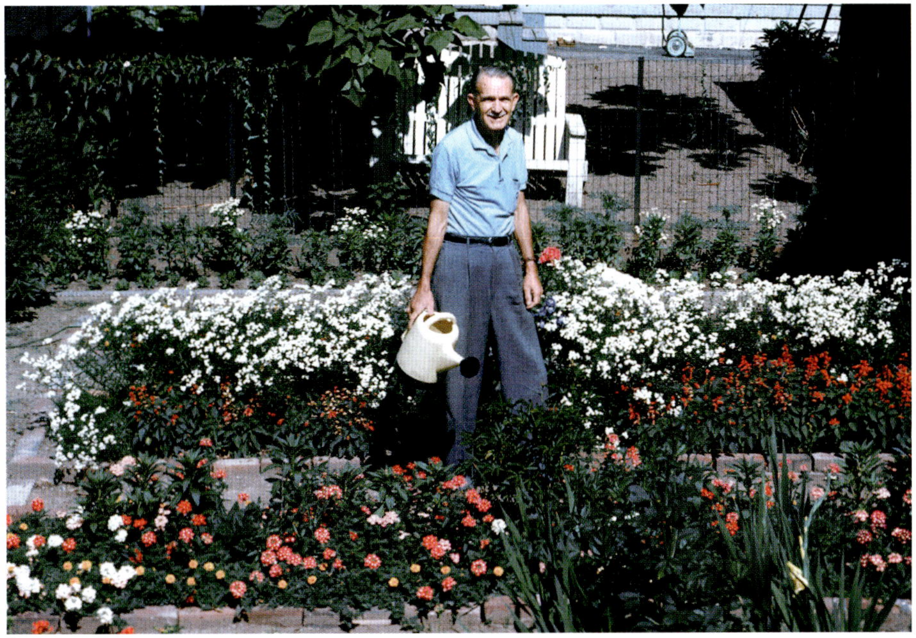

Harold's backyard garden

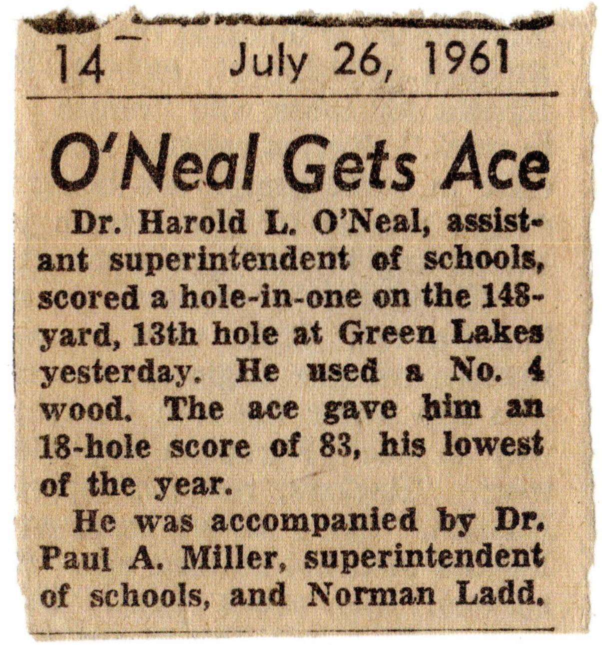

14 July 26, 1961

**O'Neal Gets Ace**

**Dr. Harold L. O'Neal, assistant superintendent of schools, scored a hole-in-one on the 148-yard, 13th hole at Green Lakes yesterday. He used a No. 4 wood. The ace gave him an 18-hole score of 83, his lowest of the year.**

**He was accompanied by Dr. Paul A. Miller, superintendent of schools, and Norman Ladd.**

present in 1954, along with two 45 rpm plastic records, the first of a 100,000 or more plastic records that would follow; new pictures for the walls, watercolors and prints; gardens full of flowers; a basketball goal in the backyard; hedges that needed to be trimmed; nice neighbors, including a mysterious man who lived across the street who rarely mingled with anyone, not because he was aloof but only because his English wasn't so good. He was Polish, and rumor had it he was famous and indeed he was, having served as the Minister Plenipotentiary for the Polish Government in exile in London during World War II. W. W. Kulski would later become one of my favorite instructors at Syracuse University.

There was time to be together, but only when it didn't intrude. In my high school years Harold and Sarah never pushed me to do anything but study; they didn't have to, because study came naturally. They never attended one of my high school baseball games, and I played for three years. Harold did get out his now rarely used Speed Graphic camera to take a picture of me with a few friends on a pick-up church league basketball team; his camera days were long over, but even if they hadn't been, he would have never interfered.

On occasion we'd toss a baseball back and forth in the driveway so I could show off a new pitch; he'd been a catcher in his youth, and managed to handle everything I threw at him and make suggestions. Harold and Sarah felt my extra-curricular activities, particularly in the sports department, were my own business, and I played almost every sport available except football, from volleyball to handball to bowling. Harold was a golfer, but when I went out with my friends to try this peculiar sport, he never suggested joining in. My friends and I could have probably used some tips, but in golf, as everything else, they never showed up to encourage

## Harold on the job

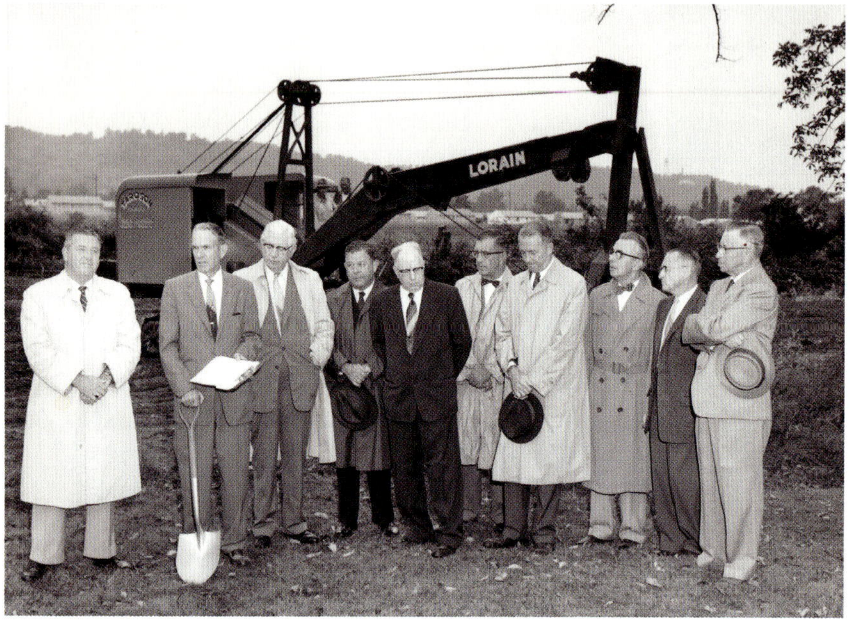


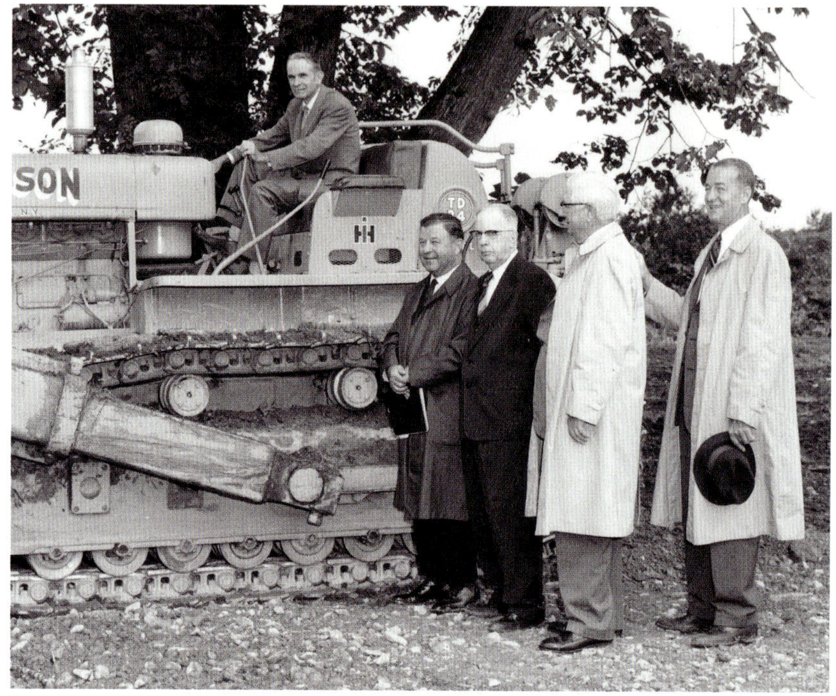


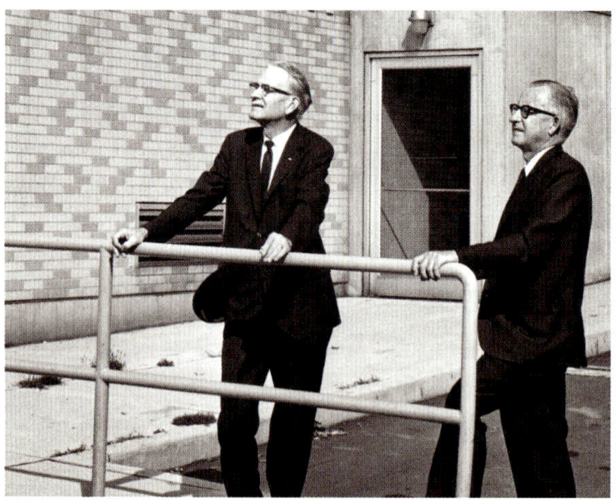

### Dr. O'Neal Promoted In Syracuse Schools

Dr. Harold O'Neal, who received his Ed.D. from I.U. in 1953, was recently advanced to assistant superintendent of the Syracuse (N.Y.) public schools. He was formerly director of census studies and research work there.

While he was at I.U., Dr. O'Neal was assistant to Dr. Harold H. Church, director of the Division of Research and Field Services, in the School of Education.

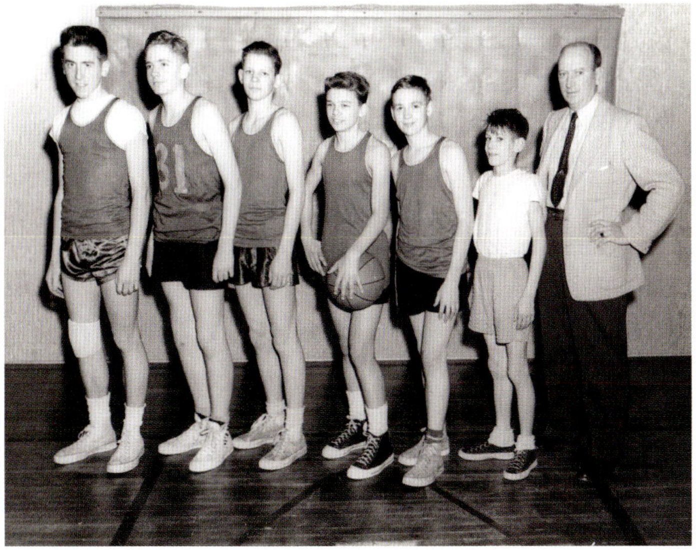


Erwin Methodist Church team (Harold's last Speed Graphic photograph)

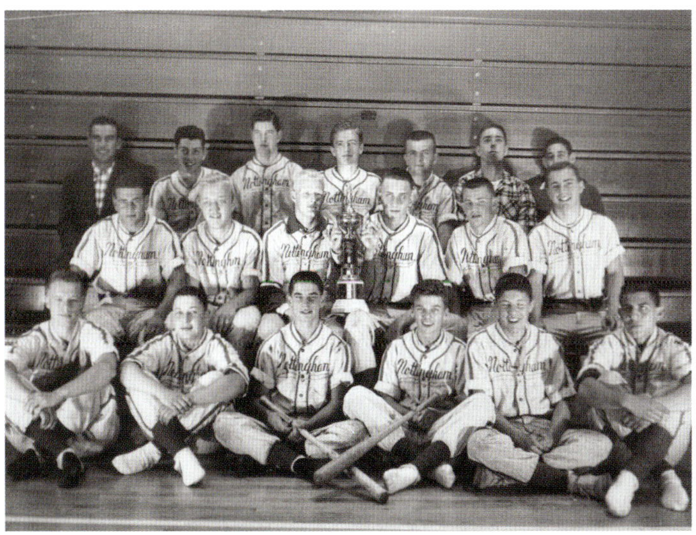

Syracuse city champions, 1956

INDIANA UNIVERSITY
BLOOMINGTON, INDIANA

March 9, 1955

Dr. Harold O'Neal
Board of Education
409 West Genesee Street
Syracuse, New York

Dear Harold:

We were very happy to learn that you can be with us this coming summer session. As I pointed out in my conversation with you, we can pay you $1500 for the summer session of eight weeks. Our summer session begins on June 15 and ends on August 12. I was glad to have the preferences of the courses you would like to teach this summer, and I shall do my best to assign you to those courses.

You will receive official confirmation of your appointment about May 1, 1955.

We all look forward to having you with us this summer.

With kindest personal regards, I remain,

Sincerely yours,

Howard

Howard T. Batchelder
Assistant Dean

HTB:rfm

me. Just like the studying, they knew they didn't have to.

There was even time for a summer in Indiana in 1955, when Harold was invited to return to Indiana University and act as a visiting professor. We returned to the "new" Hoosier Courts for a month; the big green field was still there and just as beautiful and inviting, but almost all of my old friends from two years earlier were gone, and since we had only a month there was too little time to make new ones.

The following summer there was a trip to Texas to visit family and friends. Harold made certain to route the trip so we could cross the Mississippi River at Vicksburg. He wanted to show me the Civil War battlefield he remembered from the 1930s. I had my Brownie Hawkeye camera with me, and I had no idea why he asked to stand on an old cannon for a quick snapshot. Not too long ago I found the picture of him on the same cannon, and now I do. It was part of the dream.

And so time passed for all of us. Four years of high school flew by without incident. Harold was promoted regularly, and by the time he was asked to deliver the commencement address to the graduating seniors at William Nottingham High School in June 1958, he was the second ranking administrator in the Syracuse school system. To deliver the commencement address was a dream come true, and he was thrilled to have been asked. He worked hard on it and made the most of the occasion, finding ample time to poke fun at my classmates and myself but also to put forth the principles that had guided him in his life up to that point, principles he and Sarah had tried to instill in me, principles he hoped had been installed in my classmates. These values, as much as anything else, are the main reason the dreams came true for Harold and Sarah.

He got into the meat of the speech after a few minutes of gentle ribbing, which seemed like an hour to me, but I realized it was far better to have a gentle ribbing in the high school auditorium than to be the one kid who didn't go to "released education" because my father had called the principal and said I was excused.

Harold concluded his remarks with these words:

*Now, for the few moments I have at my disposal, I want to speak most seriously to you young graduates in terms of ideal and basic values, which we, your parents, hold most dear in our everyday way of living. You see . . . ideals guide and control the institutional structure of our democratic society, and if you are in accord with our manner of living, you are then duty bound to become familiar with the basic concepts. Moral and spiritual values determine the regard men have for one another, the terms upon which they meet and mingle in their daily lives, the freedoms they demand and the restraints they are willing to impose and accept. On the other hand, attitudes and dispositions, customs and habits, the whole web of interpersonal relations . . . all these are but expressions of the ideas men live by. As our society becomes more complex, it relies less on the mores and customs and*

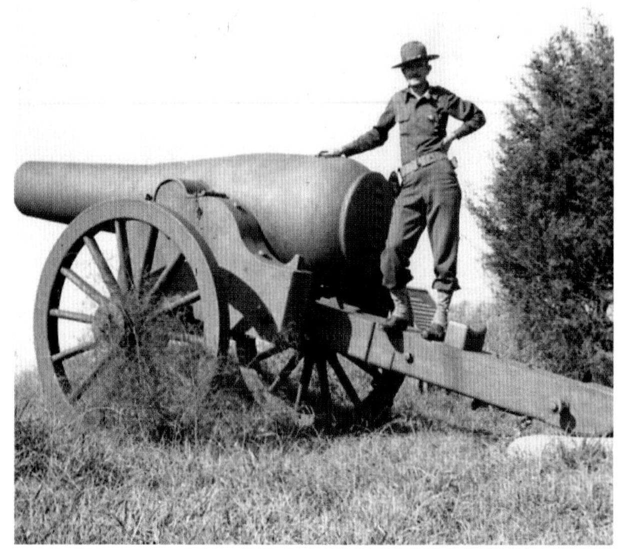

Vicksburg, 1942

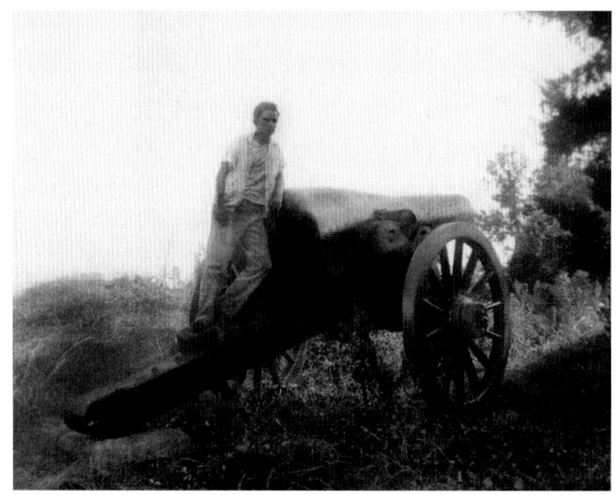

Vicksburg, 1956

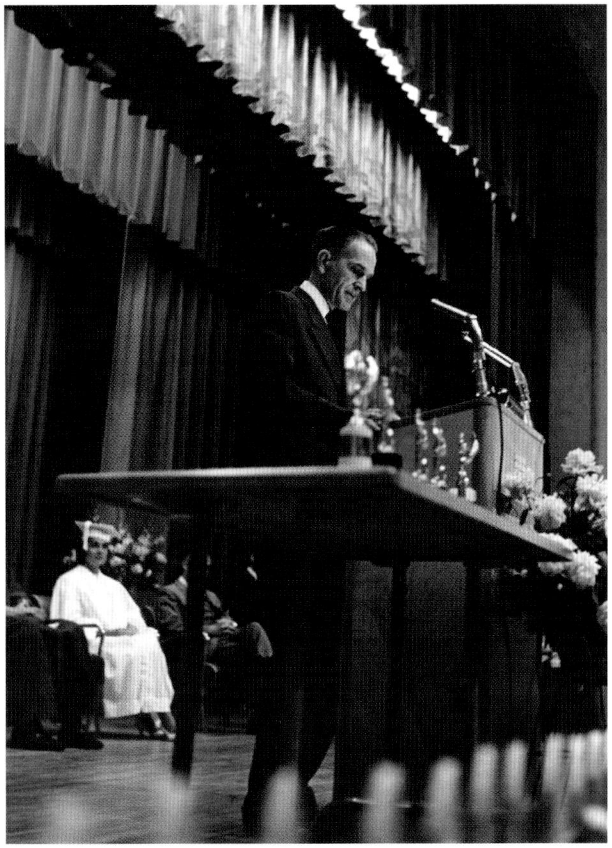

Delivering Commencement Address, June 1958

Commencement Address

Nottingham High School - June, 1958

I am both pleased and honored to be your speaker this evening, because I, too, have a personal interest in Nottingham's class of 1958. For the past four years, I have unobtrusively observed and kept up with this particular class, as my son is one of its members.

*more on an ordered pattern of social institutions. Family and community, church and state, and cultural and economic institutions become the carriers of value premises and the means of putting them into practical operation. Let me emphasize most strongly the attitude of your parents on this point, which, in time you must determine for your own well being. To us, social institutions are the servants, not the masters, of men. You must be able to make that distinction. Our democratic state makes no pretensions of being governed by some mystical law of its own being, of having a morality of its own defining, of possessing powers and prerogatives over the lives of men beyond their reach or control. In our democratic state, government is but the expression of the general will, in our United States, as proclaimed by the Declaration of Independence, it was instituted among men to safeguard their inalienable rights, and to secure life, liberty and the pursuit of happiness. . . . you young ladies and gentlemen may consider that expression rather trite for the time being, but I assure you . . . with each additional year, it will become more and more meaningful.*

*What, then, makes this way of life so important to us, and, specifically, what are these ideals to which I have been referring? Numerically there are many . . . too many for this evening's discussion. . . . But speaking for your parents I would like to acquaint you with four very important ones:*

*First: We hold that men can be free.*

*With us, freedom is more than a word. We hold that within broad limits, everyone is free in his person. Not only free in terms of what you have learned in your citizenship class, but also in terms of intellect and of conscience. Tyranny over the mind and conscience of man is tyranny at its worst. We believe in the right of every person to seek the truth where he will; to form his own convictions and to convey them to whom he will; just so long as it does not conflict with the equal rights of others. These are among the rights and freedoms we cherish and defend as part of our democratic heritage.*

*Second: We hold that freedom under law is the essential condition of a free society.*

*One of the greatest achievements of our American democracy is a legal system by which the relationships of individuals to one another and to society can be and are determined according to established rule. You must learn to live within these rules. It is this government of laws and not of men that protects the individual citizens from the caprice and injustice of irresponsible rulers.*

*Third: We hold that the price of freedom is its responsible exercise.*

*Government is an instrument of positive policy, and its authority must be commensurate with the responsibility the people, by common consent, see fit to place upon it. The price of freedom, therefore, in our country, is its responsible exercise by its citizens in their interpersonal relations, in the voluntary groups and organizations they establish to attain common purposes, and in the powers and restraints they impose on the government over which they preside.*

<u>Fourth: We hold that men have the right to be different.</u>

*Our society requires loyalty to basic democratic ideals, but within the wide framework of loyalty, it respects individual differences. This deep respect for personality is but the recognition of fundamental characteristics of human beings. Every person is a unique self, and although he can be a cooperative member of a social unity, he can never wholly surrender himself to it, can never abrogate the prerogatives of self. There is always an Ark of the Covenant in the inner recesses of each human spirit. It is for these reasons that we insist on a free market of ideas, that we will not tolerate intolerance, not enforce a narrow and rigid conformity, that we insist upon the right of dissent, that we welcome diversity of cultural patterns, and that we encourage erratic genius, and are patient with the less gifted.*

*Finally, in conclusion, let me give you the text of the message I have tried to bring to you. It is a very simple statement and consists of only five words—"Only THE FREE MAY CHOOSE." I'm quite sure you will forget most of the things I've said this evening; however, if you could make it a point to remember just those five words, "ONLY THE FREE MAY CHOOSE," I have the feeling that all your mothers and fathers in this auditorium would express their satisfaction with Nottingham's graduating class of 1958.*

*In this dual capacity which I have tried to assume this evening, may I say that we are very proud of you, and that we love you very much. In behalf of the Syracuse Board of Education, the Nottingham faculty and family, and persons present, we wish you every success. . . . Thank you.*

These were noble sentiments, particularly the fourth point. This was, after all, 1958, when there was hardly universal approval for the free market of ideas, banishing intolerance, rejecting rigid conformity, championing the right of dissent, welcoming cultural diversity, and patience with and charity for the less gifted. Indeed, these ideals are not universally tolerated in some quarters in 2018.

But life was so much simpler in 1958, and by that graduation day in June we had risen in the world to a two-car family, not one for Sarah but one for me, a shiny red Volkswagen that cost $1,630, arrived from Germany in the wilds of a place called Brooklyn, and Harold and I took the train to New York and then a subway and then a bus to fetch it and drive it back home.

Of course, I'd already visited New York City, first with my parents in November 1957 and then on my own during Easter break in 1958, when six members of the baseball team convinced Pat Stark, our coach, we should be allowed to take the trip because we could practice every afternoon in Central Park. On that trip I visited Greenwich Village, was terrified; snuck into the Metropole, saw Gene Krupa and Bobby Hackett for a minute before I was caught and thrown out for being seventeen and looking like I was twelve; saw the original productions of *West Side Story* and *My Fair Lady* on successive nights and wasn't thrown out; and never set foot

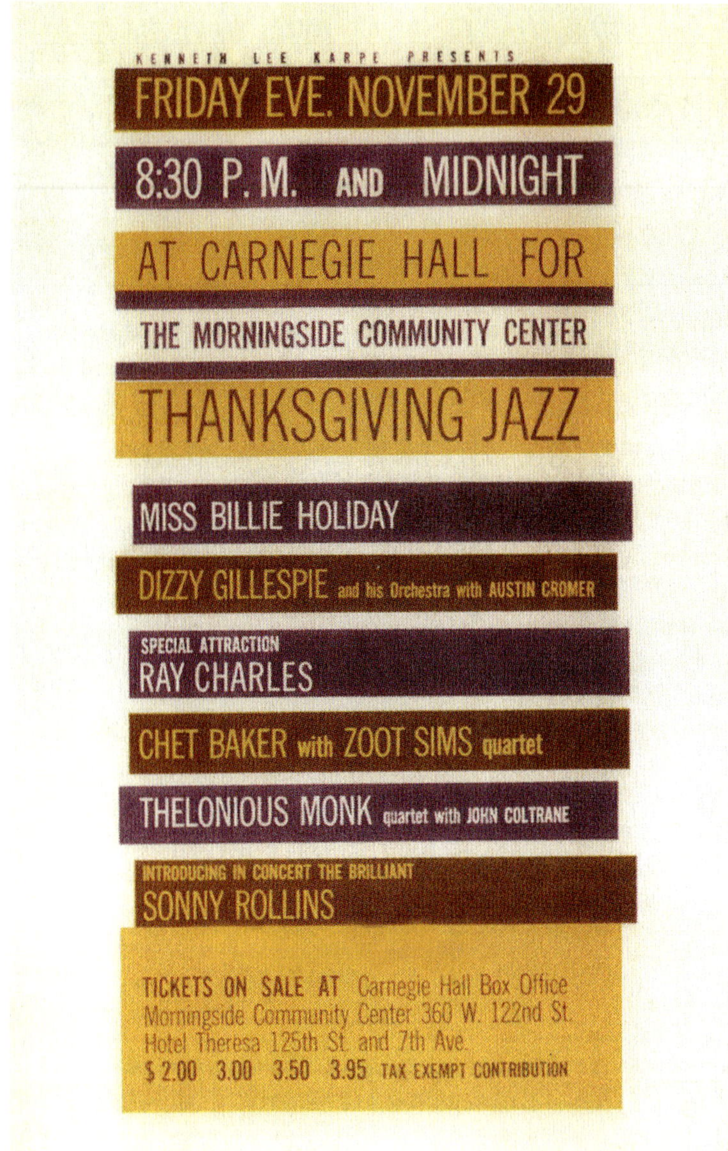


First jazz concert, 1957

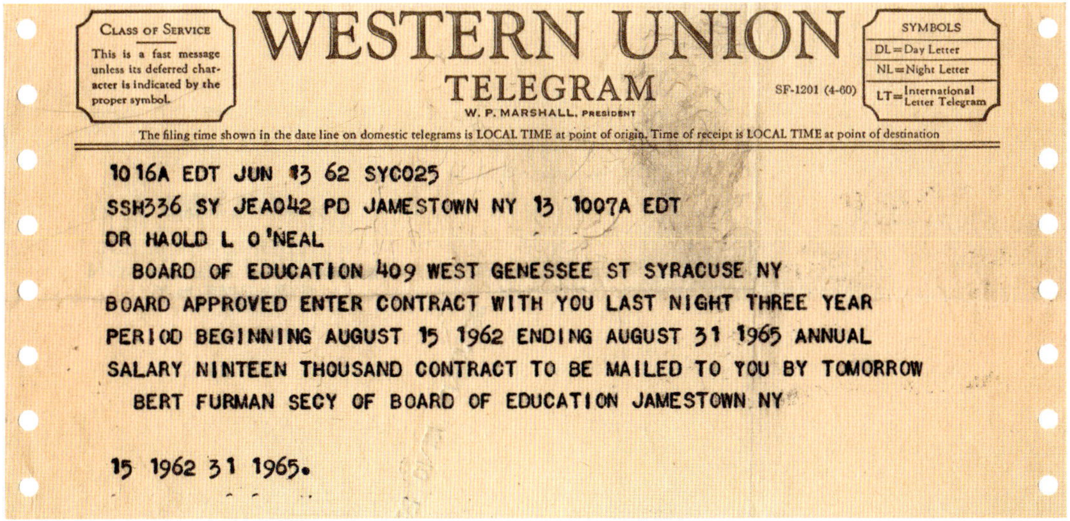

CLASS OF SERVICE
This is a fast message unless its deferred character is indicated by the proper symbol.

WESTERN UNION
TELEGRAM
W. P. MARSHALL, PRESIDENT

SF-1201 (4-60)

SYMBOLS
DL=Day Letter
NL=Night Letter
LT=International Letter Telegram

The filing time shown in the date line on domestic telegrams is LOCAL TIME at point of origin. Time of receipt is LOCAL TIME at point of destination

1016A EDT JUN 13 62 SYC025
SSH336 SY JEA042 PD JAMESTOWN NY 13 1007A EDT
DR HAOLD L O'NEAL
BOARD OF EDUCATION 409 WEST GENESSEE ST SYRACUSE NY
BOARD APPROVED ENTER CONTRACT WITH YOU LAST NIGHT THREE YEAR PERIOD BEGINNING AUGUST 15 1962 ENDING AUGUST 31 1965 ANNUAL SALARY NINTEEN THOUSAND CONTRACT TO BE MAILED TO YOU BY TOMORROW
BERT FURMAN SECY OF BOARD OF EDUCATION JAMESTOWN NY

15 1962 31 1965.

in Central Park. But those two trips were a precursor of things to come.

Harold and Sarah promised me a Thanksgiving trip to New York City if I met certain goals; I did and we went. The highlight was a concert at Carnegie Hall, my first in any concert hall anywhere, where I saw my idol, Dizzy Gillespie, with Billie Holiday along with the Carnegie debut of Ray Charles and Sonny Rollins, plus Thelonious Monk and John Coltrane together. Ten years later I would move to New York City, and nine years after my first terrifying visit to Greenwich Village I rented an apartment in the once-terrifying but now fascinating part of the city, and maintain an office-studio-apartment within half a mile of that first apartment to this day. Forty-eight years later, the John Coltrane portion of the concert was released on CD. I would be on radio and television talking about the concert, not because I am that much of an expert, but because they couldn't find anyone else who had actually been there on November 29, 1957.

**Epilogue**

Harold and Sarah were confident they'd done their job properly when, in the spring of 1958, I had been accepted to all six universities to which I had applied, and none were in Syracuse. The closest was 150 miles away, Rensselaer Polytechnic Institute, better known as RPI. MIT, Indiana University, Texas A&M, Clarkson, and Case were left in the lurch. I chose RPI because it was closest to home, and I could use my New York State scholarship. But it wasn't to be. I did poorly at RPI. I wasn't cut out to be an engineer no matter what the College Boards and my counselors had suggested, and I spent my final three years of college back home in Syracuse, sleeping in my old bedroom and walking to my classes. Harold and Sarah were confident they'd get some breathing room when I went off to RPI, but when I returned beaten to a pulp by too much advanced math and physics, they didn't complain.

I did well at Syracuse, was semi-recruited by the Central Intelligence Agency in 1960, and accepted full-time employment with them in 1962. In late December of that year Harold and Sarah and I loaded their Oldsmobile and my Volkswagen with everything we thought I might need to become a CIA Junior Officer Trainee and made our way to Washington, DC.

Harold and Sarah stuck around long enough to make sure I was settled into a one-room apartment from which I could easily commute to Langley, Virginia, to learn how to be a junior officer and launch a career in spying that would make them proud. They then headed north back to Jamestown, New York, where a few months earlier Harold had decided to close out his career in education as the Superintendent of Schools in this quiet town of 40,000.

He had seen two of his closest friends die of heart attacks in office, and he didn't want to join them on the obituary page. They had a new jewel-box of a house of a dozen gables, handmade by skilled woodworkers in the 1930s, set back from

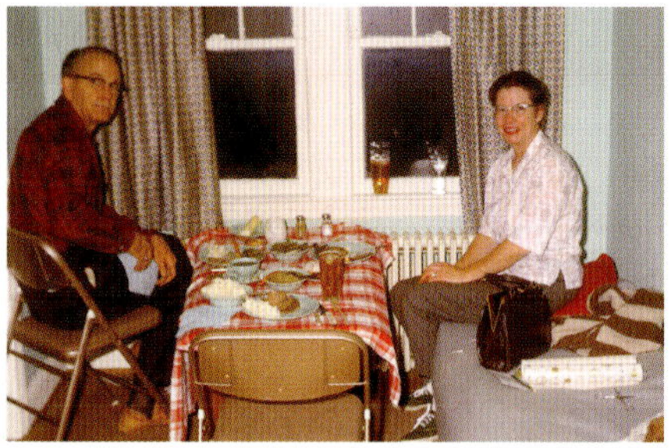

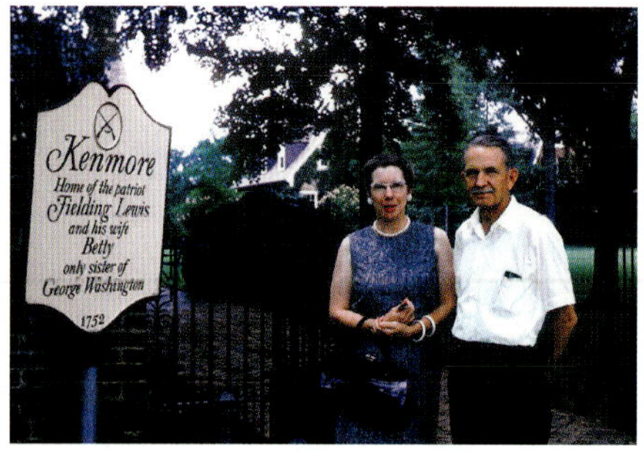


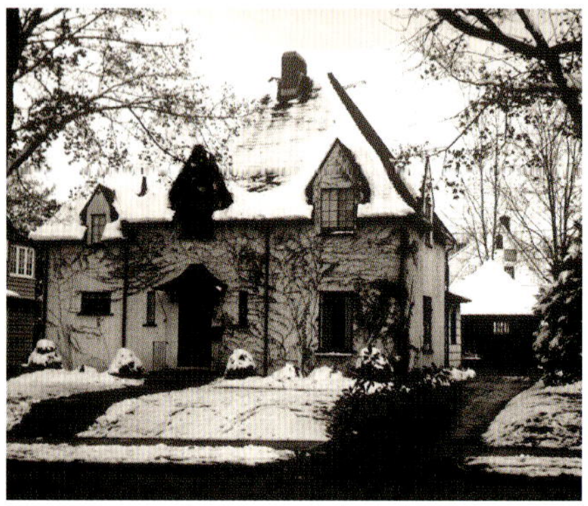

130 Arlington Avenue

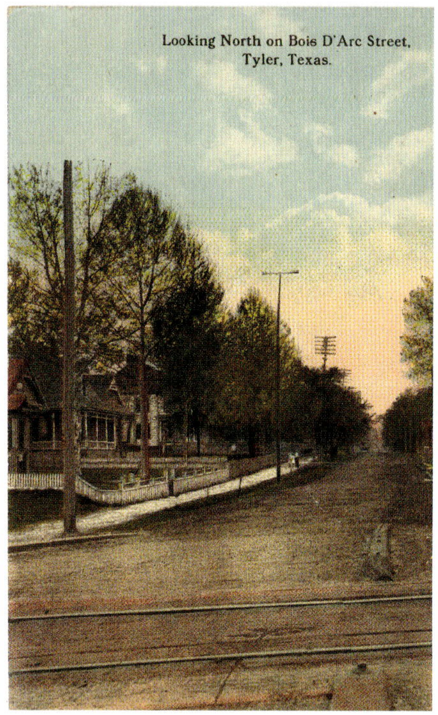


a red-brick residential street, and Sarah was intent on making it a perfect home. It was similar to one of the bungalows in her 1930s scrapbook.

They were looking forward to spending as many years as possible with one another now that all their youthful dreams had been realized and most obligations were behind them. Their goals, even though not formally set, had always been modest, goals that were achievable, and they achieved them. They had nearly six years alone together, and based on the stories they told me of their travels, vacations, and civic duties, they were wonderful years, fulfilling in every way. Their favorite escape was to drive leisurely and visit old and historic houses all over the country, usually in the south—Virginia, Georgia, along the Mississippi.

In August 1958 Harold and Sarah returned to East Texas for the first time in over a decade. It was an emotional going-home kind of trip, at least that's what Harold said when asked about it. As was his custom, he rarely volunteered personal things, but would talk about them if asked. In any event they drove into Tyler on an August afternoon. They'd probably passed through Winona, possibly had a quick look a what they'd first met in 1932, headed south on Highway 155, arrived in Tyler, made their way to Bois D'Arc Avenue and headed south, planning to see how the old family home at 508 South Bonner Avenue was holding up. They were a few blocks away when Sarah had a heart attack. Or was it?

Sarah had no history of heart trouble or any other dread diseases. She was never strong, took regular afternoon naps, and could not read for prolonged periods because her eyes were weak. She was not keen on physical exercise; did not jog, go to the gym, or take long walks. This was due to her upbringing: southern ladies of a certain era did not do that kind of thing.

Sarah was not a smoker or a drinker nor did she have other bad habits. But she was very emotional and a super romantic. It may be that all the pent-up emotions of returning after so many years, the thought of seeing strangers in the family home, the prospect of seeing old friends from the 1930s and 1940s were just too much. Lance and Alpha Verne, the two friends from the first double date in Winona thirty-six years earlier, were still very much

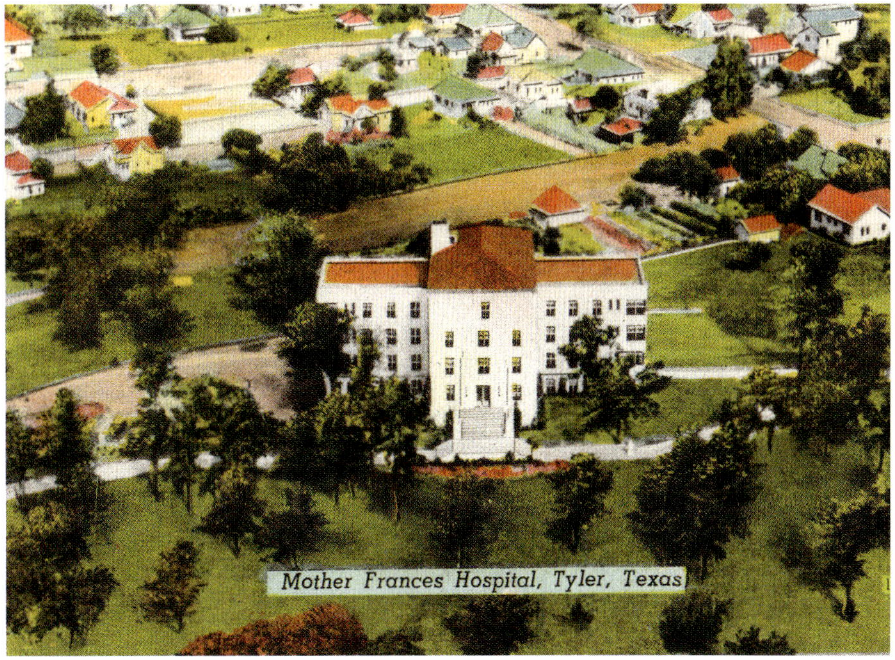


alive and probably on the must-visit list. And so all the stress hormones that were triggered by all this emotional turmoil which had probably been building day after day finally reached a climax of sorts, and these hormones weakened her heart sufficiently that the heart muscle became inoperative.

Sarah was rushed to Mother Francis Hospital, and the treating physician had probably never heard of Takotsubo Syndrome. The doctor in charge, J. Weldon Birdwell, treated it as an "ordinary" heart attack, did some tests, suggested a regimen of bed rest and return to Jamestown, where rest and a light schedule should continue. He also said that the "heart attack" was an anomaly, that she'd never have another because there was nothing wrong with her heart.

This is exactly what happened: a cautious return to upstate New York and rest. The dining room was converted into a bedroom so there would be no need for Sarah to climb stairs. All seemed well; she grew stronger and more confident, and even began to partake in her charitable work at the church and hospital. November 22 was Harold's birthday. He was fifty-eight, and they planned to celebrate it the next day, a Saturday.

On Saturday morning Sarah prepared

IN LOVING MEMORY

## Sarah O'Neal, 54, School Head's Wife Dies

Mrs. Sarah O'Neal, 54, of 130 Arlington Ave., died at 1 p.m. Saturday (Nov. 23, 1968) at W.C.A. Hospital. She was the wife of Dr. Harold L. O'Neal, superintendent of Jamestown Schools.

She was born in Tyler, Texas, Jan. 7, 1914, the daughter of Curtis A. and Beatrice Kelly Christian. She had resided in Jamestown since August, 1962, coming here from Syracuse.

Mrs. O'Neal was a member of the First United Methodist Church, and the W.S.C.S. and was a former member of the official board of the church.

She had been active in the work of the W.C.A. Hospital and other organizations prior to her illness.

Besides her husband, she is survived by a son, Harold L. O'Neal Jr., New York City; one sister, Mrs. Roy T. Will, Rock Hill, S.C.; five nieces, Sharon O'Neal, Dallas, Texas, Mrs. John Miller, Nacogdoches, Texas, Julia, Jenna and Lisa Will, Rock Hill, S.C.; two nephews, Louis Mack O'Neal, Henderson, Texas, and Chris Will, Rock Hill, S.C.

## Upsohi

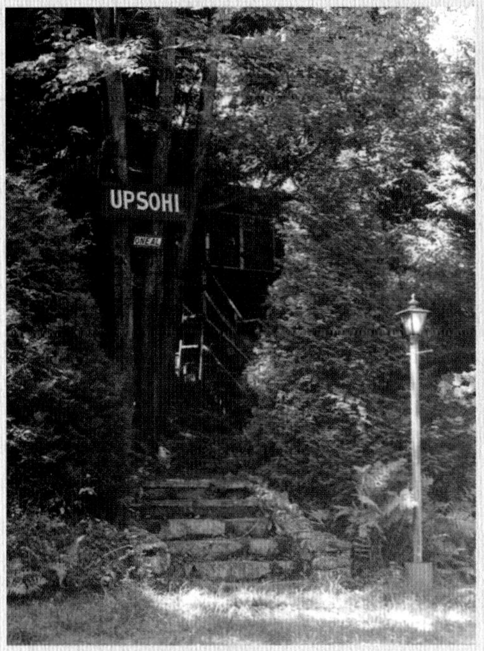
UPSOHI

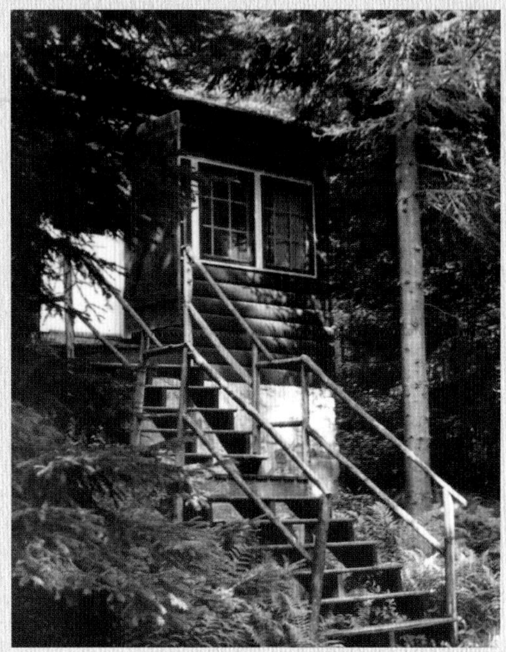

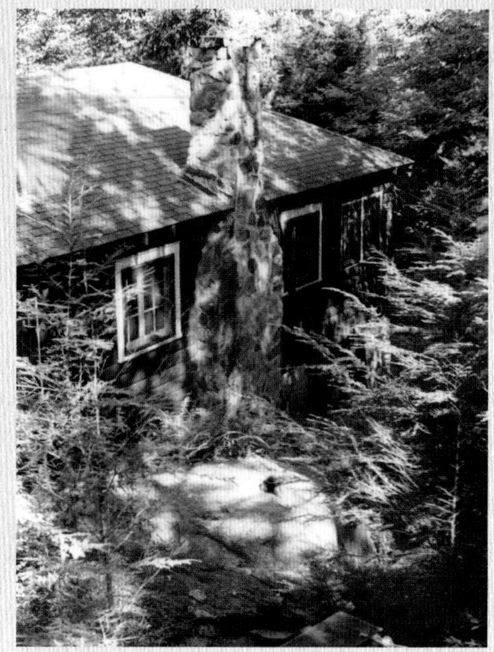

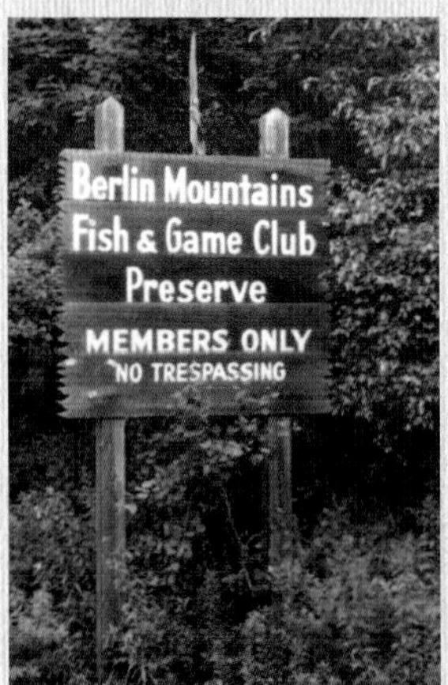
Berlin Mountains
Fish & Game Club
Preserve
MEMBERS ONLY
NO TRESPASSING

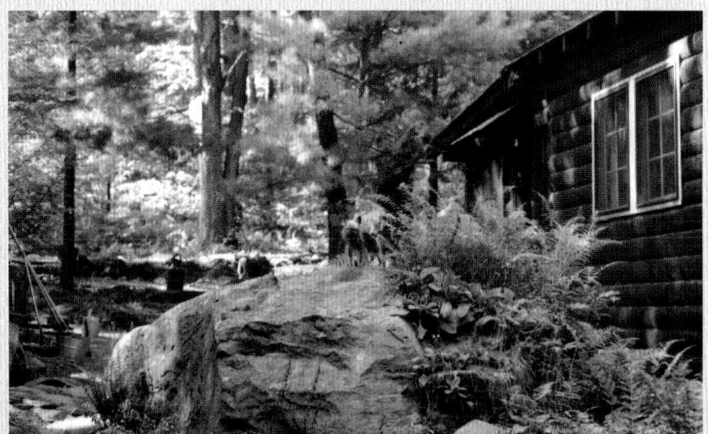

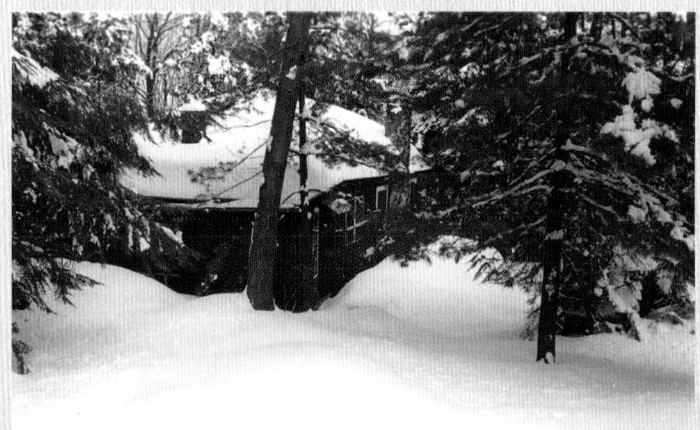

a grocery list; she planned to take the time to bake a one-day-late birthday cake. Harold went to the store for supplies and returned an hour or so later to find Sarah dead in her bed. The heart attack that was not supposed to happen had. She was fifty-four, and the dream died that day; Harold never fully recovered. But it is possible that the recipient of her eyes, if young enough, may still be seeing through them today.

I drove to Jamestown and arrived in time for the Tuesday funeral service at the First Methodist Church. Harold's brother Raymond and his wife, Evelyn, had come in from Dallas; Sarah's sister Martha had come in from North Carolina. This was the first time I'd seen them for many years. The church was filled with hundreds of people and thousands of flowers. I remember nothing about the service but vaguely recall a reception at the house of many gables on Arlington Avenue, where everyone seemed crowded into the kitchen in one corner of which, sitting on the floor, drink in hand, Harold's brother Raymond amused everyone with lighthearted stories that made the sad day somewhat better. I was happy to reconnect with Martha, a fascinating woman whom I stayed in touch with until she died thirty-five years later.

Harold remained in his position as school superintendent through the end of the school year in 1970, but troubled by the empty, possibly haunted house in Jamestown, took early retirement and spent the summer at a small lakeside cottage named Upsohi he'd purchased the year before. The cottage was in Sand Lake, near the top of Berlin Mountain in Rensselaer County, a quick train or car ride from New York City. His plan was to spend his summers in the cottage and move back into the family home in Tyler during the winter months.

He had already bought out the two tenants at 508 South Bonner Avenue and was thoroughly renovating it, hoping new cabinets, wallpaper and fixtures would keep memories of the 1930s at bay and keep whatever was left over from those days sealed carefully away in the tightly closed attic. Memories and the past were also stored in a small garage that was being cleared out and disassembled when I arrived to have my first look at his new home. I managed to rescue one old 1930s vintage baseball from the rubbish pile before the memories were dispatched to the city dump. But Harold, perhaps having had a premonition of *Scrapbooks*, had saved all the scrapbooks and important papers and photographs. I just didn't know it. I was also unaware that he'd purchased four plots in Tyler's Rose Hill cemetery, had a tombstone with the simple inscription O'NEAL carved into the white marble, and buried Sarah's ashes in Section I, Plot #111.

Harold undertook what was to be his final building project in the summer of 1970. He wanted to have his own woodworking shop, one that he could work in during the summer months and build furniture, picture frames, or whatever might come to mind. When he'd retired in Jamestown, he had been given a roomful of old and gently used powerful woodworking tools that had been used to keep the school system's furniture in good repair or to build new. Harold put the tools into storage until he built his woodshop at Upsohi. We worked on the woodshop together throughout the summer of 1970. I was amazed to see the building come together; Harold organized a lumber bill listing the materials he'd need to build the woodshop, but there never was a plan or drawings. He just built and told me what to do.

The woodshed came together before the end of the summer, and the plan was to load in the power tools from Jamestown the following summer.

In a letter dated January 12, 1971, Harold wrote about his new life back home in East Texas. He described fixing 508 South Bonner, visiting and spending holidays with his favorite cousins from the 1920s and 1930s, Maxine (Edwards), Rebecca and Elizabeth (Hays), girls he regarded as his sisters; his new rose bushes; the warm weather; a short description of how he'd get a fever if he overworked, clearly a precursor of the leukemia that would kill him in 1972; and the excitement of a trip to Mexico—one last look at Monterrey that he described like this:

*It could not have taken us 15 minutes to clear customs and we were Monterrey bound which is only 150 miles south of the border. We arrived there in early afternoon and checked in at the Gran Hotel Ancira*

Building an Upsohi workshop

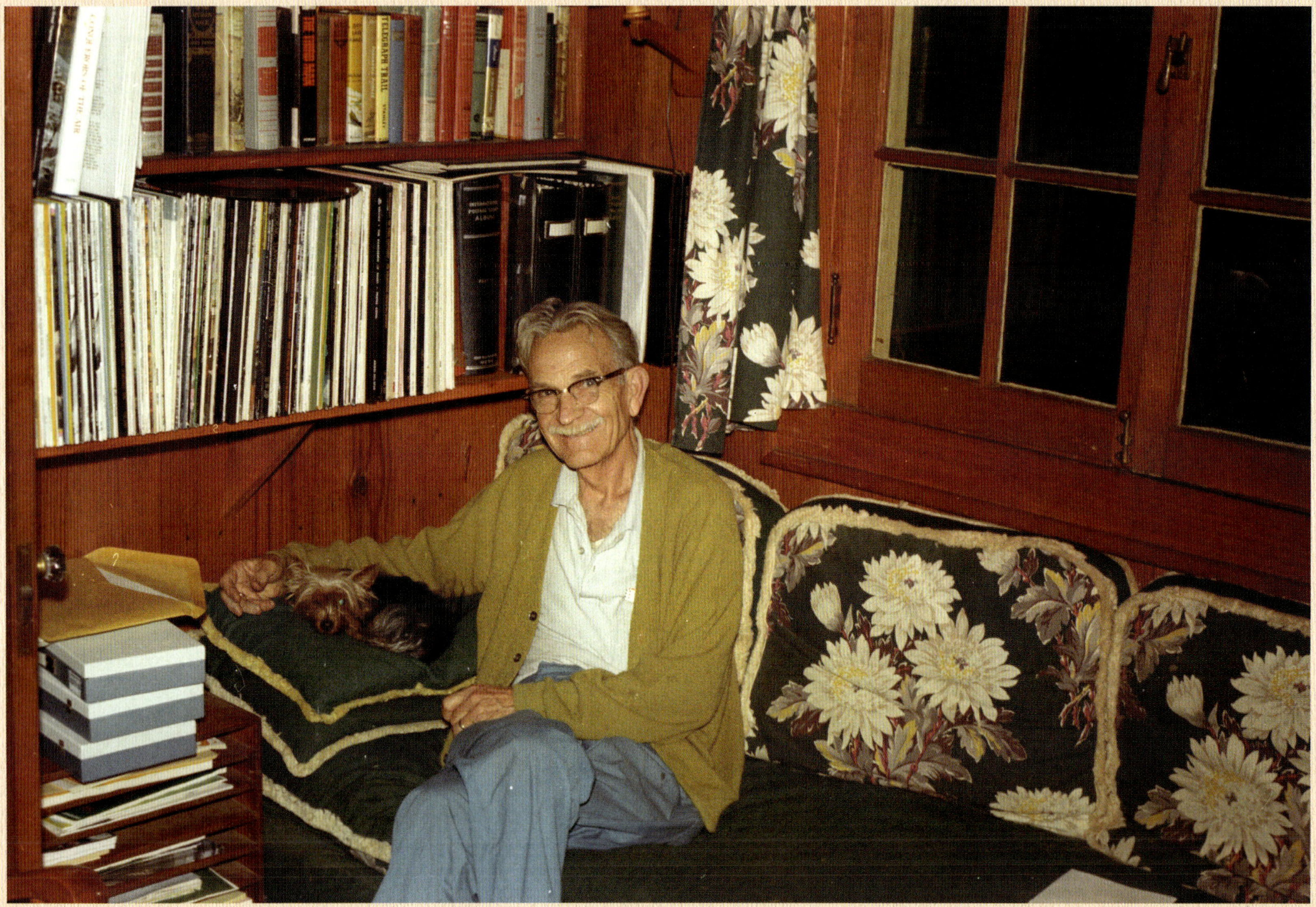

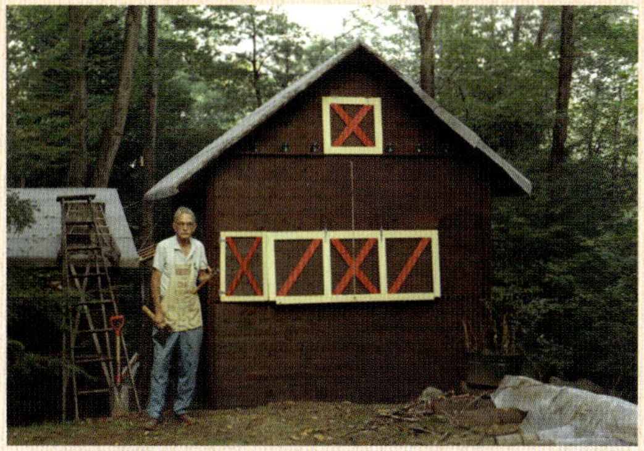

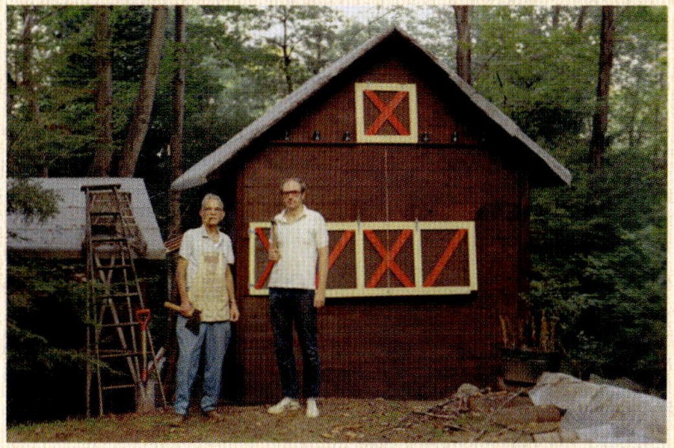

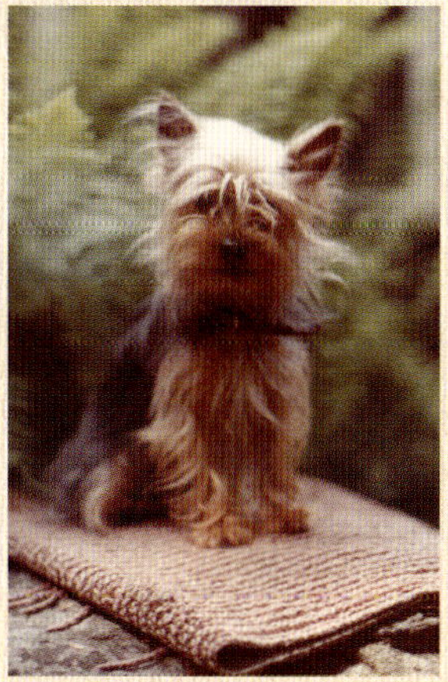

Tische

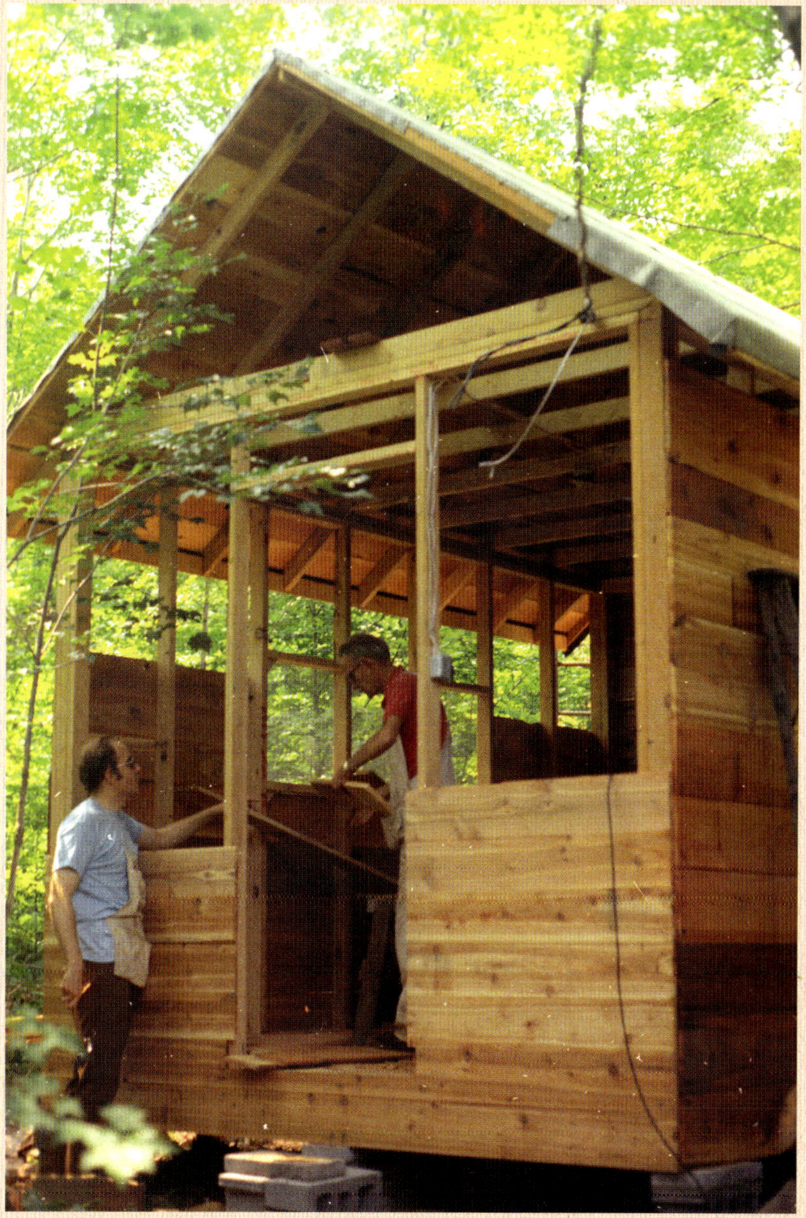

*which, in my opinion, is the best in the city. It was expensive but what the heck, I thought I'd give the kids a treat. The last of the big spenders spent $12.00 a night for our accommodations there. (Please note this was not $12.00 each but for all three of us.) Our stay at the Gran Ancira was the most delightful but I was disappointed in Monterrey. In the past Monterrey had been my favorite Mexican city. Prior to the war Sarah and I used to go there every summer up to 1939. That's 31 years ago and I remember the city as spotlessly clean with a population of 100,000. Now the population is over a million and it has become a huge industrial city. It is known as the Pittsburgh of Mexico. It's still very nice but it has grown by such leaps and bounds that it's very dirty, the traffic is something to behold, and the SMOG is so fierce from belching industrial factory smoke that you can hardly see the sun or the surrounding mountains before noon. The shopping was good. You could find anything in the world you wanted. We made quite a few purchases – some in the way of Christmas presents for each but thank goodness we didn't spend all our money there because we found goodies all over the country and we visited five states, Nuevo Leon, Coahuila, Durango, Sinaloa and Zacatecas before we were finished. . . .*

This turned out to be his last look in Mexico; he'd already said goodbye in Jamestown and Syracuse, and did the same in East Texas throughout the rest of the year. His January letter was mostly optimistic, but when Harold took early retirement it was clear he'd given up and was marking time. He began recording his fluctuations in temperature in a small notebook found in his papers; perhaps this could have been a clue if the right physician had been aware of it. He spent the summer at Upsohi, charting his fluctuations in body temperature throughout the summer and into the fall, but said nothing of it.

Upsohi was a summer cottage. It had a modest heating system, but the water had to be turned off in the early fall, because by mid to late October there were always a few freezing nights, so the water would freeze and the pipes could burst. The cottage was normally closed the first week in October, but he stayed two weeks longer that year and then returned to Tyler, but not before he'd worked a bit too hard, one day too often, closing up the cabin. His temperature began to track a little higher; he caught a cold and was increasingly weak by the time he reached Tyler. Harold contacted Dr. J. Weldon Birdwell, who

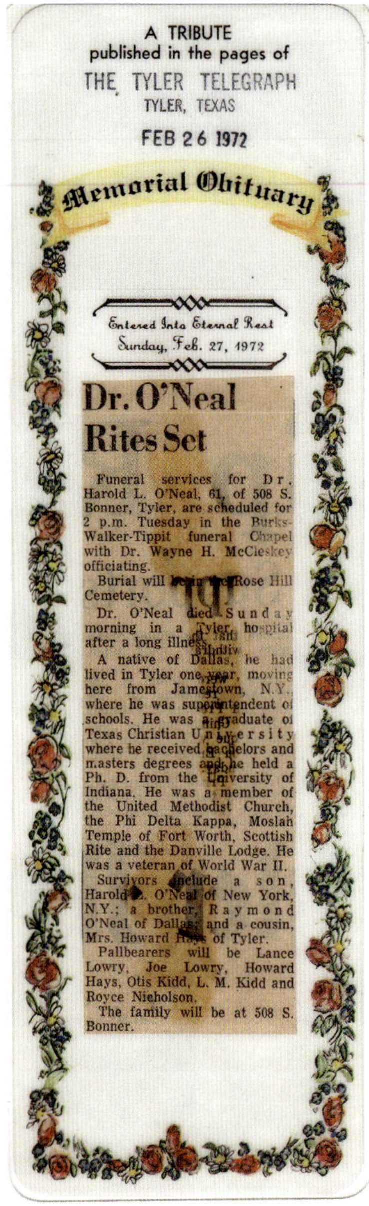
A TRIBUTE
published in the pages of
THE TYLER TELEGRAPH
TYLER, TEXAS
FEB 26 1972

Memorial Obituary

Entered Into Eternal Rest
Sunday, Feb. 27, 1972

**Dr. O'Neal Rites Set**

Funeral services for Dr. Harold L. O'Neal, 61, of 508 S. Bonner, Tyler, are scheduled for 2 p.m. Tuesday in the Burks-Walker-Tippit funeral Chapel with Dr. Wayne H. McCleskey officiating.

Burial will [illegible] Rose Hill Cemetery.

Dr. O'Neal died Sunday morning in a Tyler hospital after a long illness.

A native of Dallas, he had lived in Tyler one year, moving here from Jamestown, N.Y., where he was superintendent of schools. He was a graduate of Texas Christian University where he received bachelors and masters degrees and he held a Ph. D. from the University of Indiana. He was a member of the United Methodist Church, the Phi Delta Kappa, Moslah Temple of Fort Worth, Scottish Rite and the Danville Lodge. He was a veteran of World War II.

Survivors include a son, Harold L. O'Neal of New York, N.Y.; a brother, Raymond O'Neal of Dallas; and a cousin, Mrs. Howard Hays of Tyler.

Pallbearers will be Lance Lowry, Joe Lowry, Howard Hays, Otis Kidd, L. M. Kidd and Royce Nicholson.

The family will be at 508 S. Bonner.

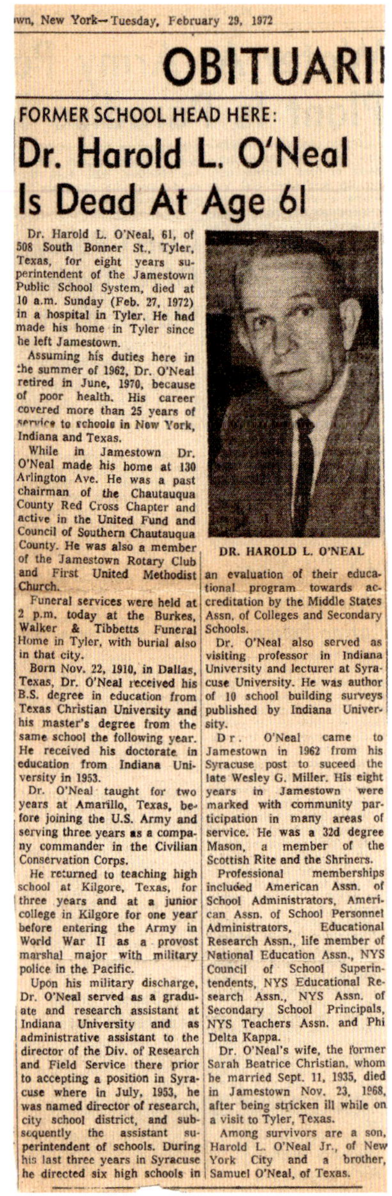
wn, New York—Tuesday, February 29, 1972

**OBITUARI**

FORMER SCHOOL HEAD HERE:

**Dr. Harold L. O'Neal Is Dead At Age 61**

DR. HAROLD L. O'NEAL

Dr. Harold L. O'Neal, 61, of 508 South Bonner St., Tyler, Texas, for eight years superintendent of the Jamestown Public School System, died at 10 a.m. Sunday (Feb. 27, 1972) in a hospital in Tyler. He had made his home in Tyler since he left Jamestown.

Assuming his duties here in the summer of 1962, Dr. O'Neal retired in June, 1970, because of poor health. His career covered more than 25 years of service to schools in New York, Indiana and Texas.

While in Jamestown Dr. O'Neal made his home at 130 Arlington Ave. He was a past chairman of the Chautauqua County Red Cross Chapter and active in the United Fund and Council of Southern Chautauqua County. He was also a member of the Jamestown Rotary Club and First United Methodist Church.

Funeral services were held at 2 p.m. today at the Burkes, Walker & Tibbetts Funeral Home in Tyler, with burial also in that city.

Born Nov. 22, 1910, in Dallas, Texas, Dr. O'Neal received his B.S. degree in education from Texas Christian University and his master's degree from the same school the following year. He received his doctorate in education from Indiana University in 1953.

Dr. O'Neal taught for two years at Amarillo, Texas, before joining the U.S. Army and serving three years as a company commander in the Civilian Conservation Corps.

He returned to teaching high school at Kilgore, Texas, for three years and at a junior college in Kilgore for one year before entering the Army in World War II as a provost marshal major with military police in the Pacific.

Upon his military discharge, Dr. O'Neal served as a graduate and research assistant at Indiana University and as administrative assistant to the director of the Div. of Research and Field Service there prior to accepting a position in Syracuse where in July, 1953, he was named director of research, city school district, and subsequently the assistant superintendent of schools. During his last three years in Syracuse he directed six high schools in an evaluation of their educational program towards accreditation by the Middle States Assn. of Colleges and Secondary Schools.

Dr. O'Neal also served as visiting professor in Indiana University and lecturer at Syracuse University. He was author of 10 school building surveys published by Indiana University.

Dr. O'Neal came to Jamestown in 1962 from his Syracuse post to suceed the late Wesley G. Miller. His eight years in Jamestown were marked with community participation in many areas of service. He was a 32d degree Mason, a member of the Scottish Rite and the Shriners.

Professional memberships included American Assn. of School Administrators, American Assn. of School Personnel Administrators, Educational Research Assn., life member of National Education Assn., NYS Council of School Superintendents, NYS Educational Research Assn., NYS Assn. of Secondary School Principals, NYS Teachers Assn. and Phi Delta Kappa.

Dr. O'Neal's wife, the former Sarah Beatrice Christian, whom he married Sept. 11, 1935, died in Jamestown Nov. 23, 1968, after being stricken ill while on a visit to Tyler, Texas.

Among survivors are a son, Harold L. O'Neal Jr., of New York City and a brother, Samuel O'Neal, of Texas.

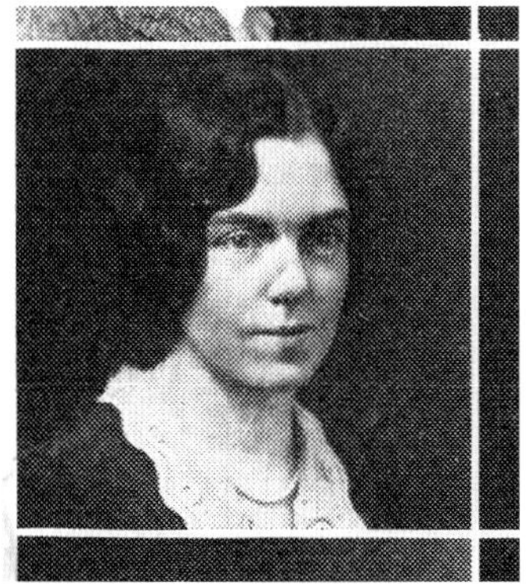

Mary Bourne, 1930

was puzzled by his condition and, unable to pinpoint the cause of Harold's weakness and temperature fluctuations, had him admitted to Mother Francis Hospital; the same one to which Sarah had been taken a few years earlier. After a month of rest and testing, they still could not determine what was wrong. I took trips to Texas in December and January, but I was inexperienced in medical matters and was useless other than to be a cheerful presence. I also began my first serious photographic project. When Harold became too tired and had to rest, I'd leave him alone and travel around East Texas for a few hours and take photographs.

I remained in touch with Dr. Birdwell by telephone on a weekly basis, hoping there might be news. I had planned to fly to Tyler at the end of February, telephoned Dr. Birdwell on February 24, a Thursday, and said I planned to fly in. He told me I shouldn't, that he thought they had found the problem, and everything was under control. I canceled my plans. On Sunday morning the telephone call came saying Harold had died that morning. I was an employee of the Central Intelligence Agency and couldn't just leave New York City on the first available flight, but I did manage to get to Tyler by the time of the funeral on Tuesday afternoon. There were notices in the Tyler and Jamestown papers.

Friends and distant relatives arranged the funeral at the Burkes-Walker-Tippet Chapel on a moment's notice. I was almost just a bystander who arrived just as the services were getting underway. One of the pallbearers was Lance Lowry (along with his son), who was part of the foursome who double dated that first night in March 1932 when Harold and Sarah met. Reverend John Gary of Starrville and his wife, Ida, sang *How Great Thou Art* and *Beyond the Sunset*. They were well past their prime, but offered heartfelt renditions. Reverend and Mrs. Gary had once resided in the now-landmarked Milburn Gary House that I'd photographed as part of of my East Texas project, and it may well have been one of the places Harold and Sarah met in Starrville.

For an hour or so many of Harold and Sarah's friends from East Texas assembled together in a small funeral chapel in Tyler, where the past came alive for a moment or two. It wasn't a large crowd—a smattering of O'Neals I didn't know; one of Sarah's teachers from the 1920s, Mary Bourne; one Crim from Kilgore; the three favorite cousins, Maxine, Rebecca, and Elizabeth; and, of course, Lance and Alpha Verne. At least these are the names that were in the memorial book supplied by Burkes-Walker-Tippet. Then it was back to the present, and we proceeded to Rose Hill where Harold was buried in Plot #112 next to Sarah in #111. No one took any photographs. There was no need. All the good ones had already been taken.

I hadn't seen Harold for about six weeks and don't know what he was like in his final days. I've often hoped he was unconscious most of the time and possibly dreaming and reliving the best of the past with Sarah, like meeting on a porch in Winona and then getting all mixed up riding in an open car under a Texas moon. And now the dream could continue forever and I'm sure it did and does, out there somewhere, maybe in some as yet unknown and undiscovered parallel universe, one reserved for the tiny fragment of time in which they lived.

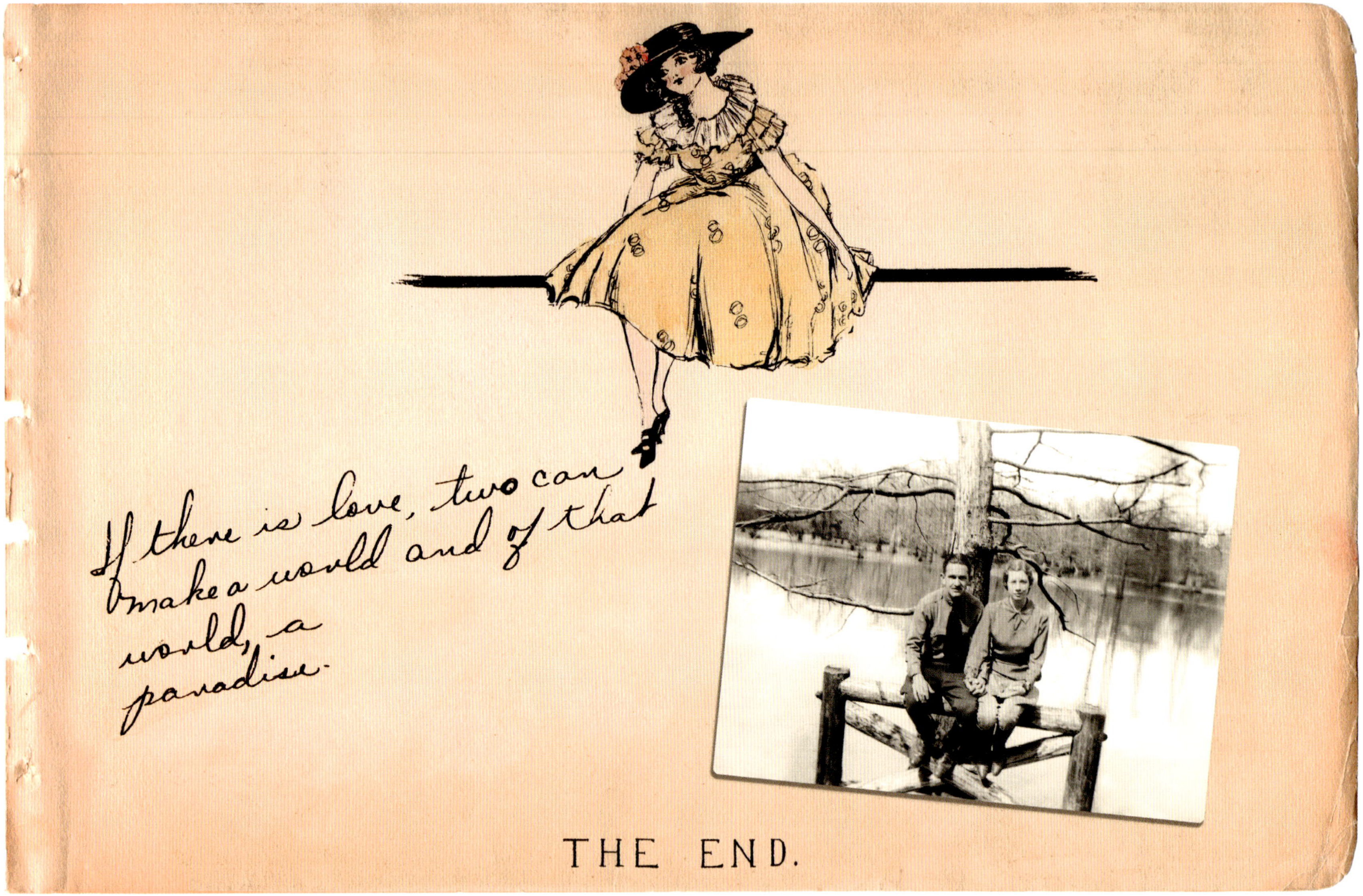
If there is love, two can make a world and of that world, a paradise.
THE END.

## The Mystery of How These Scrapbooks and Photographs Were Preserved

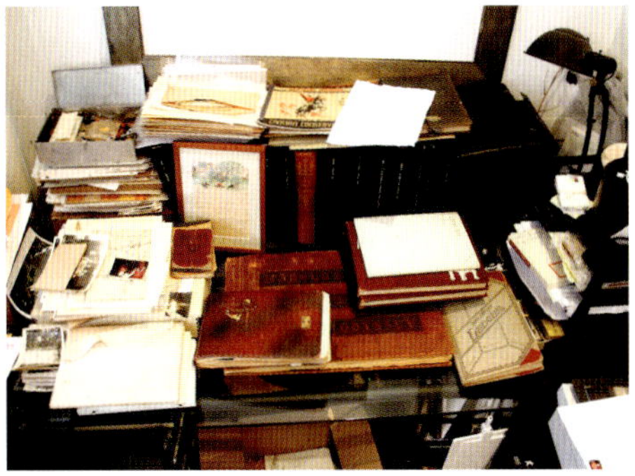

There was a great deal of raw material used to create *Preserving Lives*; seven scrapbooks compiled between the years 1920 and 1950, over a thousand loose photographs, envelopes full of newspaper clippings, programs, greeting cards, and more photographs; magazines that had been saved; high school and university yearbooks between the years 1928 and 1953 from Texas and Indiana—Tyler, Amarillo, Kilgore, Fort Worth, Bloomington; military records in 201 files, educational records all the way back to the 1920s, and even old telephone directories, postcards, letters, and tax records as old as 1878.

The mystery is how it all survived, because I was not even aware of most of this material until after Harold and Sarah died. If I had known of it, I might have asked a few questions. The oldest scrapbook and the most recently obtained is the easiest to explain. This old scrapbook was compiled in the 1920s by Harold's brother, Cecil, and kept safely by his family. It was recovered in Whitehouse, Texas, in the home of his son, Louie Mack O'Neal, courtesy of his widow, Judy O'Neal. It had remained at rest in that house for fifty years, just a few miles from where it was compiled in the 1920s.

The survival of much of the rest of the material is a mystery. Almost everything used in compiling *Preserving Lives* has traveled extensively, suffered through the cold of attics in the winter, the heat of summers, the dampness of basements, and remained largely unseen by anyone for decades. The once-white scrapbook pages yellowed over time; the acidic black pulp pages of cheap scrapbooks grew brittle; drugstore-processed photographs yellowed and faded. They were moved dozens of times throughout Texas, even surviving the catastrophic 1949 flood in Fort Worth.

Somehow room was found to move them safely from here to there in the backs of old cars, Jeeps, and crowded trailers, and then store them under beds in apartments without closets or in forgotten attics. Sarah's oldest scrapbook, the cannibalized Ledger from a drug store in Tyler, was in at least twenty-five different locations. Everything was almost soaked in a flood that ravaged their home in 1990. The water stopped four inches from the boxes in which the scrapbooks, photographs, and papers were stored.

Harold and Sarah were both romantics and saved things: scraps of paper, some with words, some with images; old photographs, clippings, and bits of sentimental memorabilia. Things from out of the past. Maybe everyone does this, or maybe they don't and when they grow old and want to remember, wish they had. But Harold and Sarah saved things and somehow miraculously the things they saved survive. I don't know why, but I like to think that deep down inside they thought that someday, someone, maybe me, would find the things they saved and perhaps write a story that would tell about their life together based on the fragments they'd left behind. Or maybe it was something else. I don't know, and there's no one left to ask.

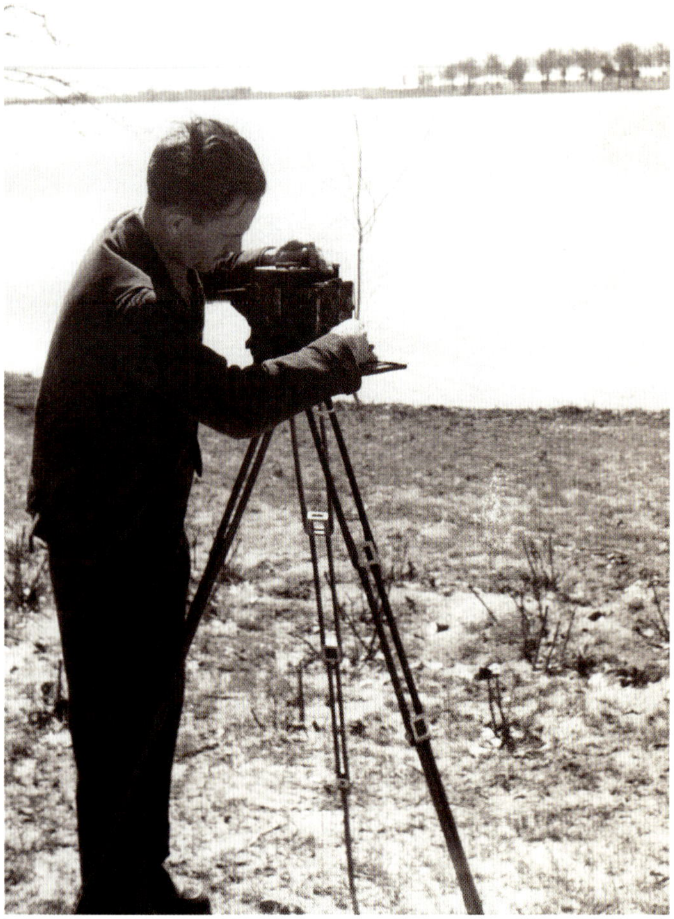

Harold, somewhere in Texas

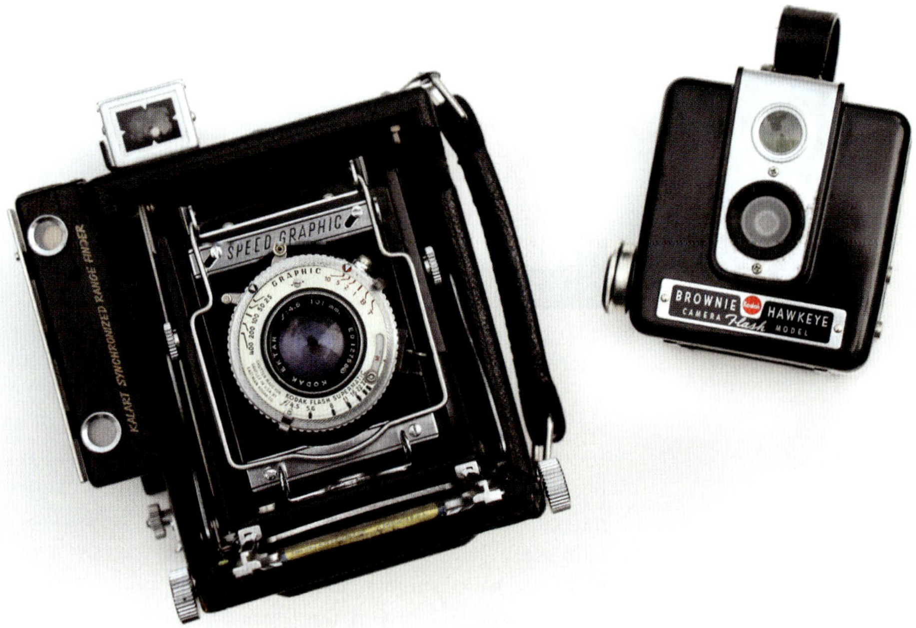


Original Speed Graphic and Brownie Hawkeye

## The Photographs

Most of the many photographs from the 1920s and 1930s reproduced in this book were taken and processed with modest equipment, usually by unknown photographers or family members in casual circumstances. There are a handful of photographs that were taken by professional photographers, and they are easy to spot; they look different—exquisite panoramas of CCC Installations and portraits by E. L. Rothwell of San Antonio or portraits presented in little folders that feature a studio name. But most of those up to World War II were taken with modest Kodak cameras, processed at the drug store or local camera shop and stuck away in albums secured by various types of mounting corners. Sometimes a few words were written on the back, a name or a date, but sometimes a few words about the event photographed.

In The Oil Patch section, nine real photo postcards taken by Jack Nolan, one of the most remarkable Texas-based oil field photographers, are included as illustrations. No one captured the energy and excitement of the East Texas oil patch as well as Nolan, and even though these postcards were not part of Harold and Sarah's scrapbooks, they have been included because they are evocative of the times during which each of them were coming of age and eventually coming together.

Sometime in 1942 Harold acquired a Leica 35mm camera. It is unclear how many rolls of film he took during his time overseas, but thirty-one rolls of black and white negatives survive. Five boxes of color transparencies also more or less survived; the Kodachromes are still beautiful, but the ANSCO photographs are now blue-green and unusable unless converted to black and white. It is also unclear how Harold managed to get his film processed: there were no camera shops in the war zone. It is likely he had friends in the Signal Corps who helped out. He probably sent the color film home to Texas.

After the war Harold traded his Leica for a 2 ¼" x 3 ¼" Speed Graphic and for a few years took carefully composed black-and-white photographs with this camera. He processed the film himself and made small 4"x 5" prints in a kitchen/darkroom. He also printed many of his World War II 35mm prints as well. I often watched him make these pictures. At some point his interest in photography waned; he took a few pictures in Bloomington, Indiana, and to the best of my knowledge, the last one he took was of my church league basketball team in Syracuse, New York, in 1954-55.

The other photographs from the 1950s and 1960s are equally anonymous, except for a handful I took with my trusty Brownie Hawkeye in the mid-1950s. Some of the photographs have been fixed with the help of Photoshop; spots were removed, and where required to present as much information as possible the photographs were evened out and color corrected, but by and large the images in this book are close to the images in the scrapbooks.

# Acknowledgments

*Preserving Lives* would not exist had it not been for the collective efforts of many people over the past one hundred years or so. Some distant relative saved the oldest item included in the book, an 1878 tax receipt, and passed it along to someone who in turn passed it and other photographs and letters and assorted pieces of paper and memorabilia that made their way into various scrapbooks and assorted binders or were saved in other fashions. Others did the same until Harold and Sarah compiled their many scrapbooks and made certain they survived for me to discover in the late 1970s.

I showed Sarah's 1932 "memory book" to Jacqueline Onassis in the early 1980s and she found it charming but didn't know what to do with the scrapbook. She encouraged me to think about it. I did, off and on, but it took me about thirty-five years to figure it out. I hope it was worth the wait.

In early 2016 I sent a blind email to Dan Williams, the director of TCU Press, and mentioned three Texas-centric projects to him. He expressed an immediate interest in the scrapbook/memoir, and of course it made perfect sense. My father attended TCU upon his return from World War II, so there was a direct link to the university.

In May of that year there was a meeting with Dan and his staff, Kathy Walton, who served as editor, Melinda Esco, the production manager, and Molly Spain, the editorial assistant. This was the team that put *Preserving Lives* together, and it is perhaps the most convivial team I have ever encountered in the world of books. Later, I worked with Rebecca Allen, the marketing coordinator, who had the book listed on Amazon several months before publication. Thanks to all of them.

There were three other people who were directly involved in creating *Preserving Lives* and three who helped indirectly. I asked Sue Brown, the president of the Kilgore Historical Preservation Foundation, to check my Kilgore chapter for accuracy. She in turn passed it along to Caleb Pirtle, a well-known authority on all things Kilgore, and my essay passed muster. Judy O'Neal of Whitehouse gave me a crumbling family scrapbook that had been assembled by Harold's older brother, Cecil, in the 1910s and 20s. It was filled with wonderful photographs and memorabilia that filled in many blanks.

On the more active participants, Ian Clifford provided invaluable expertise, and his skills in restoring photographs, tattered scrapbook pages, and eighty-year-old documents were crucial to the content of the book. Bill Brammer, who has designed many fine books for TCU Press and others, created a superlative design that captures the memories and images of the past that I found in Harold and Sarah's scrapbooks and papers and makes them visually relevant in 2018. If Dan Williams and his staff shepherded the book through production, Sherry Sereboff not only shepherded me through the production process but also served as my conscience in East Texas, as well as my guide; read the manuscript, offered good suggestions, and made certain I was on time for meetings and didn't talk too much.

Thanks are offered to all these fine people who helped make *Preserving Lives* possible.

## About the Author

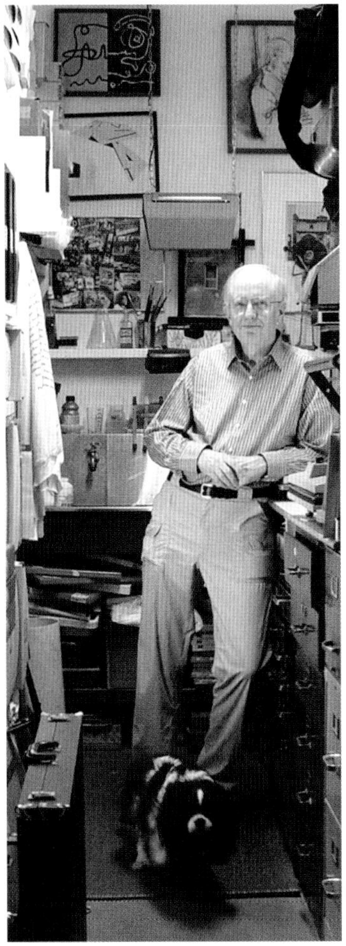

Photo by Ian P. Clifford

Hank O'Neal was born in Kilgore, Texas, in 1940. His career has included the worlds of government, education, music, photography, and literature.

O'Neal was employed by the Central Intelligence Agency from 1963 until he "retired" in 1976 and began the next phase of his life. He had heard his first jazz records when he was a teenager. He liked what he heard, and kept on listening. In the sixty years since that first awakening, he has formed two record companies (Chiaroscuro and Hammond Music Enterprises), built two recordings studios, produced over two hundred jazz LPs/CDs and one hundred music festivals (the Floating Jazz Festival, the Blues Cruise et al), published a number of books and articles on jazz, photographed most of the giants of jazz from the second half of the twentieth century, exhibited these photographs regularly, and joined and continues to serve on the boards of various non-profit organizations that serve the jazz community, including the Jazz and Contemporary Music Program of the New School (1985), the Jazz Foundation of America (1993), the Jazz Gallery (1996), and more recently the National Jazz Museum in Harlem (2008 - 2012). He continues to serve as an adviser to the Oslo Jazz Festival (1986), the Bern Jazz Festival (2005), and George Wein's New Festival Productions (2007). In 2018 all these activities continue unabated.

In 1970, O'Neal took what he considers his first serious photographs and in 1972 met Berenice Abbott, with whom he worked closely for nineteen years. About the same time he met André Kertèsz, Walker Evans, and all the other living FSA photographers and many other exceptional photographic artists who were all to influence him. His own photographs have been widely exhibited and reproduced since that time. O'Neal published his first book in 1973, but his first to gain widespread attention was *A Vision Shared* (1976). Steidl will reissue this important book in 2018. He has published seventeen books on other subjects, mostly related to photography, his own or others, music or both. In addition to *A Vision Shared*, Steidl will release four other new books by O'Neal, *You've Got To Be A Damn Sight Better Than That, Buster*, a memoir of his experiences working with Abbott; *Berenice Abbott's Maine – The Color Photographs, Maine 1960s – 1970s* (with Berenice Abbott); and *Berenice Abbott: In Her Own Words*. He was recently coeditor of the five volumes included in *The Unknown Abbott* (Steidl, 2013) and *Berenice Abbott – The Paris Portraits* (Steidl, 2015).

Since his retrospective at New York City's legendary Witkin Gallery in 1999 he has had dozens of exhibitions in both museums and commercial galleries. He is particularly proud of his three exhibitions in East Texas at the Longview Museum of Fine Arts that began in 2006. He is currently at work on a project featuring forty years of his work in East Texas along US Highway 80. He currently resides in New York City.

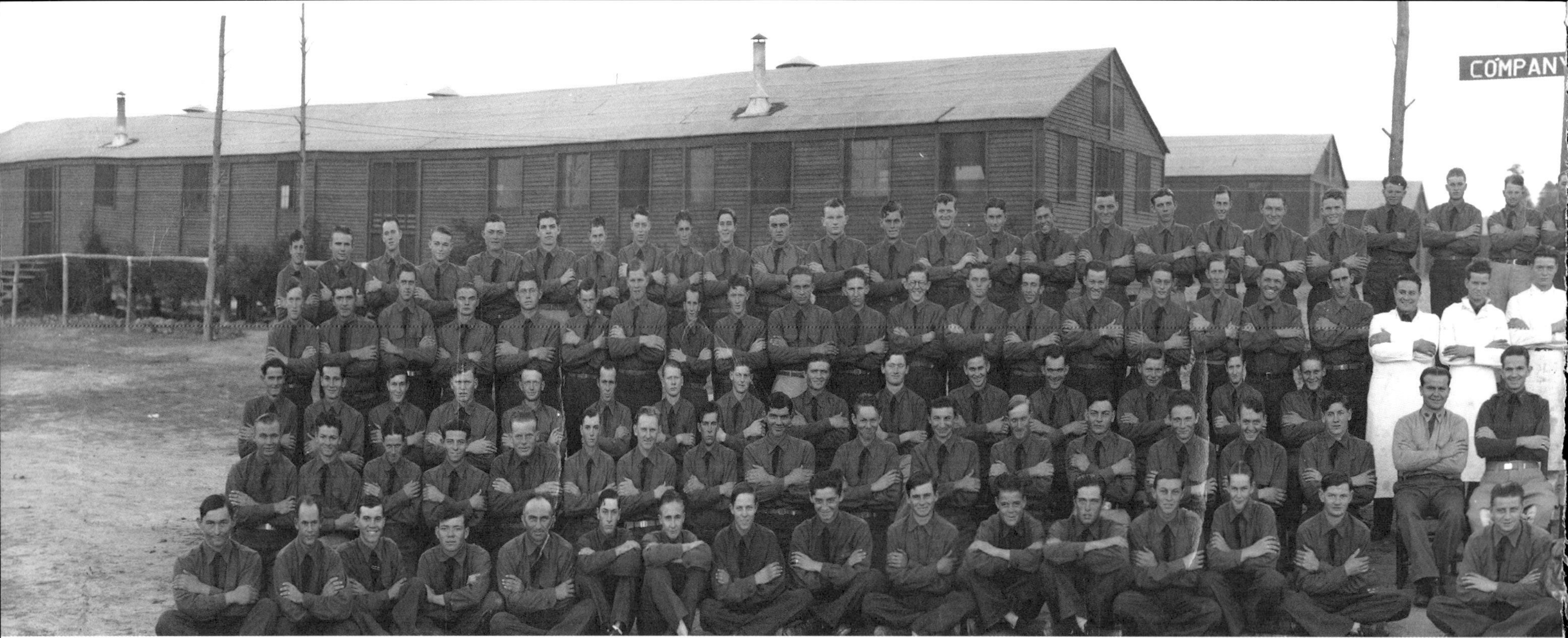
COMPANY

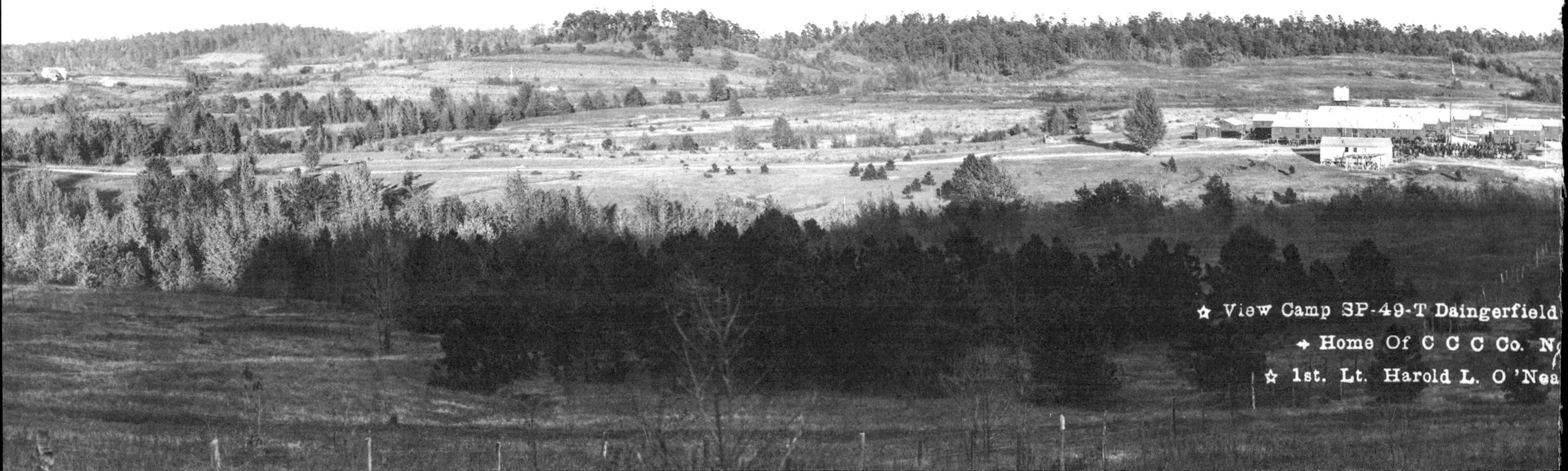
☆ View Camp SP-49-T Daingerfield
→ Home Of C C C Co. N
☆ 1st. Lt. Harold L. O'Nea